# Personal construct psychology in clinical practice

*Personal Construct Psychology in Clinical Practice* provides the first comprehensive account of the clinical applications of personal construct theory. In a single book the author brings together theoretical analyses, research findings, and descriptions of diagnostic and therapeutic approaches, amply illustrated with case material, in relation to a wide range of clinical problems. Clinicians who wish to employ methods derived from the theory, such as the repertory grid, will find guidelines set out. A further distinctive feature of the book is that it includes a thorough examination of the similarities and contrasts between personal construct theory and other major approaches to psychological disorder and its treatment.

**David Winter** is District Clinical Psychologist for Barnet Healthcare Trust and Visiting Professor in the Division of Psychology of the University of Hertfordshire. He has used personal construct psychology in his clinical research and practice for the past twenty years and has published extensively on its clinical applications.

D1125793

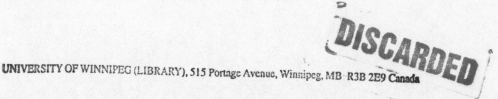

# Personal construct psychology in clinical practice

## Theory, research and applications

David A. Winter

London and New York

First published 1992
by Routledge
11 New Fetter Lane, London EC4P 4EE

Simultaneously published in the USA and Canada
by Routledge
a division of Routledge, Chapman and Hall, Inc.
29 West 35th Street, New York, NY 10001

First published in paperback in 1994 by Routledge

Typeset in Times by
NWL Editorial Services, Langport, Somerset

Printed and bound in Great Britain by
Mackays of Chatham PLC, Chatham, Kent

*British Library Cataloguing in Publication Data*
A catalogue record for this book is available from the British Library

*Library of Congress Cataloging in Publication Data*
Winter, David A., 1950–
    Personal construct psychology in clinical practice: theory, research and
    applications / David A. Winter.
    p.   cm.
    Includes bibliographical references and index.
    1. Personal construct therapy.   2. Personal construct theory.
    I. Title.
    RC489.P46W56   1994
    616.89'14 – dc20

                                                              93–47681
                                                              CIP

ISBN 0–415–00601–5 (pbk)

Our view, then, is that there is nothing in the world which is not subject to some form of reconstruction. This is the hope that constructive alternativism holds out to every man and it is the philosophical basis of the hope that a psychotherapist holds out to his client.

George Kelly

To the other Kelly in my life

# Contents

# Figures and tables

# Preface

George Kelly in 1955 put forward a psychological theory which, taking as its subject matter the whole person rather than some fragment of the person's psychological functioning, he intended to have a very wide range of applicability. That this intention was justified can be seen from a glance at any literature search on the theory, which will produce references on the application of Kelly's ideas to areas as diverse as parliamentary debate (du Preez, 1972), the pig industry (Woog, 1978), seaside resorts (Riley and Palmer, 1976), religious belief (Todd, 1988), music (Ben-Peretz and Kalekin-Fishman, 1988; Button, 1988), birth (Breen, 1975), and death (Epting and R. Neimeyer, 1984). However, the psychotherapeutic situation was, for Kelly, the area of personal construct theory's maximal potential applicability, its focus of convenience.

Nevertheless, the theory is still underused in clinical practice, and receives relatively little coverage in clinical courses. Clinicians have also often come away from reading *The Psychology of Personal Constructs*, or subsequent summaries of the theory and of its technology, feeling intellectually stimulated but somewhat at a loss as to how to apply its ideas in their work. This is doubtless in part due to the fact that the theory is presented in highly abstract terms, but it may also reflect a resistance by personal construct theorists to producing anything which might be construed as a construct theory 'cookbook', and which would therefore be antithetical to some of the basic assumptions of personal construct psychology. The present work is also not intended to provide recipes for what is ultimately a personal adventure in construction and reconstruction for clinician and client. However, in some areas, such as the interpretation of the repertory grid, it will be argued that the usefulness of a clinical procedure may be enhanced by the clinician following certain guidelines, and an attempt will be made to provide such guidelines. A further possible reason for the relative lack of attention paid by clinicians to personal construct theory is that personal construct theorists themselves have often paid little attention to developments in other branches of psychology. Therefore, in the pages that follow, as well as drawing heavily upon Kelly's original writings and attempting to provide a comprehensive review of the subsequent applications of his theory in clinical research and practice, I shall indicate how these applications may relate to, and contrast with, work conducted from other theoretical perspectives. My aim will be to demonstrate the value and potential of the personal construct theory approach in the clinical setting, in the hope that the reader may feel both stimulated by the theory and better equipped to experiment with its clinical application.

Like so many other psychology students of my generation, my own introduction to personal construct theory came in a lecture by Dr Don Bannister at a time when I was feeling particularly disenchanted with my undergraduate course. Personal construct psychology, and Don's inimitable presentation of it, provided an oasis in a desert of mechanism and reductionism, and my optimism concerning the theory remains undiminished. Sadly, Don is no longer with us, and neither is another person, Dr Brian Wijesinghe, who, although not claiming to be a personal construct theorist, in his approach to clinical practice and to life provided a clear example of Kelly's basic philosophical position of constructive alternativism. My deepest gratitude goes to these two men, and to Dr Thomas Caine, whose research programme with Brian Wijesinghe I had the good fortune to join after completing my clinical training, and who has always provided reminders of the value of openness to ideas in realms beyond the strictly psychological. Particular thanks are also due to Dr Ana Catina, who took on the unenviable task of the first reading of my manuscript, and who has been a constant source of suggestions, discussion, and encouragement.

Many other people, too numerous to mention, have, in one way or another, contributed to my interest in, and perseverance with, this project: my clients and research subjects, without whom the book would not have been written and some of whose stories, with details altered to preserve anonymity, are told in the following pages; those of my colleagues who have been open to the exploration and application of an unfamiliar approach; students whose response to this approach has been both welcoming and questioning, who have indicated to me the need for a book of this type, and some of whom have assisted me with the collection of research data; and fellow personal construct theorists who have shown interest in my work.

David Winter
St. Albans, 1990

# Personal construing:
# its nature and assessment

The handbook of clinical procedures which George Kelly produced for his students at the clinic which he directed in Kansas, after twenty years of refinement, developed into what Fillmore Sanford, his editor, termed 'an extensive exploration into a strange new land of personality theory and clinical practice' (Kelly, 1955, p. xvii). Today, some thirty-five years later, Kelly's theory may not appear much less strange to many clinicians and students. The first chapter in Part I will therefore provide an introductory guide to what may still be unfamiliar territory for some readers, a reminder of the basic concepts of the theory for those who are more familiar with it, and a preliminary discussion of the personal construct theory perspective on optimal and disordered functioning. In Chapter 2, assessment techniques employed by personal construct theorists will be presented, and discussion of the findings of research employing these techniques with 'normal subjects' will provide further indications of characteristics of the construing of the optimally functioning person, with which construing in psychological disorder may then be compared.

# Chapter 1
# The theory

Many a reader has fallen by the wayside between pages 1 and 1197 of George Kelly's *The Psychology of Personal Constructs* (1955), the two-volume magnum opus which set out the new psychology that he had fashioned out of his attempts to systematise his clinical practice. This is perhaps due not so much to the length of this first statement of personal construct theory as to the unfamiliarity of the terms in which it is couched. Although at first sight it may appear that, in the fashion of some personality theorists, this was an attempt to produce a pseudo-scientific language of neologisms, it was due more to the fact that Kelly was putting forward an alternative to existing psychologies, the terms and concepts of which he could not borrow as they would come complete with their own networks of implications. Thus, the reader will find 'no *ego*, no *emotion*, no *motivation*, no *reinforcement*, no *drive*, no *unconscious*, no *need*' (Kelly, 1955, p. x, italics in original); and that psychological disorders are classified in terms of the way in which the client makes sense of his or her world rather than using conventional diagnostic categories. When familiar terms, such as hostility, guilt, anxiety, and role, are used, they afford little comfort to the reader as they are generally defined in novel ways. As will be seen later, such a situation of finding one's well-tried concepts wanting is likely to generate anxiety, similar to that experienced by the non-mathematically inclined psychologist who opens a statistics textbook. And one way of avoiding anxiety is to close the book.

The intention of the present chapter is, therefore, to introduce the language, and the way of viewing psychological processes, 'normal' and disordered, which will be employed in the ensuing chapters. It will not attempt an extensive exposition of personal construct theory's fundamental postulate and each of its eleven corollaries since several excellent summaries of the theory, and of research bearing on it, are now available (e.g. Bannister and Fransella, 1986; Adams-Webber, 1979; Mancuso and Adams-Webber, 1982a).

## BASIC CONCEPTS

### The fundamental postulate and corollaries

The central philosophical assumption underlying personal construct theory is *constructive alternativism*, which asserts that 'all of our present interpretations of the universe are subject to revision or replacement' (Kelly, 1955, p. 15). Every theory, including personal construct theory, is just another such interpretation of the universe which, however tenaciously we may attempt to cling on to it, is likely eventually to make way for a more satisfactory alternative interpretation. This recognition that what we might regard as facts are merely expendable interpretations is perhaps particularly pertinent to the clinical field, where a client's predicament may be interpreted by clinicians in numerous different ways, where each of these views may be held with intense conviction, and where none of them may match the client's own perception of his or her situation. How much more productive some of our interchanges with our colleagues and clients might be if we adopted the stance that we are employing alternative constructions of our subject matter rather than that one of us is incorrect.

Kelly's was not a solipsistic position, inasmuch as he did not deny the existence of a real universe, albeit one that no individual can experience directly. A person's view of this universe is obtained 'through transparent patterns or templets which he creates and then attempts to fit over the realities of which the world is composed' (Kelly, 1955, pp. 8–9); in other words, he construes. Construing is an active, ongoing process in which we each constantly try to give meaning to our world and to predict future events by operating rather like a scientist: making hypotheses, testing them out, and if necessary revising them on the basis of the evidence which we collect. As stated in the words of the 'Fundamental Postulate' of personal construct theory, 'A person's processes are psychologically channelized by the ways in which he anticipates events' (Kelly, 1955, p. 47).

Kelly's 'Construction Corollary' went on to state that this anticipation of events occurs through 'construing their replications'. By searching for repeated themes in our experience of the world, we provide ourselves with a basis for predicting future events. Also central to this process of construing, according to personal construct theory, is the recognition of similarities between some events, or *elements* of the individual's world, which at the same time differentiate them from other events. In doing so, we develop a construction system which, in the words of Kelly's 'Dichotomy Corollary', 'is composed of a finite number of dichotomous *constructs*' (italics mine). Each construct can therefore be regarded as bipolar, with one pole, the *emergent pole*, indicating a way in which at least two elements are similar while its other pole, the *implicit pole*, defines their contrast with some other element or elements. For example, a psychology student may be in the habit of construing the theorists about whom he reads in terms of the distinction 'psychodynamic–behavioural'. He may fairly readily consign Freud and Jung to the former pole of this construct, contrasting them with Eysenck, whom he regards as behavioural. He may have some difficulty, however, in placing Kelly on this construct dimension; and his attempts to use the construct to make sense of his girl friend's behaviour may result in his concluding that it is not applicable to her. In personal construct theory terms, the girl friend is outside the *range of convenience* of this particular construct for this individual and, although Freud, Jung, Eysenck, and Kelly are all within its range of convenience, only the former three fall within its *focus of convenience*, the area of its maximum usefulness. While the element 'Kelly' is outside the focus of convenience of the construct, it is within its *context*, the elements between which the individual normally uses it to discriminate, and which in this case comprise psychological theorists. Kelly's (1955, p. 68) view that 'there are few if any personal constructs which one can say are relevant to everything' is expressed in the 'Range Corollary' of personal construct theory: 'A construct is convenient for the anticipation of a finite range of events only.'

Although an individual may be able to express the distinction embodied in a construct verbally, as in the 'psychodynamic–behavioural' example above, it should be remembered that the verbal labels themselves do not constitute the construct. Further, many of the ways in which people discriminate between events, their constructs, have no verbal labels: some, for example, are of the order of physiological responses. As will be discussed later, the labelling of unverbalised constructs may be a central component of therapy.

If constructs are viewed as bipolar, it follows that each construct is 'a pathway of movement' (Kelly, 1955, p. 128), and presents the individual with a choice in that a particular event may be assigned to one pole of it or the other. Kelly's (1955, p. 64) 'Choice Corollary' provides a basis for predicting the particular choice that the individual will make, stating that 'A person chooses for himself that alternative in a dichotomized construct through which he anticipates the greater possibility for extension and definition of his system'. The choice that is made will therefore be that which appears to the individual to facilitate the anticipation of future events, either by broadening the range of convenience of the construct system or by increasing its internal consistency. It is an *elaborative choice*. Implicit in Kelly's notion of choice is the rejection of a hedonistic view of human motivation: a person's choices are directed not towards maximising his or her level of pleasure but towards maximising the extent to which the world can be predicted. As we shall see later, such a view may make the sometimes puzzling, and sometimes apparently self-destructive, choices of our clients rather more comprehensible.

A person's constructs are not disparate units but rather, in the words of Kelly's (1955, p. 56) 'Organization Corollary', are organised into 'a construction system embracing ordinal relationships between constructs'. The relationships of one construct to others in the individual's construct system will indicate something of the construct's personal meaning and may allow aspects of the individual's behaviour to be predicted. For example, if our student's constructions of being 'academic', being 'boring', and being 'socially isolated' are interrelated, he might be expected not to produce a good examination performance. In stating that the construct system embraces ordinal relationships between constructs, Kelly is suggesting that its organisation is hierarchical, with some constructs subsuming others. Thus, the construct 'psychodynamic–behavioural' when applied by a psychoanalyst to different forms of therapy may be subsumed under the construct 'intensive–superficial', while itself subsuming the construct 'classical analytic–neo-Freudian' under its 'psychodynamic' pole. In personal construct theory terminology, 'intensive–superficial' is *superordinate*, and 'classical analytic–neo-Freudian' is *subordinate*, to this individual's 'psychodynamic–behavioural' construct. If the student views *all* behavioural approaches as superficial, the latter construct may be regarded as *regnant* over the former. A further distinction which may be made between constructs is in terms of whether they are *comprehensive* or *incidental*, subsuming a wide or small variety of events.

The particular relationships between a person's constructs will determine his or her predictions about the world, and these predictions may or may not be validated by subsequent events. If the person is conforming to Kelly's model of *man-the-scientist*, such experiences of validation or invalidation will lead to the strengthening or modification respectively of the predictions and constructions concerned. As stated in the 'Experience Corollary' (Kelly, 1955, p. 72), 'A person's construction system varies as he successively construes the replications of events'. For example, if our student is confronted by a number of people whom he construes as both academic and interesting, he may modify the relationships between his constructs accordingly. Similarly, if he finds that he has difficulty not only in subsuming Kelly, but also the cognitive and humanistic therapists to whose work he is exposed, with his 'psychodynamic–behavioural' construct, he may attempt to develop more adequate constructs to apply to psychological theories and therapies.

It has been questioned by some writers (e.g. Mischel, 1964) whether a construct can ever really be invalidated since events are always construed by the individual, and are likely to be interpreted in a way which is consistent with the system of constructs from which the individual's predictions were derived in the first place. As Kelly (1955, p. 13) pointed out, however, what saves the individual's constructions from being purely self-fulfilling prophecies is that 'he can usually assess the outcomes of his predictions at a different level of construction from that at which he originally makes them'. Also of note is that, although Kelly viewed people as operating like scientists, he was equally clear that they are not always good scientists. Indeed, as we shall see, to a large extent he equated psychological disorder with bad science. The apparent failure of some individuals to modify their construct systems in response to their validational fortunes is not inconsistent with Kelly's theory, and indeed the theory is able to predict which individuals, and which of their constructs, are most likely to be resistant to invalidation. For example, Kelly's (1955, p. 77) 'Modulation Corollary' states that 'The variation in a person's construction system is limited by the permeability of the constructs within whose range of convenience the variants lie'. By a *permeable* construct, Kelly is meaning one which 'will admit to its range of convenience new elements which are not yet construed within its framework' (p. 79). Our student's 'psychodynamic–behavioural' construct, for example, is relatively impermeable, being increasingly inapplicable to psychological theorists and therapies, let alone to people and events in general. If an individual's superordinate constructs are impermeable, they are unlikely to be able to subsume new constructs, and the individual may therefore show little reconstruing in response to the events with which he or she is confronted.

Not only are people not always good scientists, their construct systems are also not always completely internally consistent. If, for example, the person revises their construing of events, their new constructions may not be entirely compatible with their existing constructions. As Kelly (1955, p. 83) puts it in his 'Fragmentation Corollary', 'A person may successively employ a variety of construction subsystems which are inferentially incompatible with each other'. Therefore, in this corollary Kelly introduces the notion of a construct system being composed of separate *subsystems*. Our student may, for example, develop a subsystem of constructs concerning psychological theories and another, relatively independent, subsystem more applicable to his girl friend and other people. Any inconsistencies between subsystems may be tolerated if the individual's superordinate constructs are sufficiently permeable to subsume the inconsistent constructions. Thus, successive, apparently inconsistent, constructions of a person as cruel and kind may be resolved by applying a superordinate construct permeable enough to accommodate the notion that 'you have to be cruel to be kind' (Bannister and Fransella, 1986, p. 17). If permeable superordinate constructs are not available, the individual may employ various strategies in an attempt to cope with incompatibilities between constructions. However, as we shall see, these strategies are themselves not without their problems and, used to the extreme, may be the basis of a psychological disorder.

It will now be apparent that, as Kelly's (1955, p. 55) 'Individuality Corollary' states, 'Persons differ from each other in their construction of events'. The differences in people's behaviour in a particular situation may therefore be explained by the fact that they are viewing the situation differently. However, especially within a particular cultural group, there also tends to be a marked degree of similarity in various aspects of construing and therefore of behaviour. This issue is addressed by Kelly's (1955, p. 90) 'Commonality Corollary', which asserts that 'To the extent that one person employs a construction of experience which is similar to that employed by another, his psychological processes are similar to those of the other person'. Given that our clients' behaviour generally departs from cultural norms in some respects, the clinician who adopts a personal construct theory approach will attempt to gain an understanding of the individualistic ways of construing the world which are likely to underlie the client's behaviour. In thus attempting to view the world through the client's eyes, the clinician is laying the basis for a constructive social interaction with the client for, as Kelly's (1955, p. 95) 'Sociality Corollary' states, 'To the extent that one person construes the construction processes of another, he may play a role in a social process involving the other person'.

## New corollaries

Although there has been very little modification of Kelly's basic theory by later personal construct psychologists, some writers have proposed new corollaries in areas where the theory is not extensively elaborated, such as social interaction and the early acquisition of constructs.

For example, drawing upon the Sociality Corollary, Thomas (1979) has formulated a 'Self-awareness Corollary' and a 'Social Awareness Corollary'. The former states that 'To the extent that a person construes his own constructions of experience, he or she acquires consciousness. To the extent that a person construes his or her own *processes* of construction he or she acquires more complete awareness of themselves as a person' (p. 53, italics in original). The Social Awareness Corollary asserts that 'The forms in which a person construes his or her constructions of social interactional processes will condition their ability to consciously influence their processes of interaction with others' (p. 62). Thomas has also been concerned to apply personal construct psychology to social systems, and has proposed a 'Complementality Corollary' for this purpose. This states that 'When people share in a common pool of events including each other, but by virtue of their position sample these events differently, their constructions of experience will develop to complement each other. The complementation will produce a social system which exhibits greater complexity of stable organisation than exists in the constructions of any individual contributing to it' (p. 66). Similarly, Procter (1981) has extended the understanding of relationships which is provided by the Sociality Corollary beyond the dyad, putting forward the 'Group Corollary' that 'To the extent that a person can construe the relationships between members of a group, he may take part in a group process with them' (p. 354). He has been primarily concerned with one particular social group, the family, and his 'Family Corollary' asserts that 'For a group of people to remain together over an extended period of time, each must make a choice, within the limitations of his system, to maintain a common construction of the relationships in the group' (pp. 354–5). Procter refers to this common construction as the family construct system.

A further concern of Procter and some other workers has been the problem of whence the individual's first constructs were derived. Procter and Parry

(1978) have paid primary attention to the social origins of the child's constructs, as have Salmon (1970, 1979), who has proposed that these derive from the constructs of the child's parents, particularly the mother, and Bannister (1983a, 1985a), who has been concerned with the individual's elaboration of a construction of self through construing others and their constructions of the individual. Other writers, with the aid of new corollaries, have focussed on the biological basis of early constructs. Thus, Thomas (1979) has proposed the 'Endowment Corollaries' that '(i) Organisms are born with a set of constructions of experience (e.g. innate releaser mechanisms); and (ii) organisms are more likely to acquire certain constructions at certain critical times (e.g. imprinting)' (p. 64). Similarly, Katz (1984) has suggested the 'Origin Postulate' that 'Each individual possesses phylogenetically rooted *primitive constructs* which emerge during characteristic periods in the individual's ontogenetic development, and which serve as points of departure for the elaboration of the individual's personal constructs' (p. 318, italics in original). He has also put forward an 'Emotion Corollary' which builds on this postulate, stating that 'To the extent a person perceives an event in terms of a primitive construct and, as a necessary consequence, reacts with a psycho-physiological anticipation that is involuntary, transient, and phylogenetically predisposed, he experiences an emotion' (p. 321). As we shall see below, though, the area of emotions is one which was by no means ignored by Kelly.

## Dimensions of diagnosis and transition

As an aid to clinicians in their attempts to subsume the personal constructs of their clients, Kelly (1955) provided a set of professional, diagnostic constructs. He emphasised, however, that the range of convenience of these constructs is not limited to clients, but rather that they are 'universal axes with respect to which it is possible to plot any person's behaviour, at any time or at any place' (p. 452). Not even personal construct theorists are exempt from having their behaviour explained in terms of these diagnostic constructs, for Kelly's is a *reflexive* theory, as applicable to its users as to their clients or research subjects (Oliver and Landfield, 1962).

Some of Kelly's diagnostic constructs concern *covert construction*, that which is at a low *level of cognitive awareness*. For example, the person who is attempting to apply a construct to an element at the boundary of its range of convenience, such as our student who is trying to make sense of his girl friend's behaviour by employing the 'psychodynamic–behavioural' construct, is construing at a low level of cognitive awareness. Also included in the category of covert construction are *preverbal* constructs, those which have no consistent verbal symbols, in most cases because they were formulated in infancy, before the individual was able to use words. As many of the infant's preoccupations are often with dependency on particular people, the adult's preverbal constructs may well have similar concerns, in which case they may be described as *dependency constructs*. If used permeably, however, they may subsume elements from adult life, and they may also be elaborated into a system which includes constructs which were developed after the person could make use of words. Kelly (1955, p. 465) outlined four signs which may indicate that a person is employing preverbal constructs, namely:

(1) the client's efforts at verbalization repeatedly end up in an expression of confusion; (2) inability to verbalize the construct consistently but relatively better ability to illustrate the construct by producing the elements which make up its context; (3) appearance in dreams, the content of which the client claims he cannot remember but which, on questioning, appear to have some structure in terms of mood, number of people, movement, and so on; (4) 'recollections' of events which the client is not sure really happened.

With some constructs, one pole is more accessible than the other, the *submerged* pole often being one which might be applied to the self. For example, as we shall see in Chapter 4, some clients appear to construe other people in a uniformly favourable light, and in so doing may be exhibiting submergence of the negatively evaluated poles of some of their constructs. In Kelly's view, submergence may be a strategy by means of which a person avoids testing out a particular construct, for to do so requires the formulation of contrasting predictions on the basis of each of the construct's poles. Such a strategy may be employed, for example, if it is feared that if put to the test the construct may be invalidated or that reconstruing of the self may result. Another strategy involving low cognitive awareness of construing is *suspension*, in which a particular construction is held in abeyance, perhaps because it is incompatible with the rest of the construct system or because its implications are intolerable. As Kelly (1955, p. 473) describes it, the construction 'may be one which the person once used extensively and which he has sought to outgrow. A kind of forgetting takes place when such a structure is rejected as incompatible'. As we have seen above, apparent incompatibilities in construing may be resolved by the use of permeable superordinate constructs, and suspension of constructions may, therefore, be particularly likely to be employed as a strategy by the individual whose superordinate constructs are relatively impermeable.

Alternative strategies for dealing with incompatibilities in construing are described in another of Kelly's diagnostic dimensions, contrasting *dilation* and *constriction*. In the former case, the person extends his or her perceptual field so as to reorganise it on a more comprehensive level. To quote Kelly (1955, p. 477) again, 'when a person moves in the direction of dilation he jumps around more from topic to topic, he lumps his childhood with his future, he sees vast ranges of events as possibly related, he participates in a wider variety of activities, and, if he is a client undergoing psychotherapy, he tends to see everything that happens to him as potentially related to his problem'. For dilation to be an effective strategy, the individual must have some super-ordinate structure which will permit the organisation of the dilated field: without this, the result of dilation may, as we shall see, be chaos.

In contrast to dilation, *constriction* involves the drawing in of the outer boundaries of the perceptual field, the person coping with incompatibilities in construing by not attending to the events which present such incompatibilities. As Kelly (1955, p. 477) puts it, 'When a person moves in the direction of constriction he tends to limit his interests, he deals with one issue at a time, he does not accept potential relationships between widely varying events, he beats out the path of his daily routine in smaller and smaller circles, and he insists that his therapist stick to a sharply delimited version of his problem'. As with dilation, while constriction may be a useful strategy, it is not without its potential problems, as we shall see in Chapter 3.

In his presentation of *dimensions of transition*, Kelly discusses the constant transitions in construing which occur as the individual attempts to anticipate an ever-changing world. Awareness of the prospect of such transitions is, in Kelly's system, associated with the experience of emotion, the particular emotion concerned being determined by the particular transition with which the person is faced. For example, a person experiences *threat* when aware of an imminent *comprehensive* change in *core structures*, those constructs which govern the individual's maintenance processes and which are central to his or her identity. Thus, Kelly argued that imminent death is generally threatening because it is perceived as likely to entail fundamental changes in core constructs. According to Landfield (1954, 1955), another person may also be threatening if he or she causes the threatened individual to experience self-uncertainty either by exemplifying how the individual once was and might all too easily become again; or by appearing to expect the individual to behave in some old way. Equally, however, the prospect of behaving in some entirely new way, perhaps as a result of therapy, may be very threatening. If the anticipated change in core constructs is *incidental* rather than comprehensive, the individual's experience will be one of fear rather than threat. One aspect of core structure is the *core role*, which consists of those fundamental constructions of the construing of other people which determine the person's characteristic ways of interacting with others. Kelly (1955, p. 503) viewed the core role as 'a part one plays as if his life depended upon it' and considered that the person's 'life actually does depend upon it'. When he or she perceives an apparent dislodgement from the core role, guilt is experienced. It should be noted, however, that this need not involve the person behaving in a way which is bad in any conventional moral sense: for example, the person who has built a core role around a construction of himself or herself as unattractive to others is likely to experience guilt on the receipt of advances from other people which indicate a loss of this role. *Anxiety* was also defined by Kelly (1955) in a somewhat unusual way, namely as 'the recognition that the events with which one is confronted lie outside the range of convenience of one's construct system' (p. 495). Culture shock, at least in its 'disintegration' stage (McCoy, 1980, 1983), provides a good example of the anxiety experienced by the individual who, faced with strange new events, finds their construct system wanting. Incompatibilities in construing will lead to anxiety if the person's superordinate constructs are not sufficiently permeable to accommodate the incompatible constructions. Invalidation of a construct will also produce anxiety if, as a result, the construct is abandoned and no alternative is available. Anxiety is therefore a sign that revision of the construct system is necessary, and in Kelly's (1955, p. 894) view a negative statement of his position concerning motivation would be that 'human behaviour is directed away from ultimate anxiety'. As we have seen in discussing the Choice Corollary, the 'positive' counterpart of this statement would be that human behaviour is directed towards a more adequate anticipation of events. The 'active elaboration of one's perceptual field' which this may involve was equated by Kelly (1955, p. 508) with *aggressiveness*. Aggression may therefore be a way of dealing with anxiety by making a succession of elaborative choices in an attempt to test out constructs which may be applied to events which previously had been largely unconstruable. Hostility, by contrast, was viewed by Kelly (1955, p. 510) in more negative terms, namely as 'the continued effort to extort validational evidence in favor of a type of social prediction which has already proved itself a failure'. If a person's approach to social experiment-ation is hostile, he or she will not revise constructions of others which appear to be invalidated but instead will attempt to make other people behave in a way which validates these constructions. Hostility may thus allow the person to avoid the realisation that his or her constructions of other people's construing have been largely invalid but, if persistent, presents the risk of a breakdown of core role structure, and hence considerable guilt, if it is no longer possible to manipulate the evidence in this way.

Kelly's construction of emotions has been elaborated by McCoy (1981), who defines 'negative emotions', such as threat, fear, guilt, and anxiety, as those which 'follow unsuccessful construing' and positive emotions as 'those which follow validation of construing' (p. 97), while she classifies hostility and aggression as behaviours associated with emotion. She has provided personal construct theory conceptualisations of various emotions in addition to those which Kelly defined. For example, love is defined as 'awareness of validation of one's core structure', happiness is 'awareness of validation of a portion of one's core structure', sadness is 'awareness of the invalidation of *implications* of a portion or all of the core structure', self-confidence is the converse of guilt in that it is defined as 'awareness of the goodness of fit of the self in one's core role structure', surprise is 'sudden awareness of a need to construe events', and anger is 'awareness of invalidation of constructs leading to hostility' (McCoy, 1977, p. 121). Although we shall employ the distinction between negative and positive emotions in later chapters, this terminology should not be taken to imply that negative emotions are necessarily undesirable and should always be avoided. Indeed, the awareness of particular transitions in construing which they represent may alert the person to take steps in order to preserve the integrity of his or her construct system.

Kelly viewed the process of transition in construing as generally being cyclical in nature, and he delineated three major cycles of construction. One, the *Circumspection-Preemption-Control Cycle* (or C-P-C Cycle for short), is concerned with decision-making, and an understanding of it requires some explanation of Kelly's distinction between *preemptive*, *constellatory*, and *propositional* constructs. A preemptive construct is one which, when applied to an event, does not allow the application of any other construct to that event. The client who, having been unable to complete a work assignment, regards himself as a failure and nothing but a failure is demonstrating preemptive construing. A constellatory construct does allow an event to which it is itself applied to be viewed in terms of other constructs but, as in the use of stereotypes, it specifies the way in which these constructs are applied to the event. If our client had been exhibiting constellatory construing, to view himself as failing in a task at work may have also required him to construe himself as stupid, incompetent, worthless, unlovable, and as characterised by a host of other undesirable attributes. A propositional construct, on the other hand, does not determine what other constructs may be applied to an event to which it is applied. Propositional construing of the difficulty at work would allow the client to continue to see himself as a talented musician, a good lover, a Christian, a heavy drinker, or in terms of any other construct in his repertoire. Such construing characterises the circumspective phase of the C-P-C Cycle, in which the person surveys the various issues in a particular field. In the next stage of the cycle, however, the person construes preemptively in order to focus on one particular issue. Finally, in the Control phase, the person decides to apply one particular pole of the preemptive construct to an event.

The *Creativity Cycle* is concerned with the development of new constructions and consists of two contrasting processes, *loose* and *tight* construing. Kelly (1955, p. 484) defined loose constructs, which characterise the first stage of the Creativity Cycle, as 'those which lead to varying predictions but which, for practical purposes, may be said to retain their identity'. When the person construes loosely, as in dreams, the assignment of elements to construct poles shifts constantly. As a result, the behaviour of the loose construer may be difficult to understand and may at times appear bizarre. While loose construing allows the generation of new ideas, if these ideas are to be tested out the person must then engage in tight construing, fixing the allocation of elements to construct poles and making unvarying predictions. However, were the person to employ only tight constructions he or she could never display any originality.

A further cycle to which Kelly (1970a) refers, and which is the essence of all construing, is the Experience Cycle. In its first stage, Anticipation, a prediction is formulated concerning a particular event. Then, in the Investment phase, the person fully involves himself or herself in this anticipation. The Encounter phase consists of an open and active experiencing of the event, and the assessment of this encounter in relation to the initial anticipation constitutes the Confirmation and Disconfirmation phase. Finally, in the Constructive Revision phase, the person engages in any reconstruing which is deemed necessary following evaluation of the evidence obtained during the encounter, setting the stage for a fresh anticipation and a further Experience Cycle.

## OPTIMAL AND DISORDERED FUNCTIONING

The completion of full Experience Cycles is the mark of an optimally functioning person. As Kelly (1977) puts it, such a person is able to 'transcend the obvious' (p. 4) in arriving at 'fresh hopes never before envisioned' (p. 9), and 'to span an optimal range of loosening and tightening without breaking up the process into disjunctive thinking' (Kelly, 1980, p. 35). In the view of Epting and Amerikaner (1980), he or she is characterised by openness to interaction with the environment, having a personal construct system the boundaries of which are relatively open but which nevertheless are sufficiently well developed, and the system sufficiently hierarchically organised, that not every experience will imply changes in self-construing. The employment of hierarchies of meaning, which has been termed 'perspectivism', will allow a capacity for propositional construing, for various alternative interpretations to be placed on events, and for the tolerance of uncertainty and anxiety. In Landfield's (1980a, p. 316) view, this is 'a flexible, but not fluid, kind of structure, a system that provides some security of meaning without closing out the impact of new experience'. It will also be conducive to social competence, defined by Reid (1979, p. 251) as 'the control and articulation of circumspection and preemption in accordance with the demands of social episodes'. Further features of optimal functioning which have been delineated by Epting and Amerikaner include an orientation towards movement into the future, a balance of processes of change and of maintenance of stability, and, in the interpersonal realm, the ability to construe the constructions of others. An additional facet of their concept of optimal functioning draws on Kelly's (1955) view that it is desirable for the individual to disperse his or her dependencies appropriately amongst a number of different people. Before leaving the subject of optimal functioning, it should be noted that Warren (1989) has recently suggested that, as descriptions of 'mental health', such concepts as perspectivism are too neutral. He considers that perspectivism is only mentally healthy when the perspectivist's view of the world is characterised by egalitarianism, namely 'seeing others as equal partners, with an absence of fear and insecurity, without a need for fusion with others, and with a general tolerance' (p. 18).

The characteristics of optimal functioning delineated above essentially represent the contrast poles of constructs which define psychological disorder from the personal construct theory perspective. Kelly's (1955, p. 831) concept of a disorder as 'any personal construction which is used repeatedly in spite of consistent invalidation' implies that disorders involve failures to complete the Experience Cycle. Elaborating on this view, R. Neimeyer (1985a) suggests that the earlier in the Experience Cycle a blockage occurs the more severe is the resulting disorder likely to be. In contrast to the perspectivism of the optimally functioning person, a disorder is likely to involve 'literalism', in which the person 'prefers a fixity of construction and a lack of exceptions to how one understands a particular event or relationship' (Landfield, 1980a, p. 291), and there is likely to be preemptive or constellatory use of constructs; or 'chaotic fragmentalism', in which the person's relative lack of hierarchical structure is associated with a fragmented, inconsistent view of the world. Chaotic fragmentalism, in Landfield's view, is very similar to, and derived from, literalism, and he describes the chaotic fragmentalist as 'a literalist "of the moment"' (p. 316). Since Landfield regards a personal construct as consisting of behavioural, feeling, and value components, the literalist may act as if these components are rigidly interrelated or, in chaotic fragmentalism, totally unrelated, and in both cases the likely result will be difficulties in self-control.

Both literalism and chaotic fragmentalism may be thought of as directed towards the same ends, namely a search for unity and certainty (Landfield, 1980a). Similarly, all disorders can be considered to represent strategies by which the individual attempts to cope with invalidation and avoid uncertainty, particularly within the social context (Button, 1983a; Winter, 1990a). While the optimally functioning person is likely to make a balanced use of such contrasting strategies as are outlined in Kelly's diagnostic constructs of tight and loose construing, constriction and dilation, and preemptive and proposi-tional thinking, psychological disorder may involve a virtually exclusive use of one particular strategy and not of the converse strategy. It is this rigid use of one strategy, rather than a more flexible and cyclical interplay of strategies, which renders a disorder 'a structure which appears to fail to accomplish its purpose' (Kelly, 1955, p. 835). Nevertheless, it should be remembered that the construction processes of the client presenting with a psychological disorder, as with those of the optimally functioning individual, represent the person's best available means of anticipating events. Rather than disorders and optimal functioning being viewed as a dichotomy, they may, therefore, be considered to represent the extremes of a continuum concerning the extent to which a construction accomplishes or fails to accomplish its purpose. The particular ways in which clients may fail to accomplish their purposes will be considered in Chapters 3 and 4, but first we shall discuss how the individual's construing may be assessed and what such assessments have indicated concerning the features of individuals who function optimally.

## SUMMARY AND CONCLUSIONS

Starting from the assumption that there are innumerable possible alternative constructions of reality, Kelly's personal construct theory provides a description of how each of us construes our world. Constructs, and their interrelationships within a hierarchically organised system, form the basis for hypotheses which guide an individual's choices and actions, these being directed towards better anticipation of events. Each individual's construct system is somewhat different, and central to constructive social interaction is the attempt to understand another person's way of construing the world.

If an individual's hypotheses, and thus the constructs from which they are derived, are invalidated, they are generally revised. The process of hypothesis formulation, testing, and revision will normally face the person with frequent transitions in construing, the awareness of which is associated with the experience of emotion, the particular emotion concerned depending upon the type of transition which is involved. Optimally, construing and its transitions proceed in cyclical fashion, and involve a flexible response to new experiences, whether these be validating or invalidating, including a balanced use of strategies in response to invalidation. However, this is not the case with psychological disorder, one of the hallmarks of which is a failure to revise constructions in response to invalidation.

# Chapter 2

# Techniques for the assessment of construing

Kelly's theory has commanded rather less attention than the techniques derived from it for the exploration of an individual's construing. These techniques, and in particular the repertory grid, may appear as welcome, concrete lifelines which are clutched at before their relationship to the parent theory is fully understood or which are employed without reference to the theory. Thus, repertory grid technique can be, and has been, used to test hypotheses derived from theories other than Kelly's, to measure personality traits, and to explore general semantic dimensions rather than personal constructs. Although such applications indicate something of the flexibility of the technique, Fransella and Bannister (1977, p. 104) note that 'the practical difficulties and dangers in grid method . . . derive from the historical tendency to divorce grid methodology from personal construct theory'. Also of concern to personal construct theorists has been the extent of the reliance on repertory grid technique in empirical work based on the theory, R. Neimeyer (1985b) having found that over 96 per cent of empirical studies published by personal construct theorists over a twenty-seven-year period employed the grid as their main measure. As he states, 'This degree of methodological constriction is remarkable and may be paralleled in the history of psychology only by Skinnerian behaviorism's reliance on the operant conditioning chamber and psychoanalysis's confidence in the "psychoanalytic method" as research paradigms that pre-empt all others' (p. 116).

In view of such caveats, some personal construct theorists (e.g. Dunnett, 1988a; Fransella, 1989a) now de-emphasise the use of repertory grid technique. However, the present chapter will focus largely on this technique, acknowledging that clinicians have found it an extremely valuable method of assessment and introducing the reader to the measures which have been employed in most of the research studies to be discussed in subsequent chapters. Firstly, however, we shall consider the other, and much less widely used, assessment technique devised by Kelly.

## THE SELF-CHARACTERISATION

Kelly (1955) viewed the self-characterisation as an application of the *credulous approach* enshrined in his 'first principle' that 'if you do not know what is wrong with a person, ask him; he may tell you' (pp. 322–3). What the person is, in fact, asked to do is to write a character sketch of himself or herself in the third person, 'just as if he were the principal character in a play . . .' and 'as it might be written by a friend who knew him very *intimately* and very *sympathetically*, perhaps better than anyone ever really could know him' (p. 323, italics in original). The various components of these instructions were carefully selected in an attempt to facilitate the production of a sketch which is not superficial but in a way which minimises the threat which this might otherwise evoke.

The self-characterisation can be thought of as a method of eliciting a subject's constructions, and in particular those which are applied to the self. As will be seen below, the constructs thus elicited may then be incorporated into a repertory grid. It is more customary, however, as described by Kelly (1955, pp. 330 ff.), to apply various methods of content analysis to the charac-ter sketch. In examining a self-characterisation, the investigator may attend not only to its principal construct dimension but also to such features of the sketch as its sequence, its organisation, and indications of repetition of themes. It may also be useful to bear in mind Kelly's view that the sketch is likely to begin on relatively safe ground but to end with rather more intimate themes.

Robert, who initially attended for therapy with his wife, Ruth, following her suicide attempt, but who was eventually persuaded to seek help on his own behalf, responded to the invitation to write a self-characterisation as follows:

> You asked me to describe myself. This I will do but I find it easiest using a series of headings. I hope this will do. There is no order of importance or priority; they just come into my head.
>
> TIMID I am indeed timid in certain circumstances. I'm afraid of people and situations, particularly when it might mean putting myself under the spotlight. I certainly avoid conflict and, more worrying, contact with people who might be cleverer, more knowledgeable, more confident etc etc than I.
>
> SHY Is it the same? Certainly, I've always been shy and still am painfully so. I curl up at the thought of going into certain situations and will do almost anything to get out of some. I've always been a 'blusher' and, knowing that my embarrassment or nervousness is obvious to everyone, and that all too often it is amusing to them, I again avoid situations that might cause them.
>
> AFRAID Again, probably the same as timid, but all too often I get scared to do or say things – perhaps because I'm shy!
>
> WEAK I'm not strong at all. Again, I tell myself this is because I'm shy, because in situations in which I am comfortable I can, gradually,

become stronger as my confidence grows. As I become more confident I suppose I become more *competent* and decisive because INDECISIVENESS is another of my faults, as is

INCONSISTENCY AND DITHERING – I keep changing my mind about decisions I've made, much to other people's fury and confusion.

SEXUALITY I'm not confident about my sexuality or even, dare I say it, my masculinity? I'm sure I'm not homosexual but why am I so prepared to live a life without sexual contact? I see it as another side of my weakness, timidity, shyness and 'tolerance' of every situation and everybody. It scares me somewhat.

STUPID I sometimes think I must be stupid! I seem unable to grasp the significance of words or deeds or situations which, to others, seem obvious.

It leads me into saying things with no evil intent (or is there, deep down, as some would suggest) and then hurting my wife deeply.

MONEY I seem to have an overriding obsession about money – or rather lack of it, and the lack of security that will follow. I know that other people are worse off than we are, but I still harbour deep worries and, I suppose, quite illogical resentments when my wife spends. Illogical because I know that she doesn't waste money – indeed she is an incredible saver of pennies and pounds and that she fully realises our situation.

Why then do I get so obsessed and does it spill over into so many other things?

*PECULIAR* PRIORITIES This is also linked to odd senses of priority. For example, I worry so much about seeming to put in a fair day's work. One of our main bones of contention recently has been my membership of X Club which requires attendance at one meeting each week.

Since I often arrive at the office after 9.30 and leave at 5.00 to collect my son from Nursery I worry about taking a few hours off for the meeting, despite knowing that my wife will collect him that day if I want. Also, this question is, I suppose, linked to Money again but why do I allow work and the *feeling* that I must *justify* a certain number of hours, blind me to the real situation?

BORED AND BORING I suppose I am bored with my job although I don't always feel it.

Also, I am a boring person and this is no doubt a by-product of many other factors.

*NO FRIENDS* I think I am reasonably pleasant and can make fair relationships with people. Yet I've lost any friends I had when at school and have made no friends since. Again, I've always avoided occasions when my shyness would be put to the test so I suppose people get fed up with issuing invitations. Also, I feel I have no conversation – lack of confidence, again.

INARTICULATE I can certainly stand up and speak before an audience.

However, what I do find difficult is being able to put into words what I feel – partly, perhaps, because I cannot always be clear in my own mind about what I feel.

UNABLE TO – understand
           perceive
           analyse
           concentrate on a solution
           concentrate on anything, really

UNRELIABLE – I've become very unreliable and
FORGETFUL
TIRED – always so tired. Even wake up tired.

Altogether, I see myself as being weak, insipid, ineffectual, boring and totally unattractive either to my wife as a husband, or to others as an acquaintance or friend. Not a very nice picture.

As for any good points. Certainly not many, if any.

Kelly (1955) regarded a useful clinical psychological test not necessarily as one that produces concrete findings but as one that suggests hypotheses which may then be tested out in therapy. Such a test is therefore more likely to provide questions than answers, and Robert's character sketch may give some indication of the type of question that a self-characterisation may pose. Why, for example, does he begin the sketch with a justification of what follows? Is this typical of his initial approach to social encounters? Why does he need to compartmentalise his description of himself? Why has he not accepted the suggestion of writing the sketch in the third person, as if by a sympathetic friend? Certainly, if written by such a friend, Robert would need no enemies! Perhaps he is threatened by the notion of having a sympathetic friend. Perhaps he cannot conceive of such a friendship, the idea of which therefore generates anxiety: it is noteworthy in this regard that one of the headings in his sketch which he has highlighted is 'NO FRIENDS'. Perhaps equally anxiety-provoking for him is to view himself in a favourable light, in contrast to his well-elaborated negative self-constructions, for example the constellatory construction suggested by the links in his sketch between timidity, shyness, fear, weakness, lack of friends, and lack of sexual contact. Does the apparent inclusion of tolerance in this cluster of constructs indicate that loss of his timidity and weakness would require him to see himself as intolerant? Does the brief mention of some positive qualities (pleasantness and ability at public speaking) towards the end of the sketch indicate areas that might usefully be elaborated in therapy? Doubtless several other questions will be suggested to the reader by Robert's self-characterisation.

The investigator who employs a self-characterisation need not be limited to a purely qualitative analysis of the results, and Jackson and Bannister (1985, pp. 70–1), using the technique with children, have derived the following scores from it:

Views of others' score: 'a count of the number of times the child refers to the view taken of him or her by other people';

Personal history and future score: 'a count of the number of times the child refers to his or her past or possible future in psychological terms';

Psychological cause and effect score: 'a count of the number of times a child makes an assertion of a cause and effect kind in psychological terms';

Psychological statements score: 'a count of the number of psychological statements of any kind made by each child';

Contradictions score: 'a count of the number of pairs of themes or general assertions which were contradictory in some way';

Insight score: 'a count of the number of statements reflecting the child's awareness of his or her own shortcomings and resulting problems'.

Interrelationships between these measures indicated that children who were 'good psychologists', in that they used a large number of psychological cause and effect statements, took account of others' views, and were 'insightful', also tended to show more contradictions in their self-characterisations. Recalling our discussion of the Fragmentation Corollary, it may be that several of the features of these children's self-characterisations reflected the ability to employ relatively permeable superordinate constructs. Whatever their precise significance, however, the fact that meaningful relationships were obtained between different self-characterisation scores indicates something of their validity, as do the relationships of these scores with popularity (Jackson, 1990a) and with repertory grid measures, the latter relationships supporting the view that 'children who have a well-developed view of themselves tend also to have a well-developed view of others' (Jackson and Bannister, 1985, p. 77).

## REPERTORY GRID TECHNIQUE

### Administration

The repertory grid, which is a derivation of Kelly's (1955) Role Construct Repertory Test (Rep Test), is essentially a structured interview procedure which allows the investigator to obtain a glimpse of the world through the 'goggles' of their subject's construct system. The first step in the procedure is normally to elicit from the subject a list of 'elements', or aspects of their experience. Although these elements are often different people, this is not necessarily the case: they may be relationships (Ryle and Lunghi, 1970), facets of the self (R. Neimeyer et al., 1983a), a particular person or relationship at different points in time (Slater, 1970; Ryle and Lipshitz, 1975), parts of the body (Feldman, 1975), situations (Parker, 1981), types of job (Smith et al.,

1978), cars (Boxer, 1981), pictures (Ravenette, 1975), models of people (Salmon, 1976), or any other items in the subject's world. However, the most common procedure is to ask the subject to supply the names of people who fit certain role titles. Kelly (1955, pp. 221–2) provided a possible twenty-four role titles for this purpose, but as many of these are highly specific or include the provision of constructs to the subject (e.g. 'a person of your own sex whom you would dislike having as a companion on a trip'; 'the most intelligent person whom you know personally'), the investigator may prefer to employ a shorter list of less well-defined role titles (e.g. 'a man and woman you like'; 'a man and woman you dislike') together with the names of people of particular significance in the subject's life (e.g. 'your mother'; 'your father'; 'your spouse'; 'your therapist'). To this list may be added various aspects of the self (e.g. 'self now'; 'how you would like to be'; 'how you expect to be in a year's time'). Although there are numerous options available to the investigator in selecting grid elements, all of the elements in a particular grid should be within the range of convenience of the construct subsystem with which the investigator is concerned: this is unlikely to be the case if elements are very heterogeneous. As Yorke (1985) notes, the elements should also be chosen with a clear purpose in mind, for if this is not so they merely produce 'statistical noise'.

Having produced a list of elements, the subject is then generally given three of these, written on cards, and asked in what important way two of them are alike and thereby different from the third, this being the 'minimum context form' of the test. If he or she says that two of the elements are 'depressed', for example, the investigator will then attempt to elicit the contrast pole of this construct by asking how the subject would describe either the third element or someone who is not depressed, the latter procedure being more likely to generate bipolar constructs (Epting et al., 1971). The procedure is then repeated with another triad of elements, usually by replacing one of the elements in the first triad with the next element in the list, and is continued until a sufficient number of constructs has been elicited. In Kelly's Self-Identification grid form, the self element is retained in every triad in an attempt to elicit self-relevant constructs, while in the Personal Role Form the subject is asked questions concerning what might happen if he or she and the other two people in the triad were, for example, to spend an evening together. Various other possible combinations of elements are suggested by Kelly (1955), but the investigator who is tempted to present a subject with every possible combination of triads of elements might do well to bear in mind research findings which suggest that very few new constructs are likely to be elicited after twenty or thirty triads have been used (Hunt, 1951).

The Repertory Test is an extremely flexible procedure, and there is nothing sacrosanct about the triadic method of construct elicitation. With less intelligent subjects, or with children, a dyadic method (Salmon, 1976) may be found to be more manageable, and failing this constructs may also be elicited by asking the subject to describe each element in turn (Spindler Barton *et al.*, 1976), or even by mime in the case of deaf subjects (Baillie-Grohman, 1975). In dysarthric or dysphasic individuals, methods may be used in which, for example, the client sorts pictures of people into piles and the investigator suggests in a propositional way the constructs which may underlie the sorts (Dalton, 1988a). If the investigator's interest is in non-verbal construing, subjects may be provided with a set of materials (e.g. cards of different designs, colours, or textures) with which they can symbolise their discriminations between elements, as in R. Neimeyer's (1981) Tacit Construing Technique. If the investigator wishes to elicit superordinate constructs, Hinkle's (1965) laddering procedure may be employed. Here, the subject is first asked to which pole of a particular construct they would prefer to be assigned, and is then asked why. The reason for their preference is assumed to be a construct more superordinate than the first, and by repeating the laddering process further levels of superordinacy may be arrived at. Alternatively, if the investigator is interested in the subject's subordinate constructs, a procedure of 'downward laddering' may be adopted, the subject being asked for each construct pole how they would know that this characteristic applied to a person. A somewhat similar approach is used in Landfield's (1971) pyramid technique, in which the subject is first asked, for example, to think of the person whose company they most enjoy and to describe a characteristic of this person, as well as its opposite. They are then asked what kinds of people are described by the two construct poles thus elicited, and what characteristics describe people who are the opposite of these. The procedure may then be repeated with this new set of constructs. As Epting (1984, p. 182) remarks, this may be a particularly useful technique 'with clients who are dealing with generalizations and need to have specific concrete implications to talk about'. Constructs may also be elicited by asking an individual to fill in missing words in a passage (Karastergiou-Katsika and Watson, 1982), or by employing the various structured interview formats developed by Leitner. One such method (Leitner, 1981a) seeks to elicit the emotional, behavioural, and evaluational implications of an individual's constructs by taking the positively rated pole of each construct and asking such questions as what a person characterised by this pole might feel, what a person who feels this way might do, and why it is good to feel like this. Leitner (1985a) also describes how core constructs may be elicited by asking an individual about their earliest memories, what should be written on their tombstone, their constructions of God, significant events in their life, vivid dreams, or repetitive fantasies. Procter and Parry (1978) have examined the biographical antecedents of a subject's constructs by first eliciting a superordinate construct by laddering, and then asking the subject to think of the time in their life when they began to use this construct and to indicate from what earlier construct it evolved. The evolution of this second construct may then be traced in similar fashion. Working with children, Ravenette (1977, 1980) has also employed a number of construct elicitation techniques which may be used in their own right or as the initial stage in a grid. These include the following:

1) the child is asked to complete various sentences, such as 'The trouble with most boys is . . .' and 'They are like that because . . .';
2) the child is shown pictures of situations at school and asked such questions as who might be troubled and why;
3) the child is asked to draw pictures of times when he or she was troubled, to describe a child who would not have been troubled in such situations, to imagine when this child would have been upset, and to say when he or she was like this child;
4) in the 'Portrait Gallery' technique, the child is asked to describe and contrast drawings of a sad and happy face, to fill in other blank faces to depict various feeling states, and to say three things about each of these faces;
5) in a technique called 'the good and bad of it', which is similar to approaches employed with adult clients (Tschudi, 1977), the child is asked to say something which is bad about himself or herself and a preferred state, and then to indicate something good and bad about each of these.

It should finally be noted that formal procedures are not essential for the elicitation of a subject's constructs, which may simply be extracted from a transcript of a conversation with the individual or from written material which they have produced, such as a self-characterisation. There may be some difficulty in identifying what constitutes a construct in such material, but Woolfson (1979) has found that the most common criterion used by personal construct theorists in carrying out this task is that a judgement or contrast is being made by the subject.

Although the procedures described above are mostly designed to elicit a representative sample of the subject's constructs with minimal interference by the investigator, certain types of construct may require further questioning, particularly if the grid form of the Repertory Test is being used (see Kelly, 1955, pp. 222–3). These are the following:

a) identical constructs to those previously elicited: If the subject gives a construct which appears very similar (perhaps having the same emergent pole but a different contrast pole) to one which has already been elicited, the investigator should ask whether the two constructs do, in fact, have the same meaning for the subject. If they do, one of the constructs may be excluded from the next stage of the grid procedure.
b) situational or superficial constructs: If the client says, for example, that two elements 'live in the same town' or 'have the same colour hair', the investigator might ask for a more important similarity between them (but always bearing in mind that what is superficial for the investigator may not be superficial for the client).
c) excessively permeable constructs: Although Kelly (1955) states, following

the work of Hunt, that a similar procedure may be adopted with such constructs, it is unclear why excessive permeability per se should result in the exclusion of a construct. However, those highly permeable constructs (e.g. 'male–female'; 'married–single') which can be applied to all the elements, but only in a dichotomous fashion, cannot be employed in grid forms in which the elements are rated or ranked on the constructs (see below).

d) excessively impermeable constructs: Further questioning by the investigator is also called for if the construct elicited can be applied to very few of the elements (e.g. 'Zen Buddhist–Theravada Buddhist').

e) vague constructs: A response such as 'they're all right' would normally prompt the investigator to ask in what way this is so.

f) constructs concerning the relationships between elements: An alternative construct may also be requested if the subject's distinction between the elements is, for example, that two are members of the same family while the other is not.

g) 'peculiar' constructs: If, as Resnick and Landfield (1961) have described, the subject provides a very unusual contrast pole to a construct (e.g. 'happy–Norwegian'), it may be that what has been elicited consists of 'the emergent poles of two conflated "logical oppositions" ' (Yorke, 1985, p. 389). Further questioning may unravel the two constructs concerned, although it should always be borne in mind that an opposition which appears illogical to the investigator may be very meaningful for the subject.

If the investigator is only interested in the content of the subject's constructs, the assessment procedure may be terminated following the elicitation phase, as in Kelly's original Role Construct Repertory Test. However, the investigator who wishes, for example, to examine the structure of the subject's construct system as well as its content is likely to proceed with the grid form of this test, the next stage of which is for the subject to sort all their elements in terms of all the constructs which have been elicited. Three basic types of sorting method may be used. The subject may be asked to assign each element to one or other (or neither) pole of each of their constructs. The split-half form of this method (Bannister and Mair, 1968) requires that half of the elements are allotted to each pole of a particular construct, thus allowing the exclusion of very 'lopsided' constructs but imposing a degree of constraint on the subject's responses which may be considered unacceptable. Alternatively, and more commonly, the subject may be asked to rate or to rank the elements in terms of each construct. Advantages of the bipolar and the rating grid are that they both allow the subject the freedom of assigning more than one element to the same point on a construct dimension; and the possibility of not applying a construct to a particular element (or, in the case of the rating grid, giving a mid-point rating) if the element is beyond the construct's range of convenience.

Finally, although it is more within the spirit of Kelly's theory, and of his emphasis on the personal nature of the individual's construing, to employ a grid in which the constructs and elements are elicited from, rather than supplied to, the subject, the latter option has advantages in some circumstances. It may, for example, facilitate the making of group comparisons (e.g. Bannister, 1960; Ryle and Breen, 1972a, 1972b), or ensure that the subject's grid taps their construing of some particular area in which the investigator is interested. Various compromise solutions are possible for the investigator who has such concerns but also wishes to maximise the personal meaningfulness to the subject of the constructs and elements employed. Thus, one option is to elicit constructs and elements from the population to which the subjects belong, and then to pool a selection of these in a standard grid (e.g. Winter and Gournay, 1987). Another is to employ a grid in which some of the elements and constructs are elicited and some supplied. The investigator who supplies 'constructs' to the subject should remember, however, that what are supplied are construct labels rather than constructs, and they may carry a very different meaning for the subject than they do for the investigator. We shall return below to the question of whether to elicit or supply in order to discuss the effects which such variations in procedure may have on the results obtained from a grid.

## Alternative grid procedures

Apart from variations in the nature of the constructs or elements employed, or in the method used to sort the elements in terms of the constructs, some rather more radical departures from 'conventional' grid procedure are possible.

One of these, suggested by Kelly (1955), is the Situational Resources Repertory Test, now more commonly referred to as the Dependency Grid. In this procedure, the subject is presented with a list of difficult situations (e.g., in Kelly's original version of the test, 'The time when things seemed to be going against you – when your luck was particularly bad'; 'The time when you felt most ashamed of yourself'; 'The time when you felt jealous of someone's affection'; etc.) and asked to which of a list of people, filling various role titles, he or she might have turned for help in each situation had they been available. The resulting matrix of ticks and blanks provides, for example, an indication of whether or not the person exhibits 'undistributed dependency', turning to the same people in every situation. A quantitative method of assessing the degree of dispersion of dependency in such a grid has been proposed by Walker et al. (1988). Other variations on the procedure are asking the subject who turns to them for help in each difficult situation (Hinkle, 1965), asking who the subject would turn to if the situations were to occur now (Fransella and Bannister, 1977), and following completion of the grid asking why they would prefer to turn to certain people rather than others in each situation (Beail and Beail, 1985).

An alternative grid method which has been shown to be of value in the clinical setting (e.g. Mair and Crisp, 1968) is Hinkle's (1965) implications grid, in which the subject is questioned directly concerning the implications of their constructs (as opposed to the more indirect assessment of such implications which can be derived from a conventional repertory grid). Hinkle's original procedure was, for each construct elicited from the subject, to ask 'if you woke up one morning and realized that you were best described by one side of this construct while the day before you had been best described by the opposite side – if you realized that you were changed in this *one* respect – what other constructs of these ... remaining ones would be *likely* to be changed by a change in yourself on this one construct alone?' (p. 37, italics in original). The subject's responses are recorded in a grid matrix in which there is both a row and a column for each construct, a tick being inserted in a particular square if a change on the construct in the row in which the square is situated implies a change in the construct in the column concerned.

Derivations of implications grid procedure have been proposed. One, which was also developed by Hinkle (1965), is the resistance-to-change grid. This involves first asking the subject to which pole of each of their constructs he or she would prefer to assign the self. Each construct is then paired with every other and the subject is asked on which of the two constructs they would rather shift from the preferred to non-preferred pole if they had to make such a shift on one of the two. A resistance-to-change score may then be calculated for each construct by counting the number of times on which the subject would prefer not to shift their self-allocation on it. Another alternative, which has the dual advantages of presenting the subject with a simpler task than does Hinkle's methods and allowing the identification of implicative dilemmas in the subject's construing, is Fransella's (1972) bi-polar implications grid. Here, each pole of each of the constructs elicited from the subject is written on a card and, taking each card in turn, the subject is asked if all they knew about a person was that they were described by the characteristic written on the card, which of the other descriptions on the cards would also be expected to characterise the person. In this case, the grid matrix consists of a row and column for each construct pole, and a tick is inserted in a particular cell if a person characterised by the construct pole defining the row concerned is likely to be described by the pole in the column concerned.

It should be noted that, although in their original form the Situational Resources Repertory Test and implications grid require responses of the yes/no variety, it is quite possible to employ a rating scale in both these procedures, the subject indicating to what extent a particular person would be turned to for help in a particular situation or to what extent one construct implies another (e.g. Honess, 1978). The range of possibilities for analysis of the subject's responses would thus be increased.

Several other variations on grid procedure have been developed to explore particular domains of construing, and three of these will now be considered:

the Threat Index, the Parent Role Repertory Test, and the Interpersonal Discrimination Task. The Threat Index (Krieger *et al.*, 1974) is a method specifically developed to explore the degree to which an individual is threatened by their own mortality. It is based on the assumption, derived from Kelly's view of threat (see p. 11), that death is likely to be threatening if a considerable degree of reorganisation would be required to subsume it and the self under the same poles of the person's constructs. In the original form of the Index, the subject was presented with successive triads each including the element 'death' and two situations involving death (e.g. 'your closest friend is killed in a plane crash'; 'a homicidal maniac is on the loose and has already viciously mutilated six people in your community'). Constructs were elicited from the triads in the usual manner, and were then used as the basis for 'laddering' more superordinate constructs. Thirty constructs were obtained, and the subject's preferred pole of each recorded, together with the pole to which the elements 'self' and 'your own death' were assigned. Alternative versions of the procedure (Krieger *et al.*, 1979) involve placing the self, preferred self, and death elements on a set of provided constructs (e.g. 'predictable–random'; 'empty–meaningful').

The Parent Role Repertory Test (Mancuso and Handin, 1980) requires the subject to rate each of a series of statements concerning child rearing (e.g. 'Always try to tell a kid what is going to happen before it happens') from the perspective of each of a set of supplied parent roles (e.g. 'Joe Hooker is the kind of parent who doesn't always try hard to get his children to do what they are told to do. He's kind of easy on them'). It has been employed to evaluate the constructions of parents whose children present with developmental problems (see p. 305). Carr's (1980) Interpersonal Discrimination Task is a simplified grid procedure the focus of which is apparent in its title. The subject is first asked to name three people outside the family whom he or she likes and three he or she dislikes. The next requirement is to identify three characteristics of the self which he or she likes and three which are disliked, together with the opposites of these characteristics. Finally, for each characteristic, the subject divides a rectangle into boxes to represent the discriminations between the six others and the self (see Figure 2.1).

## Analysis

The end-product of the grid procedure will be a matrix of ticks and blanks or of numbers, as in Figure 2.2.

Various methods of analysis may be applied to such matrices. The most straightforward, and the only analyses possible if the grid form of Repertory Test is not used, involve examining the nature of the constructs and elements elicited. Kelly (1955) noted, for example, that the permeability of a construct may be indicated by its repetition with different triads, while ambivalence may be reflected by two or more constructs sharing the same contrast pole. A

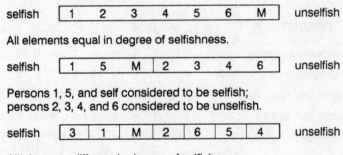

selfish | 1   2   3   4   5   6   M | unselfish

All elements equal in degree of selfishness.

selfish | 1   5   M   2   3   4   6 | unselfish

Persons 1, 5, and self considered to be selfish;
persons 2, 3, 4, and 6 considered to be unselfish.

selfish | 3 | 1 | M | 2 | 6 | 5 | 4 | unselfish

All elements different in degree of selfishness.

*Figure 2.1* Examples of responses on Interpersonal Discrimination Task
(Numbers represent people; M = self)

content analysis of the constructs elicited may also be carried out, using one
of the several systems of construct categorisation which are now available.
Perhaps the most commonly employed of these is Landfield's (1971,
pp. 166–75) classification of constructs (or, more precisely, construct poles)
in terms of the following twenty-two categories, each of which he illustrated
with numerous examples:

1 Social Interaction (Active or Inactive): 'Any statement in which face-to-
face, ongoing, continuing interaction with others is (clearly) indicated.'
2 Forcefulness (High or Low): 'Any statement denoting energy, overt
expressiveness, persistence, intensity, or the opposite.'
3 Organisation (High or Low): 'Any statement denoting either the state of
or process of structuring, planning and organizing, or the opposite. The
statement should indicate that a person either has or lacks a general trait
of structuring, organizing, and planning ability, or can be described as
organized, structured, disorganized, or unstructured.'
4 Self-Sufficiency (High or Low): 'Any statement denoting independence,
initiative, confidence, and ability to solve one's own problems or the
opposite.'
5 Status (High or Low): 'Any statement wherein references are made to
either status striving or to high prestige status symbols, or to a lack of status
striving or to low prestige status symbols.'
6 Factual Description: 'A characteristic so described that most observers
could agree that it is factual. A fact would be a characteristic not open to
question.'
7 Intellective (High or Low): 'Any statement denoting intelligence or
intellectual pursuits, or the opposite.'
8 Self-Reference: 'Any statement in which the person taking the test refers
directly to himself.'

ELEMENTS

| CONSTRUCTS | A | B | C | D | E | F | G | H | I | J |
|---|---|---|---|---|---|---|---|---|---|---|
| 1  depressed–happy | 7 | 2 | 5 | 5 | 1 | 1 | 6 | 3 | 2 | 3 |
| 2  successful–unsuccessful | 1 | 7 | 1 | 2 | 6 | 6 | 1 | 5 | 7 | 5 |
| 3  feminine–masculine | 6 | 1 | 7 | 6 | 5 | 2 | 7 | 2 | 1 | 3 |
| 4  unselfish–selfish | 7 | 2 | 6 | 6 | 7 | 2 | 7 | 3 | 1 | 2 |
| 5  honest–dishonest | 6 | 1 | 6 | 7 | 7 | 2 | 7 | 2 | 1 | 2 |
| 6  conservative–radical | 4 | 5 | 5 | 5 | 4 | 5 | 4 | 5 | 6 | 5 |
| 7  introverted–extraverted | 7 | 1 | 5 | 6 | 3 | 1 | 6 | 2 | 1 | 2 |
| 8  insecure–secure | 6 | 2 | 5 | 5 | 2 | 2 | 5 | 3 | 2 | 2 |
| 9  artistic–unartistic | 5 | 1 | 4 | 7 | 6 | 2 | 7 | 2 | 1 | 3 |
| 10  intelligent–stupid | 2 | 5 | 4 | 6 | 7 | 6 | 7 | 4 | 3 | 2 |

*Figure 2.2* Example of a completed repertory grid

Elements:    A = Self;   B = Father;   C = Mother;   D = Man I like;
E = Ideal self;   F = Husband;   G = Woman I like;   H = Brother;
I = Man I dislike;   J = Woman I dislike
(elements rated on a 7-point scale, with a high rating indicating that the left-hand pole of a construct describes the element concerned)

9 Imagination (High* or Low): 'Any statement denoting subjective activity which is supplemental to or divorced from reality, or its opposite.'

10 Alternatives (Multiple Description, Inferable Alternatives,* Open to Alternatives,* or Closed to Alternatives): 'The subject employs (a) more than one description, (b) a qualified description suggesting the possibility of other descriptions, (c) a description suggesting a strong openness, or (d) a description suggesting little receptivity to new alternatives.'

11 Sexual: 'Any direct reference to sexual behavior or implicit sexual behavior.'

12 Morality (High or Low): 'Any statement denoting religious or moral values.'

13 External Appearance: 'Any statement describing a person's appearance which may be either more objective or more subjective.'

14 Emotional Arousal: 'Any statement denoting a transient or chronic readiness to react with stronger feelings such as anger, anxiety, disgust, enthusiasm, fearfulness, grief, joy, nervousness, surprise, yearning, etc.'

15 Diffuse Generalisation*

16 Egoism (High or Low):* 'Any statement denoting self importance. High egoism may be either constructive or destructive and scoring will be more liberal – not debating whether, e.g., the conceited person really is confident.'

17 Tenderness (High or Low): 'Any statement denoting susceptibility to softer feelings towards others such as love, compassion, gentleness, kindness, considerateness, or the opposite.'

18 Time Orientation (Past, Future, or Present):[*] 'Any statement denoting a state of mind which strongly implies an individual's future orientation and expectancy, or a past orientation and expectancy. Some descriptions may imply both orientations and cannot be scored.'

19 Involvement (High or Low): 'Any statement denoting a persistent effort toward that which an individual finds more generally and internally meaningful or, restated, a high or low internal and more total commitment or dedication to and strong pursuit of an interest, occupation, way of life, philosophy, or simply the state of commitment, dedication, or lack of such.'

20 Comparatives[*]

21 Extreme Qualifiers: 'Any adjective, adverb, or phrase which makes a description extreme or suggests a high degree of the characteristic.'

22 Humour: 'Any statement specifically denoting either the ability or inability to perceive, appreciate, or express that which is funny, amusing, or ludicrous.'

Although Landfield found certain of his categories (which I have indicated by an asterisk in the above list) to have a low inter-rater reliability, and excluded them from his final system, the inclusion of these categories does permit a more comprehensive classification to be carried out. He also suggested the use of certain combined categories, viz. 'High Dogmatism' (Closed to Alternatives and High Egoism); 'High Intensity' (High Forcefulness, Emotional Arousal, and Extreme Qualifiers); 'High Structure' (High Organisation and High Involvement); 'High Social Orientation' (Active Social Interaction and High Tenderness); and 'High Concreteness' (Factual Description, Low Imagination, and External Appearance). As will be seen in subsequent chapters, his method has been used in the clinical sphere to investigate such issues as the constructs typically employed by particular client groups (Fransella, 1972; Landfield, 1976; Howells, 1979; Horley, 1988), and those which may be predictive of response to psychotherapy (Landfield, 1977; Caine et al., 1981, 1986).

The other classification systems which have been developed for the content analysis of constructs (e.g. Bieri et al., 1958; Little, 1968; Duck, 1973a) generally employ a more limited range of categories, such as 'psychological', defined by Duck (1973a, p. 84) as 'describing a character, personality or cognitive attribute of an individual'; 'role', which he defines as describing 'habitual activities or roles'; 'interaction'; and 'other'. A system has also been designed specifically to classify constructs which have been applied to situations relating to death (R. Neimeyer et al., 1984). An alternative means of assessing construct content, which has been employed by Soldz (1989), is to include in a grid supplied constructs which represent robust factors in people's ratings of others. The content of constructs elicited from an individual is then classified on the basis of their relationships with these 'marker' constructs. As Villegas *et al.* (1986) have demonstrated, constructs may also be categorised according to 'formal', rather than purely content-based, criteria, and Walker *et al.* (1988) have developed methods of differentiating constructs in terms of two formal properties, namely permeability and preemptiveness.

As well as indicating the nature of the constructs employed by a subject, visual inspection of the grid matrix may also reveal interesting features of the elements elicited (consider, for example, the subject who is unable to think of anyone who fits the role title 'a person I dislike') and of the way in which they are construed. In the case of June's grid, presented in Figure 2.2, it can be seen that the self is construed in such apparently unfavourable terms as 'unsuccessful' and 'depressed'. Information such as this, which is at a relatively high level of cognitive awareness, may normally be obtainable from a straight-forward interview, without recourse to a complex, time-consuming procedure such as the repertory grid. The grid may, however, also provide access to aspects of the client's construing at lower levels of awareness, such as may be revealed in interrelationships between the subject's elements and/or constructs. It is apparent from Figure 2.2, for example, that June construes her husband and father in very similar terms, a fact of which she may or may not be aware. Considering now interrelationships between constructs, it can be seen that she tends to construe 'feminine' people as 'unsuccessful': the implication that if she were to be successful she would have to construe herself as masculine may reflect a major dilemma for her. A similar dilemma is suggested by her construal of 'depressed' people as 'honest' and 'unselfish'.

Although 'eyeballing' a grid in this way may reveal some significant aspects of the subject's view of the world, a more precise assessment of their construing will require the investigator to have recourse to a more detailed method of quantitative analysis. Hand methods of repertory grid analysis have been devised by Kelly (1955) and others (e.g. Bannister, 1965a; Fransella, 1972; Ravenette, 1975), but have now largely been superseded by computer-ised procedures. However, the clinician who does not have easy access to a computer may, if they are using Kelly's original grid method, obtain an indication of the interrelationships between the constructs or elements in a grid by counting the number of matches between ticks and blanks in any pair of grid rows or columns. A chance level of matching can be assumed to be half of the total possible number of matches (which, if the match between two constructs is being assessed, will be half the number of elements in the grid; or, for the match between two elements, will be half the number of constructs), and, as Fransella and Bannister (1977) indicate, it is possible to calculate the probability of obtaining a particular matching score in either a conventional repertory grid or an implications grid. 'Statistically more precise' methods of assessing relationships in 'dichotomous' grids, such as the phi correlation coefficient, are discussed by Beail (1985a, p. 12). As Kelly (1955) indicated, such a grid may also be subjected to a non-parametric factor analysis. If a rating scale has been employed in the grid, a 'difference score' between two constructs can be calculated by subtracting the rating of each element on one construct from that on the other and summing these differences regardless of sign (Bannister and Mair, 1968). Alternatively, relationships between pairs of constructs may be assessed by calculating Pearson correlation coefficients between the two sets of ratings concerned, whereas if the investigator is employing a grid in which the elements are ranked Spearman correlation coefficients may be calculated. Summing the squares of all the coefficients thus obtained for a particular construct will provide a measure of the variance in the grid accounted for by that construct, and Bannister (1965a) has demonstrated that these squared relationship scores may be used to provide a plot of the construct relationships in a grid, one axis of this plot representing the construct accounting for the most variance and the other the construct which, of those not significantly correlated with the first, accounts for the highest variance. The other constructs are then plotted in terms of their relationship scores with these two constructs.

A computer program which carries out this procedure has now been produced (Higginbotham and Bannister, 1983). However, it does not provide as much information as do some other computer packages for grid analysis. Perhaps the most commonly employed of these, at least in Europe, is Slater's (1977) Grid Analysis Package. The cornerstone of this package is INGRID (Slater, 1972), a program which performs a principal component analysis of an individual grid, and, in view of its widespread availability, frequent use in the clinical setting, and the fact that several of the measures derived from it are similar to those produced by other packages, its output will now be described in some detail.

If a rating scale has been employed in the grid, the mean rating on each construct is first listed, followed by the variation about the mean and this variation expressed as a percentage of the total variation about all construct means. From the mean rating, the investigator may observe whether a particular construct is being employed in a lopsided manner, most elements being assigned to only one of its poles. As will be seen in Chapters 3 and 4, such lopsidedness in construct use may have important clinical implications. The variation about a construct mean is a measure of the extent to which the construct discriminates between elements, and therefore of its usefulness. It has been employed by some authors as a measure of superordinacy (Bannister and Salmon, 1967), although it should be noted that if only the extreme points of a construct scale are used there will be a high variation about the construct mean although the construct does not reveal subtle differences between the elements.

A measure of bias is then provided, indicating the extent of deviation of construct means from the midpoint of the rating scale; as is a measure of the variability of element assignment on the scale. This is followed by a matrix of construct intercorrelations, which of course can range from a maximum of + 1.0 to a minimum of –1.0, and which are assumed to reflect the psychological relationships between the subject's constructs. For example, the correlation of –0.90 obtained between the constructs 'feminine–masculine' and 'successful–unsuccessful' in June's grid (Figure 2.2) when it was analysed by INGRID indicated that for her success implied lack of femininity. As well as providing correlation coefficients, INGRID also calculates the angular distance between each pair of constructs, a measure with scores, which are inversely proportional to correlations, ranging from 0 to 180 degrees. This measure may be of value to the investigator who wishes, for example, to average a number of construct relationship scores, this not being permissible with untransformed correlation coefficients.

There follows a list of the sum of squares accounted for by each element, and of these scores presented as percentages of the total sum of squares. These measures essentially indicate the meaningfulness of each element for the subject, a high score suggesting that the element concerned is salient whereas a low score implies that it has been rated near the midpoint on most constructs. The analysis of elements continues with a table of the distances between each pair of elements, using an individualised scale on which a distance of 0 indicates that the two elements are construed in identical fashion, and in which distances rarely exceed 2. A distance of 1 between two elements would be expected by chance. The similarity in June's construing of her husband and father was indicated by a distance between them of 0.24, while the distance of 1.18 between her self and ideal self demonstrated that these two elements were perceived by her as somewhat dissimilar.

The results of a principal component analysis of the grid are then presented, commencing with the percentage of variance accounted for by each of the components extracted. The higher the percentage of variance accounted for by the first principal component, the more tightly organised and unidimensional is the individual's construing. That this was June's style of construing was indicated by the fact that 73.73 per cent of the variance in her grid could be accounted for by the first principal component. In a sample of normal subjects, the mean percentage of variance of the first component in a grid consisting of sixteen elements and sixteen constructs was found to be 39.4 (Ryle and Breen, 1972b), but it should be remembered that the smaller the grid the higher this percentage would be expected to be.

A table of the vectors and loadings of each element and construct on each component is next provided, and by plotting the loadings on the first two components a visual representation of the subject's construct system may be obtained. Although the position of each element is defined by the value of the two loadings concerned, it should be remembered that constructs are dimensions rather than points. Each construct is therefore displayed by drawing a straight line through the origin of the graph and the point corresponding to the construct's loadings on the two components, this latter point indicating the 'high rating' pole of the construct (e.g. the pole which has been defined by ratings of 7 on a 7–point scale). Slater (1977) suggests that the line thus drawn is extrapolated to the circumference of a circle with its centre at the origin and a convenient radius extending beyond the positions of the elements. The poles of the constructs may then be labelled, as in the plot of June's grid in Figure 2.3 (based on the element and construct loadings presented in Table 2.1), at the points where the lines representing the constructs intersect the circumference of the circle. For the sake of clarity, this circle and the lines representing constructs are not shown in Figure 2.3. It should be remembered that the plot does not provide an entirely accurate picture of the subject's construct system as, unless a three-dimensional plot is attempted, it is based only on the percentage of variation accounted for by the first two components in the grid. It can, nevertheless, provide a useful indication of interesting features of the grid which can then be verified by checking the relevant scores in the output. In June's case, for example, the similarity in her construing of her husband and father is evident from their proximity in the plot of her grid (see Figure 2.3). In general, elements in

Table 2.1 Loadings of elements and constructs on first two principal components from INGRID analysis of June's grid

| | COMPONENTS | |
| ELEMENTS | 1 | 2 |
| --- | --- | --- |
| Self | −1.09 | 0.58 |
| Father | 0.95 | −0.10 |
| Mother | −0.68 | 0.32 |
| Man I like | −0.85 | −0.05 |
| Ideal self | −0.23 | −0.93 |
| Husband | 0.80 | −0.31 |
| Woman I like | −1.19 | −0.26 |
| Brother | 0.53 | 0.14 |
| Man I dislike | 1.17 | 0.31 |
| Woman I dislike | 0.58 | 0.30 |
| CONSTRUCTS | | |
| depressed – happy | −0.82 | 0.52 |
| successful – unsuccessful | 0.92 | −0.32 |
| feminine – masculine | −0.97 | −0.03 |
| unselfish – selfish | −0.95 | −0.23 |
| honest – dishonest | −0.94 | −0.27 |
| conservative – radical | 0.71 | 0.38 |
| introverted – extraverted | −0.97 | 0.19 |
| insecure – secure | −0.89 | 0.38 |
| artistic – unartistic | −0.90 | −0.31 |
| intelligent – stupid | −0.23 | −0.87 |

|                                          |                                        |
| ---------------------------------------- | -------------------------------------- |
|       Cpt. 2 | STUPID                                 |
| DEPRESSED                                |                    CONSERVATIVE        |
|                                          |                                        |
| INSECURE                                 |                                        |
| UNSUCCESSFUL                             |                    UNARTISTIC          |
|     Self             |                    DISHONEST           |
| INTROVERTED                              |                    SELFISH             |
|     Mother   | Woman   Man I            |
|                                  | I dislike  dislike            |
|                                  |                                        |
|                                  | Brother                                |
|                                  |     MASCULINE       |

|                                          |                                  |
| ---------------------------------------- | -------------------------------- |
| FEMININE   Man I like     |            Cpt. 1                 |
|                                          | Father                           |
|   Woman I like                 |                                  |
|                                          |                                  |
|                                          | Husband                          |
| UNSELFISH                                |            EXTRAVERTED           |
| HONEST                                   |                                  |
| ARTISTIC                                 |            SUCCESSFUL            |
|     Ideal            |            SECURE               |
|     Self             |                                  |
| RADICAL                                  |            HAPPY                |
|    INTELLIGENT            |                                  |

*Figure 2.3* Plot of elements in construct space from June's grid

opposing quadrants of a subject's grid can be considered to be the most dissimilar, while those furthest removed from the origin are the most extremely perceived.

The INGRID output concludes with measures of the relationships between constructs and elements. These are first expressed as cosines, which are equivalent to correlations and thus have a range from −1.0 to +1.0, and then as degrees, which are inversely proportional to cosines. The investigator who wishes to assess how particular elements are construed by the subject may, of course, simply examine the raw data contained in the unanalysed grid, but it is sometimes argued that the more indirect level of analysis involved in the INGRID measures of relationships in component space may allow access to constructions of a lower level of awareness than are revealed in the subject's actual ratings or rankings.

As well as INGRID, the Grid Analysis Package includes programs for the analysis of pairs, and of groups, of grids. DELTA (Slater, 1968), for example, compares two grids employing the same elements and constructs. When a rating scale has been used, the DELTA output initially lists changes in the mean ratings on each construct from one grid to the next; the variation due to the differential changes; correlations between element ratings on each construct in the two grids; the results of a t-test of the significance of change in ratings on each construct; and a general correlation reflecting the overall similarity of the grids. There follows a matrix of correlations between constructs, indicating whether changes in the application of particular pairs of constructs to the elements have been in the same or opposite directions; and a list of the sum of squares of each element, high values of which reveal dissimilarity in the construing of the elements concerned in the two grids. A table of distances between elements demonstrates the degree of similarity of the changes in construing of each pair of elements, the higher the distance the more divergent the changes. Finally, a principal component analysis of change is carried out, the loadings of elements and constructs on its major components indicating the degree to which they contribute to change in the grids. If, for example, a plot of elements in construct space is derived from this analysis, the distance of an element from the origin will suggest the degree of change in construing of this element.

The DELTA program may therefore be of value to the clinician or researcher who wishes to examine differences between a client's pre- and post-treatment grids or between the grids of members of a dyad (e.g. client and therapist or husband and wife). If the investigator has collected a group of grids with the same elements and constructs, the SERIES program in the Grid Analysis Package (Slater, 1977) may be employed to provide a consensus grid, the grid of the typical member of the group, which may itself be subjected to an INGRID analysis. Further analysis by the SEQUEL program allows each individual grid in the group to be compared with the consensus grid, and provides measures of the degree of agreement in the group's use of particular constructs or perceptions of particular elements. If a pair or group of grids employ the same constructs but different elements, the COIN or ADELA programs may be used to compare them, while PREFAN allows the comparison of grids with the same elements but different constructs.

There has been a burgeoning interest in the development of computer packages for grid analysis since Slater produced his programs. Amongst the principal alternative methods which have appeared are those developed by Thomas and his colleagues (e.g. Thomas and Harri-Augstein, 1985), whose primary concern has been less the derivation of grid scores than the facilitation of 'self-organised learning' and of 'learning conversations' by, for example, encouraging grid users to reflect on their construing or on its similarities and differences with that of others. Their approach is well described by Shaw (1980, p. 14) in the following passage:

> Used as a tool within a physical science paradigm, the grid is no more than a test in the same way as a personality inventory or an attitude scale is a test. That is, the results are collated by the psychologist and interpreted by him without reference to the meaning system of the subject, who then feels

distanced from the content and less inclined to commitment. Much of the use of grids in psychotherapy and educational research has fallen into this category. However, used as a tool within a conversational paradigm, the elicitee can use the grid to become more aware of links he is implicitly making in his interaction with the world, so becoming more deeply involved and committed to the content of the grid in the elicitation stage.

To achieve such results, their package includes interactive programs such as PEGASUS which allow the elicitation, and immediate feedback of results, of a grid by computer; while FOCUS (Thomas, 1976), which carries out a cluster analysis, provides a clear visual representation, in the form of tree diagrams, of the relationships between clusters of elements or of constructs. The 'Exchange Grid' procedure (Mendoza, 1985) is designed to promote a 'heuristic encounter' (p. 173) between two individuals by requiring them each to construe the same elements using their own, and then the other's, constructs, the computer providing them with feedback on their level of agreement. Various other programs developed by this group provide additional comparative analyses of pairs or groups of grids: for example, MINUS and CORE (Shaw, 1980) compare two grids employing the same elements and constructs, CORE being an interactive program which 'allows people to uncover areas of shared understanding and agreement in a structured manner' (Shaw, 1980, p. 149). SOCIOGRIDS (Thomas, 1979) derives a 'mode grid' from a group of grids and 'socionets' indicating the pattern of commonality of construing in the group; while ARGUS elicits from an individual a set of grids, each from the viewpoint of one of the elements in the grids (these being, for example, the different roles which the person adopts or various significant people in their life), which may then be submitted to SOCIOGRIDS analysis. Used in this way, Shaw (1980, p. 100) regards ARGUS as allowing the individual to develop conversations between the various 'personalities in his head', which, following Pask (1975), she terms 'P- Individuals'.

To date, the programs produced by Thomas and his co-workers have been used more in educational and industrial settings than in clinical. However, their interactive packages suggest the, perhaps somewhat alarming, prospect of 'grid therapy' by computer. For example, had June's grid been elicited by PEGASUS, the computer would have 'informed' her that:

The two constructs you called
  successful
  masculine
are related at the 66 per cent level.

This means that most of the time you are saying successful you are also saying masculine and most of the time you are saying unsuccessful you are also saying feminine.

Think of a new person which is either successful and feminine or masculine and unsuccessful.

She would also have learnt that:

The two people father and husband are matched at the 62 per cent level. This means that so far you have not clearly distinguished between father and husband. Do you want to split these?

Had her answer been in the affirmative, she would then have been asked to 'think of a new construct which places these two people at opposite ends'. Such interventions by computer clearly not only allow subjects to become more aware of their construing but also encourage the revision of some of their constructions. In the view of Shaw and Mancuso (1987), they are more likely to be accepted by subjects as a portrayal of their own construing than if their constructs had been elicited, and results fed back, by a person rather than a computer. In addition, these authors consider that subjects are likely to be more willing to reveal idiosyncratic constructs if elicitation is by computer.

Although the variety of computer grid analysis packages available may be bewildering to the clinician who wishes to analyse grids, choice of package may ultimately be based on such considerations as the nature of the hardware and extent of funding available. For example, some programs, such as GAB (Higginbotham and Bannister, 1983) and CIRCUMGRIDS (Chambers and Grice, 1986), are free of charge, and some may be used only with a particular microcomputer, an IBM-compatible computer being necessary for CIRCUMGRIDS and one employing BASIC language for OMNIGRID (Mitterer and Adams-Webber, 1987). There is a certain amount of similarity between the analyses performed by different packages, and in general, as will be considered further below, few significant differences have been found between the results obtained from different methods (e.g. Shaw and Gaines, 1981; van der Kloot, 1981). A further similarity between the methods of analysis used is that most of them make assumptions about the nature of the grid data, such as that equal-interval rating scales are employed, which are not necessarily justified (Goodge, 1979; Yorke, 1985). Some of the more recent packages, such as FLEXIGRID (Tschudi, 1984) and CIRCUMGRIDS, include several of the principal forms of analysis developed by other workers, such as Slater, Thomas, Bannister, and Landfield. Finally, it should be noted that the investigator who wishes to analyse a grid need not necessarily have recourse to a computer program specially designed for this purpose, grids also being amenable to principal component analysis by the relevant procedure in such packages as the Statistical Package for the Social Sciences (SPSS INC, 1988).

## Alternative grid measures

A considerable range of measures has been derived from repertory grids, by either hand or computer analysis, in addition to those described above, but their relationships to Kelly's basic concepts often appear more tenuous than is claimed. There is also much overlap between the measures devised by different researchers. Some of those in most common use in the clinical sphere, the majority of which concern structural features of the construct system, will now be outlined.

### A. Measures of construct system structure

*Intensity* is a measure, developed by Bannister (1960), of the tightness of organisation in an individual's construct system. A subject's Intensity score is obtained by squaring the correlation between each pair of constructs in their grid, multiplying the result by 100, and summing all the scores thus obtained. The use of this score in exploring the predicament of the thought disordered schizophrenic is described in Chapter 3.

*Cognitive Complexity* is 'the capacity to construe social behaviour in a multidimensional way' (Bieri *et al.*, 1966, p. 185). In one of its more frequently employed forms, it involves comparing the ratings of every element on each pair of constructs in an individual's grid and assigning a score of 1 for every correspondence in ratings. The total score thus obtained is a measure of the grid's cognitive *simplicity*. Other methods of measuring cognitive complexity have also been employed, Crockett's (1965) consisting simply of totalling the number of constructs used by a subject in describing others. As Fransella and Bannister (1977, p. 61) note, cognitive complexity 'is now virtually an independent area of research', and one which has rather more in common with personality trait theories than with personal construct theory.

*Functionally Independent Construction (FIC)* is a variant on the cognitive complexity theme which was devised by Landfield (1971, 1977) to measure the degree of dissimilarity in a subject's allocation of grid elements on different constructs, or their application of constructs to different elements. A high FIC score indicates that the person is using his or her constructs in a relatively independent fashion. Landfield has employed this measure in his research on psychotherapy, and has developed computer programs to calculate it and the other structural indices which he employs (Landfield and Cannell, 1988).

*Ordination* is one of these other structural measures, and derives from Landfield's concern with assessing not only the degree of differentiation (as revealed by FIC), but also the degree of integration, or hierarchical organisation, in an individual's construing. Thus, the ordination measure was designed to assess the extent to which a subject is able to integrate their constructions by using superordinate constructs, and is calculated by multiplying the number of levels of extremity used in ratings with a particular construct, or of a particular element, by the difference between the highest and lowest ratings. The average ordination scores for constructs and for elements are then summed.

$\chi^2$ (Landfield and Schmittdiel, 1983) is essentially a refinement of the Ordination score, and measures the extent to which a subject departs from equal use of rating scale points.

*Coefficient of Variation* (Bannister, 1960) is a measure of the extent of the difference in the strength of relationships between constructs in an individual's grid. It is obtained by first calculating the total matching score of each construct with every other. The standard deviation of these scores is then multiplied by 100 and divided by their mean. Bannister's (1962a) Variability score is obtained by a similar procedure, but is less contaminated by the degree of consistency over time in the subject's construct relationships.

*Articulation* is a concept employed by Makhlouf-Norris and her colleagues (Makhlouf-Norris *et al.*, 1970; Makhlouf-Norris and Norris, 1973) in their research on obsessive-compulsive clients (see Chapter 3). Their procedure is to identify clusters consisting of constructs in an individual's grid which intercorrelate at at least the 5 per cent level of significance. If only one such primary cluster can be extracted from the person's grid, their construct system is termed 'monolithic'; if more than one cluster is identified but there are no linkage constructs significantly correlated with constructs in each cluster, it is termed 'segmented'; and if two or more clusters are joined by linkage constructs, it is regarded as 'articulated'. In the view of Makhlouf-Norris *et al.* (1970), linkage constructs usually occupy a superordinate position in the individual's system.

*Constriction* has been assessed by grids in various ways, one of the measures employed being the number of midpoint ratings which the individual gives on his or her constructs (R. Neimeyer *et al.*, 1985), indicating the extent to which constructs are felt to be inapplicable to elements. A measure of 'category constriction' employed by Ross (1985) assesses the degree to which rating scale points are used excessively, regardless of which points these are.

*Permeability* of a construct may be assessed, in a grid which allows the client the option of not applying each construct to every element, by counting the number of times that this option is *not* chosen with the construct concerned (Gottesman, 1962). In a rating grid, it could conceivably be assessed by counting the number of non-midpoint ratings on the construct.

*Mal-Distribution* (Bannister, 1962a) is a score which may be obtained from Kelly's original form of grid by, for each construct, recording the extent of the discrepancy between the subject's allocation of elements to its poles and an exact half-and-half distribution. All the figures thus obtained are then summed, giving a measure of the degree of 'lopsidedness' in the subject's construing.

*Number of Implications and Saturation* are scores which may be derived from an implications grid, in which the total number of ticks in the row referring to a particular construct can be regarded as a measure of the construct's subordinate implications (the number of constructs which it implies), while the number of ticks in the column concerned is a measure of its superordinate implications (the number of constructs which it is implied by). Saturation (Fransella, 1972) is the number of implications in the grid divided by the number of possible implications in a grid of that size.

## B. Measures of stability in construing

*Consistency* was another concept employed by Bannister (1960) in his research on schizophrenic thought disorder. In his terms, the consistent individual is one who maintains a similar pattern of relationships between constructs over time. Consistency so defined bears no necessary relationship to the consistency of element allocation on constructs. Thus, if in one grid an individual rates all 'kind' elements as 'honest', a consistent relationship between these two constructs may be maintained in a second grid even if all elements initially construed as kind are now construed as unkind, provided there has been a similar reversal in allocation of elements to construct poles on the 'honest–dishonest' construct. The Consistency score is obtained by calculating the Spearman correlation between the construct relationship scores derived from two grids.

*Element Consistency*, unlike Bannister's Consistency score, is essentially a measure of test–retest reliability of element allocation on constructs and, as will be seen in Chapter 3, was employed by Frith and Lillie (1972) and other workers in their critique of Bannister's research.

## C. Measures of self-construing

*Identification* (Jones, 1954), a measure of dissimilarity in the construing of self and others, is the average distance between self and non-self elements.

*Self-Integration*, another area considered in the Makhlouf-Norris and Norris (1973) study (see Chapter 4), also concerns the degree of dissimilarity in construing of the self and other elements. Using a grid with twenty elements, analysed by Slater's (1972) INGRID program, they defined 'actual-self isolation' as the situation in which no non-self element is at a distance of less than 0.8 from the actual self, 'ideal-self isolation' being similarly defined. In 'self-alienation', there is a distance of at least 1.2 between the actual and ideal selves, and not more than two non-self elements are more distant than this from the ideal self. Finally, in 'social alienation' all but two non-self elements are at a distance of at least 0.8 from both actual and ideal selves.

The *Self–Other Score*, derived from Carr's (1980) Interpersonal Discrimination Task (see p. 28), is the average number of persons placed in boxes separate from the self across the six constructs considered in the test.

*Self-Distinctiveness* on the Interpersonal Discrimination Task is the mean number of times that the subject places the self in a separate box, thus indicating that the self is construed as different from all other elements.

*Polarised Self-Construing* may be measured by calculating the average extremity (or deviation from the midpoint) of self-ratings on all constructs. Higher scores have been 'taken to represent greater degrees of dichotomous or absolutistic thinking about the self' (R. Neimeyer *et al.*, 1983a, p. 68).

*Cross-Sex Parental Identification* may be assessed by subtracting the distance between the self and same-sex parent elements from that between self and opposite-sex parent elements. If the figure obtained is negative, cross-sex identification is indicated (Ryle and Breen, 1972b).

*Negative Self-Construing* may be evaluated in several ways, but most simply by employing a construct scale (e.g. ranging from −6 through 0 to +6) on which a negative rating indicates that the element concerned has been construed unfavourably. The sum of negative minus positive ratings of the self provides a measure of negativity of self-construing (e.g. R. Neimeyer *et al.*, 1985).

*Variance-Based Negative Self-Construing* (Space and Cromwell, 1980) is a more complex grid measure of the degree of negativity in a subject's self-evaluation. Firstly, every construct on which the individual has rated the self negatively (in terms of the valences which they are asked to assign to their construct poles) is identified, and the self-rating on each of these constructs is converted to a standard score. Following factor analysis of the grid, each of these standard scores is multiplied by the squares of any loadings exceeding 0.30 of the construct concerned on the factors obtained. The various scores derived are then summed and expressed as a percentage of the total of negative and positive (calculated in similar fashion) variance-based self-construing.

*Death Threat* scores may be derived from the Threat Index (see p. 28) by counting the number of times on which the death element is placed at one pole of a construct and self and preferred self elements at the other, or more simply by counting the number of times on which self and death are assigned to opposite poles (Rigdon *et al.*, 1979).

## D. Measures of 'conflict' and fragmentation in construing

*Imbalance* (Slade and Sheehan, 1979) refers to the degree of logical inconsistency in the relationships between an individual's constructs, and is a concept derived from Heider's (1946) cognitive balance theory. It is assessed by considering each triad of constructs in the person's system and classifying it as 'balanced' if each of the correlations between its constituent pairs of constructs is positive, or if two are negative but one positive; and as 'imbalanced' if each of these correlations is negative, or if two are negative and one positive. That imbalanced triads are logically inconsistent may be seen from the examples in Figure 2.4: in the first, depressed people are viewed as sensitive and sensitivity is considered attractive but depression is not; while in the second, neither sensitivity nor depression is construed as attractive, but depressed people are not regarded as sensitive.

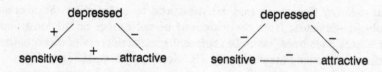

Figure 2.4 Examples of logical inconsistencies in construct relationships
Note: (signs indicate direction of relationships)

The CONFLICT computer program developed by Slade and Sheehan (1981) calculates a 'total balance value' for each construct in a grid, indicating the strength of its relationships with the pairs of constructs in each balanced triad in which it is included; a 'total imbalance value', similarly derived from imbalanced triads; and a measure of the percentage of the total imbalance in the grid accounted for by the construct. Also provided is an intensity score for each construct, arrived at by summing the construct's total balance and total imbalance values.

A somewhat similar method of assessing degree of balance in construct systems has been employed by Carroll and Carroll (1981), drawing on work by Morrissette (1958). Its major differences from Slade and Sheehan's approach are that it takes into account the valence assigned by an individual to the construct poles and elements in their grid, and that it provides balance scores for element–element and element–construct relationships as well as for relationships between constructs. Logical inconsistencies in relationships between elements, as well as in those between constructs, may also be identified by the recently developed Correlation-Test computer program (ICARUS, 1989), which includes the further refinement on the CONFLICT program that it designates triads as balanced or imbalanced on the basis of the relative strengths of the correlations concerned rather than simply their relative valences.

*Logical Inconsistency* has also been assessed by Chambers' (1983) coordinate grid, in which both columns and rows refer to role titles, which are ranked in terms of their similarity to each other. Inconsistency is assumed to be reflected in differences between rankings derived from inter-row correlations and the subject's original rankings of the role titles.

*Dilemmas*, as reflected in construct relationships, may be assessed by first identifying the direction of the relationship expected between each pair of constructs in an individual's grid on the basis of their preferred pole of each construct. If, for example, the construct pole (the pole indicated by high ratings on the construct dimension if a rating grid is employed) of each of two constructs is preferred, a positive correlation between these constructs would be expected; whereas preference for the construct pole of one and the contrast pole (the pole indicated by low ratings) of the other would suggest a negative correlation. A dilemma score can be obtained by taking each construct relationship which departs from these expectations and (if a method of analysis such as Slater's (1972) INGRID program has been employed) calculating the difference from 90 degrees of the angular distance between the two constructs concerned. A total dilemma score for the grid may be derived by summing all the individual scores thus obtained, or alternatively an average dilemma score may be calculated for constructs referring to a particular area of content. This latter method has, for example, allowed the exploration of dilemmas concerning social interaction in social skills group participants (Winter, 1987, 1988a).

*Mixed Factor-Valence Variance and Mixed Self-Valence Factor Variance* are measures developed by Space and Cromwell (1980) to assess aspects of the disequilibrium within an individual's construct system. The individual is asked to assign a positive or negative valence to each of the construct poles in their grid, which is then factor analysed. Taking each factor in turn, each construct loading on it is labelled as positive if its loading is positive and its construct pole is positively evaluated, or if both loading and evaluation are negative. Constructs where this is not the case are labelled as negative. A factor is regarded as mixed if it contains at least two positive and at least two negative constructs. The amount of variance accounted for by each mixed factor is then summed, and the total divided by the amount of variance extracted by all the factors considered and multiplied by 100 to produce the percentage of mixed factor variance.

To assess mixed self-valence variance, the subject's self-rating on each construct with a loading greater than 0.30 on a factor is considered. The factor is designated as mixed if there are at least two positive and at least two negative self-ratings on its constituent constructs. The percentage of mixed self-valence factor variance is calculated in a similar fashion to the percentage of mixed factor variance.

*Self-Conflict* may perhaps be indicated by the distance between a self element and the construct 'like me' in an individual's grid (Fransella and Crisp, 1979). I have suggested that this score might also be regarded as a measure of guilt, defined in Kelly's terms of perceived dislodgement from one's core role (Winter, 1983).

### E. Miscellaneous other measures

*Social Deviation* (Bannister, 1960) refers to the extent to which the pattern of relationships in an individual's use of particular constructs differs from that exhibited by most people. It is therefore a measure of the deviation of the content of a subject's construing from social consensus. After administering a standard grid to a sample of normal subjects, Bannister calculated the average matching scores between pairs of constructs for these subjects. A social deviation score can be calculated for an individual who completes the same grid by summing the discrepancies between his or her matching scores and those of Bannister's normal sample. A variation on this method which is independent of the strength of construct relationships in a subject's grid is the Social Agreement score, obtained by calculating the Pearson correlation between the subject's matching scores and those of the normal sample, and then squaring this correlation coefficient (Bannister, 1962a). More simply, a Social Deviation score may be derived by counting the number of times that the relationship score between two constructs in an individual's grid exceeds a level chosen to minimise contamination of the measure by differences in the strength of subjects' construct relationships, and is in the opposite direction to that in a normal sample (Bannister et al., 1971).

If the investigator is interested in the relationships between constructs other than those employed by Bannister, they may, of course, collect their own normative data for use in the calculation of social deviation scores.

*Insight* is another measure devised by Bannister (1962a), in this case to assess the extent to which a subject is aware of the relationships between constructs revealed in their grid. Having completed a grid, the subject is asked, for each construct (Bannister's original method supplied the subject with only one pole of each construct), to indicate another construct in the grid which is closest to it in meaning, together with the construct which is most opposite to it in meaning. The matching scores of all the construct pairs regarded as similar are then summed, and the matching score of each construct pair regarded as opposites is subtracted from this sum, taking into account the signs of the matching scores concerned. The score obtained is then expressed as a proportion of the sum of the matching scores in the individual's grid.

The *Overall Score* derived from Carr's (1980) Interpersonal Discrimination Task is a measure of the extent to which an individual differentiates between grid elements. It is obtained by calculating the average number of discriminations between elements made by the subject on six constructs.

The *Other–Other Score*, also derived from the Interpersonal Discrimination Task, involves, for each construct and each person, counting the number of other people, excluding the self, who are considered to differ from the person. The average number of such discriminations per person per construct is then calculated.

## Reliability and validity

Kelly rather scoffed at the traditional requirements of respectability in a psychological test, reportedly defining reliability as 'that characteristic of a test which makes it insensitive to change' and validity as 'the capacity of a test to tell us what we already know' (Bannister and Mair, 1968). On a more serious note, he indicated that he was more concerned with the consistency of a test than with its reliability, and with its usability than with its validity. As there is no standard form of the repertory grid, it is, of course, fairly meaningless to make any general statements about the grid's reliability and validity. Furthermore, Slater (1965, 1974) has pointed out that common methods of assessing the reliability and significance of a psychometric technique were designed with nomothetic tests in mind and, as such, are inapplicable to repertory grid technique except when grids constructed for general use are considered.

Perhaps in part because of Kelly's assertions, there has been, as Yorke (1985, p. 397) notes, 'a slippage towards "anything goes" as far as grid design is concerned. Put another way, a grid's validity has often been taken as axiomatic, thus leading the user away from a rigorous scrutiny of method'. In view of such concerns, which may be shared by clinicians who are considering making use of the grid in their work, we shall now consider at some length aspects of the reliability and validity of grid scores.

### Stability of grid scores

Amongst the workers who have produced counter-arguments to Kelly's views on reliability and validity, Sperlinger (1976) has remarked that if a grid does elicit significant features of an individual's construing, grids completed by the same individual at different times should show some stability. Several investigators have examined the stability of particular grid measures, Bonarius (1965) reviewing a number of such studies which have obtained test–retest correlations in the region of 0.8. Fransella (1981a, p. 173), in a later review, concludes that 'average reliabilities tend to be quite high, but the range for the individuals making up the sample is often very wide'. Other researchers have assessed the degree of stability in the constructs elicited from an individual at different times, the general finding, despite some inconsistent results (e.g. Mitsos, 1958), being of similarity in the constructs elicited on two occasions of testing even when different elements have been employed in the elicitation procedure (Hunt, 1951; Fjeld and Landfield, 1961; Sperlinger, 1976). The test–retest intervals in these studies have varied from one week to eight months, and the subjects have been clients presenting with psychological disorders, non-psychiatric patients, and 'normals'. Stability of elicited elements has also been investigated, and has been found to be equivalent to that of constructs (Pederson, 1958; Fjeld and Landfield, 1961). A further series of studies has examined the effect on reliability coefficients of varying the format of the grid (Fransella, 1965, 1976; Mair and Boyd, 1967; Bannister and Mair, 1968; Honess, 1978; Kelsall and Strongman, 1978; Beail, 1983), and the findings of such investigations have led Fransella and Bannister (1977, p. 78) to conclude that 'grids of various forms cannot be considered identical either in terms of the perceived task or in terms of results'.

Other workers have examined the effect on structural measures of varying the type of constructs and elements employed in a grid. A particular focus of the research has been the comparison of grids using supplied, and those using elicited, constructs and elements. While some studies have found little difference in the cognitive complexity scores of normal subjects derived from grids using elicited and from those using supplied constructs (Kieferle and Sechrest, 1961; Tripodi and Bieri, 1963; Metcalfe, 1974; Coleman, 1975), Barbow (1969) did find greater differentiation to be exhibited when elicited than when supplied constructs were used. To further complicate the issue, Kuusinen and Nystedt (1975a) found that the difference observed between the structuring of the two types of construct depended on the measure of cognitive complexity used. If psychological disorder is associated with an idiosyncratic pattern of construct organisation, a greater difference might be expected between the client's structuring of supplied and elicited constructs than would be observed with normal subjects. This was found to be the case by Jaspars (1963), in a study comparing neurotic and normal groups, while Caine and Smail (1967) demonstrated that neurotics apply their own constructs more differentially than supplied constructs in a grid. There is also evidence that schizophrenics and their parents structure constructs elicited from them to a greater degree than they do supplied constructs (Winter, 1971, 1975; McFadyen and Foulds, 1972), as did the subjects in a study comparing psychopaths and normal controls (Widom, 1976). A parallel series of studies has examined the effect on grid results of using supplied, rather than elicited, elements. Thus, Bannister (1962b) found that the use of facial photographs rather than people known to the subject as elements had relatively little effect on measures of the distribution of elements between construct poles, of 'insight', and of the idiosyncrasy of construct relationships, but did reduce the Intensity and Consistency scores obtained. Similarly, Williams (1971) observed that an increase in the richness of relevant cues in the elements used in a grid served to increase Intensity and Consistency scores.

It may be concluded from the above studies that, at least with psychologically disturbed individuals, only a grid using elicited constructs and elements will provide an accurate picture of the characteristics of their personal construct system. Such a conclusion is, of course, in line with Kelly's Individuality Corollary, and is supported by the consistent evidence that 'the individual prefers to express himself and to describe others by using his own personal constructs' (Bonarius, 1965) rather than constructs supplied by the investigator (Fager, 1954; Landfield, 1965; Isaacson, 1966; Delia et al., 1971). The importance to the individual of his or her own personal constructs is also indicated by research showing that constructs elicited from subjects are rated more extremely by them, or account for more variance in their element sorts, than are those supplied to them (Cromwell and Caldwell, 1962; Isaacson and Landfield, 1965; Bonarius, 1968; Stringer, 1972), although Warr and Coffman (1970), finding no difference in extremity, concluded that it is possible by careful selection to obtain a set of supplied constructs of similar meaningfulness for the subject to his or her own personal constructs. Bender (1974) explains the anomalous finding of the latter workers as being due to their employing a sequential elicitation method in which only one element in the triad is changed at a time, for this method produces constructs which load less highly on the first component of a principal component analysis and can therefore be considered less personally significant. The results of the research on rating extremity have been elevated to the status of laws by Bonarius (1977). Thus, his 'Construct Law' states that 'Ratings with personal construct scales are more extreme than ratings with extraneous contrast scales', and his 'Object Law' that 'Ratings of personal others are more extreme than ratings of extraneous others'. Such a model is in contrast to one, such as Hamilton's (1968), which sees extreme responding as a general feature of certain, more maladjusted, personality types. It perhaps shows greater consistency with the more complex approach of Landfield (1977), who has provided some support for O'Donovan's (1965) notion of normality being associated with the ability to discriminate between events of differing degrees of meaningfulness and to respond to these with corresponding levels of extremity.

Despite the findings on the effects of varying the constructs or elements in a grid, an intriguing series of research studies has suggested that certain general perceptual and conceptual processes affect construing independently of the actual constructs or elements concerned. Thus, the remarkably consistent finding that subjects use the positive poles of constructs to describe events 62 to 63 per cent of the time, rather than 50 per cent as Kelly assumed, has resulted in the 'golden section hypothesis' that such an organisation allows maximal figure–ground differentiation in construing (Adams-Webber and Benjafield, 1973; Benjafield and Adams-Webber, 1975, 1976). This hypothesis draws on Pythagoras' concept of the golden section, the most aesthetically pleasing ratio of the dimensions of a figure. That the golden section also underlies self-perception is indicated by findings that other people are construed as similar to the self 62 per cent of the time (Morse, 1965; Benjafield *et al.*, 1976; Adams-Webber, 1977a). Adams-Webber (1979) contends, from an information theory perspective, that these results suggest that our pattern of construing others is such that we are likely to pay maximum attention to negative characteristics and to differences between ourselves and others. Hargreaves (1979) has also demonstrated that a subject's construing of others, reflected in their ordering of elements on a construct, shows considerable consistency across different constructs, and he emphasises the importance of an individual's social network in determining the structure of his or her construct system.

There has been a certain amount of research examining the stability at retest of general structural features of construing. These studies have provided evidence of an increase in the level of interrelationship between constructs, and therefore in Intensity scores, from one grid to another, identical with it, completed by the same subject (Bannister, 1962a; Bannister *et al.*, 1971); and Sperlinger (1976) has similarly found the percentage of variation accounted for by the first component from principal component analysis of a grid to be a relatively unstable measure. An increase in construct relationships from one grid assessment to the next has been found to be particularly apparent when subjects have gained experience, or been given information, relevant to the events which they are construing (Adams-Webber and Mirc, 1976; Bodden and James, 1976), although findings in this area are not entirely consistent (e.g. O'Hare and Gordon, 1976). By contrast to some of the above findings, a relatively high test–retest correlation has been obtained for Crockett's (1965) measure of cognitive complexity and for Bannister's (1962a) Maldistribution and Insight scores. Studies of stability in the pattern of construct relationships over time have yielded reliability coefficients ranging from 0.60 to 0.80 (Fransella and Bannister, 1977) and an indication that the longer the test–retest interval the lower the correlation likely to be obtained (Lansdown, 1975). Levels of stability of this order have also been observed for a measure of similarity of element allotment (Watson et al., 1976).

Stability of aspects of construing of the self has been investigated by Caine and Smail (1969a), who employed a grid in which the constructs consisted of descriptions of hysteroid and obsessoid traits, chosen because they represented a personality dimension of known stability. Reasonable stability was observed over a three-month period in the relationships between the self-construct and other constructs, as well as in the application of constructs to elements. Although the reliability of the grid was not as high as that of the Hysteroid-Obsessoid Questionnaire, the authors explain this in terms of the greater complexity of grid procedure and the fact that their study did not employ elicited constructs. Sperlinger's (1976) study also examined stability of self-construing, finding a correlation of 0.95 beween the distances of the self from other elements on two occasions of testing, and that those subjects whose self-construing changed the most exhibited greater self–ideal self distance, perhaps indicating greater motivation to change, at initial assessment. A low percentage of variation accounted for by the first component from principal component analysis of the grid, and therefore a relatively loosely organised construct system, was also predictive of greater change. Low stability in construing the self, as well as in construing others, has also been related to lopsidedness in the use of an individual's constructs (Benjafield and Adams-Webber, 1975; Clyne, 1975; Cochran, 1976), and has been explained in terms of memory deficits for information coded in terms of such constructs (Adams-Webber et al., 1975). A further measure relating to self-construing, the stability of which has been examined, is the Threat Index, most studies revealing high test–retest reliability coefficients (Krieger et al., 1979; R. Neimeyer et al., 1977; Rainey and Epting, 1977).

Those of the above investigations which indicate individual differences in stability of construing would suggest that such instability may be predictable in certain people. Indeed, instability of construct relationships may be used as a diagnostic index (Bannister and Fransella, 1966), as we shall see in Chapter 3. Certain periods in a person's life might also be expected to be associated with greater instability in construing. One such period is when the person undergoes psychotherapy, and studies examining change in repertory grid scores during therapy will be reviewed in Chapter 5. That feedback of grid results may also lead to reconstruing has been demonstrated by Keen's (1977) finding of a test–retest reliability for grid scores significant at the 0.1 level when subjects were given no feedback from their initial grids but which did not approach statistical significance when they were provided with such feedback. Another period when changes in construing of an elaborative nature would be expected is childhood, and some studies of children have demonstrated an increasing use of psychological, as opposed to physical, constructs with age (Brierley, 1967; Little, 1968; Scarlett *et al.*, 1971; Duck, 1975), and use of constructs in a more complex, discriminating, logically consistent, and less lopsided, fashion by older children (Scarlett *et al.*, 1971; Applebee, 1976; Barratt, 1977; Clark and Delia, 1977; Delia *et al.*, 1979; Ritter, 1979; Vacc *et al.*, 1980; Chambers and Parsley, 1987–88). Reviewing research on the development of construing, Salmon (1970, 1976) concludes that a central feature of such development is an increase in the organisation of the construct system. Applebee (1975) has also demonstrated an increase in the consensus of children's construing, largely in terms of interrelationships between constructs, with age, while Bannister and Agnew (1977) have indicated the increasing ability of older children to identify their own constructions. Changes in construing during adolescence have been investigated by Strachan and Jones (1982), who have found that in mid-adolescence there tends to be lower self-esteem, and less identification of self and ideal self with other people, than in early or late adolescence, and that identification with parents decreases with age. Studies of developmental changes in construing in later years are relatively few, but Carr and Townes (1975) have demonstrated that, while an increase in differentiation of the self from others occurs between late adolescence and early adulthood, a consistent decrease in such differentiation is apparent thereafter.

Just as it is possible to predict the degree of stability of the construing, and therefore of the grid scores, of certain individuals, so it should be possible to predict the degree of stability of certain constructs or of certain subsystems within an individual's construct system. A construct's degree of stability would be expected to be dependent to a large extent on its validational fortunes, and there is some evidence from repertory grid research that invalidation of construing may lead to a loosening, and validation to a tightening, in construct relationships (Bannister, 1963, 1965b; Rehm, 1971). That the initial state of an individual's construct system determines the response to invalidation has been demonstrated by Crockett and Miesel (1974), who observed that subjects whose constructs were highly interrelated showed more impression change after strong than after weak invalidation, presumably because the effects of invalidation were potentially more extensive for such individuals, while the reverse was true for subjects who showed little interrelationship between their constructs. Similarly, Cochran (1977) found that subjects whose constructs were highly interrelated weakened their construct relationships following invalidation while maintaining the pattern of these relationships. By contrast, subjects whose level of construct interrelationship was low reacted to invalidation by strengthening alternative patterns of construing. In a further study, Lawlor and Cochran (1981) have also demonstrated a very high degree of loosening, and reduction in the consistency, of construct relationships as a response to invalidation in subjects with relatively tightly organised construct systems. This even extended to constructs which were not directly invalidated, suggesting that 'change on even a single construct would ramify throughout the system via strong interrelations' (p. 48) in such individuals. However, once again, subjects with relatively loosely organised construct systems did not loosen their construing further following invalidation, perhaps because their systems would then be in danger of a complete structural breakdown. It might also be expected that invalidation of the more superordinate constructs within an individual's system would be resisted because such invalidation would be likely to have extensive implications. Some evidence for this has been provided by findings that relative invulnerability of a construct to invalidation, consistency of its relationships with other constructs, and consistency of element allocation on the construct are predicted by such features of the construct as high constellatoriness (operationally defined by a high loading on the first component from principal component analysis of the grid), a high degree of grid variance accounted for by the construct, and large numbers of implications in terms of other constructs (Levy, 1956; Bannister, 1962a; Hinkle, 1965; Emerson, 1982). As Emerson (1982) points out, Mair and Boyd's (1967) failure to replicate these findings may have been due to the short test–retest interval, and while Ryle (1975) also did not obtain similar results on measuring element consistency in conventional grids, his results with dyad grids were consistent with other studies.

It seems likely that one's construing of people's behaviour is more likely to suffer invalidation than one's construing of the more predictable physical world. This may provide an explanation for findings that when physical constructs (e.g. 'tall–short') are used construing tends to be more structured and stable than when psychological (e.g. 'kind–unkind') constructs are employed, similar results being obtained when subjects' construing of objects and of people is compared (Bannister and Salmon, 1966; Bannister and Mair, 1968; McPherson and Buckley, 1970; McPherson et al., 1975). Whatever the reasons for these findings, however, they do support the view that an individual's construct system consists of various subsystems, each with its own structural properties, so that it would not be meaningful to calculate a split-half reliability coefficient for a grid unless it can be assumed that both halves tap the same subsystem. Ryle (1975) did, however, examine whether similar construct relationships would be obtained in two grids employing different elements, randomly assigned to each, and found relatively high median consistency, although there was considerable inter-subject variation.

Similarly, splitting the constructs in the Threat Index has revealed high split-half coefficients (Krieger *et al.*, 1974, 1979).

In Mair's (1964a, 1964b) view, it is more valuable to consider the degree of predictable change or predictable stability of grid measures, as in some of the research discussed above, than to attempt to assess the general reliability of a grid. In a study in which he examined whether teaching subjects the meanings of words increased grid-derived relationship scores between these words and their synonyms, as compared to those involving words the meanings of which they knew, he found that of sixty-one predictions concerning grid measures only four were unconfirmed (Mair, 1966). The predictability of change in particular grid scores is also likely to be a major concern of the clinician who carries out repeated assessments with a grid, perhaps to monitor a client's reconstruing over the course of therapy. One option which is available if predictions are made concerning change in the client's use of particular constructs or construing of particular elements is to take up Slater's (1969) suggestion of including in the grid 'control' constructs and elements where little or no change is expected, and with which the degree of change in the 'experimental' constructs and elements can be compared (e.g. Winter and Trippett, 1977). A further aspect of reliability which may be of particular concern to the clinician who attempts to predict changes in a client's grid scores on the basis of inspection of a pre-treatment grid is what Anastasi (1968) terms 'scorer reliability', the extent to which their predictions would be likely to be shared by those of another clinician who inspects the same grid. Scorer reliability may be enhanced by the provision of guidelines for the interpretation of, and prediction of change in, grid scores and, as will be discussed in Chapter 6, I have suggested some such guidelines for the prediction of changes in grid scores during therapy (Caine *et al.*, 1981; Winter, 1982, 1985a).

A final issue pertaining to reliability concerns the stability of the solutions obtained from principal component and similar analyses of grid data. The stability of the correlation coefficients which are subjected to such procedures could be questioned when the ratio of elements to constructs in a grid is, as is usually the case, less than 3:1. Careful attention to the representativeness of elements selected for the grid may, however, redress this problem. (I am indebted to John Gosling for his observations on this matter.)

*Validity of grid scores*

Internal and construct validity

A number of investigations have provided evidence of the validity of repertory grid technique by testing hypotheses derived from personal construct theory, and assumptions about grid method, without concerning themselves to any great extent with the prediction of behaviour independent of grid completion.

For example, if the grid is a valid measure of personal constructs, it would be expected that its elicitation procedure would produce constructs on which elements are more highly differentiated than they are on supplied constructs, and we have seen above that there is some evidence that this is so. Similarly, Bannister (1962b) provided support for the hypotheses that grid procedures could demonstrate that constructs within the subsystem concerned with construing of people are related to a degree above that expected by chance; and that individuals within one culture will have similar patterns of construct relationships, although not necessarily agreeing about the construing of individual elements. Slater (1974) has provided a method of assessing the significance of an individual grid by testing the null hypothesis that it is indistinguishable from a 'quasi grid' composed of an array of random numbers, and has developed the GRANNY computer program to generate and analyse such quasi grids. He has found that, provided that the constructs are meaningful to the subject and the elements are within their range of convenience, experimental grids are very rarely similar to quasi grids, the most striking difference being in the relatively large percentage of the variance accounted for by the first principal component in the experimental grids.

Mair has been concerned with the validity of certain common implicit assumptions in grid methodology. His results (Mair, 1967a) did not support the assumption that elements allotted to one pole of a construct cannot also be allotted to its contrast pole, or the assumption (Mair, 1967b) that the pattern of relationships of other constructs with a 'whole-figure' construct (e.g. 'like me in character') necessarily reflects the sorting of that figure on the constructs when it is used as an element. He states that 'grid measures will have to be used along with others in predictive studies where criteria external to these measures can be used to allow assessment of the relative adequacy of each' (p. 280). A further problem in drawing general conclusions from the way in which a particular element is construed in a grid has been highlighted by Leitner's (1988a) finding that an individual may construe another person, or the self, very differently in different contexts, for example after recalling an incident in which he or she was relating well with the person and after recalling a time when they were relating badly. Yorke (1989) has also noted the importance of taking contextual detail into account in understanding the particular meaning intended by an individual in applying a construct to a certain element. Such findings as Leitner's argue for the use of more specific elements in grids, as in the multiple self grid employed by R. Neimeyer et al. (1983a), and Ryle and Lunghi's (1969) procedure of asking a couple to construe their relationship when going well and when going badly.

Adams-Webber (1970a) has pointed out that too little attention has been given to the interrelationship of grid indices assumed to measure different variables, and has examined the discriminant validity of a few such indices. He found that cognitive simplicity and constellatoriness (the amount of variance accounted for by the largest element factor) could not be clearly distinguished from a measure of identification (the average match between self-ratings and ratings of other elements in the grid), so that there was equivalence between structural measures based on construct relationships and those based on element relationships. All the measures appeared to be concerned with the subject's tendency to construe people unidimensionally in terms of a stereotype consistent with his or her own self-concept. The high inter-correlation between measures was thought to be consistent with the internal logic of personal construct theory and the development of the grid as an instrument to explore construct–element interaction. High correlations have also been obtained between Bannister's Intensity score, the size of the first component from Slater's principal component analysis, and the first axis from Bannister's hand method of cluster analysis (Fransella, 1965); as well as between Intensity scores and low levels of imbalance in construct relation-ships in clinical populations (Sheehan, 1977; Margolius, 1980; Winter, 1983), perhaps reflecting the fact that if three constructs are very highly inter-correlated they cannot be imbalanced as defined by the Slade and Sheehan (1979) method. Other workers, however, have examined the convergent validity of different measures of cognitive complexity and have generally found this to be low (Vannoy, 1965; Irwin et al., 1967; Little, 1969; Miller, 1969; Epting and Wilkins, 1974; Orford, 1974; Kuusinen and Nystedt, 1975b; O'Keefe and Sypher, 1981), and that cognitive complexity is unrelated to Intensity (Honess, 1976). Part of this lack of correspondence between measures which are often thought equivalent may lie in a confusion between measures of the extent to which constructs differentiate between elements and those which in addition concern hierarchical relationships between constructs (Smith and Leach, 1972; Metcalfe, 1974). The results obtained with some measures may also occasionally represent artefacts of the methods used to compute them, as in the finding by Soldz and Soldz (1989) that Functionally Independent Construction scores are inflated if there is a large number of midpoint ratings in a grid. Measures of degree of structural differentiation of constructs have been found to be related to degree of abstractness or concreteness of construct content only at extremes of the differentiation dimension (Epting et al., 1972; Stringer and Terry, 1978), and the lack of a consistent relationship between these two types of measure is perhaps not surprising in that, as Honess (1976) observes, there tends to be corre-spondence between measures only when these are similarly computed. A similar situation has been found to obtain by Bannister and Salmon (1967) with measures of superordinacy of construing, their results also reflecting differences in the operational definition of this concept.

A further area of study has been concerned with the extremity of ratings on construct scales, which various investigators have found to be a valid measure of the importance to the subject of the construct or of the elements rated. For example, differences in the adjudged meaningfulness of constructs (Mitsos, 1961; O'Donovan, 1964) and their adjudged controversiality (Mogar, 1960) have been found to be reflected in differences in rating extremity on these constructs, while Tajfel and Wilkes (1964) have found rating extremity to be related to a measure of construct salience, defined in terms of earliness of occurrence of the construct in describing others and frequency of its usage. Frequency of construct repetition has in turn been related to ratings of the construct's importance by Shubsachs (1975), who regards it as a measure of superordinacy, while Lemon and Warren (1974) have demonstrated that salient traits are more central, allowing more inferences to other traits, and are more often used in characterising the self than are non-salient traits. Hasenyager (1975) has found that the use of 'Not Applicable' ratings of particular elements in a grid is related to those elements being given midpoint scores on rating scales. There is also evidence that greater extremity of ratings on construct scales is associated with greater relevance of the elements rated, defined in terms of familiarity (Koltuv, 1962), intimacy (Bonarius, 1970a), present acquaintanceship, and attractiveness (Bamber, 1972). In studies by Landfield (1977) on subjects undergoing a group experience, besides people rated most extremely by a subject being those with whom he or she felt most comfortable, was better acquainted, and rated most favourably, extremely rated people also tended to rate themselves more favourably.

One particular variant of grid procedure the construct validity of which has received considerable attention (R. Neimeyer and Moore, 1989) is the Threat Index. It will be recalled that this is considered to be a measure of the extent to which individuals are threatened by death in Kelly's (1955, p. 490) sense that 'they perceive it both as likely to happen to them and as likely to bring about drastic changes in their core constructs'. As such, it would not necessarily be expected to be highly correlated with measures of other negative emotions concerning death, such as anxiety. Although Threat Index scores have been found to show some relationship with predisposition to anxiety (R. Neimeyer, 1978), they are generally more highly correlated with measures of fear and conscious concern regarding death than with those of death anxiety (Krieger et al., 1974, 1979; R. Neimeyer et al., 1977; Epting et al., 1979; Rigdon et al., 1979; R. Neimeyer and Dingemans, 1980; Tobacyk and Eckstein, 1980; R. Neimeyer, 1985c; Ingram and Leitner, 1989), consistent with the view of Krieger et al. (1974) that the Threat Index and measures of fear of death assess an individual's construing of the relationship between his or her life and death while death anxiety relates more to autonomic arousal concerning death. In all these studies, the correlations, even when statistically significant, have been moderate, leading Rigdon et al. (1979, p. 258) to conclude that they 'support the validity of interpreting the TI as a measure of death orientation, although it apparently assesses a different aspect of death concern than do the other scales'. High Threat Index scores have also been associated with a low ability to conceive of one's mortality (Krieger et al., 1974), although not with previous closeness to one's own or a significant other's death or to illness (R. Neimeyer et al., 1977). The view that discrepancy in construing of self and death indicates threat has been considered to be supported by findings that elements which are regarded by subjects as 'terrifying' are generally allocated to the opposite, and 'comfortable' elements to the same, construct poles as the self (Krieger *et al.*, 1979; Warren and Parry, 1981). If Threat Index scores are a valid measure of death threat, they might also be expected to show some relationship with religious belief, and there is some evidence that this is so: low death threat has been linked with frequent churchgoing, belief in an afterlife, and aspects of religiosity (Krieger *et al.*, 1974; R. Neimeyer *et al.*, 1977; Tobacyk, 1984; Ingram and Leitner, 1989), although such religious affiliations as Judaism and Catholicism are associated with higher death threat than is lack of any religious affiliation (R. Neimeyer *et al.*, 1977). People who have made plans concerning their death have also been found to obtain lower death threat scores than those who have not, and, although research results are not entirely consistent, there are indications that such scores may be modified by attending a death education course (Rainey and Epting, 1977; Tobacyk and Eckstein, 1980). A further area of investigation has concerned the existentialist view, generally supported by the research evidence (Lester and Collett, 1970; R. Neimeyer and Chapman, 1980; Wood and Robinson, 1982; Robinson and Wood, 1984), that individuals who are highly dissatisfied with themselves are more likely to fear death. Their original research findings with students led Wood and Robinson to propose the 'additive model' that individuals who are characterised by low scores on both measures of self–ideal self discrepancy and death threat are less afraid of death than are those who exhibit only one of these features. However, later research with older samples has failed to reveal an interactive effect between self–ideal self discrepancy and death threat, and R. Neimeyer (1985c) suggests that this is because the two variables relate to different aspects of death concern, high death threat being associated with fear of personal death and high self–ideal self discrepancy with fear concerning death of significant others.

While the research delineating different emotional reactions to anticipations of death provides some indication of the construct validity of the Threat Index, the measure is not without its problems. As Warren and Parry (1981) point out, in its original form, in which threat is scored if the self and preferred self are allocated to one pole of a construct and death to the other, subjects who exhibit a high self–ideal self discrepancy may obtain spuriously low death threat scores. This problem may be circumvented by considering only self–death splits and disregarding the preferred self element. However, a more serious difficulty highlighted by Warren and Parry is that the range of convenience of many of the constructs employed may not encompass both 'self' and 'death' elements. They explored this problem using a grid in which all the elements used to elicit constructs for the Threat Index were rated on both supplied and elicited constructs. Principal component analysis of such grids indicated that 'self' and 'my own death' elements tended not to load on the same component, suggesting that in some subjects different construct subsystems are applicable to the self and to death. A further critique of the Threat Index has been advanced by Chambers (1986), who takes issue with its interpretation of Kelly's concept of threat, his view of which is in terms of logical incompatibilities in the implications of superordinate constructs. In addition, he suggests that a lack of differentiation between self and death, far from implying optimal functioning, may indicate a relatively simple cognitive structure whereas their differentiation may reflect an affirmation of life. Finally, he contends that the death threat hypothesis fails to acknowledge the complexity of the human encounter with death, and in particular makes the unjustified assumption that construing of the self is equivalent to construing of one's life. A rebuttal of these criticisms has been provided by R. Neimeyer (1986a), who considers that they are based on an incomplete reading of personal construct theory and of work on cognitive structure, and a selective appraisal of the Threat Index research literature. He has provided evidence that, contrary to Chambers' arguments, the extent to which individuals differentiate 'self' and 'death' elements is very highly correlated with their differentiation of death from the element 'your present life'; and that neither of these measures is correlated either with cognitive complexity or with a measure of purpose in life. Although cognitive complexity was associated with differentiation of 'self' and 'life' elements, this appeared to reflect the high correlation of both measures with self–ideal self discrepancy.

These studies of the construct validity of the Threat Index have been considered at some length because the measure is of clinical relevance, and because they indicate some of the difficulties of operationalising Kelly's concepts. Thus, although many of Chambers' criticisms of this measure have been shown by Neimeyer to have little substance, the question of whether scores on the Index or on similar measures (e.g. Leitner and Cado, 1982; G. Neimeyer and Hall, 1988) are a valid reflection of threat as defined by Kelly is perhaps deserving of further attention. Such measures make the assumption that individuals are threatened by events which they anticipate will cause them to revise substantially their view of themselves in terms of their existing construct dimensions. However, changes of self-construal of this type, often referred to as slot-rattling, were regarded by Kelly as relatively superficial since they do not necessarily involve any modification in the constructs themselves. The development of a grid measure to assess whether death implies this latter type of change in core constructs is not inconceivable, and some work along these lines is currently under way.

Finally, as well as the validity of individual grid scores, it is pertinent in this section to consider the extent to which methods of averaging a number of grids provide a valid reflection of the construing of the members of the group concerned. A major problem with, for example, Slater's (1977) consensus grid, which consists of the average ratings from subjects' individual grids, is that it takes no account of the variance in these grids and therefore may misrepresent the responses of the subjects concerned (Beail, 1984; Yorke, 1985). Principal component analysis of such a consensus grid will produce a first and second component taking up a very high percentage of its variance, but this is an artefact of the averaging method and, contrary to the assumptions of some investigators, does not indicate that the individual grids which have been averaged are tightly structured. Beail (1984) has indicated that the method employed by Higginbotham and Bannister (1983), which averages relationship scores between constructs rather than individual ratings, produces results discrepant with those of Slater's method and more in line with subjects' original responses.

Predictive and concurrent validity

That Repertory Test results may be predictive of behaviour was indicated by Kelly (1955), who noted that such results had been matched reliably with subjects' role-playing performance and Thematic Apperception Test protocols. Numerous subsequent studies have examined the capacity of grid measures to predict aspects of individuals' social behaviour. For example, Bender (1968, 1976) answered his question 'Does construing people as similar involve similar behaviour towards them?' affirmatively, although behaviour towards the people concerned was not observed directly but assessed by asking each subject and his or her spouse to construe the subject's behaviour. Knowles and Purves (1965) found that grid indices of need for approval (reflected in the relationship between constructs 'like me in character' and 'needs approval') and respect for the experimenter (reflected in the relationship between constructs 'like I'd like to be in character' and 'like the experimenter') were able to differentiate subjects high and low in conditionability in a conditioning experiment in which experimenter approval was used as the reinforcer. Salmon (1969) was rather less successful in predicting the conformity behaviour of a group of children on the basis of their grids, the only construct of any value in predicting the degree of conformity being the ideal self construct.

A considerable amount of the research in this area has employed measures of cognitive complexity. Bieri (1966, p. 14) took the view that 'a more cognitively complex individual has available a more versatile system for perceiving the behaviour of others than does a less cognitively complex person'. Some support for this argument is provided by evidence that Bieri's measure of cognitive simplicity is associated with domination of construing by an evaluative dimension (Mueller, 1974); homogeneity in evaluations of others (Wojciszke, 1979); greater vulnerability to invalidation of these evaluations (Millimet and Brien, 1980); and relative lack of attitude change after a change-producing experience (Lundy and Berkowitz, 1957). Cognitive simplicity and a similar measure devised by Adams-Webber have also been associated with assimilative projection, the tendency to construe others as similar to oneself, which has been related by Adams-Webber et al. (1972) to inaccuracy in discriminating between new acquaintances in terms of their personal constructs (Bieri, 1955; Leventhal, 1957; Adams-Webber, 1968). By contrast, cognitive complexity has been related to the ability to identify the personal constructs of another person with whom one has had a discussion (Adams-Webber, 1969); to the ability to take the role of another person (Olson and Partington, 1977); and to the combined use of positive and negative terms in describing others (Campbell, 1960; Scott, 1963). There is little evidence, however, for a relationship between cognitive complexity and accuracy in predicting the behaviour of other people. Crockett's measure of cognitive complexity has also been used in research in the area of person perception, relationships having been found with the capacity to take the perspective of another person (Hale and Delia, 1976; Clark and Delia, 1977); with persuasive and communicational ability (Delia *et al.*, 1979; O'Keefe and Delia, 1979; Hale, 1980); and with the capacity to integrate conflicting information about others, rather than forming univalent impressions of them (Nidorf and Crockett, 1965) or being influenced by recency effects (Mayo and Crockett, 1964). Similarly, it has been associated with lack of dependence on evaluative consistency, or 'balance', in learning social relationships (Press *et al.*, 1969; Delia and Crockett, 1973). The relative ease with which cognitively complex individuals can handle inconsistent information has been offered by Lawlor and Cochran (1981) as a possible explanation of the finding, discussed above, that such individuals show little loosening of construct relationships following invalidation. Cognitive complexity in the use of psychological, but not of non-psychological, constructs has also been related by Delia and O'Keefe (1976) to low Machiavellianism, and to interest in 'other persons as individuals' (p. 436). By contrast, cognitive simplicity in the construing of people when using provided (but not when using elicited) constructs has been found by Coleman (1975) to be associated with an interest in things, while interest in people was more apparent in subjects whose constructs concerning others carried many implications. That cognitive simplicity, together with an extreme response style, may be associated with less honest interactions with others has also been suggested by Chetwynd's (1977) finding of relationships between these characteristics and high scores on a measure of dissimulation.

Reviewing these various studies and other unpublished work, O'Keefe and Sypher (1981) have concluded that there is clear evidence of an association of 'advanced communicative functioning' with cognitive complexity only if the latter is assessed by means of Crockett's measure (which, it should be noted, is derived from a construct elicitation procedure rather than a repertory grid), results with other measures, such as Bieri's, being much less consistent. However, in view of relationships between Crockett's measure and measures of the 'developmental status' of an individual's construct system, such as abstractness or comprehensiveness, which are based on quality rather than number of constructs (O'Keefe and Delia, 1978, 1979; Delia *et al.*, 1979), they question to what extent findings in this area specifically reflect the effects of cognitive complexity. Nevertheless, we may tentatively conclude that the findings of several of these research studies would suggest that a complex system of psychological constructs may be predictive of facility in forming role relationships with others. That cognitive complexity in a particular construct subsystem facilitates the handling of elements within the range of convenience of that subsystem has also been demonstrated in very different spheres, as in Canter's (1970) finding of a relationship between the examination performance of architectural students and the complexity of their construing of buildings.

While it can be seen, therefore, that there is some evidence for the predictive validity of cognitive complexity measures, there have been conflicting research findings in this area. Although this may to some extent reflect differences in the complexity measures employed, it may also be due to the emphasis in most studies on construct differentiation without simultaneous consideration of the hierarchical organisation of constructs. This problem has been addressed by Landfield (1977), who, as we have seen, devised the Functionally Independent Construction measure as an index of differentiation and Ordination as a measure of hierarchical organisation. Using these measures, he has found that individuals whose construing is highly differentiated but shows little hierarchical organisation exhibit 'lower feelings of self-regard and regard for others, decreased self-meaningfulness, and less ability to predict the views of others'. Hierarchical organisation has also been associated with flexibility of disclosure, while the relationship of the latter with differentiation of construing is in the inverse direction (G. Neimeyer and Banikiotes, 1980). In addition, Berzonsky and G. Neimeyer (1988) have found high differentiation of construing in adolescents to be associated with an identity status characterised by lack of commitment, coupled with low self-esteem, these features being uncorrelated with a measure of construct integration. A further measure of 'integrative complexity' of construing has been devised by Chambers (1983), who has associated low levels of such complexity with incredulity and preemptiveness.

One area in which it has been found to be of value to discriminate between differentiation of construing, generally assessed by cognitive complexity measures, and integration, generally assessed by Intensity scores, is research on the capacity of grid scores to predict aspects of vocational decision-making. Since difficulties involving vocational choice may occasionally come to the attention of the clinician, we shall briefly consider some of the relevant research. Much of this work was initiated by Bodden, and has provided evidence that individuals whose construing of occupations is cognitively complex may be more likely to make vocational choices congruent with their personality styles (Bodden, 1970; Bodden and Klein, 1972; Harren et al., 1979; Winer et al., 1979, 1980); that judgements of liked are less complex than those of disliked occupations (Bodden and Klein, 1973); and that the provision of positive information about occupations is likely to lead them to be construed in a less complex manner (Bodden and James, 1976; Haase *et al.*, 1979; Cesari *et al.*, 1984), although this effect may not be lasting nor apparent when vocational interventions are exploration- rather than information-orientated (G. Neimeyer and Ebben, 1985). While some of these findings may at first sight appear inconsistent, Cochran (1983a) suggests that they indicate that cognitively simple individuals are more likely to make premature integrations with insufficient information, and that positive information, perhaps by providing validation of constructions concerning occupations, may strengthen an individual's integrative capacity. Subsequent research has indicated the importance of integration in facilitating effective career decision-making (G. Neimeyer *et al.*, 1985); and in promoting confidence in such decision-making when construing of occupations is highly differentiated, the generation of more career alternatives when construing is less differentiated, and an approach to career choice characterised by high 'ego development' (Nevill *et al.*, 1986). These investigations, together with studies which have found no relationship between vocational differentiation and decidedness concerning careers (Cesari *et al.*, 1982, 1984), have questioned the importance of differentiation between occupations in producing effective vocational behaviour. Indeed, Nevill *et al.* (1986) found that, under conditions of high integration, high differentiation impeded recall of vocational information. The desirability of considering both the degree of differentiation and degree of integration in investigations of vocational construing has also been indicated by findings that greater distinctiveness of interests, more advanced identity development, greater decidedness concerning careers, and greater self-efficacy in making such decisions characterise individuals whose vocational construing combines high differentiation with high integration (Winer and Gati, 1986; G. Neimeyer and Metzler, 1987a).

Since, as discussed in Chapter 1, an individual's choice behaviour was assumed by Kelly to be rooted in the characteristics of his or her construct system, it should be possible to predict on the basis of a grid the particular decisions and choices which a person is likely to make. Fransella and Bannister (1967) examined the usefulness of the grid in predicting voting behaviour and found that it was possible to make accurate predictions by considering the relationships between evaluative (e.g. 'prejudiced') and political (e.g. 'likely to vote Conservative') constructs. In addition, the grid was able to demonstrate the 'brand images' of the political parties, revealing consistencies among the subjects in the way in which they construed Labour and Conservative voters; and subjects' degree of interest in politics was positively associated with the degree of relationship they exhibited between personal and political constructs. Similarly, measures derived from Repertory Tests and grids have been found to be predictive of subjects' preferences for universities (Reid and Holley, 1972; Rowles, 1972), their attitudes towards, and frequency of visiting, particular shops (Hudson, 1974; Stringer, 1976), and their religious attitudes and affiliations (Hass, 1974; Cannell, 1985). That friendship choices may also be predicted by measures of construing is indicated by Duck's (1973a; 1973b) finding that pairs of same-sex friends, and females and their male friends, have more similar construct systems than do pairs of subjects who are not friends. Consensus on physical, as opposed to factual, constructs became a more important determinant of boys' friendship choice with increasing age, while consensus on psychological constructs was increasingly important for girls and was the major characteristic of established friendships (Duck and Spencer, 1972). These and subsequent findings (e.g. Duck and Craig, 1978) have led to the development of a filter model, which asserts that partners look for consensus at progressively deeper levels of their construct systems as a relationship progresses. Further support for this model has been provided by findings that, while similarity in attitudes predicts attraction at the beginning of a relationship, similarity at the level of structure of the construct system is more relevant in its later stages (R. and G. Neimeyer, 1983; R. Neimeyer and Mitchell, 1988).

Turning to an area of somewhat greater clinical relevance, although Griffiths and Joy (1971) found a repertory grid to be less accurate than a fear thermometer and a paired comparison forced choice scale in predicting subjects' phobic behaviour when confronted with various animals, it should be noted that the grid employed supplied constructs. Also, as we shall see in Chapter 6, the clinician who makes use of a repertory grid will rarely do so solely to assess how a particular element, such as a phobic object, is construed by a client. If this were the clinician's only concern, even if his or her orientation were personal construct theory, a more direct method such as a fear thermometer, or indeed simply asking the client, would be likely to be preferred to the far more time-consuming grid procedure.

A valid measure of personal construing might be expected to differentiate to some extent between subjects differing in terms of sex, social class, or other characteristics which may be associated with particular validational influences. Meaningful sex differences have been found in some repertory grid investigations. For example, studies of children have shown that girls employ more psychological constructs than boys, while adolescent boys are more likely to employ constructs relating to roles and behaviour (Brierley, 1967; Little, 1968). Even when construing objects, girls have been found to use more complex constructs than boys (Phillips, 1985). Landfield (1971), examining the content of the constructs elicited from men and women, found that women employed more multiple descriptions, more extreme qualifiers, and more 'high dogmatism' terms in their construing of others. He suggested that these results indicate that women are more adept at, and certain about, social construing, and perceive others more holistically. Carr (1980) has found that in an American, but not in a Malaysian, sample, females differentiated less between others than did males; and less differentiated, but more integrated, construing of occupations has also been observed in females (Bodden, 1970; Harren et al., 1979; Cochran, 1983b; G. Neimeyer and Metzler, 1987b).

However, the direction of differences between males and females in cognitive complexity scores appears to depend on the particular measures employed (Little, 1969). Other studies have considered sex differences in perceptions of parents, Giles and Rychlak (1965) demonstrating that students construed themselves as more similar to the parent of the same sex than to the opposite-sex parent, and Ryle and Lunghi (1972) also finding this to be the case in females, but not in males. They used grids with supplied constructs relating to instrumental and expressive qualities, and showed that males were construed as significantly more instrumental and less expressive than females. With male subjects, there was a significant correlation between the perceived instrumentality of one parent and the expressiveness of the other, and for the group as a whole cross-sex identification was least likely to occur when there was a large and 'appropriate' instrumental–expressive difference between the parents as construed. Similarity between parents on a 'sex-inappropriate' quality for the subject was associated with the subject seeing himself or herself as characterised by that quality. Construed resemblance to parents was related to construing of the parents as similar to each other, and the ideal self, but not the actual self, appeared to be seen as closer to the parents than to other parental generation figures. Carlson (1971) has also found that males tend to construe themselves more in terms of 'agency' than do females; while Chetwynd (1976), using grids with drawings of female physiques as elements, found that men, but not women, saw a marked difference between the roles of wife and mother, with the latter role being construed in more positive terms.

Warren (1966), comparing a working-class and middle-class sample, found that the former exhibited greater interrelationship between constructs, and interpreted his results as providing support for the hypothesis of a difference in linguistic coding (Bernstein, 1964) between these two groups. That an individual's housing conditions may influence their construing and thus their social behaviour was suggested by a grid study by Zalot and Adams-Webber (1977), who found that residents of high-rise apartments were more likely than residents of single-family homes to construe their neighbours in a complex manner and to interact with them more frequently. Ethnicity was the independent variable in Weinreich's (1979, 1983) studies of self-construing, which focussed on identity conflict, operationally defined as a function of a person's degree of identification with another and the similarity between the qualities attributed to this other and those not associated with his or her ideal self. Identity diffusion was defined as the extensiveness and magnitude of the person's identity conflicts with significant others. He found a significantly higher incidence of identity conflicts with people of their own ethnicity in minority racial groups, and particularly in girls, than in whites. Immigrant girls showed greater identity diffusion than did indigenous girls, while immigrant boys exhibited more defensive high self-esteem, tending to construe themselves and others in a globally favourable light.

The studies reviewed above provide considerable evidence of the validity of repertory grid measures in relation to a wide range of characteristics and aspects of the behaviour of 'normal' subjects, as well as giving a picture of the process of construing in such individuals. Much of the research reviewed in the ensuing chapters, which concern themselves with psychological disorder, employed repertory grid technique, and will therefore provide an indication of the validity of grid measures as indices of disorder. In addition, it will highlight features which differentiate the construing of psychologically disturbed clients from that of the normal individuals considered in the present chapter.

## The repertory grid and alternative measures

It will be apparent from the above that one of the outstanding features of repertory grid technique is its flexibility, the major limit on its range of application being the ingenuity of the investigator. It is also characterised by the rare combination which it provides of an idiographic approach coupled with objectivity in scoring, although the interpretation of grid scores may be a rather more subjective affair. Its idiographic emphasis, and the possibility of using it with illiterate people, distinguishes it from questionnaire measures, while it offers greater objectivity than most projective techniques. The face validity of many grid measures is low, and they may be able to reveal aspects of construing at low levels of cognitive awareness, thus providing access to information which is unlikely to be revealed in an interview. Last but not least, unlike many nomothetic procedures, the repertory grid is generally found to be acceptable to clients, who often remark that the procedure is an enjoyable, thought-provoking experience which is therapeutic in itself (although this does, of course, mean that the grid can be a reactive measure). A plot of elements in construct space can provide the subject with visual feedback which is relatively easy to understand and which the subject can see to be derived from his or her own responses rather than representing esoteric interpretations by the investigator.

A number of measures of semantic space and conceptual structure, particularly the semantic differential (Osgood et al., 1957) and the Q-Sort (Stephenson, 1953), show at least a superficial similarity to repertory grid technique (Bannister, 1970a). However, they are distinguished by the fact that in most cases they supply dimensions of meaning to the subject rather than eliciting them. The semantic differential makes the assumption of the generality of three specific orthogonal semantic dimensions, despite the fact that these three dimensions tend to account for only about 50 per cent of the variance in responses. It pays little attention to the subject's own personal meaning system or to the possibility that the dimensions supplied may not be applicable to the concepts under study for a particular individual. With the Q-Sort, an additional imposition on the subject is of a rating scale which ensures the same form of distribution of ratings in each study, and which Slater (1977) regards as 'unnecessarily rigid and artificial'. Further criticisms of such non-grid semantic measures are that they generally do not allow examination of the relationships between dimensions of meaning in addition to the relative placement of different concepts on these dimensions, and that they tend to employ ad hoc methods of analysis with little theoretical basis (Bannister and Mair, 1968).

## QUESTIONNAIRE MEASURES OF PERSONAL CONSTRUCT PROCESSES

Chambers and O'Day (1984) have devised a 'Personal Construct Inventory' consisting of items designed to tap anxiety (e.g. 'I often fear there is something I should know but I do not know what it is'), guilt (e.g. 'I have lately done a number of things that were not "like me"'), threat (e.g. 'Things very important to me are changing'), looseness (e.g. 'My thought is often hazy and not clearly formed'), hostility (e.g. 'Power is really more important than truth'), and preemption (e.g. 'Almost all of a person's behaviour can be predicted from knowledge of a few basic characteristics of the person'), as defined by Kelly. They report 'A cross-validation r of .84 and 6-wk. test–retest rs of .60 to .89 for the scales' (p. 554), several of which were significantly intercorrelated. In their view, the inventory could 'be useful to therapists as they diagnose and guide clients through constructional processes' (p. 554). No reports have yet appeared concerning its clinical application, although in research which is still under way my colleagues and I have found that scores on some of its subscales differentiate between neurotic clients and normal subjects, and are correlated with scores on symptom measures.

Beck (1980) has also developed an 'Experiential Learning Attitude Questionnaire' to measure Kelly's concepts of anxiety, guilt, threat, fear, hostility, and aggression. However, his paper presents no results from the use of this questionnaire.

## CONTENT ANALYSIS MEASURES OF POSITIVE AND NEGATIVE EMOTIONS

As we have seen above, various methods of content analysis may be applied to constructs elicited by such procedures as the Repertory Test. However, virtually any verbal material of a reasonable length produced by an individual may be amenable to content analysis. Although such an analysis is generally not 'theory-bound', its assumption that 'the language in which people choose to express themselves contains information about the nature of their psychological states' (Viney, 1983a, p. 559) is clearly consistent with personal construct theory. As Viney also notes, 'The value of this technique for psychologists lies in its capacity to provide accurate and consistent interpretations of people's accounts of events without depriving these accounts of their power or eloquence' (p. 560).

One of Viney's major concerns, particularly in her work with the physically ill, has been the assessment of positive and negative emotional states from responses to open-ended instructions such as the following:

> I'd like you to talk to me for a few minutes about your life at the moment – the good things and the bad – what it is like for you. Once you have started I shall be here listening to you; but I'd rather not reply to any questions you may have until a five minute period is over. Do you have any questions you would like to ask now, before we start?
>
> (Viney and Westbrook, 1981, p. 48)

Responses are generally tape recorded, and considered codable if they consist of at least fifty words.

Some of the scales which Viney and her colleagues have employed to assess negative emotions, namely Total Anxiety, Hostility Directed Outward, Hostility Directed Inward, and Ambivalent Hostility, were devised by Gottschalk and Gleser (1969), working within a psychoanalytic framework. Considering that the Total Anxiety scale did not tap anxiety as defined by Kelly (see p. 11), Viney and Westbrook (1976) have produced a scale to assess cognitive anxiety, defined as 'a reaction to inability to anticipate and integrate experience meaningfully' (p. 148), as a result of:

(a)   extremely novel stimuli, not before experienced and therefore not covered by the construct system;
(b)   extra constructs needed, but not available;
(c)   incongruous stimuli, leading to conflict within the construct system;
(d)   responses unavailable, generating uncertainty;
(e)   high rate of stimulus presentation, or any other problem interfering with cognitive processing. (p. 141)

To score a passage for cognitive anxiety, it is divided into clauses and each clause referring to any of the above categories is weighted either three, two, or one according to whether it contains self-references, references to others, or spontaneous statements of denial respectively. The weighted sum of statements indicating cognitive anxiety is multiplied by a correction factor consisting of 100/the total number of words in the passage, and added to half of the correction factor, an individual's cognitive anxiety score being the square root of the figure thus obtained. The Cognitive Anxiety scale has been found to have acceptable inter-rater reliability; to be highly correlated with measures of state, but not trait, anxiety; and to reveal higher scores in individuals faced with many new events, such as students enrolling at university, mothers describing a recent child-bearing experience, and women relocated to new housing, but lower scores if these events can be anticipated meaningfully.

To measure individuals' perceived degree of control over their lives, Westbrook and Viney (1980) have developed Origin and Pawn scales. The former concerns perceptions of one's behaviour as determined by choice, as reflected in statements concerning the individual's intentions; exertion; ability; influence over, or overcoming of, others or the environment; or causal role. High scores on the Pawn scale are reflected in statements by the individual that he or she did not intend an outcome; did not try to bring about an event; lacks ability; is controlled by external forces; or sees himself or herself as a pawn. Inter-rater reliability of the scales has been found to be satisfactory, and scores have been found to be relatively stable and to reflect the life events, such as illness, which individuals are experiencing, and their coping strategies, but to be unrelated to scores on a measure of Rotter's (1966) scale of internal–external locus of control. This latter finding is regarded as indicating that the Origin and Pawn scales are assessing changing patterns of causal perception rather than a personality trait; that Rotter's questionnaire, in contrast to these scales, 'required respondents to construe their experiences in certain predetermined ways and so to answer questions which were not necessarily meaningful to them' (Viney and Westbrook, 1981, p. 48); and the invalidity of the assumption that perceived locus of control is unidimensional.

Apart from the experience of being an 'origin', Viney and Westbrook have been concerned to assess other positive feelings, just as has Gottschalk (1974) with the Hope scale. Their Positive Affect scale (Westbrook, 1976) assesses the degree to which individuals report positive feelings, and it has been found to be reliable and to reveal higher scores in individuals who are in the process of change (Viney and Bazeley, 1977; Viney, 1980). The Sociality scale (Viney and Westbrook, 1979) assesses the individual's degree of positive inter-personal relationships, defined in terms of solidarity, people being construed as resources; intimacy, people being construed as sources of personal satisfaction; influence, people being construed as sources of power; and shared experience. It has been found to have high inter-rater reliability, and higher scores on the scale have been obtained by people who have more satisfactory relationships, by facilitators of interpersonal skills, by people undergoing transitions in which they have to relate to others, and by students who, in a dependency grid, focussed their dependencies on a few highly salient people.

Scores on all of these content analysis scales are derived in a similar manner to that on the Cognitive Anxiety scale, although omitting the weightings for degree of personal involvement. An additional score, indicating the 'cost of coping', may be obtained by taking the ratio of the Total Anxiety to the Positive Affect score (Westbrook and Viney, 1977). It has been found to discriminate women who believe that their relationship with their children is under threat from those at transitional points involving the formation of new relationships (Viney, 1980). This score, together with the individual score on each of the scales which they employ, is considered by Viney and Westbrook (1981) to constitute a means of assessment of quality of life from the respondent's viewpoint. Such a content analysis approach contrasts with most previous approaches, which attempt to assess the individual's quality of life from the observer's viewpoint, and from methods such as the repertory grid, which Viney and Westbrook (1979) consider to require greater intelligence, verbal fluency, and persistence on the part of the respondent. As we shall see in Chapters 4, 5, and 6, it may be employed to assess individuals' experience of illness or psychological disorder and their likelihood of successful rehabilitation, as well as to monitor changes over the course of therapy. A final set of content analysis scales developed by Viney and Tych (1985) for use with elderly clients is designed to assess the constructs used by clients in their communications in terms of Erikson's (1959) stages of psychosocial development.

McCoy (1981) has noted the consistency of Viney and Westbrook's methods, and of their general finding of relative independence of positive and negative affect (Westbrook, 1976), with the personal construct theory view of emotions. She has also suggested how these workers' content analysis scales might be modified in order to increase this consistency.

## ANALYSIS OF NATURALISTIC MATERIAL

As is apparent from the work of Viney and her colleagues, and as we have also seen in discussing self-characterisations, the assessment of an individual's construing does not necessarily require the use of very formal test procedures. Rosenberg (1977), for example, has demonstrated the possibility of evaluating an individual's construing of people, or implicit personality theory, by the analysis of material written by the individual or his or her 'free-response' descriptions of others. Free-response methods may also usefully be structured somewhat, as in the procedure employed by Gara and Rosenberg (1979), in which the subject is asked to provide the names of people fitting various role descriptions, and to list the traits which he or she considers to characterise these people, as well as the feelings which they engender. For every trait or feeling listed, the subject is then asked to judge whether or not it applies to each of the people under consideration. In analysing the data thus obtained, Gara and Rosenberg have been concerned to identify the *superset–subset* relationships between people for the subject, a superset being a person who, in the subject's view, possesses the same attributes as another person, the subset, in addition to other attributes. Such relationships may be examined by setting out the data relating to the two 'target people' concerned as in Table 2.2, and then calculating the phi coefficient, which equals $ad - bc / (a + c)$ $(c + d)$. Coefficients thus obtained may range from $-1$ to $+1$, and the higher a positive value the more person B is a subset of person A, whereas a negative value indicates that B is the opposite of A.

*Table 2.2* Attributions to two target people

| Person A | Person B Yes | No |
|---|---|---|
| Yes | a | b |
| No | c | d |

Yes = attribute describes the person concerned
No = attribute does not describe the person concerned

If phis are calculated for each pair of target people described by the subject, the matrix thus obtained may be entered into a cluster analysis as an aid to identifying the major supersets and subsets amongst the people concerned. Using such methods of analysis, Gara and Rosenberg were able to demonstrate the significance of supersets to their subjects, who were, for example, highly concerned about the opinions of these people. They suggest that, since supersets are described in terms of virtually every category of constructs in an individual's repertoire, it may be that they serve to provide the categories of constructs which are employed by the subject in the perception of other people. They may be regarded as the individual's *prototypes* (Rosch, 1978). Gara and Rosenberg also note the possible clinical significance of the fact that in over half of their subjects the self or the mother was a superset. In further refinements of their method of analysis, which they have applied in research on schizophrenia, they have developed ways of assessing the degree of elaboration and extent of rigidity in an individual's perception of the self and of others (DeBoeck and Rosenberg, 1988; Gara *et al.*, 1989), together with a computer program to carry out these analyses (DeBoeck, 1986).

In a variation of Gara and Rosenberg's procedure, Lehrer (1987) asks subjects to describe how they usually act, think, and feel in relation to each of a list of people. Each person is then rated in terms of the extent to which each of these various descriptions applies to him or her. Distances between people and between descriptors are then calculated. Another method, employing an interactive computer program, MYSCRIPT, requires the subject to make up a story concerning a typical interaction with each of the people, and to rate each of the people in terms of elements of the narrative structures of the various stories. Several methods of analysis are employed by Lehrer with both of these procedures in order to delineate the self as a 'narrative structure'.

Villegas *et al.* (1986) have also concerned themselves with the analysis of naturalistic material of an autobiographical nature, such as collections of letters, diaries, memoirs, and full-blown autobiographies. Their primary interest has been to indicate the core structures, or existential projects, revealed by such texts. The first stage of their analysis is to identify the elements and constructs in the text, and they suggest that the former may be defined as 'nominal groups', while in regard to the latter they focus on evaluative and relational (referring to a relationship between elements) descriptions. The constructs applied to each element are then listed, and each evaluative construct is categorised as negative, positive, or neutral. Excluding neutral constructs from the analysis, the percentages of positive and negative constructs applied to each element are counted, and in the case of 'ambivalent' elements, which are not clearly positive or negative, an attempt is made to identify situational factors which explain the variation in their construing. This situational analysis requires the identification of 'situational contextual units' within the text. Some of these, such as place of residence, may be referred to by the author; some will be defined by references to a particular element; some may be indicated by considering cultural, historical, economic, and social factors defining different periods or situations referred to in the text; and some may simply be defined in terms of periods of time. The consideration of such situational contextual units may allow an ambivalence in the construing of an element to be explained by splitting the element, for example into self in situation A and self in situation B, one of which is construed negatively and the other positively. If this is not possible, however, it may be concluded that situational factors do not account for the element's ambivalence.

The next stage in the procedure is an analysis of the relationships between constructs, excluding those which are only applied to one element. This is accomplished by calculating two phi coefficients for each pair of constructs, one to assess the extent to which construct A implies construct B and the other to assess the reverse implication. For example, in order to assess the former type of implication, a table similar to Table 2.2 would be constructed with the columns referring to construct B, the rows to construct A, and the cell entries to the number of times both constructs are applied to an element, A is applied and B is not, B is applied and A is not, or neither is applied. As in the work of Gara and Rosenberg (1979), a cluster analysis may be performed on the matrix of phi coefficients, and supersets and subsets amongst the constructs may be identified. The same procedure may then be adopted to analyse the relationships between elements in the text.

While the clinical utility of this method has yet to be explored, it is possible that it could be valuably applied to the analysis of therapy transcripts, or of self-characterisations if these were of sufficient length. Its potential in the clinical area is indicated by a report by Feixas and Villegas (1988) of its application to the diary of an anorexic woman who killed herself at the age of 33. For example, using as elements the self at different ages, it was found that the constructs used to describe herself at the age when she died had the highest degree of structural organisation but were relatively unrelated to constructs used at other ages. Also of possible relevance to her suicide was the finding that her ideal was orthogonal to a life–death dimension, and that the diary was highly logically consistent, a pattern which, as we shall see in the next chapter, is characteristic of depressives.

## SUMMARY AND CONCLUSIONS

The two major assessment methods derived from personal construct theory are the self-characterisation and the repertory grid. The former allows the exploration of a person's self-construing, and, while it is generally employed as a source of qualitative hypotheses about an individual, it may also be subjected to various quantitative analyses. Repertory grid technique is a variation on the Role Construct Repertory Test which allows the investigation of a person's construing of various aspects of his or her world, of the relationships between constructs, and of the structural properties of the construct system. It is an extremely flexible procedure, and is amenable to several forms of analysis, most of which are now available in computer programs. There is research evidence that the likely degree of stability or change of particular grid scores is predictable on the basis, for example, of the particular aspects of the individual's construing which they reflect and the general structural features of the person's construct system. Numerous studies have also provided evidence of the construct, concurrent, and predictive validity of various grid scores.

The virtually exclusive reliance of personal construct theory researchers on the repertory grid is perhaps lessening as various other assessment methods which draw upon the theory have become available. For example, laddering and pyramiding allow the elicitation of constructs at different hierarchical levels of the person's construct system; implications grids explore the interrelationships between constructs; construing processes may be assessed by questionnaire; open-ended interviews and free response methods provide material which may be subjected to content analysis and other procedures; and methods of analysis of textual material from a personal construct theory perspective are also now available. The focus of several of these methods on naturalistic material, with minimal constraints placed on the subject's responses, is very much in keeping with the spirit of personal construct theory. It is likely that the accounts and stories which people provide concerning significant events in their lives will increasingly be recognised as an invaluable source of information concerning their construing (Harvey, 1989; Mair, 1988, 1989a, 1989b).

# Part II

# Construing in psychological disorder and its treatment: a review of research

Kelly (1955) took pains to point out that his was 'not a system based upon psychopathology' (p. 831), and his presentation of disorders was in terms not of conventional nosological categories but of the diagnostic dimensions, outlined in Chapter 1, which he assumed to be applicable to the construing of any individual, whether or not he or she is considered to be psychologically disturbed. Since these dimensions are not independent of each other, a particular individual's difficulties may be usefully described in terms of more than one dimension. Kelly's resulting discussion of disorders was presented in two chapters, one on 'disorders of construction' and the other on 'disorders of transition', but it is evident that this also does not represent a clear distinction between disorders which may be characterised in terms of different dimensions since, for example, disorders involving dilation are considered in the first of these chapters while disorders involving the contrast pole of this dimension, constriction, are considered in the second. Our two chapters on disorders will not follow Kelly's original format. Rather, Chapter 3 will concern itself with disorders which may be most usefully understood in terms of structural features of the client's construing, the diagnostic dimension of dilation–constriction, or Kelly's dimensions of transition; while Chapter 4 will focus on the content of the client's construing. Finally, Chapter 5 will present the results of research on construing and reconstruction during therapy.

Although the material in this and subsequent chapters will not be ordered in terms of psychiatric diagnostic categories, these categories have been included in the index for the convenience of the reader who is more familiar with them than with Kelly's diagnostic dimensions. The reader will be enabled thereby to trace all sections of the text relevant to a particular diagnostic group defined in conventional nosological terms.

# Chapter 3

# Disorders of the structure of the construct system

That psychological well-being or its lack may be associated with structural properties of an individual's construct system has been indicated by the findings of several of the repertory grid studies discussed in the previous chapter. It has been observed, for example, that cognitive complexity facilitates various aspects of interpersonal relationships, suggesting that the person who construes very tightly may be at a disadvantage in these areas. However, it is clear that very high levels of complexity are no more conducive to psychological adjustment than are very low levels, having been associated by Sadowski (1971) with confusion, while Landfield (1977), as we have seen, has indicated the difficulties likely to be experienced by the person whose construct system is highly differentiated but poorly integrated. Such a person may be regarded as a loose construer (see p. 13), and the manifestations of loose construing in psychological disorder have been the subject of one of the largest bodies of clinical research to emerge from personal construct theory, the results of which will now be considered.

## DISORDERS INVOLVING LOOSE CONSTRUING

### Construing in 'thought disorder'

The predicament of the person whose constructs are very loosely organised was first demonstrated in a pioneering series of studies by Bannister (1960, 1962a), who examined Kelly's proposition that the thinking of some clients diagnosed as schizophrenic is characterised by loose construing. Bannister equated loose construing with weak interrelationships between constructs, and he found this, as reflected in low scores on his measure of Intensity (see p. 40), to be characteristic of the repertory grids of thought disordered schizophrenics, as was low consistency from one grid to another in the pattern of relationships between constructs.

The test which Bannister used, and which in its final version employed facial photographs as elements and supplied constructs in a grid which was completed twice by the subject, was developed into a diagnostic instrument for schizophrenic thought disorder by Bannister and Fransella (1966, 1967). In the initial validation studies for the test, thought disordered schizophrenics were differentiated from non-thought disordered schizophrenics, neurotics, depressives, and normal subjects by their lower Intensity and Consistency scores, and obtained lower Consistency scores than did organic clients. In their cross-validation study, Bannister et al. (1971) also demonstrated that Intensity and Consistency could discriminate thought disordered schizophrenics from non-thought disordered clients, except those who were brain damaged, that low Intensity was related to poor prognosis, and that thought disordered schizophrenics were also characterised by a socially deviant pattern of construct relationships. However, the results of some other studies of the test's validity have been rather less impressive. Foulds et al. (1967), for example, found that the Consistency score was significantly related, and that the Intensity score was related but not to a significant degree, to psychiatric ratings of thought process disorder in acute, but not in chronic schizophrenics; and similarly Spelman et al. (1971) demonstrated that the test could differentiate acute, but not chronic, thought disordered from non-thought disordered schizophrenics. The latter workers (Mellsop et al., 1971) reported that the Intensity, but not the Consistency, scores of manic clients differed significantly from those of thought disordered schizophrenics, while Breakey and Goodell (1972) also found that the test did not differentiate schizophrenics from manics, suggesting that this might be due to the concentration difficulties shown by both groups of clients. However, they did not specifically use thought disordered schizophrenics, and the scores of the schizophrenics were not significantly different from those of normal controls, while only the Consistency score differentiated the latter group from the manics. In another study which did not specifically concern itself with thought disordered schizophrenics, Romney and Leblanc (1975) found that the Grid Test was able to differentiate only chronic, not recently admitted, schizophrenics from other clients.

More convincing evidence of the validity of the test has been provided by Frith and Lillie (1972), by Stefan and Molloy (1982), and by McPherson et al. (1973), who showed that Intensity and Consistency, as well as measures of consistency of element allotment and of social deviation in patterning of construct relationships, differentiated thought disordered schizophrenics from non-thought disordered schizophrenics, manics, and depressives, and that each of the measures correlated with clinical ratings of severity of thought disorder in a subgroup of schizophrenics. Joensen et al. (1977) have also found the Grid Test scores of thought disordered schizophrenics to differentiate them from a range of non-thought disordered subjects, apart from organic clients. As well as its capacity to discriminate between diagnostic groups, the validity of the Grid Test has been examined in terms of its relationship with other measures, scores on the test having been related to measures of abstract conceptualisation on Rapaport's Object Sorting Test (Wright, 1973) but not to predictability of speech as measured by the Cloze Procedure (Rutter *et al.*, 1977). In addition, there is some evidence of an association between low Intensity scores and subjective distress in thought disordered schizophrenics (Livesay, 1980).

Critical attention has been paid to the Bannister-Fransella Grid Test by several other authors. For example, Phillips (1975) has raised doubts about its scoring procedure, although rightly pointing out that 'errors' in this method are essentially irrelevant when the test is used for diagnostic purposes as they were also present when the test was standardised. Cyr (1983) has proposed an alternative, mo  sensitive, method of scoring instability in grid test responses, which he found to be more highly related to ratings of thought disorder than were Intensity, Consistency, or element consistency scores. The usefulness of the test as a diagnostic instrument has been questioned by Poole (1976). While finding that clients identified as thought disordered by the test tended to be similarly assessed clinically, and that thought disordered schizophrenics were discriminated from other clients except those diagnosed as suffering from schizo-affective disorders, he reported a rate of misclassification with the test which, although lower than that obtained using base rates, is still unacceptably high. Although criticisms can be made of the retrospective nature of Poole's study, and his consequent reliance on case note diagnoses, the misclassification rate which he demonstrated was in fact little different from that in the studies mentioned above by Bannister *et al.*, Frith and Lillie, and McPherson *et al.* This means that a clinically acceptable level of misclassification has been found only in the standardisation studies for the test, which were carried out with clients whose diagnoses were clear and who would not therefore require diagnostic testing in normal clinical practice. Doubt is even thrown on this conclusion by a Bayesian analysis carried out by Allon *et al.* (1981), who found that classification levels for the test departed from chance only in the studies by Bannister *et al.* (1971) and Poole (1976), and here only because the test was better able than a random classification to identify non-thought disordered subjects. In a further study, which did not concern itself with thought disorder, Poole (1979) found that the only other symptom related to Grid Test scores in schizophrenics was the presence of ideas of reference, and that test scores were unrelated to prognosis, although he admits that the criterion variables used may have been unreliable.

Present debate centres less on the diagnostic efficiency of the Bannister-Fransella Grid Test than on the acceptability of Bannister's explanation of his results in terms of loose construing. The results cannot be interpreted on the basis of differences in such variables as age, sex, intelligence, social class, and personality factors as the independence of these from the Intensity and Consistency measures has been demonstrated (Bannister and Fransella, 1967; Kear-Colwell, 1973; Poole, 1976; Stefan and Molloy, 1982). Stefan and Molloy did find a relationship between poor memory and low Consistency scores, and Presley (1969) has suggested that the Grid Test may be primarily a measure of memory, explaining the relationship which he observed between low Intensity scores and slowness in schizophrenics' Grid Test performance in terms of the greater likelihood of forgetting prior responses when performance is slow. A similar interpretation has been offered by Romney and Leblanc (1975) for their unexpected finding that their recently admitted schizophrenic, and non-schizophrenic, subjects obtained lower Intensity scores when asked to take their time in completing the Grid Test than when urged to perform quickly, although this was not the case in chronic schizophrenics. However, their study provided no clear evidence of relationships between speed measures and Grid Test scores, and this was also the case in studies by Foulds et al. (1967) and Draffan (1972). Although Cooper (1969) found that Intensity was related to speed, in common with other investigations in this area, he was unable to differentiate thought disordered from non-thought disordered schizophrenics in terms of speed scores. A further factor which has been considered by Higgins and Sherman (1978) to be a possible basis for the Grid Test performance of thought disordered schizophrenics is low motivation. However, contrary to expectations, their attempt to increase the motivation of such clients by the promise of a monetary reward for 'doing well' on the test had the effect of reducing Intensity scores, as compared to those of a group given no incentive, despite the fact that the incentive produced enhanced performance on a card-sorting task. The authors explain this finding as being due to disruption of performance on the more complex grid task by the high arousal induced by the incentive. However, an alternative explanation may be provided in terms of the view, to be discussed further below, that loose construing is a strategy employed by the thought disordered schizophrenic to avoid invalidation of predictions. It may be that the schizophrenic client who is in a situation of high social demand, such as that in which they are offered a reward for good test performance but given no indication of what constitutes good performance except that it involves concentration and effort, will be particularly reluctant to risk invalidation and therefore more likely to construe loosely. Awareness that one's construing has been invalidated is associated by McCoy (1977) with the experience of anger, and the finding of Dingemans et al. (1983) that schizophrenics who show more anger on a mood state measure obtain lower Intensity and Consistency scores on a repertory grid test may also conceivably reflect the use of a loosening strategy by clients who have suffered particular invalidation (or who find grid administration a particularly invalidating experience) in an attempt to avoid further invalidation. Whatever the basis for this and other findings by Dingemans et al., they do at least suggest that 'much more attention should be paid in the future to mood while completing the rep grid' (p. 279).

Several other alternative concepts have been offered as providing supposedly more parsimonious explanations of Bannister's findings than does loose construing. Williams (1971), varying the elements in the

Bannister-Fransella Grid Test and finding thought disordered schizophrenics to perform poorly even when construing fictitious names and addresses, suggested that insensitivity to cues could account for their difficulties. Frith and Lillie (1972), finding that a measure of consistency in element allotment differentiated thought disordered from other clients as well as did Intensity and Consistency, suggested that their results could be explained in terms of the inability of thought disordered schizophrenics to discriminate amongst complex visual stimuli. Although Hemsley (1976) also found that both element consistency and Bannister's Consistency measure, but not Intensity, differentiated schizophrenics from depressives, his additional finding of no relationship between these scores and those on an information-processing task argued against Frith and Lillie's interpretation of their findings. These latter findings were confirmed by Van den Bergh *et al.* (1981) and, similarly, Haynes and Phillips (1973a) and Harrison and Phillips (1979), demonstrating that partialling out differences in logical consistency of grid responses between thought disordered schizophrenics and other groups removed the difference in Intensity between the groups, proposed that the performance of thought disordered schizophrenics on the Grid Test is merely a reflection of a general inconsistency in performance on all cognitive tasks. Contrasting results were obtained by McPherson *et al.* (1973), who found that partialling out of Intensity and Consistency reduced to insignificance the relationship between Element Consistency and clinical ratings of the severity of thought disorder, while the reverse was not the case. Dingemans *et al.* (1983) have also attempted to explain the grid performance of schizophrenics in terms of a cognitive deficit, namely 'episodes of attentional lapse'. They claim that this is supported by the finding, using a large grid employing twenty-two elicited elements and twenty-two elicited constructs, that an episode of marked inconsistency from one grid to another in the rating of an element on a construct is followed by a greater magnitude and duration of inconsistency in schizophrenics than in depressives or normal subjects, but one which is limited in time. Although the authors state that their results support those of Haynes and Phillips in indicating the greater importance of Consistency than of Intensity, which did not discriminate between their groups, it was in fact only Bannister's Consistency measure and not their own measure of consistency of ratings of elements which differentiated schizophrenics from depressives. Schizophrenics did, however, exhibit more changes in the polarity of their ratings than did other subjects. This study also examined differences between subclasses within the schizophrenic group, finding paranoid to be differentiated from non-paranoid, and reactive from process, schizophrenics in terms of their higher Intensity and Consistency scores, and process schizophrenics to be more likely to change the polarity of their grid ratings.

Perceptual and attentional deficits such as those described in some of the above studies could be conceptualised as resulting from a loose construct system, but much of the discussion in the literature is characterised more by acrimony than by clarification of these issues (Bannister, 1972, 1973; Haynes and Phillips, 1973b, 1973c). Further support for Bannister's position is provided by a number of additional research findings. For example, the results of his original 1960 study cannot be explained in terms of inconsistency of element allotment as the two grids completed by each subject employed different elements. Also, it has been shown that inconsistency and low Intensity of construing do not extend throughout the thought disordered schizophrenic's construct system but are more characteristic of the use of psychological than of physical constructs, even when these are applied to the same elements, and more apparent when people rather than when objects are construed (Bannister and Salmon, 1966; McPherson and Buckley, 1970; McPherson et al., 1975; Heather, 1976). As well as being more likely to exhibit thought process disorder, it has been observed that schizophrenics with loose, unstable systems of psychological constructs tend to show inappropriate or blunted affect, together with delusions or hallucinations involving disturbance of their awareness of themselves as agents, tend to use psychological constructs infrequently and to employ less extreme ratings on such constructs, and are poorer at assessing the meanings of psychological, but not non-psychological, concepts in a Word-in-Context test (Salmon et al., 1967; McPherson, 1969; McPherson et al., 1970a, 1970b, 1971a, 1971b; Bodlakova et al., 1974; Kirk, 1984). By contrast, schizophrenics with stable, coherent subsystems of psychological constructs are more likely to exhibit delusions of persecution and to fall into Foulds' (1965) category of integrated psychosis. The findings of several of the above studies are interpreted by Schnolling and Lapidus (1972) as being due to the greater complexity of the human than the object stimuli, but this criticism could not be levelled at the studies by McPherson and Buckley (1970), Heather (1976), and McPherson et al. (1975), all of which controlled for such a difference. An explanation of findings in this area in terms of cue insensitivity could also not be applied to a study such as Heather's, in which the use of people rather than photographs as elements was designed to eliminate any difference between availability of cues relating to physical characteristics and those relating to psychological characteristics. While criticisms have been levelled at the statistical procedures employed in some of these investigations (Phillips, 1977), reanalysis of the data has continued to provide support for the specificity of schizophrenic thought disorder, at least when assessed by Consistency scores (Heather et al., 1978). Nevertheless, Harrison and Phillips (1979) remain critical of much of the previous research in this area, and while their study lent some support to previous findings in terms of differences in Intensity, but not Consistency, scores between diagnostic groups, they report that such differences were largely a result of the lower Intensity scores of normal subjects than of schizophrenics when rating objects on unfamiliar physical constructs. Despite inconsistent results such as this, the overall findings of this body of research, together with Adams-Webber's (1977b) demonstration that thought disordered schizophrenics and other subjects show lower Intensity in their use of the evaluatively negative than of the positive constructs in the Grid Test, do at the very least indicate that the repertory grid performance of thought disordered schizophrenics cannot be explained in terms of a general cognitive deficit. That their performance is also not completely random, and that structural breakdown in their psychological construing is therefore not total, has been demonstrated by Draffan (1973). Nevertheless, Space and Cromwell (1978, p. 156) consider that 'whether conceptual breakdown in schizophrenia is solely a function of attention and retrieval problems, or is in at least some respects independent of it, is still an open question'.

Some additional, if rather weak, support for Bannister's explanation of schizophrenic thought disorder has also been suggested by studies which have employed alternative grid-based measures of construct organisation. For example, the report by Leitner (1981a) that schizophrenics are characterised by fragmented relationships between feelings, values, and behaviour is consistent with a formulation in terms of loose construing, as is Klion's (1988) demonstration that schizophrenics exhibit higher differentiation, and somewhat lower integration, on Landfield's FIC and Ordination measures (see p. 40) than non-schizophrenic psychiatric in-patients. High differentiation, as assessed by the FIC measure, has been related by Phillips (1976) to more eccentric, paranoid, and 'schizophrenic' responses to the Minnesota Multiphasic Personality Inventory in psychiatric in-patients, the former two characteristics also being associated with low Intensity scores from a grid employing elicited constructs and elements. Also consistent with Bannister's formulation is the finding by Space et al. (1983) that more factors are obtained by principal component analysis of the grids of schizophrenics than of those of depressives and normal subjects, although this is not true of their additional finding of no difference between the groups in the size of the first factor. Ashworth et al. (1982) did find that the three largest components from principal component analysis of schizophrenics' grids accounted for less of the variance than did those of depressives, although not differing significantly from other groups. The low level of construct interrelationship displayed by the schizophrenics in this study was indicated by the additional finding that none of their grids were 'monolithic', in the sense of containing a single large cluster of interrelated constructs (see p. 41), and any smaller construct clusters which were apparent tended not to be linked to other clusters, their construct systems being less likely to be articulated than were those of recovered depressives and medical patients. These studies are only of limited relevance to schizophrenic thought disorder, however, in that their schizophrenic subjects were not classified in terms of thought disorder. In research which did concern itself with thought disordered schizophrenics, Livesay (1983) reports the surprising finding that, although less consistent in their grid performance and in their interpersonal judgements than non-schizophrenic clients (Livesay, 1981), thought disordered schizophrenics obtained higher scores on Bieri's measure of cognitive simplicity. In attempting to explain this discrepant finding, Livesay admits that his diagnostic criteria for schizophrenic thought disorder, namely the Spitzer *et al.* (1978) system, may have been questionable, but most other studies have similarly based their diagnoses on psychiatric interviews. Perhaps of more relevance is the fact that his appears to be the only study in this area in which the schizophrenic subjects were out-patients, all of whom had had at least one previous psychiatric admission but presumably had now recovered sufficiently to be discharged. That such a group might be particularly likely to be characterised by cognitive simplicity in their construing was suggested by Klion's (1985) report that those schizophrenics in his sample whose symptoms had remitted, in common with those who appeared to be attempting to extort validational evidence for their beliefs, were characterised by low differentiation in construing.

One of the major advantages of a personal construct theory model in this area is its heuristic value, in that it necessarily provides implications about the schizophrenic process and the development of thought disorder rather than being purely descriptive. For example, the loosening or tightening of a construct subsystem would be seen in terms of its validational history. If an individual's construing of a particular element is invalidated, he or she may 'slot-rattle', allocating the element to the opposite poles of constructs from those which were originally seen to characterise it. Constant re-evaluation of elements in this way would be equivalent to a state of low element consistency, but might eventually lead to the construct system itself being regarded as inadequate, and to its modification. One such modification would be a loosening of the linkages between constructs, producing a system of the type which Bannister observed in his thought disordered schizophrenics. He hypothesised that such a system serves as a defence against further invalidation in an individual whose construing has been serially invalidated, the predictions generated from a loose system being too vague to be invalidated. This 'protective effect' of loosening in 'the thinking of certain schizophrenic clients' is described by Kelly (1955, p. 497) thus: 'The conceptualization is so loosened that they seem to have a system that still covers everything. They are not caught short of constructs. But what constructs!' In Kelly's view, such a client, particularly by the loosening of superordinate structures, 'escapes, for the time being at least, the chaos of anxiety' (p. 854). However, the cost of this strategy is indicated by drawing upon R. Neimeyer's (1985a) notion that severity of disturbance is related to the earliness of the stage at which the person's Experience Cycle is disrupted. In the habitually loose construer, the disruption occurs at the Cycle's very first stage, the person being unable to frame any coherent anticipations of events.

In a series of experiments, Bannister (1963, 1965b) tested out his serial invalidation hypothesis by attempting to produce loosened construing in normal subjects by invalidating their use of certain constructs in a facial photograph sorting task and to tighten the links between certain other constructs by validating them. In his first study, there were no significant structural changes in his subjects' construct systems, but there were changes in the content of their construing, reflected in modification of the pattern of relationships between invalidated constructs. It was felt that one of the reasons for the lack of structural changes was that no attempt was made to ensure that all the invalidated constructs were in one construct subsystem for the subject and all the validated constructs in another subsystem with little relation to the first. In further studies designed to overcome this difficulty by invalidating all the constructs used by one group of subjects and validating all those used by another group, there was significant tightening of the relationships between validated constructs but no loosening of relationships between invalidated constructs, although marked differences were observed in the reactions of individual subjects. Those whose construct systems were initially highly structured showed much more loosening in response to invalidation than did those with originally loosely structured construct systems. Bannister felt that invalidating all the constructs used by a subject would present the very threatening prospect of total loss of structure, which he or she would resist by constantly changing the pattern of construct relationships. Therefore, he carried out a final experiment in which all the constructs in one subsystem were invalidated and all those in another were validated, at last obtaining the expected result of tightening of validated, and loosening of invalidated, constructs.

In suggesting how schizophrenic thought disorder may develop, a personal construct theory analysis also carries implications for its therapeutic modification, and this was the focus of Bannister's subsequent work on his project. He and his colleagues attempted to identify residual islands of structure in the construct systems of thought disordered schizophrenics and to arrange each subject's environment in such a way that predictions in these particular areas of relatively structured construing would be validated and the linkages between constructs tightened (Bannister *et al.*, 1975). There were some changes in the predicted direction in the experimental group but no clear modification in degree of thought disorder, possibly because insufficient control was obtained over the clients' environment; or because, in devising means of validating the clients' predictions, their constructs had been operationally defined as constructs with the same verbal labels would be defined by people in general. This latter could well be an unjustified assumption for, as with the subjects in the serial invalidation experiments, distortion of the pattern of construct relationships could have occurred in the schizophrenics so that a particular construct might mean something very different to each of them than to the general population.

A formulation of the schizophrenic's response to inconsistency and invalidation which is somewhat different from Bannister's has been provided by Radley (1974a), drawing on some of the subsidiary results of Bannister's (1962a) study. One of these findings was that schizophrenics show less variability in their Intensity scores than normal subjects, thought disordered schizophrenics having a homogeneously loosely organised and non-thought disordered schizophrenics a homogeneously tightly organised system. Radley inteprets this as indicating that, whereas normal individuals have 'articulated' construct systems, consisting of interlinked clusters, the systems of schizophrenics lack the superordinate linkages which for the normal person allow some resolution of inconsistencies in their experiences. Without this means of integrating apparently incompatible information, the schizophrenic has to adopt alternative strategies in an attempt to resolve inconsistencies, and the Grid Test performance of schizophrenics could be regarded as reflecting the operation of such strategies rather than indicating some deficit in construing. As Radley puts it, 'Instead of approaching the problem of the schizophrenic process from the point of view that the schizoid person is somehow inconsistent, it might be more profitable to assume that he is attempting to maintain a consistent understanding of the events he construes' (p. 320). Elements may be constantly reallocated from one construct pole to another or, to maintain a consistent understanding of inconsistent events, the individual may adopt the strategy of allocating elements to only one pole of each construct. This tendency, which was observed by Bannister (1962a) in his sample of non-thought disordered schizophrenics, and has also been found to characterise this group by Van den Bergh et al. (1981), is one 'in which the person is actively seeking validation for his chosen construction while simultaneously avoiding evidence supportive of the contrasting construction' (Radley, 1974a, p. 322). If inconsistency is still experienced, however, the person may modify the individual constructs in his or her system such that they become more loosely formulated and idiosyncratic. Radley's analysis therefore differs from Bannister's in concerning itself with changes in the way in which the schizophrenic's constructs are applied to events, and in the resulting 'dedifferentiation' of the construct system rather than in the inter-relationships between these constructs. Formulations which, like Radley's, view schizophrenic thought disorder as an attempt to resolve internal inconsistencies within the construct system have also been provided by Space and Cromwell (1978) and by Carroll (1983), who demonstrated that the construct systems of schizophrenics classified as thought disordered on the basis of their Grid Test scores are more imbalanced than those of non-thought disordered subjects in that the interrelationships between constructs and between elements are less likely to reflect the evaluative valences of these constructs and elements for the individual (see p. 44). Like Bannister and Radley, Carroll relates her findings to those theories which view the schizophrenic as being confronted with, and having to make sense of, a family environment which is characterised by inconsistency and 'imbalance' (e.g. Bateson et al., 1956). Space and Cromwell (1978) draw similar parallels, although also making the point that 'double-bind communication is less important than the conceptual structure of the person who receives it. Some individuals develop a structure which allows them to subsume, revise, or reject conflictual communications; others develop construct clusters that make conflict self-perpetuating (that is, binding)' (p. 163).

Both Bannister's and Radley's analyses suggest, consistently with clinical observations, that prior to reaching a state of formal thought disorder, the schizophrenic may first pass through a phase of disorder in the content of construing. Repertory grid studies have also indicated that, even when there appears to be total structural breakdown, islands of relatively structured construing, idiosyncratic in content, may remain and can be tapped by grids using elicited constructs (Winter, 1971; McFadyen and Foulds, 1972). The thought disordered schizophrenic's disorder of content of construing may take the form of unusual associations between constructs, as Bannister found in his original studies and was confirmed in more recent studies (McPherson et al., 1973; Van den Bergh et al., 1981). It may also reveal itself in a shift in the focus of convenience of the construct system, as is perhaps suggested by the research, reviewed above, which has indicated a more loosely structured subsystem of psychological than of physical constructs in schizophrenics. These latter studies have been considered to be consistent with psychogenic theories of schizophrenia, which 'would predict that the disorder will be maximal in those concepts whose development is most dependent upon personal relationships, such as those to do with personality and emotions, and will be minimal in impersonal concepts, such as those to do with physical properties or appearance' (McPherson et al., 1975, p. 314).

If the schizophrenic's initial response to invalidation is to develop a subsystem of constructs with idiosyncratic interrelationships, it might be expected that little validation would be received for the predictions derived from this subsystem, so that its structure would tend to become progressively looser. Furthermore, as Kelly (1955) pointed out, the looser the individual's construing becomes, the more likely he or she is to be experienced as unpredictable and anxiety-provoking, and therefore to be avoided, by others, removing even further sources of validational evidence for his or her construing. Indeed, perhaps the only people who are not likely to withdraw from the loose construer are those whose construing is equally loose. Although it may appear that a wave of loosening is likely gradually to extend over the schizophrenic's construct system, an explanation must be provided of why some schizophrenics merely alter the content of their construing in response to invalidation, and maintain a paranoid integration, while others proceed on to structural breakdown. Bannister and Fransella (1986, p. 150) suggest that a person's reaction to serial invalidation depends on the initial state of development of the construct system: 'Thought disorder may be the fate of the person whose construct system had never developed beyond a relatively embryonic level, and paranoia may be the result of pressures on a construct system which was largely workable until traumatic interpersonal difficulties were met.' In the serial invalidation experiments, Bannister found that the more catastrophic reactions to invalidation occurred in those individuals whose construct systems were initially of high Intensity and, as we have seen in Chapter 2, similar findings have been obtained by other workers. Adams-Webber (1970b) has, therefore, put forward the view that many thought disordered schizophrenics may originally have had highly unidimensional construct systems, tightly organised under relatively impermeable superordinate constructs, but whose 'actual structure' implied 'potential chaos'. Such a construct system would have a narrow range of convenience and would be particularly susceptible to invalidation, which would lead to eventual collapse of the rigid structure. Kelly (1955) notes, however, that in such cases the person may retain vestiges of tight construction by blocking off areas of experience, or in other words by constriction. The differences in premorbid construct systems between individuals who show 'paranoid' and 'schizophrenic' reactions to invalidation have been elaborated by Lorenzini *et al.* (1989), who consider that the systems of the former individuals are poorly differentiated, highly integrated, consist of 'long chains' of hierarchically linked constructs, and become increasingly internally coherent and rigid. As they put it, 'Nothing is trivial for the future paranoid because each prediction involves even the central aspects of the system that construe the identity of the self' (p. 422). Such an individual, as Kelly (1955) described, may be seen as having highly permeable core constructs. In the view of Lorenzini *et al.*, clinical onset of paranoia follows a central invalidation of the self, to which the individual is only able to respond by extreme hostility, since no alternative constructions are available. They note that the age of onset of schizophrenia tends to be some decades earlier than that of paranoia, and therefore occurs when the individual's construct system is likely to be less well developed. On the assumption that the schizophrenic's premorbid system therefore shows little integration or hierarchical organisation, they suggest that clinical onset of schizophrenia follows invalidation of a construct central to what little hierarchical structure is present, which causes 'a fracture of the system', in which superordinate and subordinate aspects of the system are dislocated, and considerable threat. Paranoia and schizophrenia are viewed by Lorenzini *et al.* as contrasting 'solutions' to the reduction in predictive capacity of the person's system following invalidation, the paranoid reacting by 'an exaggerated "dogmatism" ', whereas the 'schizophrenic, in order not to be wrong, renounces attempting to be right' (pp. 423–4).

Findings that individuals differ in their reactions to invalidation have led Lawlor and Cochran (1981, p. 49) to conclude that 'As an unqualified assertion, the serial invalidation hypothesis is simply wrong'. The analysis of individual differences in responses to invalidation is extended by Van den Bergh *et al.* (1985) with their 'divergence hypothesis'. They propose that the completion of the Bannister-Fransella Grid Test, in which no feedback on performance is given to the subject, may itself be an invalidating experience. They also provide evidence that thought disordered and non-thought disordered schizophrenics show contrasting responses to this situation. Thought disordered schizophrenics were found to weaken the interrelationships between their constructs, obtaining lower Intensity scores, when completing the second grid in the Grid Test, while non-thought disordered schizophrenics, like normal subjects, strengthened these relationships. Furthermore, these results were found to be specific to the use of psychological constructs, when applied to people, not being apparent when grids employed physical constructs or chairs as elements. There were also indications that the strengthening of construct relationships observed in non-thought disordered schizophrenics was greater than that in normal subjects and that, like the loosening of relationships in thought disordered schizophrenics but in contrast to the results of normals, it was associated with a decrease in the variability of construct relationships and therefore in the differentiation of the construct system. Van den Bergh *et al.* interpret these findings as suggesting that both thought disordered and non-thought disordered schizophrenics attempt to avoid invalidation by 'incomplete construing' or 'loss of conjunctivity'. In the former group, this involves 'taking into account only one or a few construct aspects on a random-like basis', whereas in the latter it involves 'focusing systematically on only one or a few but always the same construct aspects' (p. 67), resulting in the lopsided construing and tightness of construct relationships observed in the non-thought disordered schizophrenics whom these workers studied. One of their further findings (DeBoeck *et al.*, 1981) was that while in most subjects the strength of relationships between pairs of constructs increased with the number of intervening constructs between the pairs in a grid, this was not so with schizophrenics. In this case, however, there was no difference between thought disordered and non-thought disordered schizophrenics.

In addition to studies of the construing of schizophrenics, there has been a certain amount of repertory grid research on the families of such individuals, which sheds some further light on the possible early validational fortunes of the schizophrenic's construing. Romney (1969) found the relatives of schizophrenics to perform no more abnormally on the Bannister-Fransella Grid Test than those of neurotics and of normal subjects when the effects of intelligence were partialled out, but his groups of relatives were very heterogeneous, ranging from clients' siblings to parents as old as 85 years, and this may have obscured differences between the groups. Cooper (1969) could not differentiate between hospitalised schizophrenics and their relatives by means of their scores on the Grid Test; and Muntz and Power (1970) found significantly more parents of thought disordered schizophrenics than parents of non-thought disordered clients to be identified as thought disordered by this test. However, a study by Liebowitz (1970) suggested that the way in which the parents of schizophrenics employ supplied constructs, such as those in the

Grid Test, may not provide a valid reflection of the structure of their *personal* construct systems. He found no difference in differentiation between the personal construct systems of parents of schizophrenics and normal subjects, but that the former group did not make such complex use of semantic differential dimensions. Similarly, I have found that, while schizophrenics obtained lower Consistency scores on the Bannister-Fransella Grid Test than non-schizophrenic clients, and their parents lower Intensity scores than the parents of other clients, there were no differences between groups, of clients or of parents, in Intensity scores derived from a grid employing elicited constructs and elements (Winter, 1975). The Bannister-Fransella Intensity scores of clients and their parents in this study were positively correlated. Even the construing of illnesses by parents of schizophrenics, as compared to that by parents of physically ill people, has been found to be loose (Liakos *et al.*, 1975). The difference between the groups was largely in the scores of mothers, and again was only apparent when subjects used supplied, rather than their own, constructs. These various findings are consistent with views of the schizophrenic's family as characterised by looseness and inconsistency in the socially shared ways of construing (e.g. Lidz, 1968). Although such structural abnormalities do not appear to extend to the family's use of their own personal constructs, additional findings of these studies, to be discussed in Chapter 4, suggest that the personal construct systems of family members may be socially deviant in content. It may perhaps be concluded that the behaviour of parents of schizophrenics in the realm of socially shared expectations is inconsistent and serially invalidating because they themselves construe loosely in this area.

## Loose construing in other client groups

Thought disordered schizophrenics do not have a monopoly on the use of loosening as a strategy for coping with invalidating life experiences, and so it should not surprise us that there are some indications of loose construing in other diagnostic groups. For example, as we have seen above, manic clients have been found in some studies to display as much inconsistency in their construct relationships as do thought disordered schizophrenics, and while one study has found manic-depressives to obtain abnormally high Intensity scores (Joensen *et al.*, 1977), another has associated high scores on the Hypomania scale of the Minnesota Multiphasic Personality Inventory with low Intensity scores (Phillips, 1976). In Kelly's (1955, p. 1039) view, however, 'the "manic's" thinking seems ... not to be loose in the sense that the "schizoid's" thinking is'. The strategy for dealing with incompatible constructions which it reflects may be more one of dilation than of loosening. The low scores obtained by brain-damaged people on the Grid Test may also not be indicative of a strategy of loose construing as employed by the thought disordered schizophrenic.

It has been suggested that repeatedly invalidating family environments have been experienced not only by individuals who develop schizophrenic thought disorder but also by emotionally disturbed children and by people, such as the victims of 'spouse abuse', who seek help because of severe marital difficulties. There is some evidence of abnormalities of construing in each of these groups which may be indicative of a loosening of constructions in response to invalidation. Thus, Reker (1974), although presenting evidence of undifferentiated construing in emotionally disturbed boys, suggests a possible basis in terms of loose construing for his additional finding that these boys were characterised by inconsistency in their construing of people over a one-week period. Abused wives have been found to display little ordinal relationship between their constructs, particularly in relation to construing of the husband (Doster, 1985), and lower Intensity scores than non-abused women on a grid employing elicited constructs (G. Neimeyer and Hall, 1988). Finally, it is conceivable that the relatively loose construing found to characterise clients referred to a family-orientated crisis intervention service, as compared to referrals to a psychiatric out-patient clinic serving the same catchment area (Winter *et al.*, 1987), was a consequence of the invalidation experienced by the former group during their family crises.

One way in which the individual may arrive at a state of loose construing, in which 'almost any response can be construed as supportive of one's anticipations' (Rivers and Landfield, 1985, p. 171), is through the use of alcohol, and Landfield (1977) has reported that there is some evidence that alcoholics have construct systems which are either very loosely or very tightly organised. Some further indication that alcoholics are characterised by loosened constructions has been provided by Chambers and Sanders (1984), who have found that the construing of such individuals tends to be logically inconsistent, a pattern which has been associated with weak construct relationships.

While loose construing may allow individuals to avoid invalidation of their predictions, a very loosely organised construct system will be able to generate few, if any, coherent anticipations of events. In such cases, the world may appear so unpredictable that the only certainty is provided by death, with the result that the person attempts to take their life (Kelly, 1961). Landfield (1976) has provided some evidence for this view with his finding that individuals who make serious suicide attempts are characterised by relatively disorganised construct systems. Although Lester (1971) failed to find any significant difference between suicidal and nonsuicidal individuals in the cognitive complexity of their construct systems, his study was unusual in that the grid which he employed was the Situational Resources Test (see p. 26).

In occupations in which the making of precise predictions is vital, the loose construer may be at a particular disadvantage, and consequently subject to stress. This may explain the finding of Crump *et al.* (1981) that, in air traffic controllers, loose construing is associated with risk of coronary heart disease.

Some evidence of a link between loose construing and distress has also been obtained in a study of church members, who were found to be more likely to request pastoral counselling if their construct subsystems relating to belief, piety, and lifestyle were fragmented (Cannell, 1985).

## DISORDERS INVOLVING TIGHT CONSTRUING

Tightening of constructions, like loosening, may be employed as a defensive strategy to counter anxiety, the tight construer building a system which is 'designed to be anxiety-tight' (Kelly, 1955, p. 849). Lifshitz (1976), for example, provides such an explanation for her finding that the construct systems of children who had lost their father before the age of 7 were less cognitively complex than those of other children. People who are under stress, which Kelly (1955, p. 792) viewed as awareness of potential threat, have also been found to become less cognitively complex (Miller, 1968).

Persistent use of tight constructions would only be a viable strategy, however, if the individual lived in an unchanging world. Since this is never the case, the persistently tight construer is likely to run into the problems which Kelly (1955, p. 849) describes as follows:

> The person's formula making has difficulty keeping up. Repeatedly, his anticipations fail to materialize. He must start discarding constructs. Anxiety finally takes over in spite of all the elaborate little preventive measures he has taken. Now he can either resort to preverbal comprehensive structures or he can constrict. The extremes of these alternatives represent the well-known choice between psychosis and suicide.

Some of these problems were indicated by the discussion in the last section of the effects of invalidation of constructions in the individual whose construct system is very tightly organised. For such an individual, the invalidation of virtually any construct may carry implications for the predictive utility of his or her core constructs and is therefore likely to be very threatening. We have also seen that the effect of persistent invalidation on a very tightly structured system may be a catastrophic loosening of constructions. As Kelly (1980, p. 34) put it, 'some of us get so tight and literal that when our thinking is finally shattered by its predictive failures we collapse into a protective looseness from which we dare not recover'. The tight construer may, therefore, be highly resistant to modifying his or her construing in the face of evidence which appears to disconfirm it, and may display considerable hostility in Kelly's sense of this term. The inability to tolerate invalidation is likely to be particularly pronounced in the person whose superordinate constructs are so impermeable that they cannot accommodate inconsistent constructions, and in Kelly's view this is the predicament of the neurotic. Whereas the optimally functioning person 'keeps opening himself up to moderate amounts of confusion in connection with his continuous revision of his construct system' and 'avoids collapse into a total chaos of anxiety by relying upon super-ordinate and permeable aspects of his system', the neurotic individual, lacking permeable superordinate constructs, 'is always fighting off anxiety' (Kelly, 1955, pp. 895–6).

The first experimental findings concerning the structural features of construing in neurotics were derived from Bannister's studies of schizo-phrenic thought disorder (Bannister, 1960, 1962a; Bannister and Fransella, 1967; Bannister *et al.*, 1971), which included control groups of neurotic clients. He claimed that 'the essence of neurotic construing is a tendency to have overtight construct relationships ... which imply a gross restriction in the number of ways in which a neurotic can view any given situation. This would mean that all situations tend to be seen as more or less exact replications of situations previously experienced and behaviour becomes consequently rigid and stereotyped' (Bannister, 1962a, p. 834). Although his consequent hypothesis that neurotics would obtain higher Intensity and Consistency scores than normal subjects was not confirmed at a statistically significant level, neurotics exhibited the highest mean Intensity score of any group in each of his four studies, and the highest mean Consistency score in two studies. In one study, they also showed significantly less variation in the strength of relationships between individual constructs than did normal subjects, indicating a lack of differentiaion of the construct system into subsystems. In the Bannister *et al.* (1971) study, which did not employ a normal control group, neurotics obtained significantly higher Intensity scores than did all other client groups and significantly higher Consistency scores than depressive, organic, and schizophrenic clients.

Bannister's studies, therefore, did not provide strong evidence of structural abnormalities in the construct systems of neurotics. However, it should be borne in mind that his neurotic samples were very heterogeneous and rather atypical of neurotic clients generally seen in clinical practice in that all his clients were sufficiently disturbed to require hospitalisation. As we have seen, the use of supplied constructs in his grids also meant that they did not necessarily provide a valid indication of the structure of his subjects' personal construct systems. Studies which have correlated neuroticism scores with grid indices in normal subjects and in neurotics undergoing psychological treat-ment (Space, 1976; Bonarius, 1977; Chetwynd, 1977; Frazer, 1980; Robertson and Molloy, 1982) have also provided little indication that they are associated with structural abnormalities in construing. Chetwynd's study did, however, demonstrate a significant relationship between neuroticism and high variability, or extreme response style, in grid responses; while links between logical inconsistency in construing and neuroticism have been reported by Chambers and Epting (1985) and Chambers (1985), who considers these findings to reflect the anxiety which results from the 'invalidation of the very processes of prediction' (p. 33) which the use of logically inconsistent constructions implies. A further area which has received some research attention, with conflicting findings, is the relationship between manifest anxiety and lopsidedness of construing, the tendency to use only one pole of a construct scale (Chetwynd, 1977; Fransella and Bannister, 1977).

Firmer conclusions concerning construing in neurotic disorder may be drawn from studies employing grids with predominantly elicited constructs and focussing primarily on neurotic out-patients prior to their therapy. A few such studies have been carried out, and have indicated that neurotic disorder is associated with tight construct organisation as reflected in the size of the first two components from principal component analysis of grids (Ryle and Breen, 1972b; Caine et al., 1981; Winter, 1988a); in Intensity scores (Winter, 1983; Bassler et al., 1989); and in the tendency to see feelings, values, and behaviours as literally related (Leitner, 1981a). Neurotic symptoms have also been associated with a tendency to make polarised judgements on construct scales (Ryle and Breen, 1972b; Margolius, 1980; Ryle, 1981), although Button (1990) did not find this tendency to characterise his sample of non-psychotic clients. In addition, I have demonstrated a relationship between neurotic symptoms and a high level of logical consistency in construct relationships (Winter, 1983) as indicated by grid analysis with Slade and Sheehan's (1979) CONFLICT computer program. The latter finding supports Kelly's assertion that neurotics do not possess the permeable superordinate constructs which would allow them to tolerate inconsistency, although it is itself inconsistent with the findings mentioned above from studies of normal subjects using a very different measure of logical inconsistency (Chambers, 1985; Chambers and Epting, 1985). A possible explanation of the difference in the results obtained with neurotic clients and with normal subjects is that in the former group logical consistency in construing is simply a reflection of very tight construct relationships since, as I have described elsewhere (Winter, 1983), more logically consistent construct relationships are likely to be identified by the CONFLICT program if the strength of construct interrelationships in a grid is generally high than if it is more moderate. Some support for this argument is provided by the finding that, while logical inconsistency of construct relationships has been found to be inversely related to the strength of these relationships in neurotic clients (Winter, 1983), this is not the case in normal subjects (Dewey and Slade, 1983), perhaps because the level of correlation between their constructs is less extreme. It should be noted, however, that in a client population of unspecified diagnosis, Chambers et al. (1986) did find evidence that logical inconsistency is not purely a structural feature of a client's construing, divorced from content, in that therapists showed some ability to discriminate the inconsistencies extracted from their clients' grids from 'bogus' inconsistencies.

A pattern of tight construing and intolerance of uncertainty might be expected to be particularly characteristic of the obsessional client, whose construct system, according to Kelly (1955, p. 89), 'is characteristically impermeable; he needs a separate pigeonhole for each new experience and he calculates his anticipations of events with minute pseudomathematical schemes'. It was surprising, therefore, that the obsessive-compulsive neurotics included in the standardisation sample for the Bannister-Fransella Grid Test tended to obtain scores indicative of very loose construing, Bannister and Fransella (1986, p. 151) observing that 'it was as if the obsessional person was living in the only world that was meaningful to them – outside the area of their obsessions all was vagueness and confusion'. As Fransella (1974) has pointed out, however, the obsessional's construct subsystem concerning the self and his or her obsessional concerns may present a very different picture, representing an island of structure amidst the 'vagueness and confusion' of a system with a generally loose organisation. A repertory grid employing elicited elements and constructs might be more likely to tap this tightly organised subsystem than would the Bannister-Fransella Grid Test. It is therefore of interest that, using such a grid, Makhlouf-Norris and her colleagues (1970, 1973), although unable to demonstrate any differences between obsessive-compulsive clients and non-psychiatric patients in the strength or consistency of their construct relationships, did find that the former group more frequently exhibited 'non-articulated' construct systems (see p. 41). However, in the absence of a control group of non-obsessional neurotics, it cannot be concluded that non-articulated systems are specific to obsessionals rather than to neurotics in general. The conclusions which can be drawn from these findings are also limited by Millar's (1980) failure to replicate them, although he did find that obsessionals were differentiated from normal subjects by their lower cognitive complexity, albeit not significantly lower than in the neurotics investigated by Ryle and Breen (1972b). Caine et al. (1981) have found neurotic clients who admit to obsessional symptoms to have relatively unidimensional construct systems; but Weeks (1985) has failed to demonstrate any relationship between non-articulated structure of the construct system and obsessionality, or any differences in this aspect of construing between groups of neurotic, arthritic, and hypochondriacal clients. The high frequency of non-articulated structures which he observed in all his groups led him to conclude that his study 'shows that non-articulated conceptual structure is not specific to obsessive-compulsive neurosis' (p. 126). It would also appear not to be specific to neurotic disorders since, as discussed above, Ashworth et al. (1982) have also observed such a pattern in clients diagnosed as schizophrenic. Non-articulated construct systems have been reported by Fisher (1985) to be common in amputees, and she suggests that this may indicate that they have tightened their construing in response to the traumatic experience of amputation. Mottram (1985) also found a high frequency of monolithic construct systems (in which there is only one major cluster of constructs) in anorexic clients, although Batty and Hall (1986) failed to observe such a pattern in a small sample of people with anorexic or bulimic symptoms. An additional finding from Mottram's study was that anorexic clients exhibited stronger relationships between constructs and more extreme ratings of grid elements than did normal control subjects. This is consistent with the observation in a non-clinical population that a rigid pattern of interpersonal construing, reflected in a poorly differentiated but highly integrated construct system, was associated with high levels of eating disorder (Heesacker and G. Neimeyer, 1989).

The finding that non-articulated construct systems characterise various client groups is consistent with the view of Mancini and Semerari (1987) that such systems are likely to show a low rate of increase in their predictive capacity, for example following invalidation. This low 'knowledge increase rate' is, for these workers, the essence of psychological disorder, and they equate awareness of it with the experience of depression. That tight construing may characterise clients diagnosed as depressive is also suggested by the view of some researchers (e.g. Ashworth *et al.*, 1982; Space and Cromwell, 1980) that tight construct relationships reflect constriction of the construct system, which Kelly felt to be a feature of depression. However, various studies have failed to differentiate depressives significantly from normal subjects or, in most cases, from other client groups (Bannister, 1960, 1962b; McPherson *et al.*, 1973; Space and Cromwell, 1980; R. Neimeyer *et al.*, 1983a, 1985; Space *et al.*, 1983; Ross, 1985; Axford and Jerrom, 1986), despite the fact that in some of the studies depressives obtained the highest mean scores of any group on measures of construct interrelationships. In one of the latter studies, by Ashworth *et al.* (1982), depressives differed significantly only from those clients (schizophrenics, alcoholics, and manics) whose construct systems might have been particularly loosely organised, and not from recovered depressives and physically ill patients.

Two studies which did demonstrate significantly tighter construct organisation in depressives than in normal subjects used rather different grid procedures from those employed in the investigations mentioned above. Silverman (1977) asked his subjects to rank the Bannister-Fransella Grid Test elements both in terms of the supplied constructs of this test and in terms of six supplied constructs relating to affect. While depressive and normal groups did not differ in their structuring of the Bannister-Fransella constructs, depressives did, as predicted, obtain significantly higher scores than the control subjects when using the affective constructs. In considering these results, however, it should be borne in mind that Silverman (p. 17) admits that his control group 'was probably of a higher socio-economic status and higher average intelligence' than his sample of depressives. The other study which has revealed structural differences between the grids of depressives and normal subjects was carried out by Sheehan (1981), who found the former group to obtain higher Intensity scores and to exhibit significantly more unidimensional and logically consistent construct systems. It is of interest that the grid which she employed was unusual in that, apart from the self and ideal self, its elements were the subject's perceptions of how various significant others construed him or her. The task which her subjects were set was, therefore, a complex one, closer to Kelly's notion of sociality as involving construing the construction processes of the other person than is normal grid procedure. It is possible, therefore, that the tight construing of her depressives indicates something of the extent of the difficulties which they may experience in interpersonal relationships. However, in a later study Sheehan (1985a) found that depressives' construing of how others construed them was less tightly organised and logically consistent than was their construing of other people.

In addition to these studies of the strength of construct interrelationships in depressives, there is some evidence that depressives and suicidal individuals, like neurotics, tend to make polarised judgements on construct scales, at least when these are applied to the self (Neuringer, 1961, 1967; Neuringer and Lettieri, 1971; Dingemans et al., 1983; R. Neimeyer et al., 1983a). Our understanding of the structural characteristics of the depressive's self-construing has also been furthered by studies which have demonstrated that the core role structure of moderately depressed individuals is less tightly organised and constellatory (R. Neimeyer et al., 1985), and less characterised by constriction in the use of rating scales and more by slot-rattling (Ross, 1985), than is that of the severely depressed or of normal subjects. A possible explanation of these findings will be considered in the next chapter.

As well as the above work with neurotics and depressives, there is some evidence of tight, undifferentiated construing in various other adult client groups and in disturbed children. Perhaps not surprisingly, the repertory grid responses of people with learning disabilities tend to reveal high inter-relationships between constructs (Wooster, 1970; Spindler Barton et al., 1976; Beail, 1985a). Heroin users have been found to display less logical inconsistency in their construct relationships than do ex-users, particularly in relation to their construing of themselves as drug users (Goggins, 1988). This, and the relationship observed between logical inconsistency and number of previous successful detoxifications, are considered by Goggins to indicate greater differentiation of construing in ex-users, who are undergoing a process of cognitive reorganisation in relation to drug use. However, as we shall see below, undifferentiated construing may be a characteristic of users of depressant drugs such as heroin, not extending to all drug users.

Low cognitive complexity in interpersonal construing has been associated with emotional disturbance in boys by Reker (1974), who also found the construing of disturbed boys to be poorly articulated in that they did not discriminate highly between people on their construct dimensions. Further-more, these findings were specific to the boys' construing of people, not extending to their construing of objects. In a further study of severely emotionally disturbed boys, Hayden et al. (1977) demonstrated that those who were rated by staff members as having the poorest social adjustment obtained the highest Intensity scores on a repertory grid test and were also least accurate in arranging a series of photographs of a boy in the correct sequence.

Those boys whose grids exhibited low total variation but high lopsidedness performed particularly poorly on this latter task. Hayden *et al.* consider that their findings point to the difficulties in appropriate social behaviour and in social prediction likely to be experienced by children whose construing is relatively undifferentiated. Such links between tight, undifferentiated construing and difficulties in interpersonal relationships are, of course, quite consistent with the research findings presented in Chapter 2 indicating that cognitive complexity is associated with facility in forming role relationships. There is some further evidence for such relationships in client populations in that tight construct organisation has been associated with inaccuracies in social skills group members' construing of the constructions of other participants in the group (Winter, 1988a), and similarly of inaccuracies in agoraphobics' predictions of their spouses' construing (Harbury and Winter, in preparation). Also not unexpected are the findings of McKain *et al.* (1988) that shy people tend to have undifferentiated construct systems, as reflected in low scores on the Functionally Independent Construction measure, and that the more fear of negative evaluation and private self-consciousness they exhibit the less they tend to make fine discriminations amongst others, as reflected in Ordination scores.

Some indication of the interpersonal difficulties which may be experienced by the person whose construing is tightly organised is also provided by studies of offenders. For example, Chetwynd's (1977) finding that cognitively simple prisoners are more likely to have committed violent offences, whereas the offences of cognitively complex prisoners were more likely to have been of a fraudulent nature, perhaps reflects the limited range of options available to cognitively simple individuals in responding to interpersonal conflict. Evidence that the construing of 'conceptually simple' prisoners becomes increasingly consistent (and presumably, therefore, tighter) during solitary confinement (Ecclestone *et al.*, 1974), an experience which might be expected to remove them from sources of social invalidation, suggests the inappropriateness of such a regime for them. Although Noble (1970), studying the construing of televised aggression in delinquents, and Howells (1983) failed to find an association between tight construct organisation and violent offending, Howells did demonstrate that 'one-off' violent offenders are characterised by lopsided construing, as will be discussed in the next chapter. Lopsided construing has also been observed by Chetwynd (1977) in prisoners who have committed theft or drug offences, and has been found to characterise clients diagnosed as psychopaths (Widom, 1976), as has polarised construing (Thomas-Peter, 1990).

## Symptom choice and the structure of the construct system

There are indications that a pattern of tight construing and intolerance of uncertainty is particularly characteristic of two of the neurotic's construct subsystems: that concerning the self and that concerning the symptoms. Thus, a high degree of logical consistency in constructs salient to aspects of the self has been associated with neurotic disorder (Margolius, 1980); and constructs concerning the neurotic's symptoms have been found to be interrelated with greater Intensity and logical consistency than are their other constructs (Winter, 1983). Similarly, in one particular neurotic group, spider phobics, constructs relating to the phobia have been shown to be more highly inter-related than are the spider constructs of non-phobic individuals (Watts and Sharrock, 1984). Studies employing listing and sorting tasks have also provided some evidence of a relatively undifferentiated conceptual structure when material relating to a person's neurotic symptoms is considered (Landau, 1980; Persons and Foa, 1984). That a pattern of particularly tight construing in the area of an individual's problems is not confined to clients diagnosed as neurotic has been demonstrated by various other studies. For example, as we have seen, Silverman (1977) has demonstrated that depressives are characterised by high Intensity of construing in the area of affect, while in a non-clinical population, restrained eaters, G. Neimeyer and Khouzam (1985) have found that severity of restraint is associated with cognitive simplicity in constructions of the self in different eating situations. Fransella (1972) has reported that, for stutterers, constructs elicited from triads of elements containing the self when stuttering carry more implications, and more superordinate implications, than do those elicited from triads including the self when fluent. However, as Adams-Webber (1979) has noted, since the number of constructs elicited by the two methods was not necessarily equal, Fransella's findings may indicate that more constructs were elicited by the former method rather than that those elicited carried, on average, more implications. Consistent with Fransella's results are Meshoulam's (1978) findings, examining stutterers' construing of speaking and non-speaking situations, that their construct systems are highly organised, and tend to include superordinate constructs concerning speech difficulty, aspects of the speech task, and arousal. However, using a similar methodology to Fransella with another client group, heroin users, Goggins (1988) failed to provide evidence that constructs relating to the self when using drugs carry more implications than do constructs relating to the self when drug-free. Indeed, for both heroin users and ex-users, the latter constructs carried significantly more implications. Goggins suggests that this result may reflect the fact that his sample of heroin users had all sought treatment, and that similar findings might not be obtained with addicts who are making no attempt to give up their habit.

More than one explanation is possible of these findings concerning the high degree of structure in the construct subsystem relating to the individual's symptoms. That most commonly employed draws upon Kelly's Choice Corollary, viewing the client as 'choosing' to construe himself or herself as characterised by the symptom because to do so carries more implications, and therefore possibilities for elaboration of the construct system, than to construe the self as symptom-free. The symptom may thus become 'the rationale by which one's chaotic experiences are given a measure of structure and meaning' (Kelly, 1955, p. 366). This view has been elaborated by Tschudi (1977), and by Fransella (1970a, 1972), who sees the symptom as a 'way of life', which will not be relinquished until an equally well elaborated alternative way of life has been developed. For example, '*a person stutters because it is in this way that he can anticipate the greatest number of events*' (Fransella, 1972, p. 58, italics in original), while in the obese woman 'No permanent weight loss will be achieved until the meaning of being a woman of normal weight is at least as meaningful to her as being a fat woman' (p. 237). Such analyses receive some support from findings with normal subjects that change towards a preferred view of the self will occur only if the implicative capacity of this view is greater than that of the present self construction (Hayden, 1979). A similar perspective has been adopted by Dawes (1985) and by Viney *et al.* (1985a) in exploring the possibility that drug dependence may result from an individual developing a construct subsystem relating to the self when 'high' which carries more implications, and therefore a more certain basis from which to antici-pate events, than the subsystem concerning the self when not in a drugged state. D. Kelly (1990) has also described how socially deviant behaviour, such as offending, and the consequent labels applied to the individual concerned, may offer some structure to the person whose core role is otherwise fragile. The predicament faced by the individuals in all these examples, however, is that in constricting their world to the area of the symptom or problem behaviour, the construct subsystem concerning this area is likely to become ever more highly structured, while at the same time the individual increasingly limits his or her opportunities to elaborate an alternative self-construction offering an equivalent degree of structure. To quote Dawes' analysis of drug abuse, 'as the new subsystem is elaborated, the individual's ability to act in the problematic situation when drug free is likely to decrease, as the implications for doing so also decrease according to Kelly's choice corollary' (p. 188).

This view of the symptom as offering the client structure and certainty is regarded by Semerari and Mancini (1987) as a homeostatic model, but one which fails to account adequately for the distress which clients' symptoms cause them. They have provided an alternative model of the vicious circle in which many neurotic clients find themselves, suggesting that whenever the client receives validation of a construction of the self as characterised by the symptom, there is a simultaneous invalidation of the anticipation of move-ment towards the ideal self. This experience of invalidation, being accompanied by such negative emotions as anxiety and threat, may then invalidate even further the client's construal of the self as strong and in control. Semerari and Mancini suggest that such a vicious circle of recursive self-invalidation is particularly likely in clients, such as the neurotic, whose construct systems are so tightly organised that they have no constructs available to construe the experience of invalidation except those which have themselves suffered invalidation. Although they consider the model to have extensive applicability, particularly with clients who find their presenting symptoms inexplicable (Gardner *et al.*, 1988), its primary utility would appear to be with clients who, as may be the case with many agoraphobics (see p. 120), have characteristically seen themselves as strong and autonomous. As I have indicated elsewhere (Winter, 1990a), only in such clients would the experience of invalidation itself be invalidating to the individual's self-construction. It should also be noted that even if the symptom does cause the client pain and suffering, this need not imply that it does not also serve some purpose such as the provision of structure, such apparent inconsistencies being explicable in terms of the notion of differences between construct subsystems (Fransella, 1972). As Kelly (1955, p. 797) noted, even if the client's symptoms provide various gains, such as disability claims or control over events, 'each of these gains may be made at the cost of losses on other fronts'.

While the 'homeostatic model' of symptoms would, therefore, still appear to be viable, one further alternative analysis is possible of findings of a high level of interrelationship between constructs concerning the client's complaint. This is that such findings indicate not a highly elaborated construct subsystem but an area of tight, inflexible construing and intolerance of ambiguity, which has itself led the individual into the difficulties which come to be presented as the symptom. For example, the spider phobic may lack 'the kind of complex, multidimensional construct system for spiders presumably necessary' for them 'to pay close, detailed attention to spiders' (Watts and Sharrock, 1985, p. 152), the depressive may be in a similar predicament in relation to construing of emotion, and restrained eaters may 'see themselves as having fewer alternatives available in relation to eating' (G. Neimeyer and Khouzam, 1985, p. 367).

One of the problems in interpreting the results of the various studies in this area is the variety of structural indices employed, some of which are primarily concerned with the differentiation of the construct system while others may bear more relation to its degree of hierarchical integration. We shall return in the next chapter to the question of the client's choice of symptoms.

## DISORDERS INVOLVING DILATION

As we have seen in Chapter 1, dilation is a strategy whereby an individual may accommodate incompatibilities in construing, but this will only be possible if there is sufficient superordinate structure in the construct system to encompass the dilated field. When this is not the case, a disorder may be presented because 'the person's exploration has outrun his organization' (Kelly, 1955, p. 846). In discussing the difficulties which may be encountered by the person who employs a strategy of dilation, Kelly notes that one way in which a dilated field may be accommodated is by increasing the permeability of certain constructs. However, the person will then be likely to experience considerable anxiety and threat if later in life he or she is faced with the prospect of abandoning these constructs, perhaps because they are found to be obsolete. In attempting to find alternative constructs which have a sufficient range of convenience to impose some order on the wide range of experiences encountered, he or she may turn to preverbal dependency constructs. Having abandoned the permeable superordinate structures which would have facilitated revision of the construct system, the person cannot afford to risk invalidation of his or her construing and therefore, instead of testing out constructions, 'looks only for the "don't you love me" facts' (Kelly, 1955, p. 858).

Dilation is particularly apparent in clients diagnosed as paranoid or manic. The delusions of the former type of client may represent a sweeping elaboration of some persecutory or grandiose construction. Similarly, the excitement of the manic client, in Kelly's (1955, p. 845) view, 'represents a kind of unmodulated spontaneous elaboration'. This may be reflected in the evidence, discussed above, of inconsistency in the construct relationships of manic individuals; and a process of dilation, in which the person tries to find a new role by incorporating the characteristics of others, is also considered by Ashworth et al. (1982) to be the basis of their finding that manic clients tend to see themselves as more similar to other people than do schizophrenic, alcoholic, or depressed clients, or recovered depressives.

Finally, it should be noted that in some individuals, and perhaps particularly those who are habitually constricted, dilation may be achieved by the use of alcohol, which becomes 'an agent for a temporary feeling of conceptual expansion' (Dawes, 1985, p. 171).

## DISORDERS INVOLVING CONSTRICTION

The individual who finds that he or she cannot structure the new experiences which result from dilating the perceptual field may 'crawl back into his shell' (Kelly, 1955, p. 847) and employ the converse strategy to dilation, namely constriction. Such a shift from dilation to constriction may be construed by the clinician as a swing from mania to depression, and it is clear that persistent use of a constrictive strategy may present as many difficulties for the individual as does persistent dilation. This is because, in disregarding confusing events, 'it may let issues accumulate which will eventually threaten a person with insurmountable anxiety' (Kelly, 1955, p. 908). As an example of such a person's predicament, Kelly considers a woman, who might be diagnosed as 'a case of involutional melancholia', who has always coped with anxiety-provoking events by restricting her activities and interests but who, when eventually faced by such changes as the menopause and the increasing independence of her children, finds herself with 'more constriction than she bargained for' (p. 905). If such a woman's response to this situation is to constrict further, the outcome may be the ultimate constriction of the construct system: suicide.

As Kelly (1961) noted, various different pathways of construing may lead towards a suicidal act. Suicide may, for example, be a 'dedicated act', in which the individual who is faced with the prospect of revoking his or her core beliefs chooses to die in the anticipation that these constructions will thereby be elaborated by others. 'Mere suicide', on the other hand, represents a final constriction of the construct system when either 'the course of events seems so obvious that there is no point waiting around for the outcome', a situation which Kelly equates with depressive fatalism, or 'everything seems so unpredictable that the only definite thing to do is to abandon the scene altogether', a response which Kelly associates with 'total anxiety' (p. 260). The personal construct theory view of suicide has been elaborated by R. Neimeyer (1984, 1985d), Stefan (1977), Stefan and Von (1985), and Stefan and Linder (1985), who, following Kelly, regard suicide as 'an experience of chaos or fatalism'. As we have seen above, a repertory grid study by Landfield (1971, 1976) provided indications of the former pattern in a small sample of serious suicide attemptors in that they showed a low degree of interrelatedness between their constructs. They also exhibited signs of constriction in that their constructs, which tended to be concrete in content, were often seen as being inapplicable to grid elements or the client was unable to decide to which pole of a construct to assign an element. Using a combined repertory grid measure of structural disorganisation and constriction, Landfield was able to demonstrate significant differences in a student population between serious suicide attemptors and clients who had made suicidal gestures or displayed suicidal ideation, clients who were receiving or had terminated psycho-therapy, and better adjusted students. However, Leenaars and Balance (1984) found that clinical psychology trainees were unable to differentiate genuine from simulated suicide notes on the basis of a classification derived from Kelly's view of suicide.

Using as a measure of constriction the overuse of particular rating scale points on a grid involving daily self-ratings, Ross (1985) found constriction to be associated with high levels of depression in moderately to severely depressed clients, although in less depressed subjects the opposite relation-ship was observed. It has been argued that if depressives are characterised by constriction, this will also be revealed in a tight, logically consistent pattern of construct relationships (e.g. Ashworth et al., 1982; Space, 1976), and research bearing on this prediction has been reviewed above. In one of the few studies which did reveal such a pattern in depressives, Sheehan (1981, p. 206) concludes that 'This picture is consistent with Kelly's notion of constriction in that the depressed person appears to have narrowed his perceptual field in order to minimize apparent incompatibilities'. Some support for the view that tight construing is indicative of a constrictive delimiting of the individual's perceptual field may be derived from research findings that clients with more unidimensional construct systems obtain higher scores on a questionnaire measure of the defence mechanism of denial (Catina *et al.*, 1988) and give more 'don't know' responses to an attitude questionnaire (Winter, 1988a). It has also been suggested that the tendency of depressives to construe themselves as dissimilar to others is a further manifestation of a constrictive strategy (Hewstone *et al.*, 1981; Ashworth *et al.*, 1982). Tight, logically consistent construing, and perceived dissimilarity of self and others, have also been found to characterise neurotic clients in general (Winter, 1985b), and so it may be that all such individuals tend to exhibit constriction. The symptoms of the phobic or obsessive-compulsive client, for example, may be regarded as clear behavioural manifestations of a constrictive process, whereby the individual finds a haven of structure in an uncertain world. Research evidence, to be discussed in the next chapter, that constructs concerning interpersonal conflict may be at a low level of cognitive awareness in the agoraphobic suggests that such clients may adopt a constrictive strategy to avoid the anxiety which would result from experiences of conflict (Winter and Gournay, 1987). This study also indicates that the constrictive process may allow the client's world to be delimited to a spouse whose construct system is very similar and who is likely, therefore, to be a constant source of validation. Those clients whose construing was most similar to that of their spouses were found to be least likely to go out alone.

Abuse of certain drugs, such as those with depressant effects, may also be associated with a constrictive strategy. This has been suggested by the finding of Penrod *et al.* (1981) that low cognitive complexity, which has been associated with a repressive defensive style (Wilkins *et al.*, 1972), differentiates heroin and barbiturate users from amphetamine users. Goggins' (1988) demonstration, discussed above, of high logical consistency in the construing of heroin users is also supportive of such a view. A further client group in which constriction may be evident consists of those suffering from organic deficits. Thus, in Kelly's (1955, p. 924) view, rigidity, perseveration, and other characteristic features of the thinking of such a client 'stem from the fact that he must now reconstrue himself in a constricted world, using as his point of departure the constructs which were once richly documented, and gradually substituting for them constructs dealing with new content and with new and limited ranges of convenience'. Kelly also indicated that the client with an organic deficit may employ constructs which have 'deteriorated' in that they have become relatively impermeable. As an illustration, he indicates that an old person's construct of 'liberal', which might once have been felt to be applicable to many people and experiences, is now in fact applied to very few of these. In his account of disorders involving organic deficit, Kelly makes it clear that an 'organic picture' is not limited to clients showing organic pathology. Such a picture merely reflects the use of a constrictive strategy in an attempt to adjust to a major change in the person's life situation, which may or may not be a result of organic factors. Similarly, Brumfitt (1985, p. 104), finding relatively unidimensional construing to be characteristic of the aphasic people to whom she administered grids in an uncontrolled study, suggests that 'the CVA patient constricts in order to cope with the chaos around him'. This is reminiscent of Fransella's (1970b) observation that, while some people whose speech has been affected by brain damage obtain scores on the Bannister-Fransella Grid Test indicative of very loose construing, others construe very tightly, perhaps in an attempt to maintain some structure when faced with the threatening and anxiety-provoking situation of loss of speech.

## CYCLES AND TRANSITIONS IN DISORDER

Research studies on the structural characteristics of the construct system in different diagnostic groups may suggest that such structural properties are largely static. However, as we have seen in Chapter 1, Kelly stressed the ever-changing, cyclical nature of construing. It may be more profitable, therefore, to view excessively loose or excessively tight construing, or exclusive use of strategies of dilation or constriction, in terms of an individual's failure to complete the Creativity and Experience Cycles and so as a process rather than a trait. As Mancini and Semerari (1987) have put it, the personal construct system in psychological disorder may more appropriately be regarded as in 'pathological evolution' than in a pathological state.

The desirability of considering the process of construing which may be operating in a disorder can be illustrated by the research on suicide discussed above. The studies of people who have attempted suicide have in most cases examined their construct systems at one particular point in time, subsequent to the attempt. Such studies can, of course, do no more than provide a basis for speculation about the state of the individual's construct system prior to his or her suicidal behaviour, how this may have differed from that of individuals who have committed suicide, and whether the suicidal person is now engaged in a process of reconstruction. It may be, for example, that the disorganisation which Landfield (1976) demonstrated in the construct systems of his serious suicide attemptors could have reflected a reaction to a major invalidation of construing in individuals whose construct systems were originally structured tightly under impermeable superordinate constructs and for whom the prospect of a breakdown in this structure was 'the instigating context of suicidal behaviour' (p. 95). In the view of R. Neimeyer (1984), such 'anxious suicide attempts' are more likely to be impulsive, and less likely to be lethal, than in the case of the depressive fatalist for whom 'self-destruction merely represents the end point in a long process of constriction' (p. 134). Like Neimeyer, Stefan and his colleagues (Stefan, 1977; Stefan and Linder, 1985; Stefan and Von, 1985), in elaborating the personal construct theory view of suicide, have also considered the likely degree of impulsivity of an individual's suicidal behaviour. Following Kelly's view of impulsivity, they regard suicidal gestures as typical of those people who tend to foreshorten the Circumspection phase of the Circumspection-Preemption-Control Cycle, and who therefore plunge too hastily into preemption and control. Suicidal ruminators, conversely, are characterised by prolongation of the Circumspection phase.

Faulty control is therefore a hallmark of, but is by no means confined to, suicidal behaviour: indeed Kelly (1955, p. 927) stated that 'all disorders of construction are disorders which involve faulty control'. Thus, impulsive behaviour may reflect an attempt to escape from uncertainty and anxiety or to avoid guilt by reverting to an old, familiar role. Landfield (1980a) has also argued that difficulties in self-control are likely to be exhibited both by individuals who rigidly equate, and by those who rigidly separate, the feeling, value, and behavioural components of personal constructs (see p. 15). The former pattern may, for example, result in a person impulsively acting out feelings or fearing that any feeling which is experienced will be acted upon; while the latter may lead to impulsivity if the person acts upon feelings without considering the implications for values or behaviour. Whatever the reasons for impulsive behaviour, if it is not followed by circumspection and evaluation, the Circumspection-Preemption-Control and Creativity Cycles will not be completed adequately and there will be little possibility of constructive revision. Impulsivity in one particular client group, those diagnosed as psychopaths, has been demonstrated by Thomas-Peter (1990), who found that, when giving non-extreme ratings on a grid, they showed a speed of response, and consequent shortness of circumspection, which is normally only associated with extreme judgements. He speculates that this indicates a simple construct system in which even apparently moderate judgements are influenced by extreme judgements at a more superordinate level.

Given the view that disorders represent a failure to complete the Experience Cycle, it may be expected that all disorders are also likely to involve the negative emotions which McCoy (1981) has associated with unsuccessful construing. As we have seen, for example, both disorders characterised by excessively loose, and those characterised by excessively tight, construing may reflect strategies directed towards the optimal anticipation of events in the face of the anxiety occasioned by an unpredictable world. This is, for example, indicated in Kelly's (1955, pp. 895–6) statement that

> A 'neurotic' person casts about frantically for new ways of construing the events of his world. Sometimes he works on 'little' events, sometimes on 'big' events, but he is always fighting off anxiety. A 'psychotic' person appears to have found some temporary solution for his anxiety. But it is a precarious solution, at best, and must be sustained in the face of evidence which, for most of us, would be invalidating.

The state which is often labelled 'free-floating anxiety' is, in Kelly's view, a reflection of a breakdown of superordinate structures. However, Bannister (1985b) makes the point that anxiety never floats entirely freely in that it is always about something, even if the client is not certain of its locus.

Disorders may involve the expression or attempted avoidance not only of anxiety but also of guilt. Some support for Kelly's notion of guilt as awareness of dislodgement from one's core role has been provided by a relationship demonstrated in neurotic clients between high scores on a guilt scale and discrepancy in the use of a self element and self construct (Winter, 1983). The serious implications of such dislodgement are reflected in Kelly's (1955, p. 909) statement that 'It is generally difficult to sustain life in the face of guilt. Some people do not even try' since 'ordinary death is less threatening to people than is the total loss of their core role' (p. 910). Following this line of argument, Nuzzo and Chiari (1987) have considered the part played by guilt in the development of cancer. They suggest that, as a result of parental hostility and attempts to impose constriction on the child, future cancer sufferers are likely to have developed as children a core role involving satisfaction of the needs, and prevention of the suffering, of other people. Invalidation of this role later in life, and consequent guilt, is responded to by hostility and constriction, involving the avoidance of deep role relationships, a construction of the self as autonomous, and a distinction between the role which is played socially and the core role. Such a person may transfer all of his or her dependencies on to any relationship or activity which allows core role validation, but may then react with constriction or extreme hostility to the loss of this relationship or activity. Nuzzo and Chiari (p. 9) speculate that this is when 'the cancer process enters the scene', involving the effects of constriction on the self/non-self distinction of the immune system, such that cancer cells come to be construed as 'self cells' and to reproduce themselves unhindered.

It will be apparent that, as well as anxiety and guilt, threat is central to many disorders. In a study of adolescents drawing upon Landfield's (1954) analysis of threat, Kasper (1962) defined this emotion as involving construal of oneself by another person in terms more characteristic of one's past than of one's current progression; construal of the self as inferior to the other's view of one; and discrepancy between one's own and another's construing of change in oneself. Such characteristics were found to differentiate poorly adjusted adolescents, and in particular a clinical sample, from better adjusted subjects. The clinical sample tended to designate a parent as their most threatening person, and saw themselves as over-rated by others, whereas the 'poorly adjusted' sample tended to see themselves as under-rated by others. Dunnett (1988b, p. 326) also suggests that the essence of phobic disorders is 'the awareness of threat produced by a single invalidational event upon a superordinate core role construct of wide range of convenience'. As an illustration, he describes a spider phobic who saw spiders as 'behaving as though I was a bit of the furniture', and therefore clearly as 'threators'. By avoiding spiders, such a person is able to preserve the core constructs under threat.

Hostility, which for Kelly was a hallmark of 'bad science' and for McCoy a behaviour associated with negative emotion, is also implicated in Kelly's view of a disorder as, in effect, a failure to take into account evidence which invalidates a particular construction. As Lester (1968) has described, the extortion of validating evidence, which is the essence of hostility, may be exemplified in behaviour, such as that of some suicidal individuals, which leads to rejection and the confirmation of a view of the self as worthless or of the world as unjust. Although aggression, and the active elaboration of construing which it involves, is regarded in more positive terms than is hostility from the personal construct theory perspective, the aggressive person may run into interpersonal difficulties if he or she does not have the patience to establish role relationships. Such individuals may, for example, experience guilt if their aggression is not found to be acceptable to their social group and is inconsistent with their core role.

Further groups of disorders which Kelly (1955) included in his discussion of disorders of transition were those involving undispersed dependency and those presenting as somatic complaints. The former are, for example, exhibited by clients who, rather than developing a range of dependency relationships of different types, try to 'get everything from everybody' (p. 914) or are looking, often with considerable hostility, for one person to satisfy every dependency. As Walker *et al.* (1988) have demonstrated, such individuals are likely to be characterised by preemptive and impermeable construing. There is also some evidence that suicidal people not only feel that they have relatively few people to depend upon in difficult situations, but are in the predicament of depending highly upon people whom they resent (Lester, 1969).

'Psychosomatic' symptoms may involve some expression of dependency constructs and generally also involve core constructs. As a result, they may 'appear as if they were something which the client requires just as urgently as he requires sustenance and safety' (Kelly, 1955, p. 868). Kelly also notes that such complaints often reflect dualistic thinking: conversion symptoms, for example, entail the client placing a preemptive 'physical' construction on some aspect of his or her life. This tendency may be particularly apparent in people who tend to construe others in objective, rather than in psychological, terms. However, such considerations will be the concern of the next chapter.

## SUMMARY AND CONCLUSIONS

Disorders may be considered to be associated with consistent invalidation of construing. Their symptoms may represent aspects of the experience of invalidation, such as the anxiety or state of arousal associated with an inability to predict events; or manifestations of the persistent and exclusive use of a particular strategy in an attempt to cope with invalidation. The various contrasting strategies which the individual may employ for this latter purpose form the basis for a taxonomy of structural disorders of construing. As we have seen in Chapter 1, however, the occasional use of such strategies is by no means a sign of a disorder: for example, loose, or indeed tight, construing may be observed not only in various client groups but in any individual who is engaging in a creative or problem-solving activity.

Much of the research in this area has concerned the excessive use of either of two strategies, loosening and tightening of construing. Investigations of the clinical manifestations of the former strategy have primarily focussed upon schizophrenic thought disorder. For example, there is a considerable amount of evidence that, at least when employing psychological constructs in common social usage, the construing of thought disordered schizophrenics is characterised by weak construct relationships and inconsistency over time in these relationships, as well as in the construing of particular elements. This may not be the case, however, when they are using their own personal constructs. Researchers have differed in the particular features of construing on which they have focussed in their attempts to explain schizophrenic thought disorder. However, it may be that apparent discrepancies between the explanations provided by different authors reflect the fact that they are focussing on different stages of the schizophrenic process: for example, low element consistency, which is considered central to the formulations of some authors, may be typical of an earlier stage of this process than is loosening of the linkages between constructs, considered central by others. Therefore, rather than necessarily being incompatible, these different formulations may merely be emphasising different aspects of the phenomenon of loose construing, just as did Kelly's original descriptions (DeBoeck, 1981).

Research findings also suggest that loose construing may result from serial invalidation of constructions, at least in individuals whose construct systems are initially tightly structured. Such invalidation may in some cases be produced by a family environment which is characterised by inconsistency, and there is some evidence that loose, inconsistent construing in schizophrenics is related to a similar pattern of construing in their parents. The adoption of loose construing as a strategy to cope with invalidation is not confined to thought disordered schizophrenics, however, and it may be associated with various other presenting complaints, ranging from the excessive use of alcohol to suicidal behaviour.

The converse strategy of dealing with anxiety, namely tight construing, has been observed in some, but not all, studies of neurotic clients, whose construing has also been found to be characteristically polarised and logically consistent. These features are particularly evident in the neurotic's construing of the symptoms and the self. Tight, logically consistent, and polarised construing of the self has also been observed in severely depressed clients. Other client groups with whom indications of tight construct organisation have been reported include people with learning disabilities, heroin users, emotionally disturbed boys, violent prisoners, and shy people.

Rather less research attention has been devoted to clinical expressions of the excessive use of the strategies of dilation and constriction. However, the former strategy has been reported to characterise clients diagnosed as manic or paranoid, while the latter has been associated with depression and suicidal behaviour, phobic and obsessive-compulsive disorders, abuse of depressant drugs, and organic deficits.

All individuals who present disorders of the structure of construing may be considered to be exhibiting failures to complete the various cycles of construing which Kelly regarded as characterising optimal functioning. Their 'unsuccessful construing' is likely to be manifested in 'disorders of transition' involving such negative emotions as anxiety, guilt, and threat, or difficulties regarding control. Disorders of transition may also be presented as failures to disperse dependencies appropriately and as psychosomatic complaints.

# Chapter 4

# The content of construing in disorder

Compared to the attention paid to structural disorders of construing, relatively little concern has been shown by personal construct theorists with disorders of construct content. Kelly (1955) himself devoted only a page to this topic in his description of different types of psychological disorder, although stating that 'Quite frequently the client's difficulty arises out of the intrinsic meaning of his personal constructs rather than out of the general form which they have assumed' (p. 935). While at first sight this apparent neglect of disorders arising from the content of the client's constructs may seem surprising, it perhaps reflects the constructive alternativist view that there are many viable alternative constructions of reality: given such a position, how could a personal construct psychotherapist regard a client's particular way of construing the world as disordered? Here lies the essential difference between the personal construct theory and cognitive approaches, a point to which we shall return later.

Nevertheless, if disorders are regarded as constructions which persist despite invalidating evidence, it may not be unexpected if such constructions are idiosyncratic in content, not being revised to accord with social consensus. It may also be the case that the content of an individual's construing will itself lead him or her into the sort of impasse which Kelly viewed as the essence of a disorder. This chapter will not adopt the view that the content of a client's construing may be disordered. The content of the construct system will, nevertheless, be seen to be very pertinent to an understanding of the client's predicament and likely response to therapy, and will be considered particularly in regard to the presenting complaint and the client's construing of himself or herself and of significant others. The chapter will conclude with a discussion of the extent to which clients display commonality and sociality in their construing.

## CONSTRUCT CONTENT AND THE PRESENTING COMPLAINT

### Predominant content of the construct system

As we have seen in Chapter 2, various systems are available for coding the content of personal constructs, and these have been employed in a few studies of clients' construing. Landfield (1976), using the system which he developed (Landfield, 1971), found that individuals who had made serious suicide attempts used more constructs of a concrete, factual nature than did his control groups. This, together with his other findings discussed in the last chapter, was considered by Landfield to be consistent with the operation of a constrictive process in those who attempt suicide. However, R. Neimeyer (1984), who reviews evidence of concreteness of content in suicide notes, points out that strictly such features of construing represent a restricted range of convenience of the construct system rather than constriction. Another group of individuals in whom an absence of abstract constructs, together with a tendency to construe others in terms of how they treat one, has been reported is the hearing impaired, although these findings may reflect limitations of vocabulary (MacDonald, 1980).

Similarly to serious suicide attemptors, alcoholics have been found to be characterised by a dearth of constructs concerning interpersonal and emotional issues, suggesting that they are likely to experience difficulties in predicting other people (Glantz *et al.*, 1981). In a study of people arrested for driving while intoxicated, Schmittdiel *et al.* (1981) found a tendency to use constructs relating to the work ethic, superficial relationships, tenderness, and maladjustment, but the conclusions which can be drawn from these findings concerning the construct systems of people with drinking problems are limited by the lack of a control group. An association between relationship difficulties and the content of the construct system has also been demonstrated by other workers. Thus, McKain *et al.* (1988) have found a relationship between shyness and the tendency to construe others in behavioural terms, this tendency itself being associated with a relative dearth of constructs concerning such 'psychological' aspects of others as their attitudes and cognitive processes. G. Neimeyer and Hall (1988), perhaps not surprisingly, found that abused women more frequently saw others in terms of a high degree of forcefulness than did non-abused women, and that they and women with other marital difficulties were less likely to construe others in terms of active social interaction than were women who were satisfied with their marriages. Studying paedophiles, Howells (1979) considered that his finding that they employed more 'egoism' constructs, particularly relating to dominance and submission, than did non-paedophile prisoners was evidence that such individuals may experience interpersonal difficulties with adults, finding them overbearing, and prefer the company of children, whom they construe as significantly less dominant. However, Horley (1988) has failed to replicate this finding, and although both studies found differences in the constructs applied to male and female grid elements these differences were not specific to the paedophile subjects. Another group of offenders studied by Howells (1983) consisted of those who had engaged in 'one-off' acts of violence, and who were found to use fewer constructs concerning obedience to the law, perhaps indicating that their offences were not committed in the context of a criminal career, than did multiple aggressive offenders and non-aggressive prisoners. Turning to a very different group of subjects, members of the Episcopal Church requesting pastoral counselling, Cannell (1985) has thrown some light upon the difficulties which these individuals were experiencing in their relationships with God in that they were characterised by a predicted dearth of constructs relating to trust. However, conclusions from this investigation are limited by the very small sample size.

Several other studies have provided evidence of relationships between particular patterns of construct content and the nature of the complaints with which clients present. Fransella (1972), for example, found that stutterers used more constructs concerning inactive social interaction than did the 'normal' students studied by Landfield; Sperlinger (1976) demonstrated that improved depressed subjects used more constructs relating to self-sufficiency than did people who had consulted their general practitioners concerning non-psychiatric problems; Spindler Barton *et al.* (1976) observed that 92 per cent of a sample of in-patients with learning disabilities, most of whom had been hospitalised because of problems involving poor emotional control, employed constructs concerning bad temper in a repertory grid; and O'Sullivan (1984) found clients presenting with agoraphobia or anxiety states to use fewer constructs relating to planning interest and ability than did normal subjects, while Schaible (1990) has reported that agoraphobic women employ more constructs relating to interpersonal control than do other female clients. In another study of neurotic clients, by Caine *et al.* (1981), 'self-sufficiency' constructs were more frequently elicited than from the individuals investigated by Landfield, Fransella, and Sperlinger, this perhaps reflecting a higher level of disturbance, and preoccupation with the need for help, in this neurotic sample. All these results are consistent with the view that 'individuals elaborate their construct systems in problem areas that are presenting them with particular difficulties; this is then reflected in the relatively large number of constructs that they have available in this area, when compared with other members of the culture' (Sperlinger, 1976, p. 346). Such an explanation of the findings would suggest that the 'problem area' is primary and results in the individual elaborating his or her construct system in that area. However, as we have seen in Chapter 3, alternative explanations are possible which propose that features of the client's construing may determine the symptoms which he or she presents, as well as their persistence. For example, it may be because the individual's construct system is highly elaborated in a particular area that he or she expresses psychological distress in a way which is consistent with these predominant constructions. Fransella's (1972) view of the symptom as a way of life is consonant with such an explanation, although the correlational nature of most of the research in this area does not, of course, allow the relative adequacy of these various constructions of the data to be evaluated.

In our study of 'personal styles in neurosis', my colleagues and I performed further analyses of construct content in support of our general thesis that clients' construing determines not only the way in which they present their complaints of psychological distress but also their preferences for, and likely response to, different forms of therapy (Caine *et al.*, 1981; Winter, 1985c). Clients referred for psychological therapies who used a large number of constructs concerning self-sufficiency were found to be more likely to see themselves as highly characterised by their symptoms and to expect their therapists to be similar to their general practitioners, both these features indicating a rather 'medical' view of their problems and of therapy, and being associated with allocation to behaviour therapy rather than group psychotherapy. Those clients who construed their symptoms, their concept of illness, and themselves in terms of lack of self-sufficiency also tended to obtain scores on a Treatment Expectancies Questionnaire (Caine *et al.*, 1982) which were indicative of expectancies favourable to medical or behavioural treatments, as did clients who construed their symptoms in terms of constructs denoting a high degree of structure. By contrast, expectancies favourable to a psychotherapeutic treatment approach were associated with construing of the self, symptoms, and illness in terms of inactive social interaction. These findings concerning constructs relating to structure and social interaction have received some support from a further study by Caine *et al.* (1986) which employed projective test measures of amenability to psychotherapy. Construct content has also been related by Caine *et al.* (1981) to two other dimensions which we have associated with treatment preference and response, namely inner/outer direction of interest and conservatism/radicalism in social attitudes. The former dimension, which is similar to Jung's concept of introversion/ extraversion, concerns the extent to which the person is predominantly concerned with his or her internal or external world. Clients who give inner-directed responses to the Direction of Interest Questionnaire (Caine *et al.*, 1982) have been generally found to prefer psychotherapeutic treatment approaches (Caine and Wijesinghe, 1976; Caine *et al.*, 1981); to give projective test responses indicative of responsiveness to such approaches (Caine *et al.*, 1986); to be open to experience and divergent in their thinking, but unexpectedly to have relatively unidimensional construct systems (Caine *et al.*, 1973, 1981); to construe their ideal selves as dissimilar to other people (Caine *et al.*, 1981); and to employ a more diverse range of constructs (Smail, 1970). Our studies of the content of these constructs have found such clients to use fewer 'Factual Description' constructs and to apply fewer constructs concerning lack of self-sufficiency to their symptoms, while tending to construe illness in terms of inactive social interaction. On the other hand, clients with conservative social attitudes, whom we have generally found to be outer-directed and to prefer medical or behavioural treatments, did tend to construe their symptoms and illness in terms of lack of self-sufficiency. These differences between clients in the content of their constructs also carried implications for the treatments to which they were allocated on the basis of clinical interviews. Clients allocated to behaviour therapy, as well as tending to be outer-directed and conservative, used more constructs concerning self-sufficiency and were more likely to construe themselves and their symptoms in these terms and in terms of high involvement, one of Landfield's 'High Structure' categories. By contrast, clients allocated to group analytic therapy, who tended to be inner-directed and radical in their social attitudes, were more likely to construe themselves and their symptoms in terms of low organisation, a 'Low Structure' category, to construe their symptoms and illness in terms of inactive social interaction, to apply 'Low Tenderness', 'Self-Reference', and 'Low Humour' constructs to their symptoms, and to obtain high scores on a grid measure of self-conflict (see p. 45) (Winter, 1983). Unexpectedly, group psychotherapy clients also used more 'Factual Description' constructs. Caine *et al.* (1981, p. 136) suggest that

> These relationships between patients' construing and their treatment allocation may have been in large part mediated by the clinician's perception of their presenting symptoms, for the latter did appear to reflect the predominant content of their construct systems. Thus, the behaviour therapy patients tended to present with more clear-cut, circumscribed symptoms, perhaps reflecting their preoccupation with 'high structure' constructs, together with symptoms involving dependency on others. By contrast, the group psychotherapy patients tended to present with much more diffuse symptoms, and particularly with difficulties in social interaction.

Examining the relationships between clients' constructions and their presenting symptoms in greater detail, employing their measures of personal styles, Caine *et al.* provided further support for these views. Thus, inner-directedness, which previously had been related by Smail (1970) to the tendency to complain of psychic, rather than somatic, symptoms, was associated with the presentation of interpersonal complaints and with high scores on measures of free-floating anxiety and hysteria. Conservatism was associated with the tendency not to present interpersonal complaints, but with high scores on measures of phobic anxiety and obsessive-compulsive symptoms. Furthermore, expectancies favourable to group psychotherapy, as measured by the Treatment Expectancies Questionnaire, were associated with the presentation of interpersonal and depressive complaints, while, as with conservatism, expectancies favourable to behavioural treatment were found to characterise clients who admitted to phobic and obsessive-compulsive symptoms. In summary, these findings revealed a difference in the predominant constructions of the world, and consequently in treatment expectancies and likely allocation, of clients presenting symptoms with an external locus, such as phobic, obsessional, and somatic complaints, and those whose symptoms have a more internal or interpersonal locus, such as diffuse anxiety, depression, and problems in relating to others. Somewhat similarly, Rowe (1987), who regards the symptoms of psychological disorder, whether 'neurotic' or 'psychotic', as the person's defences against the fear of annihilation, considers that the particular symptom into which an individual turns this fear will depend on whether he or she characteristically takes an introverted or extraverted view of the world.

Relationships between clients' presenting symptoms and the content of their personal construct systems have also been examined in terms of the extent to which clients construe people psychologically rather than objectively. Thus, it has been found, both in clients diagnosed as neurotic and those diagnosed as schizophrenic, that use of psychological rather than objective constructs in describing others is associated with the tendency to report psychological rather than somatic symptoms (Smail, 1970; McPherson, 1972; McPherson and Gray, 1976). Smail (1978, p. 51) remarks that these findings indicate that 'the patient may, so to speak, choose his "symptoms" in accordance with his personal stance towards the world'. Similarly, McPherson and Gray, drawing on Schachter and Singer's (1962) classic research, suggest that their results indicate that individuals who tend to construe psychologically will also be more likely to label bodily sensations of arousal as psychological, and that clients are particularly likely to be highly aroused as a concomitant of anxiety. From a personal construct theory perspective, a high level of arousal may be regarded as resulting from a failure to anticipate events (Mancuso and Adams-Webber, 1982b), an experience which is implicit in Kelly's definition of a disorder (Winter, 1990a).

Suggestions of an association between paucity of psychological construing and a tendency to report somatic symptoms are also evident in Leff's (1973, 1977, 1986) explanation of reported cultural differences in the extent to which symptoms are presented somatically rather than psychologically. He observed, for example, that people from 'developing countries' show less differentiation of emotional states than do those from 'developed countries', and are more likely to express distress somatically. Similarly, differences between Japanese and Caucasians in their associations to the word 'depression' have been related to differences in the way in which these races tend to present depression (Tamaka-Matsumi and Marsella, 1976). While the associations provided by Caucasians tend to refer to internal mood states such as sadness and despair, those given by the Japanese tend to refer to external objects such as storms and mountains. Marsella *et al.* (1985, pp. 301–2) conclude that

> mood aspects of depression for many non-western groups may be experienced as somatic dysfunctions and as impersonalized projections utilizing external referents. This eliminates the guilt, self-blame and

existential despair which characterizes western depressive experiences, and so insulates the non-western person from the risks of isolating him/herself from their sense of self. Thus, the non-western individual maintains his social role and is protected from the sense of loneliness and isolation that accompanies the depressive experience among westerners. The latter group, by continually referring to their inner states in personalized terms, further distance themselves from a social nexus. This accentuates and exacerbates the problem.

The relationship between modes of expression of psychological disorder in a particular culture and that culture's superordinate constructs has also been examined by Carr (1978, 1980). Using linguistic analysis, he concluded that a very abstract superordinate construct of 'appropriate versus inappropriate' behaviour characterises the Malay view of the world, and may explain the culture-bound syndrome of 'amok', involving the extremely inappropriate behaviour of indiscriminate violence and murder.

If, as discussed in the last chapter, all psychological problems serve a similar strategic function of enabling the individual to cope with invalidation, 'The particular choice of strategy may depend on commonality of construing in the person's particular context' (Button, 1983a, p. 319). The above reports of relationships between predominant constructions within a certain cultural context and the type of symptom typically presented by a member of that culture provide some support for this view. However, that care should be taken in drawing conclusions from some of the findings of 'cross-cultural research' is indicated by Fernando (1988), who notes that studies such as Leff's are not only methodologically flawed but are based on questionable assumptions such as the 'somatisation myth' concerning non-Western cultures, and the view that the particular ways of construing and of expressing feelings prevalent in Western society reflect an evolutionary superiority. Such assumptions, leading for example to the cross-cultural assessment of emotional expression using an instrument devised in London, do not rest easily with a theoretical position based on constructive alternativism.

## Construing of emotion

As we have seen in Chapter 3, several studies have explored in greater detail the relationship between use of psychological constructs and presenting symptoms in clients diagnosed as schizophrenic. As well as making use of structural measures of construct interrelationship and consistency, researchers have examined the extent to which schizophrenics spontaneously employ psychological constructs. Such clients have been found to use fewer constructs concerning traits and feelings in describing themselves and others than do normal subjects (Gara et al., 1989), and low use of psychological constructs has also been observed in schizoid children (Wolff and Barlow,

1979) and in adults who as children had been diagnosed as schizoid (Chick *et al.*, 1979). Those schizophrenics who do show a high level of psychological construing have been found to be more likely to present delusions of persecution, while limited use of psychological constructs has been associated with delusions of non-integration and with affective blunting (Dixon, 1968; McPherson *et al.*, 1970a, 1970b, 1971b; Williams and Quirke, 1972); and, in non-schizophrenic populations, with difficulties in making friends (Duck, 1973a), lack of empathy (Chick *et al.*, 1979), and, in children, with presentation of problems, perceived lack of understanding by others, and idiosyncratic construing (Jackson and Bannister, 1985). Williams and Quirke suggested that a relationship between limited psychological construing and social withdrawal may underlie its association with affective symptoms in schizophrenics, but Bodlakova *et al.* (1974), studying a mixed psychiatric in-patient sample, failed to replicate this relationship. They did, however, confirm the relationship between affective blunting and limited use of psychological constructs, as well as the finding, also observed by Rohrer (reported by Kelly, 1955), Williams and Quirke (1972), and Winter *et al.* (1991), that psychological construing is inversely associated with length of hospitalisation. The results of these various studies of schizophrenics, together with those of research employing structural measures of construing to investigate formal thought disorder, suggest that schizophrenic clients with a coherent system of psychological constructs tend to present symptoms with interpersonal content; while the lack of such a system is associated with the presentation of symptoms reflecting the meaninglessness of the client's interpersonal and emotional world.

One such symptom is affective blunting, and for some researchers it has appeared 'Paradoxical that, despite [this] . . . anhedonia, some schizophrenics are unduly sensitive to interpersonal contact' (Cutting, 1985, p. 239), as is apparent from investigations that have associated the relapse of schizo-phrenics with high levels of expressed emotion by their relatives (Brown *et al.*, 1972; Vaughn and Leff, 1976: Leff *et al.*, 1982). From the personal construct theory viewpoint, however, this finding is not paradoxical: the individual whose construing of emotion is poorly elaborated is likely not only to appear affectively blunted but to find that high levels of expressed emotion are largely outside the range of convenience of his or her construct system and are therefore anxiety-provoking. As it has been suggested that 'a schizophrenic episode is precipitated by an unassimilable incident that paralyses the schizophrenic with anxiety' (Shapiro, 1981), relapse of such an individual under conditions of high emotional expression would not be unexpected. Neither would it be unexpected that some schizophrenics would, as demon-strated by Tarrier *et al.* (1979), respond with a high degree of arousal to the presence of a highly emotionally expressive relative, or that, as has been observed in several studies, the performance of schizophrenics on various tasks is disrupted by the presence of emotional material (Chapman, 1961;

Feffer, 1961; Turbiner, 1961; Feldstein, 1962; Brodsky, 1963; Deering, 1963). Other research findings which are consistent with the view that at least some such clients have a relatively unelaborated subsystem of constructs concerning emotion are those which have indicated that schizophrenics have difficulty in accurately identifying emotions from speech (Turner, 1964; Jonsson and Sjöstedt, 1973; Bazkin *et al.*, 1978) and from facial expressions (e.g. Iscoe and Veldman, 1963; Grodin and Brown, 1967; Dougherty *et al.*, 1974; Bespalko, 1976; Harizuka, 1977; Muzekari and Bates, 1977; Cutting, 1981; Cramer *et al.*, 1989); and that they do not display the Pollyanna effect, the tendency to remember more pleasant than unpleasant items (Koh *et al.*, 1976, 1981). Further, the difficulty which some schizophrenics might have in developing role relationships is indicated by findings that they are not only deficient in the ability to construe the emotions of others but also in the ability to express emotion in such a way that it can be accurately construed by other people (Gottheil *et al.*, 1979; Andreasen *et al.*, 1981; Brown, 1981; Leff and Abberton, 1981). It should finally be noted that a very tightly organised subsystem of constructs concerning emotions, as we have seen to be characteristic of depressives (Silverman, 1977), might, of course, be no less likely to lead to emotional difficulties than is a relative absence, or very loosely organised subsystem, of such constructs.

Denial or avoidance of strong emotions or conflicts has been implicated as a causal factor in some neurotic disorders both by psychodynamically orientated theorists and by those employing more cognitive perspectives, such as attribution theory. For example, Hafner's (1977a, 1977b) studies of the marriages of agoraphobics have stressed the role played by denial of hostility in the maintenance of agoraphobic symptoms, and similarly Goldstein (1982, p. 185) asserts that agoraphobics 'go to great lengths to avoid such feelings as anger and frustration', misapprehend the causal antecedents of emotional distress, and 'label almost every state of arousal as anxiety or fear'. Goldstein and Chambless (1978) have linked the onset of agoraphobic symptoms to situations of interpersonal conflict, and Guidano and Liotti (1983, p. 225), taking a similar view, conclude that agoraphobics 'do not possess articulate cognitive structures capable of dealing with emotions', as well as observing that the wives of agoraphobic men fear the expression of aggression (Liotti and Guidano, 1976). However, as I have discussed elsewhere (Winter, 1989a), research in this area has been fraught with methodological problems and its findings are inconsistent. Nevertheless, Fisher and Wilson (1985) have provided evidence that agoraphobics show little emotional reaction to scenes of marital conflict, although this would not entirely support Goldstein's analysis as they not only experienced little anger in response to the scenes but also little anxiety. Peter and Hand (1987), although unable to demonstrate that agoraphobics deny critical feelings, did find that these clients' spouses were relatively uncritical and unable to perceive their partners' criticism of them.

Although concepts such as denial do not rest easily within a personal construct theory framework, analyses of agoraphobia such as this may be reformulated in terms of low cognitive awareness of construing in the area of interpersonal conflict and a poorly elaborated subsystem of constructs relating to emotions. More specifically, the formulations of such workers as Hafner and Goldstein would suggest that agoraphobics and their spouses may be characterised by the submergence (see p. 10) of construct poles concerning hostility and conflict and by the use of constriction to exclude situations of conflict from the perceptual field. Some support for this was provided by a repertory grid study which demonstrated that agoraphobics perceived less selfishness and anger than did non-agoraphobic neurotic clients and 'normal' people, and that similar differences obtained between the spouses of these three groups of subjects (Winter and Gournay, 1987). Agoraphobics also perceived less jealousy than did other neurotics and, together with their spouses, differentiated less than did normal subjects between grid elements in terms of selfishness, which therefore appeared to be a less superordinate construct for them. Further, the more an agoraphobic and spouse were able to differentiate between people in terms of selfishness and jealousy, the less severe were the client's phobic symptoms. The tendency of the agoraphobics to construe others in a uniformly positive light was also reflected in the finding that they construed their parents more favourably than did the normal subjects. Although high levels of differentiation between others in terms of constructs relating to interpersonal conflict were associated with low levels of phobic symptomatology, one area in which the opposite tendency was observed was marital infidelity. Infidelity therefore appeared to be a super-ordinate construct for the more disabled agoraphobics, a finding which is consistent with formulations of agoraphobia as a protective strategy which allows the phobic to avoid the possibility of acting upon fantasies of illicit sexual relationships (e.g. Hafner, 1979). Not unexpectedly, other super-ordinate constructs for the more disabled agoraphobics concerned anxiety and the ability to go out.

Research findings on two further samples have now replicated the relationships demonstrated in this study between agoraphobic symptoms and low cognitive awareness of selfishness and jealousy, favourable construal of the mother, and, in both agoraphobic and spouse, a superordinate construct of infidelity (Winter, 1989a). In attempting to understand the tendency of the agoraphobics in these studies to view significant others in a uniformly favourable light on most construct dimensions, it may be of value to consider what Kelly (1955, pp. 114–15) had to say about the individual who sees others as uniformly gentle:

There are several possibilities. Suppose the contrast to 'gentleness' in the speaker's system is something we might call 'aggressiveness'. If the speaker says that 'everyone is gentle', he avoids pointing to anyone and labeling him 'aggressive'. He may do this because he does not want to be in the position of one who is known as a seer of aggressiveness. He may do it because he cannot deal satisfactorily with aggressive people and, for the moment at least, is trying to limit his population to people he can deal with. Then there may be an implied exception in the statement; he may mean, 'Everyone *except me* is gentle'. Another interpretation is that he may feel that if anyone in the world is aggressive it would have to be himself, his own latent aggression is so great. The only way, therefore, that he can escape being the prime example of aggressiveness is to insist that everyone is gentle.

A similar interpretation is that someone close to him, such as a parent, would have to be identified as aggressive if he admitted that anyone was aggressive. To construe the parent as aggressive may have such far-reaching consequences that the better elaborative choice would seem to be to include the parent with the gentle ones, even if it means universalizing 'gentleness'. Any other interpretation on his part might shake the whole construction system which gives shape to his life role.

A few other studies of agoraphobia from the personal construct theory perspective have provided further support for the view that agoraphobics' construing of emotions associated with interpersonal conflict may present them with difficulties in this area, and have also indicated how such a pattern of construing may have developed. For example, Frazer (1980) found that agoraphobics' recollections of their family background suggested that there had been strict rules concerning the expression of emotions. It also appeared that the future agoraphobic had been protected from invalidation of construing as a child, with the result that any such invalidation experienced later in life would be particularly anxiety-provoking. While these findings provide some indication of the possible origins of a poorly elaborated sub-system of emotional constructs in the agoraphobic, it should be remembered that they are derived from a retrospective study and may therefore simply reflect the fact that an individual who employs few constructs concerning interpersonal conflict is for this reason alone likely to recall few situations involving conflict and intense emotions. In a repertory grid study of agoraphobics, clients suffering from anxiety states, and normal subjects, O'Sullivan (1985) reported that the consensus grids of these groups suggested that agoraphobics construed assertion and the expression of negative feelings more unfavourably than did the other subjects. Further findings of this study were that agoraphobics used relatively few constructs relating to change and that, apart from constructs concerning fear, few constructs were related to their self constructs. She concludes that agoraphobics have a rigid, imperm-eable core structure, and that 'agoraphobia occurs as a response of definition or constriction (because of a lack of relevant superordinate permeable constructs) to novel events implying core-structure change' (O'Sullivan, 1984, p. 251). In addition, she suggests that the higher incidence of agoraphobia amongst women may reflect a greater tendency in Western culture to protect girls than boys from experimentation and experiences of change in core structure, and therefore from opportunities to evolve permeable super-ordinate constructs. Also using repertory grid technique, Lorenzini and Sassaroli (1987, 1988) have found that agoraphobics employ fewer constructs concerning emotions, and differentiate between these constructs less, than do non-phobic neurotic clients. In their study, most of the constructs concerned were on the theme of fear versus tranquillity. The authors consider this pattern to be a result of a childhood environment in which the parents construed any state of arousal experienced by the child as a sign of illness, weakness, or danger; or, alternatively, did not allow the child the necessary solitude to experience fully his or her inner world. The agoraphobics in this study were also more likely to construe situations of exploration and change as anxiety-provoking and not associated with attachment. Lorenzini and Sassaroli suggest that this view of exploration and attachment as incompatible derives from the pre-agoraphobic child's experience of a mother who inhibited the child's exploratory, hypothesis-testing behaviour. Furthermore, they consider that the future agoraphobic often initially chooses the option of exploration and construes himself or herself as strong and independent, but that agoraphobic symptoms are then precipitated by a situation, such as a marriage or illness, which invalidates this self-construction. If the option of attachment is chosen, there will be what Bowlby (1973) terms an 'anxious attachment', and the individual's self-construction will be vulnerable to invalidation by an event such as a loss. 'Avoidance behaviour', in the view of Lorenzini and Sassaroli (1988, p. 333), 'is the exact opposite of explorative behaviour and it aims at defending the predictive skills of the subject, who gives up predicting any further because he runs the risk of not successfully predicting anything at all.' As indicated in Chapter 3, it may be regarded as a manifestation of a constrictive process by which the agoraphobic excludes situations of interpersonal conflict, which are mostly outside the range of convenience of his or her construct system, from the perceptual field and largely confines his or her interpersonal world to a relationship of mutual validation with the spouse.

It has been suggested that certain other client groups are likely to employ few constructs concerning emotions. One such group consists of those diagnosed as psychopaths, but Widom (1976) has found them to use no fewer emotional constructs than do normal subjects, and Klass (1980) has obtained similar results with sociopaths. A dearth of emotional constructs has, however, been observed by Batty and Hall (1986) in people presenting anorexic and bulimic symptoms, a finding which the authors relate to these individuals' tight control of their feelings. A further group who, it has been argued, tend not to construe their experiences in terms of emotions are those presenting with complaints of physical pain. This view is exemplified in the concept of 'alexithymia' (Nemiah and Sifneos, 1970), and has also been used to explain research findings that chronic low back pain sufferers tend to obtain low scores on depression scales (Hanvik, 1951; Forrest and Wolkind, 1974; Gentry *et al.*, 1974), suggesting to some workers that their pain is 'masked depression' (Engel, 1959; Lopez-Ibor, 1972). In a repertory grid study of people presenting with low back pain, Drysdale (1989) has provided evidence that those with chronic complaints perceived less anger than did those with acute conditions. Depression also appeared to be a less superordinate construct, and was perceived less readily, by clients whose pain was of longer duration. In an earlier grid investigation, Schonecke *et al.* (1972) found evidence of low perception of hostility, particularly in relation to people close to the individual, in clients presenting another type of 'psychosomatic' symptom, namely functional cardiac complaints. That headache sufferers may also have a poorly elaborated system of emotional constructs is perhaps suggested by research findings that such individuals tend to show little nonverbal expression of emotion when under stress (Traue *et al.*, 1985). Further, it has been observed by Pennebaker (1985) that, while inhibiting discussion of a traumatic event is associated with increased physiological activity and risk of disease, talking or writing about such an event reduces physiological arousal and the likelihood of suffering from those diseases regarded as stress-related. He suggests that these results imply that translating a traumatic event into words, or even into some non-verbal form of expression, allows the person to structure and find meaning in his or her experiences. Could it be that the person who is able to construe his or her experience in emotional terms is not only more likely, as suggested above, to place a psychological rather than a somatic interpretation on a state of high arousal but also, being better equipped to interpret experiences, is less likely to remain highly aroused and to suffer the physical ravages wrought by such a state? Such questions require further investigation from a personal construct theory perspective.

Also in need of further study are the reasons for an individual's failure to develop an elaborated subsystem of emotional constructs. Rowe (1987), in common with some of the researchers on agoraphobia, has little doubt that this has its basis in childhood experiences. Thus, she states that 'If as a child you discover that when you say to your mother, "Mummy, I'm frightened", you are ignored, punished, or humiliated but if you say, "Mummy, I'm sick", you are comforted and loved, then ... as the language of the emotions is never developed the person cannot translate bodily sensations into emotions' (pp. 159–60).

## Construing of the complaint

The client's 'choice' of a particular symptom may be further understood by considering not only the degree of elaboration, or level of cognitive awareness, of construing in the problem area but also the particular implications of constructs in this area. Thus, the literature contains many examples of the apparent dilemmas with which a client may be confronted by virtue of construing some aspect of his or her complaint in such a way that it carries 'payoffs'. In most such cases, to suffer psychological distress carries the implication for the client of being a more humane and virtuous person (Winter, 1982). For example, Rowe (1971a) described a depressed woman who divided her world into good, 'poorly' people and bad, 'well' people, and who predictably did not respond to therapy, presumably preferring to continue to see herself as poorly, with its implication that she was good. I have observed similar dilemmas in the repertory grid responses of depressed clients (Winter, 1985d), supporting Rowe's (1983a, p. 87) view that one of the propositions which enclose such clients is 'I'd rather be good than happy'. She notes, for example, that many depressives construe themselves as sensitive, and view sensitivity as carrying not only the negative implication of vulnerability but also such positive implications as being caring or creative. A similar pattern has been observed by Fransella (1972) in a stutterer whose reluctance to enter therapy was not surprising in that he construed stutterers as good and fluent speakers as bad; while Ryle and Breen (1972b) have found neurotic symptoms to be associated with a tendency to construe passivity and the need for psychiatric help as implying warmth. Ryle's (1979a) view of the predicament of neurotic individuals, similarly to Rowe's formulation of that of depressives, is that they are ensnared by 'dilemmas, traps, and snags' as a result of the constructions which they place on their world. Although in a further study he failed to confirm his hypothesis that neurotic clients would show a greater frequency of dilemmas, or false dichotomies, than normal subjects (Ryle, 1981), this may be due to the fact that dilemmas were formulated in terms of supplied constructs, which subjects may not have found personally relevant. Drysdale (1989) addressed this problem to some extent by supplying his low back pain sufferers with constructs elicited from interviews with a previous sample of such clients. He found some evidence of dilemmas associated with pain in that clients with chronic complaints showed a greater tendency to associate pain with sensitivity to others than did those with acute problems, and the longer the duration of pain the more likely it was to be associated not only with sensitivity, but also with the ability to get on well with others. However, a further study, employing elicited constructs, of a small sample of chronic pain sufferers found no difference between those whose pain was considered organic and those where it was considered psychological on a measure of positivity of construing of the self in pain, as well as on various other grid indices (Button et al., 1979). Dilemmas have also been examined in heroin users by Goggins (1988), who was unable to demonstrate that drug use carried more positive implications in terms of their own personal constructs for users seeking treatment than for ex-users. Indeed, such implications were fewest in clients who had used drugs the longest. However, the finding by Leenaars (1981) that students construed drugs more, and people less, positively when in a simulated drugged state than when in a normal state of consciousness suggests that assessments of the construing of drug users when they are not under the influence of drugs may not reflect how they evaluate drug use when they are.

Also using elicited constructs, I found that for 80 per cent of a sample of clients referred for social skills training, social competence carried some negative implications, the majority of these concerning Landfield's (1971) construct content categories of 'Low Tenderness', 'High Forcefulness', 'Low Morality', 'Closed to Alternatives', and 'High Egoism' (Winter, 1987, 1988a). Furthermore, the greater the extent of these dilemmas, the more difficulty was experienced by clients in social situations, the more likely were they to avoid such situations, and the less likely were they to construe themselves as socially competent. Such findings do not, of course, indicate whether clients who construe 'social skills' unfavourably are for this reason more likely to complain of difficulties in coping with social situations; or alternatively whether their favourable construction of 'social skill deficits' is a strategy adopted by socially unskilled clients to maintain some modicum of self-esteem in the face of awareness of their social difficulties. Such clients may, for example, be able to tell themselves that although they may be socially incompetent at least they are decent human beings. However, regardless of the direction of any causal connection between the presentation of a particular complaint and a positive construal of that complaint, it is clear, as we shall discuss further in Chapter 5, that the more favourably a person views the complaint the more resistant he or she will be to relinquishing it.

It should also now be apparent that on close examination a client's complaint may be rich with a meaning which is very different from that which it holds for the clinician who views it, for example, as a symptom of an illness. As Tschudi (1977, p. 321) puts it, 'symptomatic behaviour is behaviour which obliquely gets at the issues which are important for the person'. Like Kelly (1955), he regards the symptom as, in a sense, asking a question but one that is 'loaded' rather than 'honest' in that goals are approached indirectly and may even themselves have a false quality. His ABC model (not to be confused with the ABC framework of Ellis (1962)) regards the symptom as one pole of a construct, A, the disadvantage of the symptom as one pole of a second construct, B, and its advantage as one pole of a third, 'payoff', construct, C. That such a model may be particularly pertinent to neurotic disorders is perhaps indicated by Smail's (1978, p. 11) view of the concept of neurosis as 'a shorthand to describe a kind of strategy by which a person can deceive himself about the reasons for and aims of his conduct'.

Exploration of the personal meaning of 'socially deviant' behaviour may also be particularly useful in, for example, indicating whether socially deviant individuals construe their behaviour more favourably than does society in general. In an early grid study in this area, focussing on a paranoid schizophrenic exhibiting sadistic ideation, it is somewhat difficult to follow the logic of May's (1968) argument that if the client were potentially dangerous 'being in favour of mercy killing' would be associated with 'feeling love for the family' since 'homicide might be committed with regret rather than rage, particularly if the murderer considered that there was justification for his action' (p. 479). These constructs were, in fact, found to be correlated in the client's grid, but the subsequent prediction that this might be a characteristic feature of the construing of homicidal clients was not confirmed, perhaps not surprisingly as there are doubtless many possible roads to homicide. For example, in the case of a poisoner who was administered a grid by Howells (1978), it seemed that his actions served the desired purpose of setting him apart from society, and in particular from his parents. One study which has indicated that socially deviant individuals may be more likely than others to view their transgressions as justifiable was carried out by Klass (1980), who found that people with a history of drug abuse anticipated more negative reactions to transgressions involving harming liked than those involving harming disliked individuals, whereas normal subjects did not discriminate between different types of transgression. Explorations of the varied personal meanings of paedophiles' sexual behaviour have also been conducted from a personal construct theory perspective (Li, 1988, 1990; Needs, 1988, 1990), and have indicated that an understanding of adult sexual involvement with children requires more than a counting of the paedophile's constructs, an approach which, as we have seen, has been employed by other investigators. Li's (1988) method has been to interview paedophiles, and he describes how this has shown that 'intimate relationships with children have provided some of them with a raison d'etre to anchor their human existence' (p. 284). In view of these paedophiles' tendency not to see their sexual behaviour as pathological, it is of interest that adult females who had been sexually abused as children have also been found to construe child sexual abusers as more normal and sane than do adults with no such history (Sanderson, 1990).

A somewhat different approach to understanding the purpose served by a client's presenting problem, in this case parasuicidal behaviour, was employed by Parker (1981). Using a grid in which the elements were possible responses to crisis situations, he found that clients who had taken overdoses but were adjudged to be of low suicidal intent tended to construe an overdose as an escape from tension similar to crying and getting drunk but, in contrast to a group of high suicidal intent, as dissimilar to suicide. Similarly, in a grid study of prisoners, Watson et al. (1976) found that all the alcoholics in their sample construed getting drunk as a likely response to job loss, while the problem gamblers tended to construe gambling as a response to social stress.

Far from construing aspects of their complaints in a rather favourable light, some clients appear to view their complaints extremely negatively. On closer examination, though, it may be found that this constellatory negative construction is the stereotype which the client holds of other people who present with similar problems to their own, but that the client dissociates himself or herself from this stereotype. An early report of apparent dissociation of a client from her symptom was provided by Bannister (1965a), who observed that an agoraphobic did not relate the construct 'can go anywhere with confidence' to the other constructs in her repertory grid, including a self construct. Fransella and Adams (1966) found an even more extreme dissociation from the symptom in an arsonist, whose grid revealed a statistically significant *negative* correlation between the constructs 'like me in character' and 'the sort of person who is likely to commit arson', and a generally favourable construal of the self. This client construed the feeling he experienced when lighting a fire as associated with 'enjoying having power', believing that people get the punishment they deserve, and with his ideal self, all of which he contrasted with committing arson, and Fransella and Adams speculate that he may have construed his fire setting as the punishment of wrongdoers rather than as arson. Similar examples of the repertory grids of arsonists will be presented in Chapter 6. In her work with stutterers, Fransella (1968, 1972) has also provided evidence that, while such people tended to construe stutterers in the same negative way as non-stutterers do, they did not see themselves in this way. Hoy (1973, 1977), likewise, has found that alcoholics shared a particular negative stereotype of the alcoholic very similar to that held by the staff in his alcoholism unit and in the hospital generally, but tended not to construe themselves in these terms or as alcoholics. Similar results were obtained by McCartney and O'Donnell (1981), but Potamianos *et al.* (1985) found that alcoholics shared a less negative stereotype of the problem drinker, and one from which their degree of dissociation was less than was that of staff members. The latter workers suggest that the differences between their findings and those of previous studies may be due to the fact that their subjects were asked to evaluate 'a problem drinker' rather than 'an alcoholic', and that they studied clients referred to a general hospital for alcohol-related problems, who were therefore perhaps less dependent on alcohol and more likely to construe problem drinking in physical terms than were the alcoholics studied by Hoy and McCartney and O'Donnell. It should also be noted that, when alcoholics have been asked to evaluate the self when drunk, this has been found to be construed as more different from the sober self, and more similar to an alcoholic, than it is by non-alcoholic individuals (Partington, 1970). Perhaps the self-construing of alcoholics might best be understood, as Leitner (1988a) suggests, by comparing grids which they have completed when they have consumed various different amounts of alcohol. Heroin addicts have also been found to dissociate from their negative stereotypes of drug addiction, and, more worryingly, while these clients tended to associate methadone use with a likelihood of HIV positivity, they saw little association between HIV positivity and AIDS (Stojnov, 1990).

Further indications of dissociation from the complaint have been provided by a repertory grid study of clients referred to a psychiatric crisis intervention service, who, compared to referrals to a psychiatric out-patient clinic, construed themselves as less highly characterised by their presenting complaints, and their complaints less as signs of illness, as well as viewing treatment as less likely to change them and to make them similar to their ideal selves (Winter *et al.*, 1987). The significant others of these crisis referrals construed the clients as more highly characterised by their presenting complaints, and by unfavourable characteristics in general, than they did themselves, and showed a greater tendency to perceive the client's present state as a change from his or her previous state. It is perhaps this disjunction between the views of clients and significant others which caused general practitioners to consider these cases as 'crises' requiring more urgent attention than could be provided by the out-patient clinic.

Other workers, rather than studying specific complaints, have investigated how psychiatric in-patients construe mental illness, again with the finding that such individuals hold a negative stereotype of the mentally ill, but one from which they dissociate (Kennard, 1974; O'Mahony, 1982). In O'Mahony's study, the degree of dissociation from the stereotype was less when clients rated their 'present self' than when they rated their 'usual self', suggesting that their dissociation did not indicate that they were out of touch with the reality of their present condition. Indeed O'Mahony, like Fransella (1977), points out that those clients who dissociate from a stereotype of their particular disorder are exhibiting a normal process of construing by using a negative stereotype to define oneself by contrast with it. They are also no doubt exhibiting what workers from other perspectives have termed the 'fundamental attribution error' (Jones and Nisbett, 1972), the tendency to explain the behaviour of others in terms of personality dispositions but one's own in terms of situational factors. Dissociation from a negative stereotype, in this case of 'the disabled', has also been observed in a grid study of severely physically disabled people (Beail, 1985b). An investigation of disabled and non-disabled young people has indicated a similar pattern in that, while all construed the public image of the disabled as very negative, disabled girls viewed themselves more positively than did the non-disabled (Hayhow *et al.*, 1988).

Those clients who construe their complaints in a very negative light, but who also apply these negative constructions to themselves, may do so because they are thus able to maintain a correspondingly idealistic construction of life without the complaint. This phenomenon has been termed the 'if only syndrome' by Fransella (1972), who has pointed out that it may provide an explanation for the maintenance of apparently distressing symptoms, since the illusory belief that symptom loss would allow a client to attain all his or her ideals is tenable only as long as the symptom is retained. She observed such a pattern in stutterers and in clients with eating disorders, for whom the self when at normal weight was construed as virtually identical to the ideal self (Fransella and Crisp, 1970, 1979), although normal and neurotic women were also found to view reaching their ideal weight as implying the attainment of all their ideals. The perception of thinness by women who are concerned about their weight is an area in which research findings have been conflicting. Somewhat surprisingly, Hall and Brown (1983) found anorexic clients and their mothers to evaluate thinness less favourably than non-clients and their mothers. Munden (1982), however, was able to differentiate women with concerns about eating from those without such concerns by the anticipation of the former group that slimness would make them more like their ideal selves, in contrast to their present negative self-constructions. Evidence of the 'if only' syndrome was also obtained by Hardy (1982) with dysmorpho-phobics, who, unlike psoriatic clients and controls, imagined that they would develop ideal relationships with their parents if their most disliked body feature were 'cured'. A similar pattern was apparent in my research on agoraphobics, who imagined that after treatment they and their spouses would be more ideal than they were even before the onset of the phobic symptoms, a view which their spouses shared (Winter and Gournay, 1987). Furthermore, the more marked was this tendency in the agoraphobics, the more severe were their symptoms, perhaps because they were more resistant to testing the validity of their idealistic fantasies of what life might hold for them if only they could go out of the house. The client whose view of life without the symptom is very discrepant from his or her current self-construction is likely to be threatened by symptom loss since this will imply radical revision of core constructs. This may, perhaps, explain the observation by McKain *et al.* (1988) that, in shy people, the greater the change on other construct dimensions implied by construing themselves as non-shy, the more shy, lonely, and unassertive they were likely to view themselves as being. Similarly, G. Neimeyer and Hall (1988) interpret their finding of greater discrepancy between views of the self in and out of the marriage in women who had been abused by their husbands or were dissatisfied with their marriages than in satisfied women as indicating that the latter group are less threatened by the prospect of leaving their marriages. They conclude that, in abused and dissatisfied women, 'the marriage serves as one means of preserving the otherwise uncertain self-identity' (p. 305).

Clients' constructions of their complaints are as varied, and as relevant to the likelihood of recovery, in physical illness as in psychological disorder. As Viney (1983b, p. 1) points out, 'It is the images of illness which people build up which affect how they act when illness becomes an important aspect of their own experience.' Open-ended interviews with ill people have allowed her to identify six types of image of illness with distressing effects and three more pleasant types of image. The former are images of uncertainty, of anxiety, of anger, of helplessness, of depression, and of isolation; the latter happy and humorous images, images of competence, and images involving family and friends. Many of these images are likely to have been developed in childhood, when experiences of illness tend to be common. In recent work with men who are HIV antibody positive, Viney *et al.* (1989a) have found that, although their images revealed more indirectly expressed anger than did those of other ill people, they also displayed more images of competence and enjoyment. The association of the latter with absence of depression suggested to the authors that it was an effective coping mechanism. Physically ill clients' constructions of death have also received some research attention, and evidence has been provided that hospice clients are less threatened by death than those with temporary illnesses or cancer in remission (Hendon and Epting, 1989).

If the ill person is left with a disability, he or she may display an idealised construction of the past self, as Brumfitt (1985) observed in a grid study of aphasic people. She associated this pattern of construing with the experience of grief, defined as 'an awareness that one's core constructs are in the process of change by invalidation of their implications through loss of one of the elements' (p. 94). In the aphasic, this lost element, is, of course, the self as speaker.

Constructions of the client's condition may also be pertinent to an understanding of the situation of people with learning disabilities, but in this case, as a grid study by Vicary (1985) has indicated, others' construing of the disabled individual may be of particular relevance. She found that those mothers who saw their one-year-old child with a learning disability as very different from the child if it were developing normally were more likely to construe the imagined normally developing child as similar to a difficult child. In these mothers, 'many of the distinctions made between the child with a learning disability and the imagined child presented the child with a learning disability in a positive light – as more friendly, less selfish, more loving, etc.' (p. 362), and Vicary views this as a strategy facilitating the mother's acceptance of the handicapped child.

## CONSTRUING OF THE SELF AND OTHERS

Whether or not constructs relating to the client's complaint are core role constructs, in that they are central to his or her self-construing, the way in which the self is construed might be expected to be of particular relevance to an understanding of the client's predicament. It is not surprising, therefore, that there is a considerable body of research evidence, from both the personal construct theory and other perspectives, on self-construing in psychological disorder.

Several of these studies have examined clients' self-esteem, generally operationally defined as the similarity between the construing of actual and ideal selves, or as the tendency to apply the positively evaluated poles of constructs to the self. A consistent finding of these studies, together with one using a non-verbal technique (Ziller *et al.*, 1964), is that self-esteem is particularly low in clients diagnosed as depressive (Sperlinger, 1976; Space and Cromwell, 1980; Sheehan, 1981; Ashworth *et al.*, 1982; Space *et al.*, 1983; R. Neimeyer *et al.*, 1985; Ross, 1985; Axford and Jerrom, 1986), this, of course, being consistent with theoretical formulations and research evidence concerning depression from the cognitive perspective (e.g. Beck *et al.*, 1979). Low self-esteem has also been observed in neurotic disorders (Ryle and Breen, 1972b; Bond and Lader, 1976; Space, 1976; Fransella and Crisp, 1979; Margolius, 1980; Caine *et al.*, 1981; Winter and Gournay, 1987; Button, 1990), and amongst neurotics, agoraphobics have been found to display a particularly low level of self-esteem, especially if construing the self when alone (Lorenzini and Sassaroli, 1987, 1988). There are also reports of low self-esteem in 'one-off' violent offenders (Howells, 1983); in problematic children (Jackson, 1990b); in children taken into Local Authority foster care, particularly those who have experienced many changes of caretaker (Hicks and Nixon, 1989); and in delinquents (Bhagat and Fraser, 1970; Noble, 1971; Stanley, 1985), although Kelly and Taylor (1981) have found that engaging in one particular delinquent activity, 'taking and driving away' a car, may serve to increase the drivers' self-esteem, provided they reach home safely, while tending to have the opposite effect on that of their passengers. Other groups in which unfavourable construing of the self has been demonstrated are female (but not male) teenagers with heavy perceived weight (Worsley, 1981), and individuals presenting anorexic symptoms (Mottram, 1985; Weinreich *et al.*, 1985; Batty and Hall, 1986; Button, 1987), who appeared to Mottram to be 'unsure of what they actually want out of life' (p. 295) in that their ideal selves were construed as very dissimilar to other people. In the Weinreich *et al.* study, anorexics' current self-evaluations were lower than their past self-evaluations, and lower than those of bulimics. They also imagined that their mothers saw them in a negative light, and showed conflicted identification with these maternal metaperspectives in that they tended both to identify with, and to wish to dissociate from, the latter. Although similar results were obtained in relation to paternal metaperspectives, anorexics were not differentiated from other clients in this area. In relation to metaperspectives concerning the views of other people in general, anorexics showed higher identification conflicts than did bulimics. In another study of anorexics, using a grid method first employed with such clients by Feldman (1975), Norton *et al.* (1988) found that, compared to a sample of nurses, they were not only more dissatisfied with themselves in general but also construed their faces, hands, bellies, sexual parts, and buttocks in a more unfavourable light. Not unexpectedly, dysmorphophobic and psoriatic clients have been found, using a similar method, to be dissatisfied with their body images, although only the former group construed themselves more unfavourably than did control subjects (Hardy, 1982). Grid measures have also allowed exploration of clients' construal of various aspects of the self. For example, examining construing of the self at different points in time, Button (1990) has found non-psychotic clients to show no more temporal rigidity in their construing than do normal subjects. In depressives, negative self-construing has been found to be particularly apparent when clients are asked to construe their 'future selves' (R. Neimeyer *et al.*, 1983a, 1985), while neurotics (Ryle, 1981) and dysmorphophobics (Hardy, 1982) have been shown to construe not only themselves, but also relationships involving their significant others, unfavourably. There is also some evidence that abused women, predictably enough, are likely to construe their relationships particularly negatively (G. Neimeyer and Hall, 1988).

Although from those theoretical perspectives which take a hedonistic view of human motivation, it might appear self-evident that to construe the self unfavourably is necessarily a most undesirable state of affairs, personal construct theory would seek to consider what purpose such negative self-constructions serve for the client. It may be, for example, that they act as self-fulfilling prophecies which reduce anxiety by ensuring that the client's predictions are validated. As Makhlouf-Norris and Norris (1973, p. 287) put it, 'in neurotic patients the need for self-certainty is such that they construe the self in a way which predicts undesirable outcomes which are certain to be validated, rather than predict desirable outcomes which would be open to invalidation'. The obsessional clients whom these authors studied had been observed consistently to assign the self and ideal self to opposite poles of constellatory constructs, defined as those which were more central to their principal dimension of construing (Makhlouf-Norris and Jones, 1971), and a similar pattern of particularly low self-esteem in obsessional clients has been noted by Millar (1980). For Makhlouf-Norris and Norris, such findings suggest a view of the self as characterised by unlimited badness, a prediction which compulsive behaviour allows the obsessional to avoid testing. In many neurotic and depressive clients, however, the self is not construed in such a uniformly unfavourable light. As indicated in the previous discussion of dilemmas and 'payoffs' concerning the client's presenting complaint, it may be that the complaint allows a client to take the view that 'I may be incompetent in this sphere, and I may suffer, but at least I am virtuous'. Such observations have led Rowe (1982) to conclude that vanity may be the basis of many clients' difficulties, and that the 'gap between self and ideal-self is filled with pride which often presents itself in the guise of humility' (p. 177). In her view, 'there is no pain, no misery which some member of the human race is not prepared to put up with in order to think well of himself' (p. 173).

A client may, therefore, perceive himself or herself in terms of a mixture of negative constructions, perhaps representing the negative implications of the complaint, and positive constructions, representing its positive implications. Such a pattern of 'mixed self-valence' (see p. 45) was observed to characterise depressives more than it did other clients and normal subjects in two studies carried out by Space and his colleagues (Space and Cromwell, 1980; Space *et al.*, 1983). They interpret this finding as indicating the state of disequilibrium in self-perception of the depression-prone individual, who will consequently be particularly vulnerable to slot changes, shifting his or her construing of the self from one pole of a construct to the other, in response to new events. Such slot changes are likely to manifest themselves in mood changes, as in an oscillation between depression and mania, and if they are in a generally negative direction they may lead to the onset of a depressive episode. This may explain Rigdon's (1983) demonstration, using the Threat Index, of a marked increase in the negativity of a student's self-construing (resulting in a considerable reduction in death threat) at the time of a serious suicide attempt. Discussing such findings and research on the recall of self-referent information in depressives (Davis, 1979; Kuiper and Derry, 1981), R. Neimeyer (1984) suggests that, while the core role structure of the person who is not depressed tends to be consistently positive, the onset of depression is associated with the incorporation of negative self-constructions into the self-schema, resulting at first in a core role structure of inconsistent valency. However, the continuation of this process leads to a consistently negative core role structure in severe depression, as was perhaps reflected in Sheehan's (1981) finding of high levels of Intensity and logical consistency in depressives' construing of how others perceived them. Neimeyer further proposes that this model might account for the clinical observation that severe depressives are most at risk of suicide when their mood becomes more positive, for it is at this time that their construct systems are likely to be most fragmented. As Neimeyer points out, such an interpretation differs markedly from the normal explanation of this phenomenon in terms of the increase in energy resulting from a lifting of mood.

In subsequent research employing Functionally Independent Construction analysis of a grid in which the elements were different self roles, R. Neimeyer *et al.* (1985) were able to investigate the consistency of the self-constructions of their depressive subjects, and their results provided some indication of less coherence in the self-constructs and self-roles of moderately depressed than of more severely depressed clients, whose self-construing was more constellatory. The largest differences were, however, obtained between clients in the second and third quartiles when partitioned on the basis of scores on a rating scale for depression, those in the first and fourth quartiles obtaining intermediate scores on the grid measures. Neimeyer and his colleagues state that 'the apparent cubic trend in these findings . . . suggests that nondepressed individuals may well display greater coherence in core structure than moderate depressives, as the personal construct model would predict' (pp. 189–90). Further evidence supportive of the personal construct theory model has been provided by Ross (1985), who asked his subjects to complete a 'daily-rep test', in which they rated the self every day on a set of elicited constructs, as well as daily self-ratings, and ratings of the day's experiences, on supplied constructs. Although he found slot-rattling to be positively correlated with depression for the sample as a whole, closer examination of his data indicated a curvilinear relationship, subjects at the two extremes of the dimension of depression slot-rattling less, and therefore possibly having more coherent core role structures, than those in the middle range. Also perhaps relevant to the coherence of the core role structure in depression is research which suggests that aspects of the depressive's pessimistic view of the world, for example in relation to perceived control over positive and negative outcomes, may, in fact, reflect a greater accuracy of judgement concerning the self than is observed in non-depressed individuals (Nelson and Craighead, 1977; Alloy and Abramson, 1979, 1982). Conceivably, therefore, the tight organisation of the depressive's negative self-constructions may in part result from their greater likelihood of validation than is the case with the more optimistic constructions of the person who is not depressed.

In one of his studies, R. Neimeyer found that not only did depressives construe themselves negatively but also in very polarised, dichotomous terms, the latter tendency being associated with depression even after the effect of negative self-construing had been partialled out (R. Neimeyer, 1984; R. Neimeyer et al., 1983a). Cleaver's (1989) recent finding that women who have attempted suicide in retrospect construe how they were at the time of the attempt in a more polarised manner than the self before or after the attempt may, therefore, indicate greater depression at the time of the attempt. While Cleaver considers that his results may suggest that the suicide attempt provided these women with a heightened sense of self-identity, he also notes that 'Clarity of self-perception may indicate separateness not individuation' (p. 45). The separateness which is implicit in depressives' polarised self-constructions is reflected in the tendency of such clients, observed in several repertory grid studies, to construe the self as very dissimilar to others (Space and Cromwell, 1980; Hewstone et al., 1981; Sheehan, 1981; Space et al., 1983; Ross, 1985; Axford and Jerrom, 1986). Similar tendencies have been observed in heterogeneous samples of neurotic clients (Ryle and Breen, 1972b; Frazer, 1980; Caine et al., 1981), and particularly in those presenting obsessive-compulsive and 'anxiety state' symptoms (Millar, 1980; Caine et al., 1981), or who were allocated to behaviour therapy rather than group psychotherapy (Caine et al., 1981). Millar, however, qualifies his finding that obsessional clients construed themselves as less similar to others, and to their ideal selves, than did Ryle and Breen's more heterogeneous group of neurotics, suggesting that this may have been due to the greater severity of neurotic disorder in his in-patient sample than in Ryle and Breen's out-patients. Self–other discrimination has also been observed in psychiatric in-patients by Ziller et al. (1964), while Carr and Townes (1975), studying out-patients, found that the greater perceived dissimilarity of self and others in clients than in normal subjects only characterised clients aged 25 years and above, while in the age range from 20 to 24 years the opposite tendency was apparent. Finally, high differentiation of the self from others has been found by Harter et al. (1988) to characterise women who had suffered incestuous abuse as children, particularly if their family of origin was low in cohesion and if the abuse included intercourse.

The tendency to construe oneself as dissimilar to others has been referred to as 'self-isolation' (Makhlouf-Norris and Norris, 1973) and, in the depressive, has been regarded by Rowe (1978, 1983a, 1985a) as akin to solitary confinement in a prison consisting of propositions, or constructions, 'whereby the person sees himself as being cut off from and as choosing to be cut off from interactions with others, both people in his external reality (e.g., wife, friends) and figures in his internal reality (e.g., his God, happy memories of his dead mother, his good self, his successful future)' (Rowe, 1978, p. 235). Such propositions, in Rowe's view, are learnt by the individual during childhood, and are held as if they are axiomatic, and largely unchallengeable, rules for living. That propositions involving perceived self-isolation may lead to actual interpersonal isolation, such that a vicious circle of increasing distance from others develops, is indicated by research findings that the person who construes himself or herself as different from other people not only tends to be inaccurate in predicting the constructions of others (Winter, 1988a), but that his or her constructions are also less easily anticipated by other people (Adams-Webber, 1973). Such individuals may, therefore, make others feel anxious and less inclined to attempt to construe their construction processes and enter into a role relationship with them. The relative lack of validation of their construing by other people may conceivably provide an explanation of the finding by Dingemans *et al.* (1983) that construing of the self as very unlike other people is associated with anger. The person who perceives himself or herself as very dissimilar to others is also clearly not organising social judgements in the 'golden section ratio' (see p. 49), and there is some evidence that in normal subjects who role-play being depressed, the proportion of unlike-self judgements increases above the initial golden section baseline of 37 per cent (Rodney, 1981; Adams-Webber and Rodney, 1983; Lefebvre *et al.*, 1986). As Adams-Webber (1979) feels self-constructions in the golden section ratio to be conducive to high salience of differences between self and others, it may be that the gross distinctions which depressive and neurotic clients tend to make between self and others belie a degree of insensitivity to the precise ways in which others differ from the self. The association between high self–other differentiation and negative self-construing is consistent with Adams-Webber's (1986) model of self and other perception. Drawing on information theory, Adams-Webber (1985, pp. 65–6) also suggests that the research findings in this area indicate that 'average uncertainty in construing self and others may increase in depression and other dysphoric moods', and he relates such uncertainty to anxiety as defined by Kelly. Therefore, although we have seen in Chapter 3 that perceived self-isolation may represent a constrictive strategy by which the individual attempts to avoid uncertainties associated with social interaction (Hewstone *et al.*, 1981; Sheehan, 1981), it is unlikely adequately to serve this purpose if Adams-Webber's formulation is correct.

As well as examining clients' perceived similarity to other people in general, some researchers have considered degree of identification with particular significant figures in the client's life. There is evidence, for example, that neurotic clients construe themselves as particularly dissimilar to their parents (Ryle and Breen, 1972b), although Caine *et al.* (1981), and Frazer (1980), studying agoraphobics, found this to be the case only when clients' construing of their fathers was considered. Similarly, Schaible (1990) has found agoraphobics to construe themselves in relation to their fathers as dissimilar to their fathers in relation to them, as well as viewing the relationship with the father as unsafe. Low identification with parents was also observed in depressives by Space and Cromwell (1980). In research on delinquent boys, Noble (1971) provided an indication of their lack of adequate role models in that they showed little identification with both their fathers and their best friends, and wished to be even less like these people. Similarly, Miller and Treacher (1981) found that delinquents wished to be less similar to their significant adults, and more like television heroes. One particular aspect of identification with parents which has received some research attention is the extent to which an individual's identification with the parent of the same sex as himself or herself is greater than that with the opposite-sex parent. In a repertory grid study, I have found that clients diagnosed as schizophrenic displayed cross-sex identification to a greater degree than did non-schizophrenic clients, an even greater difference being apparent between the grid scores of the parents of these two groups (Winter, 1975). Although these findings appeared to be a function of the differences in social class between the groups, cross-sex identification has also been observed in case examples presented by Space and Cromwell (1978) of the repertory grid responses of schizophrenics. A further line of investigation has been to compare clients' construing of their relationships with various significant others. Comparing couples presenting relationship problems with normal control couples, Ryle and Breen (1972a) found that members of the former couples, who exhibited significantly higher levels of neurotic symptoms, were more likely to construe their relationship with the partner as similar to that with a parent. They also considered that when the relationship was going badly they related to the partner more as they did to a parent, while the partner related to them in a less parent-like fashion. These tendencies, interpreted by Ryle and Breen in psychodynamic terms, were more marked in relation to the parent of the opposite sex. From the personal construct theory perspective, they can perhaps be viewed as indicating an inflexible construction of intimate relationships in the members of maladjusted couples, who appear to be able to construe such relationships only in terms of constructions which they developed to anticipate their relationships with their parents.

There are some indications that the negative self-construing of the neurotic is associated with a tendency to construe the parents and others in a correspondingly positive light (Caine *et al.*, 1981), although Axford and Jerrom (1976) were unable to demonstrate any difference between depressives, other clients, and medical in-patients in the positivity of their construing of others. Favourable construing of the parents has been found to differentiate agoraphobics, but not other neurotics, from normal subjects, this being consistent with the agoraphobics' generally positive construal of others (Winter and Gournay, 1987). Idealisation of the mother has also been observed by Fransella and Crisp (1979) in anorexics. However, it is unclear whether this was to a significantly greater degree than in their normal subjects, and although Weinreich *et al.* (1985) found anorexics to regard their mothers as positive role models to a greater extent than did normal subjects, they were not differentiated from other clients in this regard. Although Button (1990) has found some evidence of negative construal of the mother in clients with non-psychotic disorders, the majority of studies in this area suggest that at least in neurotic clients, and perhaps particularly in agoraphobics, the self is characteristically defined by contrast with significant others who are construed very favourably. In similar fashion, the client's significant others may be able to validate their own positive self-construal by contrast with the client, and this may explain Hafner's (1977a, 1977b) finding of complementary patterns of self-esteem in the more disabled members of his female agoraphobic sample and their spouses, together with the finding of the Winter and Gournay study that those agoraphobics whose symptoms were more severe had spouses with higher levels of self-esteem. These results are consistent with reports of patterns of 'phobia and counterphobia' in the families of agoraphobics (Holmes, 1982), and suggest that an understanding of the purposes served by a client's complaint and negative self-construing may be elucidated by considering not only the client's own personal construct system but also what Procter (1981) has termed the family construct system. Construal of others in a highly favourable light is, of course, very vulnerable to invalidation, the possible tragic consequences of which were indicated in a repertory grid study by Howells (1983) of people who had carried out offences of extreme violence which seemed to be 'out of character'. Compared to multiple offenders and non-aggressive prisoners, such individuals were more likely to give constructs with positively evaluated emergent poles during grid elicitation, and more likely than non-aggressive prisoners to assign most elements to these positive poles. In addition, they construed the victims of their assaults, all of whom had been killed, more favourably and as more like themselves than did the multiple offenders. In Howells' view, the negatively evaluated poles of the 'one-off' violent offender's constructs tend to be submerged, but as severe interpersonal difficulties increase the individual's awareness of these construct poles, the resulting threat may lead to a violent attempt to remove the person who is the source of threat. The invalidation of the individual's favourable constructions of others may also result in slot-rattling to the submerged negative construct poles, with violence again being the possible outcome.

Although such patterns as negative self-construing and perceived dissimilarity of the self and others appear to characterise a range of neurotic and depressive clients, perhaps indicating a degree of depression in all such individuals, they are by no means observed in all clients considered to be suffering from psychological disorders. Relatively favourable self-constructions tend to be found, for example, in those clients who have not presented themselves as psychologically disturbed but have been regarded by others as such. This is often the predicament of clients diagnosed as psychotic, and Miskimins *et al.* (1971) report that in some such individuals the self–ideal self discrepancy is no higher than that of normal subjects. Riedel (1970) has obtained similar results, although his assumption that the non-verbal procedure employed allowed access to role constructs is questionable (Mancuso and Sarbin, 1972; Riedel, 1972). I have found self–ideal self distance to be significantly lower in schizophrenics than in other clients (Winter, 1975); and Kahgee *et al.* (1982) have also observed that schizophrenics, both thought disordered and non-thought disordered, rate others as similar to themselves, and apply positive and negative attributes to others, in 'golden section' proportions, as is the case with normal subjects. These workers conclude that schizophrenics 'have the same basic ability to form identifications as do normals' and 'have a more distinct notion of their own identities than has been assumed previously' (p. 323). Although Space *et al.* (1983) did find schizophrenics to identify with others to a lesser degree than did normal subjects, this was not to the extent of the alienation from others shown by depressive clients. While several of these studies would suggest a relative absence of abnormalities in the self-construing of schizophrenics, a different picture is painted by the analysis by Gara *et al.* (1987) of personal identity in schizophrenia. They regard each individual as having a multiplicity of identities, some of which are prominent, or superordinate to others. If all of a person's prominent identities are invalidated, the person is likely to attempt to enact contrasting identities, but if these latter are unelaborated the result will be a 'not-me' experience and behaviour which may be labelled as schizophrenic. Although a new identity may eventually be elaborated, this is likely to be based on global stereotypes or delusions, and to be replaced in due course by the identity of patient. The person whose system of identities is unintegrated, with few superordinate identities and consequently unelaborated identity contrasts, will be particularly at risk of schizophrenic breakdown in response to changing circumstances. Some support for these views is provided by findings that self-construing is poorly elaborated, and perceptions of self and others are stereotyped, in schizophrenics (Gara *et al.*, 1989). Also perhaps consistent with the position of Gara *et al.* is Leitner's (1981b) finding that 'chaotic fragmentalism' of construing, which he has associated with schizophrenia (Leitner, 1981a), is related to low meaningfulness of, and dissatisfaction with, the self.

Other groups in which a pattern of 'self-convergence', construing of the actual and ideal selves as very similar, has been observed are socially deviant individuals such as the arsonist studied by Fransella and Adams (1966), drug addicts and clients diagnosed as suffering from personality disorders, as well as some normal subjects (Norris and Makhlouf-Norris, 1976). Ryle (1975) and Dawes (1985) have each described the case of a drug addict who construed the self when not taking drugs in very negative terms but for whom the purpose served by drug-taking was indicated by the fact that the self when on drugs was construed as very similar to how they would like to be, and in the case of Ryle's client how she imagined her boy friend would like her to be. Some indication of abnormally favourable construing of aspects of the core role has also been observed by Breen (1975) in primiparous mothers defined as maladjusted on the basis of questionnaires and doctors' reports. She found such individuals to construe themselves as more similar to an ideal mother post-partum than during pregnancy in terms of 'maternal' but not other constructs, whereas the reverse was the case in well-adjusted mothers. Finally, in clients suffering from chronic pain, Large (1985) has found those who showed the least evidence of electromyographic correlates of pain to construe the self and ideal self as similar. He views the latter tendency as indicating denial and resistance, and speculates that it may be associated with the genesis of pain by conversion reactions rather than physiological mechanisms.

It will be evident that several different patterns of construal of the self and others have been observed in psychological disorder, and recent work by Schwartz and Garamoni (1986, 1987) provides a framework which may explain the difficulties associated with such contrasting patterns as unreservedly negative and unreservedly positive construing of the self. Their 'states of mind model' attempts to integrate research on the golden section hypothesis, cybernetic and information-processing concepts, and work from the cognitive-behavioural perspective. They classify states of mind in terms of the cognitive-behavioural notion of an 'internal dialogue' involving positive and negative cognitions. A 'positive dialogue' involves a balance of self-statements in the golden section proportion of 0.618 positive and 0.382 negative, representing a generally positive state of mind coupled with maximal attention to threat and optimum ability to cope with stress. The converse pattern, or 'negative dialogue', in which 0.618 of cognitions are negative and 0.382 positive, has been found to characterise moderately anxious and depressed people both in repertory grid research (Sheehan, 1981) and in numerous cognitive-behavioural studies, which have employed a range of methods of assessment of cognitions (Schwartz, 1986; Schwartz and Garamoni, 1986; Schwartz and Michelson, 1987). It involves maximal salience of positive events against a background of general negativity. An 'internal dialogue of conflict', in which positive and negative self-statements are symmetrically balanced, has been associated with indecision, and observed in mildly dysfunctional individuals such as those who are unassertive (Schwartz and Gottman, 1976). In contrast to these dialogic states of mind, 'positive and negative monologues' involve a predominance of positive or negative cognitions respectively, at least 0.69 of self-statements being of one valence, such that 'the dialectic process is relatively absent'. Schwartz and Garamoni consider the positive monologue to characterise manic individuals, and to be associated with denial, impulsivity, and unrealistic optimism, and the negative monologue 'severe psychopathology such as profound depression or acute panic'. These monologic states can be regarded as involving highly 'lopsided' self-construing, in contrast to the moderate lopsidedness which the model would suggest is associated with optimal functioning. Repertory grid research has provided some evidence of the difficulties likely to be faced by the person who construes in a lopsided way (Hayden et al., 1977), as will be discussed further below.

## COMMONALITY AND SOCIALITY IN CONSTRUING

It should now be apparent that the constructions which clients place on events, particularly in areas relating to their presenting complaints, may be socially deviant in that they may differ markedly from the modal constructions of others from the same culture. Such differences were examined by Bannister in his studies of schizophrenic thought disorder, the first of which provided evidence that non-thought disordered schizophrenics exhibited a more socially deviant pattern of construct relationships than did normal subjects (Bannister, 1960). Two subsequent investigations employing measures of social deviation which allowed for differences in Intensity between groups found thought disordered schizophrenics to be particularly socially deviant in their construing (Bannister, 1962a; Bannister et al., 1971), as were brain damaged clients in the later study. The further finding of this study that male clients were more socially deviant in their construing than females was speculatively linked to the higher incidence of schizophrenia in males. However, this finding was not replicated by McPherson et al. (1973) in a study which provided further evidence that thought disordered schizophrenics exhibit more socially deviant construing than do non-thought disordered schizophrenic, manic and depressive clients. Idiosyncratic construing has also been observed in unpopular children (Jackson and Bannister, 1985); and has been suggested by Jaspars (1963) to characterise neurotic clients on the basis that they exhibit a lower correlation than do normal subjects between measures from grids employing elicited and those employing supplied constructs.

Further findings of Bannister's research provide implications concerning the genesis of socially deviant patterns of construing. For example, Bannister et al. (1971) demonstrated that those clients, regardless of diagnosis, whose disturbance had a clear precipitating factor were more socially deviant than those for whom this was not the case, suggesting that the former clients may have altered the patterning of their constructs in an attempt to adapt to the traumatic events with which they had been confronted. As we have seen in Chapter 3, there is also evidence that such a change in the patterning of construct relationships may be the initial reaction of some people to an experience of serial invalidation of their construing (Bannister, 1963, 1965b; Radley, 1974a; Cochran, 1977; Lawlor and Cochran, 1981). That this reaction may involve successive shifts in the pattern of construct relationships was suggested by the association demonstrated by Bannister *et al.* (1971) between social deviation and inconsistency of relationships between constructs. Furthermore, its specificity in thought disordered schizophrenics to construing in the social realm has been indicated by the finding of Bannister and Salmon (1966) that, although such clients are more socially deviant than normal subjects in their construing of both people and objects, they exhibit relatively more social deviation when construing people.

An individual may, of course, develop a socially deviant pattern of construct relationships not only because his or her previous pattern of construing has been constantly invalidated but also as a result of constant validation of socially deviant construing. The work of Lidz (1968) suggests that the families of schizophrenics may be characterised by a mode of construing which departs from social consensus, and this was also indicated by my finding of a tendency towards cross-sex identification in such families (Winter, 1975). Liebowitz (1970) has also observed that these families may be characterised by parental confusion concerning their sons' identification patterns, and by lower self–other discrimination by parents of schizophrenics than is apparent in normal subjects. The construing of members of families of schizophrenics might be expected to be validated when it is consistent with the family's socially deviant construct system. That validation of socially deviant patterns of construct relationships may lead a person to develop such constructions has been demonstrated in an experiment by Higgins and Schwarz (1976), who found that students who were reinforced when they rated people as either kind and insincere or unkind and sincere showed a strengthening of this atypical relationship between constructs of kindness and sincerity. Furthermore, this effect was more pronounced in those subjects who were considered to be schizotypic on the basis of their responses to the Schizophrenia scale of the Minnesota Multiphasic Personality Inventory. Although Higgins and Schwarz present their demonstration of the effects of social responses on construing as an alternative to the personal construct theory model, the two explanations can be seen to be quite consistent if the reinforcement condition in this study is reconstrued as one of validation.

Some evidence of an association between socially deviant construing and socially deviant behaviour has been provided by repertory grid studies of delinquents and of clients diagnosed as psychopathic. Although Heather (1979) found that not only delinquents but also non-delinquents showed evidence of both 'subterranean' and 'conventional' values, the former implying approval and the latter disapproval of delinquent acts, subterranean values were stronger in delinquents. Widom (1976), finding that socially deviant construing characterised psychopathic clients, and in particular 'primary psychopaths', considered this to be consistent with Bannister's (1962a) finding that those of his clients whom psychiatrists rated as impulsive were most socially deviant in their construing. Furthermore, her psychopathic clients showed considerable misperception of the construing of other people when they were asked to complete grids, with situations as elements, as they imagined that people in general would complete them and these were then compared with the actual grid responses of normal subjects. A particular area of misperception concerned the construct 'dull–exciting', psychopaths imagining that other people, like themselves, would construe many situations as rather dull. Amongst the situations concerned were 'being with a friend and you are threatening to commit suicide', '"grassing on" (informing on) a close friend', and 'getting caught for a crime you didn't commit'. Psychopaths therefore not only construe idiosyncratically but fail to appreciate that other people do not share their view of the world, this perhaps providing an explanation for their difficulties in forming role relationships. The common psychiatric view that psychopaths are characterised by an absence of guilt may, similarly, represent a failure by clinicians to appreciate that the core role structure of the psychopath is often very different from their own. For example, behaviour which the clinician construes as manipulative or cruel, and which, if he or she had acted in such a way, would cause the clinician to experience guilt, may be quite consistent with the psychopath's core role. The psychopath may, therefore, be no more immune from guilt than is anyone else, but may differ from others in that finding himself or herself acting in a tender manner towards another person is the behaviour most likely to be guilt-provoking! Some support for this view has been provided by Klass (1980), who found that sociopaths with a history of drug abuse construed transgressions involving harming others as more congruent with their self-concepts than did non-sociopathic individuals with a similar history and normal subjects. Furthermore, there was evidence that subjects anticipated more negative reactions to transgressions if these were construed as discrepant with their views of themselves. The common view that psychopaths experience relatively little anxiety is more consistent with a personal construct theory analysis than their presumed lack of guilt since it may be considered to reflect the use of strategies, such as lopsided construing, which allow such clients to avoid recognising invalidation of their social construing (Widom, 1976; Hayden, 1982).

Difficulties in construing the construction processes of other people are, of course, not confined to psychopaths, and Button (1983a) regards the failure to anticipate others as a central component in all disorders. For example, he considers that the focus on control of eating in clients with eating disorders is because, in contrast to their failures to predict people, this is an area of life in which their predictions are likely to be validated (Button, 1985a). Evidence of difficulty in predicting the construing of others has also been obtained in studies of problematic children (Jackson and Bannister, 1985; Jackson,

1990a), although a subgroup of 'rebels' displayed the opposite pattern. Limited capacities for sociality, and low levels of commonality in individuals' construing, are central components of a useful taxonomy of disturbed relationships which has been provided by R. and G. Neimeyer (1985). Following Stringer (1979, p. 107), they regard 'healthy relationships' as those which 'have the characteristic of attempting to move forward another's construction processes'. 'Disrupted relationships' were once satisfactory but are characterised by failure of one or both partners to revise their constructions of each other as they each develop or as transitions in the relationship, for example the birth of a child, are encountered. These changes may lead partners to experience such negative emotions as anxiety and threat. Although an early investigation by Weigel *et al.* (1973) failed to find a relationship between low commonality in partners' adjudged meaningfulness of supplied constructs and their marital adjustment, most subsequent studies of deterioration and dissatisfaction in relationships have indicated that disrupted relationships may in their early stages be associated with low commonality between partners in construing, both in its content and in its structural features (Duck and Allison, 1978; G. and R. Neimeyer, 1981a, 1986; G. Neimeyer, 1984; G. Neimeyer and Hudson, 1985). Neimeyer and Hudson were able to demonstrate such a relationship only at the level of the content of subordinate, but not superordinate, constructs, and they suggest that it is at the subordinate level that invalidation, a major factor in marital dissatisfaction, is most commonly experienced. However, when 'functional similarity' in the application of constructs to particular elements was considered, it was only in the case of superordinate constructs that dissimilarity in application was related to marital dissatisfaction.

In contrast to disrupted relationships, 'negative relationships' are those which have always been characterised by negative emotions and which have never involved mutual validation of partners' core structures. Instead, there may be validation by contrast, as in the case of those spouses of agoraphobics who, as we have seen, may maintain a favourable self-construction by contrasting themselves with their agoraphobic partners. A predominant emotion in negative relationships is contempt, the awareness that the other person's core role is comprehensively different from one's own (McCoy, 1977).

The predicament of other individuals is an 'absence of role relationships', in that they experience 'an enduring difficulty in effectively construing other people as people' (R. and G. Neimeyer, 1985, p. 204). Such individuals may experience anxiety in many social situations, finding them largely beyond the range of convenience of their construct systems, and may adopt the constrictive response of social withdrawal. However, in the view of R. and G. Neimeyer (1985, p. 207), this will not be the case in those, such as psychopaths, who lack 'a more abstract psychological approach to relationships'. It may also be that some individuals avoid role relationships because of the risk of invalidation of core constructs, and the consequent conglomeration of negative emotions which Leitner (1985b) refers to as 'terror', which is always implicit in relationships of this nature. As Leitner has described, amongst the ways in which such avoidance may be manifested are relating to others only on the basis of social roles, being controlling or manipulative towards others, displaying hostility, or engaging in casual sexual relationships. In his view, any major, global avoidance of role relationships is indicative of psychopathology.

As we have seen in some of the research studies reviewed in this and previous chapters, certain characteristics of an individual's construct system may be associated with difficulties in construing others' constructions. For example, deficiencies in this regard are particularly apparent in those individuals whose interpersonal construct systems are relatively undifferentiated (e.g. Adams-Webber, 1969; Winter, 1988a), a feature of construing which has been observed in some studies of clients diagnosed as neurotic (Ryle and Breen, 1972b; Caine *et al.*, 1981; Winter, 1983) and depressive (Sheehan, 1981), in shy people (McKain *et al.*, 1988), and in maladjusted boys (Hayden *et al.*, 1977). In addition, we have seen that construal of the self as different from others, which has been reported in the research on neurotics and depressives, and lopsided construing, which has been observed in chronic schizophrenics (Radley, 1974a) and psychopaths (Widom, 1976), have been associated with difficulties in predicting others by Winter (1988a) and Hayden *et al.* (1977) respectively. Low accuracy in predicting aspects of the construing of others has also been observed in individuals who do not have a favourable or salient self-construction, or who are construed unfavourably by others (Landfield and Schmittdiel, 1983), although in children it has been associated with the lack of a desire to change (Jackson and Bannister, 1985). It would not be unexpected, therefore, if any of the client groups characterised by these various features of construing experienced difficulties in role relationships. As well as the evidence, discussed above, of low ability to predict others in psychopaths and maladjusted boys, Ryle and Breen (1972a) have found high levels of neurotic symptoms in men to be associated with inaccurate construing of their partners' constructions. However, the fact that a correlation in the opposite direction has been observed in women is less easy to explain. Contrary to this latter finding, Harbury and I (unpublished) have recently demonstrated that female agoraphobics were less able to predict their husbands' construing than were 'normal' women, particularly when their husbands also exhibited high levels of phobic symptoms. Furthermore, compared to normal couples, both agoraphobics and their spouses imagined that their partners would be less accurate in predicting their construing, especially if the partner displayed more neurotic symptoms. Although the relationship between sociality and cognitive complexity might suggest that couples whose construing is less complex would be more likely to be dissatisfied with their marriages, G. Neimeyer (1984) did not find this to be so, only dissimilarity between partners in their levels of cognitive complexity being associated with dissatisfaction. Nevertheless, there is evidence that partners who are able to construe each others' superordinate constructions accurately are more likely to be satisfied with their marriages, particularly if their understanding is mutual and if it applies to both the husband's and wife's constructs (G. Neimeyer and Hudson, 1985). In two studies of couples attending marital therapy groups, Wijesinghe and Wood (1976a, 1976b) have found that members of the couples were better able to predict their respective partners' construing than was the therapist, except in the area of emotional expression, this perhaps being the major problem area in these couples' relationships. Furthermore, Wood (1977) demonstrated, in the second study, that accuracy in predicting another person's construing was greater if this person's construct system was similar to the predictor's. Similar results have been obtained by Smail (1972), but the research evidence in this area is inconsistent (Corsini, 1956; O'Loughlin, 1989). Although Kelly (1955) emphasised that 'for people to be able to understand each other it takes more than a similarity or commonality in their thinking' (p. 99), it has been suggested that commonality may provide a foundation for such understanding (Richardson and Weigel, 1971; Duck, 1973a, 1979), as seemed to be the case in the individuals studied by Wood and Smail and in the children investigated by Jackson and Bannister (1985).

Commonality and sociality have been associated with more satisfactory relationships in families as well as in couples. For example, Agnew (1985) has proposed that low commonality of construing in a family may hamper a child's ability to construe others' constructions, and that autistic or violent children may be manifesting particular difficulties in this regard. Epting et al. (1979) have related mothers' construed similarity to their children to degree of maternal warmth. Studying families including an adolescent child, Harter et al. (1989) found mothers' and adolescents' satisfaction with the family to be highly related to both their commonality with, and accuracy in predicting, the construing of other family members but this tendency was less apparent in the case of fathers' satisfaction levels. Although commonality and sociality in the family may be associated with high satisfaction, they need not imply an absence of disorder, as is evident from a study of anorexic adolescents and their mothers (Hall and Brown, 1983). While these studies have concerned themselves with the construct systems of individual family members, it may also be valuable, as Procter (1981) has described, to consider the shared 'family construct system'. The family's 'disorders of negotiation' may, for example, be understood in terms of such characteristics of this system as its degree of constriction, looseness, constellatoriness, or impermeability. This approach will be discussed further in Chapters 7 and 8.

To return to the Neimeyers' classification of disturbed relationships, in 'disorganised relationships', as in individuals with an 'absence of role relationships', the person is also limited in the ability to construe others, but in this case because the construct system does not provide an adequate basis for making any predictions. As has been discussed in Chapter 3, this is the predicament of the person whose construct system is very loosely organised, perhaps providing an explanation of the finding that clients diagnosed as schizophrenic tend to be less able to predict the self-construal of others than are normal subjects (Jackson and Carr, 1955). High differentiation, coupled with low integration, of construing is for Landfield (1980a) the hallmark of chaotic fragmentalism of experiences, and has been associated by him with difficulties in construing the constructions of others (Landfield, 1977), although in a later study the combination of high differentiation and high integration appeared to pose most problems in this regard (Landfield and Schmittdiel, 1983). As in cases when role relationships are absent, R. and G. Neimeyer consider that the failures to anticipate others in disorganised relationships may be associated with anxiety, and also with bewilderment as the person modifies their peripheral constructions in response to invalidation.

As noted in Chapter 3, it is not only the 'chaotic fragmentalist' who may experience anxiety and bewilderment in personal relationships, but also people who encounter such an individual. There is some evidence, for example, that individuals whose construing is highly differentiated but poorly integrated tend not to be accurately predicted by others (Landfield and Schmittdiel, 1983; R. Neimeyer et al., 1983b), and that neither are those who construe the other people concerned unfavourably (Landfield and Schmittdiel, 1983), or who are not construed extremely by, and are therefore probably not particularly meaningful to, others (Landfield, 1977). In children, those whose peers find it difficult to understand them have been observed neither to have salient self-constructs nor to be accurate in predicting their peers' construing (Jackson and Bannister, 1985). As discussed above, lack of understanding by others is also likely to be the fate of people who, as is typical of neurotics and depressives, see themselves as very different from other people (Adams-Webber, 1973). Not only may such unpredictable individuals find themselves avoided by others but, as research findings on a client population would suggest (Catina et al., 1988), they are likely to withdraw from other people if they perceive that they are misconstrued.

## SUMMARY AND CONCLUSIONS

Research findings with a number of different client groups have indicated relationships between the predominant content of individuals' personal construct systems and the complaints with which they present, as well as the treatments to which they are subsequently allocated. A particular area of research concern has been the use by clients of constructs relating to emotions, and there is evidence that this construct subsystem is poorly elaborated in affectively blunted schizophrenics, and in agoraphobics and their spouses, who have been observed, in particular, to tend not to employ constructions concerning interpersonal conflict. This latter tendency has also been found to characterise clients suffering from chronic pain and people who have committed acts of extreme violence; and it provides an explanation of the problems manifested by these individuals.

A further body of research has indicated that for many clients the presenting complaint is construed in such a way that it carries positive implications. While other clients have been found to construe their complaints very negatively, in such cases the client may be observed to dissociate himself or herself from this negative stereotype of other people with similar complaints. They may also construe life without the complaint in a very idealistic fashion. Clients' construing of the self and significant others has also been the subject of considerable research attention. These studies have provided evidence of unfavourable self-construing in clients diagnosed as depressive, neurotic, anorexic, and delinquent, and that neurotics and depressives tend to construe the self in polarised terms and as very dissimilar to others. Research with normal subjects suggests that these latter tendencies are likely to lead to interpersonal difficulties. Much more favourable views of the self have been observed in clients diagnosed as psychotic, some of those engaging in socially deviant behaviour, and clients who present complaints of pain which appear to have no physical basis. Whatever constructions the client holds concerning the self and the complaint, they are likely to be maintained because they serve such strategic functions as enabling the person to avoid, or cope with, invalidation.

That there may be relatively litle commonality between clients' construing and that of people in general has been indicated by studies of clients diagnosed as thought disordered schizophrenics and primary psychopaths, the latter group mistakenly believing that the construing of others is similar to their own. Such failures to anticipate others' construing have also been suggested to characterise clients whose construct systems show evidence of such structural features as tight organisation and biased use of construct poles. Low commonality in a couple's construing, and a low capacity for mutual anticipation of constructions, may in some cases provide an explanation of marital difficulties.

# Chapter 5

# Explorations of therapy and reconstruction

If psychological disorders reflect particular features of construing, recovery from a disorder would be expected to necessitate a process of reconstruction. The numerous investigations which have been conducted of changes in construing during therapy therefore provide further research evidence pertinent to the personal construct theory view of psychological disorder. The findings of these investigations, which predominantly employ repertory grid technique, will be reviewed below.

## CHANGES IN THE STRUCTURE OF THE CONSTRUCT SYSTEM DURING THERAPY

Changes in structural properties of clients' construing during therapy have received rather less research attention than have changes in the content of the construct system. This is perhaps partly because of the methodological problems involved in evaluating structural changes since, as we have seen in Chapter 2, the repertory grid is a reactive measure in that the process of grid completion may itself lead to a tightening of construct relationships.

Nevertheless, some studies have attempted to demonstrate that successful therapy is associated with the development of a more optimally structured construct system. The single investigation of a therapeutic approach aiming to tighten the construct relationships of thought disordered schizophrenics failed to demonstrate an increase in the Intensity scores of the experimental group, and indeed the construct relationships of clients in this group became more unstable during therapy (Bannister *et al.*, 1975). However, as discussed in Chapter 3, various factors may have militated against the intended validational and tightening effects of the treatment procedures adopted in this study. Another client group in which, contrary to predictions, no significant increase in the strength of construct relationships was found to accompany therapy, which in this case was pharmacological, consisted of those manic clients from the 1982 study by Ashworth and his colleagues who were considered to be clinically recovered on follow-up some four months after their initial assessment (Ashworth *et al.*, 1985). Nevertheless, despite the lack of a statistically significant change, the variance accounted for by the first three principal components of these clients' grids did increase to the extent that they were no longer significantly differentiated on this measure from the depressed clients from the 1982 study, or from those members of the depressive sample who had recovered at follow-up. A 'simplification of conceptual structure' (Landfield, 1979, p. 141), as reflected in a decrease in Functionally Independent Construction and Ordination scores derived from a grid, has also been observed in problem drinkers attending an Interpersonal Transaction Group (see p. 279).

More numerous than studies of structural changes during therapy in clients whose construing is relatively disorganised are investigations of such changes in clients, for example those diagnosed as neurotic and depressive, whose construct systems have been generally considered to be tightly organised. One such study, of neurotic clients undergoing either group analytic therapy or behaviour therapy, found no evidence of reduction in the degree of logical consistency of construct relationships in those clients who improved during therapy (Winter, 1983). Bassler *et al.* (1989), although also reporting non-significant findings, have suggested that there was a tendency towards increased logical inconsistency in the construing of those of their neurotic clients who improved following psychoanalytically orientated in-patient treatment, whereas clients who failed to improve showed evidence of a reduction in the differentiation of their construct systems. Watts and Sharrock (1985) failed to observe any decrease in the degree of relationship between constructs concerning spiders in spider phobics during desensitisation treatment which appeared to be effective in reducing their anxiety. They speculate that this may reflect a desynchrony (Rachman and Hodgson, 1974) between changes in construing and those in anxiety, and that, for example, desensitisation may facilitate greater observation of spiders in such clients, which in turn may lead to a gradual differentiation of the construct subsystem concerning spiders, which would not be apparent at an immediate post-treatment assessment. Other studies of neurotic clients have been rather more successful in demonstrating a relationship between positive treatment outcome and reduction in the strength of construct relationships. For example, Raz-Duvshani (1986) found improvement on a measure of target complaints during psychoanalytically orientated psychotherapy to be associated with increases in complexity, as assessed by a range of measures of construct organisation, although not with increase in the number of constructs employed by the client in describing people. Not only did more improved clients exhibit a decrease in the degree of interrelatedness of their constructs, but those who improved less showed changes in the reverse direction, tightening their construct relationships during therapy. A study of agoraphobics undergoing behaviour therapy has also provided evidence of a reduction in the tightness of construct relationships in those clients who displayed symptomatic improvement during therapy (Winter and Gournay,

1987). A similar effect was demonstrated in the spouses of these clients, perhaps indicating that reconstruing by the spouse is a prerequisite for symptom loss by the agoraphobic. Another client group in which structural changes in construing have been observed during therapy consists of depressives who have been hospitalised. For example, Silverman (1977) found some evidence that in depressives who showed clinical remission during in-patient treatment there was a decrease in the strength of relationships between constructs relating to affect. Similarly, Ashworth *et al.* (1985) demonstrated a reduction in the tightness of construct relationships in clients whose depression lifted following pharmacological treatment. Although other studies of depressives undergoing pharmacotherapy (Sheehan, 1981), group cognitive therapy (R. Neimeyer *et al.*, 1985), and personal construct psychotherapy (Sheehan, 1985a) have failed to demonstrate a loosening of their construct relationships, the last of these investigations did find a decrease in the logical consistency of clients' construct relationships as their mood lifted, perhaps indicating an increase in the permeability of super-ordinate constructs. In a further recent study, Tibbles (1988) has examined the effects of an assessment for psychodynamic psychotherapy on depressives' construing, and has found that, contrary to predictions, their construct systems became more tightly organised and logically consistent. He concludes that this 'appeared to reflect a suspension of construing until a time when regular therapeutic intervention could be offered' (p. i).

Sheehan's (1985a) study provided some insight into the process of structural change during therapy in that, although logical inconsistency in the clients' construing initially increased markedly, it then decreased to a level which was still significantly higher than that prior to treatment. This non-linear change, and the fluctuations which she observed during therapy in scores on measures of tightness of construing, are perhaps indicative of a Creativity Cycle (see p. 13), considered by Kelly (1955) to be central to reconstruction. As will be discussed further below, repertory grid studies of group psychotherapy, although not indicating any significant overall reduction in the tightness of group members' construing, have also provided some evidence of cyclical patterns of change (Fransella and Joyston-Bechal, 1971; Winter and Trippett, 1977). If changes in structural features of construing during therapy tend to be cyclical in nature, it is perhaps not surprising that some of the studies which have compared group means on structural measures at pre- and post-treatment assessments have failed to demonstrate a significant change in scores. A rather more illuminating approach to examining structural change would seem to be serial assessment of clients on such measures at intervals over the course of therapy. Adopting this procedure with two anorexic clients, both of whom recovered from their disorder, Crisp and Fransella (1972) observed that both had very tightly organised construct systems, reflected in a 'massive first component' from repertory grid analysis. In one client, who 'continues to deal with life in a limited way' (p. 403) despite her recovery, this tightness persisted throughout treatment, the changes in her construing representing slot-rattling on her principal construct dimension. In the other, it was only after she was leuco-tomised that her construing loosened markedly, and she was then considered 'to have the opportunity of organizing her thoughts anew' (p. 405).

It might also be more productive in future research to examine changes in the structure of particular construct subsystems rather than in general structural properties of a client's system. In Sheehan's (1985a) study, more change was evident in grids which focussed on clients' self-construing than in those which concerned construing of other people, and this is not unexpected given that the depressive's core role structure is likely to be a major focus of psychotherapy. As well as constructs relating to the self, a further construct subsystem which may be particularly influenced by therapy is that relating to the symptom. It follows from Kelly's Choice Corollary, and from Fransella's (1972) notion of the symptom as a 'way of life', that successful therapy should involve a decrease in the degree of structure, and hence meaningfulness, in the client's construing of the symptom as compared to the meaningfulness of being symptom-free. The results of a single case study by Mair and Crisp (1968) are consistent with this view in that, over the course of treatment of an obese woman, during which she lost weight steadily, the number of super-ordinate implications for her of a construct concerning enjoyment of food reduced considerably, while those of a construct concerning attractiveness to the opposite sex showed a marked increase. Examining her 'way of life theory' with stutterers, Fransella (1972) found a significant increase in the number of implications for them of constructs relating to fluency over the course of personal construct psychotherapy but no change in the number of impli-cations of constructs relating to stuttering. As a result, in contrast to the pattern prior to treatment, fluency became more meaningful than stuttering for these clients. However, the fact that no significant changes were evident during therapy in saturation scores (see p. 41), which allow for the number of constructs in a grid, suggests that Fransella's findings reflect an increase in the number of constructs relating to fluency elicited from clients at the post-treatment assessment.

A further caveat which should be taken into account in considering Fransella's study is that, as discussed in Chapter 3, a very high number of implications of the constructs in a particular subsystem may mean that the subsystem is so tightly organised that it does not provide an effective basis for the prediction of events in the area concerned. To quote Honess (1979), 'the limiting case of every construct implying every other construct would render meaning*less* any attempts to anticipate events' (p. 423, italics in original). It would follow, therefore, that an increase in the number of implications of 'symptom-free' constructs is likely to be conducive to symptom loss only up to a certain optimal level of implications, but that, if construing in this area is initially very tightly organised, a loosening of constructions, and possibly a decrease in the number of implications of such constructs, may be observed to accompany a positive therapeutic outcome. The findings of research on alcoholism, although not entirely consistent, provide some support for the view that successful therapy may be associated with a tightening of construing in the area of the symptom and loosening of constructions relating to alternative ways of life. For example, Hoy (1977) found that, although the construing of alcoholism by alcoholics tightened over the course of psychotherapy, construct relationships involving constructs concerning drinking or the self tended to tighten only in clients who showed no improvement, but loosened in those who became abstinent. Heather *et al.* (1975) have also demonstrated that alcoholics who remained abstinent following group therapy showed little differentiation between a 'typical' and a 'nonbenefiting' alcoholic, while clients who relapsed distinguished more between these roles but less between them and an 'average social drinker'. The results of both these studies would suggest that if therapy is successful the alcoholic's construal of alcoholism will become relatively undifferentiated, as compared to his or her construing of alternative drinking roles.

To return to Fransella's study, her arguments would suggest that the superordinacy of constructs relating to the symptom should decrease if therapy is successful. This has been found to be the case in agoraphobics, those clients whose symptoms diminished in intensity during behaviour therapy coming to differentiate less between people in terms of whether or not they are able to go out, and their spouses showing a similar change three months after therapy (Winter, 1989a). As the ability to go out became a less superordinate construct for the clients, so the superordinacy of constructs relating to tenderness and its lack, namely 'selfish–unselfish' and 'caring–uncaring', increased, a change which was predicted in view of the association between agoraphobia and low cognitive awareness of lack of tenderness (see pp. 118–19). However, contrary to predictions were the findings that anger became a less superordinate construct for the spouses of the agoraphobics following the clients' therapy, and that at three-month follow-up assessment the superordinacy of the construct of selfishness reduced both for clients who showed symptomatic improvement and for their spouses.

## CHANGES IN THE CONTENT OF THE CONSTRUCT SYSTEM DURING THERAPY

A major focus of studies of reconstruction during therapy for psychological disorders has been on construing of the self. Self-esteem, generally considered to be indicated by similarity in construing of the 'actual' and 'ideal' self, has been a particular area of concern and has been assessed by various methods. One such method is the Q-Sort, which Meltzoff and Kornreich (1970) estimated had been used as the outcome measure in 10 per cent of all studies of psychotherapy up to the time of their review. The most consistent finding of these studies, most of which examined client-centred therapy, was that clients' self-esteem tends to increase during therapy (e.g. Sheerer, 1949; Dymond, 1954; Rudikoff, 1954; Ends and Page, 1957; Henry and Shlien, 1958; Cartwright and Vogel, 1960; Arbuckle and Boy, 1961; Hollon and Zolik, 1962; Shlien *et al.*, 1962; Dreiblatt and Weatherley, 1965; Truax *et al.*, 1966, 1968). Another method which has allowed the demonstration of positive changes in the self-concept during therapy is the semantic differential (e.g. Luria, 1959; Endler, 1961; Hafner, 1976; Kennard and Clemmey, 1976). In a few of these studies of self-perception (e.g. Fairweather *et al.*, 1960; Fairweather and Simon, 1963; Kennard and Clemmey, 1976), an apparent decrease in self-esteem was observed during treatment in some of the psychotic clients in the samples, but if, as we have seen in Chapter 4 may be the case with such clients, their self-esteem was initially high, somewhat less favourable self-construal may not have been inconsistent with a positive therapeutic outcome (Wylie, 1961).

Detailed consideration of this body of self-concept research is beyond the scope of the present review, in which I shall focus primarily on studies which have employed repertory grid technique. In one such study, each client's self-construing was examined in relation to his or her therapist's ideal self, with the finding that clients who improved during psychotherapy came to see themselves as more similar to the ideal selves of their respective therapists in terms of their own, but not their therapists', constructs (Landfield and Nawas, 1964; Landfield, 1971). Improvers' use of 'forcefulness' constructs was also found to increase by Landfield *et al.* (1961), who interpret this as indicating a greater concern with self-expressiveness. Repertory grid investigations of group psychotherapy have tended to report only moderate increases in the self-esteem of group members, or have provided insufficient information to allow the extent of such changes to be evaluated (Caplan *et al.*, 1975; Koch, 1983a). One study reported little change in the self-construing of clients diagnosed as suffering from personality disorders despite the fact that over the course of the group clients were perceived more favourably by other group members, including the therapist (Fielding, 1975). A study of encounter groups has also failed to observe an increase in the self-esteem of group participants (Lieberman *et al.*, 1973). However, using self-characterisation measures, Jackson (1990b) was able to demonstrate an increase in self-esteem, and in the elaboration of construing of self and others, in adolescents attending a personal construct therapy group. Caine *et al.* (1981) have observed an increase in the construed similarity of self and ideal self in clients diagnosed as neurotic during therapy, group analytic psychotherapy and behaviour therapy producing comparable degrees of change in this respect, but more favourable construing of the self being particularly apparent in those clients whose scores on a range of measures indicated a positive therapeutic outcome (Winter, 1982). A repertory grid study of behaviour therapy with one particular neurotic group, agoraphobics, has also demonstrated an increase in clients' self-esteem, as well as in the extent to which they were construed favourably by their spouses, over the course of therapy (Winter and Gournay, 1987). Brockman *et al.* (1987) have compared the effectiveness of cognitive-analytic therapy (see p. 158) and interpretive therapy in clients with neurotic and personality problems, finding that only the former approach produced an increase in the positivity of the clients' self-construing. Increased self-esteem has also been observed by Bassler *et al.* (1989) to accompany improvement of neurotic clients during in-patient psychotherapy, and while in improvers the salience of the self decreased from an initially high level, the reverse was the case in non-improvers.

A different approach to the examination of change in construing of the self has been adopted by Schwartz and his colleagues, who have assessed the ratio of positive to negative self-statements in clients undergoing various forms of therapy. They have found an increase in the proportion of positive self-statements during therapy, and that in the most effective therapies clients' cognitive balance following treatment tends to be a 'positive dialogue' (see p. 137) in which the positive: negative cognition ratio is in the order of the golden section, with positive cognitions predominant (Schwartz and Garamoni, 1986). Two of the studies considered by Schwartz and his colleagues concerned different treatment approaches for agoraphobia. In one (Mavissakalian *et al.*, 1983), a steady increase in the proportion of positive self-statements was apparent from pre-treatment to follow-up assessment in clients undergoing paradoxical intention therapy, while in those receiving self-statement training cognitive balance fluctuated during the follow-up period around a mean equivalent to the golden section ratio. In their analysis of the other study, by Michelson *et al.* (1985), Schwartz and Michelson (1987) found that clients changed from being characterised prior to treatment by a 'negative dialogue' (see p. 137), in which negative self-statements exceed positive by a degree approximating to the golden section ratio, to the converse state of a positive dialogue at mid- and post-treatment assessments. At three-month follow-up, these clients' positive self-statements had increased to the extent that they approached a 'positive monologue', with 0.70 of self-statements being positive. Although this exceeds somewhat the proportion of positive cognitions which would be considered optimal from an information-processing viewpoint, Schwartz and Michelson suggest that it reflects a strategy of creating a 'protective buffer' of positive cognitions which enables the agoraphobic to cope with threat. They also consider that, similarly to the developmental progression which has been observed in studies of cognitive balance in children, 'cognitive change in therapy may require an increased frequency of coping thoughts until mastery is achieved and deeper cognitive structures are modified' (Schwartz and Michelson, 1987, p. 563). However, they concede that the relatively high proportion of positive cognitions elicited from the agoraphobics may reflect the method of assessment employed, in which clients' self-statements were tape-recorded, perhaps inhibiting reports of negative cognitions. Particularly high proportions of positive cognitions at post-treatment and follow-up assessments were evident in clients who improved most during therapy, in those showing high levels of post-treatment functioning, and in those displaying concordant changes on physiological, behavioural, and anxiety measures. Differences were also apparent in the patterns of change in cognitive balance observed in the three treatment conditions considered, paradoxical intention being associated with a rapid linear increase in positive cognitions, exposure treatment with a more gradual, curvilinear pattern, and relaxation training with one which was oscillating and unstable.

The personal construct theory model of depression (R. Neimeyer, 1984), as well as that of cognitive therapists such as Beck *et al.* (1979), would predict that therapeutic improvement in depressive clients should be associated with an increase in self-esteem. Support for this view has been provided by several repertory grid studies. One of the earliest of these is largely of methodological interest in that Slater (1970, 1976) constructed a repertory grid from a depressive client's serial self-ratings on Personal Questionnaire (Shapiro, 1961) symptom scales following alternate psychotherapy and occupational therapy sessions, finding that the former treatment resulted in more favourable self-construing. Taylor and Marshall (1977) have also compared the effects of different therapies on the self-esteem of depressives, and have found this to increase, with a corresponding reduction in depression, in depressives undergoing a combined cognitive-behavioural treatment on an individual basis, these changes being greater than those in clients who received either cognitive or behavioural treatment alone. Similar changes have been observed by Sheehan (1985a) in depressives during personal construct psychotherapy, while group cognitive therapy for depressives has also been found by R. Neimeyer *et al.* (1985, p. 193) to result in 'sweeping changes in core role structure', reflected in more favourable construing of the self 'as I really am' and 'one year in the future', together with less polarised self-construing. I have provided some evidence that the increases in self-esteem which accompany reduction in depressive symptoms during group cognitive therapy are equivalent to those displayed by depressives undergoing group analytic therapy (Winter, 1985d). Increases in depressives' self-esteem during therapy have also been found not to be limited to psychological treatment approaches. For example, Klein *et al.* (1985) have provided an indication of more favourable self-construal in depressives following running therapy, and that, not surprisingly, this treatment was more likely to result in more positive construal of the self as an athlete than was group therapy or meditation-relaxation therapy. Despite its limited effects in this study, that meditation may be of value in the treatment of depressives has been indicated by the finding in a non-clinical sample of an increase in the perceived congruence of the actual self with the ideal and social selves in individuals practising transcendental meditation (Turnbull and Norris, 1982). A more common focus of investigation in clinical samples has been the effect of anti-depressant medication. In a study of depressives undergoing medical treatment, Sperlinger (1971) found that clinical improvement was associated with reconstruction, and subsequent investigations of pharmacological treatment for depression have indicated changes in clients' self-construing. Although Hewstone et al. (1981) and Ashworth et al. (1985) failed to demonstrate a significant increase over the course of in-patient treatment in the extent to which depressives construed the self and ideal self as similar, the clients in the latter study showed sufficient change on this measure that following pharmacological treatment they could no longer be differentiated from non-psychiatric patients and recovered depressives. Sheehan (1981) did observe significant reduction in self–ideal self distance in depressives over the course of drug therapy. Her clients also appeared to 'slot-rattle' on constructs relating to forcefulness, which they tended to see themselves as lacking prior to therapy while following treatment they were more likely to construe themselves as forceful. Whereas at the commencement of therapy they rated themselves negatively on their constructs approximately 62 per cent of the time, during treatment this figure reduced to approximately 38 per cent. Although Sheehan regards the latter percentage as indicating that a low level of self-esteem persists following drug therapy, it is, in fact, apparent that her clients were organising their judgements in the golden section ratio both before and after treatment, during which their 'cognitive balance' appeared to shift from a 'negative dialogue' to the 'positive dialogue' which Schwartz and Garamoni (1987) associate with optimal functioning.

Changes in self-esteem during therapy have also been examined in three studies of alcoholics by Heather and his colleagues. In the first (Heather et al., 1975), during group therapy clients were found to construe themselves less in terms of socially disapproved, alcoholic roles and more in terms of the socially approved roles of 'average drinker', 'recovered alcoholic', and 'teetotaller'. Heather et al. conclude that 'the main change occurring in the typical patient during treatment was that he regained a feeling of respectability and, hence, of self-respect' (p. 1251). However, they also found such changes on average to be unrelated to the success of treatment, and indeed that a high degree of change in self-respect, in whatever direction, tended to be associated with relapse. To explain this finding, they suggest that the alcoholic who shows considerable recovery of self-respect is in danger of seeing himself or herself as 'cured' and therefore of not appreciating the dangers of the social drinking which may be one aspect of a perceived return to normality. On the other hand, the relapse of the client whose self-respect decreases during therapy may simply reflect a reversion to behaviour which validates the individual's negative self-construction. In a subsequent repertory grid study which attempted to replicate these findings, Rollnick and Heather (1980, p. 124) reported that 'patients' constructions of themselves and other drinking friends (elements) were characterized at both admission and discharge by a single dimension which we can describe as a "self-respect/respectability" dimension, and which accounted for over 90% of the variance in the rating'. However, this conclusion is tempered by the facts that the authors employed supplied constructs, half of which related to self-respect and respectability, and that the only results which they present derive from consensus grids (see p. 37), principal component analysis of which will always produce a first component which accounts for a very high proportion of the variance (Beail, 1984). Nevertheless, constructs concerning self-respect and respectability did load more highly than those concerning social relationships on the first components of the clients' admission and discharge consensus grids. Furthermore, over the course of therapy movements of the actual and social self towards the ideal self were apparent on this component. In a further study, Heather *et al.* (1982) found greater recovery of self-respect, as indicated by changes in grid scores between admission to, and discharge from, an alcoholism unit, in clients who were abstinent at follow-up than in those who had resumed drinking, clients who were considered to have relapsed showing the least change on this measure.

Increased congruence of constructions of the actual and ideal self during therapy has generally been found to be more indicative of change in the former than in the latter aspect of self-construal (Aidman, 1951; Bowman, 1951; Butler and Haigh, 1954; Ewing, 1954; Kennard and Clemmey, 1976). Nevertheless, a study by Stefan (1977) has indicated that attempts to move an individual towards his or her ideal, by more clearly defining the behavioural implications of the latter, may lead to its rejection. That a reduction in the perceived distance between self and ideal self necessarily reflects an increase in self-esteem has also been questioned by Norris (1977), who found that such changes during young men's sentence at a Detention Centre tended to result from a 'downgrading' of the ideal self rather than a much more favourable self-evaluation. She concludes that their Detention Centre experience reduced these men's aspirations, a possibility that should be borne in mind in considering reports of greater attainability of the ideal self in young offenders following residential treatment (e.g. Lockhart, 1979). That Detention Centre experience in Norris' study also resulted in other changes contrary to those which were intended is indicated by the findings that a significantly greater number of detainees aspired to break rules on discharge than on entry to the Centre, and that rule-breaking came to be more highly associated by them with independence, a characteristic which they saw themselves as moving towards. In addition, detainees came to view themselves as more similar to their parents, but did not wish to be so. These generally unfavourable changes in construing during detention contrast with those observed by Norris (1983) in a therapeutic community for clients who would mostly be diagnosed as psychopathic. Although there was little overall indication of change in clients' self-esteem over the three months following admission, the majority came to see themselves as more independent and less rule-breaking, and improvements in self-esteem were particularly evident in those whose self-esteem was initially low. Such desirable changes in construing were related to clinical impressions of benefit from the community and, in men, were associated with frequent attendance at large and small group meetings. Another study of change during therapeutic community treatment, in this case for drug addicts, has provided further indications that reconstruing of a client's ideal self may be as appropriate a therapeutic goal as reconstruing of the actual self (Preston and Viney, 1983). In this investigation, although residents who had remained in the community construed themselves more favourably than did those with shorter lengths of stay, retesting of residents after six months revealed little change in their self-construing. Furthermore, it was found that clients tended to construe their ideal selves in terms of helplessness and self-criticism, suggesting to Preston and Viney a lack of belief by clients in their ability to cope outside the protected environment of the therapeutic community. An increase in self-esteem, but no change in construing of the ideal self, has also been observed by Bennett *et al.* (1990) in drug users during their stay at a rehabilitation centre with a Christian philosophy. These clients' identification with drug users decreased, and their identification with Christianity, and the superordinacy of the construct of religion for them, increased. However, the authors fail to indicate whether these changes were statistically significant.

As we have seen in Chapter 4, in some individuals, who appear to maintain a high level of self-esteem by dissociating themselves from their problem behaviour, a desirable change may involve a reduction in this dissociation and perhaps a corresponding increase in self–ideal self distance. Studying the changes in a sex offender over four years of forensic hospital treatment, Shorts (1985) demonstrated an increase in the extent to which he construed himself, and believed that he was construed by others, as a rapist. However, this was associated with other, apparently less desirable, changes in that the client developed a rather less negative view of rapists, and a more negative view of women. He also came to construe his ideal self in terms of dislike of married life and shyness with the opposite sex. Shorts considers this to reflect the adoption of a constrictive strategy to avoid invalidation, and to indicate that heterosocial skills training or fixed role therapy (see pp. 268 ff.) might usefully enable the client to elaborate his construing, as well as invalidating some of his less viable existing constructions. A reduction in self-esteem during psychodynamically orientated therapy, together with somewhat decreased idealisation of the therapist, has also been observed in three clients with psychosomatic complaints by Schüffel and Schonecke (1972), who associate these changes in grid scores with the clients' increasing ability to perceive hostility.

A further aspect of self-construing which has been monitored during therapy in some studies is the perceived dissimilarity of self and others. As we have seen in Chapter 4, this sense of 'self-isolation' has been found to characterise neurotic and depressive clients. It would therefore be expected to reduce during successful therapy, and this has been found to be the case in clients diagnosed as suffering from neurotic or personality disorders undergoing group psychotherapy (Fielding, 1975; Caine *et al.*, 1981; Koch, 1983a), in neurotic clients during individual behaviour therapy (Caine *et al.*, 1981) and social skills groups (Winter, 1988a), and in depressives who showed improvement during personal construct psychotherapy (Sheehan, 1985a). In-patient treatment for depression has also been found to be accompanied by construing of the self as more similar to others in one study (Hewstone *et al.*, 1981), but not in another (Ashworth *et al.*, 1985), while Button (1987) has reported a tendency towards a reduction in self-isolation, and in extreme and negative self-construing, in the members of a personal construct psycho-therapy group for clients with eating disorders. Although most of these investigations have examined the extent to which clients come to construe themselves as more similar to other people in general during therapy, some repertory grid studies have considered changes in clients' degree of identification with members of their families. For example, a single case report by Davison *et al.* (1971) describes how a client construed himself as more similar to his heterosexual twin brother, and to his father as compared to his mother, following aversion therapy for homosexuality. Caine *et al.* (1981) also considered clients' perceived similarity to their parents, finding that in those who improved during group psychotherapy and behaviour therapy there was evidence of increasing construed similarity to the mother and an increased tendency to show greater identification with the same-sex than with the opposite-sex parent (Winter, 1982). In addition, Koch (1983a) found evidence in some of the psychotherapy groups which he studied that the extent to which clients perceived their parents as similar to other group members increased, and that this tendency was associated with symptomatic improvement. Increased construed similarity to their mothers was also observed by Bennett *et al.* (1990) in drug users staying at a rehabilitation centre. Findings of increased identification with others can be considered to provide particularly impressive evidence of the effectiveness of the therapies concerned since self–other differentiation is one of the most stable of grid measures in people who are not receiving therapy (Adams-Webber, 1989a).

The studies considered above have mostly examined average changes in scores on various grid measures in samples of clients during therapy. However, the individuality of construing would suggest that the particular reconstructions which might be expected to accompany successful therapy are likely to vary from client to client. The most appropriate method of investi-gating therapeutic reconstruction may, therefore, be to predict those changes in construing which will reflect a positive treatment outcome for a particular client, and then to monitor these changes over the course of therapy. Early indications of the potential of such an approach were provided in single case studies by Bannister (1965a) and Mair and Crisp (1968). The method adopted by Morris (1977), studying a personal construct psychotherapy group, was for each therapist, at the beginning of treatment and based on the clients' grids and interview transcripts, to complete an 'ideal outcome grid' for each client as they imagined the client would respond if treatment were successful. At the end of treatment, they completed 'actual outcome grids', indicating their perceptions of how clients' construing had actually changed during therapy. Although the therapists showed considerable accuracy in these latter perceptions, many of their predictions of ideal outcome tended to be too idealistic. Three other studies have also included individualised predictions of changes in grid scores expected to accompany successful therapy, and have found these to be more likely to be confirmed than general predictions applied to every client studied (Winter and Trippett, 1977; Koch, 1983a; Caine *et al.*, 1981). Furthermore, in the Caine *et al.* study, although there was no difference in the degree of confirmation of individualised predictions and predictions of reduction in the extremity of grid scores, only the former changes were correlated with independent indices of positive therapeutic outcome. Despite such correlations, principal component analysis of change scores indicated that repertory grid and questionnaire measures were tapping different levels of change. As will be discussed further in Chapter 6, the changes in construing observed by Caine *et al.* in several of their clients involved, as well as reconstruing of the self, the resolution of dilemmas with which they were confronted by virtue of the relationships between their constructs. Anthony Ryle has pioneered the exploration of such changes in construing during brief psychotherapy which focusses on dilemmas, the relationship 'traps' in which individuals become ensnared as a result of their dilemmas, and negative implications of change (Ryle, 1975, 1979a, 1980); and during a derivation of this approach, cognitive-analytic therapy (Ryle, 1990). In one of his earlier studies, he and Lunghi demonstrated that most of the changes in grid scores (for example, an increase in the correlation between 'feminine' and 'adult' constructs) which he predicted would occur during a young woman's brief psychotherapy were confirmed (Ryle and Lunghi, 1969). There followed a series of case studies in which he also found that clients who considered their dilemmas to be resolved following therapy tended to show predicted changes in the correlations between their constructs. In addition, Brockman *et al.* (1987) have found significantly greater predicted change in construct correlations in clients receiving cognitive-analytic therapy than in those undergoing interpretive therapy. That resolution of dilemmas may also occur in therapeutic approaches which do not explicitly focus on the dilemmas concerned was apparent in the studies which I have carried out with Trippett, and with Caine and Wijesinghe, and which have investigated analytically orientated group psychotherapy and behaviour therapy. The serial assessments conducted in these studies have resulted in detailed analyses of the reconstruing of individual clients. For example, the pre-treatment grid completed by Roy, a depressive member of one of the psychotherapy groups studied by Caine *et al.*, indicated that he construed unsuccessful people as 'neurotic', but also as 'warm' and 'sensitive to others' sensitivities'. A further dilemma was indicated by his construal of 'aware', 'intellectual' people as 'depressed', 'austere', and likely not to 'think much of themselves'. As I have described elsewhere (Winter, 1982, 1985d), changes in the relationships between these constructs during psychotherapy tended to be cyclical and to precede changes on symptom measures and in construing of the self. For example, the initial decrease in the negative implications of success for him was associated with a reduction in self-esteem, perhaps because at this stage he was neither being successful nor able to attribute to himself the desirable characteristics which he had previously associated with lack of success. However, it appeared that his more favourable construal of success eventually led him to experiment with being successful, and his self-esteem subsequently increased. Other changes in construing which accompanied the reduction in his symptoms during therapy were that he came to see himself as much more similar to other people and that his initially monolithically structured construct system became 'articulated'. Melanie, who underwent group cognitive therapy, also showed changes in repertory grid scores indicative of resolution of dilemmas in that, in contrast to her pre-treatment repertory grid assessment, at termination of therapy she no longer construed happy, optimistic, sociable people as being characterised by such undesirable attributes as callousness and hardness. She was then able to see herself as neither depressed and isolated nor callous and hard, and her self-esteem increased (Winter, 1985d). While in Roy and Melanie resolution of dilemmas involving positive implications of the symptom was apparent during therapy, in other clients a reduction in some of the negative implications of the symptom may be considered desirable in that it might lead to a greater degree of self-acceptance. Such changes were evident over the course of therapy in several of the clients studied by Caine *et al.*, as in the case of the client who initially saw his presenting problem of inability to communicate as a sign of stupidity but in whom a marked change in the correlation between these constructs was apparent during group psychotherapy (Winter, 1982).

Some evidence of resolution during therapy of dilemmas which appeared to be relevant to the maintenance of clients' symptoms has also been provided in agoraphobics undergoing behaviour therapy (Winter and Gournay, 1987). Symptom reduction in these clients was found to be associated with a decrease in their tendency to construe independent people as likely to be unfaithful, an increase in the extent to which confidence implied being caring and unselfish, and a greater tendency to construe the spouse's ideal partner as able to go out. Furthermore, their spouses also came to construe the ability to go out and confidence as less highly associated with possible infidelity. However, at three-month follow-up assessment, clients were found to be increasingly concerned with infidelity, particularly if they were spending more time out of the house. Those who had shown the greatest reduction in agoraphobic symptoms also became more likely to construe independent people as uncaring. Therefore, although improvement during therapy was accompanied by an increase in the positive implications of the ability to go out, independence, and confidence, it appeared that there was a reversal of this trend during the follow-up period. While this may indicate that relapse could be expected in these clients, their spouses' construing at the follow-up assessment provided a more optimistic picture. Spouses at this time were less likely to see selfishness as an implication of independence, and the spouses of clients who had shown the greatest symptomatic improvement showed a further reduction in the degree to which they associated independence and confidence with possible infidelity, together with an increase in the extent to which they construed people who are able to go out as caring.

Studies of changes in the content of construing during therapy by Viney and her colleagues have employed not grids but the various scales for content analysis of interviews which we have described in Chapter 2. Evaluating the effects of reconstructive therapy with physically ill clients, they have found a decrease in constructions indicating anxiety, passive aggression, and helplessness, and an increase in those concerning competence (Viney, 1990). At one-year follow-up, fewer constructions concerning anxiety, depression, and anger were evident than in clients not receiving psychological therapy. Changes produced by different types of programme were also compared, and will be discussed in Chapter 7. Viney *et al.* (1989b) have used the same methodology to examine changes in elderly people following personal construct therapy, finding evidence that this resulted in a decrease in constructions concerning anxiety, depression, and indirectly expressed anger, and an increase in those concerning competence and positive feelings.

## CONSTRUING AS A PREDICTOR OF THERAPEUTIC CHANGE

From the personal construct theory perspective, it is, of course, to be expected that individuals should differ in the nature of their response to an experience such as therapy. Thus, therapy would be expected to lead to reconstruction only if it offers the client the possibility of further extension or definition of his or her construct system, and if it does not confront the client with too high a degree of such negative emotions as anxiety, threat, and guilt. Whether this is likely to be the case should be predictable from the state of the client's personal construct system prior to therapy, and several studies have examined this relationship between construing and response to therapy.

A primary concern of some of these investigations has been the structure of the client's construct system. It will be recalled, for example, that Fransella (1972) put forward the view that a stutterer is unlikely to move towards fluency if this carries fewer implications than does stuttering, and this view was supported by the findings of her study of personal construct psychotherapy with stutterers that greater reduction in disfluent speech occurred during therapy in those clients whose subsystems of constructs relating to fluency were better elaborated prior to treatment. However, her results, based on the total number of implications of 'non-stutterer' constructs, did not indicate whether the constructs relating to fluency of those clients who became more fluent carried more implications on average or whether the high total number of implications reflected the elicitation of more such constructs from these clients. Dividing her sample into 'improvers' and clients who either failed to improve during therapy or, whether or not they had shown significant improvement, terminated therapy prematurely, she also found a higher satur- ation of implications of constructs relating to stuttering at initial assessment in the latter group than in the former, although the groups did not differ in the implication saturation of their 'non-stutterer' constructs. Furthermore, examining implications of superordinate and subordinate constructs separately, she observed that prior to treatment the superordinate constructs relating to stuttering elicited from 'non-improvers' were significantly more saturated with implications than were those of improvers, but that the groups came to differ in the implication saturation of their 'non-stutterer' constructs only after several weeks of treatment, when there were significantly more such implications in the non-improvers than in the improvers. Fransella regards this as indicating a premature tightening of construing in the non-improvers. Subordinate constructs concerning both stuttering and fluency were more saturated with implications in non-improvers than in improvers prior to treatment. Fransella (1972, p. 140) concludes from this rather complex set of findings that

> A stutterer seems to stand a better chance of staying the treatment course and of improving if (a) he has a fair number of constructs and implications to do with himself as a nonstutterer to begin with and if (b) he has a sub-system of constructs for construing himself as a stutterer that is relatively permeable and so open to modification (although actual number of constructs to do with *self as stutterer* may not be very relevant).

Fransella has also been concerned with the features of construing which may be predictive of recovery in clients presenting with eating disorders. An initial report of changes in two obese clients during therapy was unable to provide support for the prediction that a tightly organised construct system would be indicative of a poor prognosis in that, although the client with such a system failed to maintain her weight loss, so did the other client, whose construct system was less unidimensional (Fransella and Crisp, 1970). In both these clients, weight change was accompanied by 'slot-rattling' in their construing of the self when overweight, which was perceived much more favourably than at initial assessment when weight was lost but very unfavourably again when the clients regained weight. Obese people were also the subject of study by Leitner and Grant (1982), who found that in those individuals for whom the construct 'overweight–not overweight' was highly ordinating, in that it had a high capacity for integrating experiences hierarchically (see p. 40), there was less weight reduction during a largely didactic treatment approach. Contrary to predictions, this relationship only held for constructions of the self now, weight reduction being unrelated to the ordinating capacity of the 'overweight' construct in relation to constructions of the self if not overweight. Leitner and Grant also considered the implications of weight loss for their subjects, finding that reduction in weight was more pronounced if it implied many changes in placement of the self on other constructs, particularly if these changes were towards a more negative self-construal. Although they consider these findings to be consistent with personal construct theory, it might have been expected that those clients who anticipated that weight loss would carry many implications, and that these would involve less favourable construal of the self, would be threatened by such a prospect. As Leitner and Grant point out, such an interpretation may be applied to their additional observation that drop-outs from treatment also tended to construe weight loss as implying a more negative view of the self.

Findings contrary to those of Leitner and Grant, in that more favourable response to treatment was apparent in clients for whom symptom loss implied less change on other constructs, have been obtained in investigations of behavioural treatment approaches by Wright (1969) and McKain et al. (1988), studying phobics and shy people respectively. Some indirect support may also be gleaned from other studies for the view that clients are more likely to change their self-construing, for example no longer seeing themselves as characterised by their symptoms, if the constructs concerned carry few implications. Thus, Varble and Landfield (1969) found that changes in the perceived discrepancy between self and ideal self during therapy were greatest on those constructs which clients considered least important, and which presumably occupied a subordinate position in their construct hierarchies. The finding by Persons and Burns (1986) that the 'dysfunctional thought' which is elicited first from a client changes less during cognitive therapy than the thought elicited last, and their suggestion that this may indicate the greater centrality to the self-concept of the first thought, may also be explained in terms of the resistance to change of constructions which carry many implications.

As well as weight reduction in obese people, Fransella's research has examined weight gain in anorexic clients during in-patient treatment. Working with Button, and using the same approach as in her study of stutterers, she found that the more implications which constructs concerning the self at normal weight carried on an anorexic's admission to hospital, the more likely was the client to have maintained her weight six months after discharge (Fransella and Button, 1983). Furthermore, there was a tendency for maintenance of weight to be associated with an increase in the implications of being of normal weight and a decrease in the implications of being thin. As well as the implications grid employed in this part of the study, Button (1983b) used a more conventional repertory grid and found a poor outcome to be more likely if the construct 'anorexic–not anorexic' was highly correlated with other constructs, and therefore highly meaningful, at discharge from hospital. The increase from admission to discharge of 'poor outcome' clients in the meaningfulness of being anorexic as compared to being of normal weight suggests, for Fransella and Button (1983, p. 115), that 'the girls who failed to maintain their weight came to see themselves more clearly as anorectic while in the hospital'. A good outcome was found by Button to be associated with an increase in meaningfulness of weight-related constructs between discharge and the first follow-up point approximately two months later, but a subsequent decrease in the meaningfulness of these constructs up to the second follow-up point, approximately eight months after discharge. Button (1983b) suggests that this may be indicative of a better outcome in those clients who admit that weight control is still important after discharge, but who later narrow the range of convenience of their weight-related constructs. As he puts it, 'we are unlikely to help the anorexic unless she has virtually abandoned weight as a solution to her problems' (p. 315). A somewhat similar pattern of relationships was observed between treatment outcome and measures of the meaningfulness of aspects of the self, high meaningfulness on admission of the self a year ago, now, at treatment weight, and 'at my thinnest' being predictive of poor outcome, but high meaningfulness at first follow-up of self at normal weight and at treatment weight being associated with good outcome, as was a decrease in the meaningfulness of these self elements between first and second follow-up points. As well as these specific measures of meaningfulness of weight-related constructs and of the self, Button considered the overall degree of tightness of the construct system, finding looser construing on admission to be predictive of good outcome, as was tightening of construing between admission and discharge. Subsequent loosening of construing between the first and second follow-up points also showed a tendency to be related to positive outcome, and Button considers his results to be consistent with Kelly's view of constructive change as involving successive processes of tight and loose construing. In addition to group data, he has provided examples of changes in the construing of individual clients over the course of his study (Button, 1985b).

The relationship between general structural aspects of construing and therapeutic outcome has also been the focus of attention in other studies. For example, Orford (1974) found that cognitive simplicity in alcoholics, assessed by a composite measure involving the unipolarity of free descriptions of others and the variance accounted for by the first two principal components derived from a grid, predicted early drop-out from a half-way house which employed a regime including regular group meetings. He suggests that this may have been due to the extremity of impression formation, and difficulty of integrating conflicting information with the impression, in cognitively simple individuals. Since the regime which he studied might have been expected to lead to reconstruing of the self in relation to others, Orford's findings are consistent with Sperlinger's (1976) demonstration that such reconstruing is less likely in people whose construct systems are low in cognitive complexity. Studying spider phobics, Watts and Sharrock (1985) found that those clients for whom constructs relating to spiders were tightly interrelated tended to show less improvement during desensitisation treatment, although this relationship fell short of statistical significance. A significant association between tight construing and poor treatment outcome has, however, been observed in agoraphobics, who have been found to spend less time out of the house following behavioural treatment if their construing prior to treatment was relatively unidimensional (Winter and Gournay, 1987). Such findings may reflect the resistance of tightly construing clients to therapeutic change and reconstruction since, most of their constructs being highly interrelated, change in any aspect of their construing is likely to have implications for core constructs and therefore to be a threatening prospect. Their predicament, as described by Fransella (1970c, p. 350), is that they have 'conceptually, only one channel along which to move'. Furthermore, any invalidation of this one dimension would leave them in the anxiety-provoking position of having no viable basis for anticipation. These considerations might imply that there should be some generality in the relationship between tight construing and poor response to therapy, and some evidence for such an association has also been provided by Carr's (1974) finding that clients who showed greater 'differentiation between conceptual dimensions' prior to psychotherapy, as measured by the number of traits considered to describe the self, considered the outcome of their therapy to be more favourable. Morris (1977), studying a personal construct psychotherapy group, found that group members whose construct systems were segmented (see p. 41), consisting of separate, unarticulated clusters, were more likely to be considered to need further treatment following the group. However, Raz-Duvshani (1986) failed to observe any relationship between tightness of construing and response to treatment in neurotic clients undergoing psychoanalytically orientated psychotherapy. Furthermore, comparing group analytic therapy and behaviour therapy, I have provided an indication of the complexity of the relationship between construct structure and therapeutic response (Winter, 1983). In this study, only in group analytic therapy was lack of improvement related to tight construing prior to treatment, reflected in high Intensity and logical consistency in relationships between constructs which did not concern the symptoms (Winter, 1983). Indeed, in behaviour therapy, the converse relationship was apparent. Constructs concerning the symptoms carried many fewer implications in terms of other constructs before treatment, and could therefore be considered less superordinate, in clients who improved during group psychotherapy than in those who did not, while again the reverse was true for behaviour therapy (Caine et al., 1981). This latter finding would appear contrary to Bannister's (1965a, p. 981) suggestion that 'the ideal subject for behaviour therapy is the learning theorist, i.e. the patient who views his symptoms as mere habits unrelated to his personal philosophy'; to

Fransella's (1972) view that clients will be resistant to removal of their symptoms if these carry many implications for them; and to some of the research findings presented above. Rather, as will be discussed further below, it seemed that those clients in the Caine *et al.* study for whom constructs relating to the symptoms were superordinate were likely to find meaningful, and to respond to, only a therapeutic approach which focussed on their symptoms. A further recent study, by McKain *et al.* (1988), has also provided indications that high complexity of construing, as reflected in Functionally Independent Construction scores, is associated with poor outcome in a cognitive-behavioural approach, in this case conducted in groups for shy people. However, this effect was apparent on only one of the seven outcome measures employed, and consideration of the interaction of Functionally Independent Construction and Ordination scores provided a more detailed picture of the relationship between structural features of construing and out-come. Although those group members who improved most were characterised by both low differentiation and low ordination of construing, members who did have highly differentiated systems, as predicted, responded more favourably if they exhibited high ordination, and vice versa.

Structural features of clients' construing may be relevant to likelihood of response to therapeutic programmes not only in those presenting with acute disorders but also in long-stay residents of psychiatric hospitals who are faced with the prospect of resettlement in the community. In two samples of such clients, we have found evidence that those who feel able to leave hospital have a more structured subsystem of constructs applicable to the social world in the community, as compared to that in hospital, than do those who feel unable to leave (Winter *et al.*, 1991), and that people outside hospital are also more salient to them. Furthermore, the more structured these clients' construct subsystems relating to life outside hospital, the more likely were they to be rated by staff members as having the necessary skills for survival in the community. They were also more likely, at interviews to which content analysis scales were applied (Westbrook and Viney, 1980; Viney and Westbrook, 1981), to express feelings of control over their lives, but also a lower experienced quality of life, at least while in hospital, than were clients whose 'outside hospital' subsystems were less structured. These findings highlight the importance of a focus in rehabilitation programmes on elaboration of clients' construing of the world beyond the hospital gates. Further support for such an approach is provided by research with elderly clients which indicates that the outcome of resettlement from hospital may be death (Aldrich and Mendkoff, 1963; Zweig and Czank, 1975), but that this tends not to be the case when the clients undergo preparatory programmes aiming to increase their ability to anticipate their new environment (Jasnau, 1967; Shultz and Brenner, 1977; Rona, 1986).

In addition to the structure of the construct system, various other aspects of construing have been associated with likelihood of response to therapy.

Kelly (1955) himself suggested that clients who employ constructs concerning 'movement' are more likely to be amenable to psychotherapy, and he also reported a finding by Rohrer that hospitalised clients who use more psychological constructs are more likely to be adjudged to be moving psychotherapeutically in the first six weeks of hospitalisation. In our study of long-stay psychiatric hospital residents, their use of psychological constructs showed some relationship with their perceived ability to leave hospital (Winter *et al.*, 1991). However, most studies of the content of the construct system in relation to response to therapy have concerned construing of the self and the presenting complaint. For example, Carr and Whittenbaugh (1969) observed that clients who construed themselves in a highly distinctive manner were more likely to be considered by their therapists to have increased their level of integration following psychotherapy. The authors speculate that this may reflect the relationship between self-distinctiveness and self-criticism, which in their view is considered favourably by therapists, or its relationship with a high level of abstraction, which they associate with a good prognosis. Similarly, Caine *et al.* (1981) found that greater improvement during group analytic therapy in clients diagnosed as neurotic was shown by those who initially construed themselves as more dissimilar to others, such constructions of personal uniqueness perhaps being particularly likely to be invalidated by this form of therapy. Clients who initially construed themselves more negatively, and who therefore presumably were more motivated to change, were also more likely to show a positive therapeutic outcome. Also investigating a group experience, the Interpersonal Transaction Group, Landfield (1977) has demonstrated a relationship between negative self-construing and a high level of reconstruction over the course of the group, although such reconstruction was less in clients whose self-construal was initially more extreme, indicating that it was more meaningful to them. A further study which has found that a high discrepancy between self and ideal self predicts a favourable response to treatment, in this case one which incorporated biofeedback, was carried out by Large (1985) on clients suffering from chronic pain. Indications that self-construal should be neither too favourable nor too unfavourable if therapy is to be successful were provided by Heather *et al.* (1982) in a study of alcoholics. Those clients who were abstinent at follow-up exhibited a self-construction at admission to, and discharge from, an alcoholism unit which was less positive than that of those clients who, although improved at follow-up, had resumed drinking, but more positive than that of clients who relapsed. Studying encounter groups, Lieberman *et al.* (1973) have found that initially negative self-construal tended to characterise not only the participants who responded well but also those who were considered to be 'casualties' of the groups, the latter individuals also tending to view other people negatively and their significant others in a differentiated fashion. With his anorexic clients, Button (1983b) also observed that an unfavourable construction of the self was associated with a poorer outcome, but that a more positive outcome was apparent in clients who construed the self now as very different from the self a year ago. Button considers the latter pattern to indicate a self-construction which is less resistant to change. Similarly, in our study of agoraphobics, Gournay and I have found a favourable construal of the self before the onset of phobic symptoms to be highly predictive of improvement during behaviour therapy, and more positive outcome at three-month follow-up to be apparent in those clients whose spouses' construal of how they were before developing phobic symptoms was favourable (Winter and Gournay, 1987). This, and Button's finding of better response to treatment when the self a year ago is construed as different from the present self, may indicate that a client is more likely to lose their symptoms during therapy if they have available an elaborated construction of an alternative, symptom-free, self based on previous experience rather than the idealistic fantasies of such a state which Fransella (1972) has observed in some of her clients. Construing of the former self has also been examined in a very different client group, amputees, with whom Fisher (1985) found that those whose rehabilitation was successful construed themselves as they were before the amputation more favourably than did clients whose rehabilitation was unsuccessful.

That the spouse's construing of the client may be predictive of therapeutic outcome, at least in agoraphobics, is consistent with findings from Hafner's research with female clients and their husbands. The multiple analyses which he has performed on the data obtained from his studies of behaviour therapy (Hafner, 1977a, 1977b, 1983, 1984; Milton and Hafner, 1979), and the diversity of measures employed to indicate such mechanisms as repression and denial, present a rather less than clear picture of the pattern of change in his subjects, although what is apparent is that the same pattern did not characterise all of these agoraphobics and their spouses. For example, dividing his sample of agoraphobics on the basis of their degree of hostility, he found that, in the more hostile group only, symptomatic improvement was accompanied by loss of self-esteem and increase in neurotic symptoms in their husbands, who tended to recover when their wives relapsed, and who, Hafner suggests, may have impeded their wives' improvement. Negative effects on husbands were most apparent after rapid symptomatic improvements in the more disabled phobic women, and occurred particularly in two groups of husbands: those who initially appeared to adapt to their wives' disability by viewing it in terms of a sex-role stereotype, and consequently seeing their wives in a much more positive light than these women saw themselves; and those, on the other hand, who were persistently critical of their wives even after their phobic symptoms had improved. Oatley and Hodgson (1987) have employed repertory grid technique in an attempt to test hypotheses, derived from Hafner's work, concerning the relationship between agoraphobics' construing of their husbands and their response to behaviour therapy. They found that clients who construed their husbands as controlling were less likely to respond to therapy if their husbands became depressed, but that grid measures of blaming, and irritation with, husbands were not predictive of treatment outcome. Gournay and I have also examined response to behaviour therapy in relation to agoraphobics' and their spouses' use of constructs relating to interpersonal conflict, emotions, and infidelity, these being aspects of construing which were central to our model of this disorder (see pp. 117 ff.). As predicted, clients for whom infidelity was a superordinate construct, in that it allowed a high degree of differentiation between grid elements, but who showed little differentiation between others in terms of anger, were less likely to show symptomatic improvement during therapy. Furthermore, if infidelity was a superordinate construct for a client's spouse, less improvement was apparent in the client at three-month follow-up. In a subsequent sample, high differentiation between others in terms of anger was again highly predictive of positive therapeutic outcome, and clients who perceived more infidelity, and differentiated between others more on this construct, showed less reduction in depression during treatment (Winter, 1989a). These relationships held constant regardless of whether the client was construing family members or other people. This was not so, however, with constructs concerning selfishness and jealousy, in that clients who differentiated highly between family members in such terms were more likely to respond positively to behaviour therapy, while the converse pattern was apparent in clients' construing of people outside the family. This would indicate that if the outside world is seen to be characterised by selfishness and jealousy, the client is less likely to venture into it, but that such ventures are more likely if these constructs are salient in construing the world at home. An additional finding of the Winter and Gournay (1987) study which was also indicative of a relationship between unfavourable construing of family members and positive treatment outcome was that clients who showed less idealisation of their mothers were very much more likely to show a reduction in the severity of their problems at three-month follow-up assessment. Unfavourable construing of, together with high identification with, their mothers has also been found to characterise drug users who do not drop out of a rehabilitation centre (Bennett et al., 1990). These clients also showed greater identification with Christianity than did dropouts, and a more superordinate construct of religion, presumably indicating that they were more sympathetic towards the Christian values of the centre.

While construal of family members in a negative light appears, therefore, to be indicative of a good prognosis in some clients, the reverse would seem to be the case in those diagnosed as schizophrenic. Employing a Family Interpersonal Perception Test with such clients and their parents, Scott and his colleagues have found that those clients who are able to live with their parents, rather than in hospital, most of the time, and who are likely to display a good outcome and not to relapse after discharge from hospital, tend to hold the same positive view of their parents as the parents do of themselves (Scott et al., 1970, 1990; Scott and Montanez, 1972; Scott and Alwyn, 1978). Not only did 'hospital-centred', poor outcome, clients view their parents less favourably, but the parents did not appreciate how negatively they were perceived. By contrast, clients who relapsed were more accurate in predicting their parents' views of them, which were generally negative, than were non-relapsing clients. A further characteristic of the families of the clients who relapsed was that at least one parent tended not to validate the other's self-construal. These various findings would suggest that a central factor in determining whether the relationship between a schizophrenic and his or her parents is tenable, and the client is unlikely to require hospital admission, is the extent to which the client validates the parents' views of themselves. Conceivably, the parents of such clients may be particularly vulnerable to, and likely to react with hostility towards, invalidation by their children, perhaps in part because they receive little validation from each other.

A further aspect of a client's construing which might be expected to be predictive of therapeutic outcome is his or her perception of the presenting problem and of the implications of its loss. I have examined such perceptions in clients who, on all outcome measures except therapist ratings of improvement, showed no significant response to social skills training (Winter, 1987, 1988a). That these clients viewed social inadequacy very differently from their therapists was indicated by a correlation of −0.35 between clients' and therapists' ratings of the clients on this construct. As discussed in Chapter 4, the clients' pre-treatment repertory grids allowed further exploration of their construing of social competence, which was found to carry negative implications in 80 per cent of clients. Some of the construct poles which these clients associated with social competence, assertiveness, and confidence are indicated in Figure 5.1, and would suggest that they may have construed their therapy as involving training in selfishness, contempt, and deceit, and that their resistance to it was, therefore, hardly surprising. This connection between their constructions of social competence and of their social skills group experience was confirmed by the finding that those clients for whom such competence tended to imply the non-preferred poles of their constructs were more likely to rate their group sessions, on the Group Climate Questionnaire (MacKenzie, 1983), as characterised by interpersonal conflict and avoidance of responsibility. Implications grid results of a further sample of social skills group clients are also providing indications that clients' constructions of social competence may be predictive of therapeutic outcome (Winter, 1990b). Figure 5.2, for example, shows that for Bill, whose questionnaire responses demonstrated an increase in social difficulties following social skills training, extraversion carried the implications of aggressiveness and insensitivity. By contrast, Fred, whose avoidance of social situations reduced markedly following treatment, construed social competence consistently positively. Another recent study, on group psychotherapy, has also indicated that clients are less likely to respond to treatment if their symptoms carry positive implications for them (Catina and Walter, 1989), while similar

| | | |
|---|---|---|
| inconsiderate | unhelpful | unsympathetic |
| selfish | having no feelings | unkind |
| impersonal | contemptuous | humiliating to others |
| uncaring | not understanding | walking over people |
| unreasonable | threatening | aggressive |
| ruthless | bossy | domineering |
| argumentative | arrogant | shouting people down |
| hard | dependent | dominating |
| demanding | impatient | unreliable |
| disloyal | dishonest | a romancer |
| talking behind others' backs | deceitful | irresponsible |
| untidy | lazy | undisciplined |
| big-headed | big-mouthed | stubborn |
| a know-it-all | pigheaded | unimaginative |
| unintellectual | non-academic | immature |

*Figure 5.1* Negative implications of social competence in social skills group members

conclusions may be drawn from an earlier demonstration, by Eastman (1978), that alcoholics are unlikely to respond to treatment if their drunk self is closer than their sober self to their ideal self.

Finally, clients' constructions of their problems have also been related to the success of rehabilitation in physically ill people. Thus, Viney and Westbrook (1982) have demonstrated that images of illness involving anxiety, depression, and anger, if directly expressed by the client, as well as sociability, are predictive of successful, and images of helplessness of unsuccessful, rehabilitation. In a further study, Viney and Westbrook (1986–7) found that the images of chronically ill people who died in the four months following assessment were characterised by less cognitive anxiety and directly expressed anger, more depression, fear of bodily damage, and guilt, and fewer shared but more recipient role relationships than those who did not die in the seven months after interview and healthy people. Compared to the ill people who did not die, those who died, together with healthy people, also expressed more good feelings. Attempting to explain these findings, Viney and Westbrook suggest that the low levels of cognitive anxiety and anger, and relatively high levels of good feelings, of chronically ill people who are anticipating death indicate that their construct systems enable them to predict what is happening to them, and that the changes which they are experiencing are not invalidating. However, their sadness and guilt indicate threats to core constructs and to their expectations of how they may relate to others.

*Bill*
Implications of Introversion–Extraversion:

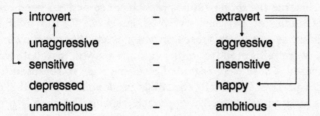

| introvert | – | extravert |
| unaggressive | – | aggressive |
| sensitive | – | insensitive |
| depressed | – | happy |
| unambitious | – | ambitious |

Social Situations Questionnaire Responses:

|  | Pre-Treatment | Follow-Up |
|---|---|---|
| Difficulty of Social Situations | 72 | 97 |
| Avoidance of Social Situations | 113 | 126 |

*Fred*
Implications of Shyness–Extraversion:

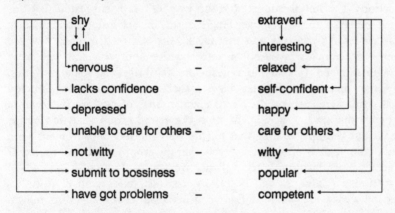

| shy | – | extravert |
| dull | – | interesting |
| nervous | – | relaxed |
| lacks confidence | – | self-confident |
| depressed | – | happy |
| unable to care for others | – | care for others |
| not witty | – | witty |
| submit to bossiness | – | popular |
| have got problems | – | competent |

Social Situations Questionnaire Responses:

|  | Pre-Treatment | Follow-Up |
|---|---|---|
| Difficulty of Social Situations | 58 | 50 |
| Avoidance of Social Situations | 94 | 61 |

*Figure 5.2* Implications grid and Social Situations Questionnaire (Trower *et al.*, 1978) results with two social skills group clients

**'Personal styles' and therapeutic outcome**

Further evidence that clients' response to therapy is likely to be determined by how they construe the therapeutic approach concerned has been provided by a series of studies of 'personal styles' (Caine *et al.*, 1981; Winter, 1985c, 1990c). The initial setting for this research was a psychotherapy clinic in which most clients were allocated to either group analytic psychotherapy or behaviour therapy. These were regarded by Caine *et al.* to represent respectively an introspective approach, focussing predominantly on the client's constructions, and an extraspective approach, viewing the client's problems largely in terms of a framework imposed by the therapist (cf. Rychlak, 1968). As discussed in Chapter 4, clients who preferred, and tended to be allocated to, the former treatment approach differed from those preferring the latter on a range of measures suggesting that the context of their construing, the events with which they were generally most concerned, predominantly concerned their internal rather than their external reality. Their therapeutic preferences therefore reflected their more general constructions of the world, their 'personal styles', and the next stage of the research examined whether positive treatment outcome would be facilitated if treatment allocation matched these constructions. The initial studies of group psychotherapy suggested that this might indeed be so, in that a longer length of stay in such groups, and positive outcome as rated by clients and therapists, was observed in clients whose treatment expectancies favoured an introspective approach and who were more 'inner-directed' (Caine and Wijesinghe, 1976). Radical social attitudes, which Caine and his colleagues have associated with an inner-directed personal style, were also predictive of client ratings of positive outcome in group psychotherapy. A subsequent study compared group analytic therapy and behaviour therapy, finding that clients who showed improvement on a range of outcome measures during psychotherapy groups exhibited treatment expectancies more favourable to introspective approaches and more radical social attitudes (Caine *et al.*, 1981). By contrast, conservative attitudes, assessed by a measure which defines conservatism as resistance to radical change (Wilson, 1975), were predictive of improvement during behaviour therapy. 'Improvers' in group analytic therapy were differentiated from 'improvers' in behaviour therapy not only by their scores on the Treatment Expectancies Questionnaire and their more radical attitudes but also by their greater inner-directedness. In addition, their repertory grid responses indicated that they construed their problems and treatment in less medical terms, viewing themselves as less ill and their therapists as likely to be less similar to their general practitioners. As we have seen above, constructs relating to their symptoms were also less superordinate, and their construct systems less tightly organised than in clients who improved during behaviour therapy.

These findings, coupled with the relationships discussed in Chapter 4 between personal styles and the content of constructs applied by a client to the symptoms and the self, suggest that aspects of clients' construing are differentially predictive of response to introspective and extraspective therapies. If a client's construing is fairly loosely structured, if his or her predominant concerns are with internal reality, social interaction, and lack of organisation, and if constructs concerning the symptoms do not occupy a superordinate position, he or she is likely to respond to a treatment approach which is introspective, interpersonally orientated, but neither highly structured nor focussed on the symptoms. If, on the other hand, constructs are more tightly organised, if the client's major concerns are with external reality, lack of self-sufficiency, structure, and opposition to radical change, and if 'symptom constructs' are superordinate, positive outcome is more likely in a therapy which is more structured, directive, and orientated towards symptom removal rather than more extensive personal change. Such relationships between positive treatment outcome and congruence of therapeutic approach with clients' constructions are consistent with the findings of previous research conceptualising such constructions in terms of psychological-mindedness (Abramowitz and Abramowitz, 1974) and internal or external locus of control (Strickland, 1978; Foon, 1987). They are also congruent with Landfield's (1971) observations that clients who prior to treatment made more use of construct poles concerning high degrees of structure, dogmatism, or concrete features of people, such as their external appearance, were least likely to improve during psychotherapy. Also unlikely to improve were female clients who used construct poles in Landfield's 'high intensity' category (concerned with forcefulness, emotional arousal, and extreme descriptions of people).

The conclusions drawn above from the investigations of Caine and his colleagues are primarily based on a comparison of group analytic and behaviour therapy. However, these treatments could be contrasted not only on the introspective–extraspective, but also on the group-individual dimension, and accordingly current research is examining clients' construing and personal styles in relation to their response to an introspective and an extraspective group therapeutic approach. Only the results from a treatment representing the latter approach, social skills training, are currently available, but, contrary to expectations, these indicated that client inner-directedness prior to treatment is highly predictive of therapist ratings of a positive therapeutic outcome and of reduction in neurotic symptoms during therapy (Winter, 1988a). Consequently, clients were interviewed to ascertain their views concerning the group sessions, which had been conducted on the skill-deficit model, teaching social skills as if they were motor skills. Not one of the interviewees mentioned training in social skills as a beneficial ingredient of therapy, the most commonly stated benefit being the opportunity which the groups provided clients to discover that other people experience difficulties similar to their own. Such an experience of 'universality' is also regarded by Yalom (1970) as a major curative factor in group psychotherapy. Therefore, since inner-directedness has been associated with the ability of clients to anticipate accurately the constructions of other therapy group members (Smail, 1972; Wood, 1977), it may be that inner-directed clients are more likely to respond to group approaches, of whatever theoretical basis, because they are more willing and able to share the perspectives of their fellows and so capitalise on the potential for universality which groups provide. A similar explanation may perhaps be provided for the unexpected finding by McKain et al. (1988) that, amongst shy people, the use of more constructs concerning behaviour was predictive of less response to cognitive-behavioural social skills groups, as assessed by increase in assertiveness. Since the frequencies of use of 'behavioural' and 'cognitive' constructs were found to be negatively correlated, these individuals may have been limited in the benefit which they could derive from their group experience by their focus on the behaviour, rather than the constructions, of themselves and other group members.

### Therapist–client commonality, sociality, and response to treatment

If congruence between clients' construing and the therapeutic conditions to which they are exposed is predictive of a positive therapeutic outcome, clients might also be expected to be more likely to respond to therapy if their construing is similar to that of their therapists. Some indirect evidence relevant to this relationship may be derived from those studies which have examined similarity between client and therapist on a range of attitudinal, personality, and demographic variables. One study which is pertinent to the work of Caine and his colleagues, since it employed the Myers-Briggs Type Indicator, one of the scales from which is highly related to the Direction of Interest Questionnaire which they employed to assess inner-directedness, found a curvilinear relationship between therapist–client compatibility and treatment outcome (Mendelsohn and Geller, 1965). On the basis of a review by Luborsky et al. (1971), Carr (1980, p. 234) concludes that 'the key to the similarity factor was found in the area of cognitive processes and not personality', but in general reviewers have noted the inconsistency in the results obtained from research in this area (e.g. Berzins, 1977; Garfield, 1986). Beutler et al. (1986, p. 275) conclude that 'the available evidence is inconclusive in establishing the presence of a relationship between initial belief similarity and subsequent improvement among clinical populations', although also that 'there is apparently a decided tendency for successful therapy dyads to be associated with the patients' acquiring therapists' belief systems, both about religious and moral attitudes and about more general concepts as well'.

Two bodies of research, by Landfield and Carr and their co-workers, have focussed more directly on commonality of construing between client and therapist. Although Nawas and Landfield (1963) failed to observe the predicted relationship between response to psychotherapy and adoption by the client of the therapist's constructs, they did find that clients who showed greater agreement with their therapists in ratings of the importance of their own constructs were more likely to show improvement (Landfield and Nawas, 1964). This latter effect was not observed when ratings of the importance of the therapists' constructs were considered. In addition, Landfield (1971) was able to demonstrate that clients showed a more favourable response to therapy if there was similarity in content between their therapists' construing and their own. Not only did clients who terminated therapy prematurely tend to use constructs of different content from their therapists, but they tended to come from dyads in which clients and therapists rated one another less extremely on the other's construct dimensions, indicating that the other's constructs were less meaningful to them. As has been reported by Ourth and Landfield (1965), premature terminators also tended to come from dyads in which therapist and client did not find each other very meaningful. Furthermore, as we have seen above, there was evidence that improved clients came to see themselves as more similar to their therapists' ideals, but only when described in terms of the clients' own constructs, leading Landfield (1971, p. 157) to conclude that 'to the extent that a therapist may plot his personal ideal in a meaningful way within the framework of his client, his client may improve'. While these findings suggested that positive outcome is facilitated when therapist and client employ similar constructs, a somewhat different picture emerged on considering the structural features of clients' and therapists' construct systems. Although initial dissimilarity between therapist and client in construct system structure was associated with premature termination of therapy, it was also related to positive outcome in those clients who remained in treatment. Landfield's explanation of these findings is that effective communication between client and therapist requires a degree of commonality in the content of their construing, but that differences between them in structural aspects of their construct systems facilitate reconstruction in the client. He considers this latter argument to be supported by the finding that the therapist–client dyads in which there was initially most divergence in structure of construing were those in which convergence in structural features, particularly due to changes in the clients, was most apparent during therapy. However, as Adams-Webber (1979) points out, if it can be assumed that therapists' construct systems are generally indicative of optimal functioning, represented on Landfield's structural measure of Functionally Independent Construction by moderate scores, the dyads in which greatest divergence between the scores of therapist and client was apparent are likely to have been those in which the clients' scores were most extreme. The greater structural change during therapy in the clients from these dyads could therefore, perhaps, be explained simply in terms of their greater 'room for improvement' on the Functionally Independent Construction dimension.

An increase in the structural similarity of the construct systems of client and therapist during psychotherapy has also been observed by Carr (1970,

1980), and in this case there was evidence that such changes were not explicable in terms of regression to the mean, and that they were more apparent in therapists than in their clients. When therapists initially differentiated more highly between people on their construct dimensions than did their clients, they tended to reduce their level of differentiation. There were no significant changes in dyads in which the client's differentiation level was initially higher than that of his or her therapist, but when differentiation levels of client and therapist were initially similar, there tended to be an increase in the therapist's level. Carr suggests that this latter trend reflected the therapists' use of finer discriminations as they attempted to understand their clients' view of the world, but that it did not necessarily result in a reduction in congruence between therapist and client since the therapist could always reduce his or her level of differentiation again when this was required to facilitate effective communication with the client. In contrast to Landfield, Carr found that clients whose construing was initially similar in structure to that of their therapists were more likely to display a positive therapeutic outcome, in terms of their own ratings of improvement and reduction in symptom levels. Explanation of this apparent discrepancy between the results of these two studies is hampered by the dearth of information which is provided on the nature of the therapies under study. What is apparent is that the treatments were comparable in duration, which was approximately twelve sessions; that Landfield's clients were undergraduates attending a student health centre while Carr's were psychiatric out-patients; and that Landfield's therapists were either members of the University Psychology Department or clinical psychology students, all with at least a year's experience as psychotherapists, while Carr's were medical students. However, although Landfield (1971, p. 27) reports that the therapists in his study espoused 'a developmental, learning approach with a de-emphasis on illness' and an acceptance that 'problems of living within oneself or with others are resolved in the context of new perspectives and alternatives, particularly related to the present and anticipated future', Carr provides no information on the approach adopted by his therapists. Apart from possible differences in the treatment approaches studied, the inconsistency in the results of Landfield and Carr may possibly be explained on the basis of the difference between the structural measures which they employed, Landfield's assessing degree of differentiation between constructs while Carr's assesses the degree to which constructs differentiate between elements (see p. 46). Carr (1974) has, in fact, found scores on his measure of differentiation within construct dimensions to be uncorrelated with those on a measure of differentiation between constructs, and that only client–therapist similarity on the former measure was associated with positive treatment outcome. The additional finding that clients whose therapists differentiated most highly amongst people on their constructs adjudged their outcome least favourably may also reflect the difference in differentiation levels between these therapists and their clients, who may 'find the articulated perceptions and interpretations of their therapists difficult to grasp, and their own limited attempts at insight even more feeble in comparison' (Carr, 1974, p. 284). However, although clients' level of differentiation amongst constructs was positively related to favourable therapeutic outcome, their differentiation within construct dimensions was not. Carr (1980) considers that his hypothesis of a relationship between therapist–client compatibility in differentiation levels and positive treatment outcome has been supported by studies using alternative measures of differentiation (McLachlan, 1972, 1974; Pardes *et al.*, 1974). His report of unpublished research which he conducted with Montgomery is harder to reconcile with this hypothesis since the therapists in this study, in contrast to those in his previous study, reduced their differentiation levels during psychotherapy. Since the clients in the second study obtained significantly higher initial differentiation levels than those in the first, Carr (1980, p. 244) concludes that 'our original view that therapists' conceptual strategy is determined in part by the differentiation level at which the patient is operating appeared to be supported'. However, it is apparent that, except in those dyads in the 1974 study in which therapists were initially much more differentiated than their clients, in both studies the overall change in therapists' differentiation levels over the course of therapy was such as to make them more discrepant from those of most of their clients. To clarify these findings, further research is necessary on clearly defined therapeutic approaches applied by experienced therapists with somewhat more homogeneous groups of clients.

It is often considered self-evident that commonality in construing between therapist and client is associated with the capacity of the therapist to construe the client's constructions, and therefore, in the words of the Sociality Corollary (Kelly, 1955, p. 95), to 'play a role in a social process' involving the client. For example, Carr (1980, p. 245) has little doubt about this, stating that 'No better validation of Kelly's sociality corollary could have been conceived' than his studies of client–therapist similarity in relation to outcome. This is despite reporting the finding that similarity between client and therapist in differentiation level was unrelated to client and therapist ratings of the extent to which therapists understood their clients' problems. As we have seen in Chapter 4, commonality in construing in a dyad need not necessarily imply that one member of the dyad will be able to anticipate the constructions of the other, and Takens (1981a) considers this to be particularly so in an asymmetric relationship such as psychotherapy, in which equal sharing of constructions is de-emphasised. Conclusions concerning therapists' understanding of their clients' construing might therefore be best derived from studies which have explored such understanding more directly. In one such study, Cartwright and Lerner (1963) found that clients were more likely to improve during client-centred therapy when an increase was apparent in their therapists' predictions of the client's self-ratings on constructs elicited from them. However, these results may have reflected the fact that the clients' therapeutic outcome was assessed by ratings made by these same therapists. A series of studies by Takens (1981a; 1981b) has also examined therapists' predictive accuracy, finding little evidence that this is a significant factor in successful therapy. Thus, in the first of these studies, he found, contrary to predictions, that group psychotherapists were better able to identify the constructs of those clients with whom they considered they had the poorest working relationships. In another investigation, conducted in a residential crisis centre, neither therapists' ability to predict their clients' self-ratings nor similarity in self-ratings between client and therapist were found to correlate with the quality of their relationship as adjudged by both client and therapist, although clients did consider therapists who accurately predicted their self-constructions to be more attractive. Subsequent studies, one of counselling trainees engaged in mock therapy sessions and one of the relationships between experienced therapists and their clients, both found therapists' predictive accuracy to be negatively correlated with ratings made from audio-tapes of their level of empathy during therapy sessions, and that commonality between client and therapist showed no relationship either with therapist empathy or with client self-disclosure. Takens (1981b) suggests that the inverse relationships which he observed between sociality and empathy may be due to a tendency of therapists who find difficulty in predicting their clients' constructions to engage in more empathic exploration as a result. The discrepancy between his findings and those of Landfield and Carr may perhaps be explained, in R. Neimeyer's (1985a) view, by differences in the procedures which they adopted, namely that he was attempting to associate commonality and sociality with aspects of the therapy process, which were not necessarily related to therapeutic outcome, and that his assessment of commonality was specifically based on similarity in the self-constructions of client and therapist rather than more general features of construing. In relation to the latter point, however, Carr (1974) did, in fact, employ a similar method in one of his studies, and was able to demonstrate that clients were more likely to regard the outcome of their therapy as favourable if they and their respective therapists construed themselves similarly. A final, recent study of therapists' construal of their clients' constructions has been carried out by Willutzki (1989). She found that, while cognitive-behavioural therapists' ability to predict the grid responses of their phobic clients was related to positive therapeutic outcome, this was not so with the ability to predict the clients' construing of their phobic situations. The implications of this latter finding, which at first sight may appear surprising, will be discussed in Chapter 8.

Other reports concerning therapists' construal of their clients' constructions mostly consist of single case studies in which grids completed by a client are compared with those completed by the therapist as he or she imagines the client would complete them. For example, Watson (1970a) applied this procedure on four occasions, two months apart, with a client who was a sexual offender, finding that he was generally unable to predict the sexual connotations which threat and anxiety carried for the client. Although his ability to predict increased somewhat over the course of the client's therapy, there was little change in the client's construing during this time. Rowe (1971b), similarly, was able to demonstrate systematic errors in a psychiatrist's prediction of his client's construing: in particular, 'The psychiatrist, whose life to that stage would suggest to the observer that he placed a high value on academic achievement, did not see how important non-academic achievement was to his patient' (Rowe and Slater, 1976, p. 142). In a later study, she found that over the course of therapy for a client who complained of difficulties in obtaining an erection, not only were there changes in the client's construing of his mother and ex-girl friend which appeared to be associated with the positive outcome of the treatment, but his psychiatrist became better able to predict his constructions, particularly with regard to his construct of fear (Rowe and Slater, 1976). This study employed a dyad grid, in which the elements are relationships, as did one by Ryle and Lunghi (1971), in which a therapist was found to be most accurate in predicting a client's construing of the relationships, those with her parents and the therapist, most focussed upon during therapy of over two years duration, but failed to percieve the degree of threat experienced by the client in the therapeutic situation.

## CONSTRUING AND THE THERAPEUTIC PROCESS

Several repertory grid studies have focussed more on elucidation of the process of psychotherapy than on evaluation of therapeutic outcome. Although examining aspects of the construing of client and therapist, these studies have in the main concerned themselves with conceptualisations of the therapeutic process derived from theories other than personal construct theory. For example, transference and countertransference have been investigated by means of repertory grid technique, and indeed Kelly (1955) himself indicated that the Repertory Test might be used in this way. An early study in this area, by Sechrest (1962), found that therapists were construed by their clients as similar to people whom they resembled in terms of age, sex, and status, but not to family members at any more than a chance level. The only change in this pattern during therapy was an increase in the extent to which clients construed themselves as similar to their therapists, and Sechrest therefore concluded that no evidence was provided for the operation of a transference process. Clients' construing of their therapists has also been examined by Tyler and Simmons (1964), who found that psychiatric in-patients construed psychologists, nurses, and activity therapists as 'persons', but doctors and social workers in terms of their task. In another study using a grid, Crisp (1964a, 1964b) was able to confirm his hypothesis that members of Social Class 1 would construe their psychiatrists as more, and their general practitioners as less, like their 'ideal dependable father' than would members of Social Class 3. He then employed the distance from the ideal dependable father as a measure of transference in a subsequent study in which neurotic clients were found to show more positive transference to a psychiatrist than did normal subjects. Turning his attention to clients receiving behaviour therapy, he made individual predictions, based on clinical judgements and psychodynamic hypotheses, of changes in transference feelings between grid assessments, finding that of fourteen such predictions all but one were confirmed. When grid-derived transference scores relating to the 'parental idealization/hostility attitude' and 'sexual attitude' were employed, he was also able to demonstrate some correspondence between changes in such attitudes during treatment and changes in the client's clinical condition (Crisp, 1966). Furthermore, in female clients, an initial positive transference was predictive of a favourable therapeutic outcome. Employing a similar method to Crisp, Houben and Pierloot (1970) found that in neurotic women receiving psychotherapy, but not in other clients, their transference towards their psychiatrists was as positive (and that towards their internists and psychologists less so) as their transference towards their general practitioners. Watson (1970b) has investigated a self-mutilating client's transference feelings towards him by means of serial grids, and, more recently, Ben-Tovim and Greenup (1983) have examined transference using a method in which grids were constructed of the ratings made by a client following successive individual psychotherapy sessions of her relationships with various significant figures including the therapist. The therapist was found consistently to be construed as relating to her in a different way to her parents, but there was more variation in the construed similarity of her mode of relating to her therapist and parents. Changes in construing of herself with her father when she was a child were found to be particularly apparent at grid assessments two weeks after the therapist had made interpretations concerning her father, but no therapeutic interventions other than interpretations were significantly associated with reconstruing of particular relationships. However, sessions at which the therapist engaged in a high degree of questioning tended to be those at which the client's construing at the post-session assessment was most different from her construing following the previous session. Another recent study which has monitored clients' construing of their therapists over the course of psycho-therapy, conducted on an in-patient basis, found that clients who failed to improve showed a tendency to idealise their therapists increasingly during therapy, but that this idealisation reduced following therapy, perhaps reflecting the clients' disillusionment (Bassler et al., 1989).

As well as its application to the study of transference, the repertory grid has also been employed by Ryle and his colleagues, as well as by Dalton (1983a), to explore therapists' countertransference feelings. In one such study, Ryle (1969) used a grid in which the elements were his psychotherapy clients at a student health centre, and found that those who were referred because of academic difficulties tended to make him bored and angry. Subsequent follow-up of these clients indicated that their treatment tended to have a less favourable outcome and to be shorter in duration than that of those who evoked sympathy from him and who he thought could work with him (Ryle, 1975). However, it appears that the ratings of success of treatment were made by Ryle himself, and so clearly could have reflected his countertransference reactions to the clients concerned. A grid method in which each element refers to a treatment session with a client has also allowed Ryle and Lipshitz (1974) to explore the relationships between Ryle's perceptions of the themes of his sessions, of his clients' transference reactions, and of his own countertransference feelings, as well as perceived changes in clients during therapy (Ryle, 1975). In addition, these workers have used grids to provide nursing staff and social work students with feedback on aspects of their construing relevant to countertransference, and the construing of the latter students will be discussed when we come to consider reconstruing by staff members during training programmes.

While the studies considered above have mostly concerned individual therapy, a considerable amount of research attention has also been devoted to the construing of clients and therapists in relation to the treatment process in group psychotherapy. For example, Watson (1970c) provided the first reports of a method in which each group member completes a grid with all the group members as elements and supplied constructs, supplemented in some cases with constructs elicited from the group. The use of a standard grid facilitated comparisons between group members and the detection of such shared constructions as operated in scapegoating or the idealisation of the therapists, examples of which are provided by Watson. The method also allowed him to identify the most salient group members and constructs, and to explore the 'emotional language' of the group. For example, he was able to demonstrate that in one group there was general agreement as to the meaning of depression and fear, but that the therapists shared one meaning of anger and the clients another. In addition, he provided a detailed examination of the construing of one particular client in relation to that of other group members. For example, her self construct was found to be highly correlated with the constructs 'like me' and 'like my mother' as employed by one of the therapists. It was not surprising, therefore, that her self-esteem was high, and Watson considers that the grids indicated a countertransference problem for the therapist, whom he viewed as unconsciously colluding with the client so that both could avoid negative feelings concerning their respective mothers.

In a subsequent study, Watson (1972) observed a common pattern in different groups of perception of considerable anxiety, anger, and affection by group members but of few similarities between group members and parents. All construct poles (only one pole of each construct was employed in the grids) were seen to characterise the groups to a greater degree by the therapists than by the clients, and the therapists' construing varied to a lesser degree in this respect, both between constructs and between occasions, than did that of the clients. Differences between clients and therapists were most apparent in relation to constructs concerning similarity to the parents, and clients' self-construing also showed greater variation over time than did that of therapists. While the principal dimension of construing employed by all the therapists tended to contrast the self, ideal self, and parents with child-like qualities, that of clients generally contrasted the self and/or one or both parents with the ideal self. Simultaneous variation was observed between occasions of testing in the extent to which members of a group applied construct poles to the group, and this variation was in different directions in different groups, suggesting that it reflected processes which were operating in particular groups. The level of variation of group members' ratings about construct means also varied from group to group, although in each case being higher for clients than for therapists, indicating that clients were giving more extreme ratings, except on a construct concerning similarity to the ideal self.

Other investigations have also revealed processes of construing in psychotherapy groups which appeared to affect most, if not all, of their members. This was the case in the psychoanalytically orientated group studied by Fransella and Joyston-Bechal (1971), in which similar fluctuations in the strength of construct relationships were apparent in the grids of group members, including a non-participating observer. An initial tightening of members' construing was followed by a marked loosening of construct relationships, which preceded changes in the ways in which members applied constructs to each other, although there was no change in the meaning of the constructs themselves, reflected in their intercorrelations. This pattern was confined to group members' construing of each other, not being evident in their scores on the Bannister-Fransella Grid Test. However, it was not apparent in the two clients who were best able to construe themselves in the same way as they were seen by other group members, and who showed most change on a measure of social adjustment. Fransella (1970d, p. 87) speculates that 'It was as if they were able to "resist" the group process and instead use it to help with their own reconstruing'. The therapist, contrary to predictions, construed those clients who saw themselves as least like they were seen by other group members as most likely to improve, and also showed a tendency to perceive clients who construed tightly as unlikely to improve. His positive evaluation of loose construing may have explained the loosening which occurred in group members between the third and ninth month of therapy, and Fransella and Joyston-Bechal suggest that the subsequent tightening which was apparent may have been a reaction to anxiety engendered by the fact that the therapist had also loosened his construing. Not surprisingly, they found that talkative people were construed as leaders in the group and as contributing usefully to discussions, but they were unable to confirm their hypothesis that the ideal self would change from being identified with the therapist to being identified with the group. In another study of a psycho-analytically orientated therapy group, although Trippett and I failed to replicate the Fransella and Joyston-Bechal finding of simultaneous changes in the tightness of group members' construing, we did, similarly to these workers, find indications of cyclical processes in construing. For example, there appeared to be an initial decrease in the consensus of meaning of constructs for members and an increase in the extent to which they differentiated between each other in terms of these constructs; these aspects of construing then remained constant for a while; and there was a reversal of the initial trends in the later stages of the group (Winter and Trippett, 1977). As in Watson's (1972) study, group members found constructs concerning similarity to parents least applicable to, and least able to differentiate between, their fellows, and showed least agreement in the meaning of these constructs. A similar pattern was observed for a construct concerning threat. Consensus in the meaning of depression for group members increased, while the opposite was the case for consensus in the meaning of anger, leading us to speculate that 'the latter construct may have initially been a rather impermeable one for the patients and that during therapy its permeability, and therefore openness to differences in application, increased, with more behavioural elements being subsumed within its range of convenience: at termination of therapy, anger was perhaps indicated by silence as well as by a raised voice, by tightly folded arms as well as by a clenched fist' (p. 346). A further similarity with Watson's study is that the similarity of clients' and therapists' grids increased somewhat over the course of the group, which, coupled with the observation that clients' construing changed more than that of the senior therapist (the other therapist failed to complete a post-treatment grid), suggested that clients 'learnt the language' of the therapists. Such increased consensus of group members' construing with that of the therapists has also been observed by Ryle and Lipshitz (1976a) to characterise those clients considered by the therapists to have changed most during group analysis, as has high emotional involvement in the group by these clients as perceived by both therapists and clients. However, a high level of recon-struction by clients, although related to symptom loss and to perceptions of change in the clients by group members, was not associated with similar perceptions by the therapists.

There is some evidence that cyclical changes in construing during group psychotherapy may be apparent not only in structural indices but in clients' construing of themselves and of other group members. Thus, Kelly (1955) reported that studies by Bieri and Lundy indicate that in the early stages of groups there is an increase, and a subsequent decrease, in the extent to which individuals construe themselves as similar to other group members. Students attending Interpersonal Transaction Groups have also been observed to show a reduction, and then an increase, in the meaningfulness of other group members, as reflected in the extremity of grid ratings assigned to them (Landfield, 1979). The processes which may operate in such groups have also been elucidated by changes in the grid scores of problem drinkers attending them, who have been found to come to construe each other more extremely and favourably, and to increase their capacity to predict each other's construing, although unexpectedly there appeared to be a decrease in the commonality of construing amongst group members (Landfield and Rivers, 1975; Landfield, 1979). Jackson (1990b) has also examined changes in members' construing of each other over the course of a personal construct therapy group for adolescents, finding an increase in their perceived ability to understand each other.

A further repertory grid investigation of a psychotherapy group, by Caplan *et al.* (1975), has demonstrated greater changes in construing of the self and the mother in clients than in therapists. Clients saw themselves as less similar to their ideal selves and their mothers than did therapists, but identification with the father, in contrast to that with the mother, tended to covary in clients and therapists. The authors also related changes in construing to themes of group sessions, finding that clients' paternal identification increased when more topics were raised in sessions, particularly when these concerned family members or other clients, while their maternal identification appeared to be unrelated to the content of sessions. The introduction of new topics, particularly concerning family members and themselves, was associated with clients construing group members as more similar to themselves and to their fathers, which Caplan and his colleagues suggest may be a result of re-enactment of family relationships in the group. Group members' self-esteem tended to increase when they talked about relatives other than nuclear family members, possibly a relatively unproblematic topic, and that of all group members decreased when sex was discussed. In the therapists, maternal identification increased when the clients talked about them, while paternal identification increased when jobs were discussed, indicating to Caplan *et al.* that they related occupational performance to their relationships with their fathers. As well as general trends, the authors also examined changes in construing in individual clients in relation to their communication in the group, finding significant relationships which varied in direction in different clients, indicating the variation in the implications for them of verbal participation in the group. Such variations were further elucidated when changes in clients' Personal Questionnaire responses were examined in relation to their grids and their verbal behaviour in group sessions (Shapiro *et al.*, 1975). The association between clients' behaviour in psychotherapy groups and changes in their construing has also been investigated in other studies. Koch (1983a), having found what he considered to be evidence of a link between therapeutic improvement and transference relationships, reflected in increased construed similarity of clients' parents, particularly their mothers, to other group members, went on to consider whether such changes in members' construing were related to their expression of affect (Koch, 1983b). Although the number of significant correlations between measures of affective expression and changes in construing was relatively few, he did find some evidence of a relationship between expression of hostility and both increase in construed similarity of group members to the mother and increased self-esteem. In one group, clients who spoke more were found to construe themselves as significantly less anxious; while amount of verbalisation in a psychoanalytically orientated group for depressive clients has been related to reconstruing of the self by Fielding (1983), who found that when clients showed greater verbal participation they were more likely to see themselves as similar to other people. Also investigating depressive clients, in a preliminary report on a much larger scale study of psychoanalytically orientated groups, Catina *et al.* (1989) have provided some evidence for their view that clients will reconstrue in response to invalidation of their self-constructions by other group members only if the group is supportive towards them, thus providing them with an overall climate of validation. One of the clients studied, whose interactions with the group were generally friendly, showed considerable change in her self-construing and a reduction in the positive implications which depression carried for her, over the course of therapy; the other, towards whom the group was much less supportive, did not fundamentally alter her self-construction and, although she reconstrued depression in a less favourable light midway through therapy, this was only a transient change.

A further method of investigating the process of group psychotherapy has been to explore the dimensions employed in construing group interactions. Initial reports of this approach (Walton and McPherson, 1968; McPherson and Walton, 1970) indicated that observers showed considerable consensus in their construing of the members of a psychotherapy group run on group-analytic lines, principal component analysis of their grids identifying a dimension which contrasted assertive, dominant group members with those who were passive and submissive; another concerned with emotional sensitivity; and a third focussing on the hindering or attainment of group goals. The authors consider these dimensions to be very similar to those which have been observed to characterise many other types of group. They may, however, reflect the way in which professionals are trained to view clients in psychotherapy rather than how the group is construed by the members themselves. Therefore, in a study of a married couples' psychotherapy group, Wijesinghe and Wood (1976a) administered grids to the clients in the group. As in the McPherson and Walton study, the first principal component of their grids tended to concern dominance and the ability to discuss problems, while the second was predominantly concerned with emotional expression, although members differed in the perceived implications of these constructs for effective group functioning. Since the constructs which were found to define the two principal components of their grids had been supplied to group members in this study, Wijesinghe and Wood (1976b) investigated another marital therapy group, but this time employing grids in which all constructs were elicited. Once again, constructs relating to discussion of problems, dominance, and emotional expression were prominent, although on this occasion they were not clearly separated on the first two principal components derived from the grids. In another study in which constructs were elicited from group members themselves, with the additional refinement that the emotional, behavioural, and evaluative implications of constructs were also elicited (cf. Leitner, 1981a), Koch (1985) found that, in members of a short-term anxiety management group and a long-term group-analytic group, 'Dimensions of "activity-passivity" in relation to "general social behaviour", "social problem solving" and "group goal facilitation" were all present, with the dimension of "intimacy-distance" also being personally relevant to group members' (pp. 314–16). The greater complexity of his procedure perhaps accounts for the fact that his results were rather less clear-cut than those of previous investigators.

## THE THERAPIST'S CONSTRUCT SYSTEM

As we have seen above, several of the repertory grid studies of psychotherapy have attempted to elucidate the therapeutic process by considering the degree of commonality between the construing of therapist and client, the therapist's ability to construe the client's constructions, and his or her construing of the client. Other investigations have considered more general features of therapists' construing rather than focussing on specific therapist–client relationships, and these will now be considered.

One area of study has been the way in which clinicians generally construe their clients. Philip and McCulloch (1968), for example, found that the constructs used by social workers to describe clients who had attempted suicide fell into two categories: those concerning the impact of the client on the social worker and those concerning the professional formulation of the case. Professionals' construing of such clients has also been examined by Costigan et al. (1987), who found that this tended to be negative, and by Platt and Salter (1987), who were unable to demonstrate any difference between staff working in a specialist centre for the treatment of self-poisoning and those working in a more conventional medical setting. However, physicians were found to construe clients who had attempted suicide more negatively than did psychiatrists, and to see the actions of these clients as more inappropriate than did nurses. Psychiatrists were more likely than physicians and nurses to impute suicidal motivation to the clients' behaviour, whereas nurses were more likely to construe it as attention-seeking. A further aspect of construing which has been studied in suicide intervention workers is death threat (see p. 28), R. Neimeyer and Dingemans (1980) finding this to be higher in such workers than in psychology undergraduates, although the groups did not differ on measures relating to concerns about the death and dying of others. One of the possible explanations of these findings suggested by the authors is that some individuals who are highly threatened by death may select suicide intervention work as a means of elaborating their construing in this area. However, G. Neimeyer et al. (1983) have found that physicians who exhibited high death threat tended to use more avoidance and denial strategies, and expected to display less psychophysiological reaction, when confronted by death. In the authors' view, the strategies adopted by these physicians served to protect their construct systems against the revision which would be necessary if death were to be included as a personal reality.

Professionals' constructions of their clients often involve psychiatric diagnostic constructs, and these were examined by Agnew and Bannister (1973), who demonstrated that consultant psychiatrists showed no more stability or inter-judge agreement when applying such constructs to their clients than when using lay descriptive constructs. Furthermore, there was overlap between the two sets of constructs, and their findings led Agnew and Bannister to conclude that psychiatric diagnosis is a 'pseudo-specialist language'. Sperber (1977) has provided some support for this conclusion in his study of child psychiatric diagnosis, in which he found that clinicians were able to construe child clients as meaningfully in terms of constructs used to describe child friends as in terms of constructs used to describe the clients, these two sets of constructs showing an equivalent degree of interrelationship when applied to clients. However, they appeared to experience more difficulty when using 'client' constructs to describe the friends than when using 'friend' constructs. Somewhat greater differences between constructs applied to clients and those applied to acquaintances have been indicated in studies by Bender (reported by Tully, 1976) and Soldz (1989), of social workers and psychotherapists respectively, in which constructs used in one domain tended to be seen as inapplicable in the other. The construct subsystem applied to clients was more differentiated in both these studies, and Soldz also found it to show more hierarchical organisation. However, Tully (1976) notes that Bender's findings indicated that the construing of clients by social workers, rather than being more complex than that of acquaintances, was less articulated, with more isolated constructs, and he considers that this reflects such characteristics of psychiatric nosology as its resistance to change. The content of this subsystem was more dominated by psychiatric terminology and less by constructs concerning emotions and self-involvement than that of the acquaintance subsystem in the Bender study, while Soldz found more constructs concerning emotional stability–instability to be applied to clients. A further study, by Leff (1978), has indicated that psychiatrists' use of diagnostic constructs is likely to be incongruent with clients' constructions of their experiences. Using a semantic differential, he found that psychiatrists differentiated between anxiety, depression, and irritability to a greater degree than clients, and in particular showed much greater discrimination between the former two emotions in terms of somatic symptoms. The extent of the discrepancy between clients' and staff members' views of the clients' conditions has been examined by Bannister (1985c), who found that 61 per cent of a sample of new admissions to a psychiatric hospital broadly agreed with hospital staff as to the cause of their breakdown, that such agreement was particularly likely if clients saw the cause of their problems in terms of internal experiences rather than external forces, but that only 43 per cent of clients received treatment which was broadly in line with what they desired. Congruence between client and staff regarding problem causation was significantly related to a good treatment outcome, but congruence between given and desired treatment was not. Considerable discrepancies in the views of clients and staff have also been indicated in a study of individuals discharged from psychiatric hospital to group homes, whose ratings of their quality of life were significantly correlated with professionals' ratings of the severity of their psychiatric symptoms (Winter *et al.*, 1991). Such findings raise doubts concerning the common practice of assessing a client's quality of life from the observer's perspective rather than from that of the client himself or herself. Maitland's (1990) study of residents' perceptions of probation hostels also provides an indication that clients may differ from staff in the issues which are salient to them in judging the quality of their accommodation.

Professional training might be expected to result in changes in trainees' construing, but a study by Gottesman (1962) of training in client-centred therapy failed to demonstrate the predicted increase in the permeability and complexity of trainees' construct systems. Nevertheless, there was some indication that trainees whose permeability increased were rated as more therapeutically able following training, and such ratings also correlated with absolute post-training levels of permeability and complexity. Following training, there was also an increase in commonality in the constructs used by trainees, but a decrease in agreement regarding the application of constructs to grid elements, perhaps reflecting the instructors' concern to discourage stereotyped responses to clients. Reconstruction during training has also been a subject of study in social work students. Indirect evidence for such changes was provided in an investigation by Lifshitz (1974), who found differences between the construing of social work students and experienced social workers, including the use of more concrete constructs by the former group and their more negative construal of needy people. However, this may have been due less to the effects of training than to the fact that the social workers were older than the students. Examining change in construing more directly, Ryle and Breen (1974a) have found that over the course of training social work students come to construe relationships less extremely and loosen the organisation of their constructs, following an initial tightening of construct relationships. This curvilinear pattern of change in construct organisation is similar to that which has been observed in trainee teachers' construing of their students' problems (Runkel and Damrin, 1961). However, Ryle and Breen suggest that the social work students in their study may have tightened their construing in the early stages of their training as a reaction to a T-group experience. Studies of a T-group by Baldwin (1972), and of a marathon encounter group for trainee group therapists by Benjafield *et al.* (1976), would suggest that any such apparent tightening may reflect the more uniformly favourable view of, and identification with, other people that is likely to result from such an experience. Investigations by Harrison (1962, 1966), conducted on individuals from a range of backgrounds attending sensitivity-training laboratories, have also elucidated the likely effects of such training. He found that participants in the laboratories showed an increase in the use of constructs concerning interpersonal processes and feelings, as opposed to concrete and instrumental constructs, this effect being greatest in individuals rated as participating actively in the training and being more apparent at follow-up than immediately after training.

An additional finding of the Ryle and Breen study was that many of the students construed their roles towards their clients as similar to their roles towards their parents, suggesting that playing a supportive role towards parents may have been a factor in the choice of social work as a career. Many also appeared to use their relationship with a tutor or supervisor as a model for clients' relationships with them. Changes in the grids of individual students were suggestive of the resolution of problems, but of changes predicted for the group as a whole the only one to be confirmed at a statistically significant level was a more favourable construal by the student of his or her relationship to the client. Furthermore, when students' grids were ranked in terms of the likelihood of the student experiencing problems, there was no correspondence between these rankings and judgements of the students made by tutors, who were found to show a high degree of consensus in their construing of the students (Ryle and Breen, 1974b). The relatively tight construing of the tutors in this study is interpreted by Tully (1976) as a reaction to the fear and threat induced by witnessing their students aggressively elaborating their construing. Grids have also been employed to examine such aspects of student nurses' construing as changes in attitudes towards clients, and the development of a professional self-image and more positive constructions of medical roles, coupled with more negative construing of low-status non-medical roles, during training (Wilkinson, 1982; Davis, 1985, 1986; Heyman *et al.*, 1983). In addition, a study of nurses' construing of what constitutes an interpersonally skilled person has generated implications for skills training in nurse education programmes (Burnard and Morrison, 1989).

Changes towards more complex, less concrete modes of construing, which would appear to accompany social work training, might be expected to be conducive to greater ability to construe the constructions of clients. The relationship between cognitive complexity and good social work practice has been stressed by Duehn and Proctor (1974) in discussing a study which associated high levels of interpersonal discrimination in social work students with the specification of more alternative interventions for clients and more transmission of information about clients dissimilar to themselves than was the case in students who discriminated less between others. However, if a training programme aims to equip students with a set of specific skills and ways of conceptualising clients' problems, and if the students are relatively unfamiliar with the area of work, it might be expected to lead to the development of tighter organisation in their construing of clients. Some support for this view is perhaps provided by Gottesman's (1962) finding of an inverse relationship between complexity of construing and the use by trainees in client-centred therapy of constructs which were similar to those used by other trainees, and which Gottesman regarded as basically 'Rogerian'. Although there was no overall change in the structure of Gottesman's subjects' construct systems during training, Zaken-Greenberg and G. Neimeyer (1986) have observed a tightening of the construing of families by trainees in structural family therapy, but only if the trainees had had little prior experience of teaching sessions on marital and family issues. Those students who had had such experience, but who did not register for the training programme, had relatively loosely organised construct systems, and the authors speculate that this may have been due to their only having been exposed to the initial stages of training, which had caused them to abandon to a large extent their existing ways of construing families but had not yet provided them with a viable alternative system of family constructs. However, Borders *et al.* (1986) were unable to demonstrate that counselling students' level of experience of training was related to aspects of the structure or content of their construct systems, although students adjudged to have higher 'ego levels' were found to employ more constructs relating to interaction in describing their clients. Cross-cultural counselling training has also received some research attention from the personal construct theory perspective by investigators using a grid method, the Cultural Attitudes Repertory Test (G. Neimeyer and Fukuyama, 1984; Fukuyama and G. Neimeyer, 1985a), in which the elements are cultural groups. As well as allowing interventions to be devised which are tailored to trainees' attitudes, this method enables the tracing of changes in participants' construing of cultural groups during training courses. Thus, some evidence has been provided of greater change in the structure and degree of conflict in construing in cross-cultural counselling trainees than in a control group, and an increase in the extent to which they recognised differences between themselves and members of other cultural groups (Fukuyama and G. Neimeyer, 1985b).

Just as training programmes may vary in their effects on trainees' construing, depending for example on the degree of directiveness and structure of the approaches which they are imparting, so the patterns of construing which facilitate effective work in a particular clinical setting may depend on the treatment approach adopted in that setting. Indications that this is the case have been provided by observations of staff reactions to transitions in the treatment philosophies adopted in their work settings, and by the research that such observations have generated. For example, as I have described elsewhere (Winter, 1985c, 1990c), the resistance of many staff to Martin's (1962) introduction of a therapeutic community in a traditional psychiatric hospital was the initial impetus for a research programme by Caine and his colleagues which commenced by considering the attitudes of staff members towards psychiatric treatment. Such attitudes not only differentiated staff working in different settings and could be modified by training experiences but, just as was later observed with clients (see p. 172), they were found to reflect staff members' fundamental constructions of the world, their 'personal styles' (Caine and Smail, 1969b; Caine, 1970, 1975; Tutt, 1970; Caine and Leigh, 1972; Panayotopoulos and Stoffelmayr, 1972; Pallis and Stoffelmayr, 1973; Caine et al., 1981; Milne, 1984; Gournay, 1986; Winter et al., 1987). Specifically, as with clients, those staff members who favoured organic treatment approaches, or who worked in settings adopting such regimes, were more conservative and 'outer-directed' than staff who favoured psycho-therapeutic approaches, or who worked in such settings as therapeutic communities or crisis intervention teams. If their core constructs are very much implicated in clinicians' views concerning treatment approaches, an explanation may be provided for their resistance to transitions in these approaches, such transitions being likely to generate negative emotions. For example, like the psychologists whom Fransella (1983, p. 92) observed defending their preferred 'models of man', 'their whole personal psychology and personal identity' may be threatened by a new therapeutic philosophy. Staff members confronted by such a transition may also find themselves having to play a role discrepant with their core role, thus experiencing guilt, or may be confronted with ways of working largely beyond the range of convenience of their constructs, and so experience anxiety. To quote Menzies' (1960, p. 108) description of change in a hospital setting, 'It implies a commitment to future events that are not entirely predictable and to their consequences, and inevitably provokes doubt and anxiety'. One such change faced by many psychiatric hospital staff, but not without some resistance, is the resettlement in the community of members of the long-stay in-patient population. Preliminary research findings have indicated that staff members opposed to this policy, compared to those who favour it, use fewer constructs to discriminate between in-patients who could and could not be discharged (Winter et al., 1991). Conceivably, if these staff members were to differentiate more highly between in-patients, they might have to construe themselves as more similar to some of the latter than they would wish to admit. Their position may therefore be as described by Fransella (1977, p. 65): 'We know we are not mad by having a very clear idea about what madness is. We resist any attempt to redefine the concept for this will reduce our ability to define ourselves.' In a further sample, staff opposed to the policy of discharging long-stay residents of psychiatric hospitals were found to construe themselves as more similar to clients whom they considered unable to be discharged than were staff favouring the policy (Winter et al., 1991). A possible explanation for this surprising finding may be provided by Landfield's (1954) exemplification hypothesis of threat (see p. 11), which, as Kelly (1955, p. 599) indicates, implies that a clinician may 'behave in an unaccepting fashion' towards a client who is reminiscent of the clinician's past role. Failure to acknowledge that a client could be discharged from hospital may be a manifestation of this lack of acceptance, as well as reinforcing the distinction between clinician and client and thus reducing the threat posed by the latter.

## SUMMARY AND CONCLUSIONS

Research findings concerning structural changes in clients' construing during therapy are somewhat inconsistent, perhaps because such changes are likely to be cyclical in nature and therefore unlikely to be demonstrated clearly by a simple comparison of pre- and post-therapy mean scores. More convincing evidence has been obtained of changes in the content of construing during therapy, particularly in studies of clients diagnosed as neurotic or depressive, for whom therapeutic improvement has tended to be accompanied by such changes as more positive self-construing, greater identification with others, and resolution of dilemmas.

A further series of studies has examined the relationship between clients' construing and likelihood of therapeutic change, finding that a positive response to psychotherapy is less likely in clients who construe tightly and whose symptoms carry many implications for them. There are indications, however, that the converse relationship may be apparent in some clients undergoing behaviour therapy, and that aspects of construing may be differentially predictive of response to 'extraspective' therapies such as this and to 'introspective' therapies. Nevertheless, in one group of clients receiving behaviour therapy, agoraphobics, tight construing has been associated with poor outcome, as have a superordinate construct of infidelity in client and spouse and the construal of family members in a uniformly favourable light. Other features of construing which have been related to lack of response to therapy are favourable construal of the self, unfavourable construal of the premorbid self, and construal of the symptom as carrying positive implications. Treatment outcome has also been investigated in relation to the degree of commonality in the construing of client and therapist, and while there is some evidence that positive outcome is facilitated by commonality at the level of construct content, findings concerning commonality on structural measures are less consistent.

Repertory grid technique has been employed to examine transference and countertransference in both individual and group psychotherapy, as well as aspects of the group process in the latter. A further focus of study has been the clinician's construct system, some studies having questioned whether psychiatric diagnostic constructs constitute a specialist language, discrete from lay descriptive constructs, while others have indicated likely areas of discrepancy in staff members' and clients' construing of the problems of the latter. There is also some evidence of reconstruing in professionals undergoing training programmes, and that, just as is the case with clients, preferences for particular treatment approaches may reflect aspects of clinicians' construing.

# Part III

# Clinical applications of personal construct psychology

Having considered personal construct theory, the techniques derived from it, and the resulting theoretical and empirical analyses of psychological disorder, we are now in a position to describe how personal construct psychology may be employed by the clinician in his or her clinical practice. In Chapter 6, the focus will be on diagnostic assessment, from the exploration of the client's personal construct system to the selection of an appropriate form of therapy. It will include numerous examples of, and guidelines for, the use of the repertory grid in clinical assessment as an aid to the clinician who wishes to employ this popular technique. Chapter 7 will present the therapeutic applications of personal construct psychology, and in Chapter 8 we shall compare these applications, and the approach to psychological disorder on which they are based, with the approaches adopted by other theoretical models. We shall conclude with a discussion of the implications of these considerations in relation to integrationist trends in the psychological therapies and the organisation of clinical services.

# Chapter 6

# The personal construct theory approach to diagnosis

For Kelly (1955, p. 775), diagnosis was 'all too frequently an attempt to cram a whole live struggling client into a nosological category' by preemptive construction of the client's behaviour. By contrast, the diagnosis made by the clinician who adopts a personal construct theory approach will be propositional and *transitive*, being primarily concerned with the avenues of movement open to the client rather than with providing a static description of his or her current predicament. In viewing psychological disturbance 'in terms of dimensions rather than in terms of entities' (Kelly, 1955, p. 831), it does not succumb to the danger of reification, the transmutation of labels and metaphors which describe groups of behaviour into 'things', which has been discussed by Rowe (1978) in relation to psychiatric diagnosis. As Kelly (1955) noted, one of the drawbacks of this latter 'disease entity' approach is that clients' difficulties may be ignored if they cannot be conveniently subsumed by one of the disease categories employed. In contrast to this approach, transitive diagnosis concerns itself with six questions, namely:

1. Exactly what is peculiar about this client, when does he show it, and where does it get him?
2. What does the client think about all this and what does he think he is trying to do?
3. What is the psychological view of the client's personal constructs?
4. In addition to the client himself, what is there to work with in this case?
5. Where does the client go next?
6. How is the client going to get well?

(Kelly, 1955, p. 779)

In attempting to answer these questions, the clinician will draw upon a range of sources of information. In addition to data obtained from more formal procedures, these will include the client's behaviour, his or her responses at interview, and descriptions of the client by others. Kelly provided various tips regarding the elicitation and interpretation of such information, some of which may not be unfamiliar to clinicians who are accustomed to carrying out behavioural analyses (e.g. Hersen and Bellack, 1981). For example, he recommended that in reporting on the client's behaviour, and the ways in which it appears deviant from the norms of the clinician, the client's primary group, and the client him/herself, the clinician should first make a precise record of the behaviour concerned, indicating how the information was obtained. Only then should the clinician place professional constructions on this information, the prior record of which will also be open to construction by other clinicians in terms of their own preferred theoretical models. Similarly, Kelly favoured the keeping of verbatim records of the client's statements in addition to the clinician's constructions of these statements. He also recommended that attention should be paid to periodicity in the client's deviant behaviour, and to phases and sequences in the behaviour. Indeed, he considered that 'The clinician who cannot detect periodicity in the deviant behavior should begin to doubt the adequacy of his own abstraction of the case. Nearly always there is *some way* in which the present deviant behavior is like behaviors which have occurred again and again in the client's life' (Kelly, 1955, p. 791, italics in original). As an aid to identifying such periodicities, he suggested that the clinician mark episodes of the deviant behaviour and other significant events on a line representing the course of the client's life. While the focus will not be on a chronicling of the client's history as if this were responsible for shaping his or her present state, historical events are nevertheless of interest in indicating, for example, the validational evidence which has been available to the client. Kelly also emphasised that the client's deviant behaviour should be considered in the context of his or her cultural, social, domestic, and occupational worlds, together with the potential threats of which the client has been aware. These latter are what in other systems would be termed stresses, and consideration of them may make the client's behaviour appear much less deviant. Further understanding of this behaviour may also be provided by considering the gains which appear to accrue from it: to give just one of the examples of such gains provided by Kelly (1955, p. 797), the client's 'expressions of guilt may prove that he is still aware of his role responsibilities'.

The complaint, defined by Kelly (1955, p. 789) as 'the layman's formulation of the clinical issues', is generally the starting point in the assessment process. Kelly considered that by attending both to the content of the complaint and to the way in which it is formulated, the clinician may gain some under-standing of the construct system of the complainant, who may or may not be the client, and that this in turn may throw some light on the development and maintenance of the complaint. In his view, the complaint 'is usually a poor formulation' in that 'it has opened no avenues to a happy solution', and it may therefore contain clues as to the impasse faced by the client. However, listening to the complaint and asking non-threatening questions concerning it are not merely ways of gathering information but also means of establishing rapport by attending to areas which the complainant considers to be important.

Whether or not the original complainant is the client, Kelly suggested that the client should always be asked to formulate his or her problem, and also to describe others' view of the problem. The client's *elaboration of the complaint* may be *uncontrolled*, not being directed by the clinician, or *controlled*. Kelly considered the former approach to be contra-indicated if the clinician is unwilling to 'see the case through'; if the client's formulation is very repetitive; if his or her construing is very loose; or if the client exhibits considerable guilt feelings, in which case continued elaboration of the loss of role which has been experienced may eventuate in hostility and paranoia or constriction and suicidal behaviour. In such cases, controlled elaboration may be more appropriate, although not providing the degree of access to the client's personal construct system which is possible with uncontrolled elaboration. The questions which Kelly (1955, p. 962) suggested could be employed in controlled elaboration were:

a. Upon what problems do you wish help?
b. When were these problems first noticed?
c. Under what conditions did these problems first appear?
d. What corrective measures have been attempted?
e. What changes have come with treatment or the passing of time?
f. Under what conditions are the problems most noticeable?
g. Under what conditions are the problems least noticeable?

These questions are 'designed to get the client (1) to place the problems, if possible, on a time line, (2) to see them as fluid and transient, and then to interpret them as responsive to (a) treatment, (b) the passing of time, and (c) varying conditions' (p. 963). By so doing, they may set the stage for therapy. Clients may also be asked to suggest the causes of their difficulties, although Kelly (1955, p. 965) considered this to be inadvisable if there is evidence of 'any combination of extreme anxiety and aggression' or 'highly systematized hostility', if 'there are some areas which the client might attempt to elaborate and which might fall apart once he started to investigate them in detail', or if the clinician 'expects the client to develop a dependency role relationship with him as a preparatory step toward later elaboration of preverbal constructs or "deep" therapy'. A further possible step in controlled elaboration is to ask clients whether they have known other people with similar complaints, what such people do about them, whether and how they are able to overcome them, and what sort of people are unable to overcome them. Such questions may enable the client to consider the complaint within socially shared, rather than purely personal, dimensions, and, by viewing the complaint as if it were someone else's, to make reconstruction in this area a less threatening prospect. However, if the client displays considerable guilt feelings, there is a danger that these may be accentuated if the client, for example, concludes that he or she is unlike, or is unable to understand, others. Yet another interview procedure for elaborating an individual's personal problems has been described by Fisher (1989a), who attempts to identify the situations which the person finds problematic, associated feelings, the emergent and submerged poles of constructs concerning these situations and feelings, and the range of convenience of the constructs concerned, this latter stage providing an indication of their hierarchical relationships. Using this procedure, Fisher has been able to reveal 'interpersonal double binds', in which an individual feels more comfortable when construing himself or herself in terms of a particular construct pole but to do so leads to interpersonal problems; 'intrapersonal double binds', which are essentially dilemmas resulting from the interrelationships between the individual's constructs; and 'intrapersonal single binds', resulting from preemptive self-construing and constellatory superordinate constructs.

Elaboration of the complaint, whether controlled or uncontrolled, is primarily directed towards eliciting what the client considers to be the problem. Nevertheless, Kelly considered that it may sometimes be advisable to confront the client concerning complaints which he or she has not mentioned. These may, for example, be complaints made by others concerning the client, or those which the clinician considers to be evident in the client's behaviour or anticipates may develop in the future. Clients may also, in reflection procedures, be confronted with the terms which they themselves commonly use to describe their complaints and asked to elaborate on these terms (e.g. 'Wound up? What do you mean by that?'). As well as helping to clarify the diagnostic picture, the use of confrontation and reflection, and indeed any elaboration of the complaint, may serve therapeutic purposes, as will be discussed further in the next chapter. Particular problems may be faced by the clinician who attempts to elaborate a child's complaints since, as Ravenette (1977, p. 264) notes, 'children do not present themselves as having problems for which they require help'. One of his solutions to this problem is to question children concerning their complaints about, or troubles with, various people, including the self, since such troubles represent invalidations of expectations and therefore provide access to the child's customary expectations. Ravenette also observes that investigation of the referrer's constructions may be as illuminating as investigation of the child's (Hayhow et al., 1988).

Diagnosis, for Kelly (1955, p. 203), was 'the planning stage of therapy', but it will be apparent from the above that often there may be no clear distinction between diagnostic assessment and the other stages of therapy. This is particularly evident when the clinician moves on from elaborating the client's complaint to elaborating the system of personal constructs of which the complaint is just one expression. Indeed, Kelly (1955, p. 976) viewed such elaboration as 'the basic task of the psychotherapist'. For example, he considered that it is likely to provide a more comprehensive picture of the alternatives facing the client and, by dilating their field of concern, to increase the material available to client and clinician as they attempt to formulate new constructs. One area on which elaboration is likely to focus is the client's self-construing. Kelly (1955) suggested that the clinician might elicit such material by saying:

> You have been telling me about the troubles you have. I intend to do all I can to help you. But if I am to help you I need to know more about *you*. I need to understand you as a person as well as understand the troubles you have. So let's lay aside your problems for a little while so that you can tell me much more about what kind of person you are. What kind of person are you really?
>
> (p. 985, italics in original)

Kelly cautioned that the clinician should not succumb to the temptation of immediately following up such an invitation by specific questions, for example about the client's family background, for these will only involve the imposition of the clinician's construing on the client. Nevertheless, it may be valuable at some point for the clinician to facilitate the process by asking more general questions to elaborate the client's construing of particular stages in his or her life. Thus, the client might be asked what kind of child he or she was; what plans for the future he or she had then; how these plans have turned out; how he or she might have done things differently; what might have been the outcome of these alternative courses of action; what kind of person he or she expects to become, for example at the age of retirement or following success-ful therapy; and what are his or her expectations of the roles of client and therapist during therapy. The clinician's primary concern in asking such questions will not be to obtain a catalogue of life events but rather a picture of the client's *life role* by attending to consistent themes in the client's constructions of what he or she considers to be salient events, and therefore to 'the thread of meaning upon which the client strings the events of his life' (Kelly, 1955, p. 799). The elaboration of the client's life-role structure in this way may, in Kelly's view, be particularly useful if the client's problems appear to reflect a lack of purpose in life.

The personal construct diagnostician's initial formulation is likely to be what Kelly (1955) termed a *structuralisation* of the client's separate behaviours in terms of the clinician's system. However, the diagnostician's subsequent, and major, concern will be to arrive at a *construction* of the constructs which are the basis for these behaviours. As the focus is, therefore, not on events but on constructions of these events, such a clinician will inevitably be concerned with contrasts (Landfield, 1980b). It will be assumed, for example, that, by defining what the client considers to be the available alternatives to his or her present behaviour, and any anxieties which accompany these alternatives, even the most apparently peculiar or self-destructive behaviour will become more comprehensible to the clinician. The client's 'strengths' will be as relevant, if not more so, to the clinician as his or her 'weaknesses', and indeed Landfield (1975) suggests that in considering the latter the clinician might most usefully ask how they could be reformulated into strengths. To quote one of his examples, 'rigidity could be translated into steadfast purpose' (p. 9). It will also be apparent that, whatever aspect of the client's construing the clinician is attempting to elaborate, his or her initial approach to the task of assessment will be to adopt a credulous attitude, 'taking what he sees and hears at face value' (Kelly, 1955, p. 173). However, only by then attempting to subsume the client's constructs with the clinician's own professional constructs can the clinician begin to enter into a role relationship with the client. In this process of construing the client's constructions, and considering the types of construction used in different areas of the client's life, the clinician may employ any of the diagnostic constructs provided by personal construct theory. These constructs, which we have described in Chapter 1, were designed by Kelly (1955) in line with various specifications. They are fertile, generating a range of hypotheses, and these hypotheses are both testable and 'should reflect a degree of optimism regarding outcomes for the client' (p. 458). The diagnostic constructs are propositional, and each may be used relatively independently of other such constructs. They are dichotomous, distinguishing between two sets of contrasting elements. They are definable, but not to the extent of being impermeable. They are characterised by temporality, being able to place elements on a time line, and by futurity, having prognostic implications. Finally, they set the stage for sociality in that they enable the construing of part of the client's construct system.

In discussing the application of his diagnostic constructs, Kelly singled out for particular attention the location of the client's areas of anxiety, constriction, and aggressiveness, the latter providing some indication of where the client is currently attempting to solve problems and of the approach which the client might adopt in tackling problems during therapy. It is also likely to be valuable for the clinician to identify areas of hostility, which may be assumed to be present if the client finds a situation highly anxiety-provoking, perceives this to be the result of his or her own social experimentation, but still seems to extort evidence for the anticipations concerned rather than aggressively exploring alternatives.

## PSYCHOLOGICAL TESTING

We have been primarily concerned above with assessment of the client's predicament by means of interview or observation of behaviour. However, Kelly made it clear that the use of more formal assessment techniques may be a valuable adjunct to this procedure since they may, for example, reveal aspects of the client's problems which are not apparent at interview. He was referring here not only to the methods which he had devised but also to those developed from other traditions, with the principal exception of those 'objective' measures which assess the client in terms of personality dimensions rather than eliciting the client's own personal constructs. For example, he considered that 'even projective testing may properly be considered a direct approach to personal constructs' (Kelly, 1955, p. 202). Thus, responses to techniques such as the Thematic Apperception Test may, if appropriately analysed, provide an insight into the client's construing of self and others, and therefore of the client's life role. The links between projective and personal construct assessments have been explored by Rowe (1973a) and Ravenette (1973), and at least one projective technique has been devised which draws upon personal construct theory (Koocher and Simmonds, 1971). Even intelligence tests, in Kelly's view, may indicate areas of anxiety and constriction, as well as the ways in which the client characteristically solves problems. However, it is with techniques specifically designed to tap the client's construing, and particularly with the interpretation of repertory grid results, that this chapter will be particularly concerned.

In devising test procedures of use to the clinician, Kelly (1955, pp. 204–5) was concerned that these should be able to fulfil five major functions, namely 'to define the client's problem in usable terms . . . to reveal the pathways or channels along which the client is free to move . . . to furnish clinical hypotheses which may subsequently be checked and put to use . . . to reveal those resources of the client which might otherwise be overlooked by the therapist . . . to reveal those problems of the client which might otherwise be overlooked by the therapist'. He also outlined various questions which should be addressed in appraising a test's clinical utility. Firstly, consideration should be given to whether the test concerns itself with the clinician's or client's yardsticks. This construct differentiates 'objective' from projective tests, although Kelly noted that these adjectives more accurately describe the clinician's use of a test than the test itself. In his view, personal construct psychology, being primarily concerned with the viewpoint of its object of study, the client, *is more objective because it is more projective* (Kelly, 1955, p. 208, italics in original). In evaluating a test's utility, the clinician should also be concerned with whether it elicits permeable constructs rather than, for example, constructs which purely concern the client's past and not the present or future. Thirdly, the clinician should consider whether the test elements, unlike those of a test such as the Rorschach, are representative of events in the client's life and therefore enable confident predictions to be made concerning the client's approach to the world. A related question is whether the test elicits role constructs, these often being central to therapeutic work, and being more likely to be tapped by a test which directly concerns itself with the construing of people than by one which, for example, involves the construing of ink blots. The clinician will also wish to know the extent to which the test, or more precisely the constructs assessed by the test, strike a balance between stability and sensitivity, being concerned with dimensions on which the client shows some consistency but is also open to change, for example during psychotherapy. A final aspect of the test with which the clinician is likely to be concerned is whether it reveals constructs which are communicable to other clinicians and are of some practical use, for example in planning treatment programmes.

Before discussing the clinical uses of assessment techniques developed from personal construct theory, lest this leads the reader to embark hastily on psychological testing with all their clients, we shall first consider some broader issues to which the clinician might do well to attend when deciding whether to administer a test. Firstly, the clinician should be aware that testing itself is likely to cause the client to reconstrue, and should consider whether the time is right for the particular reconstruction which may occur. As has been illustrated by an example provided by Button (1985b) of the use of repertory grid technique, particular caution in this regard should be exercised if test results are to be fed back to the client, who may thereby be made more aware of aspects of construing which he or she may not be ready to confront. Secondly, as Kelly also noted, testing may pose a threat to the relationship between clinician and client since, for example, it may be construed by the client as the imposition by the therapist of societal yardsticks against which the client is being measured. Kelly felt this to be a particular danger with 'objective' tests or with those projective methods, such as word-association tests, in which the client is confronted in rapid succession with a diverse range of concepts and his or her responses recorded and timed. Clearly it is less likely to be the case when a method such as the repertory grid is employed. Nevertheless, whatever type of test is administered, the clinician should phrase its introduction carefully, perhaps using the words suggested by Kelly (1955, p. 982):

> This test is to help me understand you better, how you deal with your problems in life, how I can help you deal with your troubles. I don't want to misunderstand you; I want to feel that I know you well enough to help you.

The clinician is likely to be particularly concerned about the effect of testing on the therapeutic relationship if he or she is the client's therapist, and not simply carrying out the testing in order to make recommendations concerning the client's management. Kelly considered that the earlier in therapy testing occurs, the less potentially damaging its effects on this relationship are likely to be.

## Autobiographical methods

One of the clinician's concerns in assessing a client, as noted above, will be with the client's construction of his or her life role. Attention will therefore be paid to clients' construing of their past, present, and future. A self-characterisation may elicit material which will be of value in such an assessment, and it may be profitable to ask the client to prepare character-isations of the self at different ages or a more extensive autobiography.

As indicated in Chapter 2, analysis of a self-characterisation will focus on various different aspects of it. Kelly suggested that, after an initial reading of the protocol, the clinician should consider the sequences and transitions which it reveals. Next, the organisation of the protocol will be examined, concern being paid to 'topic sentences' and to the opening sentence, which Kelly felt would reflect the greatest level of generality for the client or the safest ground from which to begin. The possible meaning of each statement in the protocol may then be considered both independently and in the context of the total protocol. Repetitions of, and linkages between, terms will be noted, and it may be suspected that repeated terms are those with a wide range of convenience or which the client is unsure that he or she can communicate verbally. The clinician may also try to gain a better understanding of the client by restating themes from the protocol in his or her own words. The topics covered by the protocol will be considered, and it will be assumed that these are likely to be areas in which the client distinguishes him/herself from others but also feels secure enough to elaborate. As Kelly (1955, p. 334) put it, 'the areas chosen are those in which the client sees enough uncertainty to make exploration interesting and enough structure to make it meaningful'. The areas covered may, however, become increasingly problematic, or increasingly specific, as the self-characterisation progresses. Themes, and especially indications of cause-and-effect relationships, will also be considered, and Kelly suggested that the latter may reveal the client's approach to therapeutic change. Of particular importance, however, will be the identification, by consideration of descriptions of similarities and contrasts, of the major dimensions and clusters of dimensions in the protocol, the client's channels of movement. The last of these dimensions to be mentioned in the protocol, in Kelly's view, is likely to reflect an intimate theme which may be addressed in the later stages of therapy. In the dimensional analysis, the clinician will attend not only to the words used by the client but also to language structure and punctuation. Finally, the clinician will apply his or her own professional constructs in an attempt to subsume the client's constructs.

Some examples of the type of hypotheses which may be generated from analysis of a self-characterisation are presented in Chapter 2, and a much more detailed illustration of such an analysis may be found in Kelly (1955). As indicated above, conclusions may be drawn from the analysis concerning the client's likely response to psychotherapy, and the clinician who is particularly interested in this issue may find it useful to employ variations on the self-characterisation procedure, such as asking clients to write character- isations of themselves as they would like to be, or as they imagine they would be if they lost their symptoms or if therapy were successful. For example, Rodney, asked to sketch how he would be without his presenting problem of inability to ejaculate, wrote as follows:

> I am relaxed about life. I enjoy life and all its every day situations. I wake in the morning refreshed from a good revitalising sleep and look forward the [sic] meet the day ahead. I get up, run a bath and enjoy grooming myself.

Cheerfully I am preparing my breakfast and make plans for the day. I have many things to do, but I am independent from routine work. I am selling my creative services and have many contracts. I am well paid and I name the price.

I am very confident and proud of my achievements. Everyday problems do not irritate me and I face every situation head on.

I enjoy having a body and feel good about my body. My body gives me pleasure instead of aches and pains. I am not ashamed to present my body publicly and I am active in some sports activities.

All the worries I have are confined to the actual problems of the day.

Rodney reported that he was unable to complete this assignment because he 'got stuck' and 'could not find the right words', and his sketch provided an indication of how he might also 'get stuck' in therapy if he saw this as likely to remove his symptom. In his view, as revealed by the sketch and by his identical ratings of 'self without symptoms' and 'ideal self' on a repertory grid, life without his sexual problem would appear to be little short of perfection, in stark contrast to his perception of his present life situation. As we have seen in Chapter 4, such an idealistic 'if only' fantasy may only be maintained if the client's symptoms are not removed, and it may therefore result in a poor response to therapy. A self-characterisation may also reveal other threats posed by therapy, as in Julia's response to the invitation to write a description of the 'new' person who might emerge if it were possible to combine positive features of two alternative roles which she initially saw as incompatible. She wrote:

What sort of personality should I like to have?
a)  Don't remove my anger – it is my fuel for life!!!
b)  Soft, rounded and feminine? Forget it!
c)  Would like to cope better, without so much 'extremism'.
d)  Don't remove my sense of humour – that is absolutely vital!

As will be apparent from these examples, and from others to be presented in the next chapter, Kelly's original self-characterisation procedure may be adapted in various ways to meet the particular diagnostic or therapeutic needs of the clinician. It need not even focus solely on the individual client but may, for example, be a characterisation of a marriage (Kremsdorf, 1985) or family, a task which may usefully be completed by each of the parties involved, or a characterisation of a child by its parents (Davis et al., 1989). However, as with all assessment procedures, the fewer the constraints imposed on the client's character sketch, the more accurate a reflection of the client's construing it is likely to be. In any case, whatever the instructions given to the client, the clinician may find that these have not been followed in the way that was anticipated. For example, Rodney, Julia, and Robert, whose self-characterisation is presented in Chapter 2, interestingly each chose not to follow the recommendation to write in the third person.

## Repertory grid technique

The repertory grid, as we have seen in Chapter 2, is also an extremely flexible procedure. The clinician who employs this technique with a particular client therefore has to make numerous decisions. Firstly, he or she must decide what variety of grid is likely to be most useful, or indeed whether to go beyond the original non-grid form of the Repertory Test, which, as an example provided by Kelly (1955) indicates, may generate useful clinical hypotheses. In using a grid, one issue which is likely to be considered is whether to elicit or to supply elements and constructs. While elicitation carries the obvious advantage of ensuring that the constructs employed in the grid are of personal relevance to the client, the clinician who is carrying out a diagnostic assessment may also wish to ensure that at least some of these constructs concern the client's problem area. Therefore, if such constructs do not appear amongst those elicited by standard means, the clinician might usefully supplement these with constructs derived from the client's description at interview of the presenting complaint. In deciding on the elements to employ, clinicians should consider whether their primary interest is, for example, in a client's construing of other individuals, of the self, of relationships, or of situations. For the purposes of diagnostic assessment, the most useful element list may often be one which includes significant other people and such aspects of the self as the self now, the ideal self, the self following treatment, the self before the presenting problem developed, and the self if the problem were to be resolved. It is unlikely that the personal construct-orientated clinician will be wishing to use the grid to arrive at a diagnosis in terms of standard psychiatric nosological categories, but if his or her primary interest is in the presence or absence of schizophrenic thought disorder, the standard Grid Test developed by Bannister and Fransella (1967), complete with cut-off points for the diagnosis of thought disorder, may be employed. Similarly, if the major concern is with the detection of neurotic psychopathology, the clinician may wish to employ a grid of the type with which Ryle and Breen (1971) were able to discriminate blindly between clients and normal subjects, reporting the following year the mean scores of neurotics and normals on measures derived from the grid, several of which significantly differentiated between these two groups.

In deciding to employ particular grid methods, clinicians may do well to consider whether the variations of the procedure which they adopt violate the assumptions which Kelly (1955) considered to underlie the repertory grid, and which are mostly directly relevant to his proposed requirements of a useful psychological test. These assumptions are that the test elicits permeable constructs; that these constructs are preexisting rather than developed during the testing; that the elements employed are representative of people in relation to whom the client must structure his or her life role; that the particular triads of elements used elicit discriminations of the kind which the client would characteristically make in structuring a life role; that a reasonable number of the constructs elicited are role constructs, reflecting the client's constructions of the viewpoints of other people and also allowing the client to construe his or her own behaviour; that all the elements fall within the range of convenience of all the constructs; that the client is sufficiently accessible to engage in the testing procedure; that the client does not shift to a different construct dimension between giving the emergent and implicit poles of a construct, so that what are in fact elicited are the emergent poles of two separate constructs; and that the verbal labels of the client's constructs are correctly understood by the clinician. The significance or otherwise of violating any of these assumptions will depend on the particular uses to which the clinician wishes to put the grid. For example, if the clinician's focus of concern is with the client's construing of various situations, the grid employed is unlikely to be designed to elicit role constructs. Similarly, if the clinician's only interest is in structural features of the client's construing, it is of little or no importance that the clinician should understand the client's construct labels.

Variations on conventional grid procedure are particularly necessary if the clinician is working with children and people with learning disabilities, and useful tips concerning the administration of grids to such clients are provided by Ravenette (1975), Salmon (1976), and Butler (1985) in the case of children, and Spindler Barton *et al.* (1976) working with people with learning disabilities. For example, Salmon notes that with younger children it is advisable to use concrete elements, such as photographs, drawings, or real objects; that simpler elicitation methods than triadic sorts are usually necessary, and that even if it is possible to use the triadic procedure this may produce more concrete constructs than are obtained by alternative methods such as sentence-completion; that it should be remembered that the range of convenience of children's constructs may be limited, so that, for example, constructs applied to other children may not be considered applicable to adults; that, as demonstrated by Wooster (1970), the contrast poles of children's constructs may not be conventional antonyms, and so both poles of each construct should be elicited (or supplied); that ranking procedures are likely to be too difficult for children below seven years of age, and should be replaced by such methods as sorting the elements in terms of each, or neither, pole of every construct; that the sorting is normally more successfully carried out by means of spatial allocation of elements than verbally; and that it may be useful to commence the sorting with a 'buffer construct', not included in the later analysis, to familiarise the child with the elements. Similar considerations apply to the use of the grid with people with learning disabilities, although Spindler Barton *et al.* have found a ranking procedure easier to employ than rating with such clients. They consider an I.Q. of 50 to be the lower limit for the successful administration of a grid.

Having chosen a particular grid format and administered the grid, the clinician's next decision will be to select a method of analysis. This decision should be based on the particular measures which the clinician wishes to derive from the grid, which in turn, as with the initial choice of grid method used, should ideally be determined by the hypotheses which the clinician is testing with the grid. All too often, however, the grid is used as a dragnet procedure, choice of method of analysis is based on availability, and as a result clinicians may eventually find themselves confronted with reams of computer output containing a seemingly overwhelming amount of information. This information is, nevertheless, perfectly manageable if it is approached in terms of a series of steps which each address specific questions. Our overwhelmed clinician may, for example, find it useful initially to produce a graphical representation of the results of the grid, such as the plot of elements in construct space which may be derived from Slater's (1972) INGRID analysis. As indicated in Chapter 2, this plot, if two-dimensional, will only be a rough picture of the client's construing but will, nevertheless, provide the clinician with clues as to those results of the analysis which it may be worth examining in more detail. The following questions may usefully guide the clinician's scanning of the graph and examination of the scores obtained from the analysis, as well as other aspects of the client's grid responses.

1. What are the structural characteristics of the client's construct system?
The particular structural properties to which the clinician attends will to some extent be determined by the method of analysis available, but he or she may, for example, wish to consider how the construct system may be characterised in terms of tightness or looseness, whether its degree of differentiation is accompanied by an appropriate degree of integration, whether it is articulated (see p. 41), whether more than one viable dimension of construing is apparent, and what is the degree of extremity of ratings on constructs.

2. What are the major dimensions of the construct system?
If, for example, a principal component analysis has been employed, the clinician should list those constructs which load most highly on, and therefore define, each of the major components. The constructs with the highest loadings on the first principal component can be considered to be superordinate and, as we have seen in Chapter 2, other measures may also be employed to indicate superordinacy.

3. What is the predominant content of the client's constructs?
As well as a general examination of the content of the constructs elicited from the client, the clinician might usefully consider certain more specific questions. For example, in their 'guidelines for hypothesizing about content', Landfield and Epting (1987) suggest that the clinician should observe whether constructs concerning social relationships are basically concrete descriptions or imply a more complex attempt to interpret other people's behaviour; how often constructs relating to social interaction are employed; whether there is 'overuse' of a particular construct dimension, this being defined by Landfield

and Epting as appearance of the construct at least 20 per cent of the time; whether there is a preoccupation with highly egocentric descriptions, which if overused indicate to Landfield and Epting lack of self-confidence; whether at least one construct contrasting openness and closure to experience has been elicited, since Kelly (1955) considered that change is facilitated if a construct relating to change is available; whether there is an emphasis on 'death, destruction, depression, confusion, withdrawal, and maladjustment', or conversely on 'patience, good-nature, forgiveness, independence, empathic feelings, an ability to withstand pressures, hopefulness, and a loving nature', Landfield and Epting (p. 126) regarding the latter concerns as 'healthier' than the former; whether the client uses constructs which are more appropriate for either an older or younger person, for example the use by an adult of constructs which predominantly concern roles, behaviour descriptions, or situations, or which are self-referent or evaluative; whether the client's constructs tend to include extreme (e.g. 'very') or moderating (e.g. 'sometimes') modifiers, over-use of which suggests to Landfield and Epting rigid problem-solving and indecisiveness respectively; whether there is an overuse of construct poles suggestive of alienation from life, and therefore of possible depression; whether any of the contrasts employed help to explain each other, as when the implicit pole more clearly indicates the implications of the emergent pole; whether in some cases only one pole of a construct has been provided, perhaps indicating that the contrast concerned is a threatening one; and whether language and contrasts which appear peculiar, and so may indicate difficulties in interpersonal communication, are employed. As an aid to this examination of the content of a client's constructs, Landfield and Epting suggest that the clinician should try to imagine what the world would be like if the client's constructs were his or her own, and wherever possible should ask clients to elaborate on their constructs.

While the guidelines provided by Landfield and Epting offer some useful indications of those aspects of construct content which may be of particular relevance in assessing a client's current predicament and likelihood of change, they also clearly reflect the authors' own values and it should be remembered that the suggested implications of, for example, the overuse of certain con-struct dimensions are hypotheses rather than fixed characterisations of the client.

4. How is the self construed?
As well as noting the construct poles applied to the self, the clinician should compare the construal of self and ideal self, examining the distance between these two elements if the analysis provides such a measure, and those particular constructs on which this distance is greatest. Construal of the self will also be considered in relation to any other self elements which have been included in the grid; to other people in general, the average distance of the self from whom provides a measure of perceived self-isolation; to significant people in the client's life, for example comparing the perceived similarity of

the self to the same-sex and opposite-sex parents; and to the stereotype of the group to which the client belongs if a suitable element has been included in the grid. Finally, consideration of the extremity of self ratings may be of value.

## 5.  How are other significant people construed?

The clinician may, for example, find it useful to consider what construct poles are applied to the spouse, and how similar is a client's construal of his or her spouse and parents. In addition, Landfield and Epting (1987) suggest that the clinician might usefully examine the degree to which clients differentiate between their parents, on the assumption that there may be an optimal level of such differentiation. They also note that the clinician should record what proportion of ratings of grid elements are positive and what proportion negative. We have seen in Chapters 2 and 4, for example, what the optimal balance in such ratings may be and what are the possible implications of construing others in a uniformly positive light.

## 6.  How is the presenting complaint construed?

If a construct pole concerning the presenting complaint has been employed, the clinician might usefully note its contrast pole and examine the correlations of this construct with others, noting whether these reveal any positive implications of the complaint or, indeed, any negative implications which appear inappropriate.

## 7.  Are there any other major areas of inconsistency, or departure from social consensus, in relationships between constructs?

Here, the clinician may note any logical inconsistencies in construct relationships, the identification of which will be facilitated if a method of analysis such as the CONFLICT computer program (see p. 44) has been employed; and any construct relationships in which the pole of a construct which is positively evaluated (either by client or clinician) is associated with the negatively evaluated pole of another construct. Such relationships may indicate dilemmas which the client faces. As Landfield and Epting (1987) indicate, departures from social consensus may be revealed not only in construct relationships but also in the valences which clients assign to construct poles.

We shall now consider how the above steps were followed in the interpretation of a client's repertory grid. This will be followed by briefer examples of the use of the grid in clinical assessment.

### Case examples

Nigel, whose behaviour at college, including experimentation with hard drugs, was regarded by his parents as increasingly self-destructive, was eventually referred for psychiatric assessment after submitting a dissertation which exhibited such loose construing as to be virtually unintelligible to his tutor. His parents initiated the referral.

A repertory grid was administered, in which the elements were himself, himself as he would like to be, himself as his parents would like him to be, himself when 'on acid', himself if he were academically successful, his parents, his brother, his girl friend, a man and woman he liked, a man and woman he disliked, and various significant people at college. Constructs elicited from these elements were as follows:

'intelligent – a book that you like would mean nothing to them';
'conventional – free';
'aware – blinkered';
'has a sense of humour – does not';
'selfish – selfless';
'vivacious – introverted';
'sensitive – callous';
'thoughtful – disinterested';
'headstrong – subservient';
'crazy – normal';
'easily affected – tough on the surface';
'neurotic – more evenly balanced';
'passive – overactive';
'self-destructive – egotistical';
'wobbly – under control'.

In addition, the construct 'a person who might take acid – would not take acid' was supplied.

The completed grid was analysed by Slater's (1972) INGRID program, from which the plot of selected elements in construct space presented in Figure 6.1 was derived. Inspection of this plot and the more detailed results of the analysis allowed the following conclusions to be drawn:

1. What are the structural characteristics of his construct system?
   The first, second, and third principal components derived from the INGRID analysis account for 41, 19, and 13 per cent of the variance respectively, suggesting that, although reasonably tightly structured, his construct system contains more than one viable dimension of construing.

2. What are the major dimensions of his construct system?
   The loadings of constructs on his principal dimension of construing indicate that it contrasts 'aware', 'thoughtful', 'self-destructive' people with those who are 'conventional' and 'egotistical'. His second major dimension concerns 'crazy', 'vivacious' people, and his third 'headstrong', 'intelligent' people. Each of these dimensions can be considered to represent some combination of desirable and undesirable qualities, at least from society's perspective, and, as we shall consider further below, may therefore point to areas of conflict for him. The construct which discriminates much the most highly between grid elements, and which

```
                      INTROVERTED      NORMAL   NO SENSE OF HUMOUR
EVENLY BALANCED       OVERACTIVE                WOULDN'T TAKE ACID
UNDER CONTROL

SENSITIVE                                              DISINTERESTED
HEADSTRONG                                      TOUGH ON THE SURFACE

                                                        CONVENTIONAL
                                                         EGOTISTICAL

INTELLIGENT                  Brother         Father
AWARE                Tutor                   Parents' Ideal Son        SELFISH
                     Girl Friend             Mother
─────────────────────────────────────────────────────────────────────────────
SELFLESS                     Ideal Self                      BLINKERED
                             Self            IMPORTANT BOOK WOULD MEAN
                                                       NOTHING TO THEM

SELF-DESTRUCTIVE
FREE

EASILY AFFECTED                                           SUBSERVIENT
THOUGHTFUL                                                   CALLOUS
                                             Self on Acid
                                                              WOBBLY
WOULD TAKE ACID                              PASSIVE      NEUROTIC
HAS SENSE OF HUMOUR   CRAZY                   VIVACIOUS
```

Figure 6.1 Plot of elements in construct space from Nigel's grid

Note: horizontal axis = Component I; vertical axis = Component II

might therefore be expected to occupy a superordinate position in his system, is 'takes acid – does not'.

3. What is the predominant content of his constructs?

He appears to be able to apply fairly complex psychological constructs to himself and others. However, some of these constructs indicate the dilemmas with which he may be faced in that neither of their poles would seem to offer a very desirable option. For example, he contrasts being self-destructive with being egotistical, being head-strong with being subservient, and being passive with being overactive. Also of interest is the contrast between being conventional and being free: elaborating on the latter pole, he said that it implied 'to choose from a spectrum of possibilities what to do – to do what I want to do and if I destroy myself in the meantime so what? I don't value life very highly.'

4. How is the self construed?

He has a fairly high level of self-esteem, the distances (see p. 34) of the self from the ideal self and the self if academically successful being 0.68 and 0.36 respectively. However, as is apparent from the fact that they fall in opposite quadrants in the plot of elements in construct space, how he would like to be is very dissimilar to how his parents would like him to be, the latter being more subservient and conventional, and less intelligent and aware. Also apparent from their positions on the plot is that the self on acid is more clearly and extremely defined than the self, these elements accounting for 9.58 and 2.84 per cent of the sum of squares respectively. Taking acid therefore appears to provide him with a degree of certainty which is not normally available in his self-construing, although, apart from becoming more vivacious, this involves seeing himself in a generally more unfavourable light.

5. How are other significant people construed?

The person who is most similar to his ideal self is the tutor to whom he submitted his dissertation, his admiration of whom reportedly extended beyond her intellectual qualities. His father appears to be the prototype of normality, conventionality, and selfishness for him, while, as can be seen from her position close to the origin of the plot of elements in construct space, he has no clear conception of his mother.

6. How is the presenting complaint construed?

The complaints of others regarding his behaviour concerned his self-destructiveness and drug-taking. However, correlations between his constructs indicate that he sees these characteristics in a very favourable light, associating them with being free, aware, thoughtful, selfless, intelligent, and having a sense of humour. In addition, he construes self-destructive people as evenly balanced and under control.

7. Are there any other major areas of inconsistency, or departure from social consensus, in relationships between constructs?

'Craziness' carries similar positive implications for him as do self-destructiveness and taking acid. Vivaciousness also appears to be associated with a certain amount of conflict for him in that several logical inconsistencies are apparent in construct relationships involving this construct. For example, as indicated in Figure 6.2, he construes intelligent people as not being vivacious and as being crazy and having a sense of humour, although he relates both of the latter characteristics to being vivacious.

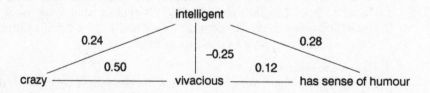

*Figure 6.2* Construct correlations indicating logical inconsistencies in Nigel's construing

A series of vignettes will now be used to illustrate further how clients' grids may elucidate their predicaments. Although each grid revealed several interesting aspects of the construing of the client concerned, the grids will be presented below in relation to those features which appeared most relevant in explaining the problems requiring assessment.

Structural characteristics of the construct system

Stella was referred for psychological assessment to assist in making the decision as to whether she should have custody of a baby whom it was suspected that she had physically assaulted. At interview, she described pregnancy and motherhood as requiring 'a totally foreign outlook to my normal self' and 'a readjustment of my senses from my academic background to being a mother'. In the elicitation procedure for her grid, she tended to use objective constructs, such as 'man–woman' and 'young–old'. When encouraged to produce more psychological constructs, these tended to be idiosyncratic, and several appeared to relate to nurturance and mothering. They included 'always in a state of movement: a feeder but always breaking up the bits of food' versus 'could be caught in still movement'; 'always seeking friendship' versus 'a mother protecting her husband, household, children, and belongings'; 'a soother' versus 'breaks up harmony'; 'wholesome' versus 'bits'; 'has too much of one thing – perhaps they can spare a bit and have enough left for themself' versus 'a person I like to see well-covered in life'; and 'jealous' versus 'in a dead sleep'. The construct 'would be a good parent – bad parent' was supplied, and the major associations for her of being a good parent were found to be being 'hot about life' and 'able to say "I hate you"'. However, few strong relationships between constructs were evident in her grid, the first principal component derived from which accounted for only 22 per cent of the variance. This picture of very loose construing was confirmed by the Bannister-Fransella Grid Test, her Intensity score of 367 and Consistency score of –0.31 on which indicated a looser structure than was observed even in the majority of the thought disordered schizophrenics in the standardisation sample for this test. It seemed, therefore, that her construct system would not provide her with an adequate basis for predicting, and responding to, the needs and behaviour of others, including her baby.

Mark's work as a journalist had recently required him to infiltrate an extremist political organisation in order that he could write an exposé of their activities. Shortly after the publication of his article, which led to the arrest of organisation members with whom he had developed friendships, he was himself arrested for shoplifting, apparently while in a fugue state. Repertory grid assessment revealed an extremely tightly organised construct system, the first principal component derived from INGRID analysis accounting for 74 per cent of the variance. This dimension contrasted 'steady', 'generous', 'daring' people, who are 'good at their work', 'know what's right and wrong', and 'would sit and talk things through and listen' with those who 'think only of themselves', 'talk about others behind their backs', 'could be swayed by their friends to do something stupid', 'might shoplift', and 'might worry about things'. It also contrasted himself and his father with members of the organisation and his stereotype of a shoplifter. It appeared, therefore, that his construct system might have been too tightly organised to enable him to tolerate the inconsistencies involved in his developing a degree of sympathy towards people about whom he would then 'talk behind their backs' to the extent that they were arrested. Faced with such apparent inconsistencies, the only option available to him, which was perhaps reflected in the shoplifting episode, may have been to slot-rattle on his major construct dimension.

Salmon (1963) was asked to assess whether a woman who had requested a sex-change operation might be helped by psychotherapy to adjust to a feminine role. She was administered two grids, in one of which the elements were photographs of men and in the other photographs of women. While the former grid revealed a highly structured subsystem of constructs, little structure was apparent in the latter. Salmon concluded, therefore, that attempts to encourage the client to view herself as a woman would be unlikely to succeed since this would require her to develop a whole new subsystem of constructs. A more appropriate therapeutic aim with such clients may be to help them acquire skills appropriate to their role following sex change. This was the approach adopted by Yardley (1976) with a male transsexual whose grid showed little correlation between 'masculine' and other constructs, these relationships decreasing even further following pre-operative training in feminine skills, which was also associated with reduction in idealisation of the self and increased identification with parents.

Major construct dimensions

Dorothy, aged 49, had taken numerous overdoses and was now an in-patient at a psychiatric hospital. The construct accounting for most variation in her grid was 'worried about me – don't care', and her major dimension of construing contrasted people who are worried about her, and are 'kind', 'well-organised', 'good parents', and have 'a keen sense of humour', with those who are 'depressed'. Her overdoses may therefore be seen as asking the question of whether or not people are worried about her. Her second principal construct dimension revealed a possible dilemma in that it contrasted people who 'get cross', and are 'catty', 'confident', 'strong', and 'clever', with those who are 'easy-going' and 'failures'. She is thus faced with a choice between being a confident, clever, but domineering (her contrast pole to 'easy-going') success or a thoughtful, friendly (contrasts to 'get cross' and 'catty') failure.

Keith's work involved him in crowd control, a task in which he had involved himself with such gusto that he had badly injured several members of the public, this having led to his referral for psychological assessment. His grid indicated that his major dimension of construing contrasted 'stupid', 'liberal', 'whingeing' 'scrotes' (which he said was a term of abuse which was short for 'scrotums') and 'Walter Mitty characters' with 'practical', 'reactionary' people, who are 'capable of making a decision'. The people towards whom he was violent were construed in the former terms and contrasted with himself and his father. His second principal construct dimension contrasted people who 'could be violent' with those who are 'soft' and 'long-winded', but 'have good morals'. Additional positive implications for him of the ability to be violent were truthfulness, practicality, shrewdness, and the abilities to make decisions, to look after oneself, and to say what one thinks. He saw himself as closer to his ideal self than any other element in his grid, and this, coupled with his constellatory construing of the members of the crowds whom he had injured and his generally favourable construal of violence, suggest that, while violence is the complaint made by others about him, he is unlikely to wish to change this aspect of his behaviour and might react in similar ways again.

As is apparent from the growing body of work in this area (Edmonds, 1979; Davies, 1985; Cochran, 1987), repertory grid technique may be of use to the clinician or counsellor whose assessment of a client is with a view to vocational guidance. For example, if the elements in a grid are jobs, the principal construct dimensions used by the client to differentiate between them may indicate the client's vocational dilemmas, as in a case described by Smith *et al.* (1978). Their client, Anthony, was found to construe jobs in terms of two major dimensions, 'outdoor–indoor' and 'bigshots–smallshots'. Although he wished to be an outdoor bigshot, he considered that his history degree was leading him towards becoming an indoor smallshot. His grid also indicated that his vocational construct system was relatively undifferentiated, which, as discussed in chapter 2, may suggest immature vocational development. Following grid completion, Anthony switched to a management sciences course which he construed as being more congruent with his ideal.

Construal of the self and alternative roles

Arthur, aged 43, had been a heavy drinker since his teens but was now threatened with the loss of his job because of his drinking. The principal construct dimension derived from his grid indicated something of a dilemma for him in that it contrasted 'intense', 'complicated' people, who are 'easily depressed' and 'aware of their limitations', with 'determined', 'headstrong' people, who 'know what they want, go out and get it, and don't care who they tread on on the way'. He saw himself when sober in the former terms, contrasting himself with disliked superiors at work. Further dilemmas were suggested by his construal of people with drink problems as intelligent, aware of their limitations, and neither vain nor headstrong. The difficulties which he will face in attempting to reduce his alcohol consumption were indicated by the fact that he viewed himself when drinking as much more similar to his ideal self, to others, and to how his superiors would like him to be than when he is sober. Elaborating on this finding, he said that drink for him is 'a big macho thing – I only feel any identity when I have a drink'.

Sylvia's agoraphobic symptoms were of some twenty years' duration. The dilemma with which she was faced appeared to be crystallised in the second principal component, accounting for 31 per cent of the variance, derived from her grid. As can be seen from Table 6.1, this dimension contrasted people who are able to go anywhere with confidence with those who are weak and unassertive, and it differentiated herself, construed in the latter terms, from her ideal self. Such a high degree of dissatisfaction with the self might normally indicate that she would be highly motivated to change. However, her construction of how her husband would like her to be was of someone even weaker, less assertive, and less able to go out than her present self. It was not unexpected, therefore, that she failed to respond to behaviour therapy and that her husband failed to attend for most of the conjoint sessions which they were offered. More surprising was the receipt of a postcard from Spain apologising for her non-attendance at one of her sessions: it transpired that her husband had been imprisoned for incest and that she had subsequently lost her agoraphobic symptoms.

*Table 6.1* Loadings of selected constructs and elements on second component of Sylvia's grid

| Constructs | Loadings |
| --- | --- |
| 'can go anywhere with confidence – cannot' | 0.95 |
| 'can stand up for self – cannot' | 0.93 |
| 'in control of self – loses control easily' | 0.91 |
| 'never gives in to anything – weak' | 0.85 |
| 'quiet – extravert' | −0.62 |

| Elements | Loadings |
| --- | --- |
| 'how I would like to be' | 0.31 |
| 'how I would be without my symptoms' | 0.30 |
| 'how I was before my symptoms developed' | 0.15 |
| 'myself now' | −1.05 |
| 'how my husband would like me to be' | −1.26 |

Edward was referred for assessment because his psychiatrist found his plans to give up a very successful career in advertising in order to become a farmer puzzling and 'unrealistic'. However, his grid indicated that these plans were perfectly comprehensible in that he viewed people who are 'successful in advertising' as 'irresponsible', 'uncaring', 'demanding', 'rude', 'unhappy', and 'unChristian'. Not surprisingly, he construed himself as a farmer more favourably than his present self.

Albert's presenting problem was fear of hell, but when interviewed he talked less about this than about Bing Crosby, describing how, ever since first hearing a Crosby song in Africa thirty-five years ago, he had modelled himself on the singer and eventually left his homeland to come to England 'on the road to Bing' with the expectation that he could become a successful 'crooner'. As he said, 'I ooze Crosby from every pore of my body', but he felt that as a result he was never able to display to others the true self which lay behind his Crosby persona. His days at work in a boring office job were spent dreaming of his eventual fame when a record company would at last respond positively to the cassettes of himself singing Crosby songs which he regularly sent them. It seemed that one hell of which he was increasingly afraid as the years passed was of a life in which it was no longer possible to maintain these fantasies. As well as 'self as a crooner', I asked him to include in his grid an alternative role which he viewed favourably, and for this he chose 'self as a social worker'. Both these roles were construed as very similar to his ideal, and the opposite of his present, self. They were also viewed more positively than Crosby, who, surprisingly, was seen as 'not clean-living', 'insensitive', and somewhat 'dishonourable'. Albert therefore imagined that, were he to become a crooner, he would outshine his idol in terms of morality. It seemed, however, that this would be at the risk of continual fear of hell and becoming 'mentally ill', since his grid revealed that these two constructs were related to being 'clean-living'.

The assessment suggested that therapy might usefully focus on elaboration of his 'self as social worker' role since this might provide a viable, positively evaluated alternative to his idealistic fantasies of crooning. He has now taken early retirement in order to return to Africa with seemingly realistic aims of engaging in social work.

Ivan, one of the people with learning disabilities whose grid results are presented by Spindler Barton et al. (1976), had an I.Q. of 56 and showed attention-seeking behaviour and difficulties in relating to others. His grid indicated that he tended not to apply his major constructs either to himself or to his friend with a learning disability, both of whom were also seen as very different from other people. In view of the relative meaninglessness of his self, it was concluded that he 'requires role-training and self-assertion plus conditioning to inquire habitually into and classify his own thoughts and actions' (p. 60).

R. Neimeyer (1985a) describes how, working with a client, Lillian, who complained of difficulty in finding an identity, he administered a grid in which the elements were photographs of herself at different periods of her life. Amongst the findings from the analysis of this grid was that considerable slot-rattling was evident between the ages of four and seven, a period during which her mother was divorced and remarried. Constructs concerning the abuse and turmoil which she had experienced during childhood were found to occupy an isolated position in her system, suggesting to Neimeyer that she employed a constrictive strategy to deal with these experiences. Her constructions of her current and future selves were also isolated from her other self-images, and their relative lack of implications indicated the difficulties which she might face in moving in the direction which they represented.

## Construal of significant others

In one of her studies of construing in clients experiencing mood changes (e.g. Rowe, 1969, 1973a), Rowe (1971c) administered a dyad grid to a young woman during a hypomanic episode and again after her recovery, a month later. Numerous differences between these grids were apparent, particularly in relation to constructs concerning anger, fear, and guilt. Her relationship with her mother was construed very differently on the two occasions, in that she perceived herself, for example, as very frightened of her when in her hypomanic state whereas after her recovery their relationship was seen by her as ideal. Rowe considers this to indicate that in the latter state the client was denying negative aspects of her relationship with her mother.

Ali's complaint was of recurring dreams in which he fought with a python, his girl friend having been injured on several occasions by his blows directed at the snake in the night. The python was included as an element in his grid, and was found to be construed as very similar to his ex-wife. Discussion of this finding led him to acknowledge that, although he tried not to think about his ex-wife, he was troubled by guilt feelings concerning his decision to terminate his arranged marriage, and in particular that he felt dislodged from his core role as a dutiful son.

Martin, aged 20, was referred as a 'diagnostic problem' after reporting that he regularly heard a woman's voice. His grid, however, indicated that this was more of a problem for other people than for him since he associated hearing voices with various characteristics which he evaluated positively, such as being 'funny', 'someone one can talk to', 'not getting angry', and 'not a straight suit-and-tie merchant'. Also, in marked contrast to his mother and to most other women whom he knew, the woman whose voice he heard was construed in a highly favourable light: for example, as someone who is 'honest', 'kind', 'not possessive', whom one 'can talk to' and 'would buy a used car from', and who 'listens to you'. He joked that he 'averaged one girl friend every $6\frac{1}{2}$ years', and it seemed that the 'woman with the voice' represented his only confidante, and that therapy might more usefully focus on helping him to relate better with women than on attempting to control his voice pharmacologically.

Ryle (1985, p. 197) reports how the grid of a woman who, after being raped, felt that she 'had lost her grip on life' indicated that she construed her relationships with the rapist and with her mother as very similar. He concludes that 'the physical assault had been experienced as analogous to mother's earlier emotional assaults'.

Beail and Beail (1985) employed dependency grids (see p. 26) to investigate the residents of a hostel for people discharged from psychiatric hospitals. All the individuals concerned were found to display undistributed dependency, with the hostel warden being the person to whom they were most likely to turn for help. It was concluded that their dependency on the warden could be reduced only if they were able to distribute their dependencies amongst other people.

One of the examples of the grids of schizophrenics presented by Space and Cromwell (1978), as well as revealing an abnormally high degree of internal consistency in construing, indicated a high degree of construed similarity to others, or 'projective assimilation', and an extremely favourable view of the self and significant others. Space and Cromwell consider that these features of her construing indicate that she is 'vulnerable to either schizophrenic fragmentation or constriction if she is put into highly complex social situations' (p. 177).

As well as examining a client's construing of other people, it may be useful to consider how others construe the client. For example, Middleton (1985) employed grids to investigate the construal of an educationally subnormal boy by his mother and teacher. Amongst her findings was that they both saw him as opposite to the type of adult whom they liked, and in the mother's case as similar to her disliked ex-husband. Middleton suggests that programmes might be devised which would enable him to behave in ways which might invalidate some of these negative constructions of him.

## Construal of situations

May, a resident in a hospital for people with learning disabilities, was thought suitable for transfer to a pre-discharge ward but seemed resistant to change and exhibited obsessional behaviour. The grid which Spindler Barton *et al.* (1976) administered to her included situations as elements, and showed that she not only construed her obsessional activities, but also surprisingly her new ward, as 'safe', 'happy', and neither 'frightened' nor 'sad', contrasting them with the village. It was concluded, therefore, that she could move to the new ward but that accompanied trips to the village might be valuable and that, as her grid also indicated a high correlation between the constructs 'safe' and 'at home', discharge from hospital should be preceded by visits to accustom her to the new environment.

Butler (1985) reports on the administration of a grid with situations as elements to Shirley, a 12-year-old with anxieties concerning going to school. This indicated that she felt at her worst when away from her mother, and provided an avenue for exploration of the separation anxieties which were being caused by her parents' increasing absences from home, and which were reflected in her presenting problem.

Construal of the complaint

Fred, a client with a learning disability, had a history of fire-setting. Laddering revealed that he regarded such behaviour as 'dangerous' and 'naughty', but he admitted that he sometimes liked to be naughty, although it carried the disadvantage that 'you might get caught and sent back to a lock-up ward'. He occasionally engaged in prostitution in public toilets, and said that the last incident of fire-setting had occurred because he had been upset by 'the man who takes me down the toilets'.

A grid was administered in an attempt to elucidate further his fire-setting behaviour. As he found the triadic method of elicitation too difficult, constructs were elicited either from dyads or from single elements. It was not possible to elicit the contrast poles of any constructs. The grid results revealed that his self-esteem was high, and that only one element was seen as more distant than himself from the element 'a person who might start fires'. The construct 'might start fires' was 'isolated' in the sense that it was not significantly related with any other construct (cf. Makhlouf-Norris and Norris, 1973), its highest correlation, of 0.38, being with 'gets angry'. This would suggest that he could start fires without this carrying any major implications for the way in which he saw himself and without any reduction in his self-esteem. Also perhaps worthy of further exploration was the fact that, although the man who takes him to the toilets was construed as very dissimilar to anyone else, the person to whom this man was seen as most similar was his father.

John, a school prefect, was very highly thought of at school and at his church until one night he broke into the church hall and burnt it down. As is apparent from the plot of elements in construct space derived from his grid (see Figure 6.3), he exhibited a similar pattern to Fred of dissociation from his fire-setting in that, of all the elements in the grid, he saw himself as the least likely to commit arson. Unlike for Fred, however, committing

```
CATTY AND BITCHY    UNANXIOUS          CLEAR THINKER       SUPERIOR
                                          UNLIKELY TO COMMIT ARSON
                                       MEMBER OF A RELIGIOUS GROUP
UNSOCIABLE
MISERABLE                                  RESPECTS AUTHORITY
NOT AS I'D LIKE TO BE
SEXUALLY            Girl I             Headmaster
   FRUSTRATED       Dislike
                                          Mother      Religious Group
                                                          Leader
UNLIKE ME                              Girl I Like   NOT STRUGGLING
                                                        TO ACHIEVE
DOESN'T THINK ABOUT                                  DOESN'T MAKE ME
   WHAT THEY'RE SAYING                                  ANGRY
```
---
```
                                                     Self
MAKES ME ANGRY      Disliked          Scout Leader         INTROVERTED
STRUGGLING TO       Teacher           Man I Admire         LIKE ME
   ACHIEVE
                    Person Who Would
                    Commit Arson
                                          Father      SEXUALLY SATISFIED
                                                      HAS STRAIGHT-
                                                         FORWARD
                                                         HUMOUR

DOESN'T RESPECT AUTHORITY                            AS I'D LIKE TO BE
                                      GOOD AT SPORTS AND ANYTHING
                                          THEY DO
UNLIKELY TO BE RELIGIOUS
   GROUP MEMBER
LIKELY TO COMMIT ARSON
         INFERIOR    MUDDLED           WORRIER       HAS FEELING
                                                     TOWARDS OTHERS
```

*Figure 6.3* Plot of elements in construct space from John's grid

Note: (horizontal axis = Component I; vertical axis = Component II)

arson did carry numerous implications, such as resenting authority, struggling to achieve, and being inferior, muddled, a loudmouth, and unlikely to be a member of a religious group. Although he also dissociated himself from his stereotype of an arsonist, these implications provided a basis for exploration of whether he might, for example, harbour unexpressed resentment towards authority and be finding his schoolwork more of a struggle than his teachers imagined.

Margaret's psychiatrist referred her for exploration of her apparent resistance to therapy, manifested, for example, in regularly precipitating a manic episode by discontinuing her medication. Her grid revealed that her principal dimension of construing contrasted caring, hard-working, ill people, like herself and her father, with selfish, domineering, well people, like her mother. It seemed, therefore, that seeing herself as ill allowed her to maintain a view of herself as a sensitive, caring person. Similarly, mania carried some positive connotations for her, herself when 'high' being construed as more similar to her ideal self than was her normal self. Her resistance to loss of her mania and to becoming 'well' was therefore hardly surprising.

Bannister (1965a) reported on an agoraphobic whose grid indicated that a construct concerning the ability to go anywhere with confidence was orthogonal to all her other constructs, suggesting that she viewed her symptom as unrelated to her personal characteristics. Subsequent grid assessments during a combined psychotherapeutic and behavioural treatment approach indicated that a marked loosening of construct relationships occurred at a point when she complained of confusion and daydreaming. That subsequent tightening involved the re-establishment of her original pattern of construct organisation rather than a new structure was attributed by Bannister to the fact that her psychotherapy was non-directive and therefore did not encourage her to revise her construing.

Another of the clients described by Bannister (1965a) was a 'frigid' woman being treated by an approach aimed at desensitising her to sexual intercourse. Serial grids, consistently with clinical impressions, revealed that this resulted in her 'no longer finding intercourse actively repugnant but merely acceptable and uninteresting' (pp. 980–1).

## Couples' construct systems

Among the variations on grid procedure which may be employed with couples, one which I have found to be particularly valuable is to elicit constructs and elements from each member of the couple separately and then to pool these in a grid which they each complete. Examination of these grids, as well as revealing significant features of their individual construing, may indicate the extent to which they are each able to use the other's constructs and the degree of commonality in their construing. If they each then complete a further grid as they imagine their partner would (cf. Ryle and Breen, 1972a), their ability to construe each other's constructions may be assessed. A less time-consuming method of carrying out such an assessment, as employed by Childs and Hedges (1980) in marital therapy, is to complete with each member of the couple a single grid in which the elements include various aspects of the self and the partner as seen by the individual himself or herself and as they each imagine the partner sees the element concerned. As in other measures of interpersonal perception (e.g. Laing et al., 1966; Drewery and Rae, 1969; Scott and Ashworth, 1969), most of which carry the disadvantage that they do not assess the respondent's own personal dimensions of construing, Childs and Hedges also asked their couple to complete ratings from the meta-meta-perspective (e.g. 'How Andrew thinks I see myself'), allowing assessment not only of the degree of mutual understanding by the couple but also of the extent to which they each appreciate the degree of understanding. Ryle and Lunghi's (1970) dyad grid may also be usefully employed with couples, in which case the two components of each relationship considered (e.g. self to wife and wife to self) are joined by lines on the plot derived from the grid. Very long 'dyad lines' are considered by Ryle and Breen (1972a) to indicate overt conflict in the relationships concerned, very short lines may indicate cosy, collusive relationships, and parallel lines indicate a similarity of the reciprocal roles in the two relationships. If all a client's dyad lines are roughly parallel, with self-to-other always at the same pole of the dyad, this may reveal 'a single higher-order scheme of which he is largely or wholly unaware' (Ryle, 1985, p. 197). Ryle also suggests that it may be useful to analyse grids consisting of self-to-other and of other-to-self elements separately, in which case differences in construct angular distances between the grids of 40 degrees or more are likely to be of psychological significance. By employing a standard set of constructs in such a grid, Ryle and Breen (1972a) are able to compare a couple's grid scores with a certain amount of normative data that they have collected. Further normative data concerning construct relationships have been provided by Ryle (1981), who considers that if an individual's score differs by more than one standard deviation from the mean score of normal subjects it is nearly always indicative of relationship difficulties (Ryle, 1985).

The examples presented by Ryle and Lunghi (1970) of the use of the dyad grid include a woman who suffered from claustrophobia and lack of sexual responsiveness. Her preference for a platonic relationship with her husband may be explained in terms of the fact that the dyad lines for her relationships with him and with her father were parallel, indicating 'unresolved Oedipal problems' to Ryle and Lunghi. The dyad grid of her husband revealed that he construed the relative positions of himself and his wife in their relationship as reversing those of his father and his mother, perhaps indicating that he took a motherly role towards his wife and colluded with her need to desexualise the relationship.

Ryle (1967) also carried out repertory grid testing on a client, Susan, and her ex-boy friend, Brian, shortly after she had made a suicide attempt, with a view to elucidating her reasons for the attempt and for their mutual attraction despite their apparent dissatisfactions with each other. She was found to construe herself as more effective and domineering than him, and similarly he construed himself as considerably weaker than her, such constructions paralleling their perceptions of the roles of males and females in their immediate families. Their relationship therefore appeared to be one of mutual validation of their socially deviant constructions of male and female roles, and Ryle considers it to be significant that Susan attempted suicide after Brian, by responding to a challenge to meet her and being unwilling to resume their relationship, had apparently invalidated her construction of him as ineffective and of herself as domineering. In Ryle's view, Susan may have considered death less painful than the revision of her construct system required by this invalidation, or have seen her suicide attempt as re-establishing her power. Reassessment of their construing following Susan's psychotherapy and the resumption of their relationship revealed few changes, and so it was not unexpected that, as Ryle (1975) reports, Susan made a subsequent suicide attempt in similar circumstances following the couple's marriage.

Jill and Jeff sought help because of her lack of sexual desire. Their grids revealed that they both saw her in a very positive light, and as firmer, stronger, and more organised than him. Correlations between constructs indicated that she found people who, unlike Jeff, are 'extraverted' and 'have libido', to be 'sexually attractive'. However, a dilemma was apparent in that she construed people who 'have libido' and are 'healthy' as rather 'inconsiderate', 'unkind', and 'unconcerned about the family', character-istics which she attributed to both their fathers. For him, sexually attractive people were 'strong', 'determined', and 'authoritative', suggesting that to be sexually attracted to her he may need to see her as the dominant partner in the relationship. There was a high degree of commonality in their construing, and further grids which they each completed as they imagined that their partner would complete them indicated that they could each accurately construe the other's constructions, although he failed to perceive that she would prefer to be less dominant. Despite possible dilemmas concerning sexuality and dominance, their mutual under-standing suggested a good foundation for marital therapy.

Celia, an actress, was referred for exploration of the possible basis of her recurrent depressive episodes with a view to indicating a focus for marital therapy. As can be seen from the plot of elements in construct space presented in Figure 6.4, her grid revealed that, unusually for someone complaining of depression, she construed herself as more similar to her ideal self, and more 'refined', 'sexually attractive', 'glamorous', 'generous', and 'able to make a sacrifice', than any other element. However, an explanation of her very favourable self-construction is provided by her romantic view of depression, which she associated with being 'refined', 'sexually attractive', 'generous', 'able to make a sacrifice', 'glamorous', 'theatrical', 'wild and free', and 'liking to dramatise'. Were she to become less depressed, she would therefore have to see herself in terms of the contrast poles of these constructs, namely as 'coarse', 'sexually unattractive', 'mean', 'selfish', 'unglamorous', 'dull and dead', 'domestic', and 'straight-forward', and as similar to her husband, Peter. Promiscuity and rebellious-

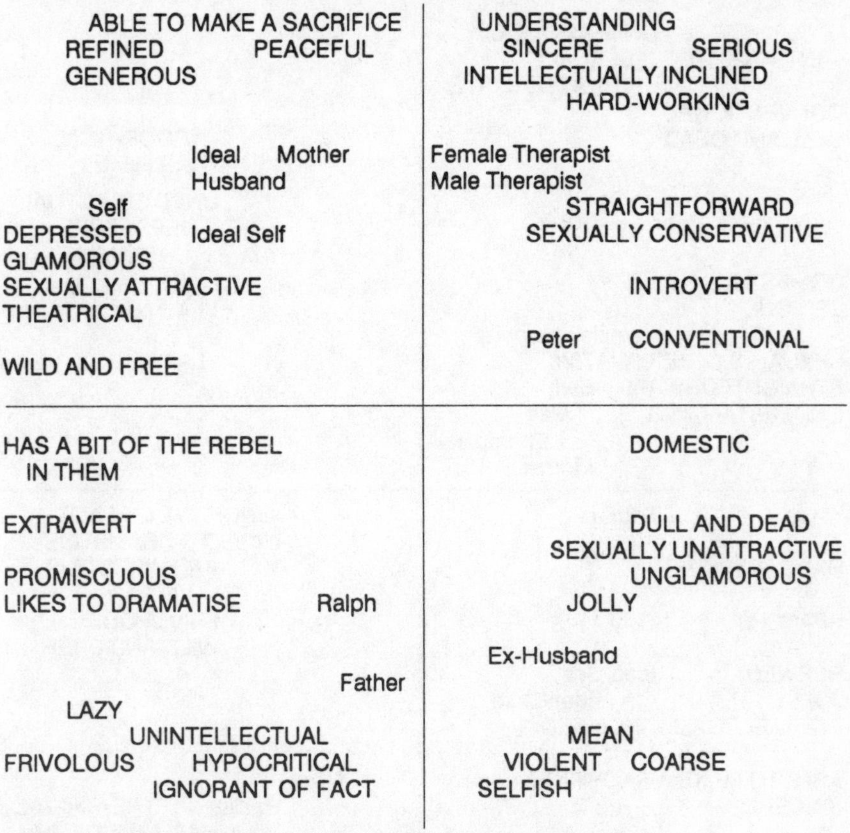

ABLE TO MAKE A SACRIFICE
REFINED                    PEACEFUL
GENEROUS

UNDERSTANDING
    SINCERE                SERIOUS
INTELLECTUALLY INCLINED
            HARD-WORKING

            Ideal     Mother
            Husband
      Self
DEPRESSED        Ideal Self
GLAMOROUS
SEXUALLY ATTRACTIVE
THEATRICAL

WILD AND FREE

Female Therapist
Male Therapist
            STRAIGHTFORWARD
            SEXUALLY CONSERVATIVE

                        INTROVERT

            Peter     CONVENTIONAL

---

HAS A BIT OF THE REBEL
   IN THEM

EXTRAVERT

PROMISCUOUS
LIKES TO DRAMATISE          Ralph

                        Father
            LAZY
            UNINTELLECTUAL
FRIVOLOUS      HYPOCRITICAL
      IGNORANT OF FACT

DOMESTIC

            DULL AND DEAD
      SEXUALLY UNATTRACTIVE
            UNGLAMOROUS
      JOLLY

Ex-Husband

            MEAN
VIOLENT     COARSE
SELFISH

*Figure 6.4* Plot of elements in construct space from Celia's grid

Note: (horizontal axis = Component I; vertical axis = Component II)

ness were also positively evaluated by her, and contrasted with being 'sexually conservative' and 'conventional'. Not surprisingly, given her construal of depression, Celia was always attracted to depressive men, and she eventually left Peter in order to live with Ralph, a very depressive character. However, this led to Peter becoming depressed, to an increase in her attraction towards him, and to her adopting a pattern in which she oscillated backwards and forwards between the two men.

Peter's grid, the plot derived from which is presented in Figure 6.5, revealed that depression carried none of the positive implications for him that it did for Celia, being associated with such characteristics as violence, selfishness, coarseness, and hypocrisy. He construed himself in a fairly favourable light, and, although he would have preferred to be more extraverted and glamorous, an obstacle to his becoming so was that

|                                                              |                                                              |
|--------------------------------------------------------------|--------------------------------------------------------------|
| UNGLAMOROUS<br>INTROVERTED  SEXUALLY<br>UNATTRACTIVE<br>CONVENTIONAL<br>DULL AND DEAD | MEAN<br><br>HYPOCRITICAL<br>SELFISH<br>UNINTELLECTUAL<br>DEPRESSED<br>COARSE |
| DOMESTIC<br>SERIOUS<br>      Female Therapist<br>SEXUALLY CONSERVATIVE<br>STRAIGHTFORWARD  Self<br>UNDERSTANDING  Male<br>      Therapist<br>      Mother | VIOLENT<br><br>LAZY |

Figure 6.5 Plot of elements in construct space from Peter's grid

Note: (horizontal axis = Component I; vertical axis = Component II)

The lower portion reads:

Father

HARD-WORKING

PEACEFUL

REFINED  Ideal Self
JOLLY  Ideal Wife
INTELLECTUALLY INCLINED

ABLE TO MAKE A SACRIFICE
SINCERE

GENEROUS

IGNORANT OF FACT
LIKES TO DRAMATISE
PROMISCUOUS

FRIVOLOUS
WILD AND FREE

Celia

Ralph  THEATRICAL
HAS A BIT OF THE
REBEL IN THEM
SEXUALLY  EXTRAVERTED
ATTRACTIVE
GLAMOROUS

extraversion and glamour were associated with his non-preferred poles of some constructs, such as being 'frivolous', 'theatrical', and 'only seeing what they want to see'. Celia was construed by him as very dissimilar to his ideal wife, who would be more 'serious', 'hard-working', 'domestic', 'intellectual', 'jolly', and 'dull and dead'. However, it seemed that he would not be particularly attracted to such a person since he associated sexual attractiveness with frivolity and rebelliousness.

Although there were some notable areas of low commonality in their construing, their predictions of each other's grids were reasonably accurate.

However, Celia was found to believe, mistakenly, that Peter's ideal wife would be mean and depressed, and that he disapproved of generosity. She eventually decided to commence psychoanalysis, but a further grid completed some two years later showed that this led to no appreciable change in her construing.

Alison, who had been diagnosed as manic-depressive, and Andrew were referred for assessment of their marital difficulties. The inclusion of the construct 'manic–depressed' in their grids allowed interesting differences in their construal of Alison's mood swings to be revealed. Mania was clearly the preferred pole of this construct for Alison, who associated it with being 'sexy', 'home-loving', and 'hard-working'. Andrew, however, viewed depression much more favourably, associating it with being 'understanding'. Also of interest was that he construed 'unpredictable', 'emotional' people as being 'sexy', suggesting that he might not altogether wish his wife to be more stable. Other constructs which carried very different implications for them were 'lone wolf – friendly' and 'treats me like a child – treats me like an adult'. For Andrew, being a lone wolf, as he construed himself, implied being 'hard-working' and 'putting the family first', while for her it was associated with aggression, selfishness, dishonesty, and disinterest. Treating someone like a child, a characteristic which Alison attributed to Andrew, was construed by her as an expression of aggression but by him as an expression of concern.

As well as essentially speaking different languages, Alison and Andrew showed little understanding of each other's construing in grids which they completed from the other's perspective. For example, Andrew mistakenly assumed that depression, being a lone wolf, and treating someone like a child meant the same for her as they did for him; and imagined that she found hard-working, aggressive people to be sexy, whereas in fact the reverse was the case. Alison failed to appreciate the extent to which Andrew felt sad and isolated, and wished to change. It was recommended, therefore, that marital therapy should focus predominantly on his dissatis-factions in the hope that this might reduce the extent to which they viewed themselves as occupying contrasting, and polarised, positions on such constructs as 'emotional–tranquil'. As may be seen from Table 6.2, their post-treatment grids indicated considerable changes in their construing, Andrew coming to see himself more favourably and as much less isolated, and viewing depression and being a lone wolf less, and emotionality more, positively. Alison also came to see both herself and Andrew in a rather more favourable light, and her construing of sexiness and depression changed markedly. However, her apparent slot-rattling from a very positive construal of mania to an even more positive construal of depression is of questionable benefit.

Table 6.2 Changes in Alison's and Andrew's grid scores during therapy

|  | Pre-treatment | Post-treatment |
| --- | --- | --- |
| *Selected measures from Alison's Grid* | | |
| Element distances: | | |
| self–ideal self | 0.94 | 0.70 |
| Andrew–ideal husband | 1.03 | 0.90 |
| Construct correlations: | | |
| 'depressed'–'hard-working' | –0.33 | 0.85 |
| 'depressed'–'home-loving' | –0.66 | 0.81 |
| 'depressed'–'understanding' | –0.10 | 0.36 |
| 'depressed'–'sexy' | –0.93 | 0.90 |
| 'sexy'–'hard-working' | –0.54 | 0.81 |
| 'sexy'–'aggressive' | –0.38 | 0.39 |
| 'sexy'–'home-loving' | –0.22 | 0.76 |
| *Selected Measures from Andrew's Grid* | | |
| % sum of squares accounted for by self | 14.68 | 7.58 |
| Element distances: | | |
| self–ideal self | 1.02 | 0.73 |
| Alison–ideal wife | 0.80 | 0.92 |
| Construct correlations: | | |
| 'depressed'–'understanding' | 0.32 | –0.18 |
| 'lone wolf'–'hard-working' | 0.42 | –0.23 |
| 'lone wolf'–'puts the family first' | 0.24 | –0.29 |
| 'lone wolf'–'understanding' | 0.19 | –0.40 |
| 'emotional'–'aggressive' | 0.43 | –0.21 |
| 'treats one like a child'–'understanding' | 0.66 | 0.12 |
| 'sexy'–'unpredictable' | 0.46 | 0.11 |

John and Ruth were undergoing sex therapy along Masters and Johnson (1970) lines because their marriage of two years was unconsummated. Therapy progressed fairly smoothly until some degree of penetration was achieved, when John appeared to lose interest completely. The basis for this apparent resistance to therapy was suggested by dyad grids which the couple completed, and in particular by the second principal component derived from John's grid, which contrasted being 'affectionate', 'frightened of hurting', and 'worrying about the least little thing' with being 'sexually attracted'. Therefore, although both John and Ruth construed their relationship when it was going well as involving more affection and fear of hurting each other than when it was going badly, John's dilemma was that feeling like this towards Ruth would be associated with feeling less sexually attracted towards her. In addition, both he and Ruth associated being sexually attracted to someone with being submissive, and this, together with his fear of hurting Ruth, suggested that it would be difficult for him to take the more dominant, forceful role in their relationship which their therapists considered would be necessary for their problem to be resolved.

The family construct system

Although there were earlier repertory grid investigations of family construct systems (e.g. Davison et al., 1971), and attempts to assess family structure by grids (Karastergiou-Katsika and Watson, 1985; Bryant, 1985; Watson, 1985; Gale and Barber, 1987), exploration of construing in families by repertory grid technique, using methods similar to those which have been employed with couples, has been pioneered primarily by Procter (1985b). His approach consists of the administration of a grid to each family member; the selection of constructs from these individual grids for use in a 'family grid', also completed by each family member, in which the elements are the family members and how the respondent imagines each member sees himself or herself and each of the others; and the completion by the family of a 'common family grid' using pooled constructs. He analyses family grids with a computer program which provides measures of perceived similarity of family members; commonality in their construing, which Procter considers may indicate coalition patterns in the family; perceived commonality, indicating the extent to which members think that they agree; sociality, or accurate perception of other members' construing; meta-commonality, comparing the predictions made by two family members concerning another's construing; and comparisons of members' self-concepts. The following example is drawn from Procter's use of such methods.

All members of Henry's family were found to employ an 'us–them' construct such that those inside the family were seen as good and those outside as bad, indicating that difficulties may be experienced if people either join or leave the family. However, his parents both included their fathers in the 'bad' cluster, placing him in the contradictory position that to be loyal to the shared family construct system he would have to reject his father. Procter considers that Henry's thought disorder may have reflected a loosening of his construing in an attempt to cope with this contradiction. He further speculates that the finding from family grids that Henry was the least agreed about member of the family may indicate that Henry, by his bizarre behaviour, was successfully making his family's construing looser and therefore more adaptive. Henry's parents underestimated the degree of disagreement in the family, suggesting to Procter that they were operating in terms of a 'family myth', but they were very accurate in predicting each other's construing. They also showed perfect agreement on how they imagined their two children viewed the family, but were mistaken in these perceptions, indicating that they may have disconfirmed their children's constructions by projecting inaccurate views upon them. All members of the family also viewed Henry and his mother as highly dissimilar, although in fact their self-constructions were very similar.

As Rowe (1973b) has indicated, anorexics' construing of their parents may be relevant to their problem. Equally so, however, may be the parents' construing of the anorexic, as Ben-Tovim *et al.* (1977) have demonstrated in reporting the results of repertory grids administered to an anorexic woman and her parents. In one set of grids, each person rated the shape of the various family members at different points in time on constructs concerning body shapes which had been elicited from them by interview. The parents then participated in a procedure whereby they each estimated the width of parts of their daughter's body, and which showed that they each tended to over-estimate her width. Her body parts at the estimated widths, and at their actual widths, were subsequently rated by the parents on the same constructs as used in the first grid, and it was found that the smaller the width of her body parts the more favourably the parents construed them. The authors speculate that such parental views may play a part in the persistence of anorexia.

## *Monitoring therapeutic change*

It will be apparent from the above examples that, in highlighting those aspects of construing which underlie a client's presenting problem, the repertory grid will indicate the nature of the reconstruction which would be expected to accompany successful therapy. As we have seen in the previous chapter, numerous studies have employed serial grid assessments to monitor such reconstruction, although relatively few have employed the idiographic approach of framing predictions of 'therapeutic' changes in construing on the basis of inspection of a client's pre-treatment grid. However, such an approach is not only within the spirit of personal construct theory but is also consistent with the view of psychotherapy researchers such as Bergin and Lambert (1978) that therapy outcome measures should be tailored to the individual client. By contrast, the employment of the same general measures of outcome with every client has been considered to exemplify what Kiesler (1966) terms the 'uniformity myths' in psychotherapy research. A further advantage of the grid as a therapy outcome measure is that scores may be derived from it which tap different levels of cognitive awareness of construing and which therefore, unlike symptom measures, are relevant to the focus of a variety of different types of therapy, ranging from those which are directed towards behavioural change to those which aim for changes at a lower level of cognitive awareness. It has therefore been found to be of value in monitoring change in treatments as varied as pharmacotherapy, behaviour therapy, cognitive therapy, psychodynamic psychotherapy, therapeutic communities, and, of course, personal construct psychotherapy (Winter, 1985a). Also, while changes in grid scores during therapy are not unrelated to other measures of change, they may detect aspects of therapeutic improvement which could not be revealed by such instruments as questionnaires (Large, 1976).

It will be apparent that, as noted by workers who have recommended the repertory grid as a research and clinical tool for psychiatric nurses (Costigan, 1985; Pollock, 1986), the technique is likely to be of value not only to the psychotherapy researcher but also to the clinician who wishes to introduce an evaluative component into his or her work. However, just as in the use of the grid in clinical assessment, a possible disincentive to the clinician or researcher who considers employing individualised grid-based outcome indices is the apparent lack of any systematic framework to facilitate the derivation of such indices from the plethora of measures provided by a grid. Therefore, on the basis of those individualised predictions of changes in construing which Caine *et al.* (1981) found tended to be confirmed in clients who responded favourably to treatment, I have produced the set of guidelines presented below, which may be of value to those who wish to make such predictions on the basis of a client's pre-treatment grid. Although the scores referred to in the guidelines are derived from Slater's (1972) INGRID computer program, with which Caine *et al.* analysed their grids, the guidelines are not limited to the use of this particular method of analysis since comparable scores may be obtained from other methods.

The following three types of construct will be considered:

Self-construct: 'like me' – 'unlike me';
Symptom construct: symptom pole (e.g. 'depressed') – contrast pole
  (e.g. 'happy');
Low desirability construct: pole describing undesirable characteristic
  (e.g. 'unkind') – pole describing desirable characteristic (e.g. 'kind').

Construing of the self

(1)   If the distance between the elements self and ideal self is initially high, it will decrease.
(2)   If there is a high relationship (cosine or correlation) between the self element or construct and a symptom construct, this will decrease.
(3)   If there is a high relationship between the self element or construct and a low desirability construct, this will decrease.

All of the above predictions concern an increase in the client's self-esteem and a reduction in the extent to which the self is construed as characterised by the symptoms. This latter is comparable to a decrease in scores on a symptom inventory, but may be of greater personal relevance to the client in that the symptoms are stated in their own terms.

(4)   If the distance between the elements self and ideal self is initially low, it will increase.

(5)    If there is a negative cosine/correlation between the self element/ construct and a symptom construct, this will become less negative.

(6)    If there is a very extreme negative cosine/correlation between the self element/construct and a low desirability construct, this will become less negative.

Predictions 4–6 concern a reduction in self-esteem, or in dissociation from the symptoms, in the client whose self-construing is much more favourable than might be considered realistic in view of their referral for psychological therapy . . . Such changes are likely to occur in the initial stages of therapy, but may be followed by some degree of recovery of self-esteem.

Self and others

(7)    If the distance between the self and a parent element is initially high, it will decrease.

(8)    If the self–opposite-sex parent distance minus the self–same-sex parent distance is equal to or less than −0.20, it will increase.

(9)    If the sum of squares accounted for by the self element is initially higher than twice the average sum of squares, it will decrease.

Predictions 7–9 were made in view of previously demonstrated associations between psychopathology and both perceived dissimilarity of the self and others and cross-sex identification (e.g. Ryle and Breen, 1972b).

Dilemmas, conflicts and non-consensual construing

(10)    If there is an extreme negative correlation between symptom and low-desirability constructs, this correlation will become less negative.

(11)    If there is an extreme negative correlation between two low-desirability constructs, this correlation will become less negative.

These correlations may indicate the dilemmas faced by a client whose presenting complaints have certain positive implications, or payoffs, for them. As has been clearly indicated in the work of Rowe (1971a), Tschudi (1977), and Ryle (1979a), therapeutic change in such an individual will require the resolution of the dilemma. Dilemmas of this type generally involve the association of the symptom with some quality of tenderness or morality. . . .

(12)    If there is a high, inappropriate correlation between a symptom construct and a low-desirability construct, this correlation will decrease.

An extreme and inappropriate negative construction of a symptom may indicate an elaborated view of the self as a failure or as ill, and thus be as indicative of psychological disorder as an inappropriate positive construction.

A reduction in such a construct correlation ... may therefore be associated with increased self-acceptance and positive therapeutic outcome.

(13)  Any other non-consensual relationship between constructs will change in the direction of social consensus.

(Winter, 1985a, pp. 163–5)

The above guidelines may help to overcome to some extent the problem of low 'scorer reliability' (Anastasi, 1968) of clinicians or researchers whose inter-pretations of a client's repertory grid results, and consequent predictions, have little basis other than their own construing. However, it will be apparent that the user of the guidelines is not entirely freed from the necessity of making subjective judgements, for example in regard to what constitutes a socially desirable characteristic or an extreme score. In regard to the former question, what is desirable for the client may not be desirable for the investi-gator, and Landfield (1979) has reported that even in a sample of 'normal' subjects a panel of judges failed to predict the valences which the subjects assigned to 15 per cent of their constructs. In attempting to employ those guide-lines which refer to the desirability of characteristics described by construct poles, the investigator may therefore wish to take the option of basing judge-ments of desirability solely on the valences assigned by the client to, or his or her ideal self placement on, the constructs concerned. In regard to what consti-tutes an extreme score on a particular grid measure, absolute criteria are hardly appropriate since judgements of extremity should take into account the extent to which a score may represent a deviation in content from social con-sensus, as well as the overall structural properties of a client's grid. For example, even a relatively low correlation of 0.3 between the constructs 'moral – immoral' and 'prepared to kill for their beliefs – not prepared to' may indicate construi-ng which is highly deviant in its content, and therefore of clinical, if not statistical, significance. Similarly, if a client's construct system is very loosely structured, a correlation between constructs of 0.3 may be worthy of note since it may represent one of the strongest construct relationships in the client's system. If absolute criteria of extremity are required, however, an extreme construct correlation may be considered to be one which attains the 5 per cent level of significance for a one-tailed test (where N is the number of elements in the grid). If the INGRID program is employed, an extreme cosine may be similarly defined, while an extreme element distance may be regarded as one which is greater than 1.50 or less than 0.50 (Slater, 1972). Alternatively, if a grid form is employed for which normative data are available (e.g. Ryle, 1981), scores which deviate by more than one standard deviation from these norms may be considered extreme and likely to become less so if therapy is successful (cf. Brockman et al., 1987).

The guidelines presented above for deriving outcome criteria from a grid have been based on the assumption that a fairly conventional grid has been administered prior to treatment, and that the same elements and constructs will be employed in a post-treatment grid. A disadvantage of such an approach is that it does not allow any assessment of whether new constructs have been developed over the course of therapy, an unfortunate omission since Kelly considered this to be the most significant reconstruing which may occur during treatment. To overcome this problem, the clinician or researcher may choose to re-elicit constructs at the post-treatment assessment and then to administer a grid which includes both the original constructs from the pre-treatment assessment together with any new constructs which have been elicited. These latter constructs may always be excluded from any subsequent analysis of the grid which produces scores, for example on structural measures, which may be affected by the increase in size of the second grid.

Further variations on grid procedure may also be of value in elucidating the process of reconstruction. One such approach, as in the study by Slater (1970) mentioned in Chapter 5, involves the completion by a client of serial ratings of one or more elements on a standard set of constructs over the course of therapy, and the inclusion of all the ratings thus obtained in a single grid. Further illustrations of the use of this procedure are provided by Ryle and Lipshitz (1975, 1976b), who have studied marital therapy with 'reconstruction grids' completed by each member of the couple, in which the two components of the couple's relationship (e.g. wife to husband and husband to wife) are rated before therapy sessions. As in the dyad grid, the components of the relationship on each occasion may be joined by a dyad line on a plot of elements in construct space derived from the grid. In the first of their examples, Ryle and Lipshitz indicate how this method revealed that a couple each came to see their reciprocal roles as more similar as therapy progressed. By dividing the data into two grids, one containing the ratings from the first half of therapy and the other those from the second half, and analysing these separately, they were also able to examine differences in construct relation-ships between these two periods. This indicated, for example, that the couple came to view dominating and attacking behaviour more, and helpful and comfort-seeking behaviour less, favourably over the course of therapy. In the second example provided by Ryle and Lipshitz, the sessional reconstruction grids, completed by the couple and the two therapists, included not only ratings of the couple's mutual relationship but also of the relationship between the therapists and of the couple's relationship with each of the therapists. In addition, the couple completed 'background grids' at longer intervals which included the same elements as in the reconstruction grids together with the relationships of the couple with their respective parents, the relationships between the parents, and the couple's relationship when going well and when going badly. Very little reconstruing was apparent in the sessional grids, in contrast to the background grids, which revealed changes by the midpoint of therapy in the couple's view of their own, and of their parents', relationships. The couple finally separated, and Ryle and Lipshitz conclude that this outcome could have been facilitated earlier had individual sessions been held with the couple at the time of the changes in the background grids. Burns *et al.* (1980) have also examined changes in construing during marital therapy, in this case conducted along Masters and Johnson (1970) lines, by obtaining ratings of each member of the couple from a couple and their therapist prior to, and following, therapy. The three sets of ratings thus obtained on each test occasion were then combined into a grid, and analysis of the two grids indicated that the partners each came to agree more with the therapist in how their spouses than in how they themselves were viewed. More interesting, particularly in view of the fact that therapy was not aiming to produce any fundamental reconstruing, is that the principal component derived from the grid changed from being largely concerned with sexual constructs to a predominant concern with communication. The treatment, incidentally, achieved its aim in that the couple were able to have sexual intercourse for the first time in the five-year history of their marriage.

## Other methods of assessing construct implications

As well as the repertory grid, other techniques described in Chapter 2, such as the implications grid, laddering, pyramiding, and Tschudi's (1977) ABC method, may be of value in the assessment procedure by revealing implicative links between a client's constructs, and we shall consider below a few illustrations of the employment of these techniques in assessing a client's presenting problem.

Ravenette (1977), for example, has employed implications grids with delinquent boys, using a procedure in which the 'constructs' in the grid are common delinquent activities. He reports how, with one client, this enabled him to demonstrate that delinquent activities were divided into two major clusters, one concerning 'adolescent', and the other 'near professional', delinquency. The activities with which he identified himself linked these two clusters, indicating that he was at a choice point in his delinquent life. Wright (1970) described how laddering enabled him to elucidate the personal meaning of a phobic client's complaint. One of this client's major fears was of being 'enclosed', which she contrasted with being 'totally relaxed'. However, laddering revealed the implicative dilemma that being totally relaxed implied that she could 'do as I please', which in turn implied 'shirking responsibility'; while being enclosed implied 'doing something I'm made to do', which, as well as negative implications such as tension, implied 'taking responsibility'. Wright considered that this client's symptoms constituted an attempted solution to her dilemma in that they allowed her to avoid doing things which she felt that she should do while at the same time not having to see herself as doing as she pleased and therefore shirking responsibilities. Laddering has also been employed by Fransella (1985a) in her clinical work, and allowed her to demonstrate, for example, that for one of her male clients being 'masculine' carried the undesirable implication of being an 'aggressive child', which he saw as implying always having to 'wear masks'.

Tschudi (1977) and Tschudi and Sandsberg (1984) also provide numerous examples of how the ABC model may reveal the implicative dilemmas underlying a client's symptoms. For example, a person's problem of being unable to handle money was found to carry such negative implications as not being able to get what one wants but also positive implications including avoidance of being 'boring, pedestrian, and trivial'. Cummins (1988) has found this method to be of value in his work in a primary care setting, for example revealing that a client's high blood pressure was construed not only as carrying various disadvantages, such as long-term strain on his body, but also such advantages as ensuring a job well done and consequent financial gain. These latter advantages provided an explanation for the client's failure to comply with the treatment programme devised by his doctor.

## SELECTION OF AN APPROPRIATE THERAPEUTIC APPROACH

As we have seen, Kelly viewed a transitive diagnosis as eventually leading to an answer to the question 'How is the client going to get well?' It is apparent that he considered that the answer would be 'with difficulty' if, during the assessment procedure, the client seems unwilling to confide, has difficulty in verbal communication or equally in acting out constructions as well as talking about them, or does not seek to validate constructions against the therapist's responses. It is also clear, however, that he would not have rejected a client for psychotherapy on such grounds as verbal inarticulacy. The personal construct-orientated assessment procedure is therefore more likely to be concerned with selecting which particular therapeutic approach may be appropriate for a client than with drawing preemptive conclusions concerning the client's suitability or otherwise for therapy in general.

In selecting a treatment approach, Kelly felt that the clinician should first consider the extent of the investment which the client is likely to make. For example, if this is not of relatively long duration, approaches which involve construct loosening or, as in exploration of the client's early history, are likely to involve preverbal dependency constructs, are best avoided. Consideration of the client's level of cognitive awareness of particular problems, and preferred mode of expression, may indicate the extent to which therapy should focus on verbal communication. The clinician, in Kelly's view, should also assess the type of transference relationship which might best be encouraged, for example whether this should be one of extreme dependency. In addition, the extent to which the treatment approaches available are likely to lead to such negative emotions as threat, fear, anxiety, and guilt will need to be considered. To take one of the examples which Kelly presents, an elderly person who is feeling guilty because of awareness of loss of former roles is unlikely to be helped by a form of psychotherapy which questions the person's whole life role even further. A further consideration will be the permeability of the client's superordinate constructions, for if this is low an approach involving loosening may result in a structural collapse of the client's system. The extent to which therapy should focus on elaboration of the complaint should also be assessed, as should what other areas should be opened up to spontaneous elaboration and aggressive exploration, bearing in mind the extent to which such aggression may be a guilt-provoking prospect. Additional questions to which Kelly considered the clinician should attend in selecting a therapeutic approach are the degree to which the client will be likely to obtain validation outside the therapy room of any new constructs developed during therapy; and the extent to which submerged poles of the client's constructs should be exposed, and are capable of being dealt with by the therapeutic approach considered.

Kelly (1955) also made it clear that the clinician should attend to the client's expectations of therapy and of the therapist, and should 'take the view that he starts with whatever limited conceptualization of psychotherapy the client is initially able to formulate. The evolvement that is psychotherapy itself must first operate within this frame' (p. 567). For example, the permeability of the client's constructions of psychotherapy will determine the extent of the changes which the client is likely to be willing to attempt during treatment. The list of possible conceptualisations of psychotherapy which Kelly provided indicate how varied these may be: psychotherapy may, for example, be seen as 'an end in itself . . . a way to obtain a fixed state of mind . . . a virtuous act . . . a means of altering circumstances . . . confirming one's illness . . . the proof of the objective difficulty of one's role . . . drastic movement within one's present construct system . . . an environment in which already imminent changes may take place . . . the ultimate state of passivity' (Kelly, 1955, pp. 569–73). Similarly, the therapist may be construed as 'a parent . . . a protector . . . an absolver of guilt . . . an authority figure . . . a prestige figure . . . a possession . . . a stabilizer . . . a temporary respite . . . a threat . . . an ideal companion . . . a stooge or foil . . . a representative of reality' (Kelly, 1955, pp. 575–81). As well as being apparent in direct statements concerning their anticipations, clients' constructions of therapy may be inferred from the nature of their presenting complaints, and the way in which these, and illness in general, are construed. For example, as we have seen in Chapter 5, if constructs relating to the complaint appear to occupy a superordinate position in the client's system, he or she is most likely to expect, and to respond to, an approach which focusses on the complaint rather than on what might appear to the client to be more peripheral, less relevant, areas of his or her life. If the client tends to apply to the problem area constructs concerning structure, lack of self-sufficiency, and objective characteristics, the most favourable response is likely to be to a structured, directive approach, whereas the use of constructs concerning problems in social interaction is more indicative of a positive outcome with an introspective, interpersonally orientated approach such as group psychotherapy. A further dimension which we have suggested the clinician might usefully consider in the treatment selection procedure is the relative emphasis on internal or external reality in the client's construing and complaints, the former emphasis suggesting expectancies favourable to, and the likelihood of a positive outcome with, an introspective, or group, treatment approach, while the latter is indicative of more favourable response to an extraspective approach (Caine *et al.*, 1981; Winter, 1985c, 1990c).

The research evidence presented in the last chapter also suggests other aspects of construing to which the clinician would be well advised to attend in deciding upon an appropriate treatment approach for a client. For example, structural characteristics of the client's construct system should be considered since if a very tight pattern of construct organisation is apparent, any intervention which invalidates the client's constructions is likely to be threatening, anxiety-provoking, and, as we have seen, may lead to a structural collapse of the entire system. However, the tightly construing client may well respond to a structured, directive approach such as behaviour therapy, which poses relatively few risks of invalidation. As Landfield (1975) notes, a client who needs the security of structure is unlikely to respond to an ambiguous, non-directive treatment approach. While a psychotherapeutic approach in which the client's constructions are likely to be challenged may be considered appropriate for the client whose construing is less tightly organised, clearly this will not be the case if the client's system is very loosely structured, when the clinician's efforts will best be directed at building up the structure of the system rather than invalidating, and loosening further, the client's few islands of structured construing. The client's construing of the self is also pertinent to treatment selection. Not only do the particular constructs which the client applies to the self indicate the role which he or she expects to play in therapy, the extent to which these constructs reveal a favourable view of the self also carry implications for response to treatment. If the self is viewed in a very favourable light, for example, little response may be expected to an approach which attempts to produce extensive personal change. If the self is viewed unfavourably and the client has no viable alternative role available, such as one which was enacted successfully in the past, an approach which does not attempt to elaborate such a self-construction will be unlikely to succeed.

As well as selecting the initial treatment approach for the client, the clinician may also draw conclusions from the assessment procedure concerning the type of therapist who would be best suited to carry out this treatment. The considerations upon which such conclusions may be based, and which are likely to include the extent to which a therapist is able to comply with the particular transferences which seem most useful with the client, may again be illustrated by a quote by Kelly (1955). He states that 'A clinician who tends to plunge his clients into childlike forms of dependency should not be assigned to a case in which the client must maintain adult-like dependency relationships. A clinician who is confused by abstract verbalizations should not be assigned to a client who must reorganize his permeable constructs' (p. 819).

As we have seen in the last chapter, there is also some research evidence that therapy may be more likely to succeed if a therapist is selected who employs similar constructs to the client's own.

As in other aspects of the assessment procedure, the features of construing which are of relevance in treatment selection decisions may be tapped by interview or by psychological testing. Thus, as indicated in Chapter 5, various repertory grid measures have been found to be predictive of the outcome of particular therapies. In addition, treatment expectancies and the extent to which an individual's construing emphasises internal or external reality may be assessed by the Claybury Selection Battery devised by Caine *et al.* (1982), and for which they provide cut-off points which they suggest may indicate the likelihood of response to an extraspective approach such as behaviour therapy on the one hand or an introspective approach such as group psychotherapy on the other. Such measures are as applicable to therapists as to clients, and may therefore provide a basis for the matching of clients and therapists.

Finally, it should be noted that in matching a client with a particular treatment approach or therapist, the clinician's concern will be with the *initial* approach adopted. However, as the client reconstrues during therapy, a change in approach may be appropriate. Although a client may well drop out of a treatment approach which is not congruent with his or her expectations, would any fundamental reconstruing be likely if the client finds that therapy continues to be entirely as expected? Would not such an approach simply validate the client's existing constructions? These issues will be considered further in the next chapter.

## SUMMARY AND CONCLUSIONS

Diagnoses made by the clinician who adopts a personal construct theory approach are transitive, indicating the avenues of movement available to a client. Diagnostic assessment will involve consideration of the client's behaviour, interview responses, and descriptions of the client by others, and may also include the use of formal test procedures. The usual sequence of stages in the assessment will be an initial focus on the elaboration of the complaint which is being presented, followed by more general elaboration of the client's personal construct system. The clinician will adopt a credulous attitude during this procedure, but will then attempt to subsume the client's constructs by the use of professional diagnostic constructs.

Amongst the formal procedures which may be used during the assessment are autobiographical methods such as self-characterisations, which may be adapted to the clinician's particular diagnostic and therapeutic concerns. Methods such as implications grids, laddering, and pyramiding may allow the tracing of implications of clients' constructs. Repertory grid technique may also be employed, and may allow the clinician to assess the structural characteristics of the client's construct system; the nature of its major dimensions;

the predominant content of the client's constructs; the client's construing of the self and significant others; his or her construing of the presenting complaint; and major areas of inconsistency or departure from social consensus in construct relationships. As well as their use with individual clients, grids may be usefully administered to couples or families, allowing the assessment of degree of commonality of construing and sociality. They may also be employed to monitor reconstruction during therapy, as by the framing of individualised predictions of desirable changes in construing on the basis of a client's pre-treatment grid, or the use of a grid in which the elements are treatment sessions.

A transitive diagnosis should lead to the selection of an appropriate treatment approach for the client. Treatment selection decisions may usefully include consideration of structural aspects of the client's construct system, including the permeability of superordinate constructs; levels of cognitive awareness of constructions; the nature and superordinacy of constructs which he or she applies to the complaint; his or her self-construing; and the relative emphasis on internal or external reality in the client's construing. Also considered will be the client's likely investment in therapy; availability of sources of validation outside therapy; the type of transference relationship which is appropriate; the client's preferred mode of expression; and his or her expectations of therapy. As in other aspects of the assessment procedure, assessment of an appropriate therapeutic approach may include both inter-viewing and the use of formal test procedures. It will result in recommend-ations concerning the initial type of intervention to be employed with the client, but with the acknowledgement that modification of the approach adopted is likely to be be required as therapy progresses.

# Chapter 7

# Personal construct psychotherapy

Therapy was viewed by Kelly (1955) as 'a psychological process which changes one's outlook on some aspect of life' (p. 186), or in other words *'the psychological reconstruction of life'* (p. 187, italics in original). Although he described its goal as *'to alleviate complaints – complaints of a person about himself and others and complaints of others about him'* (Kelly, 1955, p. 831, italics in original), he clearly did not see personal construct psychotherapy as purely having the practical aim of symptom-reduction. Indeed, his view was that 'psychotherapy should make one feel that he has come alive' (Kelly, 1980, p. 29). As Epting (1984) notes, this coming alive is a manifestation of the client beginning actively to elaborate his or her personal construct system. For him, the aims of personal construct psychotherapy are 'to help the person pour his or her creative abilities into the real world' and 'to become his or her own therapist' (p. 8).

Reconstruction during therapy may take many forms and, as will be evident from Chapter 5, may be achieved in many ways, although Adams-Webber (1986) considers that a primary focus is likely to be on the client's construing of the self, or core role reconstruction (R. Neimeyer, 1987a). We shall discuss below the various types of changes in construing which the personal construct psychotherapist may attempt to produce, and the methods which he or she may employ in order to do so.

## VARIETIES OF THERAPEUTIC RECONSTRUCTION

The varied nature of the reconstruing which may occur during therapy may conveniently be considered in terms of eight approaches to their task which Kelly (1969a, p. 231) indicated that the therapist and client might adopt. These are as follows:

(1) The two of them can decide that the client should reverse his position with respect to one of the more obvious reference axes.

The most superficial type of change in a client's construing which may result from therapy is slot-rattling, or 'contrast reconstruction' (Kelly, 1955), the construal of some person or event in terms of the opposite pole of a construct to that which was originally seen to characterise it. Its superficiality results from the fact that there is no attempt to reformulate the construct concerned, which remains as a viable pathway of movement along which the client may therefore easily slot-rattle back to his or her initial view of events. For example, the client whose self-construal switches from being 'anxious' to being 'relaxed', but who does not modify the 'anxious–relaxed' construct or its relationships with other constructs, will be likely at some stage to switch once again to the original 'anxious' self-construal.

It is unlikely that a personal construct psychotherapist will place as much emphasis on slot-rattling as do therapists of various alternative persuasions since, as Kelly (1955, p. 938) cautioned, 'it is all too likely to end up in seesaw behaviour'. However, he also noted that 'It has its place' (Kelly, 1969a, p. 231). An example of its use is provided by Agnew (1985), who, working with a 10-year-old child with alcoholic parents, who saw herself as having to take care of her younger siblings, encouraged her to experiment with a construction of the self as needing to be taken care of. Kelly enumerated several ways in which a therapist may produce a superficial movement such as this in a client's construing (Kelly, 1955). For example, by inducing threat or anxiety, the therapist may cause the client to switch to a contrasting view of events in an attempt to anticipate these more effectively. Invalidation by the therapist of the client's construing of current events, such as the therapist's own behaviour, may also lead to slot-rattling, whereas more fundamental changes may be expected if the invalidation encompasses a more extensive range of the client's experience. Other means of producing superficial change are to place the client in a situation which he or she views as requiring a contrasting role; or simply to exhort the client to behave differently.

(2)   Or they can select another construct from the client's ready repertory and apply it to matters at hand.

In Kelly's view, this is also a rather superficial approach, and one which the client is likely to have attempted already. Nevertheless, like slot-rattling, it is not without its uses. For example, the client who views his wife's persistent questioning of his actions as intrusive and critical may usefully be invited to experiment with an alternative construction of her behaviour in terms of another construct pole in his repertoire, such as 'attempting to understand me better'.

(3)   They can make more explicit those preverbal constructs by which all of us order our lives in considerable degree.

The attainment by the client of insight into his or her preverbal constructs is unlikely to be regarded by the personal construct psychotherapist as an end in itself, but rather as preliminary to testing out the constructs concerned. The therapist's initial approach to making preverbal constructs more explicit may be by methods, such as role play and various creative activities, which involve actions rather than just words. Loosening techniques (see pp. 258 ff.), such as dream reporting, may also facilitate the verbal expression of preverbal constructs. In addition, clients' level of cognitive awareness of their construing may be enhanced by increasing the permeability of their superordinate constructs and thereby their tolerance of apparently incompatible subsystems, with the result that suspended constructs may then be recovered.

(4)    They can elaborate the construct system to test it for internal consistency.

Controlled elaboration was, for Kelly (1955, p. 938), 'a way of bringing about reconstruction through clarification'. It involves consideration, and possible reorganisation, of the hierarchical relationships within the client's construct system. Its results, such as a tightening of superordinate constructs, are likely to appear 'impressive to those who always look to therapy to produce verbal consistency and "insight"' (Kelly, 1955, p. 941). The particular approaches which the therapist may adopt in attempting to elaborate the client's construing will be considered on pages 247 to 250.

(5)    They can test constructs for their predictive validity.

For Kelly (1955, p. 1123), 'discoveries one makes in therapy are similar to the discoveries one makes in the laboratory', deriving as they do from a process of experimentation with the client's constructs. An attitude on the part of the therapist which is both permissive and responsive to the client's experimentation may allow the client to dilate his or her field to experiment within the therapy room in ways which he or she might not otherwise contemplate. As we shall discuss further below, the therapist and client may also design experiments by which the predictive validity of the client's constructs may be tested outside the therapy room.

(6)    They can increase the range of convenience of certain constructs, that is, apply them more generally. They can also decrease the range of convenience and thus reduce a construct to a kind of obsolescence.

Kelly felt that increasing the range of convenience of a client's constructs may be particularly appropriate if therapy has largely focussed on the client's past and has provided the client with some understanding of the historical roots of his or her condition but not one which is sufficiently permeable to provide implications for the client's future development. For the client who is soon to terminate therapy, it may also be appropriate to focus on extension of the range of convenience of constructs which have been formulated in the treatment room. In all such cases, the therapist may attempt to increase the permeability of constructs by confronting the client with new situations to which to apply the constructs concerned. Alternatively, therapists may demonstrate to clients their own permeable use of particular constructs, these constructs can be applied to new events during enactment or some of the other approaches to elaboration to be discussed below, or therapy may focus on loosening the constructs concerned since this may allow an increase in their range of convenience. Kelly also considered that in some cases a particular element may appear to prevent the extension of a construct's range of convenience, and that the isolation of the element from the context of the construct may then increase the construct's permeability. Various examples involving increasing the range of convenience of clients' constructs have been provided by Karst (1980), the method employed in one of these being encouragement of the woman in a sexually inhibited couple to extend the application of her construct of creativity from the kitchen to the bedroom.

With other constructs employed by the client, it may appear that it would be beneficial if they were to deteriorate to a state of impermeability. This may be achieved by tightening the constructs concerned until they are very explicit, for example by binding them to particular words, times, places, people, situations, or other symbols (see p. 262). A therapist's use of such methods might include the attempt to limit a client's 'delusional material' by binding it to certain words; or the binding of a construct to a client's childhood relationship with his or her parents if it appears that the construct has been inappropriately applied to the client's adult relationships.

(7)    They can alter the meaning of certain constructs; rotate the reference axes.

As some of the examples presented in Chapters 5 and 6 demonstrate, changes in the relationships between a client's constructs, and therefore in the meaning of these constructs, may signify a resolution of dilemmas with which the individual was faced. The first stage in altering the meaning of a client's constructs, in 'getting him to shuffle some of his ideas into new combinations' (Kelly, 1955, p. 1033), is to loosen his or her construing. Loosening, as we have seen above, also has other therapeutic functions, and the techniques by which it may be facilitated will be described on pages 258 to 261.

(8)    They can erect new reference axes.

Kelly (1969a, p. 231) viewed this as 'the most ambitious undertaking of all', and as representing the most fundamental reconstruction which may result from therapy. The formation of new constructs may be facilitated by avoiding familiar or threatening elements, and instead introducing the client to new elements, which may include the therapist, a role which the client is asked to play (see pp. 268 ff.), or a story in the case of child clients. While fresh constructs are most likely to be produced if the elements concerned are not adequately anticipated by the client's existing constructs, the elements should not be totally unconstruable. On occasion, however, as Kelly suggested (R. Neimeyer, 1980) and as Rigdon and Epting (1983) demonstrated with an obsessional client who had constricted his construing of emotion, it may be useful to confront a client with a chaotic experience and then demonstrate how this may be clarified with some new construct. More generally, the formation of constructs may be facilitated by an atmosphere of experiment-ation, in which constructs are viewed propositionally and plentiful validating data are available without the client being exposed to too complex a range of influences.

## THERAPEUTIC TECHNIQUES

While personal construct psychotherapy represents a certain approach to the therapeutic enterprise rather than a specific collection of techniques, it will be apparent that various techniques may be of particular value in achieving the goals listed above. Some of these methods will now be described in greater detail.

### Palliative techniques

Although they are not in themselves designed to produce reconstruction, at certain stages in therapy it may be advisable to employ the techniques of *reassurance* and *support*. The former method involves communicating to the client a superordinate construction of his or her situation, usually expressed relatively simply rather than as a statement of the therapist's professional construction of events. It produces temporary relief from anxiety by providing the client with some structure for his or her experiences. Kelly suggested that this may be desirable if therapeutic movement is becoming so rapid that it may lead to a structural breakdown; if fragmentation of construing needs to be prevented; if the client is being encouraged to express loose constructs; if it is necessary to control anxiety between therapy sessions, for example during a break in the therapy; if the therapist wishes to prevent a chain of associations from being broken; or if the client is confronted by a temporarily traumatic situation.

Reassurance may be given in various ways. The therapist may, for example, predict certain outcomes, as when major issues have been worked upon in a particular therapy session and the therapist indicates that the client may experience some instability of mood before the next session. Similarly, a postdiction may be made, for example that the last week has been difficult for the client. Both these methods may indicate that the client's experiences, while perhaps seemingly chaotic, have some degree of consistency, as may occasions when the therapist conveys that new material which the client confides is not entirely unexpected. The structuring of therapy sessions may also be reassuring, as may the expression by the therapist of value judgements, for example that the client behaved correctly in a particular situation. However, this latter method should be used with caution since it may tend to fix the client's position with respect to the construct concerned. A further means of reassurance described by Kelly is the temporary reinstatement of a client's symptom when it appears that symptom loss has been too rapid. The example which he provides is of a girl with a limp, which she lost during psychotherapy, only to begin to present delusional material. When Kelly then suggested that she should not get rid of the limp too quickly, its return coincided with the loss of her delusional beliefs, which did not reappear even when the limp gradually disappeared.

Kelly (1955) viewed reassurance as a technique which should be used sparingly since 'it is "cheap medicine" and likely to be "habit forming"' (p. 657). It also tends to retard therapeutic movement and to perpetuate the client's maladaptive constructions. Whilst it is likely to lead to considerable dependency on the therapist, it also carries the risk of the client losing faith in the therapist if, for example, the therapist predicts a certain outcome which does not materialise. A final hazard of reassurance is that by expressing sympathy with a client's problems the therapist may unwittingly convey the message that there is no alternative to these problems.

Support is a technique which should also be used in small doses. It involves allowing the client to experiment successfully, the therapist providing some validation for the client's experimentation and enabling appropriate constructions to be developed in the therapy room before radical experiment- ation is attempted outside. Since it also entails acceptance of the client's dependencies, it may help the client to gain some understanding of the latter. Like reassurance, it may serve to stabilise the client's situation, its primary utility being with clients who are finding it hard to cope with unexpected events and who are experiencing considerable anxiety. In particular, Kelly felt it to be appropriate with clients presenting somatic symptoms who begin to express anxiety, and to be most useful at the beginning of therapy and following transitions. While it may have the effect of retarding therapeutic progress, this is unlikely to be to the same extent as does reassurance since it tends to facilitate experimentation rather than conveying to clients that they do not need to experiment since they are already adopting the correct view of events.

The therapist who wishes to be supportive towards a client should ensure that he or she is on time for appointments. Other practical means of offering support may in some cases include the provision for the client of some service, for example arrangements for a place in a psychotherapy group, admission to hospital, or writing to the Housing Department concerning the client's accommodation difficulties. Recalling material which the client produced in a previous therapy session may be experienced as supportive, as may the therapist indicating that he or she can understand the client's viewpoint or showing that he or she can apply the client's constructs to events in the way that the client would. Should the client shift his or her constructions, the supportive therapist will quickly adjust to such changes without drawing attention to any inconsistencies which they may involve, and may help the client to verbalise the new view which has been adopted. If the latter approach is employed, it should proceed slowly and with ample opportunity for the client to elaborate the therapist's statements.

## Elaborative techniques

Whereas support involves the therapist in attempting to employ the client's constructions without questioning any inconsistencies which may be apparent, in elaboration the focus is on identifying, exploring, and perhaps resolving, such inconsistencies. The therapist whose aim is the controlled elaboration of a client's system is likely to encourage the client to imagine the possible outcomes of alternative courses of action, thus elaborating the behavioural implications of the client's constructions. For example, having described how he or she, or some other person, behaved in a particular situation, the client may be asked to spell out exactly what would have happened if contrasting behaviour had been displayed. The progressive confrontation of the client with alternatives in this way essentially calls for repeated implementation of the Circumspection-Preemption-Control (C-P-C) Cycle, but with little in the way of circumspection. The therapist therefore needs to be aware that the client may choose to act on some of the alternatives considered, and may wish to emphasise to the client the importance of merely visualising different courses of action before choosing to pursue any of these. As Kelly (1955) cautioned, elaboration by means of action may result in a reduced level of cognitive awareness, and in the client developing an inflexible approach to problems as a result of foreshortening of the circumspection phase of the C-P-C Cycle. Nevertheless, he also considered that it may sometimes be of value to prescribe activities in order to facilitate elaboration of the client's construing, at both the verbal and preverbal levels, and to this end suggested the use of approaches which may appear similar to those employed by behaviour therapists. For example, he considered that the client with an unwanted habit, such as thumb-sucking, may usefully be asked to engage in the habit in a precise way at regular intervals, making notes on the experience at the end of each practice session, and with gradually increasing rest periods between these sessions. The likely results of this are a tightening of the client's constructs, an enhancement of his or her level of cognitive awareness, and the elaboration of linkages between preverbal and superordinate verbal constructs, enabling the client to choose whether or not to be the type of person who engages in the habit. In other cases, occupational, recreational, or social activities may usefully be prescribed, the client being asked to contrast experiences engendered by one type of activity with those engendered by another. R. Neimeyer (1985d) has noted the value of such approaches with constricted, depressive clients, while Selby (1988) has described her attempts to employ a personal construct theory approach to occupational therapy. Play and creative activities may occasionally be usefully employed, as in Kelly's suggestions that clients who are both impulsive and hostile may be encouraged to elaborate their hostility by modelling a pliable material such as clay, and that painting may bring about dilation in the construing of a constricted client. In such cases, the therapist's major aim is to facilitate elaboration by activating the C-P-C Cycle in relation to preverbal aspects of the client's construing. As Agnew (1985) has described, play therapy may also enable children to verbalise preverbal constructs, as well as serving such other elaborative purposes as extending a construct's range of convenience. Her example of the latter was of a boy who construed life in terms of warfare, but was gradually able, through play therapy, to extend to other relationships the notions of fair play and cooperation which he applied to games. While creative and play activities may, therefore, serve a useful purpose in therapy, they should, however, be kept within boundaries where the therapist is able to evaluate with the client the experimentation which is involved, and should not be continued past the point where it is appropriate for the client's experimentation to be conducted at a more verbal level.

It is generally advisable for elaboration of the construct system during therapy to focus on limited areas, for otherwise the likely result may be a general loosening of the client's construing. The initial focus of elaboration, particularly during the diagnostic phase considered in the last chapter, is likely to be the complaint, which provides an opportunity for exploration of areas in which the client feels anxious and confused. Moving beyond the complaint, the therapist may then attempt to elaborate other construct subsystems, thus 'broadening ... the base of the therapeutic relationship' and becoming 'more than a person who deals merely with one's symptoms' (Kelly, 1955, p. 977). Another particular area of concern, if the client's symptom, as discussed in Chapter 3, is viewed as a 'way of life' which offers some degree of structure, will be to elaborate an equally structured alternative way of life as a person without the symptom. Detailed examples of this approach may be found in Fransella's (1972) treatment of stutterers, in which, by focussing on their episodes of fluency, she elaborates their construing of themselves as fluent. As has been noted by authors who have further developed the personal construct psychotherapy approach to stuttering (Dalton, 1983b, 1987; Hayhow, 1987; Hayhow and Levy, 1989), it is also important for the stutterer during therapy to elaborate alternative ways of construing social situations other than in terms of the stuttering–fluency dimension.

A further focus for the therapist's elaborative efforts will be material which arises over the course of therapy, some of which will be considered in relation to the client's construct system in general and in order to indicate what changes may be expected in the system. In choosing the particular aspects of this material to elaborate, the therapist's attention may be drawn particularly to unexpected material; to that which may indicate therapeutic movement; to material relevant to some aspect of the construct system which is under intensive study; to material which may usefully be the focus of experimentation;

to material which the client might employ in validating any new constructs which are developed during therapy or which the therapist considers is relevant to the validation of a particular construct; and, particularly in the final stages of therapy, to material which may facilitate extension of the range of convenience of a construct.

Various approaches may be adopted in attempting to elaborate material which arises during therapy. *Recapitulation* may be employed, the last few therapy sessions being recalled by either therapist or client, perhaps with the aid of summaries of the sessions written by the client or tape-recordings, although the latter may be guilt-provoking for clients who are unable to accept their dependency on the therapist. Recapitulation is inadvisable if the client is in the process of revising constructions and might be tempted to revert to a previous view of events, and the therapist should also take care that it does not threaten the client by implying the expectation that he or she reverts to some old role which has been outgrown. However, if the therapy sessions have become rather unproductive discussions of a catalogue of incidents, review of the sessions by the therapist may be of value in that it is likely to lead to elaboration at a more superordinate level than would other- wise occur, and in particular elaboration of construing of change such that the client may be better able to countenance the prospect of further change. Such a review is essentially a form of *reflection* by the therapist, and we have seen in the previous chapter how reflection may be used to produce elaboration. In thematic reflection, for example, the therapist elaborates themes in the client's statements, asking questions which invite the client to consider the connections between separate incidents which he or she has described, and attempting in particular to understand the client's elaborative choices. As we have also seen in Chapter 6, a further method of encouraging elaboration is *confrontation*, which may be employed when the client has been elaborating the construct system in limited areas only, and the therapist deems that it is time to produce transition by introducing new problem areas. It should be used with caution, however, as, in Kelly's (1955) view, it is likely to induce threat, fear, anxiety, and guilt, which may be followed by depression and constriction; to cause loosening, and attempts to recover by using impermeable constructs, in organically deteriorated clients; and to lead to considerable hostility in those diagnosed as conversion hysterics. Another technique which the therapist may employ, either to encourage the client to deal with particular material or to steer the client away from material which he or she is not ready to explore, is *probing*. Kelly favoured the use of the delayed probe, in which the therapist questions the client concerning material which arose earlier in a session or course of sessions, rather than an immediate probe whenever the client raises an issue which appears significant. The latter approach, while of some use when directed towards relatively minor issues, is likely to involve mere ventilation of new material rather than elaboration of the client's construing of that material, and it also carries the danger that the therapist may come to be seen as waiting to pounce on the client's verbalisations. If the therapist does consider that a particular incident described by the client should be elaborated immediately, the client may be asked to cite further detail concerning the incident. This may allow it to be linked to themes of the sessions, may facilitate the testing out of constructs which are evident in the client's descriptions, may point to inconsistencies in the constructs applied to the incident, or may reveal that the incident has been used to validate constructs which are no longer useful. The client's construing of an incident may also be elaborated by asking him or her to describe events which led up to, and which followed, it; or those which are similar to, and contrast with, it. One advantage of the latter approach is that it may facilitate the verbalisation of preverbal constructs which are being expressed in the client's reported experiences. If the client is articulate, he or she may also be asked directly to verbalise constructs by citing similarities or differences between experiences which have been described. Experiences which may be of particular value for the client to construe in this way are those which have arisen at different stages during, and prior to, therapy since, as noted above, it is likely that constructs will thus be elicited that are useful pathways of movement for the client. A final way, and for Kelly (1955, p. 1025) 'One of the simplest and most effective means', of elaborating material which arises during therapy is *enactment*.

### Casual enactment

The personal construct psychotherapist who is attempting to elaborate a client's construing, or to encourage experimentation, is likely to make some use of casual enactment, informal role-playing in which both client and therapist take the parts of the client and significant or hypothetical figures in his or her life. Enactment may be of particular value in that it allows the client to experiment with alternative behaviour but to disengage core constructs from the experimentation by seeing it as only acting a part. Any threat which this behaviour might normally evoke by virtue of its inconsistency with core structures is therefore minimised. Enactment may also serve to free the client from preemptive constructs by confronting the client with a situation in which it is no longer possible to rely on such constructs. It focusses the client on the future and on the construing of others rather than on seemingly unchangeable aspects of the client's history. Finally, the procedure provides an opportunity for client and therapist to compare their construing of a situation in which they have both just been involved, and for the client to view himself or herself in perspective.

When enactment is used to elaborate an incident which the client has described during therapy, Kelly's recommendation was that the therapist, after suggesting the use of the procedure, should almost immediately take the part of a person involved in the incident, using some of the words that the client attributed to this person when describing the incident. In thus taking the initiative in a way which is aggressive, although not hostile, the therapist is following the 'first principle' of enactment that there should be 'no long preliminary discussions' (Kelly, 1955, p. 1026). Kelly's 'second principle' of enactment, when used to elaborate a construct concerning some incident recollected during therapy, was to keep it brief. In his view, an effective single episode of enactment may last no more than a minute, and generally not more than ten minutes of the first session in which enactment is used will be taken up by such episodes. When used for purposes other than elaborating material from therapy sessions, Kelly estimated that the average length of enactments is five minutes. Even if the client says very little during this brief period, he or she may still be actively participating in the enactment at a nonverbal level and gaining benefits thereby. Exchange of parts in the enactment is the 'third principle', since this ensures that neither client nor therapist is rigidly cast in a particular role and, if the enactment concerns an interaction between the client and some other person, taking the part of this latter person will facilitate the client's construing of the person's constructions. The 'fourth principle' is that the therapist should avoid caricature when taking the part of the client, tempting though it may be to give an exaggerated portrayal of some characteristic of the client of which the therapist considers that he or she is unaware.

Kelly cautions that the therapist should be alert to the possibility that the client may get into a troublesome situation during the enactment, and recommends that in such cases the enactment itself should be used to rescue the client from the situation since to terminate enactment at this point is likely only to lead to anxiety. Enactment is a powerful technique and, therefore, when it is first used the incident which is enacted should not be one which is highly anxiety-provoking for the client. It may be an incident which the client has reported, as when enactment is used for the purpose of elaboration, or a hypothetical incident, when the aim is more likely to be experimentation. If the focus is on superordinate constructs, both therapist and client may play the parts of hypothetical people, the client's lack of personal involvement with these people giving him or her greater freedom in the enactment than if the client had already developed relatively fixed constructions of the people concerned. At a later stage, significant figures in the client's life may be portrayed in such a way that reconstruing of these people is called for. Several types of scene which may be the basis of useful enactments were listed by Kelly (1955). He found that some of the most effective of these were scenes involving the client's parents or one of the parents interacting with the client. Particularly useful in allowing the client to view a parent from a fresh perspective is a scene in which the parent is younger than the client's present age. Other scenes suggested by Kelly were one in which the client has to comfort someone after a bereavement, and in which the playing of a supportive role may be elaborated; one in which everything that the client dreaded has already happened, and the focus is therefore on the client's resources in such an eventuality; one in which the client expresses aggression towards the therapist; one in which client and therapist enact respectively a psychotherapist and a hypothetical client with similar problems to the client, thus providing access to the client's expectations concerning therapy; one in which the client enacts a hypothetical close friend who is discussing the client with the therapist, which may allow the therapist to ask questions which the client might otherwise find threatening, and may be employed for several sessions until the therapist asks if the friend can bring the client to the next session to answer questions directly; and one in which the client plays the part of the therapist while the therapist plays a consultant with whom the case is being discussed. Examples of the use of this latter approach are provided by R. Neimeyer (1980) and Rigdon and Epting (1983), the first of these describing Kelly's own use of the technique. Alternatively, as Landfield (1980b) has described, a straightforward role reversal between therapist and client during a treatment session may occasionally be of value.

As R. and G. Neimeyer (1985) have indicated, enactment may be of particular value in working with a client who has problems in relationships. Thus, the client may usefully be encouraged to approach such problems as if he or she were someone who can comfortably relate to others. As we shall see on p. 302, G. Neimeyer (1985) has also applied enactment methods, both verbal and nonverbal, in treating the relationship difficulties of couples.

One of the difficulties which may arise in employing enactment is the therapist's own reluctance to be involved in a procedure which demands initiative and involves being seen in a different role by the client to that to which the therapist is accustomed. Enactment does, indeed, carry the risk that the therapist may reveal more than is in the client's interests, and Kelly considered this to be a particular danger if the therapist is hostile towards the client since this hostility may be displayed during the enactment. Therapists or clients who place great value on sincerity may also find it difficult to participate in enactment, but Kelly (1955) was rather dismissive of such concerns. A final difficulty in employing the technique is that a client, particularly one with a tendency to 'acting out', may drop out of role during the enactment, but it may be possible to control this by the therapist remaining in cast himself or herself and continuing to respond as if the client were still playing the assigned part.

## Use of formal assessment procedures during therapy

Apart from their use in diagnosis, formal assessment techniques may occasionally be employed by the personal construct psychotherapist to achieve such therapeutic ends as controlled elaboration of a client's personal construct system. For example, as any clinician who has employed repertory grid technique will know, the completion of a grid often has a considerable impact on a client, and represents 'a confrontation likely to have therapeutic repercussions' (Kelly, 1955, p. 980). As Rowe (1976, p. 6) puts it,

> when we ask a client to consider the implicit pole of a core construct, to make differentiations about his loved ones of a kind always forbidden by his family's mores, we are asking him to undertake activities which may change him. When we ask a client to do a WAIS or EPI, we are asking him questions the answers of which he knows he knows or he knows he does not know. In giving a grid we may ask our client questions the answers of which he does not know he knows, and, when he discovers what he knows, this discovery changes him.

For example, Ryle and Lipshitz (1975), describing a couple who became more able to express 'negative feelings', and whose reconstruction grids (see p. 234) indicated an increased tolerance of such feelings, during marital therapy, speculate that these changes may in part have been due to the couple being forced to acknowledge denied feelings by the testing procedure.

While the monitoring of therapy by repertory grid testing may, therefore, have adventitious therapeutic effects, the grid may also be used in a planned way specifically with a view to elaborating a particular construct subsystem. This was the case with Rodney, whose presenting complaint was inability to ejaculate, and whose anxiety concerning sexual situations appeared to reflect his lack of a sufficiently structured subsystem of constructs to enable him to anticipate such situations. One approach to elaborating his construal of sexuality was to ask him to keep a daily record of the frequency of, and degree of pleasure associated with, his sexual urges, and these records provided further evidence for the formulation of his problem in that there was a significantly reduced frequency of sexual urges in the weeks following those therapy sessions at which his verbalisations revealed high levels of cognitive anxiety when rated by Viney and Westbrook's (1976) procedure. When anxious concerning sex, he appeared to adopt a constrictive strategy and, as he put it, 'dismissed thinking about it', restricting even further opportunities for the elaboration of a subsystem of sexual constructs. Therefore, in a further attempt to elaborate this subsystem, he was administered a grid which required him to think about sex in that it involved the rating of various sexual situations on constructs elicited from triads of these situations. As I have described elsewhere, this grid indicated that he construed several such situations in terms of tedium, fear, uneasiness, and feelings of unreality, but this was no longer the case when a repeat grid assessment was carried out at a later stage in therapy, during which he reported that he had developed the ability to masturbate to orgasm (Winter, 1988b). Repertory grid technique may be used for similar therapeutic purposes with a client who places himself or herself outside the range of convenience of constructs, perhaps tending to give the self midpoint ratings when completing a standard grid. In such a case, it may be of value to administer a grid, such as the 'Role Rating Questionnaire' employed by R. Neimeyer *et al.* (1983a), in which all the elements are aspects of the self and which may therefore serve to elaborate self-construing.

Not only does repertory grid testing itself require the client to elaborate his or her construing, but the raw data which it provides may usefully be given to the client to reflect upon (Landfield, 1980b), and features of construing identified by grid analysis may be used as a focus for further elaboration and experimentation during therapy. Honess (1982), for example, has described how exploration with an individual of logical inconsistencies in his implications grid responses facilitated elaboration of his self-construing. An implications grid, in addition to the sexual situations grid and a more conventional grid, also proved to be of value with Rodney, in that it revealed such negative implications of sexuality as 'game-playing', deceptiveness, and insensitivity. It was then possible to focus on testing out these constructions by asking Rodney to try to think of people who were able to combine sexual competence with a sensitive and open manner of relating to others. The people concerned were subsequently discussed, with a view to the elaboration of a more favourable construal of sexuality, and as can be seen from Figure 7.1, a repeat implications grid indicated that sexual responsiveness was no longer seen as necessarily carrying negative implications. Jankowicz and Cooper (1982) provide further examples of the use in counselling of this procedure of 'elaboration of elements' which differentiate two highly related constructs, and note that the converse procedure of 'elaboration of constructs' may also be useful, the client being asked to think of a construct which differentiates two elements viewed as very similar. Numerous other reports of the use of the grid to focus therapy may be found in the literature (e.g. Rowe, 1976; R. Neimeyer, 1987a), many of these being provided by Ryle and his colleagues. Ryle's (1979a) particular concern, as discussed in Chapter 4, has been the identification, from grid results or clinical material, of clients' 'dilemmas, traps, and snags', which then become target problems in therapy and may form the basis of rating scales by means of which therapeutic change is monitored.

It will be apparent from the above examples that repertory grid technique may enhance a client's self-knowledge. It should be noted that, in common with other techniques that have this capacity, it may be used not only to elaborate a client's self-construction but also to provide sufficient awareness of covert constructions that the individual may be enabled to become a 'personal anarchist', overthrowing and transcending 'institutionalised' self structures (McWilliams, 1988). The grid may also provide clues, on which it may sometimes be of value for subsequent therapeutic endeavours to focus, as to the possible origins of particular constructions or complaints. With Rodney, for example, his mother's role in his difficulties was indicated by the finding from his grid that two women with whom he had wished to have a sexual relationship but had been unable to be on more than platonic terms were construed as very much more similar to his mother than were two women

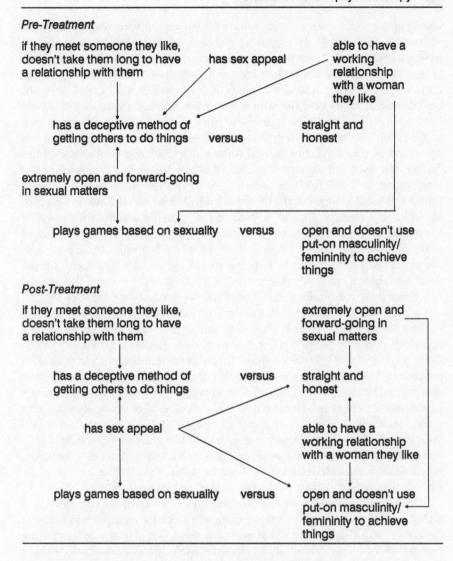

*Pre-Treatment*

if they meet someone they like, doesn't take them long to have a relationship with them

has sex appeal

able to have a working relationship with a woman they like

has a deceptive method of getting others to do things   versus

straight and honest

extremely open and forward-going in sexual matters

plays games based on sexuality   versus

open and doesn't use put-on masculinity/ femininity to achieve things

*Post-Treatment*

if they meet someone they like, doesn't take them long to have a relationship with them

extremely open and forward-going in sexual matters

has a deceptive method of getting others to do things   versus

straight and honest

has sex appeal

able to have a working relationship with a woman they like

plays games based on sexuality   versus

open and doesn't use put-on masculinity/ femininity to achieve things

*Figure 7.1* Implications of sexual responsiveness in Rodney's pre- and post-treatment implication grids

with whom he had had sexual intercourse. In the case of Stanley, who presented with difficulties in obtaining an erection, his grid indicated that he anticipated that loss of his sexual problem would not only make him much less honest and lovable but also much more like his father (Winter, 1988b). This enabled identification of the probable origins of his negative constructions of sexuality in his childhood perceptions of his father becoming 'ridiculous' when flirting with women. With Julia, who presented with phobic anxieties, which she felt unable to explain, concerning noise from her neighbour's house, a grid revealed that her neighbour was construed as very similar to her father. Discussion of this finding led her to recall occasions from her childhood when her father returned home from long periods at sea, and when she was displaced from sleeping with her mother but lay awake in the neighbouring room listening to her parents arguing. In the case of a child molester, reported by Needs (1988), a grid indicated that the self when depressed was construed as very similar to the self when 8 years old, and exploration of this finding led to discussion of the client himself being the victim of sexual molestation as a child. While such tracing of the historical roots of clients' difficulties would not generally be regarded by the personal construct psychotherapist as a therapeutic end in itself, it may provide a client with a way of construing an experience, such as Julia's panic on hearing noises in the house next door, which itself has become a source of considerable anxiety because the client finds it inexplicable. Explorations of the client's past such as those described above may also serve as a preliminary to such therapeutic procedures as time-binding, as will be discussed further on pages 314 to 315.

As has been indicated by research findings presented in Chapter 2, and one of the examples in Chapter 6, one particular type of intervention for which a repertory grid may provide a focus is vocational guidance (Edmonds, 1979; Cochran, 1983a, 1987; Davies, 1985). Not only may it indicate areas of conflict concerning vocational choice, which may then be subjected to therapeutic exploration, but also, by revealing structural properties of vocational construing, it may indicate the type of intervention which is most likely to be effective with a particular client. For example, Nevill et al. (1986) suggest that, if a grid indicates that a client's construing is highly integrated but poorly differentiated, exploratory interventions might serve a useful loosening function, but that such interventions are likely to be anxiety-provoking for the client whose vocational construct subsystem is less well integrated.

Various additional possibilities for the therapeutic use of repertory grid technique are available if a couple or family is being treated. Some of the variations on grid procedure which may be of value in such cases, as by allowing exploration of a couple's ability to construe each other's constructions, have been described in Chapter 6, and they will be discussed further on pages 300 to 301. We shall also consider a technique in which a couple complete repertory tests in interaction with each other (Bonarius, 1977). Although this method may be employed with a pair of strangers, it was designed for use with people who already know each other. In such conditions, it is likely to lead to a greater experience of self-disclosure, although this has not been found to be reflected in the type of constructs which the participants produce (Eland et al., 1979).

Just as grids may usefully identify, and allow therapy to focus upon, areas in which a couple misconstrue each other's views, so they may enable a therapist to locate his or her own misperceptions of a client's constructions and to refocus therapy accordingly. This may be illustrated by an example provided by Bannister and Bott (1973), in which a psychotherapist predicted the relationships between constructs which would be revealed in the grid of a client who was an amputee. The therapist's errors largely centred on a mistaken belief that the client saw how he used to be as similar to his ideal self. This belief had been associated with attributing the client's problems to his disability, which had been the primary focus of psychotherapy. The grid findings led to therapy focussing more on the interpersonal difficulties which the client had faced even before his amputation, and a subsequent grid which he completed revealed an increase in his self-esteem.

As well as being of therapeutic value in its own right, a grid may, as Rowe (1976) has illustrated, provide an initial point of departure for the use of laddering in therapy. For example, finding that a young man's grid indicated that he wished to be less self-confident, Rowe asked why he preferred to be shy, his contrast pole to self-confidence. It transpired that shyness for him implied being likeable, and that he would prefer to be liked than to be respected. Rowe then asked the client's parents to choose between being liked and respected, and the finding that they both chose the former provided a basis for their increased understanding of their son's stealing as a way of financing outings with his friends and thereby ensuring that he was liked. As a result, they agreed to review the amount of pocket money which he received. Rowe's (1976, 1978) use of laddering, with or without a grid as a starting point for this, has also allowed her to trace with her depressed clients the positive implications which depression carried for many of them. Laddering has also been employed in psychotherapy by Fransella (1972, 1985a), who has illustrated how the procedure may allow clients to identify the implicit poles, and the implications, of their constructs. She describes, for example, a client who preferred to be 'not masculine' since this implied that he could 'be, without strings', which in turn implied being 'without a mask', but for whom the discovery of these implicative connections was a source of disquiet and appeared to be a starting point for reconstruction (Fransella, 1981b, 1985a). Other methods which may be usefully employed during psychotherapy to identify construct implications are Landfield's (1971) pyramid procedure and Tschudi's ABC procedure (Tschudi and Sandsberg, 1984; Dawes, 1985; Winter, 1987; Selby, 1988). For example, Landfield has described how the former procedure was used with a client presenting with somatic symptoms at a point when both she and her therapist were becoming discouraged by her lack of progress. Several pyramids were completed, and the client was also asked to sort the constructs thus elicited, the procedure leading to the client becoming more involved in therapy and more prepared to discuss problems other than her somatic complaints.

A further formal procedure which, as described by several workers (Fransella, 1981b, 1985a; Epting and Amerikaner, 1980; Kremsdorf, 1985; G. Neimeyer and Hudson, 1985; Stefan and Von, 1985; Dalton, 1983b, 1987;

Browning, 1988; Jones, 1988; Ryle, 1990), has therapeutic as well as diagnostic uses is the self-characterisation. For example, having elicited a self-characterisation in the usual way with a client who presented the complaint of vomiting when under stress, Fransella (1981b) discussed the self-characterisation with the client, and then defined her therapeutic task as 'to help him discover who he "really" is as well as just who he "feels" he is; to help him tighten his construing ... and yet retain the ability to fantasise and dream and be creative; to help him get into action and so test out his true worth' (p. 222). With these ends in mind, she asked him in subsequent sessions to write various characterisations which invited him to elaborate alternative constructions of himself. These included descriptions of himself as he would be in ten years' time; as he would be if he stopped vomiting; and as he would be if he were a success. The last of these self-characterisations enabled him to discover that he no longer particularly wished to be a success, but instead to be 'ordinary'. While a self-characterisation may, therefore, be employed to allow a client to elaborate how he or she might be without a particular symptom, it is clear from Fransella's description of her client that even to imagine such a change in the self may be threatening and anxiety-provoking.

## Loosening

Kelly (1955, p. 1060) regarded loosening as 'one of the most important procedures in the psychotherapist's armamentarium'. He described its major functions as follows:

> (1) The shifting of elements in the construct context represents an incipient movement in the construction system. The result is that new experience is produced and new responses are elicited from one's associates. (2) The shifting permits certain elements to come into the field of one's attention which might otherwise be firmly ruled out by logic-tight construction. (3) Looseness permits some extension of the construct's range of convenience. (4) Sometimes the loosening tends to make the construct more permeable to new experience.
>
> In psychotherapy loosening serves certain special purposes. (5) It is a way of getting the client to recall events he would not otherwise think of. (6) It is a way of getting him to shuffle some of his ideas into new combinations. (7) By encouraging loosening the therapist can sometimes elicit an approximate verbal expression of a preverbal construct. (8) Finally, loosening may help release a client from the cul-de-sac of a preemptive construct. As the client loosely applies the preemptive construct, he may find that shifting its context admits new elements to which other constructs are also applicable.

(p. 1033)

Loosening may be brought about in four main ways. *Relaxation* exercises may be taught to the client, or relaxation may be facilitated by the therapist's relaxed manner and the physical setting in which therapy is conducted. *Chain association* may be employed, the client being asked to say whatever comes into his or her mind. With the client who is learning to construe loosely or who finds such spontaneous verbalisation difficult because of a preemptive construction of what therapy entails, the therapist may suggest that the client simply lets his or her mind wander, discussing later where these wanderings have led; or alternatively may offer a particular starting point, such as a word or sound, for the client's associations. Kelly considered that access to preverbal material may be provided by asking the client either to let his or her mind wander away from a starting point, a technique which may indicate the submerged poles of the client's constructs relating to the initial point of the associations; or, similarly, to stay away from important issues in his or her associations. Further guidance by the therapist may be required when chain association is to be employed to loosen some particular tight construction of the client's. The therapist may say, for example:

But how does all of this *feel* to you? What is it reminiscent of? What does all of this vaguely resemble? Does this feel like something you have told or experienced before and yet cannot quite put your finger on? You are telling the facts – let's not deal with facts just now, let's deal with deeper meanings, with pressures, with lurking anxieties, with vague uneasiness, with yearnings, with ideas that are hard to put into words.

(Kelly, 1955, p. 1036, italics in original)

A third way of producing loose constructions is *recounting of dreams,* since 'Dreams represent about the most loosened construction that one can put into words' (Kelly, 1955, p. 1037). In order to elaborate a dream, the therapist may ask specific questions, such as whether the dream was happy or sad, whether there were people involved in it, or what other experiences similar to the dream the client has had. If the client is still not able to remember the dream's content, the client may be asked to think about it for a while and then to let his or her mind wander, reporting the resulting thoughts. Kelly noted that a slow tempo is usually required for such elaboration of dream content. A further technique which he suggested is to ask clients to note down their dreams as soon as they wake. Some of the loose constructions reported in dreams may represent material at a low level of cognitive awareness. For example, dreams which the client recalls as vague, and involving visual imagery rather than conversation, may express preverbal constructs. Others may reveal suspended elements or the submerged poles of constructs, as when the client dreams that he or she is engaging in behaviour which contrasts markedly with the client's characteristic self-construction. In these latter cases, the dream may presage the client's experimentation with contrast behaviour, perhaps in an impulsive manner. A particular type of dream which

Kelly (1955) considered normally expresses some new behaviour with which the client is about to experiment, and indicates a transition in the client's construing, is the 'mile-post dream'. Such dreams tend to be vivid and to incorporate material from many previous dreams and therapy sessions, indicating that they involve comprehensive, superordinate constructions. Kelly noted that 'a therapist should be prepared to enter a new phase of treatment whenever such a dream is reported' (p. 1044).

The final method of producing loosening which was described by Kelly is *uncritical acceptance*, when the therapist passively attempts to employ the client's constructs without questioning the internal consistency of the constructions involved. The therapist, by indicating to the client that he or she understands the loose constructions which are being verbalised, offers some validation of these constructions. As in the other methods described above, the therapist's primary concern will be to facilitate loosening of the client's construing rather than with the content of the loose material produced, and close questioning concerning this material is likely to be counter-productive in that it may serve only to tighten construing once again. For the same reason, the personal construct psychotherapist will normally resist making any interpretations of the client's loose constructions, at least until it seems that tightening of these may be desirable. Interpretations which provoke anxiety or threat in the client are particularly likely to result in the client resorting to tightening, as are some remarks by the therapist in which a new element apppears to be introduced into the context of a loose construct. The example which Kelly (1955) provides of the latter situation is of a therapist making a remark about a client's teenage daughter after the client has been expressing loose constructions concerning sexual matters. Distracting elements from some other source, such as noises outside the therapy room, may also stop the client in his or her loosening tracks. A further interference to loosening may occur when a loose construct expressed by a client superficially resembles a tight construct, to which the client then switches his or her attention. In such a case, the therapist should not also become distracted by the tight construct but, having noted the transition in the client's construing, should attempt to focus again on the client's loose constructions. If, however, the client appears to be very threatened by the loose construing engendered by a particular approach, the therapist would be well-advised not to persist with this approach. More productive alternative approaches may be for the therapist to suggest that the client enacts the part of a person who construes loosely, or to switch the focus of loosening to a context which is less threatening. It is also, of course, advisable to focus on relatively unthreatening material when the therapist is initially encouraging the client to loosen constructions.

R. Neimeyer (1988a) has usefully extended Kelly's description of loosening strategies by indicating how these may include variations of aspects of the therapy process as well as particular techniques. For example, various 'environmental conditions', such as individual therapy in a setting which offers privacy, subdued lighting, and comfortable seats, are conducive to loose construing. In relation to therapist behaviours, this is also true of such nonverbal behaviours as reclining in a chair with a wandering gaze and an open posture; such 'coverbal' behaviours as slow, quiet speech in incomplete sentences; and such verbal behaviours as use of metaphors, lack of precision in speech, and the asking of questions which are open-ended or which concern feelings. Neimeyer also lists various loosening techniques, which, in addition to those described by Kelly, include guided imagery, artistic expression, fixed-role therapy, brainstorming, and hypnotherapy.

## Tightening

Once a client's constructs have been loosened, and subsequently realigned, it is, of course, necessary for the structure to be tightened again if the client is to complete a Creativity Cycle and the predictive capacity of the revised pattern of constructs to be put to the test. Like loosening, Kelly (1955) regarded tightening as having several major functions. As well as enabling the client to define his or her predictions, and therefore facilitating experimentation, it stabilises the client's psychological processes and therefore may make him or her less confused and confusing. It facilitates the development of hierarchical organisation in the client's construct system by, for example, defining subordinate constructions precisely in order that superordinate constructs which subsume them may then be developed. Finally, it may allow constructs which are serving little or no useful purpose to be reduced to a state of impermeability.

Various techniques may be used to bring about tightening of a client's construing, including many of those discussed under the heading of elaboration, of which tightening is one form. The client may be asked to make judgements about his or her statements or behaviour by, for example, thinking how what he or she has said in a session differs from what has been said previously. Similarly, he or she may be asked to summarise, either during the session or as a written exercise between sessions, what has been discussed. If a written summary has been prepared, further tightening is likely to result if the client reads it to the therapist at the next session, with the therapist occasionally asking for clarification of particular sections. Tightening may also be produced by asking the client to place constructions in a historical context by, for example, trying to recall when he or she first had similar thoughts. Alternatively, the client may be asked who else thinks in the same way or, more directly, may simply be asked to be more explicit. The client's constructions may be challenged, the way in which this is done depending on the degree of threat which it is considered that the client can tolerate. Thus, Kelly's (1955, p. 1071) suggested challenges ranged from the relatively unthreatening ' "I don't want to misunderstand you, so could you go back over what you were just saying?" ' to ' "Bosh!" "When are you going to start talking sense?" '. The use of enactment may also require the client to tighten constructions in order that they may be acted upon. If the therapist is enacting the part of the client or of a significant figure in his or her life, questioning the client concerning the accuracy of the portrayal may be a particularly effective means of tightening the client's construing of the person concerned. A further method of tightening constructions is to ask the client how two events are similar but different from a third, and then to assign other events to the two poles of the construct thus elicited. Since this is the basic repertory grid procedure, it will be evident that grid testing is likely to tighten constructions, and we have seen in Chapter 2 that completion of a grid tends to strengthen the interrelationships between the subject's constructs. Tightening is also likely to result if the client is asked for the validational evidence for certain constructions, or what would make him or her see a particular situation differently. A final method of tightening constructs is to apply the binding techniques developed to reduce the constructs concerned to a state of impermeability. For example, in *word binding* the therapist asks the client to name constructs and keep to the chosen names; in *time binding* a construct is regarded as an anachronism which was applicable only to the time when it was formed; and in *person binding* a construct is viewed as convenient only for anticipating a particular person. As I have described elsewhere (Winter, 1988b), my use of these techniques has included, in clients presenting with sexual problems, the binding of negative constructions of sexuality to their childhood perceptions of their parents. Similarly, G. Neimeyer (1987a) has indicated how such an approach may be employed with the individual who was sexually abused as a child.

As in his discussion of loosening, R. Neimeyer (1988a) lists various environmental conditions, nonverbal, coverbal, and verbal therapist behaviours, and techniques which may promote tightening. In his view, group therapy, lack of privacy, bright lighting, and upright seats are conducive to tight construing. He also indicates that the therapist who wishes a client to construe tightly may facilitate this by leaning forward in the chair, maintaining eye contact, or note taking, as well as by loud, fast speech, in which sentences are correctly formed, literal, and precise, and any questions are not open-ended but consist of requests for information. Techniques which Neimeyer considers may be usefully employed for the purpose of tightening include self-monitoring of behaviours or thoughts, practising of new skills, planning experiments to test particular hypotheses, and the provision of interpretations.

Kelly noted various difficulties which may arise in attempting to tighten a client's construing. For example, although it may appear that the client's use of a particular construct has become more consistent, it may be only the word symbols used for the construct which are relatively constant while the construct itself remains loose. If word symbols for particular constructs are completely lacking, however, the constructs being preverbal, an even more difficult problem is posed for the therapist who is aiming to tighten constructions. Tightening may also have undesirable effects, such as preemptive thinking or the reduction of the permeability or comprehensiveness of a construct when this was not the therapist's intention. In such cases, and those in which it has not proved possible to produce constructs which are both tight and superordinate, the result of tightening may be a client who only appears able to think in a very concrete manner. If a client's loose construing has served as a protection against anxiety, as with the impulsive person who by construing loosely avoids being confronted with the incompatibilities in his or her actions, the therapist needs to be prepared for the anxiety which is likely to result from tightening. The therapist may also find it difficult to tighten the construing of the client who tries to constrict his or her world to the therapeutic relationship and expects the therapist to understand every communication, however vague. Kelly notes that in such cases, even when the therapist does understand the client's loose construction, he or she should ask the client to be more explicit. If the client tends to 'act out' constructions rather than tightening and verbalising them, the therapist may in some cases usefully explore the client's hostility by asking what reaction the client is expecting and why. Tightening is also likely to be resisted by the client who risks considerable losses if particular constructions are tightened and put to the test. That the therapist should not always be too insistent on tightening such a client's constructions is illustrated by Kelly's (1955) description of a client diagnosed as a conversion hysteric whose therapist, with a view to conducting medical tests, forced him to tighten his construing by making explicit his beliefs concerning the illness from which he suffered. The client attempted suicide on the night before he was due to receive the test results. As a general rule, the therapist should consider tightening to be premature if it is unclear what might be the results of the client testing out the tightened construct, or if the client does not have available a viable alternative construction to which to turn should this construct be invalidated. In the latter case, the client's reaction may be one of hostility, and Kelly remarks that if this involves an attempt to extort validation from the therapist it may also result in the therapist becoming hostile.

Over a course of psychotherapy, if it is being fruitful, a client is likely to pass through several Creativity Cycles or, as Kelly described it, to weave back and forth between tightening and loosening. For example, although the personal construct psychotherapist will normally use dream reporting for the purpose of loosening a client's constructions without being too concerned to place an interpretation on the loose constructions thus produced, it may eventually be desirable to complete the Creativity Cycle by tightening these constructions and elaborating their linkages with other areas of the client's construing. As O'Donovan (1985) has described, the therapist may even resort to computer analysis of the interrelationships between elements in the client's dream, and between these elements and significant elements of the client's waking life. Kelly cautions that it is inadvisable to weave too rapidly between tightening and loosening in the early stages of therapy, although in general it may enable the client to cope better between sessions if constructions are tightened somewhat at the end of sessions, or of a series of sessions before a break. As therapy proceeds, and the client's facility in construing creatively increases, he or she is likely to be better able to engage in shorter Creativity Cycles.

### Facilitating experimentation

Having tightened his or her constructs, the client will be able to frame specific hypotheses on the basis of these constructs, and then to put these hypotheses to the test. The therapist may facilitate the experimentation concerned by confronting the client with a new situation, either during therapy sessions or in 'real life': thus, 'the therapy room can be a laboratory and the client's community a field project' (Kelly, 1955, p. 1067). For example, enactment of hypothetical situations may be employed, or the client may be encouraged to enter a new social environment, to join a therapy group, to adjust to some planned change in the therapy sessions, or even to enter hospital for a while in order to try out new behaviours and thereby test out the constructs concerned. Kelly (1955, p. 1131) also suggested that the therapist 'provide the client with the tools of experimentation': for example, if the client's manner of social interaction appears to be such as to be likely to limit severely his or her opportunities for social experimentation, the therapist might consider that teaching rudimentary 'social skills' is an appropriate first step in facilitating experimentation. Similarly, Fransella (1972) has reported that very severe stutterers failed to benefit from her approach focussing on the construing of fluency, and that in such cases it may be be advisable initially to use mechanical speech aids in order to equip the client with some means of experimentation in speaking situations.

Like any good research supervisor, the personal construct psychotherapist will encourage the client to make predictions, for example concerning the consequences of alternative ways of behaving. The client may even be asked to keep a diary in which the client's hypotheses, and results of experi-mentation, are recorded (Epting and Amerikaner, 1980). He or she may also be asked to make interpretations of, or to enact, the viewpoints of other people, such as how they see themselves and how they see the client, and to express these interpretations as testable hypotheses. Kelly suggested that the client should be encouraged to make negative as well as positive predictions, anticipating the worst outcome of an experiment with a view to lessening the anxiety which may result if the outcome is indeed unfavourable. With clients who view themselves as victims of their biographies, it may be useful for the therapist to elaborate in what ways their pasts would have had to differ for them to be able to behave differently. A possible outcome of formulating such biographical hypotheses is that 'As the structuration of the new behaviour becomes increasingly clear, and the more plausible it becomes, the more likely the client is to forget himself and actually do what, supposedly, he "cannot do" ' (Kelly, 1955, p. 1134). Two final methods of encouraging experimentation outlined by Kelly are to suggest directly that the client tries something out to see what the results might be; or to place the client in a social situation where others are engaged in an activity in which the client is skilled or interested, and which, since the client is likely to have a structured system of constructs relating to the activity concerned, is likely to induce minimal anxiety.

Perhaps the feature of personal construct psychotherapy which is most conducive to experimentation is the *invitational* mood (Kelly, 1964) in which it is conducted. This is the mood of hypothesis, of make-believe, of approaching an event *as if* some new construction of it were correct. Kelly drew upon Vaihinger's (1924) philosophy in suggesting this 'as if' approach, which he saw as reducing the threat occasioned by the new construction sufficiently for its implications to be pursued. For example, it may be used to facilitate the client's exploration of the possibility that a symptom carries certain advantages (Tschudi and Sandsberg, 1984). Several avenues of research have provided indications of the potential value of the 'as if' approach. It has been demonstrated, for example, that, when given the protection of make-believe, individuals are easily able to enact convincingly either pole of a construct, even if the enacted pole contrasts with the way in which the individual has always been characterised (Hudson, 1970; Crockett, 1985). There is also evidence that imagination of a particular scenario leads individuals to modify their expectations and behaviour in the direction of the imagined scene (Carroll, 1978; Gregory *et al.*, 1982; Anderson, 1983). For example, a person who has imagined giving blood is more likely to do so subsequently than one who has imagined an alternative scene. Such findings are explicable in terms of Kelly's Choice Corollary if it is assumed that imagining a certain behaviour serves to elaborate construing of that behaviour, and they have clear therapeutic implications. For example, R. Neimeyer (1985d) suggests that mood induction techniques may be usefully employed to enable depressives to imagine aspects of a more positive role, with a view to them subsequently behaving as if such a role were possible. When individuals have been asked to role-play particular moods or states, ranging from being depressed or 'stoned' to being similar to their ideal selves, characteristic changes in their construing of themselves and others have been observed (Benjafield and Adams-Webber, 1975; Leenaars, 1981; Adams-Webber and Rodney, 1983; Lefebvre *et al.*, 1986). While both imagining a particular change in behaviour and enacting the new role may, therefore, facilitate reconstruing, a study by Radley (1974b) has indicated that the former approach is likely to lead to less change than the latter. He found that, compared to students who wrote descriptions of hypothetical characters and of how they might change if they became more like these characters, students who also enacted the characters in written form were more prepared to change in their direction. This effect was most marked when the enacted characters represented the students' least preferred poles, which it was assumed that they were not spontaneously elaborating prior to the experiment. Furthermore, statements written by students from the perspective of the enacted character were rated by them as more useful than statements written from their own perspective. Radley's results point to the therapeutic value of one particular personal construct psychotherapy approach, fixed-role therapy, which we shall discuss on pages 268 to 275.

The 'as if' approach, as Mair (1977a) has noted, is exemplified by the use of metaphor, which may be employed in therapy to facilitate elaboration of construing and experimentation. Working with heavy smokers, Mair (1970a, 1977a) has invited them to think of cigarettes as if they were people. He also reports how a stammerer, invited to consider his stammer as if it were a person, viewed it as a boy who had been imprisoned in a small room for a long time and wanted to be heard. He was then invited to *be* this boy in order to explore the boy's construing. Similarly, other workers have employed metaphors in treating depression, a term which is itself, of course, a metaphor. For example, Jones (1985) reports how she and her client approached therapy *as if* the client were depressed, and *as if* her depression were potentially creative. Rowe (1978, 1983b) has also provided numerous examples of the use of metaphor in exploring clients' experience of depression, which in her view may be more easily described in an image than in words. She regards the metaphors that individuals create as the basis for the axioms and myths, usually constructed in childhood, which guide their lives. These myths are likely to include the individual's beliefs concerning death, and, as Rowe (1982) considers that these are core constructs which determine how the individual approaches life, she asks her clients early in therapy whether they view death 'as the end or as a doorway to another life' (Rowe, 1983b, p. 34). She is also concerned to identify whether clients' metaphors, myths, and metaphysical beliefs imply courage or despair, a dimension which she sees as indicative of coping or not coping with life.

A specific therapeutic application of metaphor which Mair (1977b) has proposed is to invite the client to consider the self as a community of selves, and to explore the parts played in the community by these different selves, perhaps by 'becoming' each of the characters for a while. The different selves are regarded as vantage points from which the individual can act, and therefore ways of obtaining various perspectives on events. With one client, a heavy smoker, the members of this community held 'political offices' such as Foreign Secretary and Home Secretary, and during therapy the client curbed some of their individual powers, by for example requiring that all requests for help from other 'communities' were discussed 'in Cabinet' before being granted. He then discovered that, for the first time, he could be by himself without feeling lonely, since he was always in the company of the various members of his community, and his cigarette consumption reduced. Another client, a stutterer, viewed his community as composed of 'hard line' and 'soft line' political factions, and began to speak in a more relaxed manner with the advent of a 'middle group' in the community. Hayhow *et al.* (1988) have described how the problems of motherhood may usefully be explored by considering the mother's community of selves. In addition, as Burr and Butt (1989) have noted, the use of hypnosis may be viewed in terms of the hypnotist addressing members of the client's community of selves, and encouraging experimentation with such metaphors as 'going deeper and deeper'. Rather than the imposition of ideas upon a passive and suggestible subject, the personal construct hypnotherapist will view it as an invitation to propositional thinking, in which the client will accept suggestions only if these can be subsumed within, and are elaborative of, the client's existing system of constructs (Procter and Brennan, 1985; Procter, 1989).

Humour, in Viney's (1985b) view, may serve similar therapeutic functions to the use of metaphor. It essentially involves a novel alternative construction of some event, such as a client's problem, but one which, unlike a metaphor, is generally incongruous with the individual's characteristic construction of the event. Viney therefore considers that its most important therapeutic effect is 'a freeing of the client from the self-imposed limitations of a single-reality world' (p. 239), but notes that to be effective client and therapist should share the meaning of the humorous construction employed. If humour is introduced by the client, Kelly (1955) considered it to be indicative of 'quick movement and reversed construction' (p. 643), and he warned that the therapist should note which constructs are involved in the movement concerned.

It will be apparent that personal construct psychotherapy is in some ways a playful enterprise (Epting, 1984). It will also not be unexpected that such an approach may be employed relatively easily with children, since they are natural experimenters, who are not likely to require such elaborate procedures as those described above to support their experimentation (Agnew, 1985). However, the responses of adult clients to attempts to encourage experimentation may in some cases be less than enthusiastic. Such attempts are, of course, likely to run into difficulties with hostile clients who are only interested in proving themselves right. There is also a danger that anxious clients who are experimenting with major constructions may be faced with yet more anxiety and confusion by the outcomes of their experiments, even when such outcomes seem favourable to the observer. As we have discussed in Chapter 4, some clients develop an elaborated negative view of themselves: if the experimentation of such a client leads to a much more favourable self-construction, the relative lack of structure of this alternative may be most anxiety-provoking. Threat is also likely to be produced if the outcome of a client's experiment implies fundamental changes in his or her construing. Persistence with experimentation in the client for whom the experiment generates considerable anxiety or threat may cause the client to react by constriction, hostility, or loosening of constructions. The client who is experiencing guilt may feel too dislodged from his or her core role to imagine that experimentation will alter this situation, and Kelly suggested that in such a case the client should develop a role relationship with the therapist before beginning to experiment. However, the client who is very dependent on the therapist may be reluctant to experiment outside the therapy room, viewing all validational evidence as deriving from the therapist. Reluctance to experiment may also derive from the client viewing the outcomes of experiments as final, and as stifling continued elaboration, rather than as leading to alternative constructions and yet further experimentation. It will be apparent, therefore, that, before suggesting a particular experiment, the therapist should ensure that the client is well prepared and that the experimentation is neither premature nor too far-reaching in its implications. Finally, the therapist should also have sufficient familiarity with the social milieu in which the experiment is to be carried out for him or her to be able to interpret its results.

**Fixed-role therapy**

Having been influenced by Moreno's (1959) psychodrama, as well as by other writers, Kelly (1955) devised one particular enactment-based method of experimentation, fixed-role therapy, which is often regarded as the therapeutic procedure most closely identified with personal construct theory. The therapist who employs this technique will usually first ask the client to write a self-characterisation, which Epting (1984) suggests should be at least two paragraphs in length and may usefully be written in the form of a letter to the therapist from a close friend of the client (Epting and Nazario, 1987). The client may also complete other assessment procedures, such as a repertory grid. Drawing on the material thus derived, and on his or her conversations with the client, the therapist then drafts a fixed-role sketch depicting a new personality which it is considered that it may be desirable for the client to enact. Six basic considerations underlie the writing of the sketch, which Kelly tended to do in conjunction with a panel of clinicians but which, as Epting and Nazario (1987) report, may also be done in conjunction with the client, preferably after some initial drafting by the therapist. Firstly, the sketch should not be regarded as an attempt to correct all the client's minor faults but should demonstrate an acceptance of the client coupled with the development of some major theme which it may be of value for the client to explore. For example, the theme of a sketch which Kelly (1955, p. 375) provided as an example of the procedure was *'the seeking of answers in the subtle feelings of other people rather than in literalistic dispute with them'* (italics in original). The sketch should not contain too many themes, for it is then likely to be difficult to remember and to enact. Kelly's second suggested feature of a fixed-role sketch is that it should require the client to experiment with sharply contrasting behaviour, provided that this does not entail the client 'slot-rattling' on constellatory constructs, with consequent far-reaching implications for the client's self-construing in terms of other constructs in his or her system. This emphasis on contrast therefore does not mean that the fixed-role sketch should be of a person who is the complete opposite of the client when viewed in terms of the client's constructs, and as will be evident from our discussion of varieties of therapeutic change it is likely to be far more profitable for the sketch to introduce some new construct, orthogonal to the client's major existing construct dimensions. As Bonarius (1970b, p. 216) remarks, 'the main role dimension must cross the main construct dimension of the patient at right angles. Were these two dimensions related in an oblique way, there would be the chance that the patient might rotate the role and align it to his own construct. He might subsume the role-playing under his personal construct system and would not experience a really new approach to his life situation.' Nevertheless, some personal construct psychotherapists, such as Viney (1981), have based fixed-role sketches on the preferred poles of clients' existing constructs. The third desired feature of a fixed-role sketch listed by Kelly was that it should include more permeable constructs, conducive to movement, than does the client's self-characterisation. Two further requirements are that the sketch should present hypotheses which are testable, taking into account the validational opportunities available to the client, and that the new constructs which it introduces will allow the client to subsume the construing of others. Finally, in writing the sketch, the therapist should bear in mind that during its enactment the client should be protected by the 'make-believe' nature of the exercise: the character portrayed should be given a new name which is acceptable to the client, appropriate to the client's cultural group, and perhaps symbolic of a major quality of the character, rather than the client's own name; and the sketch should not include direct comparisons with the client. In addition to the above characteristics of the sketch, Epting and Nazario (1987) recommend that it should not portray an ideal person who never makes mistakes.

A brief illustration may serve to highlight some of these features of a fixed-role sketch:

Tom's difficulties in social situations constituted a major theme of his self-characterisation, in which he described the last twenty years of his life from the perspective of a friend. For example, focusing on the period after he left University, he wrote:

'By this time our friendship has changed in that I through another ex school mate met up with a crowd of guys who were into real ale, computers. Tom became an outsider who would try to mix in but found it difficult.

I think he was trying to sort his life out and was trying and aiming for all sorts of things and never really settling down. I remember making a comment that I thought he was screwed up. By this time was was (sic) settled, earning good money and really enjoying life. Tom on the other hand because of his problems was never good company. My social life was really going well but Tom seems to be wanting something different. I was content in mixing mostly with blokes and socialising with their girlfriends. I think Tom was fed up with male company and longed for a girlfriend ... When met a girl called Kate I hardly saw him but presumed he was happy and perhaps more settled. I met her on a couple of occasions at a party but he did not seem to be happy with her. When he finished with her he came back into my social scene but more often than not was quiet, depressed and somehow we couldn't talk about the same things again. He would be with the group of mates for 1 week then disappear for a couple of weeks ... He seems to worry a lot particularly over if he will ever get married and have children. I tell him that is not worth worrying about.'

The picture presented by his self-characterisation was, therefore, of someone who had increasingly constricted his concerns around his search for a mate, to the detriment of his other social relationships. Repertory grid testing, Tschudi's (1977) ABC procedure, and conversation with him also highlighted other difficulties which he faced in such relationships, particularly on occasions when he might be required to be assertive. For example, assertiveness was associated by him with such characteristics as being demanding and unreasonable, and extraversion carried similar negative implications. In arguments, he considered that there was always 'a right and wrong opinion', 'a winner and a loser', and, as he was usually convinced that he was right, he rarely took the trouble to consider the perspective of the other person. He also complained of feeling socially isolated at work since he was more 'refined' and of 'a higher social class' than his workmates. The fixed role that was written for him included curiosity in others as a major theme, and presented mixing with people of a different background as an opportunity to develop this curiosity. Similarly, it attempted to reframe some of what he tended to construe as impediments as possible sources of strength, while incorporating his acknowledged strengths, such as abilities at tennis. It deliberately omitted specific mention of relationships with the opposite sex. It read as follows:

'Roy Taylor's philosophy of life very much reflects his approach to his favorite sport, tennis: it's not whether a player wins or loses that's important but whether they've played the game to the best of their ability. Whether at work or at play, he believes that if a job is worth doing it's worth doing well, and he brings to everything that he does a certain passion and conviction, which cannot fail to earn your respect. Although you might perhaps think that this would make him appear a little too serious and intense, once you get to know him you soon realize that his main concern is to live life to the full and that this includes having fun as well as working hard. Life doesn't always run smoothly for him, of course, but when he has a disappointment he always seems able to learn something from it, and to look to the future rather than brooding on his present or past misfortunes.

One of his greatest strengths at tennis is his ability to anticipate the moves of the other players, be they his opponents or doubles partners. In other areas of his life, he also always tries to see the world through the eyes of the people with whom he comes into contact, perhaps because he has mixed with people from so many different walks of life. His lively curiosity in what makes other people tick is usually reciprocated and leads him, almost before he knows it, into some very rewarding relationships. He also, of course, has his fair share of disagreements with others, but when this happens he always makes an effort to understand the other person's point of view, even though he might not accept it. Because of this, he has a reputation both for commitment to those causes that are close to his heart and tolerance of the right of others to hold different opinions.'

(Winter, 1987, p. 118)

Having prepared the fixed-role sketch, the therapist carries out an acceptance check with the client, asking the client whether the sketch depicts the sort of person whom the client would like to know and who seems real. The therapist thereby discovers whether the character portrayed is likely to be threatening to the client or appears implausible. If so, the sketch, or sections of it, may need to be rewritten. After eventually arriving at a sketch which is acceptable to the client, the therapist next initiates the client in the therapy procedure, indicating both the nature of the experimentation which the client will be asked to carry out and also that the therapist will provide some degree of reassurance and support during the exercise. The way in which Kelly (1955, pp. 384–5) introduced the procedure to a client, Ronald Barrett, who was asked to portray a character called Kenneth Norton, was as follows:

'For the next two weeks I want you to do something unusual. I want you to *act* as if you were (Kenneth Norton). We will work it out together. For two weeks try to forget that you are (Ronald Barrett) or that you ever were. You *are* (Kenneth Norton)! You *act* like him! You *think* like him. You *talk* to your friends the way you think he would talk! You *do* the things you think he would do! You even have his interests and you *enjoy* the things he would enjoy!

'Now I know this is going to seem very artificial. We expect that. You will have to keep thinking about the way (Kenneth) would do things rather than the way (Ronald) might want to do them.

'You might say that we are going to send (Ronald) on a two weeks' vacation and let him rest up. In the meantime (Kenneth) will take over. Other people may not know it but (Ronald) will not even be around. Of course you will have to let people keep on calling you (Ronald), but you will think of yourself as (Kenneth). After two weeks we will let (Ronald) come back and then see what we can do to help him.

'Let us arrange to talk this over every other day.' (The clinician sets up the schedule of appointments.)

'Now that copy of Kenneth's character sketch is for you to keep. Keep it with you all the time and read it over at least three different times a day, say, when you get up, some time during the day – perhaps when you eat lunch – and when you go to bed.

'Now let us do some rehearsing.'

The situations on which rehearsals of the role with the therapist focus generally follow a progression from those involving relatively superficial relationships to those which are more likely to generate anxiety and threat. For example, Kelly suggested that the first rehearsal session might consider various work situations, the second situations involving casual relationships with companions of the same sex as the client, the third situations involving the spouse or someone of the opposite sex, the fourth situations involving parents, and the fifth situations concerning the client's life orientation and plans, while the final session in the series is devoted to general discussion and review of the experiment. As in other forms of enactment, during rehearsal sessions the client and therapist alternate in playing the fixed role and the particular person with whom the character in the role is interacting, and they each comment on how faithfully the other portrayed the role. Following the first such session, the therapist will remind the client of the instructions to play the role constantly and to read the character sketch regularly, may advise the client not to reveal to others that he or she is playing a role since this will generally reduce the value of the exercise, and will suggest that the client try to create the type of situations that have been rehearsed. The next session will normally commence with a discussion of the client's experiences in these situations, which may be enacted again in the session. This careful rehearsal of very specific situations guards against the client commencing the role too generally and riskily before there has been adequate preparation. Although the rehearsal sessions are frequent, some of them need only be relatively brief (Epting and Nazario, 1987).

In introducing the fixed role, and discussing it subsequently, the therapist should take care not to present it as how the client ought to be but rather as describing a character whom it might be useful for the client to pretend to be for a while. The primary aim of this form of therapy is not the transformation of the client into some ideal person envisaged by the therapist but, by encouraging experimentation with a new role which is likely to elicit new reactions from others, to demonstrate that the client need not be trapped in his or her autobiography, and to provide 'one good, rousing, construct-shaking experience' (Kelly, 1955, p. 412). Therefore, it need not matter if the client enacts the fixed-role sketch in a way that is different from what the therapist envisaged, provided therapist and client are able to formulate constructs which provide a rationale for the client's behaviour while experimenting with the role. In such cases, the therapist may modify his or her own interpretation of the fixed role so that it is more consistent with the client's interpretation. Whether therapist and client have modified the role or not, the therapist should demonstrate acceptance of the character portrayed by showing an understanding of how he or she feels. In the final session, in which the client, no longer in the fixed role, can discuss any issues which have arisen during the experiment, the therapist will generally let the client 'take the floor' while limiting himself or herself to expressions of encouragement.

Kelly made it clear that the therapist who expects a client to take on a fixed role with enthusiasm and ease is likely to be disappointed. Indeed, if the client is able to slip smoothly and rapidly into the role, it probably means that the role is too similar to the client's initial outlook to lead to any substantial reconstruing. At times the client may challenge the therapist by asking for a demonstration of how the role may be employed to deal with a particularly difficult situation, but by taking up the challenge and enacting the situation the therapist may be able to provide just such a demonstration. While there may be few direct statements by the client that the role is proving to be of value, its likely effectiveness may be indicated when the client spontaneously considers how the character in the role might deal with a particular situation, remarks that the role has begun to feel like the client's real self, forgets his or her reason for initially requesting help, makes fresh interpretations of other people, or engages in behaviour which appears inconsistent with his or her self-characterisation and which is not seen as 'just acting'. However, Kelly cautions that if this new behaviour suggests that the client's movement has been solely within his or her original construct system it may indicate that the therapist has exerted too much pressure on the client to change, with potentially catastrophic results. Furthermore, if early in therapy the client's spontaneous elaboration of the role is leading him or her to behave in ways which may be looked back upon with embarrassment, it may be advisable for the therapist to protect the client by making a comment which provides a reminder of the 'make-believe' nature of the behaviour. If, on the other hand, the client persistently fails to employ the fixed role and continually discusses some issue unrelated to it, such as his or her presenting complaint, there may be little to be gained by pursuing this form of treatment. Further indicators that fixed-role therapy is unlikely to be effective are the client's use of mixtures of old and new constructs, and failure to perceive the contrast between the fixed role and the client's former role, or the implications of the fixed role, despite the therapist's efforts to demonstrate these. Criticism of the role by the client need not be an unfavourable sign, however, since at least in criticising the role the client is having to construe it, and the criticisms themselves may provide a useful focus for enactment. Kelly suggested that it may be especially valuable for the critical client at the end of therapy to enact particular scenes in both the fixed role and the client's role prior to therapy.

Personal construct psychotherapy is sometimes preemptively construed as consisting of nothing but fixed-role therapy. However, just as repertory grid technique is only one of the assessment methods which may be employed by the personal construct psychotherapist, so fixed-role therapy is just one of several therapeutic techniques of which such a therapist may make use, and which may be of value to some clients at some times but is by no means regarded as a universal panacea. Kelly (1973) himself indicated that he used it in not more than one out of fifteen cases, although it is also apparent that he felt that it may be of value with a wide variety of clients, including people with learning disabilities and those diagnosed as schizophrenic, manic, or depressive. He considered, however, that the procedure may be particularly useful in certain situations (Kelly, 1955). Firstly, since it may require only two weeks to complete a fixed-role therapy programme, such an approach may be particularly valuable when the therapist has little time available. It may also be the treatment of choice when the therapist wishes to avoid entering into a highly dependent transference relationship with the client, or when therapist and client are likely to have unavoidable nonclinical interactions. Since it is less likely to harm a client than are other forms of therapy, in that the client is not asked to change himself or herself, it may be a particularly appropriate technique for inexperienced therapists to employ. It is also appropriate in those cases in which the client's difficulties involve particular social situations and events as these situations will provide much validational material for the client's experiments with the fixed role. When another form of therapy needs to be terminated, fixed-role therapy may be usefully employed in view of its focus on the present and future rather than the past, and on the client's experimentation in the outside world rather than continued dependency on the therapist. As Epting and Nazario (1987) point out, it may also provide a useful way out of an impasse in therapy. A particular group of clients with whom it may be of value consists of those who are somewhat out of touch with everyday reality, either because they are intellectualisers or have what might be regarded as schizoid tendencies. It is also particularly useful with those clients who appear defensive regarding therapy since it allows them the protection of 'make-believe' for their experimentation. Finally, it may provide a relatively quick means of assessing a client's readiness to change and likelihood of benefiting from a longer-term form of therapy.

Apart from Kelly's (1955) original descriptions of the use of fixed-role therapy, published examples of the use of the technique are, as Adams-Webber (1981) notes, relatively few. Bonarius (1970b) has described its use with a client who complained of depression, Karst and Trexler (1970) have studied its application to the treatment of speaking anxiety, Landfield (1980b) has used it to help a law student cope with mock trials, Viney (1981, 1987) has reported how it was employed together with other techniques in the personal construct psychotherapy of a client presenting with anxiety, and in another who felt helpless following a myocardial infarction, and Butt and Bannister (1987) have made use of it with a client who found it difficult to relate to others. Skene (1973) has also used the method with a man, of 'borderline subnormal' intellect, who was admitted to psychiatric hospital following illegal homosexual acts with adolescents, and whose homosexual behaviour appeared to decrease, and to be replaced by heterosexual behaviour, over the course of fixed-role therapy, despite the fact that the fixed role was not concerned with sexual orientation. Some of the applications of the technique have employed variations of Kelly's original procedure. For example, as we shall discuss further below, adaptations of fixed-role therapy for use in a group setting have been reported by Kelly (1955) himself and by Epting and Amerikaner (1980), while Kremsdorf (1985) has employed the method in marital therapy. A particular derivation of the technique is 'variable role therapy', developed by Epting and Suchman, in which therapist and client create a series of mini fixed roles, each designed to tackle a specific problem faced by the client (Epting, 1984). Epting and Nazario (1987, p. 287) report that 'By the end of some sessions the therapy room was almost completely filled by these extra characters'.

## Group psychotherapy

Group treatment approaches may be particularly facilitative of experimentation since they generally provide opportunities for a greater variety of social experiments, of anticipations of the construing of others, and of validational evidence than is possible if the 'laboratory' contains only the client and therapist. Furthermore, the experiments may be better controlled than if they were carried out in the less protected environment of the world outside the therapy room. Amongst the likely benefits which Kelly indicated that the client may derive from interacting and experimenting with other group members are the development of a more comprehensive role, and the discovery of variations in the degree of permeability and comprehensiveness of his or her constructs. Another particularly beneficial effect of group therapy is that, especially if the group is heterogeneous, it is likely to facilitate the revision of preemptive and constellatory constructs. For example, the client who holds a rigid stereotype of homosexuals may find that his or her constellatory construction does not readily apply to homosexual members of the group. A further advantage of a group treatment approach, in Kelly's view, is that it allows the client, early in therapy, to disperse his or her dependencies.

As with other writers on group psychotherapy, Kelly (1955) considered that therapy groups pass through various stages of development, and he regarded different therapeutic approaches as being appropriate at different stages. The initial focus of a group, in his view, should be the *initiation of mutual support*, such that each group member comes to feel that at least one other member is attempting to construe events as he or she does. Because of the potentially threatening nature of the group situation, Kelly felt that until this occurs the therapist should steer group members away from revealing very disturbing material. Mutual support may be facilitated by, after clients have described particular experiences, asking other group members how they would have felt in the same situations. However, Kelly's preferred method at this stage of the group was enactment, normally conducted in pairs, every group member except the therapist being asked after each enactment to indicate with which of the participants in the enactment he or she identified. The situation should then be reenacted, with the participants exchanging roles, and group members again being asked for their identifications and the reasons for these. Although hypothetical stressful or guilt-provoking enactment situations may be employed in order to strengthen support, Kelly felt it inadvisable in the early stages of the group for these to be very similar to clients' actual life situations. As an example of the type of enactment situation which might be valuable, Kelly suggested one in which one of the participants had an argument several hours earlier with their 'problem child' son, who stormed out of the house. The other participant arrives at the house to inform the boy's parents that he or she has knocked him over while driving home from a social engagement. Each participant is asked to leave the group room while the other is briefed on his or her part, and therefore neither knows the full background to the enactment. As in individual psychotherapy, enactments need not be lengthy, but Kelly considered that an enactment should not be discontinued until each participant has had to behave in a spontaneous, unrehearsed manner. It should be remembered that enactment is being employed not to teach clients particular ways of behaving, but rather to facilitate experimentation and mutual support. With the latter purpose in mind, the therapist may usefully encourage clients to discuss the degree of support which they experienced from other group members, and should take note of instances where particular clients remain unsupported following enactments or where cliques begin to form.

Kelly termed the second phase of group psychotherapy the *initiation of primary role relationships*, group members beginning to construe each other's construction processes. To facilitate this phase, the therapist may ask non-participating group members to say how they imagine participants felt during enactments, or how they might themselves have felt if participating, the participants then commenting on the accuracy of the other members' perceptions. If this procedure indicates that a particular group member shows little commonality of construing with others, the member may be asked to participate in reenactments of the situations which have been portrayed previously with a view to exploration of the similarities and contrasts between his or her construing and that of other group members. Enactment may also be employed at this stage of therapy to encourage participants to step into other group members' shoes by portraying situations involving these members. As with other enactments, there should be exchange of parts, which will demonstrate that there may be various alternative constructions of the person portrayed. Both this latter person and the participants in the enactment may feel threatened by the procedure, and Kelly advised that the therapist should help the group to understand the nature of this threat. The therapist should also be alert to such expressions of hostility as the portrayal of a caricature of another group member. Kelly's suggestions were that, as well as preventing too much expression of hostility by ensuring that the hostile client feels supported, the therapist may allow the client's caricature to be invalidated and then ask the client to reenact the part, or may suggest that the client plays the part in two contrasting ways. The client may thus reveal both poles of the construct underlying the caricature, discussion of which may facilitate consideration of the difficulty which the client is facing in forming a role relationship with the person portrayed.

The third of Kelly's phases of group development is the *initiation of mutual primary enterprises*, in which group members devise and carry out experiments within the group based on their construing of each other's views. The therapist may usefully emphasise the latter aspect of the experimentation by asking group members how other members may be helped by, or be helpful in, their proposed enterprises. In its fourth phase, the group is primarily concerned with *exploration of personal problems*, by either discussion or enactment by group members of incidents from their own lives and from those of other members. The purpose of discussion at this stage will generally be to formulate hypotheses and design experiments, which may then form the basis of enactments. Enactment may be particularly useful if the hostility or aggression of one member is very threatening to others, in which case the client may be asked to portray these feelings, the use of role play allowing his or her impulsivity and guilt to be controlled and helping to preserve the client's role relationship with the group. The enactment of the client by another group member carries the further advantage that the client, when instructing the other member concerning the portrayal, will be forced to word-bind the constructs underlying these feelings. In the next phase of group psychotherapy, the focus moves to the *exploration of secondary roles*, clients' roles in the outside world. Clients at this stage will begin to attempt to construe the outlooks of people outside the group, and this may be facilitated by sociodrama techniques or by discussion of similarities and differences between 'outsiders' and group members, clients thereby increasing the permeability of their role constructs. In the group's final stage, there is *exploration of secondary enterprises*, as clients experiment in the outside world and report the results of their experiments to the group.

Although personal construct theory has been employed by several clinicians to inform their practice of group psychotherapy, there would appear to have been few attempts to make use of Kelly's particular model of group development in this work. This is perhaps because of therapists' discomfort with the degree of structure which the model appears to impose on group sessions or, despite Kelly's note that his phases of development may well overlap in particular group sessions, because of the construal of these phases as an invariant sequence which does not seem to apply to clinicians' groups. For example, Morris (1977, p. 121) reports that the therapists in a personal construct psychotherapy group 'found that, despite their attempts to regulate the move from one phase to another, certain members of the group would jump the gun and initiate activities relevant to other phases. In those situations therapists occasionally had to revert to assessing each person's individual needs and encouraging them or not accordingly. On the whole, however, therapists felt satisfied with the progress of the group, and felt that they learned from it too'. Llewelyn and Dunnett (1987) also discuss their discomfort with aspects of Kelly's model of group psychotherapy, and in particular with its emphasis on enactment. They have introduced various modifications to the personal construct approach to group psychotherapy. Their initial focus is on the establishment of cohesiveness, which is facilitated by warm-up exercises. They then attempt to encourage self-disclosure and permeability of construing by asking group members, in pairs, to discuss particular issues, members then describing to the group the viewpoints of their partners in this exercise. Next, interactions between group members are considered, with a focus on the utility of particular constructs, and Kelly's concepts of hostility and aggression are explained to the group. This is followed by the encouragement of active experimentation in group sessions and by the completion of a group grid, facilitating group members' understanding of their social roles. The concept of slot-rattling, and the view that there may be more productive ways of changing, is also explained to them at this stage. The therapists may disclose some aspects of themselves in order to model experimentation, and then in the final stage of the group the members are asked to set each other homework assignments, the outcome of these experiments in the outside world being reported back to the group. Llewelyn and Dunnett also employed other techniques, such as self-characterisations and laddering, in group therapy, but it is clear from their descriptions of their groups that the attempt to operate in terms of predetermined stages was no more successful than Morris' therapists' application of Kelly's model of the group process. They report, for example, that 'the group members were bringing such important material so quickly that we were having to devise the structure as we went along' (Dunnett and Llewelyn, 1988, p. 196). Although they regarded the groups as having therapeutic benefits, and although favourable reports have been provided by the members of such groups (e.g. Dodds, 1985), they conclude that personal construct theory was of value only in understanding and working with the problems of individual members. In understanding the group process, it 'seemed less helpful than more traditional approaches', and 'its use does not seem to change how the group as a whole works' (Dunnett and Llewelyn, 1988, p. 200).

Other workers, without necessarily attempting to employ a developmental model of group phases, have usefully applied personal construct theory approaches in a group setting. For example, although Dunnett and Llewelyn

(1988, p. 200) found that the use of grids in their groups was experienced as 'constricting and authoritarian', more favourable reports of the employment of grids in the group setting have been provided by Kerrick-Mack (1978) and Batty and Hall (1986). Kerrick-Mack considers that grids may be of particular use in groups for adolescents, where they may facilitate awareness of group members' own construing and that of others without engendering too much anxiety in the process. The use of experiential and role-play exercises to explore social aspects of construing in a non-client group has been reported by Procter and Parry (1978), some of their procedures being of possible utility with clients. As we have seen above, fixed-role techniques may also be employed in a group setting. Kelly's group fixed-role therapy approach involved roles being provided for the members by the therapist, and members being aware of each other's roles. Epting and Nazario (1987) have modified this procedure by dividing the group into pairs, and asking partners to exchange self-characterisations and to add a paragraph to the other's characterisation, completing a role which, if plausible, the other then enacts. In their 'multiple role group', one of numerous group procedures which they employ, Epting and Amerikaner (1980) ask members to enact various roles relating to a particular theme, such as 'maleness'. However, the most well elaborated personal construct approach to groups, apart from Kelly's own, is Landfield and Rivers' (1975) Interpersonal Transaction (IT) Group, which aims to facilitate the development of role relationships. These workers' original groups were characterised by two basic features. At the beginning and end of each session, all group members wrote on slips of paper how they felt, and did not feel, at that particular time, the procedure therefore eliciting their emotional constructs. Each member then attached this 'Mood Tag' to their clothes and circulated amongst the other members. The other basic feature of such groups is that most of the interactions take place in dyads. At every group, members are given general instructions on what to share in these interactions, each of which lasts for six to eight minutes before the members rotate to new dyads, the procedure continuing until each member has interacted in a dyad with every other. In the first such dyadic interaction, Landfield and Rivers asked group members to use gestures to communicate something about themselves to each other. Members are told that during the dyadic interactions they should try to understand each other without being critical. The aim of these instructions is to produce an unthreatening atmosphere, in which group members are given the freedom to share whatever they wish concerning a general topic but not to be invalidated while doing so. Furthermore, the structuring of the group sessions serves to reduce anxiety while, as Landfield (1979) notes, the brevity of interactions also minimises anxiety and threat. In later sessions of cohesive groups, the total time spent in dyadic interaction may be reduced, perhaps by asking members each to interact with one person whose viewpoint they know well and another whose views are much less familiar (R. Neimeyer, 1988b). After the dyadic exercise at each session, and before group members complete their second Mood Tags, there is a group discussion of the experience for at least fifteen minutes.

Amongst the advantages of the IT procedure, R. Neimeyer (1988b) notes that it tends to produce rapid self-disclosure in a cohesive climate on issues which can be selected for their therapeutic relevance. It facilitates a comparable level of participation by all members, who also each have the opportunity to interact in both listening and disclosing roles. Neimeyer emphasises the importance of careful selection of topics for the dyadic interactions, which will generally concern issues of increasingly specific relevance to the clients' problem areas as the sessions progress. For example, in a group for problem drinkers, Landfield and Rivers (1975) gave 'Who are you' as the topic for the first verbal dyadic interaction, while in the sixteenth of the twenty sessions the topic was 'Why I should drink the way I do and why I should not drink the way I do'. The latter topic illustrates a further feature of useful issues for dyadic discussion, namely that they should generally be framed in terms of a contrast. R. Neimeyer (1988b) provides a list of topics which may be of value to IT Group leaders, and he also suggests the following bridging questions to facilitate the transition from the dyadic to the plenary stage of the group:

1. What sorts of things did you find out about other group members during your conversations?
2. Whose experience did you most identify with?
3. In what ways did you and other group members differ?
4. Did you hear anything that surprised you?
5. Did you find that what you had to say changed or developed in any way over the course of the conversations?
6. How did the conversations influence the way you think about the topic?
7. Is there anything you would like to explore further?
8. What questions do you have at this point for other group members?
9. How did the things you discussed relate to the problem (e.g., depression, incest) that brought you in?

(R. Neimeyer, 1988b, p. 187)

Also of value to the IT Group leader will be Neimeyer's suggestions of variations in the group structure, interaction topics, and bridging questions which may help to resolve problems which arise in a group. These possible ways of dealing with problems familiar to all group leaders are listed in Table 7.1.

Another procedure involving interaction in pairs is Mair's (1970b) 'conversational approach'. While not specifically designed for use in groups or, indeed, in therapy, this may be easily adapted to a group psychotherapy setting. In this approach, a pair of individuals each write two character sketches of themselves, the contents of one of which will not be disclosed while the other is shared with the individual's partner in the exercise. Each also writes two character sketches of the other on the same basis. After

Table 7.1 Modifications in IT group format to resolve common group problems

| Problem | Structure | Dyad topic | Bridging questions |
| --- | --- | --- | --- |
| Needy group members | Both therapists participate in rotating dyads as means of giving more individual attention to members. | Ways I can give help to others and seek help from them. | Whose needs were most like your own? Whose needs surprised you? |
| Some members not sharing in dyads | Interrupt each dyadic interaction at halfway point and explicitly switch roles of speaker and listener. | Things I share easily and things that are harder to share. | Did you find yourself sharing more as the dyads continued? What kind of atmosphere made it harder to open up? |
| Group is dealing with one severely disturbed member | Arrange ancillary individual contact with therapist. | Times I feel 'together' and times I feel like I'm 'falling apart'. | Did the dyads help you see more of your own hidden weaknesses? Your own hidden strengths? |
| Multiple absences | Monitor degree of criticism of others in dyads, and reassert 'rule' of nonconfrontative sharing, if needed. | Positive and negative reactions to the group so far. | How would the group have been different if everyone were here? What would you have said to the members not present? |
| Anticipated problems with termination | Plan 'graduation' for last session to facilitate leave-taking. | What would I most like to say to each group member? | Whose message was easiest to accept? Whose was most challenging? |

Reproduced with permission from Neimeyer, R.A. (1988b) 'Clinical guidelines for conducting Interpersonal Transaction Groups', *International Journal of Personal Construct Psychology*, 1, 181–90.

exchanging their 'public' character sketches of each other, the pair record their reactions to how they are described, ask the other to elaborate on points which are unclear, and perhaps note how they are dealing with the information which they have received and how they imagine the other may be dealing with new information. In the next stage of the procedure, each partner questions the other concerning the evidence on which their descriptions of each other are based and the further evidence which the other would require to be more certain about the conclusions drawn in the sketch. The final stage involves each partner making inferences about the other on the basis of the sketch written by the other. These same steps may then be followed in relation to the participants' 'public' sketches of themselves, allowing discussion of similarities and differences between participants' views of themselves and how they are seen by the other. At all stages in the procedure, and after the session, participants are encouraged to note down points which arise, including thoughts which they would not wish to share with the other. Mair suggests that the procedure is likely to lead each participant to engage in experimentation following the session to test out hypotheses developed in the encounter. In subsequent sessions, the participants, using a similar procedure to that in the first, may focus on their anticipations of how the other made use of their encounter in the intervening period.

As Agnew (1985) has noted, the value of group treatment approaches is not confined to adult clients. Working with children, she introduced the group as a 'Magic Garden', 'a changing place where the familiar and unfamiliar lived together' (p. 242). Sessions focussed on 'superordinate problems and issues' provided by the therapists, for example that frightening things can become good things, and in some sessions props such as puppets were also provided. However, the aim of the group was not that the children would be led towards a particular view of the world, but rather 'that the experience would allow each child to discover the richness of his ideas and the power of his action and that we would all learn something about touching each other's worlds' (p. 242). Jackson (1990b) has also described a personal construct therapy group for adolescents which made use of a variety of structured exercises, including the sharing of self-characterisations, drawing, games, discussion of stories, behavioural experiments, enactment of scripted plays and of role-play situations, and reflection on the group experience by such means as video recordings.

Before closing our discussion of personal construct psychotherapy in a group setting, the composition and other structural features of therapy groups should be considered. It will be apparent that a fairly heterogeneous group is more likely to be conducive to experimentation, to the revision of preemptive and constellatory constructs, and to the development of more comprehensive constructs than one in which members are from similar backgrounds and tend to share particular constructions of the world. The latter type of group, although providing considerable support, may only serve to validate group members' existing constructions, and in Kelly's view its clients may be more likely to require additional forms of treatment. Exposure to the uniform constructions of clients in a homogeneous group may also pose dangers for the therapists, as indicated by my finding that the leaders of a cognitive therapy group for depressives both showed a reduction in self-esteem over the course of therapy (Winter, 1985d). Nevertheless, group formats such as the IT Group may be usefully adapted to the goals of therapy with particular client groups, and the IT procedure has been found to be of value in homogeneous groups of problem drinkers (Landfield and Rivers, 1975; Landfield, 1979; Rivers and Landfield, 1985), clients with eating disorders (Button, 1985a, 1987), and incest victims (Alexander *et al.*, 1989), while my colleagues and I are experimenting with its use in elaborating the construing of interpersonal conflict in agoraphobics. For problem drinkers, IT groups are likely to provide a rare opportunity for a validating social interaction, a focus on change towards sobriety, and a less blocked use of the Circumspection-Preemption-Control Cycle than is usually the case in such individuals (Rivers and Landfield, 1985). That incest victims may also be particularly likely to benefit from homogeneous groups is indicated by Alexander and Follette (1987), who note that such groups provide an opportunity for individuals who may not previously have revealed their backgrounds to others to experience commonality with other members and consensual validation. These authors, who report their use of a personal construct approach to such groups, note that it is equally important for the clients to acknowledge their differences since incestuous families tend to be characterised by members' limited ability to perceive and understand subtle differences between their viewpoints and those of others. It should also be noted that, as is apparent from Button's (1987) description of his eating disorders group, the focus of a homogeneous group need not always be on the clients' shared problem area, and indeed our discussion of the symptom as a way of life indicates the importance of attention to areas other than the problem area in such groups. This may be relatively easily achieved in an IT Group by the use of dyadic interaction topics relating to more general themes and to life without the symptom. An alternative approach, which has been employed with groups of stutterers, is for the initial sessions to focus on the teaching of techniques to produce fluency; and the later sessions, which aim to prevent relapse, to employ a personal construct theory model focussing on experimentation with fluency and elaboration of clients' construing of themselves as fluent speakers (Dalton, 1983c; Evesham and Fransella, 1985; Evesham, 1987). Dalton suggests that the clients selected for such groups should have some degree of fluency, or the ability to achieve it through the use of a technique; an interest in their self-development, and not just in the development of fluency; and an interest in the needs of others. She does not consider it advisable to include clients with 'interiorised' stuttering, in which a stutter is concealed by various mechanisms, in stutterers' groups, but Levy (1987) has found homogeneous groups for such clients to be a useful source of support. The first stage of her groups involves identification of the features of stuttering by, for example, the use of self-characterisations. The second stage is concerned with the reconstruing of, or desensitisation towards, stuttering such that the client may stutter more openly without finding this particularly unpleasant. As well as the use of various speech techniques, it may include 'voluntary stuttering' tasks. The final focus of the group is on experimentation, with, for example, enactment exercises within group sessions, and group members setting each other tasks involving variation of their behaviour outside the therapy room. Other clients who, it has been argued, might benefit from the support provided by homogeneous groups are drug addicts (Dawes, 1985) and suicidal individuals (Stefan and Von, 1985), and personal construct group psychotherapy has also been employed with couples (G. Neimeyer, 1987b), as we shall discuss on p. 302. With suicidal people, a group approach may be of particular value in reducing preemptive construing, and the method adopted by Stefan and Von, with the intention of facilitating positive anticipations of the future, is to ask group members to describe their 'ideal house'. In less structured homogeneous groups than those described above, and perhaps particularly in groups organised on a self-help basis, it may be more difficult to deflect the group away from issues which are likely only to elaborate even further group members' ways of life as sufferers from a particular symptom. Nevertheless, Batty and Hall (1986), describing a personal construct theory approach to self-help groups for people with eating disorders, demonstrate that such a group need not be dominated by concern with food and weight. Alcoholics Anonymous groups were also considered by Kelly (1955) to serve a valuable function in many cases by providing a new role for the individual for whom loss of the alcoholic role is a guilt-provoking prospect. Similarly, Rivers and Landfield (1985) indicate that such groups may offer their members a useful set of constructions which, as a temporary measure, may help the individual cope with the initial uncertainty of an unfamiliar state such as sobriety. As Dawes (1985) has pointed out, however, in discussing therapeutic communities, transition from the group to the outside world will not be facilitated if the new constructs developed are not permeable to events beyond the context of the group. Finally, it should be noted that self-help groups may be of value with the parents of such clients as children with special needs (Cunningham and Davis, 1985), or who stutter (Hayhow, 1987), since these parents may be more willing to compare their constructions with those of others who are in a similar situation than with professionals.

Varying degrees of structure have been employed in the groups discussed above, from the relatively controlled format of the IT Group to the freer discussion evident in Alexander and Follette's groups. It seems possible that different types of client are likely to benefit from groups of high and low structure, the greater control over experiences of invalidation, anxiety, and threat which is possible in structured groups perhaps making them more appropriate for the tightly construing client. As Landfield (1979) points out, however, even an IT Group may be perceived as so lacking in structure as to be highly anxiety-provoking for a tight construer unless very concrete discussion topics are chosen. G. Neimeyer and Merluzzi (1982), drawing on experimental evidence (G. Neimeyer et al., 1979; G. Neimeyer and Merluzzi, 1979), suggest that, as a general rule, initial structuring of a group is likely to facilitate 'systematic information exchange' involving self-disclosure and, in particular, the use, and testing out, of abstract, psychological constructions of others. This in turn, in the view of these authors, is likely to lead to enhancement of the ability of group members to construe each others' construction processes, and hence increased group cohesion. As well as the differential selection of clients for alternative types of group, the therapist will also be concerned with whether a client's construing is such that he or she is likely to benefit from group approaches in general. Thus, in selecting clients for a group, Kelly regarded the primary consideration as their readiness to construe the viewpoints of others, and as we have seen in Chapter 5 this appears to be related to an inner-directed 'personal style'. He also considered that a potential group member should have some permeable constructs which are comprehensive enough to be applied to a range of other people, should use some constructs relating to dependency, but relatively few relating to factual descriptions of others, and should not construe too tightly. Such considerations were, for Kelly (1955), more important than clients' verbal facility or degree of disturbance, and indeed, contrary to the opinions of some writers, he felt that 'group psychotherapy may be the treatment of choice for seriously disturbed clients' (p. 1156). I have also argued that, from a personal construct theory perspective, it may be the treatment of choice for depressed clients (Winter, 1985d, 1989b), despite the fact that, as R. Neimeyer (1985e) has noted, depression is often considered one of the exclusion criteria for group therapy. The possible utility of a group approach to the treatment of depressives is indicated by the various features of construing which, as we have seen in previous chapters, have been found to characterise such clients: namely, constriction, low self-esteem, a bleak view of the future, perceived dissimilarity to others, socially deviant constructions in which depression carries positive implications, and polarised self-construing. Thus, the constricted depressive, if the constriction is not too extreme, may benefit from the dilation and experimentation which are encouraged by group therapy. As Yalom (1970) has noted in discussing the group curative factors of 'altruism' and 'interpersonal learning', group therapy may demonstrate to clients of low self-esteem that they have something of worth to offer others, and that the reactions of others towards them become increasingly favourable as their 'interpersonal distortions' lessen. He also considers that, for the client whose view of the future is pessimistic, the group may instil hope as the client witnesses the recovery of other members. For clients who consider themselves to be very different from other people, the group offers 'universality' and 'a "welcome to the human race" experience' (Yalom, 1970, p. 10). Finally, particularly if heterogeneous, the group is likely to result in invalidation of clients' non-consensual constructions of depression, and of the preemptive or constellatory constructions likely to be reflected in their polarised construing of themselves.

A personal construct psychotherapy group, in common with many other types of group, will generally consist of some ten members, including the therapists. Ideally, all members will commence treatment at the same time, since late arrivals may receive relatively little support and may make it difficult to follow a planned sequence of group sessions, as in an IT Group. The group will generally be short-term: IT Groups, for example, rarely last for more than twenty sessions. Llewelyn and Dunnett (1987) regard the brevity of personal construct therapy groups, which is made possible by the emphasis on transfer of experimentation from within the group to the outside world, as one of the major advantages of this approach. Finally, the personal construct group psychotherapist will generally not frown upon social interaction between members outside the group, viewing this as a further opportunity for experimentation, and may also not be averse to the provision of refreshments during or following group sessions. Indeed, the democratic approach of some such therapists may even extend to allowing group members to set their own rules for the group and to invite their friends to sessions (Bannister, 1983b; Jackson, 1990b).

Koch (1985, p. 326) concludes his review of the personal construct theory approach to group psychotherapy with the statement that 'Although many would . . . elaborate it into a form of therapy in its own right, this does not appear to have as great an advantage as suggesting it as an approach which could be used to encompass and understand many therapeutic approaches'. Such a conclusion seems unnecessarily pessimistic. Although personal construct group psychotherapy has not been extensively elaborated, and may on occasion not seem dissimilar to other approaches (Dunnett and Llewelyn, 1988), there would seem to be considerable potential for the further development of a range of group treatment methods, perhaps varying along such dimensions as degree of structure, which are firmly rooted in personal construct theory.

## Emotive-reconstructive therapy

Morrison (1987) has described how his dissatisfaction with the behavioural treatment approach led him to develop the method of emotive-reconstructive therapy, which he now conceptualises in personal construct theory terms. For example, he views it as aiming to elaborate clients' construing of particular past events and to extend the range of convenience of the constructs concerned. It is also apparent that the loosening and realignment of constructs are aspects of his procedure.

The view of psychological disorder on which this form of therapy is based is that clients exhibit an 'inability to construe themselves and others in a congruent, personally satisfying manner' (Morrison and Cometa, 1977, p. 294), and that their inadequate constructions and roles arise as strategies to cope with the stress occasioned by events inconsistent with their construct systems. Such inadequate strategies are particularly likely to be developed in childhood, when the individual's construct system is not sufficiently complex or permeable to enable the construing of events in a propositional manner.

For example, the child confronted with events which appear to invalidate a preemptive construction of a parent as loving may reduce the stress which this involves by construing the self as bad, enactment of this role allowing maintenance of the belief that the parent would behave lovingly if only the child were good. The child may also be under pressure to adopt some dysfunctional role and way of construing which has been passed down in the family heritage (Morrison, 1977).

The first phase of emotive-reconstructive therapy aims to enable the client, by means of such techniques as imagery, hyperventilation, Gestalt therapy methods such as cushion-pounding, and enactment, to reexperience the stress of the past event which it is assumed led the client to develop a dysfunctional role and associated constructs. A typical procedure is for the client to focus in imagination, with eyes closed, for up to 30 minutes on some place, object, or person, with particular emphasis on sensory recall, for example of the smells, noises, and colours accompanying the event. The event concerned may be selected with reference to the client's presenting problem: thus, a client who has been unable to complete a grieving process may be asked to focus on the death or burial of the significant other concerned (Morrison, 1978, 1981, 1986). During and following the recreation of the stress associated with the past event, the therapist assists the client to verbalise adequate constructs which will reduce this stress. The second phase of treatment focusses on the integration of the experience, such that the client is able to reconstrue the past event and ultimately his or her life. Morrison and Cometa consider that this then enables the suspension of the constructs which had previously been employed to cope with the stress.

Morrison and Cometa report that the duration of emotive-reconstructive therapy rarely needs to be longer than fifteen sessions. In view of its stressful nature, they also point out that before the end of a therapy session, the therapist should offer the client support by self-disclosure and reassurance; and that the client will need to be highly motivated. Despite this latter requirement, Morrison and his colleagues have reported successful applications of the method with a range of clients (Morrison, 1979, 1980a, 1980b, 1981; Morrison and Cometa, 1979, 1980; Morrison and Heeder, 1984, 1984–5; Morrison and Holdridge, 1984; Morrison et al., 1981, 1983a, 1983b).

## TREATMENT APPROACHES FOR PARTICULAR PROBLEMS

With a wide range of techniques in their treatment repertoires, personal construct psychotherapists are able to adapt their approaches to the needs of particular clients, or to address specific problems which arise over the course of therapy. An indication of which techniques may be appropriately employed in treating particular disorders of construing has been provided above, but it may be useful to provide some guidelines concerning ways of approaching certain problems.

## The loose construer

Clearly, if the therapist considers a client's disorder to have a basis in excessively loose construing, tightening techniques are likely to figure prominently in therapy. However, if the client, as with many loose construers, has withdrawn from others, the therapist's initial concern will simply (or, often, not so simply) be to make contact. This, as Kelly points out, involves the therapist construing the client sufficiently well to play a role in relation to him or her, and to behave in a way which is predictable to the client, thereby coming within the range of convenience of the client's role constructs.

Several hazards are likely to be faced in working with such clients, and the therapist should not embark too hastily or indiscriminately on tightening, and putting to the test, the client's constructs. Instead, it should be remembered that loosening has served a purpose for the client, such as the reduction of anxiety. If constructs are suddenly tightened, tested, and then invalidated, the result, particularly if the constructs are comprehensive, is likely to be considerable anxiety, to which the client may respond by constriction. A good example of this danger is provided by Leitner (1980), whose premature tightening of one of the loose superordinate constructs of his client led her to terminate therapy for a while. Equally, however, as the client begins to tighten constructions, there is a danger that he or she will attempt a too extensive dilation and apply constructs too rapidly to unpredictable people and events, with the result that loosening occurs once again. If the client has not re-established the social role which is likely to have been lost as a result of loosening and social withdrawal, too rapid dilation is also likely to lead to confrontation with this dislodgement from role, and therefore to guilt. And, in Kelly's view, the client may then attempt to cope with this guilt by adopting a 'paranoid role'.

## The tight construer

Treatment of the client whose constructions are excessively tight is also not likely to be a straightforward matter of applying loosening techniques. Attention should normally first be paid to developing the therapeutic relationship 'as a bridge which spans the unpredictable vicissitudes of life' (Kelly, 1955, p. 850), and which may be viewed in terms of less literalistic constructs than the tight construer is initially likely to employ. To achieve such ends, the therapist may provide support when the client becomes anxious, and may encourage a certain amount of constriction, which may even involve hospitalisation. As the research results presented in Chapter 5 would suggest, a relatively structured approach to treatment is likely to be most acceptable to the tightly construing client, at least in these early stages of therapy.

If the therapeutic relationship has not been very firmly established, the therapist, rather than concentrating on loosening, may decide to focus on the less anxiety-provoking approach of increasing the permeability of the client's tight constructs. When loosening is employed, as with tightening in the loose construer, it should not be applied too extensively. Since the tight construer 'will see loose constructs as much like no constructs at all' (Kelly, 1955, p. 850), extensive loosening is likely to lead to considerable anxiety. As the client's tight constructs are likely to have been impermeable, loosening may also result in rapid dilation. Faced with anxiety and dilation, the client may respond by constriction, hostility, or preemptive construing. Kelly noted that the therapist is also likely to be confronted with various other problems in working with the tight construer, ranging from guilt reactions to dealing with constructions at a low level of cognitive awareness.

Once the therapist has successfully enabled the client to loosen constructions, the client will need to be shown how to tighten constructs once again, and to weave back and forth between tight and loose construing. Experimentation will need to be facilitated, and the client gradually encouraged to carry out these experiments in the outside world rather than depending solely on his or her relationship with the therapist.

### The dilated client

In the example which he provided of treatment of a client whose disorder involved dilation, Kelly (1955) offered a few tips which may be of some general utility in treating such clients. Firstly, he suggested that it might be useful occasionally to accept the client's constructions of the therapist as omnipotent, while at the same time indicating that any such omnipotence will not be used to change the client in a way which he or she does not wish. Kelly also noted that the dilated client is likely to apply any new 'insights' developed during therapy in an indiscriminate fashion, and that one of the therapist's main tasks will be to help the client to develop small islands of structure. It may also be of value to focus on the development of a new, comprehensive, superordinate system of constructs, while encouraging the verbalisation and testing of any preverbal constructs on which the client had previously relied. Finally, hospitalisation may be considered to help the client to constrict his or her field, but the clinician should then be sure before recommending discharge that the client has developed a sufficiently structured system of constructs to be able to handle a dilated field. If this is not the case, Kelly cautions that the likely result may be suicide.

### The constricted client

The client who has characteristically kept anxiety under control by constriction should also, of course, not be encouraged to dilate too rapidly by, for example, being placed immediately in a psychotherapy group. Instead, relatively 'safe' means of dilation will first have to be discovered, and Kelly (1955) suggested that this may in some cases include such creative activities as painting, experimentation and elaboration of construing at a more verbal level being reserved for a later stage of therapy. Kelly even acknowledged that electroconvulsive therapy may have temporary beneficial effects with the highly constricted client who is at risk of constricting further to the point of suicide. His explanation of this phenomenon was that ECT produces 'a sudden constriction of the whole perceptual field, followed by a rapid redilation of the immediate field but a slower dilation of the more remote field' (p. 905). In his view, it is this redilation which is the major active ingredient of ECT, and he recommended that psychotherapy be employed in conjunction with ECT to control the dilation and help the client to develop a system of constructs which can provide some structure for the client who is confronted with a redilated field. It may be hoped that the personal construct psychotherapist will find some less drastic means than ECT of treating the constricted client, and that this is so is indicated by Sheehan's (1985a, 1985b) psychotherapy for depressives, employing an approach which focusses upon dilation, and R. Neimeyer's (1985d) suggestion of the use of activity scheduling and mood induction techniques to dilate the construing of such clients. However, Kelly's example of the use of ECT provides a further reminder that, far from plunging the client immediately into a dilated field, the therapist may in some cases help the client to constrict further before gradually embarking on dilation.

As well as depressives, another group of clients who, as we have seen in Chapter 3, are likely to be characterised by constriction are those suffering from organic deficits. Kelly regarded a major goal of therapy with such clients as the development of constructs which allow the client to span the seemingly very different events of the past, present, and future. Conveying a wish to understand the client's experience may be particularly important, as in Brumfitt and Clarke's (1983) approach with aphasic people. As Green (1986) has indicated in his account of work with brain-injured adolescents, therapy with these clients is also likely to involve dealing with such issues as guilt and impulsivity.

### The anxious client

The personal construct psychotherapist would not necessarily view anxiety as an undesirable state, but rather as 'a harbinger of change' (Kelly, 1955, p. 836). In some cases, such as the client who construes so loosely as to be diagnosed as schizophrenic, the presence of some anxiety may indicate that the client still retains a sufficient degree of contact with 'reality' to be amenable to a conventional psychotherapeutic approach. Nevertheless, if a client's anxiety is such as to be likely to impede therapeutic movement, the therapist may take direct steps to ameliorate it by using any of a number of strategies. To quote

Kelly (1955) again, 'When anxiety stifles adventure, then it is time to do something about it' (p. 1111). The strategies which may then be employed include provision of support or reassurance; encouragement of constriction; encouragement of dilation, with a view to development of comprehensive constructs which will help to reduce anxiety; loosening of constructions, so that they become less vulnerable to invalidation; tightening of some constructs, so that clearer predictions are generated; binding of constructs, and anxieties, to particular times or situations; encouragement of short-range experimentation to facilitate the structuring of the construct system; encouragement of circumspection, and therefore of alternative perspectives on situations; encouragement of preemption, as a basis for action; or encouragement of weeping, and consequently acceptance of a role for the client which is structured in terms of dependency constructs. The last of these options, and indeed any attempt to control anxiety by encouraging dependency on the therapist, should not be chosen lightly. For example, as Kelly (1955) pointed out, if the client is hostile as well as anxious, it may lead to the therapist being expected to validate all the client's constructions, with the result that therapy will probably be a very lengthy affair. In regard to the encouragement of weeping, Kelly also differentiated between ten different types of weeping, some of which are more appropriate to encourage than others. Persistent weeping which is accompanied by constriction and withdrawal may, for example, lead to such loss of structure that there is a risk of suicide.

During a session, if anxiety becomes, or is likely to become, excessive, the therapist may deal with it in various ways in addition to the broad strategies outlined above. These include rigid structuring of the session; leading the session into an area in which the client's construing is well structured; ensuring that there is adequate time to complete reconstruction in a particular area before moving on to another; conversely, increasing the tempo of the session so that there is insufficient time to generate much anxiety about a particular topic; differentiating between different types of anxiety reported by the client; informing the client that anxiety may be anticipated at particular stages of therapy, thus binding the anxiety to those stages; asking the client to introspect about the experience; and encouraging preemption concerning, and therefore encapsulation of, the client's anxieties, although this may hamper any later reconstruction of the anxieties concerned.

### The hostile client

It will be apparent from Kelly's definition of hostility that psychotherapy with the hostile client is likely to be beset with difficulties. Such a client will generally be reluctant to experiment, and will not be seeking to develop more adequate constructions but rather will be expecting the world to fall into line with his or her existing constructions. Faced with a hostile client, the therapist will wish to understand which of the client's predictions are being invalidated, and will need to beware of the counter-hostility which the client may provoke (Soldz, 1983). Kelly viewed the therapist's primary task as to produce aggression, perhaps by gradually encouraging experimentation in circumscribed areas. He suggested that, as a first step, it may be valuable to attempt to limit the client's hostility to particular topics, which are only discussed in therapy and in relation to which the therapist is willing to make some concessions, such as always being prepared to listen to what the client has to say. Next, opportunities should be provided for aggressive exploration in areas where this is unlikely to result in either anxiety or a high degree of guilt. Such exploration will usually be limited to the therapy sessions at first, and Kelly even found such methods as clay modelling, in which the client is given some freedom to manipulate the environment, to be of use at this stage of therapy. When the client begins to experiment in the 'real world', the therapist will need to be attentive to the possible effects on those close to the client, and Kelly suggested that such experimentation should not be attempted until the client has some ability to engage in role relationships. Finally, after developing a viable alternative way of construing, the client may be helped to see the extent of his or her hostility. However, before the therapist confronts a client with the realisation that his or her view of the world is based on a hostile misinterpretation of events, it will be as well to ensure that the client has begun to develop a new core role. If this has not occurred, the client who discovers that his or her ways of relating to others have been based on misperceptions of these people will be faced with loss of core role and therefore considerable guilt.

### The guilty client

Kelly (1955, p. 891) viewed guilt as 'an ever present hazard in psychotherapy': for example, it may be produced in the client who reveals highly emotionally loaded material, and thereby becomes very dependent on the therapist, or who elaborates his or her complaint, and loss of role, in an uncontrolled way. We have seen above how guilt may be minimised by, for example, encouraging the client to experiment in a way, such as enactment, which does not imply dislodgement from the client's core role. Experimentation through the medium of discussion with the therapist, rather than by action, may serve a similar purpose. A rather more direct way of reducing guilt is the reconstruction of the client's core role, for example by facilitating behaviour based on the client's construing of the constructions of others. The perspectives of those others with whom the client's core role is primarily defined will be likely to be a central focus of therapy, which may usefully involve enactment of the people concerned. The guilty client may also be profitably encouraged to develop alternative roles, as by vocational guidance or providing useful activities for an in-patient during his or her hospital stay.

Group psychotherapy is often another very effective means of enabling a client to feel less dislodged from his or her core role, and therefore reducing guilt. Also useful in some cases may be the development of a comprehensive role relationship with the therapist, which may be facilitated by frequent therapy sessions focussing on many different areas of the client's life.

Kelly considered that, in working with children, the control of guilt by development of the client's role relationship with the therapist may be particularly valuable. Turning to the other end of the age spectrum, elderly people may be especially likely to feel guilty due to loss of role, and this is therefore one client group with which the therapist would be well-advised to avoid any questioning of the client's life role and consequent further exacerbation of the client's guilt. Instead, with the elderly client, 'it is extremely important that the significance of his earlier life be carefully preserved and enhanced' (Kelly, 1955, p.925). Such arguments perhaps provide a justification for the use with elderly people of techniques, such as reminiscence therapy (Lewis and Butler, 1974), which may be likely to strengthen clients' core role identification and, to use Hill's (1988) terms, may perhaps help to reawaken 'dormant' constructs. Elaborating on the functions of reminiscence in the elderly, Viney et al. (1989c) point out that it may provide a necessary validation for constructs at a time at which numerous changes and losses have resulted in a dearth of external sources of validation. Mourning may be considered to serve a similar function (Hoaglands, 1984; Woodfield and Viney, 1985; Viney et al., 1989c), allowing the bereaved person to retain some predictability in a construct system disrupted by loss, and lessening guilt by reducing the discrepancy between core constructs and past behaviour. As Viney and her colleagues note, however, reminiscence and mourning in therapy should be accompanied by attempts to develop new external sources of validation.

It should finally be noted that, as Kelly (1969b) indicated, and as R. Neimeyer and Harter (1988) have found in working with women who were sexually abused as children, guilt rarely responds to therapeutic absolution by, for example, disputing the client's blameworthiness. The alternative approach which the latter authors have adopted is firstly to invite the woman to consider her moral reprehensibility from a variety of perspectives; if she still sees herself as in some way responsible for the abuse, to accept this as a hypothesis; to consider current episodes in which she may also be inviting abuse; and to design experiments in which she behaves as if she were no longer deserving of abuse. Neimeyer and Harter also discuss the importance of viewing guilt as a 'signal of the need to revise the implicative links of core structures to resolve inconsistencies in the system and to allow the person to deal elaboratively with new experiences' (p. 178).

## The threatened client

Threat, like guilt, may often be produced by psychotherapy, as we shall consider further below. For example, it is likely to result if there is an attempt to force rapid change on the client. Amongst the ways in which Kelly suggested that threat may be controlled are that any new constructs developed in therapy should initially be formulated in contexts not involving the client and their family; and that when these constructs come to be applied to the self, the initial focus should be on the past self or on some defined area, such as the client's behaviour during therapy. Enactment methods may also be as useful in minimising the threat provoked by therapy as they are in minimising guilt.

## The client with a disorder of control

In working with a client whose disorder is reflected in failure to complete the C-P-C Cycle adequately, the therapist's basic task will be to facilitate experimentation. The particular approach adopted will depend on the stage in the cycle at which the client is 'stuck'. If the client's problem is one of indecisiveness, due to failure to move beyond the circumspection phase or, because of the apparent incompatibility of the choices available, to move beyond preemption, the therapist may encourage the client to disregard implications of choices until control is attained (Dunnett, 1985). If the circumspection phase is foreshortened, and the client acts impulsively, because a situation is viewed from one perspective only, the most appropriate approach may be elaboration of the construct concerned during therapy. As Dunnett (1985) notes, if the client appears to base decisions on only one, highly permeable, superordinate construct, the development of a wider range of superordinate constructs will be a major therapeutic goal. If the impulsivity represents an attempt to escape anxiety, therapy may also usefully focus on the development of superordinate constructs which will allow apparent incompatibilities in construing, and anxiety, to be tolerated. If the client's impulsive actions result from difficulty in choosing a preemptive issue, enactment of the various options open to the client may be usefully employed. If the impulsivity is basically a problem of 'bad timing', the focus of therapy may be the client's social experimentation. Therapy with an impulsive client always carries the danger that the client's experimentation may be carried out in an impulsive manner, and the therapist should pay particular attention to exerting some control on the impulsivity of the client's experiments outside the therapy room.

One particular manifestation of a disorder of control may be a suicide attempt, and Stefan and Von (1985) have discussed the task of the therapist with suicidal individuals. They note that therapy should begin soon after the suicide attempt, for this will be a time of reconstruing. The constructions of the client and significant others concerning the attempt should be discussed, and the attempt should be 'word-bound' and 'time-bound' as a strategy which may have served some purpose for the individual at the time but is no longer relevant to present circumstances. Similarly, R. Neimeyer (1988c) notes the importance of helping the suicidal client to formulate the question which is being enacted in his or her behaviour, including demands made on the therapist. Stefan and Von suggest that, if the client has difficulty in articulating constructions concerning the attempt, he or she may be usefully asked to describe pictures or write characterisations depicting the self at particular times. If the client is one who anticipates chaos (see p. 101), they consider that therapy should focus on helping the individual to develop a self-construction as capable and in control, and should employ tightening procedures. On the other hand, with the client whose suicide attempt reflects a view of life as highly determined, loosening techniques may be employed with a view to the development of alternative, propositional constructions which will allow the individual to experience more avenues of movement and control of his or her destiny.

### The client with undifferentiated dependency

The most direct approach in working with a client whose dependencies are undifferentiated is to document this lack of differentiation by citing instances of it to the client. The danger of such an approach, as Kelly points out, is that the client's response to the 'insight' which has been offered may be to slot-rattle to behaviour which is construed as independent, and that this construction of independence may be derived from the client's childhood view of adult behaviour rather than being based on role relationships. Such a rapid provision of insight is also likely to lead to threat and panic if the client has not been helped to develop alternative ways of relating to others. A more gradual approach, focussing on experimentation with social relationships but not on core constructs, and both on the differential construing of dependencies and the identification of resources which may match them (Kelly, 1969c), is therefore generally desirable. Undifferentiated dependency, in Kelly's view, is often associated with hostility, and therefore encouraging such a client to experiment, and to accept the results of the experimentation, may be no easy matter. It is also likely that the client's dependencies on the therapist will have to be differentiated, so that some of them may be gradually dispersed amongst other people.

### The client presenting with somatic complaints

Kelly viewed a primary aim of therapy with the client who presents somatic symptoms as being the development of permeable, comprehensive, but not necessarily verbal, constructs which the client may use to 'bridge the gap' between mind and body. The major ingredients of therapy in such cases may not be verbal, but instead the therapist 'has to deal with interpersonal relationships rather than word symbols . . . to be able to enact various parts as if he were a child's playmate . . . to be able to do role playing skillfully and sympathetically . . . to be aware of the therapeutic effectiveness of genuine role relationships' (Kelly, 1955, p. 923).

Clients diagnosed as physically ill are by no means unsuitable for personal construct psychotherapy. As Viney (1983b, 1983c, 1985a) and Skenderian (1983) have described, the way in which they respond to their predicament will depend upon the 'images of illness' which they have developed, and which may be based on their experiences of illness as children. For example, Viney considers that images involving uncertainty, helplessness, isolation, anxiety, anger, and depression all make people more vulnerable towards illness, but while the first three of these images tend to impede recovery, the last three, if expressed by clients, may facilitate recovery. Recovery, in her view, is also more likely in the client whose images of illness involve certain positive features, such as competence and good relationships with family and friends. It follows from this perspective that it may be valuable for a therapist to help an ill client to identify, express, and possibly to reconstrue, his or her images of illness. Such therapeutic efforts are likely to involve assisting clients who are faced with uncertainties, changes in core constructs, and role dislodgement to cope with the negative emotions which they experience, and which may be evoked by the prospect of recovery from illness as well as by that of physical deterioration. A therapist may, for example, assist the ill client to anticipate events, including death, and to find an adequately structured new role. The latter process may be facilitated by group approaches, which are likely to help reduce the client's sense of isolation. Also of value in enabling clients to construe themselves as more competent may be training in ways of coping with illness, including the use of imagery, and ways of coping with anxiety, such as relaxation exercises (Viney, 1987a). A further useful therapeutic focus may be the constructs employed by members of the ill person's family, since Viney considers that greater ability to cope with illness is likely if these are flexible and conducive to autonomy amongst family members. Finally, it may be productive to work with the images of professionals which underlie clinical policies likely to hamper recovery. As Viney (1983b, p. 45) notes, 'It is important to remember that people – whether they be debilitated, in pain or almost comatose – continue to try to make sense of what is happening to them. To render this more difficult for them by deception or withholding information from them is to frustrate them and generate more anger-laden images'. She also emphasises the importance of validation by staff of clients' constructs, and indicates the desirability of reversal of the tendency of staff to validate clients' constructions of themselves as helpless more than those of themselves as competent. However, perhaps the primary task of the personal construct psychotherapist in working with carers is to assist them in construing the constructions of their clients rather than preemptively viewing them as sick or disabled (Bannister, 1981).

Viney (1983b) has suggested that a language of illness which tends to employ verbs rather than, as at present, nouns may be conducive to greater attention being paid to psychological and social processes in illness and a reduction in the use of unnecessary surgical procedures. A similar view is taken by Kenny (1987), whose radical personal construct theory perspective on cancer complainants is that they are actively 'doing' cancer. He has found that such people are often highly preoccupied with past events, in contrast to their poorly elaborated anticipations of the future, particularly of the future self. Such an individual's future role enactment, in his view, is that of a dead person, and he or she may often, before developing cancer, visualise and elaborate a construction of the self as a victim of illness. In working with cancer complainants, Kenny initially elaborates the meaning of cancer for them, paying particular attention to articulation of the preverbal constructs that are likely to be implicated in the illness, and facilitating this process by asking them to keep diaries. He describes how, in one such client, he also elaborated the construct system of her family, who tended to communicate and compete with each other by means of illness experiences, by asking her to map family members onto the body on the basis of the symptoms which they each regularly experienced. He then viewed his therapeutic task as to disintegrate the client's individual and family construct systems by interacting with her, and by enabling her to interact with the family, in ways which were orthogonal to these respective systems. Specifically, such interactions were seen as providing her with an alternative to 'conversations for illness'. His interventions with the client, as with others with cancer, encompassed the physical, psychological, and spiritual levels. Viewing her cancer as a way of drawing a boundary between herself and her family which her very permeable construct system had not previously provided, he also focussed, with the aid of enactment, on the creation of an alternative boundary. Various other methods of facilitating experimentation and controlled elaboration were also employed, and during shiatsu sessions she became aware of preverbal constructions concerning family members which allowed her to reconstruct her past and thus her future. She subsequently consulted Tibetan physicians, whose investigations with Western and Oriental methods revealed no trace of cancer.

## The client whose construct system is socially deviant in content

The therapeutic approach with a client whose disorder is primarily manifested in the content of his or her construct system may include imparting of information, assisting the client to formulate new constructs, and experimentation which is designed to invalidate some of the client's existing constructs and to validate new constructs. Group psychotherapy may be a particularly useful means of providing such experiences of invalidation and validation. An alternative approach is reduction of the client's socially deviant constructs to impermeability, perhaps by applying the binding techniques described on page 262.

With the client whose construing is so deviant as to lead to a diagnosis of 'paranoia', Kelly considered that it may be useful in some cases to place the client in a position of considerable dependency on others, with which the construction of the social world as hostile is incompatible. The focus of therapy will then be on the development of permeable, comprehensive, super-ordinate constructs which will allow the client to experiment and, if necessary, to revise constructions to accommodate the results of the experimentation. In working with the client who is regarded as deluded, the personal construct psychotherapist will take the view that the client's 'fictitious perception will often turn out to be a grossly distorted construction of something which actually does exist' (Kelly, 1955, p. 8), and which may be understood if the therapist attempts to adopt this construction and to explore what predictions might follow from it. Dunnett (1988c) also emphasises the importance of exploring the meaning of a client's beliefs, rather than discounting them as delusional. One of the clearest examples of such an approach is provided by Bannister (1985d), who describes how he originally tried unsuccessfully to adopt the alternative approaches of humouring deluded clients, rational argu-ment, or ignoring 'delusional talk'. Humouring such clients, in his view, does not allow the client to discover that some constructions are more valid than others; ignoring delusional talk may mean that the therapist has to ignore virtually everything that the client says, and also does not prepare the client for the way in which other people will be likely to respond to him or her; and rational argument generally fails because of the client's hostile reaction to the evidence with which he or she is confronted. As Lorenzini *et al.* (1989) point out, invalidation of the paranoid client's delusional system by the therapist will generally not be possible until an alternative system is available since the delusional system is developed precisely so that the client may resist invalid-ation which would leave the client with no adequate basis for the prediction of events. Bannister's attempt to employ a personal construct psychotherapy approach with deluded clients involved focussing on the superordinate themes which were reflected in their delusions, and then devising appropriate experiments with the clients. For example, with a client who believed that doctors were conspiring with lorry drivers to have him run over, Bannister discussed the client's apparent belief that the doctors disliked him, and arranged for him to talk with the doctors concerned about their attitude towards him. As Bannister (1985d, p. 173) puts it, 'All delusions have an assertion in them which can be abstracted, which in itself is not unreasonable. The only "unreasonable" things are the concrete elaborations of the delusion.' He felt that one of the purposes served by delusions is that they allow the client to maintain a distance from others, and to test out which other people may be trusted. Trust in the therapist may, therefore, take a long time to develop, and consequently therapy with such clients may be a lengthy process.

## The client with difficulties in sociality

It is self-evident that the major focus of therapy for the client who has difficulty in forming role relationships will be to encourage the client to see the world through the eyes of others. This may be achieved, for example, by enactment of another person or by group treatment approaches, particularly those, such as the Interpersonal Transaction Group, which emphasise understanding the viewpoints of others. Working with children who stutter, Hayhow (1987) has also facilitated their construing of the constructions of others by setting exercises, such as making a book about the family, which require the child to ask others questions about themselves.

As R. and G. Neimeyer (1985) suggest, individuals with difficulties in sociality may usefully be taught particular strategies of developing relationships, such as the filter sequence, progressing from more to less superficial areas of construing, indicated by Duck's (1973b, 1979) research. In Reid's (1979) view, however, any such practical methods for enhancing social competence should 'have as their primary objective the elaboration of the superordinate system through which the individual appraises the demands of his social world and his capacities to meet those demands' (p. 249). Reid puts particular emphasis on training the individual to differentiate between occasions when it is appropriate to apply loose construing and circumspection to social events and those when tight construing and preemption are called for. He advocates the use of techniques which enhance the person's superordinate perspective on his or her social construing. For example, he considers that provision of feedback on the person's social behaviour and on their constructions of this behaviour may help them to construe the outcomes of these constructions.

The task facing the therapist in working with clients who are terrified by role relationships has been described by Leitner (1985b). For example, with one such client, whose ways of dealing with this terror included fragmentation of the self into seven different personalities, one of Leitner's (1987) aims was to facilitate reconstruing in relation to core role constructs which could be preserved from invalidation only by avoidance of role relationships. At termination of therapy, the reduction in the client's fragmentation was reflected in grid scores indicating a decrease in the meaningfulness of his various personalities. With all such clients, the development of a role relationship with the therapist is likely to be of central importance, and Leitner (1988b) cautions that, having been deeply wounded in previous role relationships, they are likely to be very sensitive to any sign that the therapist is retreating from a role relationship with them.

## Couples as clients

G. Neimeyer (1985) also emphasises the development of the role relationship between therapists and clients in work with couples, and has described the wide variety of techniques which may be employed in such work, including various of the methods derived from personal construct theory which we have discussed above. Thus, as we have seen in Chapter 6, several variations on grid procedure have been found to be of value in marital therapy, as by allowing exploration of a couple's ability to construe each other's constructions. For example, grid administration enabled Childs and Hedges (1980) to demonstrate that a couple shared a common language, which might provide them with a basis for discussion of their difficulties during therapy. Despite the similarity in meaning of their constructs, there were significant areas of misperception, such as the husband's failure to appreciate the similarity in their goals for the future, and it was decided to focus therapy on areas, such as various forms of emotional expression, in which the grids indicated that they shared common goals but perhaps did not fully appreciate this commonality. While therapy achieved its intended result of the husband defining achievable goals for himself, an unanticipated outcome, confirmed by a repeat grid assessment, was that these goals diverged from how his wife would like him to be, with a resultant deterioration in the couple's relationship. McCoy (1980) has also made use of repertory grids in marital counselling, but in this case focussing on a particular type of problem, culture shock in marriages between non-Chinese women and Chinese men in Hong Kong. Grids have allowed her to identify such aspects of the culture shock process as polarisation of a wife's construing of Chinese and non-Chinese people, and to chart wives' progress through the stages of her model of the transition experiences which constitute culture shock (McCoy, 1983). Further ingenious adaptations of grid procedure in a marital therapy context have been described by G. Neimeyer (1985), who has helped couples to discern patterns in their relationships by employing a grid in which the elements are chapter sketches for an autobiography of the relationship; and by Bannister and Bott (1973), working with a couple whose marriage was unconsummated. At various points over the course of therapy, this latter couple completed individual grids and a 'duo grid', which they completed together. As all grids employed the same elements and constructs, it was possible to correlate the duo grid with each individual grid completed at the assessment session concerned, this providing an indication of which partner's construct system was dominant in that it had most strongly influenced the duo grid. This procedure allowed the couple's sexual difficulties to be more clearly understood since they were found to be sexually active only when the wife's construing was dominant. The couple's individual grids also revealed various negative implications of sexuality, the wife associating sexual attractiveness with immorality and the husband interest in sex with being unartistic. Therapy therefore focussed on invalidation of these constructions, together with validation of the association revealed in the husband's grid between fear of sex and selfishness. In addition, since the wife's sexual constructs showed little relationship with other constructs, attempts were made to elaborate her construing in this area. Such interventions appeared to be effective in that the couple's level of sexual interest increased, and a repeat grid assessment indicated that sexual interest and attractiveness no longer carried negative implications for them, and that the wife saw them both as keener on sex and her husband as more attractive. However, he no longer construed fear of sex as selfish, and the interrelationships between his sexual constructs diminished. In view of the positive changes which appeared to have occurred, the therapists switched to a more behavioural approach 'on the assumption that the construing problems were largely solved and that, given more frequent and energetic "practice", the couple would achieve intercourse' (p. 170). However, in fact their sexual activity subsequently declined and a further grid assessment indicated an increase in the negative implications which sexual attractiveness carried for the husband, and a decrease in the extent to which he saw himself as keen on sex and to which his wife saw him as sexually attractive. A final grid completed by the husband before termination of therapy showed no substantial change, while the wife's final grid indicated further reduction in the correlations of her sexual constructs. In retrospect, the authors consider that the switch to a behavioural approach was premature, and that further exploration of such aspects of the couple's construing as the husband's view of control and their construal of each other's constructions, aided by the use of alternative grid procedures, might have been advisable.

Yet another application of repertory test procedure in marital therapy has been Kremsdorf's (1985) use of the Reptest Interaction Technique (Bonarius, 1977) to facilitate a couple's construing of each other's constructions. In the first stage of the technique, the couple, taking turns, choose, and describe to each other, a list of elements other than themselves who fit various role titles. The second stage involves the partners alternating in formulating a construct on the basis of each of a number of triads of their elements. Thirdly, the partners take turns to sort all their respective elements in terms of each of their constructs; and finally, each applies the constructs to the self and the partner. At each stage of the procedure, discussion of the meaning of the couple's constructs and their application to elements is encouraged.

Various other assessment procedures have been usefully employed in personal construct therapy with couples. For example, as an adaptation of the self-characterisation procedure, each member of a couple has been asked to write a characterisation of their relationship, which may then be shared and discussed with the partner (Kremsdorf, 1985; G. Neimeyer and Hudson, 1985). Laddering has been used to allow partners to discover that, despite their differences at the subordinate level, their superordinate values may be similar (G. Neimeyer, 1985); and the ABC model may be employed to trace the payoffs of a couple's problems (Tschudi and Sandsberg, 1984). Another procedure which may enable a couple to identify their central differences of opinion, as well as areas of agreement which were perhaps previously unappreciated, has been developed by Slater et al. (1989). This involves the partners each listing their arguments concerning a particular issue, and then each completing a 'logical equivalence matrix' in which their own and their partner's arguments are compared with each other. The use of genograms (Bowen, 1978) may allow a couple to appreciate how their constructions of earlier relationships may be influencing their view of their current relationship, and, together with relationship histories (Satir, 1987), may help the couple to develop a shared theory of their relationship (Wile, 1981) which will enable them to anticipate their interactions. Also useful in this regard, in the view of G. Neimeyer and Hudson (1985), are shared experimentation and Kagen's (1972) Interpersonal Process Recall technique, in which a couple is videotaped in interaction and then they view, and comment upon, the tape.

Experimentation during marital therapy may be facilitated by the use of behavioural contracts (R. Neimeyer, 1986b), and G. Neimeyer's (1985) work with couples has also employed behavioural methods. These include 'love days' (Jacobson, 1977), used to increase levels of validation at subordinate levels of the partners' construct systems; and monitoring of behaviour in one's partner which represents the opposite of a complaint made about the partner (R. Neimeyer and G. Neimeyer, 1985). In addition, G. Neimeyer (1987b) has made use of personal construct group psychotherapy with couples, since he considers that 'the group context would seem ideally suited to the reconstruction of intimate role relations' (p. 127). The techniques used in his groups include brainstorming, for example of ways in which a couple might approach their arguments; and enactment, for example of a 'student–teacher' relationship in a couple whose previous interactions suggested a 'parent–child' relationship. He has also asked each member of a couple to enact the other, and employed nonverbal enactment methods, some of which draw upon family sculpting techniques. In one such procedure, the opposing walls of the therapy room are designated in terms of the contrasting poles of some construct (e.g. 'powerful–powerless'), and partners asked to position themselves as they think appropriate between these poles (G. Neimeyer, 1985). Another method which he has used is to ask group members to line up behind whichever member of a couple they identify with concerning a particular issue, each member of the couple then stating their position and giving up their chair to the person behind them who can elaborate on this position, the process continuing until all have participated. A further enactment procedure which has been adapted for use with couples is fixed-role therapy, Kremsdorf (1985) finding that, although the partners' awareness of each other's roles contravenes Kelly's recommendation that others should not know that the client is role-playing, it allows rigid patterns in a marriage to be broken and, by facilitating rapid feedback on the new behaviour enacted, enables partners' motivation to be maintained. He has also involved children in the therapy process by asking them to play roles complementary to those of their parents.

## The family as client

Rather than focussing on the construing of an individual client, or the individual construct systems of a couple of clients, the therapist may occasionally attempt to produce change in a 'family construct system' (Procter, 1981). This system is viewed by Procter as the family's common reality, which provides the avenues of movement open to its members and the slots which they may occupy. It follows that one of the aims of family therapy is to arrive at a family system composed of constructs which are sufficiently permeable to allow the development of new behaviour and the making of elaborative choices by family members, as well as adequate opportunities for new members to join the family network. As Procter notes, this system should be appropriate to the ages of the family members.

The basic types of technique employed by the personal construct family therapist may be similar to those employed in the individual therapy situation, although the way in which they are applied may differ. For example, the therapist will initially accept the family construct system by 'flowing with, encouraging and utilizing the sequences and contingencies of the interaction process' (Procter, 1981, p. 360). In so doing, the therapist acknowledges that the family's way of being represents an elaborative choice and that their alternative, which is often submerged, is likely to be a state of affairs, such as a marital conflict, which they would consider to be even worse (Procter, 1985a). Whole-figure constructs may be usefully identified and explored, as when it appears that the 'shadow' of some mad ancestor is falling upon a particular family member, who is construed by other members as virtually identical with this person (Scott and Ashworth, 1969). Alternatives and linkages within the system may also be traced by asking the family to indicate similarities and contrasts between its members, and their patterns of interaction. A particular method which, in the view of Dallos and Aldridge (1987), may reveal family constructions is the Milan group's technique of circular questioning, in which every family member is asked to state their perception of the relationship between two other members, who are then compared with a third member. These authors identify family constructs from videotapes of interviews with the family, taking particular note of how other family members respond when a member uses a certain construct. As well as observing that circular questioning may be employed to elicit constructs from a family, Alexander and G. Neimeyer (1989) consider that methods developed by Kantor (1985), such as position claims and time line sculptures, may be viewed as ways of articulating preverbal constructions within the family. In the former technique, each member is asked to state the problem from a personal, biased position, the implications of which are elaborated with the therapist; while in the latter each member is asked to walk along an imaginary time line, indicating verbally and nonverbally critical incidents in the relationship beween them. Repertory tests may also be usefully administered to family members, following which each member may be asked to say what they can about the constructs of another (Doster, 1980).

If it seems that the family construct system is very loose, tightening may be attempted by focussing on specific issues, assigning brief, structured tasks, or linking fragmented acts, and the family may be helped to appreciate that looseness is an aspect of creativity. If few discriminations are made on constructs within the family boundary, as in those families of agoraphobics in which everyone in the family is construed as good and contrasted with outsiders, the therapist will focus on 'elaborating the main construct, differentiating the people in the family and in the external social network' (Procter, 1981, p. 362). The therapist may reframe an issue in terms of some new construct which can be subsumed by the family's superordinate constructs, and as Dallos and Aldridge (1987) note, prior tracing of the implications of constructs within the family system will indicate how the reframe might best be presented. Alternatively, each member may be offered a new construction which allows experimentation with fresh roles and negotiation of a new family construct system. Enactment and methods borrowed from structural family therapy may be employed with a view to elaboration of the family construct system, with members perhaps being assigned to new 'slots' in the system in order to elaborate them. Other tasks may be set to facilitate experimentation, including paradoxical tasks which, while offering reassurance by validating the family reality, prevent members opting for habitual choices and therefore are likely to lead to the development of new alternatives. For example, Procter (1981) notes that forbidding physical contact in a couple presenting with a sexual problem, by validating their lack of sexual interaction, may allow them to experiment with new ways of relating to each other. Procter also suggests the use of various additional techniques, drawn from alternative schools of family therapy, to produce particular changes in the family construct system. Metaphor may be employed to change some superordinate construct without arousing the negative emotions which may result from working directly on this construct's subordinate implications. Massage may be used as a metaphorical technique, and other methods focussing on the body, such as bioenergetic techniques, may help to elaborate what Procter (1981) terms 'within-boundary constructs'. Techniques such as sculpting may be used to validate some new construction. If there is a homeostatic situation in which a family member sees himself or herself as totally bad and another member as totally good, the therapist may borrow Kleinian strategies, asking the member to give examples of the good–bad distinction and then gradually differentiating between them. For example, as the member comes to see that 'some of her attributes are bad, some downright appalling' (Procter, 1981, p. 364), and that there are similar gradations in the goodness of the other member's attributes, the polarisation between them will be reduced.

It will be apparent that the family construct therapist's interventions may, depending on the particular family, focus on family members' actions or on the constructs underlying these actions. As illustrated in the numerous examples provided by Procter (1981, 1985a, 1987), the flexibility of the approach includes the possibility of individual sessions to elaborate constructs in a particular family member with a view to creating a change in the family construct system. Similarly, as Kelly (1955) described, the personal construct psychotherapist's goal in working with one member of a family may be to induce change in another member. Two of the cases described by Procter (1985a, 1987) involve families including a mute member, who in terms of traditional nosological categories might have been diagnosed as schizophrenic. In both families, dramatic changes occurred and the mute individual began to speak, but it seemed that in one case this was due to the family accepting the therapists' reconstruction of their problem, while in the other it involved rejection of this reconstruction and the polarisation within the family being replaced by polarisation between the family and the therapists.

A different application of the personal construct theory perspective to work with families, in that it focusses on parent training, has been developed by Mancuso and his colleagues (Mancuso and Handin, 1980, 1983; McDonald and Mancuso, 1987). In this approach, parents are encouraged to consider their own constructions, particularly those concerning parenting, and the constructions of their children, and if necessary to reconstrue their parenting roles. The particular role which is encouraged is one in which the parent 'recognizes and anticipates differences in adult–child construing of events and reflects this knowledge in parenting behavior' (McDonald and Mancuso, 1987, p. 176). In particular, the parent is helped to moderate the novelty experienced by the child, protecting the child from the high degree of arousal occasioned by extensive failures to anticipate events (Mancuso, 1977). By contrast, in Mancuso's view, children who are presented as management problems tend to have a history of being forced into novel situations by their parents, and of their consequent difficulties in anticipating events being met with coercive parental reprimands. As a result, the parents are construed by their children as not being useful, and indeed enhancing arousal even further, when the child experiences anticipatory failure. Mancuso and his colleagues have given particular attention to reprimand, which they see as initially producing an experience of failure to anticipate, with consequent arousal, but one which should then lead to a reconstruction which reduces arousal (Mancuso and Allen, 1976; Mancuso, 1979a; Handin and Mancuso, 1980). The type of reprimand which they encourage parents in their training programme to employ is one based on consideration of the child's perspective and an attempt to reduce discrepancies between the construing of parent and child. The child may thus be enabled to view the parent as moderating the child's failures to anticipate, and as a result may be less likely to avoid adults.

Assessment of the parents' constructions of parenting roles in Mancuso's training programmes may include the use of the Parent Role Repertory Test (see p. 28), the results of which may provide a focus for training. The programme then involves a period of interaction between the child and therapist, in which the therapist draws the parents' attention to aspects of the child's construing, and the parents viewing videotapes of themselves in interaction with their children. The therapist indicates aspects of these tapes which validate or invalidate the parents' constructions of their role, and encourages experimentation with new ways of relating to the child. As Kirkland *et al.* (1986) have indicated, an alternative method of exploring parents' construing of interactions with infants is to administer a grid with photographs of these interactions as elements.

It may also be of value for a personal construct psychotherapist to work with a client's parents if the client has a learning disability. From a personal construct theory perspective, the transitions involved in the birth of any child may be seen to face parents with a range of emotions, not all positive (O'Reilly, 1977). However, if the child is diagnosed as having a learning disability, threat, guilt, and anxiety may be particularly apparent as the parents confront this sudden invalidation of their constructs concerning parenting, their response to which may be a hostile denial of the disability (Davis, 1983; McConachie, 1985). Therefore, as Davis and Cunningham (1985) point out, one of the therapist's major tasks with them may be to negotiate a construction of their situation which will guide their experimentation with the child. The parents may also be enabled to construe the child's constructions, and thereby to view the child's behaviour from a fresh perspective and to change their own behaviour accordingly. To quote one of the examples provided by Davis and Cunningham, parents who reconstrued their child's hand-flapping as a communication of excitement rather than stereotyped behaviour were then able to communicate to the child in the same way. In the view of these authors, even the use of behaviour modification principles may provide parents with a more viable alternative means of construing the child, as well as facilitating the child's anticipation of its parents' actions (Davis, 1984; Cunningham and Davis, 1985). However, as Hayhow (1987) points out in discussing counselling with parents whose children begin to stammer, the extent of the task involved will be largely determined by the parents' ability to adjust their construct systems in response to new experiences with their children.

At the other end of the age spectrum, Viney *et al.* (1988) have developed a personal construct psychotherapy approach for the families of elderly people whose psychosocial functioning is inhibited by the family construct system. Although the methods employed are similar to those used by other family construct therapists, the content of the constructs concerned may be somewhat different. For example, there is an initial focus on losses experienced by the elderly person which affect the family; and an emphasis is placed on the development of constructs which convey respect and acceptance of the elderly family member, and acknowledgement of the roles which the latter may play within the family system. There must also be an awareness of the likely differences in the personal construct systems of elderly family members and younger therapists, as well as caution not to focus excessively on constructs, such as those concerning competence or intimate relationships, which may be more relevant to earlier stages of 'psychosocial maturity'. As in work with other families, however, Viney *et al.* also emphasise the importance of encouraging alternation between tight and loose construing; the recognition and expression of anxiety and anger in response to invalidation of construing; and the negotiation of changes in family roles and constructs.

## The social system as client

As with families, institutions and societies may be considered to have construct systems (Berger and Luckmann, 1966), and, as Button (1985c) has indicated, may vary in the extent to which they are able to function optimally by, for example, completing cycles of construing. They will also differ in the extent to which they are conducive to the optimal functioning of their members, a point which has been emphasised by writers who have stressed the egalitarian values of personal construct theory, implicit in its basic assumption of constructive alternativism. For example, Warren (1989, pp. 18–19) considers that 'mental health is best thought of in terms of an individual operating in a social context which stresses enquiry, exploration, and dialogue, rather than knowledge, "the truth", or ready-made answers'. Personal construct theory therefore stands in opposition to 'cognitive imperialism', the imposition of the views of inhabitants of one world on those of another (Berger, 1976; Tschudi and Rommetveit, 1982). As Bannister (1979, pp. 31–2) asserts, 'the values of personal construct theory are not consonant with the values of any political theory which prescribes the nature of reality or which makes truth, in any form, the particular possession of a group', and 'the political and psychological intent of construct theory is the total diffusion of power'. For Bannister (1983b, p. 149), 'the explicit purpose of psychotherapy can become the destruction of the non-reciprocal power relationship which is its starting point. 'Cure' can be defined as reaching a level at which the client can effectively contest the psychotherapist's view of life'. He, like Smail (1987), looks forward to a time when the therapeutic and care-taking qualities of communities are such that the, inevitably non-reciprocal and unequal, roles of client and therapist are no longer necessary. It will be apparent, therefore, that, as Epting (1984, p. 191) observes, personal construct 'therapy clearly takes a position opposing social and political oppression', and that its practitioners will favour any social system which facilitates the elaboration of its members' construing, provided that this is not at the expense of constriction of some other individual. Nevertheless, personal construct theorists have occasionally been criticised for over-emphasising the individual's freedom of choice at the expense of adequate consideration of the social and political constraints on this freedom (Procter and Parry, 1978; Salmon, 1990), as well as ethical concerns, such as Li (1990) has discussed in relation to the sexual abuse of children. As Salmon (1990) notes, the theory might usefully take more heed of the fact that some constructions within a particular society are considered more equal than others, some individuals having a 'warranted voice' (Gergen, 1989). In her view, the psychotherapist's concerns may need to be less with individual construing and reconstruing than with 'deconstructing the dominant discourse'.

Personal construct psychotherapists might be expected to be concerned with fostering egalitarian values in institutions or social systems of which they are members, and to apply concepts derived from Kelly's theory in understanding, and attempting to modify, these systems. This will, for example, be the case in the clinical team, where there will be a focus on construing the constructions of other team members and appreciating, and minimising, the threat and anxiety with which transitions may face them (Dunnett, 1988c; Winter et al., 1991). The personal construct theorist may also act as a consultant to other organisations, and while such work may at first sight appear far removed from clinical concerns, it may serve to promote optimal functioning in the organisations concerned and their members, and so play a role in the prevention or alleviation of psychological disorder in the latter. As Fransella et al. (1988) have described, the interventions concerned may range from therapeutic work with individual members of an organisation's staff to methods, such as repertory grid technique (Stewart and Stewart, 1981), which provide managers and staff with insight into their own constructions and those of their colleagues. The increasing application of personal construct psychology in educational settings (e.g. Pope and Keen, 1981), as well as perhaps in itself playing a role in the development of a society which is more tolerant of alternative constructions, may provide approaches which can usefully be applied in a variety of institutional contexts. For example, methods of encouraging self-organised learning rather than dependence on the directions of others have been used to facilitate management styles which emphasise the more equal partnership of managers and staff (Randall and Thomas, 1988).

A further area of concern for the personal construct psychologist may be the analysis and attempted resolution of conflict between social groups, or between different factions within an institution. Such work may usefully draw upon some of the techniques described above in the discussion of interventions with couples and families (e.g. Slater et al., 1989). As du Preez (1988) notes, there should be a focus on identifying the core constructs of the conflicting groups, which, as in his analysis of the superordinate constructs of opposing parties in South African parliamentary debates (du Preez, 1972), may be found to be incompatible. He also emphasises the importance of viewing conflicts within their historical context, with due attention to the 'primal myths' of the groups concerned. The aim of intervention, in his view, will be to convert conflict into competition. Similarly, Rowe (1985b) indicates that attempts at conflict resolution should not necessarily aim to eliminate differences, which may serve the purpose of allowing the individuals or groups concerned to define themselves by contrast with others, but rather should emphasise attempts to understand the constructions of those with whom one is in conflict, forgiveness, and a view of 'strangers' as simply being different rather than as dangerous enemies.

## MOVEMENT, AND 'RESISTANCE' TO MOVEMENT, IN THERAPY

### Signs of movement

As we have discussed in Chapter 6, formal assessment procedures may reveal a client's reconstruing during therapy. However, as Kelly described, indications of movement may be obtained without the necessity of resorting to formal procedures. One such indication is the 'Aha' phenomenon, the surprise shown by the client when an appropriate construction is found for a particular element. Another is the spontaneous documentation by the client of elements which may be subsumed by a new construct: if these elements are drawn from the client's experiences in the 'outside world' after the construct has been formulated, it may be assumed that the client is employing the construct in daily life. Mood changes in the client may also be indicative of restructuring of constructs, provided that they are not accompanied by marked behavioural changes, in which case they are likely to reflect slot-rattling. Experimentation with new behaviour in a therapy session may be a particular indication of forthcoming reconstruction, and a further sign of movement is the client's report that his or her present behaviour contrasts with earlier behaviour, although Kelly cautions that this may occasionally indicate a 'flight into health' by the client who is threatened by treatment. Reconstruing may also be indicated if the client ceases to mention a particular complaint, or if new material is evident in the client's loose constructions. Finally, the client's summaries of treatment sessions may reveal whether reconstruing has occurred.

Other signs may indicate to the therapist that a client's apparent insight does not represent an entirely adequate new construction. This may be so, for example, if the new construct is articulated in a loose or erratic manner; if the documentation of its elements is bizarre or suggestive of highly preemptive construing; or if it is applied in a very rigid fashion. In addition, as noted above, if the client exhibits sharply contrasting behaviour, it may be suspected that there is avoidance of the threat of therapy rather than any fundamental reconstruing. Kelly suggested that when it transpires that a new construction is inadequate, the reason may be that the client had seized upon the construction in an attempt to deal with either his or her own anxiety or the therapist's apparent anxiety. Alternatively, the therapist may have seized too rapidly upon some 'insight' of the client's which was no more than a very loosely formulated construction.

## 'Resistance' to therapy

Like various other concepts commonly employed by psychotherapists, Kelly did not regard resistance as a particularly useful notion, and indeed it has been suggested, from the personal construct theory perspective, that a therapist who labels a client as resistant may merely be responding in a hostile manner to the invalidation of his or her constructs by the client (Leitner, 1985b; Fransella, 1989b). Kelly's (1955) view was that the client who appears resistant, and 'who exasperates the therapist by his failure to deal with what the therapist wants him to, or by his refusal to see things the way the therapist so clearly sees them, is not necessarily warding off the therapist as a person; more likely he is demonstrating the fact that his construct system does not subsume what the therapist thinks it should' (p. 1101). In other words, like other aspects of the client's behaviour, lack of response to a therapist's efforts may be a perfectly comprehensible, albeit often hostile, reaction given the client's particular way of construing events. Various possible reasons for 'resistance' will be apparent in the discussion above of therapy with particular types of client, as well as in the research findings presented in Chapter 5 concerning features of construing predictive of response to therapy. These reasons may be conveniently summarised in terms of the avoidance of the negative emotions which therapy may engender, although equally, and more positively, they may be seen to be based in the client's choice of what seems to be the best available means of anticipating events.

A particular negative emotion which may be experienced by the client at the prospect of therapeutic change is anxiety. As we have seen above, this may be the case, for example, with the loose construer whose therapist engages in tightening, with the tight construer whose constructs are invalidated or loosened in therapy, or with the constricted client whose perceptual field is suddenly dilated. It will also be the case if the client has no well-elaborated alternative to his or her present state, as with psychiatric in-patients who are unable to anticipate life outside hospital (Winter *et al.*, 1991), or those clients described by Fransella (1972) whose symptoms offer them a more meaningful 'way of life' than would be available without them. For such clients, 'even an obviously invalid part of a construction system may be preferable to the void of anxiety which might be caused by its elimination altogether' (Kelly, 1955, p. 831). They are operating on the assumption that better the devil you know than the one you don't know (Rowe, 1982; Butt and Bannister, 1987). Even if a structured, and desirable, alternative to the symptom does seem to be available, this, as Kelly (1955, p. 977) notes, 'is likely to be unrealistically drawn and oversimplified'. For example, as Fransella (1972) has reported, the client's construction of life without symptoms may be an idealistic fantasy which can be maintained only as long as the symptoms persist. However, as we have seen in Chapter 5, if the client has available a favourable construction of the self as he or she was before developing symptoms, a favourable construction of a future symptom-free self may be more realistic, and therapeutic change therefore more likely (e.g. Button, 1983b; Winter and Gournay, 1987). This was not so with Crispin, an ageing hippy whose agoraphobic symptoms commenced at the end of the 1960s, and whose repertory grid indicated that, while he imagined that he would become virtually identical to his ideal self if he lost his phobic symptoms, his construal of himself before his symptoms developed was of an irresponsible, self-centred person (Winter, 1988c, 1989). By dropping out of a behavioural treatment programme, he was able to avoid testing out the fantasy that symptom loss would enable him to become more ideal than he had ever been (including, incidentally, finding fame and fortune as a folk guitarist). A further finding of our research on agoraphobia has been that clients who do not appear to have a usable construct of anger are less responsive to behaviour therapy, perhaps because situations of interpersonal conflict, with which they are more likely to be confronted if they are able to go out, would as a result be more unpredictable, and therefore anxiety-provoking, to them (Winter and Gournay, 1987; Winter, 1989a).

Therapy may also be a guilt-provoking prospect for the client if it is anticipated to lead to dislodgement from his or her core role. This may explain, for example, the poor response to social skills training of clients for whom social competence carried such negative implications, inconsistent with their core roles, as selfishness and deceit (Winter, 1987, 1988a). As we have seen in previous chapters, several similar examples have been reported of resistance to, or relapse following, therapy in clients whose symptoms appeared to be integral to a favourably construed core role (e.g. Rowe, 1971a, 1982, 1983c, 1987; Catina and Walter, 1989a). Rowe (1982) considers the predicament of such clients to be similar to that of Rilke (1946), who refused to have his devils driven out by undergoing psychoanalysis lest his angels were to leave with them. Resistance may be particularly likely if the client's positive construction of his or her symptoms is shared by other members of the family, as in some of the agoraphobics studied by Gournay and myself in the research discussed in Chapter 5. For example, repertory grids completed by Joan, an agoraphobic, and Jack, her husband, revealed that they both associated the ability to go out with the risk of marital infidelity. While Joan initially responded well to behaviour therapy, Jack's post-treatment grid indicated that, not unexpectedly, as his wife's symptoms reduced in intensity the super-ordinacy of his construct of infidelity increased and his self-esteem decreased. Predictably, follow-up assessment three months later showed a reversal of these changes in Jack's construing as his wife's self-esteem decreased once again (Winter, 1988c). A further possible cause of guilt during therapy, inde-pendent of how the client construes his or her symptoms, is the recognition of dependency on the therapist by the client whose core role has involved independence from others. Such a client may be made to feel particularly guilty by a supportive therapist. Since therapy involves the development of role relationships, it may also evoke the terror which Leitner (1985b), as we have seen in Chapter 4, has associated with such relationships. On the other hand, termination of therapy may confront the client with the meaninglessness of a life in which role relationships are avoided. It will not be surprising if the client who is in such a predicament approaches therapy with an ambivalence which may be labelled as resistance.

If therapy seems to imply a comprehensive change in core constructs the client will feel threatened, and again resistance may be expected. As discussed in Chapter 5, this, together with the loss of structure and consequent anxiety likely to result from construct invalidation during therapy, may explain the poor response to therapy observed in some studies in clients whose construct systems are very tightly organised (e.g. Carr, 1974; Orford, 1974; Button, 1983b; Winter and Gournay, 1987). An explanation in terms of resistance to threat may also be offered for findings of poor response to therapy in clients for whom symptom loss implies considerable change on other constructs (Wright, 1969; McKain et al., 1988). The provision of insight is often threatening and, as Mair (1979) has described, being known by the therapist may be a threatening prospect because it may involve the client in coming to know that much of his or her past behaviour has been a hostile concealment of the truth. Clients may also be threatened in therapy by coming to feel that there is no solution to their problems, which Kelly cautioned may be an unintended effect of the provision of reassurance and sympathy by the therapist. Threat may result if the client is introduced to new elements from which a construct is elicited which is incompatible with the client's existing constructs. As Kelly (1955) describes, it may also occur if the therapist attempts to change the client's identification, or lack of identification, with a parent since this is likely to have numerous implications. It follows from Landfield's (1954) 'expectancy hypothesis' that a particular source of threat in therapy may be an apparent expectation by the therapist that the client should behave in some way, perhaps by being dependent or tearful, which typifies an old, abandoned role. Kelly (1955) also noted, however, that any expectation of substantial change in the client, whether or not this involves regression to past behaviour, will be threatening. To quote him,

> Clients are frequently most threatened by their therapists just before making major shifts in their outlooks. They may appear to fight defensively against the therapist's efforts. They may complain that they are worse off. They may show hostility towards the therapist. They may appear to be unusually obtuse to obvious interpretations. They may generally thrash about in a disturbing manner on the eve of accepting a newly structured version of themselves.

> (p. 492)

Particularly clear examples of threat leading to relapse during a client's therapy are provided in Fransella's (1972) description of her treatment of a stutterer who relapsed at such times as when he could clearly imagine being fluent, when he came to discover that the implications of fluency were not entirely positive, and when he visited his parents, who expected him to be as he had been before the changes which had taken place during therapy.

The personal construct psychotherapist will generally not be perplexed if, as in Fransella's client, relapse or apparent resistance to therapy occasionally occurs following what seem to be signs of progress during treatment. For example, the client who has habitually viewed himself or herself as a failure will be likely to find the sudden prospect of success unpredictable and therefore anxiety-provoking, requiring behaviour inconsistent with the core role and therefore guilt-provoking, or likely to lead to comprehensive reorganisation of core constructs and therefore threatening. In such a client, movement towards success may well be resisted. In working with the resistant client, the personal construct psychotherapist will be concerned to identify the nature of the anxiety, guilt, or threat which therapy produces, and will select interventions with a view to minimising these negative emotions and modifying the constructions which underlie them, perhaps taking into account some of the considerations which we have discussed above in relation to the treatment of the anxious, guilty, or threatened client. Interventions will, therefore, be 'ecologically sound', in that they will foster the evolution of the client's construct system but not be disruptive of its integrity (R. Neimeyer and Harter, 1988). Two examples, concerning clients whom I have described in greater detail elsewhere (Winter, 1987, 1988a, 1990a), will illustrate this approach.

Alan was referred for exploration of what his therapist considered to be his resistance to behaviour therapy, stating that 'in the past there have been some encouraging responses to the behavioural method before he has eventually closed down the barriers'. His presenting problem, of some twenty years' duration, was annoyance and anxiety engendered by other people's mannerisms, as a result of which he had given up his job and severely constricted his interpersonal world. It appeared, therefore, that situations involving annoyance with others' mannerisms might confront him with incompatibilities in his construing, which he avoided by constriction. Repertory grid assessment revealed several such incompatibilities: for example, becoming 'easily wound up' was associated by him with perfectionism and ability to solve one's problems, but while these latter characteristics were associated with intelligence, becoming easily wound up was associated with stupidity. A further construct which presented him with a dilemma, in that he could not decide which of its poles he preferred, contrasted workaholics with layabouts. His prototype for the workaholic pole of this construct, which was laden with negative implications, appeared to be a father whom he considered to have been neglectful. His own tendency when working, however, was to work very hard. It appeared, therefore, that his symptoms, requiring him to give up work, allowed him to avoid the guilt which might be provoked by either construing himself as a workaholic, with all that this implied for him, or to stop work with no valid reason for so doing and therefore to be construed as a layabout. A further possible reason for his resistance was his fantasy that he would 'enjoy life fully' were it not for his symptoms, since this appeared to overlook his marital conflicts and his wife's suicidal behaviour.

Given the above constructions, it was not surprising that Alan resisted a therapeutic approach which involved exposing him to annoying manner- isms and to the prospect of working once again. However, attempts to elaborate a construction of working without being a workaholic did not meet with very much more success since for him it implied 'sloppiness and rubbishy work', the preferable option to which was not to work at all. The alternative approach which has been adopted with him is to 'time bind' the 'workaholic–layabout' construct to his childhood constructions of his father, and to attempt to develop new constructions, and in particular more permeable superordinate constructs which might provide some resolution of the apparent incompatibilities in his construing.

Tom also had a very long history of resistance to therapy, which had involved individual and group analytic psychotherapy, and more recently social skills training. Research assessments indicated that his symptom levels increased over the course of this latter treatment, his lack of response to which was explicable in terms of the fact that his grid indicated that social competence carried more negative implications for him, these increasing during treatment, than for any other client included in the study. For example, his contrast pole to assertiveness was to be 'reasonable', and he also construed assertive extraverts as 'demanding' and 'aggressive': to have become more assertive and extraverted would therefore have involved considerable dislodgement from his core role. He labelled himself as schizophrenic, and had vainly attempted to have this label confirmed by psychiatric diagnosis or by being accepted for membership by self-help groups for schizophrenics. The anxiety with which loss of his problems would confront him was reflected in his statement that if he were not schizophrenic life would be 'a mystery'.

Personal construct psychotherapy with him involved four major components. Firstly, controlled elaboration of his complaints, using Tschudi's (1977) ABC procedure, allowed tracing of the implications of assertiveness for him and his discovery of such inconsistencies that, although he construed being reasonable as implying being perceived as 'a good bloke', he did not consider that he was seen as such despite always being reasonable and unassertive. Secondly, since he tended to view arguments in terms of 'right and wrong opinions', more propositional construing, and the view that there may be alternative constructions of reality, was encouraged by helping him to take the perspectives of others.

Time-binding of his negative constructions of assertiveness and extra-version was attempted by indicating how these had once helped him to comprehend his mother's behaviour, but were not applicable to his present relationships. Finally, by focussing on episodes when he considered that he had been assertive, a more assertive self-construction was elaborated. It was hoped that this would afford him with as much certainty as did his view of himself as 'schizophrenic'.

Questionnaire and repertory grid assessment at the end of therapy revealed a marked reduction in Tom's level of discomfort in social situations, neurotic symptoms, and, perhaps most significantly, in the negative implications which extraversion and assertiveness carried for him.

Butt and Bannister (1987) have also described how clients, similar to Tom, who are resistant to social skills training might be assisted by a personal construct psychotherapy approach in which they are helped to consider whether they have been 'asking the best questions'. For example, Kevin, who feared men's violence and consequently behaved in a very submissive manner, did not feel comfortable with the assertive role which had been provided for him by social skills training. To explore his apparent resistance to change, he was asked to rate various target behaviours, such as 'talking back in an argument', in terms of certain of his core role constructs, such as being 'under-standing'. This exercise revealed that achievement of his target behaviours implied moving away from the preferred poles of core role constructs. After these results were conveyed to Kevin in terms of the costs and benefits of change, a further course of social skills training was attempted, and resulted in him seeing himself as both more extraverted and more inconsiderate. Not surprisingly, subsequent targets were completed less successfully, and the focus of therapy accordingly switched to the exploration of alternative construc-tions of events, construal of the constructions of hostile men, and of how such a man would view Kevin as having to change in order to become like him, and questioning of the evidence for some of the constructions which thus became apparent. Finally, fixed-role therapy was employed, the role involved being of a person who was understanding but not submissive. His interpersonal relationships began to improve, and it was soon possible to terminate therapy.

Before leaving the subject of 'resistance', two further possible bases for a client's lack of response to therapy should be mentioned. One is that, as indicated above, the construing of the client's significant others may be as much a factor as is the client's own construing. As Rowe (1982) has noted, it is not only the client but also those close to him or her who may feel anxious, threatened, or guilty at the prospect of therapeutic change in the client. Another relevant factor concerns the client's expectations of therapy for, as the research results discussed in Chapter 5 would suggest, a client is particularly likely to resist a therapeutic approach which is inconsistent with his or her view of the world or a therapist the content of whose construing differs markedly from the client's own. As Kelly (1955, p. 567) points out, the personal construct psychotherapist will, therefore, 'make an effort to subsume the client's construction of psychotherapy ... this does not mean that the clinician must adopt the client's construction of psychotherapy, but it does mean that he must be able to utilize it'.

While personal construct theory provides the therapist with a way of understanding, and of attempting to reduce, 'resistance' which indicates an ambivalence towards therapy, it leaves the therapist in a dilemma in the case of clients who are being seen at the request of people other than themselves and who resist therapy because they have no wish to change. In most such cases, the personal construct psychotherapist may accept the client's viewpoint as a valid alternative construction, and not intervene, but this is a perilous course when the clients concerned seem likely to endanger themselves or others. Fransella (1985b) has explored this dilemma in relation to anorexic clients.

## THE THERAPEUTIC RELATIONSHIP AND ITS CONTEXT

The way in which the personal construct psychotherapist responds to the 'resistant' client exemplifies basic features of the therapeutic relationship in this treatment approach. Firstly, by demonstrating acceptance of the client, attempting to use the client's constructions, and by taking a credulous attitude to the latter, the therapist indicates that these constructions will not be suddenly dismantled during therapy, and indicates an attitude of respect, or reverence, for the client (Davis, 1984; Leitner, 1988b). A similar message is conveyed by therapy being conducted in an invitational mood rather than in terms of the prescription of 'better' ways of behaving or thinking. It is acknowledged that, like research students, clients are the experts in their particular fields of interest – themselves – but that therapists, like research supervisors, may offer useful expertise in the formulation and testing of hypotheses. Personal construct psychotherapy therefore involves client and therapist working together as co-experimenters.

Nevertheless, it is clear from his use of such constructs as 'limited–adequate', 'misperceptions' (Kelly, 1955), and 'preconceived sophistries' (Kelly, 1969d) to describe clients' expectations of therapy that Kelly was not entirely accepting of all of his clients' constructions. In particular, as Epting (1984) observes, the personal construct psychotherapist will not consider to be productive a conception of the therapeutic relationship 'characterized by the expert therapist having to administer a treatment to a rather passive client' (p. 14) and 'never wants to get into the position where she is directing the therapy' (p. 96). The personal construct psychotherapist will not, however, adopt a fixed mode of relating to clients, but instead 'The client must be given an opportunity to cast the therapist in whatever dramatic parts his reconstructive adventures require' (Kelly, 1955, p. 619). For this reason, Kelly did not consider that therapists should reveal much about themselves to, or engage in social contacts with, their clients. Such revelation is likely to lead to a *primary transference*, in which the therapist is construed preemptively by the client, and is therefore limited in the roles which he or she may play during therapy; and there is likely to be undiscriminating dependency on the therapist, and consequent difficulty in terminating therapy and in generalising experimentation from the therapy room to the outside world. More desirable, in Kelly's view, was a *secondary transference*, in which the client transfers on to the therapist various role constructs which have been applied to other figures in the client's life. On becoming aware of such a transference, the therapist should encourage the client to formulate, and test, hypotheses concerning it; and in general should use the transference to help the client to develop role relationships with the figures whom it involves. For example, Leitner (1980) has described how a highly threatened client was gradually able to test out some of her constructs in her relationship with him, at one point by successively casting him in four different roles, and responding to him accordingly.

The constructs on which transferences are based may be highly constellatory or preemptive, impermeable, and preverbal, as in the case of dependency constructs. The client may still be helped to verbalise and test such constructs, provided that the therapist is not seduced into remaining forever in the role of the all-knowing and all-providing expert. However, if a primary transference is involved, such testing is difficult since the therapist appears to constitute the whole realm of the dependency constructs, which will therefore not easily be seen as having been transferred from other figures. A further danger of a primary dependency transference is that it may induce a counter dependency transference from the therapist, who comes to apply impermeable, preemptive, unverbalisable constructs to the client, and whose dependency on the client may be manifested, for example, in attempts to limit the extent to which the client experiments outside the therapy room. The unhelpful nature of a primary transference led Kelly (1955) to recommend that, on becoming aware of such a transference, the therapist 'should take definite and positive measures to resolve it immediately' (p. 685). One of the methods of so doing which he suggested was to behave in a rigid, repetitive way, reducing the client's opportunities for elaborating his or her constructions concerning the therapist. Primary transferences may also be controlled by the use of enactment, so that therapy sessions come to involve the client relating not to the therapist as such but to other people portrayed by the therapist.

Transferences, in Kelly's view, proceed in cycles, each of which initially involves the elaboration and testing by the client of particular role constructs, and some dependence on the therapist, which reduces when the reconstruction concerned is completed. At the ending of a transference cycle, the therapist will decide whether another cycle should be commenced, and if so what particular transferences it should involve. Kelly's (1955) rule was '*either to plan a new cycle or to terminate the series with the second conference after the first clear sign of a transference break*' (p. 683, italics in original). Transference cycles vary in length, depending on characteristics of the client and the type of therapeutic approach employed. They are, for example, likely to be long with clients who have difficulty in verbalising their expectations of therapy, and with older clients, and short if an approach, such as fixed-role therapy, is adopted in which some new construction is offered to the client alongside his or her existing constructions. If the therapist wishes to accelerate a transference cycle, the use of loosening techniques and support should be avoided, and sessions should focus on the present rather than the client's past, on low levels of abstraction, and on constructions which are not central to the client's core role. The therapist should employ highly structured sentences, should use the same language every time a particular issue is discussed, and should encourage experimentation in the outside world rather than in therapy sessions. Enactment, and in particular fixed-role therapy, were regarded by Kelly as particularly useful methods of drawing a transference cycle to a close.

Kelly made various other recommendations concerning the way in which therapy sessions should generally be conducted. He stated, for example, that they should be held in a room which is relatively free of distractions. He conducted his own sessions in a room in which he and the client were separated by a desk, which he felt allowed them to focus their attention on each other's faces, and by a distance of some six to eight feet. The therapist's manner, in his view, should be relaxed but mentally receptive and responsive, and the rhythm and volume of his or her speech should generally be attuned to that of the client. The therapist should also attempt to use terms employed by the client, if necessary asking the client's assistance in finding the right word. However, sessions should not always be allowed to proceed at the client's pace. While a slow tempo may be necessary if the client is dealing with elements which are difficult to construe or is seeking verbal labels for constructs, at times the therapist may consider that the session is getting nowhere and that the client's perceptual field could usefully be broadened. Rapid questioning may then be employed, this generally being acceptable to the client if it concerns recent incidents, although it should be followed by therapist and client attempting to structure the material which has thus been generated. Conversely, the client who has been talking rapidly but unproductively may be asked to relax and think about the one thing which, on looking back upon the session, he or she would most like to have said; to state thoughts in single words rather than sentences; or to summarise, perhaps with the aid of a recording of the session, the meaning of what has been said.

Each therapy session, in Kelly's view, should be planned at least to the extent that the therapist knows the direction in which he or she wishes the client to move, as well as what the client should be steered away from in the session. The therapist's subsequent notes on the session should indicate the client's current position in relation to the overall plan of therapy, material which requires further exploration, and predictions concerning the client's likely behaviour prior to the next session. If these predictions are reasonably accurate, Kelly considered that the therapist may allow himself or herself greater flexibility in adhering to the plans of sessions. He recommended, however, that the therapist's plan should generally determine how the session is initiated rather than the client being allowed to dictate the course of the session. In the early sessions, the therapist is likely to be concerned with imparting his or her expectations of therapy to the client, pointing out that the therapeutic relationship is likely to be different from relationships which the client has previously experienced, and will be a situation in which the client may, without risk of criticism, raise issues which are hard to verbalise or which the client would not consider discussing outside the therapy room. Kelly also prepared clients for the loosening or anxiety which may occur during therapy, and advised them not to make major decisions while in treatment or to discuss their sessions with other people. The latter advice was given in order that the client would not feel trapped into making definite decisions on the basis of constructions which he or she is only beginning to explore. Kelly did consider, however, that with children or adolescents it may sometimes be useful if they discuss the sessions with their parents. A final component of his preparation of clients for therapy was often to point out that they would ultimately have to take the initiative in solving their problems.

Kelly's sessions were generally 45 minutes in length, although when he employed group psychotherapy, or play therapy with children, sessions were of up to two hours duration. The frequency of sessions was to some extent determined by the degree of disorganisation and experimentation with which the client was to be faced, with a session being held every other day if an approach such as fixed-role therapy was employed. Breaks in therapy were carefully handled, the general rules being that they should not occur at times when the client is engaging in considerable experimentation, and that sessions immediately prior to and following breaks should not involve loosening and probing. Kelly also considered that these latter techniques, and invalidation of the client's constructs, should be avoided in the final three sessions of therapy. The sessions prior to termination, in his view, should be more widely spaced, the final session should be not more than fifteen minutes in length, and it should be understood that the client may request a further appointment in the future if necessary. The duration of a course of personal construct psychotherapy will vary with the nature of the client's disorder and the approach adopted, being more lengthy if a dependency transference has been encouraged or if much loosening has been involved. With its emphasis on continuing experimentation in the outside world, it is generally considered to be conducive to relatively brief therapy (Llewelyn and Dunnett, 1987). However, the importance of enough time being provided for the client to elaborate adequately any new constructions which have been developed during therapy has been noted by Fransella (1972), who found an increase in the relapse rate of her stutterers when she attempted to accelerate the treatment process. On the other hand, she pointed out that there may sometimes be a danger of treatment being too lengthy in that it may encourage a client to view situations in terms of his or her complaint longer than is desirable, and more recently, coupled with an increasing emphasis on adequate time spent on diagnosis, she has come 'to wonder what is holding us up' if a client's therapy lasts for as many as twenty sessions (Fransella, 1989a, p. 128). The therapist who wishes to ensure that experimentation proceeds at an adequate rate may find the use of renewable treatment contracts to be of value.

While Kelly's recommendations concerning the therapeutic relationship and the structure of sessions provide valuable general guidelines for therapeutic practice, they should, of course, be viewed in a historical context. For example, few, if any, personal construct psychotherapists nowadays would conduct their sessions from behind a desk! Some present day personal construct psychotherapists (e.g. Dunnett and Llewelyn, 1988) appear to be more prepared to reveal aspects of their own lives to their clients than was Kelly, and, for example, Rowe (1978), who refers to her treatment sessions as 'conversations', describes how disclosing her own views to a client may serve to demonstrate that alternative constructions of a situation are always possible. Understanding of the therapeutic relationship from a personal construct theory perspective has also recently been advanced by Semerari (1989), who considers that effective therapeutic relationships proceed in three phases. In the first of these, the client construes the therapist as the validating agent (Landfield, 1988) of his or her constructions. In the next phase, a construction of the therapist acts as an internalised source of advice and interpretation of events, but is not integrated with the remainder of the client's construct system. Finally, the subsystem symbolised by the therapist becomes integrated into the client's system, and the client comes to attribute to himself or herself constructions which may previously have been attributed to the therapist.

## REQUIREMENTS OF THE PERSONAL CONSTRUCT PSYCHOTHERAPIST

The qualities of an ideal personal construct psychotherapist are essentially those of the optimally functioning person, described in Chapter 1. The therapist, to use Epting's (1984, p. 11) term, should be able to make his or her 'best human qualities' available for the client to validate constructs against. Various other specific characteristics are of particular importance in the personal construct psychotherapist. He or she should, for example, have a construct system, such as is provided by Kelly's professional constructs, which enables the subsuming of the very varied construct systems of clients. Without a system of this type, the therapist's only available options in construing a client may be to identify with, or to transfer his or her dependencies on to, the client. The therapist's personal construct system should have been elaborated sufficiently, and applied to a sufficient range of experiences, to facilitate alertness to a wide variety of cues. This alertness will also be facilitated if the therapist formulates hypotheses as propositional constructs rather than in preemptive or constellatory fashion. Propositional construing will enable the therapist to be creative, and Kelly emphasised that the therapist's creativity should be such as to involve experimentation on the basis of unverbalised hunches. As well as being creative, the therapist should be sufficiently versatile to place himself or herself in the position of a varied range of clients, and to predict the nature of the validations which are likely to be available in a client's primary group and cultural background. Verbal skill is necessary, particularly when attempts are made to label unverbalised constructs, to formulate new constructs, or to speak in the client's language. An aggressive approach, emphasising active experimentation, is also desirable. Perhaps nowhere are these requirements of creativity, versatility, verbal ability, and encouragement of experimentation, coupled with acting skill, better exemplified than in fixed-role therapy. The necessary requirements for a successful personal construct psychotherapist have also been considered by Landfield (1980b), who suggests that such an individual should have a personal construct system which is both highly differentiated and highly integrated, and is likely to employ constructs 'one pole of which will suggest some interest in or concern about (1) openness to experience, (2) sociality and warmth of interaction, (3) independence, (4) ethical values, (5) emotionality, and (6) energy or forcefulness of expression and activity' (p. 128).

Many of the qualities required in the personal construct psychotherapist may be considered to be reflections of a world view which has come to be termed *constructivism* (see p. 343): as Mancuso (1979b, p. 304) remarks, 'A counselor who cannot integrate his world from a constructivist position, could hardly be expected to be of value in aiding another person to work from a constructivist position'. This, and our discussion of the social system as client, may suggest that the personal construct psychotherapist should hold particular values. Kelly (1955, p. 608) describes this value system as 'a kind of liberalism without paternalism', in which the 'clinician is not only tolerant of the varying points of view represented in his clients, but . . . is willing to devote himself to the defense and facilitation of widely differing patterns of life'. That this need not necessarily, however, involve exhorting the client to share the therapist's values is indicated by Landfield's (1971, p. 7) assertion that 'To do so might be considered a sign of incompetence or even an index of unethical behaviour'. He considers that Kelly's 'focus is no less value laden than a minutely detailed prescription of how one must live since there are people and patients who do not want freedom. Structures of freedom may be value laden and possibly even coercive for some individuals, as value laden and coercive as structures of authoritarianism'. It may perhaps be concluded that, as O'Sullivan (1988) notes in considering therapy from a feminist perspective, while it is impossible for the therapist to adopt a value-free state, the decision to approach therapy in terms of a specific set of values should rest with the client and not the therapist.

Semerari (1989) has pointed out that the therapeutic relationship is by definition emotional since it aims to produce transitions in the client's construing. A further requirement for the therapist is, therefore, that he or she should feel comfortable with the intense emotions which are likely to be experienced by the client undergoing psychotherapy (Leitner, 1985b, 1988b). Transitions during psychotherapy will be faced by both client and therapist, and indeed Epting (1984, p. 13) suggests that 'the most effective psychotherapies are those in which not only the client changes, but the therapist changes as well'. Psychotherapy may, therefore, be a hazardous affair for the therapist as well as for the client, and Kelly considered that a clear construction of the psychotherapeutic role is necessary if the therapist is to have the courage and persistence to persevere in the face of hazards. These latter, like the reasons for a client's resistance to therapy, may be viewed in terms of anxiety, threat, and guilt. Anxiety may be faced, for example, by the therapist who employs loosening techniques and whose constructs are not sufficiently permeable to structure the loose constructions thus produced. It follows from Landfield's (1954) hypotheses that threat is likely to be experienced by the therapist if the client exemplifies a way of construing that the therapist could all too easily adopt, or expects the therapist to behave in a way which he or she has not long outgrown. The solutions at which the client arrives for particular problems may be threatening to the therapist for similar reasons, and Kelly (1955, p. 607) cautioned that 'the clinician should not try to stake his whole personal system on the outcomes of his client's experimentations', but should use these only to validate his or her role as a clinician. As we have suggested in Chapter 5, threat and guilt may also be experienced by the therapist who engages in a treatment approach incompatible with his or her core constructs. For example, if the therapeutic relationship with a particular client turns out to be very different from the therapist's original construction of such a relationship, the therapist may experience guilt, as may the therapist who, when a client fails to respond to treatment, feels that he or she is not adequately fulfilling the therapeutic role. Enactment procedures, requiring as they do that the therapist steps out of his or her characteristic role with a client, may be very uncomfortable for some therapists.

Not only may psychotherapy lead to negative emotions in therapists as well as clients, but the responses of therapists to these emotions, just like those of their clients, may involve such strategies as hostility, constriction, or impulsivity. These strategies may, for example, be manifested by the therapist who prematurely and preemptively affixes some diagnostic label, such as 'psychotic', to a client; who insists that a client gets better; who seeks in hostile fashion to blame a client's family for the client's lack of response to treatment; whose enactments of a client are mere caricatures; who avoids significant issues in therapy; who is late for sessions; who impulsively reduces a client's problem to a single dimension; or who, as Leitner (1988b) has described, uses techniques in order to retreat from, rather than to foster, a role relationship with the client. It is perhaps the avoidance of such potentially destructive strategies, by the reinforcement of a view of therapy as an essentially scientific enterprise, that is the primary goal of training and supervision in personal construct psychotherapy.

## Training of personal construct psychotherapists

Kelly, in 1955, was scathing about the training of most psychotherapists, seeing them as 'being trained like witch doctors, with reliance placed primarily on long apprenticeships, unquestioned doctrines, and empathic "relationships"' (p. 1179). He viewed the principal features of training in personal construct psychotherapy as the development in the therapist of a professional construct system and a view of the therapeutic role as that of 'professional scientist'. In addition, he made it clear that the trainer will also be concerned with the trainee's construct system as a whole, both its verbal and preverbal aspects. He equated the elaboration of the latter with the development of the trainee's intellectual and emotional insight respectively. One of the trainer's concerns will be the identification of the trainee's areas of hostility, and of constructions which appear to require revision before the trainee is considered ready to practise psychotherapy. In view of the attention paid to the trainee's personal construct system, Kelly felt that personal construct psychotherapists should be taught in very small groups. A further desirable component of training in personal construct psychotherapy may be a focus on skills in experimentation, but with a view to the therapist then passing these skills on to clients rather than using them in order to experiment upon clients (Mair, 1970b).

Although it was not considered by Kelly to be essential that personal construct psychotherapists should themselves have undergone psychotherapy, he did feel that this is often beneficial, particularly if the therapy concerned is personal construct psychotherapy. For example, it allows particular techniques to be demonstrated, and provides an experience of being in the client role which may better equip trainees to develop role relationships with their future clients. While it may help trainees to see parallels between themselves and their clients, Kelly considered that this is only likely to be beneficial if therapists come to view their clients as passing through stages which they themselves have satisfactorily negotiated. It is also likely to be of value if therapists are thus enabled to appreciate that their construing processes are essentially the same as those of their clients (Kenny, 1988a). It will generally not be helpful, however, if a therapist views himself or herself as still grappling with the same problems as is a client, or as having solved a similar problem when the similarity is, in fact, only superficial. Psychotherapy may of course help trainees to resolve particular problems, and finally it may allow trainees to discover what roles clients are likely to cast them in.

Of particular value if a trainee receives psychotherapy is a requirement that he or she write a summary of each session, indicating not only what was said but what the trainee felt reluctant to say (Kenny, 1988a), as well as the trainee's feelings within and between sessions. Training and trainee psychotherapist may also usefully abandon their therapist and client roles at the end of each session to review the content of the session and the techniques employed during it. Other features which may differentiate the trainee's therapy from that of an 'ordinary' client is that the therapist may have to be more aggressive in encouraging the trainee to deal with problems, and that it may be more difficult for the trainee to disperse dependency away from the therapist, particularly if the therapist is also the trainee's supervisor. Kelly considered it inadvisable for a psychotherapist to be receiving psychotherapy at the same time as practising it, since counter dependency transferences on clients might then be particularly likely. Also problematic in his view was personal psychotherapy at the same time as trainees are engaged in educational programmes, since it may then be difficult to consider the peripheral constructs developed in the latter experience in isolation from the core constructs which are the concern of the former. Group psychotherapy for trainees was viewed by Kelly as involving fewer such problems than an individual approach since it entails wider support for the trainee, less likelihood of loose construing, and therefore greater protection for core structures. As in psychotherapy for any client, the appropriate point at which to terminate the trainee's therapy needs to be chosen carefully, and Kenny (1988a) suggests that it should be at a time when the trainee's construct system has reached a new level of organisation, but certainly not at a point at which the trainee, in becoming more aware of his or her actions, temporarily loses the ability to act spontaneously.

In supervising trainees' first cases, Kelly considered that the supervisor should make use of the systems with which the trainees are most familiar. He tended to ask trainees to monitor, and occasionally enact, each other's sessions, which were tape recorded; and to present reports on each of their own sessions including the session's plan, its factual content, a professional construction of this content, and predictions of the client's behaviour prior to the next session. Although some recommendations were made in supervision, it was also made clear that the ultimate decision as to how to conduct a particular session was the trainee's. Kelly also, of course, emphasised the importance of trainees trying to gain a glimpse of the world as their clients might experience it, no matter how disturbed these clients might appear to be. Thus, he stated that

I urge students, for example, who want to investigate 'schizoid' thought to have a round of experience with it themselves. They should talk to their teammates, trying out their hunches about what it is to be a 'schizoid' thinker. And they should ask their teammates to do the same thing and report what they observe and what they experience. Then they should see how others react to 'schizoid' thought. And, lest the possibility should escape them, they should check their portrayals with experts, that is with 'genuine schizophrenics' and the professors who study them.

(Kelly, 1969e, p. 132)

As we have seen in Chapter 5, repertory grids in which clients, or relationships with clients, are elements (e.g. Ryle and Lipshitz, 1974), or which are completed from the perspective of the client, may provide a useful means of facilitating trainees' exploration of their construing of clients.

Clearly, access to such equipment as video-recorders has presented possibilities for the training and supervision of personal construct psychotherapists which were not available to Kelly. However, little has been written on the training of personal construct psychotherapists since Kelly's original descriptions, and formal courses of training in this approach are very few. One exception is the programme offered by the Centre for Personal Construct Psychology, in London, a forerunner of the courses offered by which is described by Fransella (1980). Working with clinicians with allegiances to a range of theoretical orientations, she adopted an approach which included formal teaching, homework assignments, case presentations, and experiential activities. She believes strongly that personal therapy should not be a requirement for trainees, and instead, like Dunnett (1988d), emphasises how the reflexivity of personal construct theory allows those who employ it to become their own therapists (Fransella, 1989a). In his 'radical constructivist' model, Kenny (1988a) has also elaborated on Kelly's original approach to training by drawing on the work of Maturana and Varela (1980) and on the notion of 'self-organised', rather than 'dependent', learning (Thomas and Harri-Augstein, 1983). He has emphasised that such a model of training does not focus upon the transmission of information and particular skills, but instead upon 'the unpacking and explication of the trainee's ontology of observing' (Kenny, 1988a, p. 152). In her workshops for professionals, Rowe (1983b) also focusses on examining core constructs, using such exercises as asking participants to list what they consider the five major virtues and five major vices, or their beliefs about death. One of the values of such an approach, as she has indicated, is that therapists may thereby discover fundamental ways in which they are likely to differ from many of their clients, for example in beliefs concerning life after death and, therefore, how life before death should be lived. Death should, of course, be a major concern in training programmes for clinicians working with clients who have illnesses which may be life-threatening. Considering physicians' responses to the death of clients, G. Neimeyer et al. (1983) suggest that, to reduce death threat, the clinician should be assisted to construe his or her professional role as that of helper rather than healer; while, to reduce death anxiety, strategies which increase the personal or professional meaning of death should be encouraged.

Finally, it should be noted that the learning process does not, of course, cease at the end of a formal training programme, and the importance of continuing supervision of therapy cases, as well as more personal support for professionals, has been stressed by Jones (1988), Viney *et al.* (1988), and Dunnett (1988c, 1988d).

## THE EFFECTIVENESS OF PERSONAL CONSTRUCT PSYCHOTHERAPY

Numerous single case reports have now appeared which indicate positive changes on various measures during personal construct psychotherapy in a range of client groups. However, relatively few studies have been carried out which involve any statistical evaluation of the outcome of this form of treatment. One of the first of these, by Karst and Trexler (1970), compared the effectiveness of fixed-role therapy and rational-emotive therapy with clients presenting with public-speaking anxiety. Both treatment groups were found to show greater anxiety reduction than an untreated control group, but clients receiving fixed-role therapy exhibited significantly greater improvement on an anxiety scale than did those receiving rational-emotive therapy. Furthermore, on a Fear Survey Scale, and on an item from this scale concerning public-speaking anxiety, only the fixed-role therapy group improved significantly more than the control group. Clients in the fixed-role therapy group also rated their treatment as more helpful than did those in the rational-emotive therapy group. While the results of this study are encouraging, it should be noted that the fixed-role therapy procedure adopted differed in several respects from that described by Kelly: for example, the roles adopted were specifically designed for public speaking by the clients themselves, who were asked to enact them 'to the extent possible' (Karst and Trexler, 1970, p. 362). A further, analogue, study of fixed-role therapy, by Todd (1973), also employed a procedure which differed from Kelly's in that students were asked to play roles which were the *opposite* of how they saw their personalities. Male extraverts and female introverts were found to change significantly in degree of extraversion, and the former group to show a reduction in neuroticism, during treatment. Also far removed from Kelly's original method was the role-playing procedure adopted by Lira *et al.* (1975) in a study of snake phobics which has been quoted by Epting and Nazario (1987) as an investigation of fixed-role therapy. Here, the role to be enacted was that of a person who contrasted markedly with the clients, being 'a snake hobbyist who impressed friends with the ease and expertise that he/she displayed while handling snakes' (Lira *et al.*, 1975, p. 609). Clients receiving this treatment approach, compared with those treated by modelling, those exposed to a videotape of a snake, and a no-treatment group, developed greater ability to approach a snake. Clients in the role-play condition also showed significantly less fear, and more positive attitudes towards snakes, at post-treatment assessment than did those in the modelling condition, and their gains were maintained at two-month follow-up.

One of the major early studies of personal construct psychotherapy was carried out with stutterers by Fransella (1972). As we have seen in Chapter 5, she found that her treatment approach had its intended effect of elaborating the implications of fluency for her clients, whose rates of speaking and reading increased, and disfluencies decreased, significantly over the course of treatment. Thirteen out of sixteen stutterers studied showed at least a 50 per cent reduction of disfluencies on one of the measures employed. Follow-up data on nine of the sample over an interval ranging from nine months to three years showed that only one failed to maintain his improvement. As such a low relapse rate is generally not found in treatments of stuttering, but methods involving training in speech techniques and behaviour modification are generally briefer than the therapy described in Fransella's study, an attempt was made by Evesham and Huddleston (1983) to combine the advantages of these two types of approach. Treatment commenced with a two-week residential course, the first week of which focussed on training in speech techniques, while the second focussed on experimentation with, and elaboration of construing of, fluency. These latter concerns also characterised twenty subsequent group sessions, initially held on a weekly basis, then fortnightly, and finally monthly. Stutterers treated by this method showed less improvement at post-treatment assessment than did those whose treatment programme was of the same structure but focussed throughout on speech techniques (Evesham and Fransella, 1985). However, some improvement was evident in all clients, and the difference between the groups may have been an artefact of the greater initial severity of the stutters of members of the 'technique' group. As predicted, stutterers in this latter group showed a significantly higher relapse rate at eighteen-month follow-up assessment than did those in the group which incorporated personal construct psychotherapy. The authors note that the repertory grids, laddering, and self-characterisations which were completed as assessment procedures by both groups appeared themselves to produce reconstruing, and that had they not been employed the difference in relapse rates between the groups might have been even greater.

The effectiveness of personal construct psychotherapy has also been assessed with various other client groups. Bannister et al. (1975), evaluating their method of serial validation of the construing of thought disordered schizophrenics, which we have discussed earlier, compared clients treated by this method with a control group consisting of thought disordered schizophrenics whose clinicians were told that the clients were in a 'total push regime' and should be treated as special. The only significant difference between the groups at any of the four eight-monthly assessment points was a lower score for the experimental group on a measure of lethargy and dejection at the fourth assessment. Similarly, the groups' change scores differed significantly on only one measure at the fourth assessment. In view of the number of outcome measures used, these differences would have been expected on a chance basis. Nevertheless, when within-group changes were examined, the experimental group showed significant improvement on nine measures and deterioration on two, while the control group improved on three and deteriorated on two. While there was significant improvement in the experimental group on some measures which might asssess thought disorder, such as a conceptual dysfunction score derived from a structured interview, this was not the case on measures from the Grid Test of Thought Disorder, on one of which deterioration was apparent. The authors therefore give a 'not proven' verdict on their results and, as we have seen on page 83, suggest reasons why their treatment might have been less effective than intended. Somewhat more encouraging findings regarding the effectiveness of personal construct psychotherapy, in this case focussing on the dilation of construing in depressives, were obtained by Sheehan (1985a). She found a significant decrease in her clients' levels of depression and in the negativity of their self-construing and self–ideal self distance over the course of treatment, a tendency for them to construe themselves as more similar to others, and an increase in their capacity to tolerate logical inconsistency in their construing. Although no control group was included in Sheehan's study, it is of interest to compare its results with those of her previous study of depressives under-going pharmacological treatment, who also showed a significant reduction in depression and increase in self-esteem but no change on the measure of logical inconsistency (Sheehan, 1981). It is conceivable, therefore, that, while enhanced self-esteem may result from both pharmacological and personal construct therapy, only the latter approach can produce the increase in the permeability of superordinate constructs which is necessary if logical inconsistencies in construing are to be tolerated. Also of some relevance to an evaluation of personal construct psychotherapy with depressives is the study by R. Neimeyer et al. (1985) of group cognitive therapy since their groups employed 'an amalgam of personal construct and cognitive interventions' (R. Neimeyer, 1985d, p. 100), although seeming to emphasise the latter. Clients in such groups showed greater reduction in depressive symptoms, suicidal ideation, negative construing of themselves 'as they really were' and in the future, and polarised self-construing than did waiting list controls.

A few other empirical studies have examined the effects of a personal construct theory approach in a group setting. Morris (1977) reports that the repertory grids of five of the eight members of a personal construct psychotherapy group at retest were highly related to the grids which their therapists had predicted they would produce if their outcome had been ideal. Jackson (1990b) observed that, compared to a control group, the adolescents attending her therapy group, which focussed on the construing of self and others, made significant gains on self-characterisation measures of self-esteem and of being a 'good psychologist'. They also showed improvements on interview measures, on checklist responses indicating the view of the adolescent by himself or herself and by his or her father, and, as with control group members, on a personality and adjustment inventory. In addition, therapy group members considered each other less hard to understand following therapy, made more psychological statements about themselves, and made more cause-and-effect statements, which the author considered to reflect the group's focus on anticipation. The other reported studies on personal construct psychotherapy groups have concerned the Interpersonal Transaction Group. Employing this approach with twenty problem drinkers, Landfield and Rivers (1975) found that at six-month follow-up after a group experience lasting for twenty weeks, 'only one alcoholic member was known to have been drinking' (Landfield, 1979, p. 144). Grid measures indicated that members' construing became less differentiated over the course of treatment, and that they came to see each other more meaningfully and in a more positive light, and increased their ability to predict other members' construing. No significant changes were evident in the grids of a control group of students who underwent the same procedure (e.g. Mood Tags) as the Interpersonal Transaction Group members for its first four sessions, but were not seen again for another fourteen weeks.

A series of studies by Viney and her colleagues have applied content analysis of clients' verbalisations to examine the effects of treatment programmes employing personal construct theory approaches. They have reported, for example, that crisis intervention counselling based on a personal construct psychology model for people hospitalised with medical problems produced reductions at discharge from hospital in anxiety, indirectly expressed anger, and helplessness, and an increase in expressions of competence (Viney et al., 1985b). The counselled clients, compared to those who had not received counselling, also showed reductions in anxiety, indirectly expressed anger, and depression from discharge to long-term follow-up, and the effects of the programme appeared to be independent of the number of counselling sessions and the level of experience of the counsellor. Viney et al. (1985c) also compared three programmes, each designed for a particular type of client, the first aiming to reduce anxiety and depression, the second to make expression of anger more direct, and the third to increase feelings of competence. Some evidence was provided of the differential effectiveness of the second and third programmes, but not of the first, and clients in the third programme also displayed more depression at follow-up. As well as examining the psychological effects of their programmes, they have investigated effects on the physical recovery of clients, finding that counselled clients spent fewer days on antibiotics, and were quicker to return to normal temperature and to oral food intake, than were clients who were not counselled (Viney et al., 1985d). In addition, there was evidence of lower health care costs in the counselled group following treatment (Viney et al., 1985e). A further area of concern for Viney et al. (1989b) has been the evaluation of personal construct psychotherapy for elderly people presenting with psychological problems.

Sixty such clients were randomly assigned to either a treatment group or a contrast group the members of which were not offered therapy until the end of the data-collection period. Content analyses of interviews indicated that the treatment group, compared to the contrast group, showed significant decreases in anxiety, particularly concerning death and disability, depression, and indirectly expressed anger, coupled with increases in competence and good feelings. At post-treatment assessment, the treatment group showed less evidence of anxiety and depression than did a criterion group of psychologically and physically healthy old people, despite having been significantly more anxious than this group prior to treatment. Although the number of visits made by treated clients to health professionals unexpectedly increased immediately following therapy, this appeared to be a result of encouragement during therapy to use such visits in order to obtain information, and it decreased at follow-up (Viney, 1986). The treated clients also reported fewer physical symptoms following therapy than did those who did not receive psychotherapy.

The studies by Viney *et al.*, the investigation of serial validation of thought disordered schizophrenics' construing by Bannister *et al.* (1975), the research by Evesham and Fransella (1985) on stutterers, and Jackson's (1990b) study of a therapy group for adolescents are the only published reports of the outcome of personal construct psychotherapy which have employed adequate comparison groups. While such groups were also employed by Karst and Trexler (1970), Todd (1973), Lira *et al.* (1975), and R. Neimeyer *et al.* (1985), their investigations are not accurately described as outcome studies of personal construct psychotherapy but rather of treatment methods which make some use of techniques developed from personal construct theory. This also applies to the reports by Morrison and his colleagues of reductions in problem behaviours and anxiety, and more positive self-construing, following emotive-reconstructive therapy (Morrison and Teta, 1978; Morrison *et al.*, 1981, 1983a, 1983b; Morrison and Heeder, 1984; Morrison and Holdridge, 1984); and those of the effectiveness of cognitive-analytic therapy in promoting reconstruing in psychiatric out-patients (Brockman *et al.*, 1987) and control of diabetes (Ryle, 1990). Clearly, considerably more research needs to be undertaken on the effectiveness of therapy conducted from the personal construct theory perspective.

## SUMMARY AND CONCLUSIONS

Personal construct psychotherapy is a process of reconstruction. This reconstruing may take many forms, ranging from the relatively superficial change of slot-rattling on the client's existing constructs to much more fundamental transitions involving altering the meaning of these constructs or forming new constructs. The techniques which may be employed to promote reconstruction are also very varied. The palliative techniques of reassurance and support may occasionally be used to reduce anxiety temporarily and, in the latter case, to facilitate successful experimentation. Elaborative techniques will be employed if the therapist wishes to explore with the client the implications of his or her constructs, perhaps with a view to identifying inconsistencies in the client's construing. Such techniques may include enactment procedures, which also allow relatively unthreatening experimentation with new behaviour; the use of formal assessment procedures, such as repertory and implications grids, laddering, and self-characterisations; and, if the focus is on the construing of past events, emotive-reconstructive therapy. The therapist is also likely at times to be concerned with the loosening or tightening of a client's construing, and may employ various contrasting strategies, and variations of his or her own behaviour and of the therapeutic environment, to achieve these ends. A major emphasis of therapy is also likely to be experimentation, which may be facilitated by conducting therapy in an invitational mood; by confronting the client with new situations; by the use of metaphor and humour; or by fixed-role therapy, in which for a brief period the client enacts a role based on a sketch written by the therapist. Group treatment approaches may also facilitate social experimentation, although Kelly's model of the development of therapy groups has rarely been employed by later personal construct group therapists. A more commonly used method is the Interpersonal Transaction Group, in which the interactions largely take place in dyads. In addition to individual and group treatment modalities, personal construct approaches may be applied with couples and families, and their application to larger social systems is also beginning to be elaborated.

The personal construct psychotherapist's selection of techniques will be based on his or her diagnostic assessment of the client's construct system, which will also indicate the hazards which may be anticipated during the client's therapy. Some of these hazards will be manifested in what therapists of other persuasions might term resistance, but will be viewed by the personal construct psychotherapist as understandable reactions to the negative emotions associated with transitions produced by therapy. Therapeutic interventions will be chosen with a view to minimising such emotions. The therapeutic relationship will be one in which a credulous attitude, and respect, is conveyed to the client. Although a primary transference, in which the therapist is construed preemptively, will not be encouraged, a secondary transference, in which role constructs previously applied to other figures are transferred onto the therapist, may allow the client to test out relevant hypotheses. Therapy sessions will generally be planned in advance, and therapy will usually be relatively brief.

As well as having a professional construct system which enables clients' construct systems to be subsumed, the therapist should be able to construe propositionally, and should be tolerant of a wide range of constructions, as well as of strong emotions. Such requirements may be focussed upon during training. Although personal therapy for trainees is not considered essential, personal construct theory may be applied reflexively by the trainee or trained therapist in the examination of his or her own construing.

Despite numerous single case reports of positive treatment outcome in a wide range of clients, there is a dearth of controlled research on the effectiveness of personal construct psychotherapy. Those few controlled investigations which have been conducted have produced encouraging findings concerning the outcome of this treatment approach when applied with stutterers, physically ill people, adolescents, and the elderly, and inconclusive results in relation to the treatment of thought disordered schizophrenics.

# Chapter 8

# Personal construct theory and alternative constructions of psychological disorder and therapy

It will be apparent from our discussion of personal construct psychotherapy that a very wide variety of techniques, some developed within alternative theoretical frameworks, may be employed in this treatment approach. Indeed, Kelly (1969f) viewed it as 'a way of getting on with the human enterprise' which 'may embody and mobilize all of the techniques for doing this that man has yet devised' (p. 221). Consequently, as Fransella (1972, p. 231) remarks, it may be that 'if one observed a dozen people who say they are doing "personal construct psychotherapy", they will seem to have very little in common'. She and Bannister have pointed out that, for example,

> a personal construct psychotherapy might well include behaviour therapy methods if, for instance, the client was having difficulty in tightening construing in a given area. It might include a psychoanalytic type of free association if the patient had difficulty in loosening constructs. But the personal construct psychotherapist would retain throughout the view that clients are essentially experimental scientists in their own right, rather than people to be manipulated by the behaviour therapist or absolved by the analyst.
>
> (Bannister and Fransella, 1986, p. 118)

In other words, the apparent eclecticism of the therapeutic approach is only at the level of the techniques employed, not extending to the theoretical concepts used in interpreting the client's predicament and selecting appropriate techniques.

It may be concluded, then, that, as Karst (1980, p. 167) puts it, 'PCT is one of a small set of theories which can afford to be technically eclectic, is technically fertile, and still remains rationally integrated'. Nevertheless, there has been a tendency in the literature to identify personal construct theory with those other approaches from which it might borrow techniques, subsuming its concepts within those of more familiar theories and overlooking the distinctiveness of its basic assumptions. Kelly (1969f) himself expressed his puzzlement at the various ways in which his theory had been classified, and described how it has 'been accused of being both cognitive and existential' and 'has also been categorized by responsible scholars as an emotional theory, a learning theory, a psychoanalytic theory (Freudian, Adlerian, and Jungian – all three), a typically American theory, a Marxist theory, a humanistic theory, a logical positivistic theory, a Zen Buddhistic theory, a Thomistic theory, a behaviouristic theory, an Apollonian theory, a pragmatistic theory, a reflective theory, and no theory at all' (Kelly, 1970a, p. 10). Since some of these constructions of the theory are still employed, this chapter will attempt to delineate the similarities and contrasts between personal construct theory and other common approaches to the understanding and treatment of psychological disorder. We shall conclude by considering the extent to which it is possible, or desirable, to integrate personal construct theory and alternative approaches to clinical practice.

## PERSONAL CONSTRUCT THEORY AND OTHER APPROACHES TO PSYCHOLOGICAL DISORDER

### The behavioural approach

Kelly (1969f) was highly amused on finding a book which described him as a learning theorist, a classification which he regarded as 'patently ridiculous' (p. 216). Nevertheless, in an *Introduction to Clinical Psychology* published some twenty years after Kelly presented this paper, behaviour therapy and personal construct theory still appear as strange bedfellows in a category of 'learning orientation' (Sundberg *et al.*, 1983).

Kelly's amusement at being considered a learning theorist reflects his rather disparaging views of such theories. For example, in his initial presentation of personal construct theory, he made it clear that it involved 'the discarding of much of what has been accumulated under the aegis of learning theory' (Kelly, 1955, p. 37), not least the concept of learning itself, which he regarded as central to all human functioning and not a specific type of psychological process. Holland (1970) has summarised the features of behaviourism to which Kelly drew attention in rejecting this approach as that

it is deterministic; it is the dominant psychology of our time; it is manipulative; it is static and fails to account for or register the explosive change now taking place in the human world; it assumes that the future of all men, except psychologists, must be a repetition of the past; it generally regards a fulfilled prediction as a pinned down fragment of ultimate truth; it is Darwinian; it assumes primordial beginnings and blind drive.

(p. 117)

To expand on one of the items in this list which has been emphasised by other personal construct theorists (e.g. Bannister, 1970b), some of Kelly's most scathing criticisms of the behavioural approach were reserved for his discussion of the psychotherapeutic relationship, with regard to which he commented that 'a psychopath is a stimulus-response psychologist who takes it seriously' (Kelly, 1969f, p. 220). Such a person may attempt to modify another's behaviour without taking into account the constructions underlying this behaviour: in short, he or she does not attempt to form role relationships with others but instead adopts 'a strictly manipulative approach to human relations' (Kelly, 1969c, p. 202). A further criticism of learning theory, which has also been noted by other authors (e.g. Landfield, 1970), is that, unlike personal construct theory, it is not reflexive, in that it may 'account for all kinds of human behaviour *except* the formulation of learning theory' (Bannister and Fransella, 1986, p. 4).

Despite the views indicated above, Kelly was not averse to the use by personal construct psychotherapists of techniques designed to change a client's behaviour, and suggested that 'the key to therapy might be in getting the client to get on with a new way of life without waiting to acquire "insight"' (Kelly, 1969d, p. 59). He accepted that reconstruing may occasionally be facilitated by modifying a client's behaviour or symptoms, as indicated by his statement that 'Sometimes it is more feasible to try to produce personality readjustments by attacking the symptoms than by going directly after the basically faulty structures. Thus some of the cue elements upon which those structures have been resting are removed before the structures themselves are attacked' (Kelly, 1955, pp. 995–6). For Kelly, behaviour therapy was essentially a way of encouraging experimentation, and all that is wrong with it, in his view, is that, as usually conducted, it fails to appreciate that the principal investigator in the experiment is the client rather than the therapist (Kelly, 1970b). He considered, for example, that a procedure such as systematic desensitisation is well designed to enable the client to become his or her own experimenter. The personal construct psychotherapist may, therefore, be no less interested in the client's behaviour than is a behaviour therapist but would consider this behaviour not in terms of what conditioned it but in terms of what questions it is asking. For example, Kelly (1969g, p. 19) viewed his clients' symptoms not as bad habits but as 'urgent questions, behaviourally expressed, which had somehow lost the threads that lead either to answers or to better questions'. Such an approach regards behaviour as 'man's independent variable in the experiment of creating his own existence' (Kelly, 1969g, p. 36). Its focus is not solely on the behaviour but on the person's experiment, for, as Kelly (1969h, p. 137) put it, 'To look only at "behaviours" is to lose sight of man'.

It should be noted that many behaviour therapists now also take the view that their approach is one which encourages the client to experiment. For example, exposure of a phobic or obsessive-compulsive client to situations which he or she had previously avoided has been viewed by some authors (Seligman and Johnston, 1973; Meyer *et al.*, 1974; Rachman, 1983) as serving to disconfirm the client's expectancies that catastrophic consequences might result from such confrontation. The work of Rachman and his colleagues (Rachman and Levitt, 1985; Rachman and Lopatka, 1986a, 1986b) on the prediction of panics by fearful people, and the greater increase in fear following an unpredicted than a predicted panic, is also not inconsistent with the view of the person as an experimenter. Much of Rachman's recent work attempts to address inadequacies of traditional learning theory models in, for example, accounting for the acquisition and maintenance of various disorders, delineating the theoretical basis of behavioural treatment, and explaining the fact that in many clients residual problems persist following such treatments. It is of interest that his arguments, such as that exposure is not a necessary condition for fear reduction since the latter can occur, for example, as a result of purely cognitive interventions (de Silva and Rachman, 1981, 1983), have been firmly rejected by some learning theorists (Boyd and Levis, 1983). However, their counter-arguments, drawing upon such concepts as generalisation and exposure to internal cues, only indicate that Kelly (1969i) was correct in viewing learning theory as being as untestable as its proponents have generally accused psychoanalysis of being.

Nevertheless, behavioural techniques may be employed without the attendant trappings of learning theory and, as we have seen in the last chapter, specific uses of behavioural techniques in personal construct psychotherapy include the employment of relaxation exercises to produce loosening in construing (Kelly, 1955); the employment of behavioural analyses or self-monitoring techniques to produce tightening (R. Neimeyer, 1986b); the setting of homework exercises with a view to elaborating a particular construct subsystem or testing out certain constructions (R. Neimeyer, 1985a; Winter, 1988b); the use of activity scheduling as a means to achieve controlled elaboration of the construct system (Kelly, 1955; R. Neimeyer, 1985d); the use of behavioural contracts in marital therapy to resolve dilemmas in construing (R. Neimeyer, 1986b) or increase validation at subordinate levels of the system (G. Neimeyer, 1985); the prohibition of physical contact in a couple presenting with a sexual problem, in order to validate not relating sexually and to facilitate experimentation with new ways of relating (Procter, 1981); and the encouragement of dilation by exposing a client to situations which he or she had previously avoided (Viney, 1981; Dunnett, 1985). We have also seen, in Chapter 5, that repertory grid investigations have provided evidence of the potential of behavioural approaches to facilitate reconstruction. In one of these studies (Caine et al., 1981; Winter, 1983), indications were provided of the features of construing which characterise clients who are likely to benefit from such approaches, namely tightly organised, logically consistent construct systems in which the symptoms carry many implications; construal of the self as ill and of treatment in terms of a traditional doctor–patient relationship; and a predominant concern with external reality. Furthermore, it appears that such characteristics may be particularly evident in clients who present circumscribed symptoms with an external focus, such as phobias. Agoraphobics, for example, have been found to express preferences for a behavioural approach (Norton *et al.*, 1983), to which they are more likely to respond the more external their locus of control (Michelson *et al.*, 1983). However, while a behavioural intervention may be an acceptable initial treatment approach for such clients, and may, as we have seen, lead to some reconstruing, our research has also indicated that following behaviour therapy agoraphobics become increasingly aware of the possible negative implications of their growing independence (Winter and Gournay, 1987; Winter, 1989a). This would support the view of Tschudi and Sandsberg (1984) that the primary value of behavioural techniques may be a diagnostic one in that they may make apparent the advantages of the client's symptom. It would also suggest that, if used, symptom-orientated interventions should be a preliminary to more direct work on the client's construing, as in the treatment approach for stutterers developed by Evesham and Fransella (1985). Such an approach may also be advisable because, if the focus of therapy does not extend beyond the client's symptoms, it may simply serve to elaborate further the 'way of life' which, as Fransella (1972) has described, the symptoms may provide for the client. This may perhaps explain Willutzki's (1989) unexpected finding that behaviour therapists' ability to predict their phobic clients' construing of phobic situations, in contrast to their prediction of clients' construing of non-phobic situations, was not related to positive therapeutic outcome. Thus, it may be that the ability of a behaviour therapist to anticipate his or her client's construing of symptom-related situations is achieved by focussing almost exclusively on symptoms and ignoring other aspects of construing, the consideration of which would be more likely to eventuate in a positive outcome.

Lest there remains any impression of a basic commonality between the behavioural and personal construct approaches, it should be emphasised that the use of a behavioural intervention by a personal construct psychotherapist will always be in the context of facilitating some particular change in the client's construing and of considering the meaning to the client of any behavioural change which is produced. This contrasts markedly with the mechanistic, reductionist assumptions apparent in most behavioural approaches, as I have described elsewhere in relation to those approaches which attempt to teach social skills as if they were motor skills (Winter, 1987, 1988a) and those forms of sex therapy which view the client's complaint as a technical problem (Winter, 1988b). By failing to consider the purpose served by the complaint, such approaches may underestimate the threat, guilt, and anxiety likely to result from its too rapid elimination, and this may be the basis of 'therapeutic errors' (R. Neimeyer, 1987b). For example, the transience of changes produced by social skills training based on the skill-deficit model (Twentyman and Zimering, 1979) is not surprising when it is considered that such approaches generally do not take into account the negative constructions of social skills which may be held by the clients concerned (see p. 169). As

Kelly (1955, p. 594) remarked, 'if the clinician tells the client to be "self-confident" the client may look around within his repertory of constructs and decide that the clinician is talking about something the client would be more likely to call "conceited"'. Likewise, Needs (1988) has indicated the importance of considering the meaning to the client of the behaviour in which they are being trained, suggesting that the tendency of offenders to reject assertiveness training may reflect the role which aggressiveness plays in validating their core constructs. As Karst (1980) notes, in discussing assertiveness training programmes, what is required are changes at the level of 'deep structure', rather than the 'surface structure' changes, such as slot-rattling, likely to be involved in skills training or other behavioural approaches. Nevertheless, Landfield (1980a) points out that such procedures may entail useful 'training in contrast', such that, for example, the habitually passive person is able to experience himself or herself behaving assertively or the anxious person is able to experience relaxation. The person may then be better able to choose one or other pole of the construct concerned in a particular situation. In his view, it is only when behaviour therapy is approached in a 'literal' manner (see p. 15) that the result is likely to be slot-rattling by the client and, for example, persistently assertive or relaxed behaviour even when such behaviours are inappropriate. Karst (1980) even considers that operant programmes may be usefully employed to promote reconstruing, but the examples which he presents concern specific techniques employed in such programmes, such as clients or their carers keeping records of situations in which the problem behaviour occurs, rather than full-blown applications of operant conditioning principles. These latter behaviour modification programmes may in some cases serve only to validate constructions concerning control which were largely responsible for the client's problems in the first place (Gara, 1982). In the view of Mancuso and his colleagues (Mancuso and Handin, 1980; McDonald and Mancuso, 1987), they also contrast markedly with the personal construct theory approach in that they are based on a mechanistic paradigm. Although they may occasionally be effective in, for example, allowing parents to reconstrue a child's problem behaviour as meaningfully related to its context rather than in terms of a disease model (Davis, 1984; Cunningham and Davis, 1985; Davis and Cunningham, 1985), as well as in changing the child's construing of its parents, these results are more likely to be achieved by a programme, such as those developed by Mancuso, which is explicitly based on a 'contextualist' paradigm. It should be noted, however, that Mancuso's approach is not without criticism from a constructivist perspective (Fisher, 1990).

Even if it does appear that a behavioural approach has similar concerns to personal construct psychotherapy, this similarity may be more apparent than real. For example, although behavioural therapists may be much concerned with the client's anxiety, they are likely to conceptualise, and therefore to treat, this anxiety in a fundamentally different manner than would personal construct psychotherapists. This may be illustrated by considering sex therapy, in which a behavioural approach might regard a client's anxiety as due to the anticipation of failure, whereas from a personal construct theory perspective it might be viewed as due to 'the anticipation of successful sexual performance in the person whose construct system cannot encompass the implications of such success' (Winter, 1988b, p. 84). Whatever the basis of a client's anxiety concerning sexual performance, this anxiety may be exacerbated even further by those highly performance-orientated approaches to sex therapy which carry 'implicit demands to conform and perform' (Lazarus, 1980, p. 151). Such approaches exemplify a further basic difference between behaviour therapy, as traditionally practised, and personal construct psychotherapy, namely that the former approach tends to be directed towards normatively defined goals whereas in the latter treatment goals and the means of achieving them tend to be more personal, taking into account the possibility that normative behaviour may be quite discrepant with the client's core constructs. Indeed, the aim of personal construct psychotherapy may be not to develop some particular new behaviour or construction in the client but rather to encourage experimentation and the possibility of employing alternative constructions, whatever these may be. As Epting (1984, p. 14) puts it, 'the most important issue is the nature of the voyage itself rather than any specific destination'. Fixed-role therapy illustrates this approach, and is regarded by Adams-Webber (1979, p. 130) as 'based on a radical form of "behaviorism" ' in which the client formulates and tests out hypotheses. It does not generally involve the client role playing the therapist's prescription of how he or she should be, as in approaches sometimes employed by behaviour therapists. Therefore, although the latter approaches, such as the procedure of role-playing of orgasms by inorgasmic women (Lobitz and LoPiccolo, 1972), are sometimes presented as analogous to fixed-role therapy, this suggests a misconception of fixed-role therapy.

Such considerations as the above have led Fransella (1970d, p. 65), whose own clinical psychology training was behavioural in emphasis, to conclude that behaviour therapists are 'amongst the worst offenders' of those therapists who tend to impose their own constructions on clients while largely ignoring the clients' own views of events. In Rychlak's (1968) terms, theirs is an *extraspective* approach, viewing the client from an external perspective rather than from the client's own perspective, as in the *introspective* approach of personal construct theory. The view that behavioural approaches do not focus sufficiently on the client's personal construction of his or her complaint may appear inconsistent with the common claim that such approaches contrast with psychoanalysis in taking clients' complaints seriously and at face value. However, as Butt and Bannister (1987, p. 146) note in a discussion of Butt's increasing dissatisfaction with behaviour therapy and adoption of a personal construct theory approach, 'although we must take the client's initial complaint seriously, we must not confuse this with taking it at face value. The therapist would be wise to assume that even a client with an apparently simple spider phobia is expressing a fear about a number of things, including spiders.' More precisely, while the personal construct psychotherapist's *initial* approach will be to take the client's complaints at face value, the consequent application of the therapist's professional constructions to these complaints may include, for example, considering aspects of them, such as their strategic functions, which may be at a low level of cognitive awareness for the client. This essential difference between the behavioural and personal construct theory approaches is exemplified in the so-called 'neurotic paradox' of behaviour which is 'at one and the same time self-perpetuating and self-defeating' (Mowrer, 1950). Such persistence of apparently self- destructive behaviour is very difficult to explain from the perspective of a theory which takes a hedonistic view of human motivation, but poses no such problems for one which regards people's actions as directed towards the better anticipation of their world, and towards validation of predictions, whether these be pleasant or unpleasant, rather than reinforcement. Thus, for Kelly (1969i, pp. 84–5),

> there is no neurotic paradox. Or, to be more correct, the paradox is the jam certain learning theorists get themselves into rather than the jam their clients get themselves into . . . the behaviour of a so-called neurotic client does not seem paradoxical to him until he tries to rationalize it in terms his therapist can understand. It is when he tries to use his therapist's construc-tion system that the paradox appears. Within the client's own limited construction system he may be faced with a dilemma but not with a paradox.

In other words, if the therapist looks beyond the client's symptoms and complaints to the purpose which these may serve for him or her in anticipating events, the client's behaviour will appear no more puzzling than will that of any other individual.

The concept of 'resistance to therapy' can be considered a variation on that of the neurotic paradox, for if it is perplexing that a client repeatedly behaves in a self-defeating manner it will be equally perplexing if he or she appears to resist a therapist's efforts to modify such behaviour. The responses of behaviour therapists to this perplexity have included fining clients for non-compliance with their treatment contracts (e.g. Lobitz and LoPiccolo, 1972) and Salter's (1949, p. 68) advice that resistant clients should 'be chased from the office with a broomstick'. As we have seen in the last chapter, however, the personal construct psychotherapist will view clients who appear to resist therapy as 'behaving perfectly reasonably *from their own perspective*' (Fransella, 1985a, p. 300, italics in original), and will therefore attempt to understand, and perhaps attempt to modify, this perspective, rather than cajoling, coercing, or rejecting the client.

In view of the above discussion, it may be no surprise that Dryden's (1984) analysis of various individual therapies showed the behavioural approach to be that which, in terms of various underlying dimensions, is most dissimilar to personal construct psychotherapy; and that the personal construct theorists who responded to the survey by R. Neimeyer *et al.* (1986) on the future of the theory viewed integration with behaviour therapy as the least likely of all the possibilities for therapeutic integration which they were asked to consider. Indeed, rather than integrating with behavioural approaches, Fransella (1978) has suggested that personal construct theory should subsume behaviour therapy and, borrowing behavioural techniques, develop a 'personal construct behaviour therapy'. As she has stated in relation to the 'cognitivisation' of behaviour therapy, to be discussed further in the next section, 'If behaviour therapy is up for grabs – we must be in there doing the grabbing' (p. 6).

## The cognitive approach

The behavioural approach of which Kelly was so critical is, of course, one to which few post-'cognitive revolution' behaviour therapists would subscribe, except perhaps the inappropriately named radical behaviourists. Kelly's anticipation of the trends which were to occur in this and other areas of psychology has been noted by various authors (Mischel, 1980; Goldfried, 1988), and debts to him have been acknowledged by several of those who have developed cognitive approaches to therapy (Mahoney and Arnkoff, 1978; Beck *et al.*, 1979; Ellis, 1979; Guidano and Liotti, 1983). Since it first appeared until the present day, the most popular classification of personal construct theory has been that it is 'cognitive' (e.g. Bruner, 1956; Mehrabian, 1968; Southwell and Merbaum, 1971; Patterson, 1980; Pervin, 1980). Goldfried (1988), seeing basic commonalities between personal construct theory and those theories which make use of such concepts as expectancies (e.g. Bandura, 1977) and schemata, considers, in relation to personal construct psychotherapy, that 'the parallels to cognitive-behaviour therapy, as well as to other orientations, are numerous' (p. 325). Indeed, it is included in a recent edited volume presenting several cognitive-behavioural approaches to psychotherapy (Dryden and Golden, 1986), where personal construct theory is described as 'one of the original wellsprings of cognitive therapy' (R. Neimeyer, 1986b, p. 256).

It is necessary, therefore, to emphasise that, although Kelly may well have been more sympathetic to some current cognitive approaches than he was to S–R theory, he was at pains to repudiate claims that his was a cognitive theory. The very term cognition was one for which he had little use, viewing its differentiation from emotion as contrasting markedly with his more holistic view of the person. He pointed out, for example, that

The psychology of personal constructs is built upon an intellectual model, to be sure, but its application is not intended to be limited to that which is ordinarily called intellectual or cognitive. It is also taken to apply to that which is commonly called emotional or affective and to that which has to do with action or conation. The classic threefold division of psychology into cognition, affection, and conation has been completely abandoned in the psychology of personal constructs.

(Kelly, 1955, p. 130)

By contrast, such book titles as *Cognitive Processes and Emotional Disorders* (Guidano and Liotti, 1983) and *Cognitive Psychology and Emotional Disorders* (Williams *et al.*, 1988) betray cognitive theorists' continuing distinction of cognition from emotion, as well as a seemingly more negative view of the latter in that disorders are described as emotional rather than cognitive.

The independence of personal construct theory and psychotherapy from cognitive theories and therapies has also been asserted by several post-Kellian personal construct theorists (e.g. Bannister, 1977; McCoy, 1977; Epting, 1984; Bannister and Fransella, 1986; Viney *et al.*, 1988). As R. Neimeyer (1985b, p. 126) states, in his sociohistorical analysis of personal construct psychology, 'most leaders within PCT are at best lukewarm concerning the prospects for meaningful collaboration with cognitive-behavior theorists, and at worst are openly antagonistic to such collaboration'. However, he also found this not to be a universal stance amongst personal construct theorists, and his later survey of members of the Clearing House for Personal Construct Theory (R. Neimeyer *et al.*, 1986) indicated that they considered incorporation into the theory of concepts from cognitive psychology to be a not altogether unlikely prospect. Neimeyer (1985d) himself makes use of the cognitive concept of schema, which has been regarded as equivalent to a cluster of constructs (Hayden, 1982), in his work on depression, and his comparison of personal construct therapy with 'other cognitive approaches' (R. Neimeyer, 1986b, p. 233) suggests that he considers it to be one such approach. However, that the use of cognitive concepts does not necessarily imply an alignment with cognitive therapy is evident in the writings of Mancuso, who, while employing cognitive notions, emphasising the cognitive aspects of Kelly's theory, and regarding constructs as 'atomic schemata' (Mancuso, 1970; Mancuso and Ceely, 1980), considers cognitive therapists to be 'full of hogwash' (R. Neimeyer, 1985b, p. 125) since their work is mechanistic and not cognitive.

In order to explain the differences between those personal construct theorists, like R. and G. Neimeyer, who favour cross-fertilisation between personal construct and cognitive approaches, employ cognitive concepts, and have published in cognitively orientated journals and edited volumes, and those, like Leitner, who 'see very serious dangers in identifying ourselves too closely with these very recent cognitive approaches to personality and psychotherapy' (R. Neimeyer, 1985b, p. 125), it is necessary to explore in greater detail the bases for these contrasting positions, and to distinguish more clearly between the range of approaches within cognitive psychology, as well as between cognitive theories and therapies. R. Neimeyer's (1985b) analysis again provides an indication of the reasons for the different stances taken by personal construct theorists concerning cognitive approaches, since he suggests that those who favour some degree of integration may be taking the pragmatic view that this is the only way to have an influence on psychology. On the other hand, those who oppose any such integration tend to do so because of incompatibilities at the metatheoretical level between the personal construct and cognitive approaches. For example, essential differences between the notions of schema and personal construct have been noted by some writers (e.g. Dalton, 1988b), and Epting (1988, p. 58) wonders 'how self-conscious and aware we should be ... of using terms from cognitive theories along with, or in the place of, theoretical formulations derived from personal construct theory. An example might be the use of the term schema as an equivalent substitute term for personal construct system. Other examples from the general field of information and cognitive theory would include terms such as encoding, accessing, retrieving, and so on. All of these terms are legitimately mechanistic in theoretical origin and quite devoid of the telic qualities incorporated in personal construct formulations'. Epting also agrees with Salmon (1970) and Rychlak (1981) that, while there are some commonalities between personal construct and Piagetian theory, an essential difference is that the latter approach takes an absolutist view of reality.

Such metatheoretical issues have been elucidated by analyses of the philosophical traditions reflected in personal construct theory. Warren (1985a), for example, identifies parallels between the theory and Spinoza's model of the person, and concludes that Kelly's 'is a "cognitive psychology" at a level of comprehensiveness and subjectivity that makes the label "cognitive" as useless as it is difficult to delineate' (p. 17). He sees no objection to the investigation by personal construct theorists of 'cognitive processes', and the use of cognitive terminology, as if these processes could be identified. Jahoda (1988, p. 3) also regards Kelly as 'a cognitivist in the modern sense of the term', which involves a concern with 'the entire content of the black box' and does not exclude the emotional and conative aspects of the person. Mahoney's (1988a) analysis delineates the distinction between *constructivism* and *realism*, the former term referring to *'a family of theories that share the assertion that human knowledge and experience entail the (pro)active participation of the individual'* (p. 2, italics in original). While Mahoney traces the philosophical lineage of constructivism to Vico, Kant, and Vaihinger, he states that 'In the realms of personality theory and psychotherapy, there is ... little doubt that George A. Kelly was the pioneer constructivist' (p. 27). As well as its emphasis on proactive cognition, and integration of thought, feeling, and action, other defining features of constructivism, in Mahoney's view, are its concern with 'morphogenic nuclear structure', in which core processes dictate the peripheral expressions of these processes; and self-organising development, 'the assertion that individual human systems organize themselves so as to protect and perpetuate their integrity, and they develop via structural differentiations selected out of their trial-and-error variations' (p. 9). In the clinical field, the major difference between constructivist and realist therapeutic approaches is that the former are concerned with the *viability* of the client's view of the world while the latter, reflected in the 'rationalist' cognitive therapies, are concerned with its *validity*, the client's difficulties being assumed to result from 'cognitive errors'. Rather than simply disputing the client's beliefs and exhorting him or her to adopt the therapist's purportedly more valid and rational constructions, constructivist therapies therefore 'typically attempt to foster creative evolution of the construct system as a whole' (Harter, 1988, p. 355). Although not attempting to inculcate particular beliefs in the client they do, as Mancuso (1979b, p. 303) points out, promote 'the acceptance of a particular personal epistemology', namely constructivism. They involve what Mahoney (1988b) terms process-level therapeutic work, the concern of which is by no means solely with modification of particular cognitions but instead *'invites deeply felt and intensely emotional experiments in being'* (p. 305, italics in original). As Epting (1984, p. 85) notes, in discussing Rowe's (1978) therapy with depressive clients, 'This approach is a far cry from simply giving the clients new things to say to themselves as would be the case in a "rational" therapy. Instead, the very existential grounding of the client is examined in order that new constructions can be chosen by the client.' Even the pursuit of rationality, and the development of a 'completely self-consistent person' (Epting, 1984, p. 34) is not a goal which personal construct psychotherapy would share with the rationalist therapies. As Rowe (1980, p. 9) has noted, 'there's more to being human than being logical', and indeed, as we have seen in Chapter 3, a highly logical pattern of construct organisation may simply indicate that an individual's construct system lacks the permeability at a superordinate level which would allow inconsistencies at more subordinate levels to be tolerated. For such an individual, therefore, a decrease in the apparent rationality of his or her thinking might be considered by a personal construct psychotherapist to indicate a positive therapeutic outcome. In any case, as Kelly (1977) suggested, a therapist's construal of a client as irrational may simply indicate the inadequacy of the therapist's anticipations of the client, rather than indicating the inadequacy of the client's thinking. A clearer understanding of the client's construction processes might, therefore, allow such a therapist to appreciate the client's own logic.

As will now be apparent, cognitive therapy can no longer be considered a uniform therapeutic approach, and, as Carmin and Dowd (1988, p. 15) have described, 'there seems to have been a significant evolution of most of the cognitive psychotherapies from the molecular perspective to the meta-cognitive'. These latter approaches, focussing on cognitive structures and processes, contrast less markedly with personal construct psychotherapy than do 'molecular' approaches, focussing purely on the content of 'cognitive events'. Most dissimilar to personal construct theory are those approaches which view cognitions simply as mediating between stimuli and responses, and which therefore share the mechanistic assumptions of S–R theory. Rationalist therapies, as we have seen above, are also based on fundamentally different assumptions to personal construct theory, as may be exemplified by rational-emotive therapy. Although it has been presented as representing a radical alternative approach to the behavioural paradigm, in that the person is seen as 'a social agent who actively constructs his own experiences and generates his own goal-directed behaviour on the basis of those constructs' (Trower, 1984, p. 4), descriptions of the approach suggest that it is far from radical. Indeed, Schroeder and Rakos (1983, p. 125), commenting on Trower's 'agency approach', consider that 'the emphasis on cognitive restructuring suggests an orientation towards conformity'. Dismissing the client's constructions as mere irrationalities, the rational-emotive therapist will encourage the client to replace them with a fixed set of 'rational' cognitions. If the client resists this approach, it may be seen by the rational-emotive therapist as indicating that the therapist's persuasive efforts have been insufficiently forceful. For example, Ellis (1980, p. 256) states that resistance may be due to 'the therapist's engaging in . . . therapy in a namby-pamby, passive way instead of vigorously getting after clients'. Therefore, although rational-emotive and personal construct therapies have been considered to be similar by some authors (e.g. Meichenbaum, 1977), and although Ellis (1977) himself acknowledges an overlap between his and Kelly's ideas, there are, as Ellis also points out, marked differences in therapeutic practice between the two approaches. Indeed, a comparative analysis of therapist behaviour in ten different treatment methods has indicated that of all the methods considered rational-emotive therapy was the approach which, for example by its didactic style, is most dissimilar to personal construct psychotherapy (Dryden, 1984). Nevertheless, Dryden (1987, p. 57) considers that 'RET therapists have much to learn from the work of George Kelly', such as an understanding of resistance to change based on what clients contrast with their negative feelings. However, the use of fixed-role therapy in rational-emotive therapy by Dryden and Ellis (1987) is very different from a personal construct theory approach in that it involves giving clients the prescription to act as if they were thinking rationally. The approach of Wessler (1984), a renegade from the rational-emotive therapy camp, is much more in keeping with the personal construct theory perspective, as evidenced by his statement that 'what appears to be unrewarding behaviour may actually satisfy the "need to predict accurately" and the security it brings' (p. 136).

While Beck's (1976) cognitive therapy, as Harter (1988) notes, has more in common with the 'collaborative research' approach of personal construct psychotherapy than does rational-emotive therapy, it is still based on the assumption that the client is suffering from cognitive distortions which need to be corrected. Nevertheless, Leitner (1982) considers that the methods of both Beck and Ellis may be useful ways of attacking literal relationships between behaviours, feelings, and values. A final type of cognitive approach which is far removed from personal construct psychotherapy is that which attempts to change the client's self-statements, for example from negative to positive, and which may be viewed as promoting slot-rattling rather than fundamental changes in the client's construing (Huber and Altmaier, 1983).

It is such cognitive approaches as these which are characterised to varying degrees by what Sarason (1978) terms the 'three lacunae of cognitive therapy', namely a relative inattention to the client's cognitive history, differences in the levels of accessibility of cognitions, and the interactions between cognitions. As G. and R. Neimeyer (1981b) note, such lacunae are not apparent in the personal construct theory approach. For example, although personal construct psychotherapy is unlikely to focus to any great extent on the past, it may involve exploration of the historical roots of constructions, perhaps as a preliminary to time-binding these constructions (see p. 262). In addition, the personal construct psychotherapist is, of course, likely to be very much concerned with differences in the levels of cognitive awareness of a client's constructions, with preverbal as well as the verbal constructs which are the main concern of the cognitive therapist, and with interrelationships between constructs. It should be noted, however, that such concerns are now also apparent in some contemporary cognitive approaches, such as those drawing upon attachment theory (e.g. Guidano and Liotti, 1983; Beck and Emery, 1985), in some cases together with biological perspectives (Gilbert, 1984), and which therefore appear to have plugged some of the gaps which were identified by Sarason. That some of these approaches are essentially constructivist is indicated by Guidano's (1987, p. 216) statement that 'psychotherapy based on such a perspective does not aim at persuading clients to adopt other standards for truth, but rather at helping them to recognize, understand, and better conceptualize their own personal truth'.

Finally, in comparing and contrasting personal construct and cognitive approaches, a distinction should be made between cognitive psychology and cognitive therapy since there often appears to be relatively little connection between the two. Indeed, Williams *et al.* (1988, p. 12) consider that 'for the time being, cognitive psychology promises to contribute more to the general understanding of emotional disorders than to advance in clinical techniques'. As has been briefly discussed in previous chapters, some of the research findings from this tradition, for example concerning such areas as information processing, attributions, and prototypes are of clear relevance to personal construct theory, and the clinical practice not only of the cognitive therapist but also of the personal construct psychotherapist may be enriched by drawing upon this work.

## Psychoanalytic theories

Kelly's discussions of psychoanalysis are a mixture of appreciations of Freud as a clinician and rather scornful criticisms of psychoanalytic theory. For example, he describes how, when commencing his clinical practice, he re-read Freud and became a 'Freudian', but found that even when he fabricated 'insights' and made 'preposterous interpretations', some of them proved very effective (Kelly, 1969d). In his view, the benefit which these interpretations afforded clients was that they provided an explanation which they could use as 'a fresh approach to life' (p. 54). Kelly, in this passage, is demonstrating his opposition to what he considered the tendency of psychoanalysts to give interpretations to clients as if they were absolute truths rather than hypotheses providing a basis for experimentation. Indeed, he predicted that the view that psychoanalytic theory offers absolute truths, coupled with the difficulties in validating its concepts experimentally, would result in it being 'condemned to end its days as a crumbling stockade of proprietary dogmatism' (Kelly, 1969i, p. 67). His view that psychoanalysis essentially is not a scientific theory, but that instead it consists of 'rubber hypotheses', is, of course, shared by other critics. However, it has been questioned both by those who have subjected psychoanalytic hypotheses to traditional experimental test (e.g. Fisher and Greenberg, 1978; Kline, 1981; Fonagy, 1982) and by others who have noted that there may be alternative constructions of what constitutes scientific method (e.g. Warren, 1983). A further reason for Kelly's disaffection with psychoanalysis was another common criticism of this approach, namely its apparent inapplicability to the problems of many of the clients, often very socially deprived people, with whom he was dealing. Indeed, it has been suggested that the necessity of adapting his treatment approach to the needs of these clients was a major determinant of the theory which he developed (Zelhart and Jackson, 1983).

Describing his growing disenchantment with psychoanalysis, Kelly (1969d, p. 58) writes that 'the more we understood what was actually happening the less useful was our lexicon of psychodynamic terms'. In particular, while he regarded personal construct theory as an 'all-out dynamic theory' (Kelly, 1969i, p. 89), in that it regards the person as constantly in motion, he also considered it 'completely nondynamic' (Kelly, 1969f, p. 217) in that this motion is not dependent on any forces, libidinal or otherwise. People are viewed by the theory as active, rather than inert bodies requiring propulsion into action, and there is no place in the theory for the hydraulic model of the person favoured by psychoanalysts. In denying that there was any place either for the notions of ego, superego, and id, which he dismissed as anthropomorphisms, Kelly was rejecting the view of the person as essentially bad which is implicit in these concepts. He also rejected the psychoanalytic view of such emotions as guilt and hostility. For example, he pointed out that while difficulties in toilet training may dislodge a person from his or her core role and therefore produce guilt, so may a wide variety of other experiences. Likewise, the notion that hostility is an attempt to extort validational evidence for constructions is in marked contrast to the psychoanalytic view of it as a destructive force which could be turned against the self if not directed towards others (Kelly, 1969j). Aggression, similarly, was not regarded by Kelly, as it is by psychoanalysts, as an aspect of hostility. These differences between the psychoanalytic and personal construct theory views of hostility and aggression were perhaps reflected in the results of a factor analysis of the Q-sorts carried out by Kelly and seven other personality theorists on statements concerning a clinical case protocol (Kelly, 1963a). The second factor from the analysis distinguished between aggression and hostility, and contrasted Kelly's responses with those of a Freudian and a Jungian. There is somewhat greater commonality, however, between the personal construct theory view of anxiety and that of such psychoanalysts as Rycroft (1968, p. 15), who considers that 'Anxiety is the expectation of something as yet unknown'.

As we have seen, Kelly did not employ the concept of the unconscious, although he did acknowledge that some constructions may be at a low level of cognitive awareness. In his view, 'If the client does not construe things in the way we do, we assume that he construes them in some other way, not that he really must construe them the way we do but is unaware of it' (Kelly, 1955, p. 467). Nevertheless, he considered that some of his concepts, such as preverbal constructs, submergence, suspension, and impermeability, 'cover some of the same ground' as the unconscious (Kelly, 1955, p. 466). Indeed, Kelly's (1955, p. 474) description of the recovery during therapy of a phobic client's constructions concerning sibling rivalry, previously suspended because they 'were so wholly embedded in the threatening structure of hostility', would not be altogether out of place in a psychoanalytic text. Fransella (1982) has elaborated on the relationship between the concepts of levels of awareness and of the unconscious by drawing upon Polanyi's (1958) notions of focal and subsidiary awareness, and of tacit knowing. She suggested, for example, that one has subsidiary awareness of such aspects of one's construct system as submerged construct poles and preverbal construing, and that only suspended elements are totally unavailable to consciousness. Epting (1984) has also noted that, while the distinction between conscious and unconscious may imply a difference in the processes characterising these two realms, the concept of levels of awareness requires no such assumption.

The psychoanalytic concept of defence mechanisms has also been reframed in personal construct theory terms by writers from both theoretical backgrounds. Kelly himself considered defences to be 'not just ... kinds of perversity toward the therapist, but ... genuinely vulnerable points in the construct system' (quoted in R. Neimeyer, 1980, p. 80). Discussing particular defence mechanisms, he suggested that repression and reaction formation are explicable in terms of the notion that constructs consist of contrasting poles, and that, for example, 'there are instances in which the person is so self-involved with a construct that he avoids expressing its contrasting aspect lest he misidentify himself' (Kelly, 1955, p. 71). He also considered that the concepts of suspension and submergence may provide an explanation of such phenomena, but without requiring the assumption that the material which is at a low level of awareness is intolerable because of its unpleasantness. However, as Rychlak (1981) made clear, threatening or anxiety-provoking events may not be easily recalled because of the lack of appropriate constructs to structure them, this being precisely the reason why they are threatening and anxiety-provoking in the first place. Rychlak also considered the personal construct theory view of projection to be that it is 'a special form of hostility, in which the person insists on naming what another's motives are despite all evidence to the contrary' (p. 726). Introjection, in personal construct theory terms, would be seen as taking over the constructs of a particular group; incorporation as the construing of others as like oneself; and regression as behaviour that reflects preverbal or immature constructions. The primary contributor to this area from the psychoanalytic tradition has been Ryle (1978), who considers that 'defence mechanisms ... can be reformulated in terms of the predominance of certain restricted constructions of events, and of certain rigidly maintained plans for action, resulting in the exclusion of alternative interpretations and plans. The alternative unacted plans may remain "on store" and, because untested, unchanged' (p. 589). For example,

> repression, denial, dissociation, isolation, and undoing represent examples of the selective perception and selective accommodation of perceptions to the whole structure of meaning of the individual's personal construct system. Reaction formation, reversal, and turning against the self, and sublimation, similarly represent particular examples of the selection of programmes or plans of action ... The more primitive defences described in object-relations theory as projection, projective identification, and splitting, represent in cognitive terms confused boundaries between self and others.
>
> (Ryle, 1978 pp. 589–90)

Ryle (1975, 1985) has made considerable use of the repertory grid in his work, and considers that the grid can provide access to defence mechanisms and to other unconscious mental processes. For example, he suggests that splitting may be indicated by highly polarised construing of the self or a significant other, the split-off aspects of whom may be revealed by considering the contrast poles to those applied to the self or the other. Two further defence mechanisms which Ryle considers may be revealed by a repertory grid are repression and denial of negative feelings, which may be indicated by an individual providing few constructs concerned with such feelings (or, presumably, providing few elements to fit such role titles as 'a person I dislike'), being able to provide only the 'positive' poles of such constructs, or not differentiating between grid elements in terms of the constructs concerned. As we have seen in Chapter 4, the use of grid indices of this type has provided an understanding of such disorders as agoraphobia and psychosomatic complaints which is not incompatible with the psychodynamic view. Similarly, it has been suggested that denial is indicated by the low distances between self and ideal self in the grids of clients in whom there is little apparent physical basis for their complaints of chronic pain (Large, 1985). As well as his suggested grid indices of defence mechanisms, Ryle also considers that unconscious fantasy processes may be reflected in a grid by non-consensual construct relationships, of the type which he has elaborated in his later work on 'dilemmas, traps, and snags' (Ryle, 1979a). Finally, he suggests that unresolved Oedipal problems may be indicated in a grid by the association of appropriate sex-role characteristics with negative attributes; by construing of the self as similar to opposite-sex elements; and, in the dyad grid (see p. 223), by client's and spouse's reciprocal roles either repeating the reciprocal roles of the client and a parent or reversing the reciprocal sex roles of the client's parents.

There has now been a certain amount of consideration by other authors of defence mechanisms from a personal construct theory perspective. For example, splitting has been viewed by Procter (1981) as similar to fragment-ation, and the strategies with which the Kleinian therapist attempts to resolve it as involving the development of a superordinate construct which can subsume the split poles. He also, similarly to Ryle, regards the phenomena referred to as repression as perhaps indicating lack of elaboration of the construct system in an area such as interpersonal conflict; and projection as possibly reflecting the definition of oneself by contrast with some other figure. Gardner *et al.* (1988), considering the view that clients often repress the conflicts which underlie their symptoms, conclude that such an explanation is unnecessary since the difficulty experienced by clients in tracing the roots of their symptoms may be the result of the invalidation of the constructs on which such an understanding could be based. Apart from such theoretical analyses, some empirical work has also been carried out on the relationship between defence mechanisms and features of construing. Two of these studies have employed the Repression-Sensitization Scale (Byrne *et al.*, 1963), which discriminates repressors, who tend to deny and avoid threat and conflict, from sensitisers, who tend to be very vigilant to such situations and to employ intellectual and obsessive defences. Wilkins *et al.* (1972), working with students, found that repressors were less cognitively complex than both sensitisers and subjects who scored in the intermediate range on the scale, while Carr and Post (1974), following up work by Altrocchi (1961), associated sensitisation in a client population with high differentiation of the self from others on negative dimensions. In their study of choice of drugs, Penrod *et al.* (1981) have also obtained findings suggestive of a link between interpersonal cognitive differentiation and defensive style in that depressant users, whose principal defences are presumed to be repression and denial, showed lower differentiation than stimulant users, who are considered to employ defences of intellectualisation and sensitisation. A further feature of construing which has been considered to indicate a rigid defensive style is literal relating of values, feelings, and behaviours, Leitner (1981b) finding this to be associated with an extreme view of the self and a tendency, reflected in a low self–ideal self discrepancy, not to admit to dissatisfaction with this view. However, the most extensive work in this area has been carried out by Catina *et al.* (1988, 1991), whose approach has been to relate clients' repertory grid scores to those on a questionnaire measure of defence mechanisms (Ehlers and Peter, 1989). Consistently with the Wilkins *et al.* study, denial was associated with tight construing, and also with a tendency to view the self as similar to how one is construed by others, perhaps indicating the avoidance of social feedback which invalidates the individual's self-construction. In addition, and unexpectedly, denial was related to variation in the application of emotional constructs to grid elements, as well as to construal of the past and ideal selves as dissimilar. Rationalisation was associated with variation in the use of emotional constructs and with extreme construing of grid elements, suggesting that it involves a strategy of making clear-cut distinctions between events. This defence was also related to construal of the past self as dissimilar to the ideal. 'Turning against the object' was found to characterise those clients who showed high variation in their use of emotional constructs and who imagined that others construed them as dissimilar to how they would like to be. Rather than simply suggesting that defence mechanisms may be operationalised in grid terms, the authors have attempted to conceptualise them as ways of dealing with persistent invalidation, particularly of self-construing, which may involve hostility and the long-term use of particular strategies of construing such as constriction and tightening rather than of the cyclical interplay of strategies which Kelly associated with optimal functioning.

A further area of some apparent similarity between the formulations of personal construct theorists and psychoanalysts, particularly such concepts as 'secondary gain', is the notion that a client's presenting problem may have implications for him or her, perhaps at a low level of cognitive awareness, which are not entirely negative (see Chapter 4). For example, the suggestion that by being agoraphobic a client may in some cases avoid construing himself or herself as potentially unfaithful (see p. 118) is consistent with psycho-dynamic formulations (e.g. Abraham, 1955), while the view that other clients may associate their depression or anxiety with tenderness is reminiscent of Rycroft's (1968, p. 113) statement that 'a tendency to feel anxious may be used as evidence of sensibility, of being a more tender plant than ordinary mortals'. However, the personal construct psychotherapist differs from the psycho-analyst in that symptoms are not viewed as necessarily having any *particular* symbolic significance, nor the function of compromise gratification of some *particular* desires. Similarly, while the view that the client's symptoms may serve some purpose for him or her would imply that therapy may well be resisted by the client, the personal construct theory and psychoanalytic perspectives on resistance, as we have seen in Chapter 7, are very different. As Kelly (1955, p. 1101) points out in discussing resistance, 'Since we do not employ a defensive theory of human motivation, the term does not have the important meaning it must necessarily assume for the psychoanalysts.'

Superficial similarities between personal construct psychotherapy and psychoanalysis may be apparent not only in some of their concepts but also in some of the procedures employed by therapists from the two schools. As Kelly (1955) pointed out, psychoanalytic therapy nearly always involves loosening techniques. He questions the assumption of psychoanalysis 'that there is only one acceptable kind of psychotherapeutic procedure for producing mobility' (p. 213), and, as we have seen in Chapter 7, while loosening may be an appropriate approach with some clients it is clearly contra-indicated with others. Nevertheless, when a personal construct psychotherapist does wish to loosen a client's construing, he or she may well turn to a technique which is more usually associated with psychoanalysis, albeit not necessarily with the same therapeutic aims as in the analyst's use of the technique. For example, personal construct psychotherapists, as we have seen, are not averse to discussing their clients' dreams, but rather than viewing these as sources of repressed material, they will regard the enterprise as one of allowing the client to produce loose, or preverbal, constructions, or as providing access to submerged construct poles. Kelly points out, for example, that Freud's observation that in dreams ideas are often expressed in terms of their opposites is explicable simply in terms of the notion that constructs consist of contrasting poles. Constructs which emerge during exploration of dreams or other loosening procedures will not be regarded as the client's 'true feelings' but rather as hypotheses to be tightened and tested. As Epting (1984, p. 126) remarks, the emphasis is 'on the extension and creation of meaning rather than an excavation of something buried in the unconscious which contains the meaning of the material'. The concern will be less with the content of the material than with the process of construing which is involved, and generally there will be no attempt to interpret the symbolism of dream elements, Kelly (1955, p. 1040) viewing this as 'usually an attempt of the therapist to impose his own construct system upon the client'.

Symbolism, in personal construct theory, refers to the representation of a construct by a particular element. Thus, in early childhood, the child's parents may become the symbols (or, to use more 'cognitive' terms, the prototypes or supersets) of several constructs: for example, Rodney's (see pp. 254–5) mother symbolised virtuous suffering for him, while his father symbolised irresponsible hedonism, and later in life he applied this construct to sexual situations. As Kelly (1955) noted, this is very different from the psychoanalytic view that the child introjects his or her parents. Nevertheless, the personal construct psychotherapist who traces the symbols of a client's constructs, perhaps by exploring the client's past history, may appear to be operating in a similar manner to a psychoanalyst. Any such concern with the past is 'both because it is the stuff which the client's construct system must have been designed to make sense out of, and because the way the past is now seen is a cue to the way the present is now seen, and a forecaster of the way events which are about to happen will first be seen' (Kelly, 1955, pp. 591–2). The personal construct psychotherapist will generally be much more concerned with the present and the future than with the past, and for Kelly (1955) there were

> only three ways in which dealing with the past can be considered therapeutically defensible: (1) it may clarify the constructs under which the client has been operating and thus enable the client and the therapist to judge what the implications for the future are, (2) it may enable the client to reduce certain constructs to a state of inoperativeness by making them concrete – that is, impermeable to the embracing of additional elements – or (3) it may provide an array of elements out of which new constructs may be *created*.
>
> (p. 380, italics in original)

Therefore, unlike the psychoanalyst who explores a client's past, the personal construct psychotherapist will 'not conceptualize this part of his role as eliciting catharsis or as dealing with hidden dynamic forces' (Kelly, 1955, p. 592), the client's childhood will not be viewed in terms of the extent to which a fixed sequence of developmental stages has been successfully negotiated, and the client will not be regarded as a 'victim of his biography' (Kelly, 1955, p. 208). Indeed, Kelly considered that one of the dangers of the 'backward elaboration' of the client's construing favoured by psychoanalysis is that it might reinforce the client's construction of himself or herself as a victim of the past. Soldz (1988) suggests that the relative lack of emphasis by personal construct psychotherapists on the client's childhood experiences may reflect the tendency of such therapists to employ short-term therapies, and is less apparent in those, such as Leitner (1980, 1987), who engage in longer-term treatments. A concern with childhood experience is also apparent in the work of Lorenzini and Sassaroli (1987, 1988), who draw upon Bowlby's (1969, 1973, 1980) ideas to explain the childhood development of such constructions as the view, apparent in some agoraphobics, that exploration and attachment are incompatible. Finally, regression has been considered by some personal construct psychotherapists to serve a useful therapeutic purpose in, for example, promoting loosening and countering impermeability (Green, 1987; Procter, 1989).

While psychoanalytic procedures generally involve loosening, this is not the case with interpretation, which is likely to tighten a client's construing. In attempting to facilitate reconstruing, personal construct psychotherapists may at times also appear to be offering interpretations to their clients, but Kelly (1955) indicated that a major difference from the psychoanalytic approach is that 'it is always the client who interprets, not the therapist' (p. 1090). By contrast, he considered that psychoanalytic interpretations tend to involve providing the client with some new, ready-formed construction. The client may then be regarded as showing insight if he or she accepts the new construction, or as showing resistance if he or she does not. Kelly notes, however, that conformity with the therapist's construction does not necessarily imply that this construction was previously below the level of the client's conscious awareness and has been brought to the surface. For the personal construct psychotherapist, insight is 'the comprehensive construction of one's behavior' (Kelly, 1955, p. 917), but the construction concerned is not necessarily one which the client has adopted from the therapist. For example, enactment procedures may allow the client to arrive at more explicit interpretations of his or her own constructions, and Kelly (1955) considered that one of the reasons why such procedures are less than popular with psychoanalysts is that the constructions concerned are those of the client and not of the analyst.

A somewhat greater similarity between psychoanalysis and personal construct psychotherapy is apparent in their use of the concept of transference, and indeed Kelly (1955, pp. 662–3) borrowed this term because he considered that 'Much of what we have to say regarding the use of transference, as indeed much of what we have already said about therapeutic technique, has been said by those who approach therapy from the standpoint of psychoanalysis'. However, he also considered the psychoanalytic use of the term to be 'altogether too loose for our purposes' (Kelly, 1955, p. 1100). Transference, in his view, was central to all construing, since this always involves an individual transferring a construct from his or her repertoire on to a situation or person. More specifically, transference may be considered to be 'the tendency of any person to perceive another prejudicately as a replicate of a third person' (Kelly, 1955, p. 1100), or as a subset of this third person (Gara and Rosenberg, 1979). It is therefore a feature not only of the client–therapist relationship but of all interpersonal relationships, and 'is not necessarily pathological' (Kelly, 1955, p. 1100). Semerari (1989) takes a similar view, regarding transference as involving the application to the therapist, or to another significant person who takes on the role of validating agent, of constructs which were developed in the context of the client's relationship with his or her first validating agents.

As we have seen in the last chapter, Kelly considered that primary transferences should be discouraged and, as a result, shared the psychoanalytic view that the therapist should be a somewhat ambiguous figure. He also agreed that the preemptive construction of the therapist which may be involved in transference can be used in therapy to allow the client to reconstrue his or her relationship with other significant figures. However, he parted company with psychoanalysts on what he felt to be their view that an authoritarian therapist–client relationship, with childlike dependencies being transferred onto the therapist, was 'an essential feature of the transference which is so useful in therapy' (Kelly, 1955, p. 578). Bannister (1970b, p. 243) has likened this preferred therapist–client relationship in psychoanalysis to that between priest and penitent, and as 'one of condescension, of superiority, of paternalism'. Rather than viewing the client's transference relationship with the therapist as necessarily reflecting, and leading to the exploration of, his or her relationship with a parent, the personal construct psychotherapist will be more concerned to identify the particular preemptive constructs and dependencies which are being transferred on to the therapist. If 'transference interpretations' are made, they may be seen as serving to decrease the range of convenience of the client's construing of the therapist (Karst, 1980), such that he or she will no longer be seen in the same terms as some other significant figure in the client's life. As Leitner (1982) has pointed out, these and other psychoanalytic interventions may also be viewed as serving to move the client from literalism or chaotic fragmentalism towards a perspectivist position.

In discussing similarities in technique between personal construct and psychoanalytic therapies, mention should also perhaps be made of the common use by therapists of both persuasions of group treatment approaches. Although the particular approaches concerned are likely to differ in important respects, some of the curative processes which have been considered to operate in analytic groups, as we have discussed in Chapter 7, are not incompatible with the aims of personal construct psychotherapy (Koch, 1985; Winter, 1985d, 1989b). However, such similarities are more apparent in those group approaches in which group members are facilitated to arrive at their own interpretations (e.g. Foulkes, 1964; Yalom, 1970) than in methods closer to traditional psychoanalysis, in which the group receives interpretations from the analyst. As Llewelyn and Dunnett (1987) point out, in contrast to the latter type of group, the leaders in a personal construct psychotherapy group are merely viewed as 'additional data for the client's own experimentation' (p. 255), although also modelling the process of experimentation and offering concepts which may allow clients to interpret their own behaviour. An additional distinction which these authors make between the personal construct and the traditional analytic approach to group psychotherapy is that the former approach encourages discussion of events outside the group whereas the latter tends to regard such discussion as an avoidance of issues within the group.

Just as personal construct psychotherapists have borrowed techniques developed within the psychoanalytic tradition, some psychoanalytic therapists have also found repertory grid technique to be of value in focussing their therapy, in exploring its process, and in demonstrating the reconstruing which may result from it (see Chapter 5). Indeed, Rowe (1973a, p. 19) has been led to assert: 'Take heart, Freud is not dead. He is alive and well and living in Patrick Slater's computer.' Kelly (1955) himself, in introducing the grid, noted that it could be used by a psychoanalytically orientated clinician to reveal such problems as Oedipal conflicts. The primary proponent of this approach has been Ryle (1975), who considers that in feeding back grid results to a client one is 'carrying out a process indistinguishable from that aspect of psychotherapeutic interpretation which is concerned with "making the unconscious conscious"' (p. 57). In his later work (see Chapters 4 and 7), often with the aid of repertory grid technique, he defines the constructions underlying a client's problems in terms of 'dilemmas, traps, and snags' (Ryle, 1979a), which are then used as a focus of therapy in which the goal is *to achieve a change in the terms through which his experience is construed* (p. 50, italics in original). While this method is primarily intended to be of value to psychoanalytic therapists, Ryle notes that his formulations of dilemmas, traps, and snags make no reference to psychoanalytic concepts but instead are generally couched in the client's own language. His approach to achieving the therapeutic goals defined with a particular client, and which was originally described as focussed integrated active psychotherapy (Ryle, 1980) but has been refined into 'cognitive analytic therapy' (Ryle, 1990), may also incorporate methods other than the purely psychoanalytic, including behavioural and cognitive techniques. Indeed, he views the terminology which he has employed, and which draws on both personal construct theory and cognitive models of information-processing, as providing the basis of a common language for the psychotherapies (Ryle, 1978, 1982). He considers that personal construct theory pays insufficient attention to the organisation of action and of construing (Ryle, 1989), addressed in his model by the concept of 'procedures', sequences of behavioural and mental processes. In the view of Adams-Webber (1989b), however, the model lacks a coherent theoretical basis.

A final area with which Kelly (1955) concerned himself in his writings on psychoanalysis was the training of analysts. In particular, he regarded the requirement that analysts are themselves psychoanalysed as providing them with 'a form of direct professional lineage to Freud' (p. 1178), and an indoctrination in psychoanalytic concepts which is likely to lead to rigidity in the therapist's professional constructions of clients. Nevertheless, as we have seen in Chapter 7, Kelly was not averse to therapists undergoing therapy if this is viewed in terms of facilitating the development of role relationships with clients and the learning of particular techniques, although he opposed the practice of therapists treating clients while at the same time receiving therapy themselves.

Just as is the case in some of the writings of Kelly and later personal construct theorists concerning behavioural approaches, Ryle (1975) notes that there has been a tendency to caricature psychoanalysis and to ignore more recent work within the psychoanalytic tradition. As Appelbaum (1969, p. 21) remarked, Kelly's 'broadsides are against a piece of psychoanalytic theory that was discarded in the 1920s'. Ryle proposes that the fact that, despite espousing constructive alternativism, 'adherents of personal construct theory display postures of such ungenerous incomprehension, suggests that there may be a need for a construct like "the unconscious" ' (p. 53). Similarly, Holland (1970) considers that Kelly's accounts of Freudian theory reflect a defensiveness which was perhaps based in anxieties concerning the inadequacies of personal construct theory, in comparison to psychoanalysis, in providing an understanding of such areas as childhood development. While some post-Kellian personal construct theorists, such as Bannister and Fransella

(1986), are, indeed, very dismissive of psychoanalysis, others, such as Viney (1981, 1987b), note various common features of the two theories, and their respective therapeutic approaches: namely, that they both consider therapeutic goals to involve change in experience as well as behaviour, both emphasise reflexivity, and both are concerned with intentions and meanings. Although Viney (1990) accepts such psychoanalytic notions as the equation of depression with anger turned against oneself, she also contends that the phenomeno-logical roots of personal construct theory are very different from the mechanistic roots of psychoanalysis, and that while the meanings with which personal construct psychotherapy is concerned are the client's, in psycho-analysis they may be the meanings which the analyst brings to the therapeutic situation (Viney, 1987b). Something of a shift from a concern with personal meanings to one with universal meanings is apparent in the writings of Rowe (1978, 1982, 1983a, 1987, 1989), who seems to have seen no necessary incom-patibility in employing both personal construct and psychoanalytic concepts in her explanations of clients' problems, but whose later work appears to draw less heavily on the former concepts. In this work, there is an emphasis on childhood experiences, on assertions that constructions with a certain content are always to be found in particular clients, such as depressives, and on the use of the distinction between extraverted and introverted types as an explanation for a wide range of clinical phenomena.

The post-Freudian psychoanalytic work which Ryle (1975) suggests is worthy of greater attention by personal construct theorists encompasses not only his own preferred approach of object-relations theory (Fairbairn, 1952) but also ego psychology (Rapaport, 1959) and views of psychoanalytic theory as a theory of meaning (Rycroft, 1970). It should also be noted that, although the analysis of Q-sorts referred to earlier revealed no relationship between the sorts completed by Kelly and by a Freudian, there was much greater corres-pondence of Kelly's views with those of an Adlerian (Kelly, 1963a). Other workers have also noted compatibilities between personal construct theory and more recent elaborations of psychoanalysis. For example, Warren (1983) indicates that developments in French psychoanalytic thought (Ricoeur, 1970; Lacan, 1977), including the reading of Freudian biological, energy, and other concepts as symbols, suggest a common location of psychoanalysis and personal construct theory within a phenomenological perspective and a common emphasis on a hermeneutic approach to therapy. In his view, shared by Bieri (1986), each of these theories 'is concerned with language and with meaning, and each accords the individual a central and an active role. Equally, and contrary to what has become practice, the real psychoanalytic therapy is a process of enquiry into meanings; a mutual search rather than interpretation coming down from on high in the form of "stone tablets"' (p. 12). It should be noted here that, although Kelly's writings do often appear to consider Freudian concepts as if they referred to concrete entities, at other points he does acknowledge that they could be viewed symbolically, and criticises 'those who follow Freud concretistically with no real appreciation of the propositional use of many Freudian constructs' (Kelly, 1955, p. 298). An example of the latter would be use of the tripartite personality structure concept as a 'community of selves' metaphor (Mair, 1977b). As Schafer (1976) has described, psychoanalytic constructs may also be expressed in terms of an 'action language' which, since it presents the person as active and purposive, is rather more consistent with personal construct theory.

Soldz (1986, 1988), in his analysis of similarities between personal construct psychology and recent variations of psychoanalysis, has focussed on a different set of contemporary psychoanalytic ideas from those discussed by Warren. In his view, all of the approaches which he considers reflect constructivist tendencies, since the 'person is no longer viewed as simply a victim of forces outside awareness', and there is 'an emphasis on basing theory on an understanding of the perspective or point of view of the patient' (Soldz, 1986, p. 54). For example, he regards the psychoanalytic phenomenology of Atwood and Stolorow (1984), with its emphasis on 'structures of experience', its notion of psychological health as involving a balance of accommodation and assimilation, and its view of transference as an example of 'organising activity', as being essentially compatible with personal construct theory. Object-relations theory, with its view that the individual constructs representations of personal relationships, is also regarded by Soldz as consistent with constructivist approaches, although Dryden's (1984) analysis of similarities and differences between different approaches has indicated that personal construct psychotherapy differs markedly from Kleinian therapy, and more so than from Freudian therapy, in terms of therapist behaviour. Another method which Soldz considers to be essentially constructivist is Peterfreund's (1983) heuristic approach to psychoanalysis, with its emphasis on mutual discovery of personal meanings by client and analyst rather than a dogmatic, stereotyped analytic approach. Also considered by Soldz is control-mastery theory (Weiss et al., 1986), which regards the client as entering analysis with an unconscious plan to test and invalidate a pathogenic belief resulting from childhood experiences; and the modern psychoanalytic school (Spotnitz, 1976), which provides techniques which allow the analyst to work with severely disturbed clients without premature invalidation of the client's core constructs. For example, the technique of 'joining', which involves the therapist agreeing with the client, may provide the necessary validation to encourage elaboration of construing and experimentation, while 'object-orientated questions', which concern someone or something outside the client, may also allow clients to elaborate their construing of others and of others' constructions. In addition, Soldz (1987a) describes how the modern psychoanalytic therapist regards resistance in a less pejorative light than is apparent in those psychoanalytic writings which have been criticised by Kelly, and is also in agreement with Kelly in viewing insight as not necessary for therapeutic change. Soldz (1987a), whose therapeutic approach with severely disturbed clients is informed both by modern psychoanalytic theory and by personal construct theory, considers that such clients tend to be characterised by hostility, and that their therapy generally needs to be of several years' duration. Although concluding that integration of psychoanalysis and personal construct psychology is unlikely, Soldz (1988, p. 345) suggests that each theory may gain from cross-fertilisation with the other. In his view, the gains for personal construct theory are likely to be in the areas of the importance of bodily experience, of childhood development, and of primitive constructions. On the other hand, the gains for psychoanalysis might be in the areas of the process of change, structural features of construing, and the personal construct theory view of emotions.

## Systemic approaches

Apart from childhood development, the other major area in which personal construct theory was not extensively elaborated by Kelly is that of social processes. Indeed, Procter and Parry (1978, p. 157) remarked that 'as construct theorists, we are forced to admit that our theory fails to take adequate account of the social nature of meanings and values'. More recently, however, much greater attention has been paid by personal construct theorists to the individual's social world (e.g. Stringer and Bannister, 1979), Procter (1981, 1985a) himself having been the pioneer of such work in the clinical sphere.

Procter's primary area of interest is family therapy, and he considers the fact that such treatment approaches began to be developed at about the same time as personal construct theory as reflecting their common basis in 'American pragmatism'. He states, for example, that 'They share the optimism that things can be changed and the belief that action that leads to change is of the most fundamental importance' (Procter, 1981, p. 350). In common with Mahoney (1988b), he also regards such aspects of personal construct theory as its concern with process rather than content as being epistemologically compatible with systems theory. The areas of commonality between these two theories have been highlighted by Procter's development of a 'family construct psychology' which, as we have discussed in previous chapters, includes the notion of a family construct system. Procter notes, for example, that both family construct psychology and systems theory would predict the occurrence of such phenomena as the 'transfer of illness' from one family member to another as the first member begins to improve; as well as the 'homeostatic' relapse which may be observed in a family if the reconstruing at subordinate levels reflected in behavioural change does not extend to superordinate levels of the system.

Procter has also discussed similarities and differences between family construct psychology and the work of particular family therapists, pointing out, for example, that an essential difference between the concepts of family construct system and of 'family myth' (Ferreira, 1963) is that the latter implies an inaccurate construction whereas family construct psychology makes no such assumption. Dallos and Aldridge (1987) also note that such concepts as family myth and script are based on a deterministic model, and that the latter concept may more usefully be viewed in terms of the transmission of sets of constructs from one generation to the next. Procter sees greater similarities between his approach and the work of Minuchin (1974), whose notion of boundaries can be viewed in terms of the existence of constructs which discriminate, and thus form a boundary, between particular systems or subsystems. Similarly, Procter considers that 'enmeshment', as described by Minuchin, may reflect constellatory family constructs, a lack of within-boundary constructs, or a family construct system which is more appropriate to an earlier developmental level. He relates Minuchin's concept of 'disengagement' to excessive impermeability of within-boundary constructs, which will not, for example, subsume new behaviour; and to fragmentation of the family construct system. As we have seen in Chapter 7, Procter has also noted that many of the techniques employed by structural family therapists such as Minuchin, as well as by strategic therapists such as the Milan group (Selvini-Palazzoli *et al.*, 1980) and Erickson (Erickson and Rossi, 1979), may be subsumed by family construct psychology. Amongst the techniques which he considers are reframing, various enactment methods, and the use of paradox and metaphor.

The links between personal construct theory and the work of family therapists have been further considered by Alexander and G. Neimeyer (1989) and Alexander (1988), who distinguishes between 'family cognitions', the beliefs held by each family member about every other member, and 'family constructs', the family's shared beliefs. Drawing upon the family therapy literature, she describes how these latter constructs may be maintained by family rituals; by the fact that they are often implicit and abstract, and as a result relatively untestable; or by their occasional lack of complexity and permeability. She considers that intervening at the level of family constructs may produce more far-reaching changes than intervening at the level of family cognitions, and that such interventions may be achieved by the use of various family therapy techniques.

Not only are some of the techniques developed within alternative family therapy traditions consistent with a reconstructive therapy model, but, as Epting and Amerikaner (1980) point out, the systems theory view of the desirability of systems maintaining open but adequate boundaries is compatible with personal construct psychotherapy goals of optimal functioning. However, many of the procedures developed by family therapists on the basis of systems theory do not rest altogether easily with a personal construct theory approach. Such procedures are based on the assumption that 'intervention must be forceful or disguised since, having reached some sort of homeostasis in their interaction, partners are likely to resist therapeutic efforts that threaten this equilibrium' (G. Neimeyer, 1985, p. 202). As a result, families are subjected to various manipulations, double binds, and paradoxical injunctions, or receive authoritative prescriptions from therapists who may themselves be complying with the 'higher authority' of consultants observing the session from behind a one-way screen and broadcasting instructions via an intercom. Thus, while such systems theory concepts as homeostasis imply a view of resistance, consistent with personal construct theory, as involving not stubborn opposition but an understandable attempt to preserve the organis- ation of the system, they have also led some workers to a view of the therapist– family relationship as essentially adversarial (Wile, 1981). To explore whether this need be so, it is necessary to consider in somewhat greater detail the assumptions underlying the work of various family therapists.

As Harter (1988) has indicated, family therapies, like the other therapeutic approaches which we have considered in this chapter, differ in the extent to which their epistemological assumptions are essentially constructivist. For example, as noted above, the basic assumptions of those approaches which consider dysfunctional families to be characterised by mythical or distorted beliefs are realist rather than constructivist, and the structural approaches have also been considered to display realist assumptions (Keeney and Sprenkle, 1982). While Selvini-Palazzoli et al. (1980) and Watzlawick et al. (1974) are classified by Harter as 'constructive family theorists', and are also viewed as such by Loos and Epstein (1989), she regards the less than constructivist assumptions reflected in many of their techniques as indicating a failure of work on treatment strategies to keep pace with developments at a theoretical level. She notes that in their more recent work Selvini-Palazzoli et al. acknowledge that prescriptive approaches may not be necessary in family therapy. As examples of the movement away from the use of prescriptive techniques, Harter has drawn attention to those approaches which view the therapist less as a prescriptive agent than as part of the therapist–family system (Bateson, 1974; Keeney, 1979; Dell, 1982; Rosenbaum, 1982). Similarities between the work of some of the theorists concerned and Kelly's ideas have also been noted by Foley (1988), and by Feixas et al. (1987) in their discussion of what they consider to be the common constructivist epistemo- logical foundations of personal construct psychology and systems theory.

The trends in family therapy described by Harter may usefully be viewed in terms of the distinction between emphasis on first-order and on second-order cybernetics (von Foerster, 1981). In the former type of approach, the concern is with observation of a system, whereas in the latter the observer is regarded as part of the system, and as inevitably affecting what is observed. The shift from first-order to second-order concerns is considered by Loos and Epstein (1989) to be exemplified by Bateson's (1972, 1978) initial emphasis on the functionality of symptoms in maintaining family structure, and later rejection of this notion because of its lack of attention to the role of the observer. These workers also consider Procter's earlier writings, with their emphasis on the homeostatic functions of the family construct system, to reflect a first-order cybernetic position. By contrast, they note Kelly's concern with client and therapist jointly arriving at a construction of events, and cite the work of Andersen (1987) and Goolishian and Anderson (1987) as examples of the 'conversational coconstruction of realities' in family therapy. Andersen neatly reverses the practice of a consultancy team observing family therapy sessions by allowing clients to observe the deliberations of the family therapy team, and then to discuss these with the team. Unlike the view of many family therapists that systems create problems, Goolishian and Anderson consider that problems define the systems with which they work, and which are determined by people who are communicating about the problems concerned. Elaborating on this view, Loos and Epstein note that the relevant system for treatment in a particular case will vary as the definition of the problem changes. They regard the goal of therapy as being 'to maintain a conversation until what was originally defined as a problem is no longer viewed as a problem by those in communication about it' (p. 161). They do not consider that the therapist should attempt to maintain a neutral position in this conversation, and remark that 'the debate in the family therapy field over whether therapists are manipulative interventionists is meaningless, since every conversational act is an act of influence' (p. 162).

Finally, we should note that as well as the distinction between realists and constructivists, it is possible to distinguish between critical and radical constructivists (Mahoney, 1988a), the former acknowledging the existence of a real world while the latter do not accept that constructions reflect an objective reality. Although Kelly could be regarded as a critical constructivist, similarities have been noted between his approach and that of the biologist and systems theorist Maturana, who considers himself a *radical* radical constructivist in that rather than accepting that there are multiple alternative constructions of experience he maintains that at a given moment only one construction of experience is possible, determined by the structure of the living system concerned (Maturana and Varela, 1980; Kenny, 1988b, 1989; Fisher, 1989b). Such ideas, Maturana's notions of living systems as organisationally closed, as conserving their organisational invariance, and as self-creating, and his emphasis on the dialogical construction of meaning have implications for family therapy (Dell, 1982). Thus, Loos and Epstein consider their focus on the co-evolution of meaning by therapist and family to be consistent with Maturana's views, and similarly Kenny (1988b, p. 42) notes that it follows from this position that a therapist can never transmit instructions to a client but can only be 'a source of perturbations in the other's medium', the client's response to which will be determined by the structure of his or her system. A further therapeutic implication noted by Kenny is that the therapist's interactions should be orthogonal to the system, such that if the system is a family therapeutic interaction should be through dimensions which are not constitutive of the family. He also considers the various therapeutic strategies suggested by Kelly in terms of the extent to which they are likely to have an effect on the organisation of the system. Despite these applications of Maturana's ideas by family construct therapists, Viney *et al.* (1988) note that Maturana's view that all systems are closed is not entirely compatible with a personal construct theory approach.

Work on the links between personal construct theory and recent developments in systems theories has largely focussed on commonalities between the two approaches and the possible extension of personal construct psychology by, for example, drawing upon Maturana's work. Equally, however, as Feixas (1989) has indicated, there may be scope for development of our under-standing of broader systems by extending Procter's analysis of them in terms of the properties which personal construct theorists have described in relation to individual personal construct systems. Reiss (1981), for example, has described how these latter ideas contributed to his work on the family's development of a paradigm for the organisation of information.

## Existential and humanistic approaches

While, as we have seen, Kelly's criticisms of other approaches were often based on their assumptions of realism, his rejection of existentialism, in contrast, was in part because he equated 'extreme existentialism' with phenomenology and with the view that 'since we know reality only in the dubious terms of our own construction of it, there is no point in assuming that it exists at all, except as a figment of our imagination' (Kelly, 1969g, pp. 23–4). Kelly regarded such a view as leading to the pessimistic conclusion that the person 'experiences the absolute freedom that only utter emptiness can guarantee the human soul' (p. 24). He also remarked that his was not a phenomenological theory because, rather than simply leading to a description of an individual's constructions, it emphasises that these constructions should be subsumed by those of the observer or therapist (Kelly, 1955).

Holland (1970) considers that many of Kelly's writings (e.g. Kelly, 1969e) display a lack of familiarity with existentialism and phenomenology and a misunderstanding of such existential concepts as 'being in the world'. He also suggests that Kelly's style in describing existential and phenomenological approaches suggests a reaction to the change in core structures, and therefore threat, which might be posed by construing himself as an existentialist. In describing Kelly as a 'reluctant existentialist', Holland notes various similarities between personal construct theory and existentialism. These are a concern to question labels and to break out of existing categories; emphases on the person's responsibility for his or her construing, and on the importance of human experience; a similar model of interpersonal perception; and rejection both of the disease entity view of psychological disorder and of the concept of motivation. Holland (1970, p. 132) concludes that 'Kelly in trying to look without preconceptions at human experience, exemplified the phenomenological method which is the basis of existentialism', and that his writings display the same characteristics of individualism and subjectivism for which he criticised the existentialists. Patterson (1980) has also classified Kelly's viewpoint as basically phenomenological, while Smail (1978, p. 31) considers personal construct theory to be 'certainly the most profound and sophisticated attempt so far to elaborate the phenomenological position in psychological terms'. Finally, Rychlak (1981), distinguishing between sensory and logical phenomenologists on the basis of their respective emphases on the sensory and conceptual organisation of knowledge, places Kelly in the latter category.

That an association between personal construct theory and existentialism and phenomenology is not unwelcome to all personal construct psychologists is indicated by Epting's response to R. Neimeyer's (1985b, p. 124) question concerning linkages to the cognitive therapies. He stated that his 'interests lie in the direction of elaborating PCT in the direction of phenomenological and existential positions within psychology, just because I believe they're bigger ideas than the ones being pursued in cognitive psychology'. Elsewhere, he has described personal construct psychotherapy as 'a kind of phenomenological-existential-behaviourism' (Epting, 1984, p. 8) and 'a tough phenomenology' (p. 187). Here he is indicating that the concern of this form of psychotherapy with the client's subjective experience involves making this experience explicit and measurable. In addition, Epting notes a similarity between personal construct theory and existentialism in their emphases on choice and commitment. Another personal construct theorist who considers that there is no inconsistency between this theory and phenomenology is Warren (1985b), and indeed one of his conclusions is that 'in having regard to the therapist's own construing, the therapeutic aspect of personal construct theory comes as close as an intervention process can to the phenomenological method' (p. 262).

Various additional similarities and differences between personal construct theory and existentialism may be noted. Both approaches take a holistic view of the person, who is also seen as constantly changing. In addition, the importance attached by the existentialists to meaning, and the notion that neurosis may result from a perceived lack of meaning in life (Frankl, 1969), are consistent with the personal construct theory view of individuals as being primarily concerned with structuring their experiences, and as becoming anxious when they are unable to do so. Frankl's (1961) idea that when there is an existential vacuum, symptoms rush in to fill it is also not dissimilar to Kelly's belief that symptoms may provide some structure and meaning for a person's experiences, while Frankl's technique of paradoxical intention may be usefully employed to allow clients to develop an alternative, more distanced, construction of their symptoms (Meshoulam, 1978). Comparing personal constructs and existential a priori categories, with particular reference to Bannister's (1960) and Binswanger's (Needleman, 1968) analyses of schizophrenia, Levy (1975) concludes that 'the model of mind structure differs but the fundamental epistemological assumptions are very similar' (p. 379). Authenticity, which existential therapists would regard as a characteristic of the optimally functioning person (van Deurzen-Smith, 1984), has been related by Epting and Amerikaner (1980) to the notion of committed encounter, which Kelly (1970a) regarded as a central component of the Experience Cycle. The concept of the individual's 'existential project' has also been related by Villegas and Feixas (1985) to the notion of core constructs. Less compatible with personal construct theory is the existential position that conflict and anxiety necessarily stem from confrontation with what Yalom (1980, p. 8) terms the 'givens of existence', namely death, freedom, isolation, and meaninglessness. This notion of anxiety as involving a confrontation with the human condition, and as having to be endured, exemplifies the existential view of feelings as involving revelation of the nature of the world rather than, as in Kelly's approach, awareness of aspects of one's construing. The concern of some existential therapists (e.g. van Deurzen-Smith, 1984) with the client's 'true self' is also somewhat at odds with the personal construct theory view of psychotherapy as involving self-creation rather than self-discovery. Indeed, Kelly (1964) considered that if one never strove to become anything other than oneself, it would be 'a very dull way of living' (p. 147). Finally, a difference in therapeutic practice between personal construct and existential therapists is that the former are likely to employ more directed activities, such as role-playing, in their sessions (Dryden, 1984).

While the development of existentialism as a school of philosophy may be traced to the writings of various European thinkers, such as Kierkegaard (1941), Nietzsche (1969), Husserl (1952), Sartre (1948), Heidegger (1949), and Camus (1956), its popularisation in psychology is generally associated with the work of those American psychologists, such as Rogers (1951), Maslow (1965), and Perls (1969), who pioneered the humanistic psychology movement (Yalom, 1980). This 'third force' in psychology developed in the 1950s in opposition to the determinism and reductionism of the dominant behavioural and psychoanalytic traditions, and its compatibility with personal construct theory may be seen in its 'basic postulates', namely: 'Man, as man, supersedes the sum of his parts ... Man has his being in a human context ... Man is aware ... Man has choice ... Man is intentional' (Bugental, 1964, pp. 23–4). The basic characteristics of the humanistic orientation delineated by Bugental also display considerable commonality with personal construct theory. These characteristics are that 'Humanistic psychology cares about man ... values meaning more than procedure ... looks for human rather than nonhuman validations ... accepts the relativism of all knowledge ... relies heavily upon the phenomenological orientation ... does not deny the contributions of other views, but tries to supplement them and give them a setting within a broader conception of the human experience' (pp. 24–5).

As Yalom (1980) notes, one of the major differences between the American humanistic approaches and the European existential tradition is the more optimistic view of the human condition in the former. While this optimism is also shared by Kelly, that he was no more accepting of the humanistic assumption that people are essentially good than he was of the psychoanalytic assumption that they are essentially bad is clear from his discussion of what he terms the 'humanist paradox' (Kelly, 1969k). This is what he saw as the conflict between the humanistic views that people should be encouraged to express themselves freely and to be audacious, but that in doing so they should not be permitted to suppress other people's freedom. Kelly noted that one solution to this paradox is to assume that free expression of one's true self will always result in harmony with others who are similarly expressing themselves. However, he concluded that 'it appears to me to be as presumptuous to regard man as naturally good as it is to label him as inherently evil. Moreover, we are still much too busy sorting out good from evil to be altogether clear about which is which, or whether man is wholly one or the other' (p. 284). His own solution to the humanist paradox was to draw upon his distinction between aggression and hostility, and to point out that 'It is the hostile, and not necessarily the aggressive enterprise, that must be guarded against' (p. 288). As Giorgi (1981) has described, Kelly's sympathy with the humanistic movement was also tempered by criticism of the anti-intellectualist tendencies of this movement.

Some personal construct theorists, such as Epting (1984, p. 185), are in no doubt that 'Personal Construct Psychotherapy is a humanistic approach to therapy'. Amongst his bases for this conclusion are the personal construct psychotherapist's concern with personal experience; the view of the person as creating meaning rather than having it imposed on him or her by the world; and the similarity between the humanistic notion of self-actualisation as a central component of personal growth and Kelly's concept of the elaborative choice. There are, however, major differences between these two latter ideas, including deterministic elements in the concept of self-actualisation (Davisson, 1978). Feixas and Villegas (1985) have elaborated on the similarities between humanistic and personal construct approaches, and have noted the emphasis on creativity, albeit conceptualised in rather different ways, by followers of both approaches. The humanistic therapy movement has, however, witnessed a mushrooming of treatment methods, similarities between which and personal construct psychotherapy are often by no means apparent. Rowan (1976, 1981) has lent some clarity to this area by describing what he considers to be the basic commonalities between the various humanistic approaches. Those from his list which, at least to some extent, are not inconsistent with personal construct psychotherapy are the emphasis on exploring what lies behind a client's surface behaviour; the encouragement of the client to act in new ways; the acknowledgement of the importance of the therapist–client relationship; the rejection of the psychoanalytic view of the importance of encouraging the client's transference on to the therapist; the use of group therapy approaches; the rejection of the medical model; the rejection of a mechanistic approach to the client; and preference for research paradigms which emphasise the subjective experience of the people under study. Items from Rowan's list which may be considered to reflect areas in which personal construct psychotherapy could usefully be elaborated further are emphases on guided imagery and on bodily awareness. A final three items which are less compatible with the personal construct theory view are the emphasis on the desirability of therapists undergoing the same therapy as their clients, this being an issue on which, as we have seen, personal construct psychotherapists do not take a firm position; the focus on ecstasy and the use in therapy of 'a lot of gratification' (Rowan, 1981, p. 63); and the belief in the real self. Also distinguishing personal construct psychotherapy from the humanistic therapy approach is the concern of the former with structural properties and processes of construing.

A further characteristic which Weiner (1980) considers to be shared by humanistic and personal construct therapies is an essentially democratic client–therapist relationship. However, it should be noted that the methods employed by humanistic therapists sometimes appear to display the very characteristics which such therapists strongly criticise in other approaches. As Smail (1978, p. 37) has put it, humanistic psychologists 'have often mindlessly applied the same mechanistic and deterministic assumptions in pursuit of their own goals, without apparently becoming aware of the paradox involved in doing so'. It is also apparent that some humanistic therapists adopt a very directive, authoritarian style which seems inconsistent with the basic assumptions of the humanistic movement (Lieberman *et al.*, 1973). Such approaches are, of course, far removed from personal construct psychotherapy.

Commonalities have been noted between the goals of one particular form of humanistic therapy, Gestalt therapy, and those of personal construct psychotherapy. For example, Epting and Amerikaner (1980) consider that the Gestalt goals of 'closure' and 'finishing of unfinished situations' (Perls, 1969), and techniques used to achieve these ends, may be viewed in terms of completion of the Experience Cycle. Similarly, Leitner (1982) regards Perls' emphasis on the holistic integration of feelings, values, and actions as being consistent with the personal construct psychotherapy goal of perspectivism. In his view, 'most Gestalt techniques ... reduce the relatedness between feelings, values, and behaviours' (p. 311), and so may be of particular value with literalistic clients. Dryden's (1984) comparison of individual therapy approaches has also indicated considerable similarities in the behaviour of Gestalt and personal construct therapists. However, despite such commonalities, Viney (1981) notes that personal construct psychotherapy does not share Gestalt therapy's emphasis on retrieval of experiences of which the client is no longer aware, although this is not the case with one particular variant of the approach (Morrison and Cometa, 1977), which makes use of Gestalt techniques. Neither does personal construct psychotherapy share some of the more psychoanalytic assumptions of transactional analysis, another approach occasionally classified as a humanistic therapy. However, Kelly (1963b) was not unsympathetic towards transactional analysis, the notion of life script (Berne, 1964) bears some similarity to that of core constructs, and Tschudi (1977) has drawn on Berne's (1964) descriptions of the 'games people play' in his analysis of the positive implications of clients' symptoms.

The humanistic approach which has received most attention from personal construct theorists is the client-centred therapy of Carl Rogers, whom Kelly succeeded as Director of Training in Clinical Psychology at Ohio State University and whose ideas had similar origins to Kelly's, being developed on the basis of clinical concerns (Adams-Webber and Mancuso, 1983). Kelly (1955) himself was critical of some aspects of the client-centred approach, and Rogers (1956), in turn, was much less appreciative of Kelly's writings on therapy than of the presentation of his theory. He considered that Kelly viewed therapy as 'almost entirely an intellectual function', in which, contrary to his view of the client as a personal scientist, 'the wisdom all lies in the mind of the therapist'; that there was a 'lack of any sense of depth in his discussions of therapy'; and that the examples which he presented of his therapeutic approach 'seem to describe but superficial change' (pp. 64–5). However, as Adams-Webber (1981) has pointed out, Rogers' discussion of such personal construct psychotherapy approaches as fixed-role therapy suggests a less than complete understanding of this form of therapy. To some extent, though, Rogers' discomfort with some of Kelly's views on therapy may reflect what Rychlak (1981) identifies as the different 'motives to therapy' of these two theorists, Rogers' being primarily 'ethical', and Kelly's primarily 'scholarly'.

Despite their differences, various commonalities between personal construct and client-centred therapy are evident, and indeed, of all the individual therapy approaches considered by Dryden (1984), client-centred therapy was found to be the most similar to personal construct psychotherapy in its basic assumptions. For example, there may appear to be some similarities between Rogers' 'uncritical acceptance' of the client and Kelly's 'credulous approach', and between the importance which Rogers attached to therapist empathy and that which Kelly attached to therapists construing their clients' construction processes. However, Kelly (1955) pointed out that his position, unlike that of client-centred therapy, was that although therapists should attempt to use their clients' constructs, they should not necessarily accept clients' views of themselves. He also did not share the Rogerian emphasis on therapist genuineness, believing that the therapist should not reveal much of himself or herself during treatment and indeed should choose particular roles to play in relation to the client. As he remarked, 'The client comes to the therapist, not to watch him be "sincere" for an hour, but to get help!' (Kelly, 1955, p. 1153). Neither, of course, did Kelly consider that the therapist should eschew the application of diagnostic constructs to the client, as he felt had been the case with some client-centred therapists. The non-directive approach of the client-centred therapist was also the subject of some discussion by Kelly, who regarded it as a method of uncontrolled elaboration of construing. As we have seen in Chapter 7, he considered this to be valuable at times but contra-indicated at others. In particular, he was critical of the Rogerian notion that growth is equated with self-realisation, and necessarily results from the nondirective approach, given adequate therapeutic conditions. As Leitner (1989) notes, he saw the person as less passive than did Rogers, and considered that 'the individual does not merely reach a terminal state of adjustment through the unfolding of an inner potentiality, but he is continuously adjusting to a changing scene by means of *an organized succession of formulated plans*' (Kelly, 1955, p. 401, italics in original). As a result, he was 'more inclined to urge the client to experiment with life and to seek his answers in the succession of events which life unveils than to seek them within himself' (p. 402). His concern with the directionality of the growth process has been echoed by Bannister (1965a), who has indicated that the nondirective approach, in that it does not offer the client possible alternative constructions of his or her world, may be unlikely to lead to any fundamental reconstruing. Bannister and Kelly appear to disagree, however, on the likely effects of the client-centred approach on the structure of the client's construct system. While Kelly (1955) considered that the reflection of feeling which is central to this approach is likely to lead to tighter, more precise constructions by the client, Bannister's (1975) view was that the nondirective approach generally encourages loosening of construing. Rogers' own belief that loosening is a desirable aspect of the therapeutic process has been noted by Fransella (1970d). He related such loss of rigidity to greater openness to experience, leading Epting and Amerikaner (1980) to regard his notion of the optimally functioning person as being consistent with the personal construct theory view. Also consistent with such a view, and with the therapeutic goal of perspectivism, are such Rogerian notions as that therapy should counter both the fragmentation of significant experiences and the literalistic relationships of values to feelings and behaviours which are reflected in 'conditions of worth' (Leitner, 1982).

Although client-centred therapy may be of value in tackling literalisms, the avoidance by some client-centred therapists of any intervention which might challenge their clients is itself considered by Landfield (1980a) to reflect a literalist view of the therapeutic role, and the rigid translation of a warm, accepting attitude into a particular pattern of behaviour by the therapist. Landfield (1980b) observes that, as well as being more active than the traditional client-centred therapist, the personal construct psychotherapist will show greater variety of approach. He notes, however, that contemporary client-centred therapists are more flexible in their styles and techniques (Landfield, 1980a), and the greater commonality of such developments with personal construct psychotherapy has also been remarked upon by Epting (1984) and Takens (1987). The latter writer considers that personal construct and client-centred theories are compatible in their phenomenological viewpoint, idiographic orientation, emphasis on individual experience, concern with the self, viewed as constantly changing, and self in relation to others, and view of the client as an expert on his or her own problems. However, he considers that the personal construct psychotherapist is more active and task-orientated than the traditional client-centred therapist, whereas this difference is less apparent in the three post-Rogerian client-centred approaches which he considers: the cognitive-reflective, experiential, and interactional therapeutic methods. In the first of these, the therapist goes beyond simply reflecting back to the client his or her understanding of what the client expressed, but acts as a 'surrogate information processor' by responding in a way which leads the client to elaborate and reorganise constructions (Rice, 1974; Wexler, 1974). Although Takens considers this approach to have 'much in common with the basic tenets of Personal Construct Psychology' (p. 4), Smail (1978) regards it as an example of the intrusion of mechanistic assumptions into a school which was originally developed as a reaction against mechanism. In the second new development discussed by Takens, the experiential approach (Gendlin, 1974), the emphasis is on the client attending to bodily 'felt meanings' and, by a process of 'focussing', attaching labels to, and eventually accepting, the feelings concerned. This focussing technique is one which Epting (1984) feels could usefully be appropriated by personal construct psychotherapists who are concerned with the articulation of preverbal constructs. Takens (1987) also draws attention to the interplay of loosening and tightening in this approach, as well as in the interactional approach. In the latter, one of the therapist's tasks is to identify the client's self-defeating style of interaction and, rather than responding in a complementary fashion, to suggest to the client hypotheses about this style for which the client can attempt to obtain validational evidence by changing his or her communication patterns (Kiesler, 1982). Takens considers that the three approaches on which he focuses share the goal of attempting to set in motion again intra- and interpersonal processes which have become stuck, as well as emphasising the importance of the therapeutic relationship and of the here and now. He suggests not only that the techniques involved could be of value to personal construct psychotherapists, but that client-centred therapists who employ these approaches might usefully borrow procedures from personal construct theory in order to expedite the therapeutic process. For example, he considers that repertory grid technique might be used to facilitate reflection upon one's construing or as a component of the focussing process, and that enactment methods might usefully be incorporated in the interactional approach.

Takens' suggestions are consistent with Kelly's (1955, p. 42) view that 'it is possible to combine certain features of the neophenomenological approaches with more conventional methodology'. Kelly (1969h) later asserted that such a combination is not only possible but 'crucial', stating that 'humanistic psychology needs a technology through which to express its humane intentions' (p. 135). In that personal construct theory brings together such characteristics, often considered to be contrasting and incompatible, we may agree with Epting (1984, p. 187) that it 'has both a heart and a head' and, to borrow Rychlak's (1977) term, may be classified as a 'rigorous humanism'.

## Medical and biological approaches

Although our primary concern in this chapter is with similarities and differences between personal construct theory and other psychological approaches in the clinical field, Kelly's opposition to the medical model should briefly be re-emphasised. As we have seen in previous chapters, he did not view clients' complaints in terms of pathology or traditional nosological categories, which he considered to involve preemptive construction of clients. He also did not consider the preemptive tendencies of the medical model to be limited to diagnostic practices, and expressed concern at 'professional medicine's attempt to preempt the field of psychiatry' (Kelly, 1955, p. 185).

It should be noted that, in criticising the medical model, Kelly was not rejecting the view that clients' problems may be construed in physical terms. Indeed, he was at pains to make it clear that 'any event may be viewed either in its psychological or in its physiological aspects' (Kelly, 1955, p. 11), and suggested that 'we might be more effective as clinicians if we routinely applied both psychological and physiological systems at the outset rather than applying one only after the other has been shown to be inadequate' (p. 921). A client's problems might, for example, be alternatively viewed in terms of the invalidation of particular constructions or the state of arousal which, as Mancuso and Adams-Webber (1982b) have indicated, is likely to be associated with such failures to anticipate. Similarly, depression may be considered in terms of constructions which serve to isolate the individual or metabolic changes which, in Rowe's (1978) view, may result from this isolation if it is prolonged. Physiological processes may be viewed as aspects of construing or, to use Procter's (1989) term, as 'organismic constructs', and it has even been suggested that cells may be regarded as construing, so that, for example, clients suffering from cancer may be invited to encourage their cells to reconstrue (Fransella, 1989a).

The psychological and physiological construct systems do, however, have different ranges of convenience, and Kelly noted, for example, that the labelling of a client's complaint by a physician as 'psychosomatic', a term which he considered to be 'systematically meaningless' (p. 577), often represents a vain attempt to subsume within the physiological system a problem which is barely within this system's range of convenience. To take a physiological perspective on a problem may also, as Bannister (1968) has described, represent an avoidance of contact with the person whose problem it is. In deciding whether a problem should be approached psychologically or physiologically, Kelly considered that the primary consideration should be the pragmatic one of the client's likely response to each type of intervention. His acknowledgement that a physical treatment approach may sometimes be of value even extended to a somewhat grudging acceptance of the occasional utility of electroconvulsive therapy as an aid to constriction, to the establishment of contact with a loose and withdrawn client, or to the recovery of suspended elements. Dawes (1985) has also indicated that anti-depressant or anxiolytic drugs may induce reconstruing of the self or of other events, and some research evidence of such effects has been provided in Chapter 5. While Dawes notes that the continued use of drugs is likely to reduce the client's ability to anticipate events when drug-free, he also points out, drawing on the findings of McPherson and Gray (1976), that if a client construes their complaint in physical terms he or she may be more likely to respond to a physical than to a psychological treatment approach. In the view of Gara *et al.* (1987), anti-psychotic medication may also be of value in promoting reconstruing of the self. As we have seen in Chapter 4, these workers regard schizophrenics as being characterised by poorly elaborated self-constructions, and they consider that the effects of medication, together with other aspects of the mental health system, allow such clients to develop coherent identities as patients. Therefore, if relapse is not to occur, the client should be helped to elaborate an alternative viable identity prior to discontinuation of medication.

As well as specific physical treatments, Kelly discussed the likely effects of psychiatric hospitalisation on the client's construing. He considered that psychiatric hospitalisation may provide a constrictive release from anxiety, albeit one that may involve dislodgement of a client from his or her social role, and therefore guilt. However, as we have seen in Chapter 4, hospitalisation may lead to a reduction in the client's ability to anticipate his or her psychological world (Williams and Quirke, 1972; Bodlakova *et al.*, 1974; Winter *et al.*, 1991), and the development of a system of constructs which may be applicable to events within hospital but would not be conducive to survival in the community (Spindler Barton *et al.*, 1976). It has been viewed by Bannister and Fransella (1986, p. 149) as 'an impressive experiment in serial invalidation, likely to disrupt all but the most well-articulated construct system'. Bannister has been the most forthright critic of the medical model from the personal construct theory perspective, his rejection of psychiatric diagnosis as a 'pseudo-specialist language' (Agnew and Bannister, 1973) contrasting markedly with his previous construction of a test to assist in the diagnosis of schizophrenic thought disorder (Bannister and Fransella, 1967). Bannister's (1985c) primary objections to the medical model are that it is likely to produce:

1. a deflecting of attention from the person: the personal meaning of the questionable behaviour and experience is bleached out by regarding it as 'symptomatic' of illness; for example, a 'depression' is something to be cured rather than a personal experience to be understood and learned from,
2. the inducing of passivity and irresponsibility in the patient since he or

she is neither to be blamed for having contracted the 'illness' nor to be expected to play any important part in its cure, this being a matter for medical expertise, and

3. the encouragement of irresponsibility in the community around the patient, since the notion of 'illness' locates the problem *inside* the patient and does not recognise that the problems lie between people.

(p. 3, italics in original)

Bannister did not deny, however, that some clients may construe their complaints in such a way that they are likely to respond to a physical treatment approach. Thus, he and Mair (1968, p. 213) write that 'If the patient regards his condition as an "illness" of mysterious origin, unrelated to his present outlook or past way of life, or if he has been persuaded by the hospital to accept such a view, then he may well respond to equally mysterious electricity or equally mysterious chemicals as the appropriate agents of recovery.'

Finally, it should be noted that, although Kelly opposed the biological reductionism of the medical model, that a biological approach need not be reductionist is indicated by the recent constructivist trends in biology (Varela, 1979; Maturana and Varela, 1980). As we have seen above, the implications of such trends for personal construct psychology are beginning to be elaborated.

## DIMENSIONS OF THEORY AND THERAPY

These comparisons and contrasts between the personal construct theory and alternative approaches have highlighted the construct poles which may be considered to characterise personal construct psychology and its clinical applications. Our construing of this approach may be further elaborated by drawing upon the dimensions which other authors have employed to differentiate between various theories of personality and schools of therapy.

### The theory

Rychlak (1968) has suggested five 'fundamental dimensions' for the classification of theories. The first of these concerns the degree of abstraction in theory formulation, and poses no problems for the classification of personal construct theory, which was stated in highly *abstract* terms. Rychlak's second dimension contrasts realism and idealism, differentiating those theorists who believe in the existence of an external world independent of the observer and those who do not. His placement of personal construct theory on this dimension seems to have changed in that, while he initially considered it closer to the idealist than the realist pole, in a later analysis he concluded that Kelly 'essentially accepted a realistic view of the world' (Rychlak, 1981, p. 712). The pole to which personal construct theory is allocated will, however, depend on with what approach it is being contrasted, as may be seen by drawing upon Mahoney's (1988a) discussion of constructive metatheory. Thus, compared with a rationalist approach, Kelly, the *constructivist*, may be considered to be an idealist. However, compared to radical constructivists, he, as a *critical constructivist* (see p. 362), may be considered a realist.

Personal construct theory may also be viewed as occupying an intermediate position on Rychlak's 'objective–subjective' dimension, which bears some similarity to Allport's (1946) distinction between nomothetic and idiographic approaches. As we have seen in discussing humanistic therapies, while Kelly was certainly much concerned with the individual's subjective experience, he attempted to understand such experience in terms of general principles of human functioning. His position is more clear-cut, however, on Rychlak's fourth dimension of 'introspection–extraspection', which concerns respectively the extent to which a theorist formulates constructs from the point of view of the object of study or of the observer. In taking the constructions of his or her clients or research subjects seriously, and seeing all people as scientists, the personal construct theorist is clearly adopting an *introspective* approach. Finally, in terms of Rychlak's dimension of 'formal versus informal' theories, personal construct theory may be readily assigned to the former pole.

A further set of ten dimensions which distinguish between personality theories has been proposed by Corsini (1977), and as part of his comparison of different therapeutic approaches Dryden (1984) asked a leading personal construct theorist, Fransella, to apply these to the theory. The first dimension, 'objective–subjective', combines elements of Rychlak's dimension of the same name with his 'extraspective–introspective' distinction, and it is not surprising, therefore, that Fransella classified personal construct theory as *subjective*. She also construed it as *holistic*, viewing the person as an indivisible whole, rather than elementaristic; as *personal*, dealing with the single individual, rather than apersonal; as *dynamic*, seeing the individual as a learner and not as a reactor as in static theories; as *exogenistic*, not viewing the person as having a biological constitution as in endogenistic theories; and as *indeterministic*, seeing the person as having self-direction, rather than deterministic. Dimensions on which she considered that the theory occupied an intermediate position were quantitative versus qualitative; concern with the past versus concern with the future; cognitive versus affective; and concern with the unconscious versus concern with the conscious.

Finally, the personal construct theory approach may be usefully construed in terms of the different world views delineated by Pepper (1942). As Sarbin (1977) and Sarbin and Mancuso (1980) have indicated, in these terms the theory may be aligned with *contextualism*, the position that an event should be viewed within its total present context, which is regarded as an ever-changing pattern of relationships. Such a perspective stands in marked contrast to mechanism, with its root metaphor of the machine, exemplified in psychology by the behavioural approach. However, in that it emphasises the individual's construing of his or her context, Crockett (1982) considers that the theory is rather less a contextualist than what Pepper terms an organicist position.

## The therapeutic approach

As well as classifying their theories, Dryden (1984) asked the representatives of the various schools of therapy which he considered to classify their therapeutic behaviour on various dimensions. Fransella's view of personal construct psychotherapy was that, in terms of therapist relationship style, it is informal rather than formal; impersonal rather than self-disclosing; and intermediate in terms of therapist involvement and support. In terms of therapeutic focus and structuring of sessions, she considered it to be characterised by low structuring and therapist control of sessions; a focus on awareness now; a concern with unconscious awareness; and an intermediate position on the dimensions broadband versus narrowband goals and high versus low preplanning of sessions. She also classified it as high on use of directed activity, and on the particular activities of role-playing, systematic problem-solving, and structured imagery, but low on the use of free association and rewards and penalties, and intermediate on the encouragement of physical release and activity. Finally, in terms of expressive and evocative dimensions of therapist behaviour, she rated it as high in its use of clarification and questioning, low in its use of interpretations, advice-giving, and teaching, and intermediate in verbal activity level, use of reflections, and reframing of clients' communications.

Several of the features of personal construct psychotherapy delineated by Fransella may be considered to reflect the concrete expressions of more superordinate constructivist assumptions. These assumptions, which were touched upon in our discussion of alternative treatment approaches, have been outlined by Mahoney (1988b). Firstly, there is the view of people as 'dynamic processes that participate in their own ongoing development' (p. 302). Problems, which may be experienced by therapists just as by their clients, are viewed 'not as isolated anomalies requiring technical correction, but as indications that the individual may be operating at the edges or limits of his or her own current psychological viability' (p. 305). Treatment goals are therefore likely to be creative rather than corrective (Harter, 1988), and personal rather than normative (Winter, 1988b), involving the exploration of alternative constructions which may facilitate the development of the client's system rather than the replacement of existing constructions by others which conform more closely to normative standards. The client's problems are also not regarded as solely 'emotional', but instead emotions are seen as knowing processes, any apparent disruptive effect of which on behaviour is a reflection of systemic restructuring. From the constructivist perspective, problems are the person's attempts at adaptation, and may reflect deep structural processes. The focus of therapy is, therefore, likely to shift from the problem, via concern with patterns in the client's problems, to the level of process, in which the concern is with the constructions which perpetuate these patterns. As noted by Goldfried (1988), therapy will include both 'bottom–up' and 'top–down' interventions, in contrast to behaviour therapy, which tends exclusively to employ the former, and psychoanalysis, which tends solely to use the latter. The constructivist therapist will also expect that any attempt to change core structures will be met with resistance, which will be viewed as a natural, self-protective process that should be worked with, rather than against. The therapeutic relationship in this approach is a collaborative one, providing sufficient safety to allow exploration of alternative possibilities which may entail more viable constructions of the world. In Mahoney's (1988b) view, constructivist psychotherapy is therefore 'a very intimate and personalized exchange between human beings' (p. 308), not the impersonal activity which might be suggested by Fransella's classification of personal construct psychotherapy on this dimension.

## ECLECTICISM, INTEGRATION, AND CONSTRUCTIVE ALTERNATIVISM

Currently the major debate between personal construct psychotherapists, as evidenced by papers and symposia at recent international conferences on the theory (Alexander, 1987; R. Neimeyer, 1987c; Soldz, 1987b; Leitner, 1989; Leitner and Dunnett, 1989; R. Neimeyer, 1989), concerns the integration of personal construct and other approaches. A foretaste of this debate has been provided in our discussion on cognitive therapies, but it is perhaps best approached by considering again the issue of eclecticism.

As indicated at the beginning of this chapter, personal construct psycho-therapy may be characterised as technically eclectic, to use a term coined by Lazarus (1967) to describe an approach which borrows techniques from other theoretical systems but without accepting the assumptions on which these techniques are based. The personal construct psychotherapist selects particular techniques, and conceptualises their mode of action, in terms not of the theory from which they were derived but of personal construct theory. As such, he or she differs from some other therapists who also consider themselves to be technically eclectic. These include Lazarus (1980) himself, whose 'multimodal therapy' is based on not one but three theories, with little in the way of a 'congruent framework' (Dryden, 1986, p. 356). Similarly, the theory which Ellis (1975) claims underlies the selection of the bewilderingly wide range of techniques which he employs may be seen as no more than 'a collection of loosely related and poorly elucidated propositions' (Mahoney, 1979, p. 177).

Although survey results would suggest that eclecticism is 'the modal orientation of psychologists' (Norcross, 1986, p. 4), over a third of whom subscribe to it, the dominant eclectic approach is not technical but synthetic eclecticism, in which an attempt is made to integrate different theories. For example, as we have seen, Ryle (1978) has attempted such an integration by employing cognitive psychology as a 'common language' for the psycho-therapies. A further variety of eclecticism, to which 10 per cent of eclectic psychologists admit, is atheoretical, involving the use of such techniques as are necessary, without any theoretical considerations.

In terms of the three types of eclecticism delineated by Norcross, R. Neimeyer (1988a) would agree that personal construct psychotherapy is technically eclectic. However, he considers that as this therapeutic approach has developed the character of its eclecticism has also evolved, and may now best be described as 'theoretically progressive integrationism', the goal of which is 'to elaborate a *coherent theory* that both *explains* and *constrains* effective interventions' (p. 290, italics in original). It involves two integrative dialectics, one between theory and practice, allowing each to be developed by drawing upon the other; and one with other theories that share a compatible metatheory. The metatheoretical assumptions of such theories would be expected to include what we might regard as the two most superordinate characteristics delineated above in describing personal construct theory, namely constructivism, particularly of the critical variety, and contextualism. Therefore, while theoretically progressive integrationism may allow not only methods but also concepts of other approaches to be borrowed, it differs from synthetic eclecticism in that it specifies that such methods and concepts must be limited to those which share particular basic assumptions. Neimeyer also points out that it is a perspectivist view, differing from those, promoted by Ryle (1978) and Norcross (1986) respectively, that assert that eventually a common language or a common paradigm will unify therapeutic practice. He considers that such an assertion is inconsistent not only with constructive alternativism but with the notion that language in part determines our view of reality. As Goldfried and Safran (1986) have remarked in commenting on the proposals by Ryle and other workers for a unifying cognitive language, 'cognitive psychology is more than a language. It is a paradigm for under-standing human functioning ... it is thus *vital to identify the metatheoretical assumptions that underly cognitive psychology* and to evaluate how adequate they are to capture the various domains of human functioning focused on by different forms of psychotherapy' (pp. 467–8, italics in original).

The desirability or otherwise of an eclectic approach may usefully be considered not only at the level of therapy with an individual client but also in relation to a pattern of service organisation. As we have seen in Chapter 7, personal construct psychotherapy makes considerable demands on the adaptability of the therapist, who will be required to adopt a range of alternative roles and therapeutic styles depending on the particular client and stage of therapy. However, to expect a personal construct psychotherapist to be a therapeutic Jack of all trades may be unrealistic since, as discussed in Chapter 5, therapists are likely to find some patterns of relating to clients more comfortable and less threatening than others. A personal construct therapy service might, therefore, ideally be staffed by therapists differing in their preferred therapeutic styles, each client being allocated to that therapist whose style seems most likely to be effective given the nature of the reconstruing which appears desirable and the client's expectations of therapy. While all the therapists concerned would ideally share basic constructivist and contextualist assumptions, I have suggested elsewhere that such a service, in a less ideal setting such as the British National Health Service, might even employ therapists of different theoretical persuasions (Winter, 1985c, 1990c). In accepting that numerous viable alternative constructions of therapy may be held by both clients and therapists, a service of this type may be considered to be firmly rooted in constructive alternativist principles. It would also be consistent with Kelly's (1955, p. 391) assertion that 'Almost any type of therapy seems to work in some cases', which was supported twenty years later by the 'Dodo bird verdict' of Luborsky et al. (1975) that 'Everybody has won and all must have prizes', as well as by more sophisticated subsequent metaanalyses of comparative outcome studies (e.g. Smith and Glass, 1977; Smith et al., 1980; Shapiro and Shapiro, 1982). As we have seen in Chapter 5, for example, there is evidence that a wide range of therapeutic approaches may produce reconstruing, and that the approach which is likely to be effective with a particular client may be determined by features of the client's construct system. Such findings suggest that there may be little justification for excluding any approach from a therapeutic service. In addition, they are often considered to be supportive of the argument that the so-called non-specific factors may, in fact, be the major active ingredients of therapies; and that the primary characteristic of a successful therapeutic approach is that it is consistent with the client's expectancies, and thus provides the client with a plausible means of understanding how his or her problems developed and how they may be resolved (Frank, 1973, 1982; Caine et al., 1981). As Harter (1988) points out, these latter arguments rarely provide an account of the nature of the healing process which is set into motion by a correct match between therapeutic approach and client expectancies. She argues, however, that, from a personal construct theory perspective, a successful therapy is likely to be one which provides a client with a viable alternative construction of his or her difficulties without either directly challenging core constructs or being beyond the range of convenience of the client's construct system (R. Neimeyer and Harter, 1988). It will neither be so much in accord with the client's expectancies that it simply validates existing constructions, nor so far removed from, or confrontative to, these constructions as to be highly anxiety-provoking or threatening. It is on such considerations that treatment allocation decisions in a therapeutic service may be usefully based, regardless of the particular therapeutic approaches which are represented in the service.

Those personal construct theorists who oppose any movement towards integration do so largely because they fear dilution of the radicalism of Kelly's ideas and of the unique components of his theory. However, the danger of not drawing upon developments within other theoretical traditions is to perpetuate an intellectual isolationism which has been viewed by others as indicating tight, preemptive construing on the part of personal construct theorists (Pervin, 1973), and which limits possibilities for the elaboration of the theory. R. Neimeyer (1985b) considers that this isolationism served an important function at an early stage in the development of personal construct psychology, but that 'the present challenge is that of revitalization through integration with other disciplines' (pp. 114–15). As we have seen in our consideration of these other disciplines, recent constructivist and contextualist trends within them now allow personal construct theorists to be much more charitable towards them than was Kelly, and increasingly to perceive commonalities with them in addition to the inevitable contrasts. We may, therefore, agree with Tyler (1985, p. 19) that 'Personal construct psychology fits well into the framework of the new psychology that is taking shape'. Although discussions of integration have largely focussed on the cognitive therapies, such commonalities would seem to be particularly apparent with systems approaches, which might continue to provide personal construct psychotherapy with ways of profitably extending their concerns beyond the individual construer; and with humanistic approaches, which might offer personal construct psychotherapy a less impersonal therapeutic style, a more experiential form of therapy (cf. Leitner, 1988b), and some useful non-verbal techniques. Despite recent work in these areas, the cognitive, psychodynamic, biological, and particularly the behavioural approach are less compatible with personal construct psychotherapy at the metatheoretical level, although there is still much to gain by drawing upon work in each of these fields. To take just one of several examples from cognitive psychology, research, reviewed by Williams *et al.* (1988), on judgemental biases both in normal individuals and in those presenting with psychological disorder has clearly demonstrated phenomena which may be subsumed by such Kellian concepts as hostility, and which are likely to have implications for the practice of personal construct psychotherapy. However, such work has been largely ignored by personal construct psychotherapists, as indeed by cognitive therapists. The personal construct psychotherapist may also continue to gain from the psychoanalyst an enhanced understanding of the origins of a client's constructions, and from the behaviour therapist useful methods of encouraging experimentation, while the effects of persistent invalidation may be usefully considered from a biological perspective. There are also indications that attention might profitably be paid to work in areas, such as linguistics and literary criticism, traditionally viewed as much further removed from psychotherapy (Mair, 1989a, 1989b). In order to take full advantage of developments in other fields, the personal construct theorist will, of course, need to appreciate that a wide variety of methodologies, and not just those which have generally been associated with the theory, may provide insights into the process of construing. For example, as Howard (1988) notes, there has been an underuse by personal construct theorists of methodologies developed within other constructivist approaches.

To be open to the possibility that the concepts and approaches of personal construct theory may be elaborated by cross-fertilisation with other approaches is to be consistent with the constructive alternativist position that all theories are ultimately expendable. The occasional apparent resistance of many personal construct theorists, including Kelly himself, to such developments is not unexpected, given the anxiety and threat which would be likely to result from awareness of the expendability or need for modification of cherished constructions, and from acknowledging 'the limits of our knowing' (R. Neimeyer, 1988a, p. 295). As I have suggested elsewhere (Winter, 1990c), it is the threat associated with constructive alternativism that has perhaps rendered personal construct theory less than popular amongst clinicians. To follow this principle would, after all, require one to take seriously not only the possibility that the constructions of one's clients, but also those of clinicians of alternative persuasions, may be as valid as one's own. It would also require the challenging of hierarchical institutional structures and their replacement by democratic patterns of organisation, implying equal validity of the constructions of all members of a team, as Bannister attempted to implement at the Bexley Hospital Psychology Department (1980). As Mahoney (1988b) remarks, *'the psychological demands of constructive metatheory are unsurpassed by those of any other contemporary perspective*. No other family of modern theories asks its adherents to maintain such a degree of self-examining openness, to so painstakingly tolerate and harvest (rather than eliminate) ambiguity, or to so thoroughly question both the answers and the questions by which they inquire. It is not easy to be a constructivist' (p. 312, italics in original). That contextualism, the other basic assumption of personal construct theory, is no less demanding has been indicated by Sarbin (1977), who points out that

> Models that flow from the root metaphor of contextualism may appear to reflect chaos – especially to the mechanistically inclined. The latter tries to avoid chaos by simplifying the object of study, by fragmentation, by ecological impoverishment, and by striving for replicability. But chaos is a relative term. Episodes in a drama might appear chaotic to a scientist who looks at the blurred actors through an out-of-focus high-powered microscope. But the human condition must be lived in episodes that are not arbitrarily simplified, fragmented, ecologically impoverished, or replicable.

If, as the 'new physics' has demonstrated, even the physical world is characterised by uncertainty (Heisenberg, 1963; Capra, 1975; Zukav, 1979), how much more so must this apply to our understanding of the psychological world. Any attempt by a clinician to cling to certainty and to a particular set of constructions is, therefore, as doomed to failure as are the similar attempts by our clients. To quote Rowe (1982, pp. 208–9),

It takes courage to live with uncertainty and responsibility, but the alternatives are hardly attractive. If we insist that our construction of reality is the true and only one, we condemn ourselves to suffering. If we try to force other people to accept our one and only construction of reality, then we condemn both them and us to suffering. If we accept that our constructions are structures and not reality itself, and that each person has his own construction of reality, then we have to live with uncertainty. But we can choose to define that uncertainty as either prison or freedom. I prefer freedom.

This book, which has been too long in the writing, is published in the expectation that many of the ideas which it presents will now have been superseded by alternative constructions. However, it is written in the hope that it may persuade the reader, whether or not he or she was initially committed to personal construct theory, that any threat which is posed by fully embracing the constructive alternativist position also carries with it the promise of adventure and of endless fresh constructions, and that any anxiety and uncertainty which accompanies commitment to a constructivist and contextualist perspective is an inevitable and necessary concomitant of creativity and growth. Personal construct theory does not offer the security and comfort of a fixed set of dogmas and prescriptions, and even its formal structure of fundamental postulate and corollaries is not immutable, much as we may occasionally wish it to be so. What the theory does offer, however, is a flexibility, and openness to refinement and elaboration, which is likely to ensure its continuing applicability to the ever-changing problems confronted by the clinician.

## SUMMARY AND CONCLUSIONS

While personal construct psychotherapy may employ techniques developed within other treatment approaches, this does not imply similarities at the theoretical level with the approaches concerned. For example, although the personal construct psychotherapist is not averse to the use of techniques which focus upon changing a client's behaviour, these would be viewed as a means of encouraging experimentation. The contrasts between the personal construct theory and behavioural approaches are exemplified by Kelly's rejection of the concept of learning, and by the reductionistic and mechanistic assumptions implicit in behaviour therapy. Personal construct theorists have also been critical of the manipulative nature of the behaviour therapist–client relationship, and of the lack of reflexivity in learning theory. While behavioural approaches may promote reconstruing, research would indicate that they should be regarded as preliminary to a more direct focus on the client's construing and on the meaning of the behavioural changes produced. Although such concerns have been introduced into behaviour therapy by the cognitive revolution, the cognitive approach to therapy still exhibits marked contrasts with personal construct psychotherapy. Thus, the latter approach does not distinguish cognition from emotion or conation, does not view the client as irrational or as making cognitive errors which require correction, and is more concerned to focus upon the process of construing than on the content of the client's constructions. There are, however, many different varieties of cognitive approach, and while personal construct theory contrasts markedly with those based on realist assumptions, it may be classified as a constructivist approach, with similarities to other such approaches. There are also common-alities, and possibilities for cross-fertilisation, between the personal construct theory approach and work in experimental cognitive psychology.

Numerous contrasts have been noted between the personal construct theory and psychoanalytic approaches. These include the tendency of some psychoanalysts to offer interpretations as if they were absolute truths rather than hypotheses; their use of hydraulic metaphors; and their focus on the client's past. Rather than employing a concept of the unconscious, Kelly regarded constructions as being of different levels of cognitive awareness, but some of the defence mechanisms described by psychoanalysts have been reframed in personal construct theory terms, and both theories would also consider that a client's symptoms may sometimes carry positive implications for him or her. The personal construct psychotherapist may also at times employ similar procedures to the psychoanalyst, particularly in order to produce loosening in construing. Both theories also make use of the concept of transference, although in a somewhat different manner. It has been suggested that there is greater commonality between personal construct psychotherapy and some post-Freudian psychoanalytic approaches, such as those which emphasise the symbolic nature of psychoanalytic concepts.

Applications of personal construct psychotherapy to families show similarities to systems approaches both in technique and in some of the theo-retical concepts employed. However, the assumptions underlying the work of family therapists range from the realist to the constructivist, and only the latter approaches can be considered to be compatible with personal construct theory. Similarities have also been noted between personal construct psycho-therapy and existential and humanistic approaches. For example, they share a holistic view of the person, reject mechanistic assumptions, and generally involve a democratic relationship between therapist and client. Differences between existential and personal construct theory approaches include the existential view of negative emotions as involving confrontation with aspects of the human condition; and the notion of the true self. Personal construct psychotherapy, with its emphasis on analysis of the structure and process of construing, may be considered a rigorous humanism.

A client's difficulties may be alternatively construed in psychological or physical terms, and, for example, invalidation of constructions may usefully be viewed in terms of the state of heightened arousal which is likely to be associated with it. The use of physical treatment procedures, and other common features of the use of the medical model, such as psychiatric hospitalisation, may produce reconstruing, although some of these effects may reduce the client's capacity to anticipate events in his or her social world, and may lead the personal meaning of the client's complaints to be ignored.

Amongst the major characteristics which may be attributed to personal construct psychotherapy are that it is constructivist, contextualist, introspective, and holistic, and aims for creative and personal, rather than corrective and normative, goals. It has generally been regarded as a technically eclectic approach, although some personal construct psychotherapists now employ not only techniques derived from other approaches but also concepts borrowed from those approaches with which it is compatible at a meta-theoretical level. Such approaches will be characterised by constructivism and contextualism, and since there are now trends in these directions in most of the major models of therapy, opportunities for personal construct theorists to draw upon work carried out within other traditions are likely to increase.

# References

Abraham, K. (1955) *Clinical Papers and Essays on Psychoanalysis*, Hogarth, London.

Abramowitz, S.I. and Abramowitz, C.V. (1974) 'Psychological-mindedness and benefit from insight-oriented group therapy', *Archives of General Psychiatry, 30*, 610–15.

Adams-Webber, J. (1968) 'Construct and Figure Interactions within a Personal Construct System: an Extension of Repertory Grid Technique', unpublished PhD thesis, Brandeis University.

Adams-Webber, J.R. (1969) 'Cognitive complexity and sociality', *British Journal of Social and Clinical Psychology, 8*, 211–16.

Adams-Webber, J.R. (1970a) 'An analysis of the discriminant validity of several repertory grid indices', *British Journal of Psychology, 61*, 83–90.

Adams-Webber, J.R. (1970b) 'Actual structure and potential chaos' in D. Bannister (ed.), *Perspectives in Personal Construct Theory*, Academic Press, London.

Adams-Webber, J. (1973) 'The complexity of the target as a factor in interpersonal judgement', *Social Behavior and Personality, 1*, 35–8.

Adams-Webber, J. (1977a) 'The golden section and structure of self-concepts', *Perceptual and Motor Skills, 45*, 703–6.

Adams-Webber, J. (1977b) 'The organization of judgements based on positive and negative adjectives in the Bannister-Fransella Grid Test', *British Journal of Medical Psychology, 50*, 173–6.

Adams-Webber, J.R. (1979) *Personal Construct Theory: Concepts and Applications*, Wiley, Chichester.

Adams-Webber, J.R. (1981) 'Fixed role therapy' in R. Corsini (ed.), *Handbook of Innovative Psychotherapies*, Wiley, New York.

Adams-Webber, J. (1985) 'Construing self and others' in F. Epting and A.W. Landfield (eds.), *Anticipating Personal Construct Psychology*, University of Nebraska Press, Lincoln, Nebraska.

Adams-Webber, J.R. (1986) 'Self-construct perspectives in psychotherapy' in I.M. Hartman and K.R. Blankstein (eds.), *Perception of Self in Emotional Disorder and Psychotherapy*, Plenum, New York.

Adams-Webber, J.R. (1989a) 'Some reflections on the "meaning" of repertory grid responses', *International Journal of Personal Construct Psychology, 2*, 77–92.

Adams-Webber, J.R. (1989b) 'Resorting to applied psychology in psychotherapy', *International Journal of Personal Construct Psychology, 2*, 239–43.

Adams-Webber, J. and Benjafield, J. (1973) 'The relation between lexical marking and rating extremity in interpersonal judgements', *Canadian Journal of Behavioral Science, 5*, 234–41.

Adams-Webber, J., Benjafield, J., Doan, B., and Giesbrecht, L. (1975) 'Construct

Maldistribution, Memory for Adjectives and Concept Utilization', unpublished MS, Brock University.

Adams-Webber, J. and Mancuso, J.C. (1983) 'The pragmatic logic of personal construct theory' in J. Adams-Webber and J.C. Mancuso (eds.), *Applications of Personal Construct Theory*, Academic Press, Toronto.

Adams-Webber, J. and Mirc, E. (1976) 'Assessing the development of student teachers' role conceptions', *British Journal of Educational Psychology, 46*, 338–40.

Adams-Webber, J. and Rodney, Y. (1983) 'Relational aspects of temporary changes in construing self and others', *Canadian Journal of Behavioral Science, 15*, 52–9.

Adams-Webber, J.R., Schwenker, B., and Barbeau, D. (1972) 'Personal constructs and the perception of individual differences', *Canadian Journal of Behavioral Science, 4*, 218–24.

Agnew, J. (1985) 'Childhood disorders or the venture of children' in E. Button (ed.), *Personal Construct Theory and Mental Health*, Croom Helm, London.

Agnew, J. and Bannister, D. (1973) 'Psychiatric diagnosis as a pseudo-specialist language', *British Journal of Medical Psychology, 46*, 69–73.

Aidman, T. (1951) 'An Objective Study of the Changing Relationship between the Present Self and Wanted Self Pictures as Expressed by the Client in Client-Centred Therapy', unpublished PhD thesis, University of Chicago.

Aldrich, C.K. and Mendkoff, G. (1963) 'Relocation of the aged and disabled: a mortality study', *Journal of the American Geriatric Society, 11*, 185–94.

Alexander, P.C. (1987) 'The integration of family therapy perspectives in personal construct theory', paper presented at 7th International Congress on Personal Construct Psychology, Memphis.

Alexander, P.C. (1988) 'The therapeutic implications of family cognitions and constructs', *Journal of Cognitive Psychotherapy, 2*, 219–36.

Alexander, P.C. and Follette, V.M. (1987) 'Personal constructs in the group treatment of incest' in R.A. Neimeyer and G.J. Neimeyer (eds.), *Personal Construct Therapy Casebook*, Springer, New York.

Alexander, P.C. and Neimeyer, G.J. (1989) 'Constructivism and family therapy', *International Journal of Personal Construct Psychology, 2*, 111–21.

Alexander, P.C., Neimeyer, R.A., Follette, V., Moore, M.K., and Harter, S. (1989) 'A comparison of group treatments of women sexually abused as children', *Journal of Consulting and Clinical Psychology, 57*, 479–83.

Allon, R., Stewart, M.F., Lancee, W.J., and Brawley, P. (1981) 'Conditional probabilities and the grid test for schizophrenic thought disorder', *British Journal of Social and Clinical Psychology, 20*, 57–66.

Alloy, L.B. and Abramson, L.Y. (1979) 'Judgement of contingency in depressed and non-depressed students: sadder but wiser?', *Journal of Experimental Psychology, 108*, 441–85.

Alloy, L.B. and Abramson, L.Y. (1982) 'Learned helplessness, depression and the illusion of control', *Journal of Personality and Social Psychology, 42*, 1114–26.

Allport, G.W. (1946) 'Personalistic psychology as a science; a reply', *Psychological Review, 53*, 132–5.

Altrocchi, J. (1961) 'Interpersonal perceptions of repressors and sensitizers and component analysis of assumed dissimilarity scores', *Journal of Abnormal and Social Psychology, 62*, 528–34.

Anastasi, A. (1968) *Psychological Testing*, Macmillan, Toronto.

Andersen, T. (1987) 'The reflecting team: dialogue and metadialogue in clinical work', *Family Process, 26*, 415–28.

Anderson, C.A. (1983) 'Imagination and expectation: the effect of imagining behavioural scripts on personal intentions', *Journal of Personality and Social Psychology, 45*, 293–305.

Andreasen, N.C., Alport, M., and Martz, M.J. (1981) 'Acoustic analysis: an objective measure of affective flattening', *Archives of General Psychiatry, 38*, 281–5.

Appelbaum, S.A. (1969) 'The accidental eminence of George Kelly', *Psychiatry and Social Science Review, 3*, 20–5.

Applebee, A.N. (1975) 'Developmental changes in consensus in construing within a specified domain', *British Journal of Psychology, 66*, 473–8.

Applebee, A.N. (1976) 'The development of children's responses to repertory grids', *British Journal of Social and Clinical Psychology, 15*, 101–2.

Arbuckle, D.S. and Boy, A.V. (1961) 'Client-centered therapy in counseling students with behavioral problems', *Journal of Counseling Psychology, 8*, 136–9.

Ashworth, C.M., Blackburn, I.M., and McPherson, F.M. (1982) 'The performance of depressed and manic patients on some repertory grid measures: a cross-sectional study', *British Journal of Medical Psychology, 55*, 247–56.

Ashworth, C.M., Blackburn, I.M., and McPherson, F.M. (1985) 'The performance of depressed and manic patients on some repertory grid measures: a longitudinal study', *British Journal of Medical Psychology, 58*, 337–42.

Atwood, G.E. and Stolorow, R.D. (1984) *Structures of Subjectivity*, Academic Press, Hillsdale, NJ.

Axford, S. and Jerrom, D.W.A. (1986) 'Self-esteem in depression: a controlled repertory grid investigation', *British Journal of Medical Psychology, 59*, 61–8.

Baillie-Grohman, R. (1975) 'The Use of a Modified Form of Repertory Grid Technique to Investigate the Extent to which Deaf School Leavers Tend to Use Stereotypes', unpublished MSc dissertation, University of London.

Baldwin, R. (1972) 'Change in interpersonal cognitive complexity as a function of a training group experience', *Psychological Reports, 30*, 935–40.

Bamber, M. (1972) 'Threat and Meaningfulness in the Development of Friendship', unpublished Master's thesis, University of Missouri.

Bandura, A. (1977) 'Self-efficacy: toward a unifying theory of behavior change', *Psychological Review, 84*, 191–215.

Bannister, D. (1960) 'Conceptual structure in thought-disordered schizophrenics', *Journal of Mental Science, 106*, 1230–49.

Bannister, D. (1962a) 'The nature and measurement of schizophrenic thought disorder', *Journal of Mental Science, 108*, 825–42.

Bannister, D. (1962b) 'Personal construct theory: a summary and experimental paradigm', *Acta Psychologica, 20*, 104–20.

Bannister, D. (1963) 'The genesis of schizophrenic thought disorder: a serial invalidation hypothesis', *British Journal of Psychiatry, 109*, 680–6.

Bannister, D. (1965a) 'The rationale and clinical relevance of repertory grid technique', *British Journal of Psychiatry, 111*, 977–82.

Bannister, D. (1965b) 'The genesis of schizophrenic thought disorder: re-test of the serial invalidation hypothesis', *British Journal of Psychiatry, 111*, 377–82.

Bannister, D. (1968) 'The myth of physiological psychology', *Bulletin of the British Psychological Society, 21*, 229–31.

Bannister, D. (1970a) 'Concepts and personality: Kelly and Osgood' in P. Mittler (ed.), *The Psychological Assessment of Mental and Physical Handicap*, Methuen, London.

Bannister, D. (1970b) 'Psychological theories as ways of relating to people', *British Journal of Medical Psychology, 43*, 241–4.

Bannister, D. (1972) 'Critiques of the concept of "loose construing": a reply', *British Journal of Social and Clinical Psychology, 11*, 412–14.

Bannister, D. (1973) 'Reply to Haynes and Phillips', *British Journal of Social and Clinical Psychology, 12*, 324–5.

Bannister, D. (1975) 'Personal construct psychotherapy' in D. Bannister (ed.), *Issues and Approaches in the Psychological Therapies*, Wiley, London.

Bannister, D. (1977) 'The logic of passion' in D. Bannister (ed.), *New Perspectives in Personal Construct Theory*, Academic Press, London.

Bannister, D. (1979) 'Personal construct theory and politics' in P. Stringer and D. Bannister (eds.), *Constructs of Sociality and Individuality*, Academic Press, London.

Bannister, D. (1981) 'Construing a disability' in A. Brechin, P. Liddiard, and J. Swain (eds.), *Handicap in a Social World*, Hodder & Stoughton, London.

Bannister, D. (1983a) 'Self in personal construct theory' in J. Adams-Webber and J.C. Mancuso (eds.), *Applications of Personal Construct Theory*, Academic Press, Toronto.

Bannister, D. (1983b) 'The internal politics of psychotherapy' in D. Pilgrim (ed.), *Psychology and Psychotherapy: Current Trends and Issues*, Routledge & Kegan Paul, London.

Bannister, D. (1985a) 'The experience of self' in F. Epting and A.W. Landfield (eds.), *Anticipating Personal Construct Psychology*, University of Nebraska Press, Lincoln.

Bannister, D. (1985b) 'The free-floating concept of anxiety' in E. Karas (ed.), *Current Issues in Clinical Psychology* (vol. 2), Plenum Press, New York.

Bannister, D. (1985c) 'The patient's point of view' in D. Bannister (ed.), *Issues and Approaches in Personal Construct Theory*, Academic Press, London.

Bannister, D. (1985d) 'The psychotic disguise' in W. Dryden (ed.), *Therapists' Dilemmas*, Harper & Row, London.

Bannister, D., Adams-Webber, J.R., Penn, W.I., and Radley, A.R. (1975) 'Reversing the process of thought disorder: a serial validation experiment', *British Journal of Social and Clinical Psychology, 14*, 169–80.

Bannister, D. and Agnew, J. (1977) 'The child's construing of self' in J.K. Cole and A.W. Landfield (eds.), *Nebraska Symposium on Motivation 1976*, University of Nebraska Press, Lincoln.

Bannister, D. and Bott, M. (1973) 'Evaluating the person' in P. Kline (ed.), *New Approaches in Psychological Measurement*, Wiley, London.

Bannister, D. and Fransella, F. (1966) 'A grid test of schizophrenic thought disorder', *British Journal of Social and Clinical Psychology, 5*, 95–102.

Bannister, D. and Fransella, F. (1967) *A Grid Test of Schizophrenic Thought Disorder: A Standard Clinical Test*, Psychological Test Publications, Barnstaple.

Bannister, D. and Fransella, F. (1986) *Inquiring Man* (3rd edition), Croom Helm, London.

Bannister, D., Fransella, F., and Agnew, J. (1971) 'Characteristics and validity of the Grid Test of Thought Disorder', *British Journal of Social and Clinical Psychology, 10*, 144–51.

Bannister, D. and Mair, J.M.M. (1968) *The Evaluation of Personal Constructs*, Academic Press, London.

Bannister, D. and Salmon, P. (1966) 'Schizophrenic thought disorder: specific or diffuse?', *British Journal of Medical Psychology, 39*, 215–19.

Bannister, D. and Salmon, P. (1967) 'Measures of Superordinacy', unpublished MS, Bexley Hospital.

Barbow, P.I. (1969)) 'Some Aspects of the Reliability of the Repertory Grid Technique', unpublished MSc thesis, Queen's University, Belfast.

Barratt, B. (1977) 'The Development of Organizational Complexity and Structure in Peer Perception', unpublished MS, Harvard University.

Bassler, M., Krauthauser, K., and Hoffmann, S.O. (1989) 'Evaluation of the therapeutic process during inhospital psychotherapy within the horizon of repertory grid technique, a follow-up study with 138 patients', paper presented at 3rd European Conference on Psychotherapy Research, Bern.

Bateson, G. (1972) *Steps to an Ecology of Mind*, Ballantine, New York.

Bateson, G. (1974) 'Draft: scattered thoughts for a conference on "Broken Power"', *Co-evolution Quarterly, 4*, 26–7.

Bateson, G. (1978) 'The birth of a matrix double bind and epistemology' in M. Berger (ed.), *Beyond the Double Bind: Communication and Family Systems, Theories and Techniques with Schizophrenics*, Brunner/Mazel, New York.

Bateson, G., Jackson, D.D., Haley, J., and Weakland, J. (1956) 'Toward a theory of schizophrenia', *Behavioral Science, 1*, 251–64.

Batty, C. and Hall, E. (1986) 'Personal constructs of students with eating disorders: Implications for counselling', *British Journal of Guidance and Counselling, 14*, 306–13.

Bazkin, E.F., Komeva, T.V., and Lonachenko, A.S. (1978) 'The ability of emotional perception in schizophrenic patients' in R.W. Rieker (ed.), *Applied Psycholinguistics and Mental Health*, Plenum Press, New York.

Beail, N. (1983) 'Equivalence of grid forms: a case report', *British Journal of Medical Psychology, 56*, 263–4.

Beail, N. (1984) 'Consensus grids: what about the variance?', *British Journal of Medical Psychology, 57*, 193–5.

Beail, N. (1985a) 'An introduction to repertory grid technique' in N. Beail (ed.), *Repertory Grid Technique and Personal Constructs: Applications in Clinical and Educational Settings*, Croom Helm, London.

Beail, N. (1985b) 'Using repertory grid technique with severely physically disabled people' in N. Beail (ed.), *Repertory Grid Technique and Personal Constructs: Applications in Clinical and Educational Settings*, Croom Helm, London.

Beail, N. and Beail, S. (1985) 'Evaluating dependency' in N. Beail (ed.), *Repertory Grid Technique and Personal Constructs: Applications in Clinical and Educational Settings*, Croom Helm, London.

Beck, A.T. (1976) *Cognitive Therapy and the Emotional Disorders*, International Universities Press, New York.

Beck, A.T. and Emery, G. (1985) *Anxiety Disorders and Phobias: A Cognitive Perspective*, Basic Books, New York.

Beck, A.T., Rush, A.J., Shaw, B.F., and Emery, G. (1979) *Cognitive Therapy of Depression*, Guilford, New York.

Beck, J.E. (1980) 'Learning from experience in sensitivity training groups: a personal construct theory model and framework for research', *Small Group Behaviour, 11*, 279–96.

Bender, M.P. (1968) 'Does construing people as similar involve similar behaviour towards them?', *British Journal of Social and Clinical Psychology, 7*, 303–4.

Bender, M.P. (1974) 'Provided versus elicited constructs: an explanation of Warr and Coffman's (1970) anomalous finding', *British Journal of Social and Clinical Psychology, 13*, 329–30.

Bender, M.P. (1976) 'Does construing people as similar involve similar behaviour towards them? A subjective and objective replication', *British Journal of Social and Clinical Psychology, 15*, 93–6.

Benjafield, J. and Adams-Webber, J. (1975) 'Assimilative projection and construct balance in the repertory grid', *British Journal of Psychology, 66*, 169–73.

Benjafield, J. and Adams-Webber, J. (1976) 'The golden section hypothesis', *British Journal of Psychology, 67*, 11–16.

Benjafield, J., Jordan, D., and Pomeroy, E. (1976) 'Encounter groups: a return to the fundamental', *Psychotherapy: Theory, Research and Practice, 13*, 387–9.

Bennett, G., Rigby, K., and Owers, D. (1990) 'Assessment of psychological change within a residential rehabilitation centre for drug users' in P. Maitland (ed.), *Personal Construct Theory Deviancy and Social Work*, Inner London Probation Service/ Centre for Personal Construct Psychology, London.

Ben-Peretz, M. and Kalekin-Fishman, D. (1988) 'Applying PCP to constructs related to music' in F. Fransella and L. Thomas (eds.), *Experimenting with Personal Construct Psychology*, Routledge & Kegan Paul, London.

Ben-Tovim, D.I. and Greenup, J. (1983) 'The representation of transference through serial grids: a methodological study', *British Journal of Medical Psychology, 56*, 255–62.

Ben-Tovim, D., Hunter, M., and Crisp, A.H. (1977) 'Discrimination and evaluation of shape and size in anorexia nervosa: an exploratory study', *Research Communications in Psychology, Psychiatry, and Behavior, 2*, 241–53.

Berger, P. (1976) *Pyramids of Sacrifice*, Anchor Books, New York.

Berger, P.L. and Luckmann, T. (1966) *The Social Construction of Reality*, Doubleday, New York.

Bergin, A.E. and Lambert, M.J. (1978) 'The evaluation of therapeutic outcomes', in S.L. Garfield and A.E. Bergin (eds.), *Handbook of Psychotherapy and Behavior Change: An Empirical Analysis* (2nd edition), Wiley, New York.

Berne, E. (1961) *Transactional Analysis in Psychotherapy*, Grove, New York.

Berne, E. (1964) *Games People Play*, Penguin, Harmondsworth.

Bernstein, B. (1964) 'Elaborated and restricted codes', *American Anthropologist, Special Publication, 66*, 2–55.

Berzins, J.I. (1977) 'Therapist–patient matching' in A.S. Gurman and A.M. Razin (eds.), *Effective Psychotherapy. A Handbook of Research*, Pergamon, Oxford.

Berzonsky, M. and Neimeyer, G.J. (1988) 'Identity status and personal construct systems', *Journal of Adolescence, 11*, 195–204.

Bespalko, I.G. (1976) 'Peculiarities in the perception of mimicry in schizophrenic patients connected with the disturbance of probable evaluations' in R.W. Rieker (ed.), *Applied Psychodiagnostics and Mental Health*, Plenum Press, New York.

Beutler, L.E., Crago, M., and Arizmendi, T.G. (1986) 'Research on therapist variables in psychotherapy' in S.L. Garfield and A.E. Bergin (eds.), *Handbook of Psychotherapy and Behavior Change* (3rd edition), Wiley, New York.

Bexley Hospital Psychology Department (1980) 'The evolution of democracy in an NHS psychology department: Bexley Hospital Psychology Department', *Newsletter of the British Psychological Society Division of Clinical Psychology, 28*, 24–30.

Bhagat, M. and Fraser, W.I. (1970) 'Young offenders' images of self and surroundings: a semantic enquiry', *British Journal of Psychiatry, 117*, 381–7.

Bieri, J. (1955) 'Cognitive complexity–simplicity and predictive behavior', *Journal of Abnormal and Social Psychology, 51*, 263–8.

Bieri, J. (1966) 'Cognitive complexity and personality development' in O.J. Harvey (ed.), *Experience, Structure and Adaptability*, Springer, New York.

Bieri, J. (1986) 'Beyond the grid principle', *Contemporary Psychology, 31*, 672–4.

Bieri, J., Atkins, A.L., Briar, S., Leaman, R.L., Miller, H., and Tripodi, T. (1966) *Clinical and Social Judgement*, Wiley, New York.

Bieri, J., Bradburn, W.M., and Galinsky, M.D. (1958) 'Sex differences in perceptual behavior', *Journal of Personality, 26*, 1–12.

Bodden, J. (1970) 'Cognitive complexity as a factor in appropriate vocational choice', *Journal of Counseling Psychology, 17*, 364–8.

Bodden, J. and James, L.E. (1976) 'Influence of occupational information giving on cognitive complexity', *Journal of Counseling Psychology, 23*, 280–2.

Bodden, J. and Klein, A. (1972) 'Cognitive complexity and appropriate vocational choice: another look', *Journal of Counseling Psychology, 19*, 257–8.

Bodden, J.L. and Klein, A. (1973) 'Cognitive differentiation and affective stimulus value in vocational judgements', *Journal of Vocational Behaviour, 3*, 75–9.

Bodlakova, V., Hemsley, D.R., and Mumford, S.J. (1974) 'Psychological variables and flattening of affect', *British Journal of Medical Psychology, 47*, 227–34.

Bonarius, J.C.J. (1965) 'Research in the personal construct theory of George A. Kelly' in B.A. Maher (ed.), *Progress in Experimental Personality Research* (vol. 2), Academic Press, New York.

Bonarius, J.C.J. (1968) 'Personal constructs and extremity of ratings' in *Proceedings XVIth International Congress of Applied Psychology*, Swets & Zeitinger, Amsterdam.

Bonarius, J.C.J. (1970a) 'Personal Construct Psychology and Extreme Response Style', unpublished PhD thesis, University of Groningen.

Bonarius, J.C.J. (1970b) 'Fixed role therapy: a double paradox', *British Journal of Medical Psychology, 43*, 213–19.

Bonarius, J.C.J. (1977) 'The interaction model of communication: through experimental research towards existential relevance' in J.K. Cole and A.W. Landfield (eds.), *1976 Nebraska Symposium on Motivation*, University of Nebraska Press, Lincoln.

Bond, A. and Lader, M. (1976) 'Self concepts in anxiety states', *British Journal of Medical Psychology, 49*, 275–9.

Borders, L.D., Fong, M.L., and Neimeyer, G.J. (1986) 'Counseling students' level of ego development and perceptions of clients', *Counselor Education and Supervision, 26*, 36–49.

Bowen, M. (1978) 'Theory in the practice of psychotherapy' in P. Guerin (ed.), *Family Therapy*, Gardner, New York.

Bowlby, J. (1969) *Attachment and Loss. Vol. 1, Attachment*, Hogarth, London.

Bowlby, J. (1973) *Attachment and Loss. Vol. 2, Anxiety and Anger*, Hogarth, London.

Bowlby, J. (1980) *Attachment and Loss. Vol. 3, Sadness and Depression*, Hogarth, London.

Bowman, P.H. (1951) 'A Study of the Consistency of Current, Wish and Proper Self Concepts as a Measure of Therapeutic Progress', unpublished PhD thesis, University of Chicago.

Boxer, P.J. (1981) 'Reflective analysis' in M.L.G. Shaw (ed.), *Recent Advances in Personal Construct Technology*, Academic Press, London.

Boyd, T.L. and Levis, D.J. (1983) 'Exposure is a necessary condition for fear-reduction: a reply to de Silva and Rachman', *Behaviour Research and Therapy, 21*, 143–50.

Breakey, W.R. and Goodell, H. (1972) 'Thought disorder in mania and schizophrenia evaluated by Bannister's Grid Test for Schizophrenic Thought Disorder', *British Journal of Psychiatry, 120*, 391–5.

Breen, D. (1975) *The Birth of a First Child. Towards an Understanding of Femininity*, Tavistock, London.

Brierley, D.W. (1967) 'The Use of Personality Constructs by Children of Three Different Ages', unpublished PhD thesis, University of London.

Brockman, B., Poynton, A., Ryle, A., and Watson, J.P. (1987) 'Effectiveness of time-limited therapy carried out by trainees: comparison of two methods', *British Journal of Psychiatry, 151*, 602–10.

Brodsky, M. (1963) 'Interpersonal stimuli as interference in a sorting task', *Journal of Personality, 31*, 517–33.

Brown, G.W., Birley, J.L.T., and Wing, J.K. (1972) 'Influence of family life on the course of schizophrenic disorders: a replication', *British Journal of Psychiatry, 121*, 241–58.

Brown, S-.L. (1981) 'Dissociation of pleasure in psychopathology', *Journal of Nervous and Mental Disease, 169*, 3–17.

Browning, H. (1988) 'Speculative adventures: the social work setting' in G. Dunnett (ed.), *Working with People: Clinical Uses of Personal Construct Psychology*, Routledge, London.

Brumfitt, S. (1985) 'The use of repertory grids with aphasic people' in N. Beail (ed.), *Repertory Grid Technique and Personal Constructs: Applications in Clinical and Educational Settings*, Croom Helm, London.

Brumfitt, S.M. and Clarke, P.R.F. (1983) 'An application of psychotherapeutic techniques to the management of aphasia' in C. Code and D.J. Müller (eds.), *Aphasia Therapy*, Edward Arnold, London.

Bruner, J.S. (1956) 'You are your constructs', *Contemporary Psychology, 1*, 355–7.

Bryant, R. (1985) 'Families and repertory grids – a brief introduction with comments on Karastergiou-Katsika and Watson', *Journal of Family Therapy, 7*, 251–7.

Bugental, J. (1964) 'The third force in psychology', *Journal of Humanistic Psychology, 4*, 19–26.

Burnard, P. and Morrison, P. (1989) 'What is an interpersonally skilled person?: a repertory grid account of professional nurses' views', *Nurse Education Today, 9*, 384–91.

Burns, T., Hunter, M., and Lieberman, S. (1980) 'A repertory grid study of therapist/couple interaction', *Journal of Family Therapy, 2*, 297–310.

Burr, V. and Butt, T. (1989) 'A personal construct view of hypnosis', *British Journal of Experimental and Clinical Hypnosis, 6*, 85–90.

Butler, J.M. and Haigh, G. (1954) 'Changes in the relationship between self-concepts and ideal concepts consequent upon client-centered counseling' in C.R. Rogers and R.F. Dymond (eds.), *Psychotherapy and Personality Change*, University of Chicago Press, Chicago.

Butler, R.J. (1985) 'Towards an understanding of childhood difficulties' in N. Beail (ed.), *Repertory Grid Technique and Personal Constructs: Applications in Clinical and Educational Settings*, Croom Helm, London.

Butt, T. and Bannister, D. (1987) 'Better the devil you know' in W. Dryden (ed.), *Key Cases in Psychotherapy*, Croom Helm, London.

Button, E. (1983a) 'Personal construct theory and psychological well-being', *British Journal of Medical Psychology, 56*, 313–22.

Button, E.J. (1983b) 'Construing the anorexic' in J. Adams-Webber and J.C. Mancuso (eds.), *Applications of Personal Construct Theory*, Academic Press, New York.

Button, E. (1985a) 'Eating disorders: a quest for control?' in E. Button (ed.), *Personal Construct Theory and Mental Health*, Croom Helm, London.

Button, E. (1985b) 'Women with weight on their minds' in N. Beail (ed.), *Repertory Grid Technique and Personal Constructs: Applications in Clinical and Educational Settings*, Croom Helm, London.

Button, E. (1985c) 'Societal and institutional change: beyond the clinical context' in E. Button (ed.), *Personal Construct Theory and Mental Health*, Croom Helm, London.

Button, E. (1987) 'Construing people or weight?: an eating disorders group' in R.A. Neimeyer and G.J. Neimeyer (eds.), *Personal Construct Therapy Casebook*, Springer, New York.

Button, E. (1988) 'Music and personal constructs' in F. Fransella and L. Thomas (eds.), *Experimenting with Personal Construct Psychology*, Routledge & Kegan Paul, London.

Button, E. (1990) 'Rigidity of construing of self and significant others, and psychological disorder', *British Journal of Medical Psychology, 63*, 345–54.

Button, E.J., Curtis-Hayward, K., Marcer, D., and Larson, A.G. (1979) 'The personal implications of chronic pain' in D.J. Oborne, M.M. Gruneberg, and J.R. Eiser (eds.), *Research in Psychology and Medicine* (vol. 1), Academic Press, London.

Byrne, D., Barry, J., and Nelson, D. (1963) 'Relation of the revised repression-sensitization scale to measures of self-description', *Psychological Reports, 13*, 323–34.

Caine, T.M. (1970) 'Appendix I' in D. Boorer, *A Question of Attitudes*, King's Fund Hospital Centre, London.

Caine, T.M. (1975) 'Attitudes to patient care in OT students', *Occupational Therapy, 38*, 239.

Caine, T.M., Henley, S., Moses, P., Shamni, S., Smith, H., and Winter, D.A. (1986) 'A new projective test: the Caine- Marteau-Dympna Test (CMD) ', *British Journal of Medical Psychology*, 59, 157–64.

Caine, T.M. and Leigh, R. (1972) 'Conservatism in relation to psychiatric treatment', *British Journal of Social and Clinical Psychology*, 11, 52–6.

Caine, T.M. and Smail, D.J. (1967) 'Personal relevance and the choice of constructs for the repertory grid technique', *British Journal of Psychiatry*, 113, 517–20.

Caine, T.M. and Smail, D.J. (1969a) 'A study of the reliability and validity of the repertory grid technique as a measure of the hysteroid/obsessoid component of personality', *British Journal of Psychiatry*, 115, 1305–8.

Caine, T.M. and Smail, D.J. (1969b) *The Treatment of Mental Illness: Science, Faith and the Therapeutic Personality*, University of London Press, London.

Caine, T.M., Smail, D.J., Wijesinghe, O.B.A., and Winter, D.A. (1982) *Claybury Selection Battery Manual*, NFER-Nelson, Windsor.

Caine, T.M. and Wijesinghe, B. (1976) 'Personality, expectancies and group psychotherapy', *British Journal of Psychiatry*, 129, 384–7.

Caine, T.M., Wijesinghe, O.B.A., and Winter, D.A. (1981) *Personal Styles in Neurosis: Implications for Small Group Psychotherapy and Behaviour Therapy*, Routledge & Kegan Paul, London.

Caine, T.M., Wijesinghe, B., and Wood, R.R. (1973) 'Personality and psychiatric treatment expectancies', *British Journal of Psychiatry*, 122, 87–8.

Campbell, V.N. (1960) 'Assumed Similarity, Perceived Sociometric Balance, and Social Influence', unpublished PhD thesis, University of Colorado.

Camus, A. (1956) *The Rebel: An Essay on Man in Revolt*, Knopf, New York.

Cannell, J.E. (1985) 'Pastoral psychology: A personal construct perspective' in F. Epting and A.W. Landfield (eds.), *Anticipating Personal Construct Psychology*, University of Nebraska Press, Lincoln.

Canter, D. (1970) 'Individual response to the physical environment', *Bulletin of the British Psychological Society*, 23, 123.

Caplan, H.L., Rohde, P.D., Shapiro, D.A., and Watson, J.P. (1975) 'Some correlates of repertory grid measures used to study a psychotherapeutic group', *British Journal of Medical Psychology*, 48, 217–26.

Capra, F. (1975) *The Tao of Physics*, Fontana/Collins, London.

Carlson, R. (1971) 'Sex differences in ego functioning: exploratory studies of agency and communion', *Journal of Consulting and Clinical Psychology*, 37, 267–77.

Carmin, C.N. and Dowd, E.T. (1988) 'Paradigms in cognitive psychotherapy' in W. Dryden and P. Trower (eds.), *Developments in Cognitive Psychotherapy*, Sage, London.

Carr, J.E. (1970) 'Differentiation similarity of patient and therapist and the outcome of psychotherapy', *Journal of Abnormal Psychology*, 76, 361–9.

Carr, J.E. (1974) 'Perceived therapy outcome as a function of differentiation between and within conceptual dimensions', *Journal of Clinical Psychology*, 30, 282–5.

Carr, J.E. (1978) 'Ethno-behaviorism and the culture-bound syndrome: the case of amok', *Culture, Medicine and Psychiatry*, 2, 269–93.

Carr, J.E. (1980) 'Personal construct theory and psychotherapy research' in A.W. Landfield and L.M. Leitner (eds.), *Personal Construct Psychology: Psychotherapy and Personality*, Wiley, New York.

Carr, J.E. and Post, R. (1974) 'Repression-sensitization and self–other discrimination', *Journal of Personality Assessment*, 38, 48–51.

Carr, J. and Townes, B. (1975) 'Interpersonal discrimination as a function of age and psychopathology', *Child Psychiatry and Human Development*, 5, 209–15.

Carr, J.E. and Whittenbaugh, J. (1969) 'Sources of disagreement in the perception of psychotherapy', *Journal of Clinical Psychology*, 25, 16–21.

Carroll, J.S. (1978) 'The effect of imagining an event on expectations for the event: an interpretation in terms of the availability heuristic', *Journal of Experimental and Social Psychology, 14*, 88–96.

Carroll, R.C. (1983) 'Cognitive imbalance in schizophrenia' in J. Adams-Webber and J.C. Mancuso (eds.), *Applications of Personal Construct Theory*, Academic Press, Toronto.

Carroll, W.K. and Carroll, R.C. (1981) 'Cognitive balance in personal construct systems' in H. Bonarius, R. Holland, and S. Rosenberg (eds.), *Personal Construct Psychology: Recent Advances in Theory and Practice*, Macmillan, London.

Cartwright, D.S. and Vogel, J. (1960) 'A comparison of change in psychoneurotic patients during matched periods of therapy and no-therapy', *Journal of Consulting Psychology, 24*, 121–7.

Cartwright, R.D. and Lerner, B. (1963) 'Empathy, need to change and improvement in psychotherapy', *Journal of Consulting and Clinical Psychology, 27*, 138–44.

Catina, A., Gitzinger, I., and Hoeckh, H. (1991) 'Defence mechanisms: an approach from the perspective of personal construct psychology', *International Journal of Personal Construct Psychology*, in press.

Catina, A., Tschuschke, V., and Winter, D. (1989) 'Self-reconstruing as a result of social interaction in analytic group therapy', *Group Analysis, 22*, 59–72.

Catina, A. and Walter, E. (1989) 'What is a successful therapy?', paper presented at 1st European Congress of Psychology, Amsterdam.

Catina, A., Winter, D., and Hoeckh, H. (1988) 'Defence strategies: a cognitive approach to a psychoanalytical construct', paper presented at 4th European Conference on Personality, Stockholm.

Cesari, J.P., Winer, J.L., and Piper, K.P. (1984) 'Vocational decision status and the effect of four types of occupational information on cognitive complexity', *Journal of Vocational Behavior, 25*, 215–24.

Cesari, J.P., Winer, J.L., Zychlinski, F., and Laird, I.O. (1982) 'Influence of occupational information giving on cognitive complexity in decided versus undecided students, *Journal of Vocational Behavior, 21*, 224–30.

Chambers, W. (1983) 'Circumspection, preemption and personal constructs', *Social Behavior and Personality, 11*, 33–5.

Chambers, W.V. (1985) 'Logical consistency of personal constructs and choice behavior', *Psychological Reports, 57*, 190.

Chambers, W. (1986) 'Inconsistencies in the theory of death threat', *Death Studies, 10*, 165–76.

Chambers, W.V. and Epting, F.R. (1985) 'Personality and personal construct logical inconsistency', *Psychological Reports, 57*, 1120.

Chambers, W. and Grice, J.W. (1986) 'Circumgrids: a repertory grid package for personal computers', *Behavior Research Methods, Instruments, and Computers, 18*, 468.

Chambers, W.V. and O'Day, P. (1984) 'A nomothetic view of personal construct processes', *Psychological Reports, 55*, 554.

Chambers, W.V., Olson, C., Carlock, J., and Olson, D. (1986) 'Clinical and grid predictions of inconsistencies in individuals' personal constructs', *Perceptual and Motor Skills, 62*, 649–50.

Chambers, W.V. and Parsley, L. (1987–8) 'Cognitive development, integrative complexity and logical consistency of personal constructs', *Psychology and Human Development, 2*, 7–11.

Chambers, W. and Sanders, J. (1984) 'Alcoholism and logical consistency of personal constructs', *Psychological Reports, 54*, 882.

Chapman, L.J. (1961) 'Emotional factors in schizophrenic deficit', *Psychological Reports, 9*, 564.

Chetwynd, S.J. (1976) 'Sex differences in stereotyping the roles of wife and mother' in P. Slater (ed.), *The Measurement of Intrapersonal Space by Grid Technique. Vol.1. Explorations of Intrapersonal Space*, Wiley, London.

Chetwynd, J. (1977) 'The psychological meaning of structural measures derived from grids' in P. Slater (ed.), *The Measurement of Intrapersonal Space by Grid Technique. Vol.2. Dimensions of Intrapersonal Space*, Wiley, London.

Chick, J., Waterhouse, L., and Wolff, S. (1979) 'Psychological construing in schizoid children grown up', *British Journal of Psychiatry, 135*, 425–30.

Childs, D. and Hedges, R. (1980) 'The analysis of interpersonal perceptions as a repertory grid', *British Journal of Medical Psychology, 53*, 127–36.

Clark, R.A. and Delia, J.G. (1977) 'Cognitive complexity, social perspective-taking, and functional persuasive skills in second- to ninth-grade children', *Human Communication Research, 3*, 128–34.

Cleaver, J. (1989) 'Fourteen Female Self-Poisoners: A Multi-Variable Study', unpublished BA dissertation, Middlesex Polytechnic.

Clyne, S. (1975) 'The Effect of Cognitive Complexity and Assimilative Projection on Preference for the Definitive or Extensive Role in an Elaborative Choice Situation', unpublished MA thesis, University of Windsor.

Cochran, L. (1976) 'Categorization and change in conceptual relatedness', *Canadian Journal of Behavioral Science, 8*, 275–86.

Cochran, L.C. (1977) 'Inconsistency and change in conceptual organization', *British Journal of Medical Psychology, 50*, 319–28.

Cochran, L. (1983a) 'Conflict and integration in career decision making schemes', *Journal of Vocational Behavior, 23*, 87–97.

Cochran, L. (1983b) 'Seven measures of the ways that deciders frame their career decisions', *Measurement and Evaluation in Guidance, 16*, 67–77.

Cochran, L. (1987) 'Framing career decisions' in R.A. Neimeyer and G.J. Neimeyer (eds.), *Personal Construct Therapy Casebook*, Springer, New York.

Coleman, P.G. (1975) 'Interest in personal activities and degree of perceived implication between personal constructs', *British Journal of Social and Clinical Psychology, 14*, 93–5.

Cooper, J.R. (1969) 'A Factor-Analytic Study of the Grid Test of Schizophrenic Thought Disorder', unpublished Dip Clin Psychol dissertation, University of Newcastle upon Tyne.

Corsini, R.J. (1956) 'Understanding and similarity in marriage', *Journal of Abnormal and Social Psychology, 52*, 327–32.

Corsini, R.J. (ed.) (1977) *Current Personality Theories*, Peacock, Itasca, Ill.

Costigan, J. (1985) 'Personal construct psychology: a theoretical and methodological framework for nursing research', *Australian Journal of Advanced Nursing, 2*, 15–23.

Costigan, J., Humphrey, J., and Murphy, C. (1987) 'Attempted suicide: a personal construct theory exploration', *Australian Journal of Advanced Nursing, 4*, 39–50.

Cramer, P., Weegmann, M., and O'Neill, M. (1989) 'Schizophrenia and the perception of emotions: how accurately do schizophrenics judge the emotional states of others?', *British Journal of Psychiatry, 155*, 225–8.

Crisp, A.H. (1964a) 'An attempt to measure an aspect of "transference"', *British Journal of Medical Psychology, 37*, 17–30.

Crisp, A.H. (1964b) 'Development and application of a measure of "transference"', *Journal of Psychosomatic Research, 8*, 327–35.

Crisp, A.H. (1966) '"Transference", "symptom emergence", and "social repercussion" in behaviour therapy', *British Journal of Medical Psychology, 39*, 179–96.

Crisp, A.H. and Fransella, F. (1972) 'Conceptual changes during recovery from anorexia nervosa', *British Journal of Medical Psychology, 45*, 395–405.

Crockett, W.H. (1965) 'Cognitive complexity and impression formation' in B.A. Maher (ed.), *Progress in Experimental Personality Research* (vol. 2), Academic Press, New York.

Crockett, W.H. (1982) 'The organization of construct systems: the organization corollary' in J.C. Mancuso and J.R. Adams-Webber (eds.), *The Construing Person*, Praeger, New York.

Crockett, W. (1985) 'Constructs, impressions, actions, responses, and construct change: a model of processes in impression formation' in F. Epting and A.W. Landfield (eds.), *Anticipating Personal Construct Psychology*, University of Nebraska Press, Lincoln.

Crockett, W.H. and Meisel, P. (1974) 'Construct connectedness, strength of disconfirmation and impression change', *Journal of Personality, 42*, 290–9.

Cromwell, R.L. and Caldwell, D.F. (1962) 'A comparison of ratings based on personal constructs of self and others', *Journal of Clinical Psychology, 18*, 43–6.

Crump, J.H., Cooper, C.L., and Maxwell, V.B. (1981) 'Stress among air traffic controllers: occupational sources of coronary heart disease risk', *Journal of Occupational Behaviour, 2*, 293–303.

Cummins, P. (1988) '"What can I do for you?" Personal Construct Psychology in primary care' in G. Dunnett (ed.), *Working with People: Clinical Uses of Personal Construct Psychology*, Routledge, London.

Cunningham, C. and Davis, H. (1985) *Working with Parents: Frameworks for Collaboration*, Open University Press, Milton Keynes.

Cutting, J. (1981) 'Judgement of emotional expression in schizophrenics', *British Journal of Psychiatry, 139*, 1–6.

Cutting, J. (1985) *The Psychology of Schizophrenia*, Blackwell, Oxford.

Cyr, J.J. (1983) 'Measuring consistency with the grid test', *British Journal of Clinical Psychology, 22*, 219–20.

Dallos, R. and Aldridge, D. (1987) 'Handing it on: family constructs, symptoms and choice', *Journal of Family Therapy, 9*, 39–58.

Dalton, P. (1983a) 'Major issues for the therapist' in P. Dalton (ed.), *Approaches to the Treatment of Stuttering*, Croom Helm, London.

Dalton, P. (1983b) 'Psychological approaches to the treatment of stuttering' in P. Dalton (ed.), *Approaches to the Treatment of Stuttering*, Croom Helm, London.

Dalton, P. (1983c) 'Maintenance of change: towards the integration of behavioural and psychological procedures' in P. Dalton (ed.), *Approaches to the Treatment of Stuttering*, Croom Helm, London.

Dalton, P. (1987) 'Some developments in individual personal construct therapy with adults who stutter' in C. Levy (ed.), *Stuttering Therapies: Practical Approaches*, Croom Helm, London.

Dalton, P. (1988a) 'Personal Construct Psychotherapy and speech therapy in Britain: a time of transition' in G. Dunnett (ed.), *Working with People: Clinical Uses of Personal Construct Psychology*, Routledge, London.

Dalton, P. (1988b) 'Personal meaning and memory: Kelly and Bartlett' in F. Fransella and L. Thomas (eds.), *Experimenting with Personal Construct Psychology*, Routledge & Kegan Paul, London.

Davies, R. (1985) 'Using grids in vocational guidance' in N. Beail (ed.), *Repertory Grid Technique and Personal Constructs: Applications in Clinical and Educational Settings*, Croom Helm, London.

Davis, B.D. (1985) 'Dependency grids: an illustration of their use in an educational setting' in N. Beail (ed.), *Repertory Grid Technique and Personal Constructs: Applications in Clinical and Educational Settings*, Croom Helm, London.

Davis, B. (1986) 'The strain of training: being a student psychiatric nurse' in J. Brooking (ed.), *Psychiatric Nursing Research*, Wiley, London.

Davis, H. (1979) 'Self-reference and the encoding of personal information in depression', *Cognitive Therapy and Research, 3*, 97–110.

Davis, H. (1983) 'Constructs of handicap: working with parents and children', *Changes, 1*, 37–9.

Davis, H. (1984) 'Personal construct theory: a possible framework for use', *Mental Handicap, 12*, 80–1.

Davis, H. and Cunningham, C. (1985) 'Mental handicap: people in context' in E. Button (ed.), *Personal Construct Theory and Mental Health*, Croom Helm, London.

Davis, H., Stroud, A., and Green, L. (1989) 'Child characterization sketch', *International Journal of Personal Construct Psychology, 2*, 323–37.

Davison, K., Brierley, H., and Smith, C. (1971) 'A male monozygotic twinship discordant for homosexuality: a repertory grid study', *British Journal of Psychiatry, 118*, 675–82.

Davisson, A. (1978) 'George Kelly and the American mind (or why has he been obscure for so long in the U.S.A. and whence the new interest?)' in F. Fransella (ed.), *Personal Construct Psychology 1977*, Academic Press, London.

Dawes, A. (1985) 'Construing drug dependence' in E. Button (ed.), *Personal Construct Theory and Mental Health*, Croom Helm, London.

DeBoeck, P. (1981) 'An interpretation of loose construing in schizophrenic thought disorder' in H. Bonarius, R. Holland, and S. Rosenberg (eds.), *Personal Construct Psychology: Recent Advances in Theory and Practice*, Macmillan, London.

DeBoeck, P. (1986) *HICLAS Computer Program: Version 1.0*, Psychology Department, Katholieke Universiteit Leuven, Leuven.

DeBoeck, P. and Rosenberg, S. (1988) 'Hierarchical classes: model and data analysis', *Psychometrika, 53*, 361–81.

DeBoeck, P., Van den Bergh, O., and Claeys, W. (1981) 'The immediacy hypothesis of schizophrenia tested in the Grid Test', *British Journal of Clinical Psychology, 20*, 131–2.

Deering, G. (1963) 'Affective stimuli and disturbance of thought processes', *Journal of Consulting Psychology, 27*, 338–43.

Delia, J.G. and Crockett, W.H. (1973) 'Social schemas, cognitive complexity, and the learning of social structures', *Journal of Personality, 41*, 413–29.

Delia, J.G., Gonyea, A.H., and Crockett, W.H. (1971) 'The effects of subject-generated and normative constructs upon the formation of impressions', *British Journal of Social and Clinical Psychology, 10*, 301–5.

Delia, J.G., Kline, S.L., and Burleson, B.R. (1979) 'The development of persuasive communication strategies in kindergarteners through twelfth-graders', *Communication Monographs, 46*, 241–56.

Delia, J.G. and O'Keefe, B.J. (1976) 'The interpersonal constructs of Machiavellians', *British Journal of Social and Clinical Psychology, 15*, 435–6.

Dell, P.F. (1982) 'Beyond homeostasis: toward a concept of coherence', *Family Process, 21*, 21–41.

de Silva, P. and Rachman, S. (1981) 'Is exposure a necessary condition for fear-reduction?', *Behaviour Research and Therapy, 19*, 227–32.

de Silva, P. and Rachman, S. (1983) 'Exposure and fear-reduction', *Behaviour Research and Therapy, 21*, 151–2.

Dewey, M.E. and Slade, P.D. (1983) 'The Relationship between Conflict and Complexity', unpublished MS, University of Liverpool.

Dingemans, P.M., Space, L.G., and Cromwell, R.L. (1983) 'How general is the inconsistency in schizophrenic behavior?' in J. Adams-Webber and J.C. Mancuso (eds.), *Applications of Personal Construct Theory*, Academic Press, Toronto.

Dixon, P.M. (1968) 'Reduced Emotional Responsiveness in Schizophrenia', unpublished PhD thesis, University of London.

Dodds, J. (1981) 'Applying construct theory in groups, with Sue Llewelyn', *Changes, 3*, 138.

Doster, J.A. (1980) 'Personal construction and human interaction' in A.W. Landfield and L.M. Leitner (eds.), *Personal Construct Psychology: Psychotherapy and Personality*, Wiley, New York.

Doster, J.A. (1985) 'A personal construct assessment of marital violence: some preliminary findings' in F. Epting and A.W. Landfield (eds.), *Anticipating Personal Construct Psychology*, University of Nebraska Press, Lincoln.

Dougherty, F.E., Bartlett, E.S., and Izard, C.E. (1974) 'Responses of schizophrenics to expressions of the fundamental emotions', *Journal of Clinical Psychology, 30*, 243–6.

Draffan, J.W. (1973) 'Randomness in grid test scores', *British Journal of Medical Psychology, 46*, 391–2.

Draffan, J.W. (1972) 'Speed of function, thought process disorder and flattening of affect', *British Journal of Psychiatry, 120*, 183–7.

Dreiblatt, I.S. and Weatherley, D.A. (1965), 'An evaluation of the efficacy of brief-contact therapy with hospitalized psychiatric patients', *Journal of Consulting Psychology, 29*, 513–19.

Drewery, J. and Rae, J.B. (1969), 'A group comparison of alcoholic and non-alcoholic marriages using the interpersonal perception technique', *British Journal of Psychiatry, 115*, 287–300.

Dryden, W. (ed.) (1984) *Individual Therapy in Britain*, Harper & Row, London.

Dryden, W. (1986) 'Eclectic psychotherapies: a critique of leading approaches' in J.C. Norcross (ed.), *Handbook of Eclectic Psychotherapy*, Brunner/Mazel, New York.

Dryden, W. (1987) *Current Issues in Rational-Emotive Therapy*, Croom Helm, London.

Dryden, W. and Ellis, A. (1987), 'Rational-emotive therapy: an update' in W. Dryden (ed.), *Current Issues in Rational-Emotive Therapy*, Croom Helm, London.

Dryden, W. and Golden, W. (eds.) (1986) *Cognitive Behavioural Approaches to Psychotherapy*, Harper & Row, London.

Drysdale, B. (1989) 'The construing of pain: a comparison of acute and chronic low back pain patients using the repertory grid technique', *International Journal of Personal Construct Psychology, 2*, 271–86.

Duck, S.W. (1973a) *Personal Relationships and Personal Constructs: A Study of Friendship Formation*, Wiley, London.

Duck, S.W. (1973b) 'Similarity and perceived similarity of personal constructs as influences in friendship choice', *British Journal of Social and Clinical Psychology, 12*, 1–6.

Duck, S.W. (1975) 'Personality similarity and friendship choices by adolescents', *European Journal of Social Psychology, 5*, 351–65.

Duck, S.W. (1979) 'Personal constructs in the development and collapse of personal relationships', paper presented at 3rd International Congress on Personal Construct Psychology, Breukelen.

Duck, S.W. and Allison, D. (1978) 'I liked you but I can't live with you: a study of lapsed friendships', *Social Behavior and Personality, 8*, 43–7.

Duck, S.W. and Craig, G. (1978) 'Personality similarity and the development of friendship: a longitudinal study', *British Journal of Social and Clinical Psychology, 17*, 237–42.

Duck, S.W. and Spencer, C. (1972) 'Personal constructs and friendship formation', *Journal of Personality and Social Psychology, 23*, 40–5.

Duehn, D. and Proctor, E.K. (1974) 'A study of cognitive complexity in the education for social work practice', *Journal of Education for Social Work, 10*, 20–6.

Dunnett, G. (1985) 'Construing control in theory and therapy' in D. Bannister (ed.), *Issues and Approaches in Personal Construct Theory*, Academic Press, London.

Dunnett, G. (1988a) 'Myths, methods and technique' in G. Dunnett (ed.), *Working with People: Clinical Uses of Personal Construct Psychology*, Routledge, London.

Dunnett, G. (1988b) 'Phobias: a journey beyond neurosis' in F. Fransella and L. Thomas (eds.), *Experimenting with Personal Construct Psychology*, Routledge & Kegan Paul, London.

Dunnett, G. (1988c) 'Enlarging horizons: Personal Construct Psychology and psychiatry' in G. Dunnett (ed.), *Working with People: Clinical Uses of Personal Construct Psychology*, Routledge, London.

Dunnett, G. (1988d) 'Working with oneself', in G. Dunnett (ed.), *Working with People: Clinical Uses of Personal Construct Psychology*, Routledge, London.

Dunnett, G. and Llewelyn, S. (1988) 'Elaborating personal construct theory in a group setting' in G. Dunnett (ed.), *Working with People: Clinical Uses of Personal Construct Psychology*, Routledge, London.

du Preez, P. (1972) 'The construction of alternatives in parliamentary debate: psychological theory and political analysis', *South African Journal of Psychology, 2*, 23–40.

du Preez, P. (1988) 'What might psychologists tell politicians about intergroup conflict' in F. Fransella and L. Thomas (eds.), *Experimenting with Personal Construct Psychology*, Routledge & Kegan Paul, London.

Dymond, R.F. (1954) 'Adjustment changes over therapy from self-sorts' in C.R. Rogers and R.F. Dymond (eds.), *Psychotherapy and Personality Change*, University of Chicago Press, Chicago.

Eastman, C. (1978) 'The Self-Identity and Drinking Motivation of Alcoholics and Social Drinkers', unpublished PhD thesis, University of Birmingham.

Ecclestone, C.E., Gendreau, P., and Knox, C. (1974) 'Solitary confinement of prisoners: an assessment of its effects on inmates' personal constructs and adrenocortical activity', *Canadian Journal of Behavioral Science, 6*, 178–91.

Edmonds, T. (1979) 'Applying personal construct theory in occupational guidance', *British Journal of Guidance and Counselling, 7*, 225–33.

Ehlers, W. and Peter, R. (1989) *Selbstbeurteilung von Abwehrkonzepten*, PZK, Ulm.

Eland, F.A., Epting, F.R., and Bonarius, H. (1979) 'Self-disclosure and the Reptest Interaction Technique' in P. Stringer and D. Bannister (eds.), *Constructs of Sociality and Individuality*, Academic Press, London.

Ellis, A. (1962) *Reason and Emotion in Psychotherapy*, Lyle Stuart, New York.

Ellis, A. (1975) 'The rational-emotive approach to sex therapy', *The Counseling Psychologist, 5*, 14–21.

Ellis, A. (1977) 'The basic clinical theory of rational-emotive therapy' in A. Ellis and R. Grieger (eds.), *Handbook of Rational-Emotive Therapy* (vol. 1), Springer, New York.

Ellis, A. (1979) 'The theory of rational-emotive therapy' in A. Ellis and J.M. Whiteley (eds.), *Theoretical and Empirical Foundations of Rational-Emotive Therapy*, Brooks/Cole, Monterey.

Ellis, A. (1980) 'Treatment of erectile dysfunction' in S.R. Leiblum and L.A. Pervin (eds.), *Principles and Practice of Sex Therapy*, Tavistock, London.

Emerson, E. (1982) 'The prediction of change in repertory grids', *British Journal of Medical Psychology, 55*, 241–6.

Endler, N.S. (1961) 'Changes in meaning during psychotherapy as measured by the Semantic Differential', *Journal of Counseling Psychology, 8*, 105–11.

Ends, E. and Page, C. (1957) 'A study of 3 types of group psychotherapy with hospitalised male inebriates', *Quarterly Journal of Studies of Alcohol, 18*, 263–77.

Engel, G.L. (1959) ' "Psychogenic" pain and the pain prone patient', *American Journal of Medicine, 26*, 899–918.

Epting, F.R. (1984) *Personal Construct Counseling and Psychotherapy*, Wiley, New York.

Epting, F.R. (1988) 'Journeying into the personal constructs of children', *International Journal of Personal Construct Psychology, 1*, 53–61.

Epting, F. and Amerikaner, M. (1980) 'Optimal functioning: a personal construct approach' in A.W. Landfield and L.M. Leitner (eds.), *Personal Construct Psychology: Psychotherapy and Personality*, Wiley, New York.

Epting, F.R. and Nazario, A., Jr. (1987) 'Designing a fixed role therapy: issues, technique, and modifications' in R.A. Neimeyer and G.J. Neimeyer (eds.), *Personal Construct Therapy Casebook*, Springer, New York.

Epting, F.R. and Neimeyer, R.A. (eds.) (1984) *Personal Meanings of Death: Applications of Personal Construct Theory to Clinical Practice*, Hemisphere/McGraw-Hill, New York.

Epting, F.R., Rainey, L.C., and Weiss, M. (1979) 'Constructions of death and levels of death fear', *Death Education, 3*, 21–30.

Epting, F.R., Suchman, D.I., and Nickeson, C.J. (1971) 'An evaluation of elicitation procedures for personal constructs', *British Journal of Psychology, 62*, 513–17.

Epting, F.R. and Wilkins, G. (1974) 'Comparison of cognitive structural measures for predicting person perception', *Perceptual and Motor Skills, 38*, 727–30.

Epting, F.R., Wilkins, G., and Margulis, S.T. (1972) 'Relationship between cognitive differentiation and level of abstraction', *Psychological Reports, 31*, 367–70.

Epting, F.R., Zempel, C.E., and Rubio, C.T. (1979) 'Construct similarity and maternal warmth', *Social Behavior and Personality, 7*, 97–105.

Erickson, M.H. and Rossi, E.L. (1979) *Hypnotherapy: An Exploratory Casebook*, Irvington, New York.

Erikson, E.H. (1959) 'Growth and crises of the healthy personality', *Psychological Issues, 1*, 50–100.

Evesham, M. (1987) 'Residential courses for stutterers: combining technique and personal construct psychology' in C. Levy (ed.), *Stuttering Therapies: Practical Approaches*, Croom Helm, London.

Evesham, M. and Fransella, F. (1985) 'Stuttering relapse: the effects of a combined speech and psychological reconstruction programme', *British Journal of Disorders of Communication, 20*, 237–48.

Evesham, M. and Huddleston, A. (1983) 'Teaching stutterers the skill of fluent speech as a preliminary to the study of relapse', *British Journal of Disorders of Communication, 18*, 31–8.

Ewing, T.N. (1954) 'Changes in attitude during counseling', *Journal of Counseling Psychology, 1*, 232–9.

Fager, R.E. (1954) 'Communication in Personal Construct Theory', unpublished PhD thesis, Ohio State University.

Fairbairn, W.R.D. (1952) *Psychoanalytic Studies of the Personality*, Tavistock, London.

Fairweather, G.W. and Simon R. (1963) 'A further follow-up comparison of psychotherapeutic programs', *Journal of Consulting Psychology, 27*, 186.

Fairweather, G.W., Simon, R., Gebhard, M.E., Weingarten, E., Holland, J.L., Sanders, R., Stone, G.B., and Reahl, J.E. (1960) 'Relative effectiveness of psychotherapeutic programs: a multidimensional criteria comparison of four programs for three different patient groups', *Psychological Monographs, 74*, 492, whole no.

Feffer, M.H. (1961) 'The influence of affective factors on conceptualization in schizophrenia', *Journal of Abnormal Psychology, 63*, 588–96.

Feixas, G. (1989) 'Approaching the individual and the system', paper presented at the 8th International Congress on Personal Construct Psychology, Assisi.

Feixas, G., Cunillera, C., and Villegas, M. (1987) 'PCT and the systems approach: a theoretical and methodological proposal for integration', paper presented at 7th International Congress on Personal Construct Psychology, Memphis.

Feixas, G. and Villegas, M. (1985) 'Kelly as humanist?', paper presented at 6th International Congress on Personal Construct Psychology, Cambridge.

Feixas, G. and Villegas, M. (1988) 'Ellen West: an analysis of the autobiographical material of a disturbed eater', paper presented at 17th European Conference on Psychosomatic Research, Marburg.

Feldman, M.M. (1975) 'The body image and object relations: exploration of a method utilizing repertory grid technique', *British Journal of Medical Psychology, 48*, 317–32.

Feldstein, S. (1962) 'The relationship of interpersonal involvement and affectiveness of content to the verbal communication of schizophrenic patients', *Journal of Abnormal Psychology, 64*, 39–45.

Fernando, S. (1988) *Race and Culture in Psychiatry*, Croom Helm, London.

Ferreira, A.J. (1963) 'Family myth and homeostasis', *Archives of General Psychiatry, 9*, 457–63.

Fielding, J.M. (1975) 'A technique for measuring outcome in group psychotherapy', *British Journal of Medical Psychology, 48*, 189–98.

Fielding, J.M. (1983) 'Verbal participation and group therapy outcome', *British Journal of Psychiatry, 142*, 524–8.

Fisher, D.D.V. (1989a) 'Personal problems: eliciting problem-operative constructs', *International Journal of Personal Construct Psychology, 2*, 55–64.

Fisher, D. (1989b) 'Kelly and Maturana', paper presented at 8th International Congress on Personal Construct Psychology, Assisi.

Fisher, D.V. (1990) 'Construing action as effective: a review of Mancuso's position', paper presented at 2nd British Conference on Personal Construct Psychology, York.

Fisher, K. (1985) 'Repertory grids with amputees' in N. Beail (ed.), *Repertory Grid Technique and Personal Constructs: Applications in Clinical and Educational Settings*, Croom Helm, London.

Fisher, L.M. and Wilson, G.T. (1985) 'A study of the psychology of agoraphobia', *Behaviour Research and Therapy, 23*, 97–108.

Fisher, S. and Greenberg, R.P. (1978) *The Scientific Evaluation of Freud's Theories and Therapy*, Basic Books, New York.

Fjeld, S.P. and Landfield, A.W. (1961) 'Personal construct theory consistency', *Psychological Reports, 8*, 127–9.

Foley, R. (1988) 'Kelly and Bateson: antithesis or synthesis?' in F. Fransella and L. Thomas (eds.), *Experimenting with Personal Construct Psychology*, Routledge & Kegan Paul, London.

Fonagy, P. (1982) 'The integration of psychoanalysis and experimental science: a review', *International Review of Psychoanalysis, 9*, 125–45.

Foon, A.E. (1987) 'Review: locus of control as a predictor of outcome of psychotherapy', *British Journal of Medical Psychology, 2*, 99–108.

Forrest, A.J. and Wolkind, S.N. (1974) 'Masked depression in men with low back pain', *Rheumatology and Rehabilitation, 13*, 148–53.

Foulds, G.A. (1965) *Personality and Personal Illness*, Tavistock, London.

Foulds, G., Hope, K., McPherson, F., and Mayo, P. (1967) 'Cognitive disorder among the schizophrenias: I The validity of some tests of thought-process disorder', *British Journal of Psychiatry, 113*, 1361–8.

Foulkes, S.H. (1964) *Therapeutic Group Analysis*, Allen & Unwin, London.

Frank, J.D. (1973) *Persuasion and Healing* (2nd edition), Johns Hopkins University Press, Baltimore.

Frank, J.D. (1982) 'Therapeutic components shared by all psychotherapies' in J.H. Harvey and M.M. Parks (eds.), *Psychotherapy Research and Behavior Change*, American Psychological Association, Washington, DC.

Frankl, V. (1961) 'Dynamics, existence and values', *Journal of Existential Psychiatry, 2*, 5–16.

Frankl, V. (1969) *The Will to Meaning: Foundations and Applications of Logotherapy*, Plenum Press, New York.

Fransella, F. (1965) 'The Effects of Imposed Rhythm and Certain Aspects of Personality on the Speech of Stutterers', unpublished PhD thesis, University of London.

Fransella, F. (1968) 'Self concepts and the stutterer', *British Journal of Psychiatry, 114*, 1531–5.

Fransella, F. (1970a) 'Stuttering: not a symptom but a way of life', *British Journal of Communication Disorders, 5*, 22–9.

Fransella, F. (1970b) 'Construing and the Dysphasic', unpublished MS.

Fransella, F. (1970c), 'Measurement of conceptual change accompanying weight loss', *Journal of Psychosomatic Research, 14*, 347–51.

Fransella, F. (1970d) '. . . And then there was one' in D. Bannister (ed.), *Perspectives in Personal Construct Theory*, Academic Press, London.

Fransella, F. (1972) *Personal Change and Reconstruction*, Academic Press, London.

Fransella, F. (1974) 'Thinking in the obsessional' in H.R. Beech (ed.), *Obsessional States*, Methuen, London.

Fransella, F. (1976) 'The theory and measurement of personal constructs' in K. Granville-Grossman (ed.), *Recent Advances in Clinical Psychiatry*, Churchill Livingstone, London.

Fransella, F. (1977) 'The self and the stereotype' in D. Bannister (ed.), *New Perspectives in Personal Construct Theory*, Academic Press, London.

Fransella, F. (1978) 'Personal construct theory or psychology?', in F. Fransella (ed.), *Personal Construct Psychology 1977*, Academic Press, London.

Fransella, F. (1980) 'Teaching personal construct psychotherapy' in A.W. Landfield and L.M. Leitner (eds.), *Personal Construct Psychology: Psychotherapy and Personality*, Wiley, New York.

Fransella, F. (1981a) 'Repertory grid technique' in F. Fransella (ed.), *Personality: Theory, Measurement and Research*, Methuen, London.

Fransella, F. (1981b) 'Nature babbling to herself: the self characterisation as a therapeutic tool', in H. Bonarius, R. Holland, and S. Rosenberg (eds.), *Personal Construct Psychology: Recent Advances in Theory and Practice*, Macmillan, London.

Fransella, F. (1982) 'Personal meanings and personal contructs' in E. Shepherd and J.P. Watson (eds.), *Personal Meanings*, Wiley, London.

Fransella, F. (1983) 'Threat and the scientist' in G.M. Breakwell (ed.), *Threatened Identities*, Wiley, London.

Fransella, F. (1985a) 'Individual psychotherapy' in E. Button (ed.), *Personal Construct Theory and Mental Health*, Croom Helm, London.

Fransella, F. (1985b) 'Death by starvation: whose decision?' in W. Dryden (ed.), *Therapists' Dilemmas*, Harper & Row, London.

Fransella, F. (1988) 'PCT: still radical thirty years on?' in F. Fransella and L. Thomas (eds.), *Experimenting with Personal Construct Psychology*, Routledge & Kegan Paul, London.

Fransella, F. (1989a) 'A fight for freedom' in W. Dryden and L. Spurling (eds.), *On Becoming a Psychotherapist*, Tavistock/Routledge, London.

Fransella, F. (1989b) 'Obstacles to change' in W. Dryden and P. Trower (eds.), *Cognitive Psychotherapy: Therapeutic Stasis and Change*, Cassel, London.

Fransella, F. and Adams, B. (1966) 'An illustration of the use of repertory grid technique in a clinical setting', *British Journal of Social and Clinical Psychology, 5*, 51–62.

Fransella, F. and Bannister, D. (1967) 'A validation of repertory grid technique as a measure of political construing', *Acta Psychologica, 26*, 97–106.

Fransella, F. and Bannister, D. (1977) *A Manual for Repertory Grid Technique*, Academic Press, London.

Fransella, F. and Button, E. (1983) 'The "construing" of self and body size in relation to the maintenance of weight gain in anorexia nervosa' in P.L. Darby (ed.), *Anorexia Nervosa: Recent Developments in Research*, Liss, New York.

Fransella, F. and Crisp, A.H. (1970) 'Conceptual organisation and weight change', *Psychotherapy and Psychosomatics, 18*, 176–85.

Fransella, F. and Crisp, A.H. (1979) 'Comparison of weight concepts in groups of a) neurotic b) normal and c) anorexic females', *British Journal of Psychiatry, 134*, 79–86.

Fransella, F., Jones, H., and Watson, J. (1988) 'A range of applications of PCP within business and industry' in F. Fransella and L. Thomas (eds.), *Experimenting with Personal Construct Psychology*, Routledge & Kegan Paul, London.

Fransella, F. and Joyston-Bechal, M.P. (1971) 'An investigation of conceptual process and pattern change in a psychotherapy group over one year', *British Journal of Psychiatry, 119*, 199–206.

Frazer, H. (1980) 'Agoraphobia: Parental Influence and Cognitive Structures', unpublished PhD thesis, University of Toronto.

Frith, C.E. and Lillie, F.J. (1972) 'Why does the repertory grid test indicate thought disorder?', *British Journal of Social and Clinical Psychology, 11*, 73–8.

Fukuyama, M.A. and Neimeyer, G.J. (1985a) 'Using the Cultural Attitudes Repertory Technique (CART) in a cross-cultural counseling workshop', *Journal of Counseling and Development, 63*, 304–5.

Fukuyama, M.A. and Neimeyer, G.J. (1985b) 'Measuring cross-cultural attitudes using the Cultural Attitudes Repertory Technique', paper presented at 6th International Congress on Personal Construct Psychology, Cambridge.

Gale, A. and Barker, M. (1987) 'The repertory grid approach to analysing family members' perception of self and others: a pilot study', *Journal of Family Therapy, 9*, 355–66.

Gara, M.A. (1982) 'Back to basics in personality study – the individual person's own organization of experience: the individuality corollary' in J.C. Mancuso and J.R. Adams-Webber (eds.), *The Construing Person*, Praeger, New York.

Gara, M.A. and Rosenberg, S. (1979) 'The identification of persons as supersets amd subsets in free-response personality descriptions', *Journal of Personality and Social Psychology, 37*, 2161–70.

Gara, M.A., Rosenberg, S., and Cohen, B.D. (1987) 'Personal identity and the schizophrenic process', *Psychiatry, 50*, 267–9.

Gara, M.A., Rosenberg, S., and Mueller, D.R. (1989) 'Perception of self and others in schizophrenia', *International Journal of Personal Construct Psychology, 2*, 253–70.

Gardner, G.G., Mancini, F., and Semerari, A. (1988) 'Construction of psychological disorders as invalidation of self-knowledge' in F. Fransella and L. Thomas (eds.), *Experimenting with Personal Construct Psychology*, Routledge & Kegan Paul, London.

Garfield, S.L. (1986) 'Research on client variables in psychotherapy' in S.L. Garfield and A.E. Bergin (eds.), *Handbook of Psychotherapy and Behavior Change* (3rd edition), Wiley, New York.

Gendlin, E.T. (1974) 'Client-centered and experiential psychotherapy' in D.A. Wexler and L.N. Rice (eds.), *Innovations in Client-Centered Therapy*, Wiley, New York.

Gentry, W.D., Shows, W.D., and Thomas, N. (1974) 'Chronic low back pain: a psychological profile', *Psychosomatics, 15*, 174–7.

Gergen, K.J. (1989) 'Warranting voice and the elaboration of the self' in J. Shotter and K.J. Gergen (eds.), *Text of Identity*, Sage, London.

Gilbert, P. (1984) *Depression: From Psychology to Brain State*, Lawrence Erlbaum, London.

Giles, P.G. and Rychlak, J.F. (1965) 'The validity of the role construct repertory test as a measure of sexual identification', *Journal of Projective Techniques, 29*, 7–11.

Giorgi, A.P. (1981) 'Humanistic psychology and metapsychology' in J.R. Royce and L.P. Mos (eds.), *Humanistic Psychology*, Plenum Press, New York.

Glantz, M., Burr, W., and Bosse, R. (1981) 'Constructs used by alcoholics, non-psychotic out-patients and normals', paper presented at 4th International Congress on Personal Construct Psychology, St. Catharines, Ontario.

Goggins, S. (1988) 'An Examination of the Construing of Drug Dependence and Abstinence by Heroin Addicts going through Detoxification and Ex-Heroin Addicts going through Rehabilitation using an Implication Grid Technique', unpublished BSc dissertation, University of Surrey.

Goldfried, M.R. (1988) 'Personal construct therapy and other theoretical orientations', *International Journal of Personal Construct Psychology, 1*, 317–27.

Goldfried, M.R. and Safran, J.D. (1986) 'Future directions in psychotherapy integration' in J.C. Norcross (ed.), *Handbook of Eclectic Psychotherapy*, Brunner/Mazel, New York.

Goldstein, A.J. (1982) 'Agoraphobia: treatment successes, treatment failures and theoretical implications' in D.L. Chambless and A.J. Goldstein (eds.), *Agoraphobia: Multiple Perspectives on Theory and Treatment*, Wiley, New York.

Goldstein, A.J. and Chambless, D.L. (1978) 'A reanalysis of agoraphobia', *Behavior Therapy, 9*, 47–59.

Goodge, P. (1979) 'Problems of repertory grid analysis and a cluster analysis solution', *British Journal of Psychiatry, 134*, 516–21.

Goolishian, H. and Anderson, H. (1982) 'Language systems and therapy: an evolving idea', *Psychotherapy: Theory, Research, and Practice, 24*, 524–38.

Gottesman, L.E. (1962) 'The relationship of cognitive variables to therapeutic ability and training of client centered therapists', *Journal of Consulting Psychology, 26*, 119–23.

Gottheil, E., Exline, R.V., and Winkelmeyer, R. (1979) 'Judging emotions of normal and schizophrenic subjects', *American Journal of Psychiatry, 136*, 1049–54.

Gottschalk, L.A. (1974) 'A hope scale applicable to verbal samples', *Archives of General Psychiatry, 30*, 779–85.

Gottschalk, L.A. and Gleser, G.C. (1969) *The Measurement of Psychological States through the Content Analysis of Verbal Behavior*, University of California Press, Berkeley.

Gournay, K. (1986) 'A pilot study of nurses' attitudes with relation to post-basic training' in J. Brooking (ed.), *Psychiatric Nursing Research*, Wiley, London.

Green, D. (1986) 'Impact on the self: head injury in adolescence', *Constructs, 4*, 1–6.

Green, D. (1987) 'The stigma of incest: an experiment in personal construct psychotherapy', paper presented at 7th International Congress on Personal Construct Psychology, Memphis.

Gregory, W.L., Cialdini, R.B., and Carpenter, K.M. (1982) 'Self-relevant scenarios as mediators of likelihood estimates and compliance: does imagining make it so?', *Journal of Personality and Social Psychology, 43*, 89–99.

Griffiths, R.D. and Joy, M. (1971) 'The prediction of phobic behaviour', *Behaviour Research and Therapy, 9*, 109–18.

Grodin, M. and Brown, D.R. (1967) 'Multivariate stimulus processing by normal and paranoid schizophrenic subjects', *Psychonomic Science, 8*, 525–6.

Guidano, V.F. (1987) *Complexity of the Self: A Developmental Approach to Psychopathology and Therapy*, Guilford, New York.

Guidano, V.F. and Liotti, G. (1983) *Cognitive Processes and Emotional Disorders*, Guilford, New York.

Haase, R.F., Reed, C.F., Winer, J.L., and Bodden, T. (1979) 'Effect of positive, negative, and mixed occupational information on cognitive and affective complexity', *Journal of Vocational Behavior, 15*, 294–302.

Hafner, R.J. (1976) 'Fresh symptom emergence after intensive behaviour therapy', *British Journal of Psychiatry, 129*, 378–83.

Hafner, R.J. (1977a) 'The husbands of agoraphobic women: assortative mating or pathogenic interaction?', *British Journal of Psychiatry, 130*, 233–9.

Hafner, R.J. (1977b) 'The husbands of agoraphobic women and their influence on treatment outcome', *British Journal of Psychiatry, 131*, 289–94.

Hafner, R.J. (1979) 'Agoraphobic women married to abnormally jealous men', *British Journal of Medical Psychology, 52*, 99–104.

Hafner, R.J. (1983) 'Marital systems of agoraphobic women: contributions of husbands' denial and projection', *Journal of Family Therapy, 5*, 379–96.

Hafner, R.J. (1984) 'Predicting the effects on husbands of behaviour therapy for wives' agoraphobia', *Behaviour Research and Therapy, 22*, 217–26.

Hale, C.L. (1980) 'Cognitive complexity–simplicity as a determinant of communication effectiveness', *Communication Monographs, 47*, 304–11.

Hale, C.L. and Delia, J.G. (1976) 'Cognitive complexity and social perspective-taking', *Communication Monographs, 43*, 195–203.

Hall, A. and Brown, L.B. (1983) 'A comparison of the attitudes of young anorexia nervosa patients and non-patients with those of their mothers', *British Journal of Medical Psychology, 56*, 39–48.

Hamilton, D.L. (1968) 'Personality attributes associated with extreme response style', *Psychological Bulletin, 69*, 192–203.

Handin, K.H. and Mancuso, J.C. (1980) 'Perceptions of the functions of reprimand', *Journal of Social Psychology, 110*, 43–52.

Hanvik, L.J. (1951) 'MMPI profiles in patients with low back pain', *Journal of Consulting Psychology, 5*, 350–3.

Hardy, G.E. (1982) 'Body image disturbance in dysmorphophobia', *British Journal of Psychiatry, 141*, 181–5.

Hargreaves, C. (1979) 'Social networks and interpersonal constructs' in P. Stringer and D. Bannister (eds.), *Constructs of Sociality and Individuality*, Academic Press, London.

Harizuka, S. (1977) 'Perception of schizophrenic patients in classifying pictures of facial expression', *Japanese Journal of Psychology, 48*, 231–8.

Harren, V.A., Koss, R.A., Tinsley, H., and Moreland, J.R. (1979) 'Influence of gender, sex-role attitudes, and cognitive complexity on gender-dominant career choices', *Journal of Counseling Psychology, 26*, 227–34.

Harrison, A. and Phillips, J.P.N. (1979) 'The specificity of schizophrenic thought disorder', *British Journal of Medical Psychology, 52*, 105–18.

Harrison, R. (1962) 'The impact of the laboratory on perceptions of others by the experimental group' in C. Argyris (ed.), *Interpersonal Competence and Organizational Effectiveness*, Irwin, Homewood, Ill.

Harrison, R. (1966) 'Cognitive change and participation in a sensitivity-training laboratory', *Journal of Consulting Psychology, 30*, 517–20.

Harter, S. (1988) 'Psychotherapy as a reconstructive process: Implications of integrative theories for outcome research', *International Journal of Personal Construct Psychology, 1*, 349–67.

Harter, S., Alexander, P.C., and Neimeyer, R.A. (1988) 'Long-term effects of incestuous child abuse in college women: social adjustment, social cognition, and family characteristics', *Journal of Consulting and Clinical Psychology, 56*, 5–8.

Harter, S., Neimeyer, R.A., and Alexander, P.C. (1989) 'Personal construction of family relationship: the relation of commonality and sociality to family satisfaction for parents and adolescents', *International Journal of Personal Construct Psychology, 2*, 123–42.

Harvey, J.H. (1989) 'People's naive understandings of their close relationships: attitudinal and personal construct perspectives', *International Journal of Personal Construct Psychology, 2*, 37–48.

Hasenyager, P. (1975) 'The Relationship between Neutral Responses on the Role Construct Repertory Test versus the Extremity Rating Scale', unpublished MS, University of Nebraska.

Hass, L. (1974) 'Personal Construct Systems and Theological Conservatism: A Study of Conservative Lutheran Pastors', unpublished PhD thesis, University of Nebraska.

Hayden, B. (1979) 'The self and possibilities for change', *Journal of Personality, 47*, 546–56.

Hayden, B.C. (1982) 'Experience – a case for possible change: the modulation corollary' in J.C. Mancuso and J.R. Adams-Webber (eds.), *The Construing Person*, Praeger, New York.

Hayden, B., Nasby, W., and Davids, A. (1977) 'Interpersonal conceptual structures, predictive accuracy and social adjustment of emotionally disturbed boys', *Journal of Abnormal Psychology, 86*, 315–20.

Hayhow, R. (1987) 'Personal construct therapy with children who stutter and their families' in C. Levy (ed.), *Stuttering Therapies: Practical Approaches*, Croom Helm, London.

Hayhow, R., Lansdown, R., Maddick, J., and Ravenette, T. (1988) 'PCP and children' in F. Fransella and L. Thomas (eds.), *Experimenting with Personal Construct Psychology*, Routledge & Kegan Paul, London.

Hayhow, R. and Levy, C. (1989) *Working with Stuttering: A Personal Construct Approach*, Winslow Press, Bicester, Oxon.

Haynes, E.T. and Phillips, J.P.N. (1973a) 'Inconsistency, loose construing and schizophrenic thought disorder', *British Journal of Psychiatry, 123*, 209–17.

Haynes, E.T. and Phillips, J.P.N. (1973b) 'Schizophrenic thought disorder, loose construing, personal construct theory and scientific research', *British Journal of Social and Clinical Psychology, 12*, 323–4.

Haynes, E.T. and Phillips, J.P.N. (1973c) 'A rejoinder', *British Journal of Social and Clinical Psychology, 12*, 325.

Heather, B.B., McPherson, F.M., and Sprent, P. (1978) 'The analysis of interactions in experiments on the specificity of schizophrenic thought disorder: a reply to Phillips', *British Journal of Social and Clinical Psychology, 17*, 379–82.

Heather, N. (1976) 'The specificity of schizophrenic thought disorder: a replication and extension of previous findings', *British Journal of Social and Clinical Psychology, 15*, 131–7.

Heather, N. (1979) 'The structure of delinquent values: a repertory grid investigation', *British Journal of Social and Clinical Psychology, 18*, 263–75.

Heather, N., Edwards, S., and Hore, B.D. (1975) 'Changes in construing and outcome of group therapy for alcoholism', *Journal of Studies of Alcohol, 36*, 1238–53.

Heather, N., Rollnick, S., and Winton, M. (1982) 'Psychological change among in-patient alcoholics and its relationship to treatment outcome', *British Journal of Alcohol and Alcoholism, 17*, 90–7.

Heesacker, R.S. and Neimeyer, G.J. (1989) 'Assessing Object Relations and Social Cognitive Correlates of Eating Disorder', unpublished MS, University of Florida.

Heidegger, M. (1949) *Existence and Being*, Henry Regnery, Chicago.

Heider, F. (1946) 'Attitudes and cognitive organisation', *Journal of Psychology, 2*, 107–12.

Heisenberg, W. (1963) *Physics and Philosophy*, Allen & Unwin, London.

Hemsley, D.R. (1976) 'Problems in the interpretation of cognitive abnormalities in schizophrenia', *British Journal of Psychiatry, 129*, 32–5.

Hendon, M.K. and Epting, F.R. (1989) 'A comparison of hospice patients with other recovering and ill patients', *Death Studies, 13*, 567–78.

Henry, W.E. and Shlien, J.M. (1958) 'Affective complexity and psychotherapy: some comparisons of time-limited and unlimited treatment', *Journal of Projective Techniques,* *22,* 153–62.

Hersen, M. and Bellack, A.S. (eds.) (1981) *Behavioral Assessment: A Practical Handbook,* Pergamon, New York.

Hewstone, M., Hooper, D., and Miller, K. (1981) 'Psychological change in neurotic depression', *British Journal of Psychiatry, 139,* 47–51.

Heyman, R., Shaw, M.P., and Harding, J. (1983) 'A personal construct theory approach to the socialization of nursing trainees in two British general hospitals', *Journal of Advanced Nursing, 8,* 59–67.

Hicks, C. and Nixon, S. (1989) 'The use of a modified repertory grid technique for assessing the self-concept of children in Local Authority foster care', *British Journal of Social Work, 19,* 203–16.

Higginbotham, P.G. and Bannister, D. (1983) *The GAB Computer Program for the Analysis of Repertory Grid Data,* High Royds Hospital, Menston, W. Yorkshire.

Higgins, K. and Schwarz, J.C. (1976) 'Use of reinforcement to produce loose construing: differential effects for schizotypic and non-schizotypic normals', *Psychological Reports, 38,* 799–806.

Higgins, K. and Sherman, M. (1978) 'The effect of motivation on loose thinking in schizophrenics as measured by the Bannister-Fransella grid test', *Journal of Clinical Psychology, 34,* 624–8.

Hill, E.A. (1988) 'Understanding the disoriented senior as a personal scientist' in F. Fransella and L. Thomas (eds.), *Experimenting with Personal Construct Psychology,* Routledge & Kegan Paul, London.

Hinkle, D. (1965) 'The Change of Personal Constructs from the Viewpoint of a Theory of Construct Implications', unpublished PhD thesis, Ohio State University.

Hoaglands, A. (1984) 'Bereavement and personal constructs: old theories and new concepts' in F. Epting and R.A. Neimeyer (eds.), *Personal Meanings of Death: Applications of Personal Construct Theory to Clinical Practice,* Hemisphere, London.

Holland, R. (1970) 'George Kelly: constructive innocent and reluctant existentialist' in D. Bannister (ed.), *Perspectives in Personal Construct Theory,* Academic Press, London.

Hollon, T.H. and Zolik, E.S. (1962) 'Self-esteem and symptomatic complaints in the initial phase of psychoanalytically oriented therapy', *American Journal of Psychotherapy, 16,* 83–93.

Holmes, J. (1982) 'Phobia and counterphobia: family aspects of agoraphobia', *Journal of Family Therapy, 4,* 137–52.

Honess, T. (1976) 'Cognitive complexity and social prediction', *British Journal of Social and Clinical Psychology, 15,* 23–31.

Honess, T. (1978) 'A comparison of the implication and repertory grid techniques', *British Journal of Psychology, 69,* 305–14.

Honess, T. (1979) 'Children's implicit theories of their peers: a developmental analysis', *British Journal of Psychology, 70,* 417–24.

Honess, T. (1982) 'Accounting for oneself: meanings of self-descriptions and inconsistencies in self-descriptions', *British Journal of Medical Psychology, 55,* 41–52.

Horley, J. (1988) 'Cognitions of child sexual abusers', *Journal of Sex Research, 25,* 542–5.

Houben, M-.E. and Pierloot, R.A. (1970) 'Possibilities and limitations of Kelly's grid technique in the differentiation of transference towards therapeutical figures', *Psychotherapy and Psychosomatics, 18,* 61–6.

Howard, G.S. (1988) 'Kelly's thought at age 33: suggestions for conceptual and methodological refinements', *International Journal of Personal Construct Psychology, 1,* 263–72.

Howells, K. (1978) 'The meaning of poisoning to a person diagnosed as a psychopath', *Medicine, Science and the Law, 8,* 179–84.

Howells, K. (1979) 'Some meanings of children for pedophiles' in M. Cook and G. Wilson (eds.), *Love and Attraction*, Pergamon, Oxford.

Howells, K. (1983) 'Social construing and violent behavior in mentally abnormal offenders' in J.W. Hinton (ed.), *Dangerousness: Problems of Assessment and Prediction*, Allen & Unwin, London.

Hoy, R.M. (1973) 'The meaning of alcoholism for alcoholics: a repertory grid study', *British Journal of Social and Clinical Psychology, 12*, 98–9.

Hoy, R.M. (1977) 'Some findings concerning beliefs about alcoholism', *British Journal of Medical Psychology, 50*, 227–35.

Huber, J.W. and Altmaier, E.M. (1983) 'An investigation of the self-statement systems of phobic and nonphobic individuals', *Cognitive Therapy and Research, 7*, 355–62.

Hudson, L. (1970) *Frames of Mind*, Penguin, Harmondsworth.

Hudson, R. (1974) 'Images of the retailing environment: an example of the use of the repertory grid methodology', *Environmental Behavior, 6*, 470–94.

Hunt, D.E. (1951) 'Studies in Role Concept Repertory: Conceptual Consistency', unpublished MA thesis, Ohio State University.

Husserl, E. (1952) *Ideas*, Collier, New York.

ICARUS (1989) *Correlation-Test: Version 1.00*, ICARUS EDV, Schifferstadt.

Ingram, B.J. and Leitner, L.M. (1989) 'Death threat, religiosity, and fear of death: a repertory grid investigation', *International Journal of Personal Construct Psychology, 2*, 199–214.

Irwin, M., Tripodi, T., and Bieri, J. (1967) 'Affective stimulus value and cognitive complexity', *Journal of Personality and Social Psychology, 5*, 444–8.

Isaacson, G.S. (1966) 'A Comparative Study of the Meaningfulness of Personal and Common Constructs', unpublished PhD thesis, University of Missouri.

Isaacson, G.S. and Landfield, A.W. (1965) 'Meaningfulness of personal versus common constructs', *Journal of Individual Psychology, 21*, 160–6.

Iscoe, I. and Veldman, D.J. (1963) 'Perception of an emotional continuum by schizophrenics, normal adults and children', *Journal of Clinical Psychology, 19*, 272–6.

Jackson, S. (1990a) 'A self-characterisation: development and deviance in adolescent construing' in P. Maitland (ed.), *Personal Construct Theory Deviancy and Social Work*, Inner London Probation Service/Centre for Personal Construct Psychology, London.

Jackson, S. (1990b) 'A PCT therapy group for adolescents' in P. Maitland (ed.), *Personal Construct Theory Deviancy and Social Work*, Inner London Probation Service/Centre for Personal Construct Psychology, London.

Jackson, S.R. and Bannister, D. (1985) 'Growing into self' in D. Bannister (ed.), *Issues and Approaches in Personal Construct Theory*, Academic Press, London.

Jackson, W. and Carr, A.C. (1955) 'Empathic ability in normals and schizophrenics', *Journal of Abnormal Psychology, 51*, 79–82.

Jacobson, N.S. (1977) 'Training couples to solve marital problems: a behavioral approach to marital discord. Part I. Problem solving skills', *International Journal of Family Counseling, 5*, 22–31.

Jahoda, M. (1988) 'The range of convenience of personal construct psychology – an outsider's view' in F. Fransella and L. Thomas (eds.), *Experimenting with Personal Construct Psychology*, Routledge & Kegan Paul, London.

Jankowicz, A.Z.D. and Cooper, K. (1982) 'The use of focussed repertory grids in counselling', *British Journal of Guidance and Counselling, 10*, 136–50.

Jasnau, K.F. (1967) 'Individualized versus mass transfer of non psychotic geriatric patients from mental hospitals to nursing homes, with special reference to their death rate', *Journal of the American Geriatric Society, 15*, 280–4.

Jaspars, J.M.F. (1963) 'Individual cognitive structure' in *Proceedings of 17th International Congress on Psychology*, Washington, DC.

Joensen, E., Lund, Y., and Richardt, C. (1977) 'A comparison between the Grid Test of Schizophrenic Thought Disorder and diagnostic psychological testing', *Scandinavian Journal of Psychology, 18*, 153–6.

Jones, E.E. and Nisbett, R.E. (1972) 'The actor and the observer' in E.E. Jones, D.E. Kanhouse, H.H. Kelley, R.E. Nisbett, S. Valins, and B. Weiner (eds.), *Attribution: Perceiving the Causes of Behavior*, G.L.P., New Jersey.

Jones, H. (1985) 'Creativity and depression: an idiographic study' in F. Epting and A.W. Landfield (eds.), *Anticipating Personal Construct Psychology*, University of Nebraska Press, Lincoln.

Jones, H. (1988) 'Personal Construct Psychology and counselling: a personal view' in G. Dunnett (ed.), *Working with People: Clinical Uses of Personal Construct Psychology*, Routledge, London.

Jones, R.E. (1954) 'Identification in terms of Personal Constructs', unpublished PhD thesis, Ohio State University.

Jonsson, C-.O. and Sjöstedt, A. (1973) 'Auditory perception in schizophrenia: a second study of the intonation test', *Acta Psychiatrica Scandinavica, 49*, 588–600.

Kagen, N. (1972) *Influencing Human Interaction*, Michigan State University, East Lansing.

Kahgee, S.L., Pomeroy, E., and Miller, H.R. (1982) 'Interpersonal judgements of schizophrenics: a golden section study', *British Journal of Medical Psychology, 55*, 319–26.

Kantor, D. (1985) 'Couples therapy, crisis induction, and change' in A.S. Gurman (ed.), *Casebook of Marital Therapy*, Guilford, New York.

Karastergiou-Katsika, A. and Watson, J.P. (1982) 'A new approach to construct elicitation for a grid test', *British Journal of Clinical Psychology, 21*, 67–8.

Karastergiou-Katsika, A. and Watson, J.P. (1985) 'A comparative study of repertory grid and clinical methods for assessing family structure', *Journal of Family Therapy, 7*, 231–50.

Karst, T.O. (1980) 'The relationship between personal construct theory and psychotherapeutic techniques' in A.W. Landfield and L.M. Leitner (eds.), *Personal Construct Psychology: Psychotherapy and Personality*, Wiley, New York.

Karst, T.O. and Trexler, L.D. (1970) 'Initial study using fixed role and rational-emotive therapy in treating speaking anxiety', *Journal of Consulting and Clinical Psychology, 34*, 360–6.

Kasper, S. (1962) 'Measurement of adjustment in adolescents: an extension of personal construct theory and methodology', *Psychological Monographs, 76*, 1–32.

Katz, J.O. (1984) 'Personal Construct Theory and the emotions: an interpretation in terms of primitive constructs', *British Journal of Psychology, 75*, 315–27.

Kear-Colwell, J.J. (1973) 'Bannister-Fransella grid performance: relationships with personality and intelligence', *British Journal of Social and Clinical Psychology, 12*, 78–82.

Keen, T.R. (1977) 'TARGET – teaching appraisal by repertory grid techniques', paper presented at 2nd International Congress on Personal Construct Psychology, Oxford.

Keeney, B.P. (1979) 'Ecosystemic epistemology: an alternative paradigm for diagnosis', *Family Process, 18*, 117–29.

Keeney, B.P. and Sprenkle, D.H. (1982) 'Ecosystemic epistemology: critical implications for the aesthetics and pragmatics of family therapy', *Family Process, 21*, 1–19.

Kelly, D. (1990) 'A personal construct psychology perspective on deviance' in P. Maitland (ed.), *Personal Construct Theory Deviancy and Social Work*, Inner London Probation Service/Centre for Personal Construct Psychology, London.

Kelly, D. and Taylor, H. (1981) 'Take and escape: a personal construct study of car "theft"' in H. Bonarius, R. Holland, and S. Rosenberg (eds.), *Personal Construct Psychology: Recent Advances in Theory and Practice*, Macmillan, London.

Kelly, G.A. (1955) *The Psychology of Personal Constructs*, Norton, New York.

Kelly, G.A. (1961) 'Theory and therapy in suicide: the personal construct point of view' in M. Farberow and E. Shneidman (eds.), *The Cry for Help*, McGraw-Hill, New York.

Kelly, G.A. (1963a) 'Nonparametric factor analysis of personality theories', *Journal of Individual Psychology, 19*, 115–47.

Kelly, G.A. (1963b) 'Look who's talking', *Contemporary Psychology, 8*, 189–90.

Kelly, G.A. (1964) 'The language of hypothesis: man's psychological instrument', *Journal of Individual Psychology, 20*, 137–52.

Kelly, G.A. (1969a) 'Personal construct theory and the psychotherapeutic interview' in B. Maher (ed.), *Clinical Psychology and Personality: The Selected Papers of George Kelly*, Wiley, New York.

Kelly, G.A. (1969b) 'Sin and psychotherapy' in B. Maher (ed.), *Clinical Psychology and Personality: The Selected Papers of George Kelly*, Wiley, New York.

Kelly, G.A. (1969c) 'In whom confide: on whom depend for what?' in B. Maher (ed.), *Clinical Psychology and Personality: The Selected Papers of George Kelly*, Wiley, New York.

Kelly, G.A. (1969d) 'The autobiography of a theory' in B. Maher (ed.), *Clinical Psychology and Personality: The Selected Papers of George Kelly*, Wiley, New York.

Kelly, G.A. (1969e) 'The strategy of psychological research' in B. Maher (ed.), *Clinical Psychology and Personality: The Selected Papers of George Kelly*, Wiley, New York.

Kelly, G.A. (1969f) 'The psychotherapeutic relationship' in B. Maher (ed.), *Clinical Psychology and Personality: The Selected Papers of George Kelly*, Wiley, New York.

Kelly, G.A. (1969g) 'Ontological acceleration' in B. Maher (ed.), *Clinical Psychology and Personality: The Selected Papers of George Kelly*, Wiley, New York.

Kelly, G.A. (1969h) 'Humanistic methodology in psychological research' in B. Maher (ed.), *Clinical Psychology and Personality: The Selected Papers of George Kelly*, Wiley, New York.

Kelly, G.A. (1969i) 'Man's construction of his alternatives' in B. Maher (ed.), *Clinical Psychology and Personality: The Selected Papers of George Kelly*, Wiley, New York.

Kelly, G.A. (1969j) 'Hostility' in B. Maher (ed.), *Clinical Psychology and Personality: The Selected Papers of George Kelly*, Wiley, New York.

Kelly, G.A. (1969k) 'The threat of aggression' in B. Maher (ed.), *Clinical Psychology and Personality: The Selected Papers of George Kelly*, Wiley, New York.

Kelly, G.A. (1970a) 'A brief introduction to personal construct theory' in D. Bannister (ed.), *Perspectives in Personal Construct Theory*, Academic Press, London.

Kelly, G.A. (1970b) 'Behaviour is an experiment' in D. Bannister (ed.), *Perspectives in Personal Construct Theory*, Academic Press, London.

Kelly, G.A. (1973) 'Fixed role therapy' in R.M. Jejevich (ed.), *Direct Psychotherapy: 28 American Originals*, University of Miami Press, Coral Gables.

Kelly, G.A. (1977) 'The psychology of the unknown' in D. Bannister (ed.), *New Perspectives in Personal Construct Theory*, Academic Press, London.

Kelly, G.A. (1980) 'A psychology of the optimal man' in A.W. Landfield and L.M. Leitner (eds.), *Personal Construct Psychology: Psychotherapy and Personality*, Wiley, New York.

Kelsall, P.N. and Strongman, K.T. (1978) 'Emotional experience and the implication grid', *British Journal of Medical Psychology, 51*, 243–52.

Kennard, D. (1974) 'The newly admitted psychiatric patient as seen by self and others', *British Journal of Medical Psychology, 47*, 27–41.

Kennard, D. and Clemmey, R. (1976) 'Psychiatric patients as seen by self and others: an exploration of change in a therapeutic community setting', *British Journal of Medical Psychology, 49*, 35–54.

Kenny, V. (1987) 'Family somatics: a personal construct approach to cancer' in R.A.

Neimeyer and G.J. Neimeyer (eds.), *Personal Construct Therapy Casebook*, Springer, New York.

Kenny, V. (1988a) 'Changing conversations: a constructivist model of training for psychotherapists' in G. Dunnett (ed.), *Working with People: Clinical Uses of Personal Construct Psychology*, Routledge, London.

Kenny, V. (1988b) 'Autopoiesis and alternativism in psychotherapy: fluctuations and reconstructions' in F. Fransella and L. Thomas (eds.), *Experimenting with Personal Construct Psychology*, Routledge & Kegan Paul, London.

Kenny, V. (1989) 'Kelly and systems', paper presented at 8th International Congress on Personal Construct Psychology, Assisi.

Kerrick-Mack, J. (1978) 'The role construct repertory grid as a process for facilitating self-awareness and personal growth' in F. Fransella (ed.), *Personal Construct Psychology 1977*, Academic Press, London.

Kieferle, D.A. and Sechrest, L.B. (1961), 'Effects of alterations in personal constructs', *Journal of Psychological Studies, 12*, 173–8.

Kierkegaard, S. (1941) *Concluding Unscientific Postscripts*, Princeton University Press, Princeton.

Kiesler, D.J. (1966) 'Some myths of psychotherapy research and the search for a paradigm', *Psychological Bulletin, 65*, 110–36.

Kiesler, D.J. (1982) 'Interpersonal theory for personality and psychotherapy' in J.C. Anchin and D.J. Kiesler (eds.), *Handbook of Interpersonal Psychotherapy*, Pergamon, New York.

Kirk, J.W. (1984) 'Psychological construing and meaningfulness in schizophrenia', *British Journal of Medical Psychology, 57*, 153–8.

Kirkland, J., Johns, D., Lambourne, R., and Black, S. (1986) 'Picgrids as a technique for investigating parent–infant interaction', *Early Child Development, 24*, 1–15.

Klass, E.T. (1980) 'Cognitive appraisal of transgression among sociopaths and normals', *Cognitive Therapy and Research, 4*, 353–67.

Klein, M.H., Greist, J.H., Gurman, A.S., Neimeyer, R.A., Lesser, D.P., Bushnell, N.J., and Smith, R.E. (1985) 'A comparative outcome study of group psychotherapy vs. exercise treatments for depression', *International Journal of Mental Health, 13*, 148–77.

Kline, P. (1981) *Fact and Fantasy in Freudian Theory*, Methuen, London.

Klion, R.E. (1985) 'The construing of schizophrenic and non-schizophrenic psychiatric in-patients', paper presented at 6th International Congress on Personal Construct Psychology, Cambridge.

Klion, R.E. (1988) 'Construct system organization and schizophrenia: the role of construct integration', *Journal of Social and Clinical Psychology, 6*, 439–47.

Knowles, J.B. and Purves, C. (1965) 'The use of repertory grid technique to assess the influence of the experimenter–subject relationship in verbal conditioning', *Bulletin of The British Psychological Society, 18*, 23A.

Koch, H.C.H. (1983a) 'Correlates of changes in personal construing of members of two psychotherapy groups: changes in affective expression', *British Journal of Medical Psychology, 56*, 323–8.

Koch, H.C.H. (1983b) 'Changes in personal construing in three psychotherapy groups and a control group', *British Journal of Medical Psychology, 56*, 245–54.

Koch, H.C.H. (1985) 'Group psychotherapy' in E. Button (ed.), *Personal Construct Theory and Mental Health*, Croom Helm, London.

Koh, S.D., Grinker, R.R., Marusarz, T.Z., and Forman, P.L. (1981) 'Affective memory and schizophrenic anhedonia', *Schizophrenia Bulletin, 7*, 292–307.

Koh, S.D., Kayton, L., and Peterson, R.A. (1976) 'Affective encoding and consequent remembering in schizophrenic young adults', *Journal of Abnormal Psychology, 85*, 56–66.

Koltuv, B.B. (1962) 'Some characteristics of intrajudge trait intercorrelations', *Psychological Monographs, 76*, 552.

Koocher, G.P. and Simmonds, D.W. (1971) 'The animal and opposite drawing technique: implications for personality assessment', *International Journal of Symbology, 2*, 9–12.

Kremsdorf, R. (1985) 'An extension of fixed-role therapy with a couple' in F. Epting and A.W. Landfield (eds.), *Anticipating Personal Construct Psychology*, University of Nebraska Press, Lincoln.

Krieger, S.R., Epting, F.R., and Leitner, L.M. (1974) 'Personal constructs, threat, and attitudes towards death', *Omega, 5*, 229–310.

Krieger, S.R., Epting, F.R., and Hays, C.H. (1979) 'Validity and reliability of provided constructs in assessing death threat: a self-administered form', *Omega, 10*, 87–95.

Kuiper, N.A. and Derry, P.A. (1981) 'The self as a cognitive prototype: an application to person perception and depression' in N. Cantor and J.F. Kihlstrom (eds.), *Personality, Cognition and Social Interaction*, Erlbaum, Hillsdale, NJ.

Kuusinen, J. and Nystedt, L. (1975a) 'Individual versus provided constructs, cognitive complexity and extremity of ratings in person perception', *Scandinavian Journal of Psychology, 16*, 137–48.

Kuusinen, J. and Nystedt, L. (1975b) 'The convergent validity of four indices of cognitive complexity in person perception', *Scandinavian Journal of Psychology, 16*, 131–6.

Lacan, J. (1977) *The Four Fundamental Concepts of Psychoanalysis*, Norton, New York.

Laing, R.D., Phillipson, H., and Lee, A.R. (1966) *Interpersonal Perception*, Tavistock, London.

Landau, R.J. (1980) 'The role of semantic schemata in phobic word interpretation', *Cognitive Therapy and Research, 4*, 427–34.

Landfield, A.W. (1954) 'A movement interpretation of threat', *Journal of Abnormal and Social Psychology, 49*, 529–32.

Landfield, A.W. (1955) 'Self predictive orientation and the movement interpretation of threat', *Journal of Abnormal and Social Psychology, 51*, 434–8.

Landfield, A.W. (1965) 'Meaningfulness of self, ideal, and other as related to own versus therapist's personal construct dimensions', *Psychological Reports, 16*, 605–8.

Landfield, A.W. (1970) 'High priests, reflexivity and congruency of client-therapist Personal Construct systems', *British Journal of Medical Psychology, 43*, 207–12.

Landfield, A.W. (1971) *Personal Construct Systems in Psychotherapy*, University of Nebraska Press, Lincoln.

Landfield, A.W. (1975) 'The complaint: a confrontation of personal urgency and professional construction' in D. Bannister (ed.), *Issues and Approaches in the Psychological Therapies*, Wiley, London.

Landfield, A. (1976) 'A personal construct approach to suicidal behaviour' in P. Slater (ed.), *The Measurement of Intrapersonal Space by Grid Technique. Vol.1. Explorations of Intrapersonal Space*, Wiley, London.

Landfield, A.W. (1977) 'Interpretive man: the enlarged self-image' in J.K. Cole and A.W. Landfield (eds.), *1976 Nebraska Symposium on Motivation*, University of Nebraska Press, Lincoln.

Landfield, A.W. (1979) 'Exploring socialisation through the Interpersonal Transaction Group' in P. Stringer and D. Bannister (eds.), *Constructs of Sociality and Individuality*, Academic Press, London.

Landfield, A.W. (1980a) 'The person as perspectivist, literalist, and chaotic fragmentalist' in A.W. Landfield and L.M. Leitner (eds.), *Personal Construct Psychology: Psychotherapy and Personality*, Wiley, New York.

Landfield, A.W. (1980b) 'Personal construct psychotherapy: a personal construction' in A.W. Landfield and L.M. Leitner (eds.), *Personal Construct Psychology: Psychotherapy and Personality*, Wiley, New York.

Landfield, A.W. (1988) 'Personal science and the concept of validation', *International Journal of Personal Construct Psychology, 1*, 237–49.

Landfield, A.W. and Cannell, J. (1988) 'Ways of assessing functionally independent construction, meaningfulness, and construction in hierarchy' in J. Mancuso and M. Shaw (eds.), *Cognition and Personal Structure*, Praeger, New York.

Landfield, A.W. and Epting, F.R. (1987) *Personal Construct Psychology: Clinical and Personality Assessment*, Human Sciences Press, New York.

Landfield, A.W. and Nawas, M.M. (1964) 'Psychotherapeutic improvement as a function of communication and adoption of therapist's values', *Journal of Counseling Psychology, 11*, 336–41.

Landfield, A.W. and Rivers, P.C. (1975) 'An introduction to interpersonal transaction and rotating dyads', *Psychotherapy: Theory, Research, and Practice, 12*, 366–74.

Landfield, A.W. and Schmittdiel, C.J. (1983) 'The Interpersonal Transaction Group: Evolving measurements in the pursuit of theory' in J. Adams-Webber and J.C. Mancuso, *Applications of Personal Construct Theory*, Academic Press, Toronto.

Landfield, A.W., Stern, M., and Fjeld, S. (1961) 'Social conceptual processes and change in students undergoing psychotherapy', *Psychological Reports, 8*, 63–8.

Lansdown, R. (1975) 'A reliability study of the 8 × 8 repertory grid', *Journal of the Association of Educational Psychologists, 3*, 24–5.

Large, R.G. (1976) 'The use of the role construct repertory grid in studying changes during psychotherapy', *Australian and New Zealand Journal of Psychiatry, 10*, 315–20.

Large, R.G. (1985) 'Prediction of treatment response in pain patients: the Illness Self-Concept Repertory Grid and EMG feedback', *Pain, 21*, 279–87.

Lawlor, M. and Cochran, L. (1981) 'Does invalidation produce loose construing?', *British Journal of Medical Psychology, 54*, 41–50.

Lazarus, A.A. (1967) 'In support of technical eclecticism', *Psychological Reports, 21*, 415–16.

Lazarus, A.A. (1980) 'Psychological treatment of dyspareunia' in S.R. Leiblum and L.A. Pervin (eds.), *Principles and Practice of Sex Therapy*, Tavistock, London.

Leenaars, A. (1981) 'Drugs and people: repertory grid structure and the construal of two different types of targets', *Journal of Clinical Psychology, 37*, 198–201.

Leenaars, A.A. and Balance, W.D.G. (1984) 'A logical empirical approach to the study of suicide rates', *Canadian Journal of Behavioral Science, 16*, 249–56.

Lefebvre, V.A., Lefebvre, V.D., and Adams-Webber, J. (1986) 'Modeling in experiment on construing self and others', *Journal of Mathematical Psychology, 30*, 317–30.

Leff, J. (1973) 'Culture and the differentiation of emotional states', *British Journal of Psychiatry, 123*, 299–306.

Leff, J. (1977) 'The cross-cultural study of emotions', *Culture, Medicine and Psychiatry, 1*, 317–50.

Leff, J.P. (1978) 'Psychiatrists' versus patients' concepts of unpleasant emotions', *British Journal of Psychiatry, 133*, 306–13.

Leff, J. (1986) 'The epidemiology of mental illness across cultures' in J.L. Cox (ed.), *Transcultural Psychiatry*, Croom Helm, London.

Leff, J.P. and Abberton, E. (1981) 'Voice pitch measurements in schizophrenia and depression', *Psychological Medicine, 11*, 849–52.

Leff, J., Kuipers, L., Berkowitz, R., Eberlein-Kies, R., and Sturgeon, D. (1982) 'A controlled trial of social intervention in the families of schizophrenic patients', *British Journal of Psychiatry, 141*, 121–34.

Lehrer, R. (1987) 'Characters in search of an author: the self as a narrative structure' in J. Mancuso and M. Shaw (eds.), *Cognition and Personal Structure*, Praeger, New York.

Leitner, L.M. (1980) 'Personal construct treatment of a severely disturbed woman: the case of Sue' in A.W. Landfield and L.M. Leitner (eds.), *Personal Construct Psychology: Psychotherapy and Personality*, Wiley, New York.

Leitner, L.M. (1981a) 'Psychopathology and the differentiation of values, emotions, and behaviours: a repertory grid study', *British Journal of Psychiatry, 138*, 147–53.

Leitner, L.M. (1981b) 'Construct validity of a repertory grid measure of personality styles', *Journal of Personality Assessment, 45*, 539–44.

Leitner, L.M. (1982) 'Literalism, perspectivism, chaotic fragmentalism and psychotherapy techniques', *British Journal of Medical Psychology, 55*, 307–18.

Leitner, L.M. (1985a) 'Interview methodologies for construct elicitation: searching for the core' in F. Epting and A.W. Landfield (eds.), *Anticipating Personal Construct Psychology*, University of Nebraska Press, Lincoln.

Leitner, L.M. (1985b) 'The terrors of cognition: on the experiential validity of personal construct theory' in D. Bannister (ed.), *Issues and Approaches in Personal Construct Theory*, Academic Press, London.

Leitner, L.M. (1987) 'Crisis of the self: the terror of personal evolution' in R.A. Neimeyer and G.J. Neimeyer (eds.), *Personal Construct Therapy Casebook*, Springer, New York.

Leitner, L.M. (1988a) 'Contextual shifts in interpersonal constructions' in F. Fransella and L. Thomas (eds.), *Experimenting with Personal Construct Psychology*, Routledge & Kegan Paul, London.

Leitner, L.M. (1988b) 'Terror, risk, and reverence: experiential personal construct psychotherapy', *International Journal of Personal Construct Psychology, 1*, 299–310.

Leitner, L.M. (1989) 'Me Too Iguana: on the relationship between PCP and psychology', paper presented at 8th International Congress on Personal Construct Psychology, Assisi.

Leitner, L.M. and Cado, S. (1982) 'Personal constructs and homosexual stress', *Journal of Personality and Social Psychology, 43*, 869–72.

Leitner, L. and Dunnett, G. (1989) 'Unique contribution of personal construct psychology to counselling and psychotherapy', symposium at 8th International Congress on Personal Construct Psychology, Assisi.

Leitner, L.M. and Grant, C.H. (1982) 'Obesity, personal constructs, and amount of weight loss', *Psychological Reports, 50*, 491–8.

Lemon, N. and Warren, N. (1974) 'Salience, centrality and self-relevance of traits in construing others', *British Journal of Social and Clinical Psychology, 13*, 119–24.

Lester, D. (1968) 'Attempted suicide as a hostile act', *Journal of Psychology, 68*, 243–8.

Lester, D. (1969) 'Resentment and dependency in the suicidal individual', *Journal of General Psychology, 81*, 137–45.

Lester, D. (1971) 'Cognitive complexity of the suicidal individual', *Psychological Reports, 28*, 158.

Lester, D. and Collett, L. (1970) 'Fear of death and self–ideal discrepancy', *Archives of the Foundation of Thanatology, 21*, 130.

Leventhal, H. (1957) 'Cognitive processes and interpersonal predictions', *Journal of Abnormal and Social Psychology, 55*, 176–80.

Levy, C. (1983) 'Group therapy with adults' in P. Dalton (ed.), *Approaches to the Treatment of Stuttering*, Croom Helm, London.

Levy, C. (1987) 'Interiorised stuttering: a group therapy approach' in C. Levy (ed.), *Stuttering Therapies: Practical Approaches*, Croom Helm, London.

Levy, L.H. (1956) 'Personal constructs and predictive behaviour', *Journal of Abnormal and Social Psychology, 53*, 54–8.

Levy, S.M.E. (1975) 'Personal construct and existential a priori categories', *Journal of Phenomenological Psychology, 5*, 369–88.

Lewis, M.I. and Butler, R.N. (1974) 'Life review therapy: putting memories to work in individual and group psychotherapy', *Geriatrics, 29,* 165–73.

Li, Chin-Keung (1988) 'PCT interpretation of sexual involvement with children', in F. Fransella and L. Thomas (eds.), *Experimenting with Personal Construct Psychology,* Routledge & Kegan Paul, London.

Li, Chin-Keung (1990) 'Ethics, politics and paedophilia: the relevance of George Kelly' in P. Maitland (ed.), *Personal Construct Theory Deviancy and Social Work,* Inner London Probation Service/Centre for Personal Construct Psychology, London.

Liakos, A., Papacostas, I., and Stefanis, C. (1975) 'A repertory grid investigation of the concept of illness by parents of schizophrenic patients', *British Journal of Psychiatry, 126,* 354–9.

Lidz, T. (1968) 'The family, language, and the transmission of schizophrenia' in D. Rosenthal and S.S. Kety (eds.), *The Transmission of Schizophrenia,* Pergamon, Oxford.

Lieberman, M.A., Yalom, I.D., and Miles, M.B. (1973) *Encounter Groups: First Facts,* Basic Books, New York.

Liebowitz, G.D. (1970) 'Conceptual Systems in Schizogenic Families', unpublished PhD thesis, University of Rochester.

Lifshitz, M. (1974) 'Quality professionals: does training make a difference? A personal construct theory study of the issue', *British Journal of Social and Clinical Psychology, 13,* 183–9.

Lifshitz, M. (1976) 'Long range effects of father's loss: the cognitive complexity of bereaved children and their school adjustment', *British Journal of Medical Psychology, 49,* 189–97.

Liotti, G. and Guidano, V.F. (1976) 'Behavioral analysis of marital interaction in agoraphobic male patients', *Behaviour Research and Therapy, 14,* 161–2.

Lira, F.T., Nay, W.R., McCullough, J.P., and Etkin, W. (1975) 'Relative effects of modeling and role playing in the treatment of avoidance behaviors', *Journal of Consulting and Clinical Psychology, 43,* 608–18.

Little, B.R. (1968) 'Factors affecting the use of psychological versus non-psychological constructs on the Rep. Test', *Bulletin of the British Psychological Society, 21,* 34.

Little, B.R. (1969) 'Sex differences and comparability of three measures of cognitive complexity', *Psychological Reports, 24,* 607–9.

Livesay, J.R. (1980) 'Heightened subjective distress as an indicator of the severity of thought disorder', *Psychological Reports, 46,* 1323–6.

Livesay, J.R. (1981) 'Inconsistent interpersonal judgement in thought-disordered schizophrenia', *Psychological Reports, 49,* 179–82.

Livesay, J.R. (1983) 'Cognitive complexity–simplicity and inconsistent interpersonal judgement in thought disordered schizophrenia as assessed by Bieri's repertory grid', paper presented at 5th International Congress on Personal Construct Psychology, Boston.

Llewelyn, S. and Dunnett, G. (1987) 'The use of personal construct theory in groups' in R.A. Neimeyer and G.J. Neimeyer (eds.), *Personal Construct Therapy Casebook,* Springer, New York.

Lobitz, W.C. and LoPiccolo, J. (1972) 'New methods in the behavioral treatment of sexual dysfunction', *Journal of Behavior Therapy and Experimental Psychiatry, 3,* 265–71.

Lockhart, W.H. (1979) 'Illustrations of the use of self-identity plots to measure change with young offenders', *Journal of Adolescence, 2,* 139–52.

Loos, V.E. and Epstein, E.S. (1989) 'Conversational construction of meaning in family therapy: some evolving thoughts on Kelly's Sociality Corollary', *International Journal of Personal Construct Psychology, 2,* 149–67.

Lopez-Ibor, J.J. (1972) 'Masked depressions', *British Journal of Psychiatry, 120*, 245–58.

Lorenzini, R. and Sassaroli, S. (1987) *La Paura della Paura: un Modello Clinico delle Fobie*, Nuova Italia Scientifica, Rome.

Lorenzini, R. and Sassaroli, S. (1988) 'The construction of change in agoraphobia' in F. Fransella and L. Thomas (eds.), *Experimenting with Personal Construct Psychology*, Routledge & Kegan Paul, London.

Lorenzini, R., Sassaroli, S., and Rocchi, M.T. (1989) 'Schizophrenia and paranoia as solutions to predictive failure', *International Journal of Personal Construct Psychology, 2*, 417–32.

Luborsky, L., Chandler, M., Aurbach, A., and Cohen, J. (1971) 'Factors influencing the outcome of psychotherapy: a review of quantitative research', *Psychological Bulletin, 75*, 145–85.

Luborsky, L., Singer, B., and Luborsky, L. (1975) 'Comparative studies of psychotherapies: is it true that "everybody has won and all must have prizes"?', *Archives of General Psychiatry, 32*, 995–1008.

Lundy, R.N. and Berkowitz, L. (1957) 'Cognitive complexity and assimilative projection in attitude change', *Journal of Abnormal and Social Psychology, 55*, 34–7.

Luria, Z. (1959) 'A semantic analysis of a normal and a neurotic therapy group', *Journal of Abnormal and Social Psychology, 58*, 216–20.

McCartney, J. and O'Donnell, J.P. (1981) 'The perception of drinking roles by recovered problem drinkers', *Psychological Medicine, 11*, 747–54.

McConachie, H. (1985) 'How parents of young mentally handicapped children construe their role' in D. Bannister (ed.), *Issues and Approaches in the Psychological Therapies*, Academic Press, London.

McCoy, M.M. (1977) 'A reconstruction of emotion' in D. Bannister (ed.), *New Perspectives in Personal Construct Theory*, Academic Press, London.

McCoy, M. (1980) 'Culture-shocked marriages' in A.W. Landfield and L.M. Leitner (eds.), *Personal Construct Psychology: Psychotherapy and Personality*, Wiley, New York.

McCoy, M.M. (1981) 'Positive and negative emotion: a personal construct theory interpretation' in H. Bonarius, R. Holland, and S. Rosenberg (eds.), *Personal Construct Psychology: Recent Advances in Theory and Practice*, Macmillan, London.

McCoy, M. (1983) 'Personal construct theory and methodology in intercultural research' in J. Adams-Webber and J.C. Mancuso (eds.), *Applications of Personal Construct Theory*, Academic Press, Toronto.

McDonald, D.E. and Mancuso, J.C. (1987) 'A constructivist approach to parent training' in R.A. Neimeyer and G.J. Neimeyer (eds.), *Personal Construct Therapy Casebook*, Springer, New York.

MacDonald, P.J. (1980) 'Is personal construct theory useful in studying the hearing-impaired?', *Journal of the British Association of Teachers of the Deaf, 4*, 161–7.

McFadyen, M. and Foulds, G.A. (1972) 'Comparison of provided and elicited grid content in the grid test of schizophrenic thought disorder', *British Journal of Psychiatry, 121*, 53–7.

McKain, T.L., Glass, C.R., Arnkoff, D.B., Sydnor-Greenberg, J.M., and Shea, C.A. (1988) 'Personal constructs and shyness: the relationship between Rep Grid data and therapy outcome', *International Journal of Personal Construct Psychology, 1*, 151–67.

MacKenzie, K.R. (1983) 'The clinical application of a group climate measure' in R. Dies and K.R. MacKenzie (eds.), *Advances in Group Psychotherapy: Integrating Research and Practice*, International Universities Press, New York.

McLachlan, J.F. (1972) 'Benefit from group therapy as a function of patient–therapist match on conceptual level', *Psychotherapy: Theory, Research, and Practice, 9*, 317–23.

McLachlan, J.F. (1974) 'Therapy strategies, personality orientation, and recovery from alcoholism', *Canadian Psychiatric Association Journal, 19*, 30–5.

McPherson, F.M. (1969) 'Thought-process disorder, delusions of persecution and "non-integration" in schizophrenia', *British Journal of Medical Psychology, 42*, 55–7.

McPherson, F.M. (1972) '"Psychological" constructs and "psychological" symptoms in schizophrenia', *British Journal of Psychiatry, 120*, 197–8.

McPherson, F.M., Armstrong, J., and Heather, B.B. (1975) 'Psychological construing, "difficulty" and thought disorder', *British Journal of Medical Psychology, 48*, 303–15.

McPherson, F.M., Barden, V., and Buckley, F. (1970a) 'Use of psychological constructs by affectively flattened schizophrenics', *British Journal of Medical Psychology, 43*, 291–3.

McPherson, F., Barden, V., Hay, A.J., Johnstone, D.W., and Kushner, A.W. (1970b) 'Flattening of affect and personal constructs', *British Journal of Psychiatry, 116*, 39–43.

McPherson, F.M., Blackburn, I.M., Draffan, J.W., and McFadyen, M. (1973) 'A further study of the Grid Test of Thought Disorder', *British Journal of Social and Clinical Psychology, 12*, 420–7.

McPherson, F. and Buckley, F. (1970) 'Thought-process disorder and personal construct subsystems', *British Journal of Social and Clinical Psychology, 9*, 380–1.

McPherson, F., Buckley, F., and Draffan, J. (1971a) 'Psychological constructs, thought-process disorder, and flattening of affect', *British Journal of Social and Clinical Psychology, 10*, 267–70.

McPherson, F., Buckley, F., and Draffan, J. (1971b) '"Psychological" constructs and delusions of persecution and "non-integration" in schizophrenia', *British Journal of Medical Psychology, 44*, 277–80.

McPherson, F.M. and Gray, A. (1976) 'Psychological construing and psychological symptoms', *British Journal of Medical Psychology, 49*, 73–9.

McPherson, F.M. and Walton, H.J. (1970) 'The dimensions of psychotherapy group interaction: an analysis of clinicians' constructs', *British Journal of Medical Psychology, 43*, 281–90.

McWilliams, S.A. (1988) 'On becoming a personal anarchist' in F. Fransella and L. Thomas (eds.), *Experimenting with Personal Construct Psychology*, Routledge & Kegan Paul, London.

Mahoney, M.J. (1979) 'A critical analysis of rational-emotive theory and therapy' in A. Ellis and J.M. Whitely (eds.), *Theoretical and Empirical Foundations of Rational-Emotive Therapy*, Brooks/Cole, Monterey.

Mahoney, M.J. (1988a) 'Constructive metatheory: I. Basic features and historical foundations', *International Journal of Personal Construct Psychology, 1*, 1–35.

Mahoney, M.J. (1988b) 'Constructive metatheory: II. Implications for psychotherapy', *International Journal of Personal Construct Psychology, 1*, 299–315.

Mahoney, M. and Arnkoff, D. (1978) 'Cognitive and self-control therapies' in S. Garfield and A. Bergin (eds.), *Handbook of Psychotherapy and Behavior Change* (3rd edition), Wiley, New York.

Mair, J.M.M. (1964a) 'The concepts of reliability and validity in relation to construct theory and repertory grid technique' in N. Warren (ed.), *Brunel Construct Theory Seminar Report*, Brunel University, Uxbridge.

Mair, J.M.M. (1964b) 'The derivation, reliability and validity of grid measures: some problems and suggestions', *Bulletin of the British Psychological Society, 17*, 55.

Mair, J.M.M. (1966) 'Prediction of grid scores', *British Journal of Psychology, 57*, 187–92.

Mair, J.M.M. (1967a) 'Some problems in repertory grid measurement: I. The use of bipolar constructs', *British Journal of Psychology, 58*, 261–70.

Mair, J.M.M. (1967b) 'Some problems in repertory grid measurement: II. The use of whole figure constructs', *British Journal of Psychology, 58*, 271–82.

Mair, J.M.M. (1970a) 'Experimenting with individuals', *British Journal of Medical Psychology, 43*, 245–56.

Mair, J.M.M. (1970b) 'The person in psychology and psychotherapy: an introduction', *British Journal of Medical Psychology, 43*, 197–205.

Mair, M. (1977a) 'Metaphors for living' in J.K. Cole and A.W. Landfield (eds.), *1976 Nebraska Symposium on Motivation*, University of Nebraska Press, Lincoln.

Mair, J.M.M. (1977b) 'The community of self' in D. Bannister (ed.), *New Perspectives in Personal Construct Theory*, Academic Press, London.

Mair, M. (1979) 'The personal venture' in P. Stringer and D. Bannister (eds.), *Constructs of Sociality and Individuality*, Academic Press, London.

Mair, M. (1988) 'Psychology as storytelling', *International Journal of Personal Construct Psychology, 1*, 125–37.

Mair, M. (1989a) *Between Psychology and Psychotherapy: a poetics of experience*, Routledge, London.

Mair, M. (1989b) 'Kelly, Bannister, and a story-telling psychology', *International Journal of Personal Construct Psychology, 2*, 1–14.

Mair, J.M.M. and Boyd, P. (1967) 'A comparison of two grid forms', *British Journal of Social and Clinical Psychology, 6*, 220.

Mair, J.M. and Crisp, A.H. (1968) 'Estimating psychological organization, meaning and change in relation to clinical practice', *British Journal of Medical Psychology, 4*, 15–29.

Maitland, P. (1990) 'Residents' perceptions of their probation hostel' in P. Maitland (ed.), *Personal Construct Theory Deviancy and Social Work*, Inner London Probation Service/Centre for Personal Construct Psychology, London.

Makhlouf-Norris, F. and Gwynne Jones, H. (1971) 'Conceptual distance indices as measures of alienation in obsessional neurosis', *Psychological Medicine, 1*, 381–7.

Makhlouf-Norris, F., Jones, H.G., and Norris, H. (1970) 'Articulation of the conceptual structure in obsessional neurosis', *British Journal of Social and Clinical Psychology, 9*, 264–74.

Makhlouf-Norris, F. and Norris, H. (1973) 'The obsessive compulsive syndrome as a neurotic device for the reduction of self-uncertainty', *British Journal of Psychiatry, 122*, 277–88.

Mancini, F. and Semerari, A. (1987) 'Temporal becoming and psychopathology: some notes', paper presented at 7th International Congress on Personal Construct Psychology, Memphis.

Mancuso, J.C. (ed.) (1970) *Readings for a Cognitive Theory of Personality*, Holt, Rinehart & Winston, New York.

Mancuso, J.C. (1977) 'Current motivational models in the elaboration of personal construct theory' in J.K. Cole and A.W. Landfield (eds.), *1976 Nebraska Symposium on Motivation*, University of Nebraska Press, Lincoln.

Mancuso, J.C. (1979a) 'Reprimand: the construing of the rule violator's construct system' in P. Stringer and D. Bannister (eds.), *Constructs of Sociality and Individuality*, Academic Press, London.

Mancuso, J.C. (1979b) 'Counseling from a personal construct perspective', *International Journal for the Advancement of Counseling, 1*, 303–13.

Mancuso, J.C. and Ceely, S.G. (1980) 'The self as memory processing', *Cognitive Therapy and Research, 4*, 1–25.

Mancuso, J.C. and Adams-Webber, J.R. (eds.) (1982a) *The Construing Person*, Praeger, New York.

Mancuso, J.C. and Adams-Webber, J.R. (1982b) 'Anticipation as a constructive process:

the fundamental postulate' in J.C. Mancuso and J.R. Adams-Webber (eds.), *The Construing Person*, Praeger, New York.

Mancuso, J.C. and Allen, D.A. (1976) 'Children's perceptions of a transgressor's socialization as a function of a type of reprimand', *Human Development, 19*, 277–90.

Mancuso, J.C. and Handin, K.H. (1980) 'Training parents to construe the child's construing' in A.W. Landfield and L.M. Leitner (eds.), *Personal Construct Psychology: Psychotherapy and Personality*, Wiley, New York.

Mancuso, J.C. and Handin, K.H. (1983) 'Prompting parents towards constructivist caregiving practices' in I.E. Sigel and L.M. Laosa (eds.), *Changing Families*, Plenum Press, New York.

Mancuso, J.C. and Sarbin, T.R. (1972) 'Schizophrenia, personal constructs and Riedel's constructs', *Journal of Abnormal Psychology, 79*, 148–50.

Margolius, O. (1980) 'Conflicts in Construing the Self: Differences between Neurotics and Normals', unpublished MSc dissertation, North East London Polytechnic.

Marsella, A.J., DeVos, G., and Hsu, F.L.K. (1985) *Culture and Self: Asian and Western Perspectives*, Tavistock, London.

Martin, D.V. (1962) *Adventure in Psychiatry*, Cassirer, Oxford.

Maslow, A.A. (1965) 'A philosophy of psychology: the need for a mature science of human nature' in F. Severin (ed.), *Humanistic Viewpoints in Psychology: A Book of Readings*, McGraw-Hill, New York.

Masters, W.H. and Johnson, V.E. (1970) *Human Sexual Inadequacy*, Churchill, London.

Maturana, H.R. and Varela, F. (1980) *Autopoiesis and Cognition*, Reidel, Boston.

Mavissakalian, M., Michelson, L., Greenwald, D., Kornblith, S., and Greenwald, M. (1983) 'Cognitive-behavioral treatment of agoraphobia: paradoxical intention vs. self-statement training', *Behaviour Research and Therapy, 21*, 75–86.

May, A.E. (1968) 'An assessment of homicidal attitudes', *British Journal of Psychiatry, 114*, 479–80.

Mayo, C. and Crockett, W.H. (1964) 'Cognitive complexity and primacy-recency effects in impression formation', *Journal of Abnormal and Social Psychology, 68*, 335–8.

Mehrabian, A. (1968) *An Analysis of Personality Theories*, Prentice-Hall, Englewood Cliffs, NJ.

Meichenbaum, D. (1977) *Cognitive Behavior Modification*, Plenum Press, New York.

Mellsop, G.W., Spelman, M.S., and Harrison, A.W. (1971) 'The performance of manic patients on the Grid Test for Schizophrenic Thought Disorder', *British Journal of Psychiatry, 118*, 671–3.

Meltzoff, J. and Kornreich, M. (1970) *Research in Psychotherapy*, Atherton Press, New York.

Mendelsohn, G.A. and Geller, M.H. (1965) 'Structure of client attitudes towards counseling and their relation to client–counselor similarity', *Journal of Consulting Psychology, 29*, 63–72.

Mendoza, S. (1985) 'The exchange grid' in N. Beail (ed.), *Repertory Grid Technique and Personal Constructs: Applications in Clinical and Educational Settings*, Croom Helm, London.

Menzies, I.E.P. (1960) 'A case-study in the functioning of social systems as a defence against anxiety', *Human Relations, 13*, 95–121.

Meshoulam, U. (1978) 'There is more to stuttering than meets the ear: stutterers' construing of speaking situations' in F. Fransella (ed.), *Personal Construct Psychology 1977*, Academic Press, London.

Metcalfe, R.J.A. (1974) 'Own versus provided constructs in a reptest measure of cognitive complexity', *Psychological Reports, 35*, 1305–6.

Meyer, V., Levy, R., and Schnurer, A. (1974) 'The behavioural treatment of obsessive-compulsive disorders' in H.R. Beech (ed.), *Obsessional States*, Methuen, London.

Michelson, L., Mavissakalian, M., and Meminger, S. (1983) 'Prognostic utility of locus of control in treatment of agoraphobia', *Behaviour Research and Therapy, 21*, 309–13.

Michelson, L., Mavissakalian, M., and Marchione, K. (1985) 'Cognitive-behavioral treatments of agoraphobia: clinical, behavioral, and psychophysiological outcomes', *Journal of Consulting and Clinical Psychology, 53*, 913–25.

Middleton, J. (1985) 'So where does this leave Simon? A mother's and a teacher's perspective of an ESN(M) boy' in N. Beail (ed.), *Repertory Grid Technique and Personal Constructs: Applications in Clinical and Educational Settings*, Croom Helm, London.

Millar, D.G. (1980) 'A repertory grid study of obsessionality: distinctive cognitive structure or distinctive cognitive content?', *British Journal of Medical Psychology, 53*, 59–66.

Miller, A.D. (1968) 'Psychological stress as a determinant of cognitive complexity', *Psychological Reports, 23*, 635–9.

Miller, A. (1969) 'Amount of information and stimulus value as determinants of cognitive complexity', *Journal of Personality, 37*, 141–57.

Miller, K. and Treacher, A. (1981) 'Delinquency: a personal construct theory approach' in H. Bonarius, R. Holland, and S. Rosenberg (eds.), *Personal Construct Psychology: Recent Advances in Theory and Practice*, Macmillan, London.

Millimet, C.R. and Brien, M. (1980) 'Cognitive differentiation and interpersonal discomfort: an integration theory approach', *Journal of Mind and Behavior, 1*, 211–25.

Milne, D. (1984) 'The relevance of nurses' characteristics in learning behaviour therapy', *Journal of Advanced Nursing, 9*, 175–9.

Milton, F. and Hafner, R.J. (1979) 'The outcome of behaviour therapy for agoraphobia in relation to marital adjustment', *Archives of General Psychiatry, 36*, 807–11.

Minuchin, S. (1974) *Families and Family Therapy*, Tavistock, London.

Mischel, T. (1964) 'Personal constructs, roles and the logic of clinical activity', *Psychological Review, 71*, 180–92.

Mischel, W. (1980) 'George Kelly's anticipation of psychology' in M.J. Mahoney (ed.), *Psychotherapy Process: Current Issues and Future Directions*, Plenum Press, New York.

Miskimins, R.W., Wilson, L.T., Braucht, G.N., and Berry, K.L. (1971) 'Self-concept and psychiatric symptomatology', *Journal of Clinical Psychology, 27*, 185–7.

Mitsos, S.B. (1958) 'Representative elements in role construct technique', *Journal of Consulting Psychology, 22*, 311–13.

Mitsos, S.B. (1961) 'Personal constructs and the semantic differential', *Journal of Abnormal and Social Psychology, 62*, 433–4.

Mitterer, J. and Adams-Webber, J. (1987) 'OMNIGRID: a program for the construction, administration, and analysis of repertory grids' in J.C. Mancuso and M.L.G. Shaw (eds.), *Cognition and Personal Structure: Computer Access and Analysis*, Praeger, New York.

Mogar, R.E. (1960) 'Three versions of the F scale and performance on the semantic differential', *Journal of Abnormal and Social Psychology, 60*, 262–5.

Moreno, J.L. (1959) 'Psychodrama' in S. Arieti (ed.), *American Handbook of Psychiatry*, Basic Books, New York.

Morris, J.B. (1977) 'Appendix I. The prediction and measurement of change in a psychotherapy group using the repertory grid' in F. Fransella and D. Bannister (eds.), *A Manual for Repertory Grid Technique*, Academic Press, London.

Morrison, J.K. (1977) 'The family heritage: dysfunctional constructs and roles', *International Journal of Family Counseling, 5*, 54–8.

Morrison, J.K. (1978) 'Successful grieving: changing personal constructs through mental imagery', *Journal of Mental Imagery, 2*, 63–8.

Morrison, J.K. (1979) 'Emotive-reconstructive therapy: changing constructs by means of mental imagery' in A.A. Sheikh and J.T. Shaffer (eds.), *The Potential of Fantasy and Imagination*, Brandon, New York.

Morrison, J.K. (1980a) 'Emotive-reconstructive therapy: a short-term psychotherapeutic use of mental imagery' in J.E. Shorr, J. Connelly, G. Sobel, and T. Robin (eds.), *Imagery: Its Many Dimensions and Applications* (vol. 2), Plenum Press, New York.

Morrison, J.K. (1980b) 'Homosexual fantasies and the reconstructive use of imagery', *Journal of Mental Imagery, 4*, 165–8.

Morrison, J.K. (1981) 'Using death imagery to induce proper grieving: an emotive-reconstructive approach' in E. Klinger (ed.), *Imagery: Concepts, Results, and Applications* (vol. 2), Plenum Press, New York.

Morrison, J.K. (1986) 'The emotive-reconstructive use of imagery to induce psychotherapeutic grieving' in A.A. Sheikh (ed.), *Death before Life: Growth Potential of Death Imagery*, Baywood, New York.

Morrison, J.K. (1987) 'A psychotherapist at the crossroads: a personal and professional turning point' in W. Dryden (ed.), *Key Cases in Psychotherapy*, Croom Helm, London.

Morrison, J.K., Becker, R.E., and Heeder, R. (1983a) 'Individual imagery psychotherapy vs. didactic self-help seminars: comparative effect on problem behaviors', *Psychological Reports, 52*, 709–16.

Morrison, J.K., Becker, R.E., and Heeder, R. (1983b) 'Anxiety reduction: comparative effectiveness of imagery psychotherapy vs. self-help seminars', *Psychological Reports, 53*, 417–18.

Morrison, J.K., Becker, R.E., and Isaacs, K. (1981) 'Comparative effectiveness of individual imagery psychotherapy vs. didactic self-help seminars', *Psychological Reports, 49*, 923–8.

Morrison, J.K. and Cometa, M.S. (1977) 'Emotive-reconstructive psychotherapy: a short-term cognitive approach', *American Journal of Psychotherapy, 31*, 294–301.

Morrison, J.K. and Cometa, M.S. (1979) 'Emotive-reconstructive therapy and client problem resolution: periodic accountability to the consumer' in J.K. Morrison (ed.), *A Consumer Approach to Community Psychology*, Nelson-Hall, Chicago.

Morrison, J.K. and Cometa, M.S. (1980) 'A cognitive, reconstructive approach to the psychotherapeutic use of imagery', *Journal of Mental Imagery, 4*, 35–42.

Morrison, J.K. and Heeder, R. (1984) 'Follow-up study of the effectiveness of emotive-reconstructive therapy', *Psychological Reports, 54*, 149–50.

Morrison, J.K. and Heeder, R. (1984–5) 'Feeling-expression ratings by psychotherapist as predictive of imagery therapy outcome: a pilot study', *Imagination, Cognition, and Personality, 4*, 219–23.

Morrison, J.K. and Holdridge, S. (1984) 'Emotive-reconstructive therapy and the resolution of artists' problem behaviors and negative self-constructs: a pilot study', *Psychological Reports, 54*, 505–6.

Morrison, J.K. and Teta, D.C. (1978) 'Simplified use of the semantic differential to measure psychotherapy outcome', *Journal of Clinical Psychology, 34*, 751–3.

Morrissette, J.O. (1958) 'An experimental study of the theory of structural balance', *Human Relationships, 11*, 239–54.

Morse, E. (1965) 'An Exploratory Study of Personal Identity based on the Psychology of Personal Constructs', unpublished PhD thesis, Ohio State University.

Mottram, M.A. (1985) 'Personal constructs in anorexia nervosa', *Journal of Psychiatric Research, 19*, 291–5.

Mowrer, O.H. (1950) *Learning Theory and Personality Dynamics*, Ronald Press, New York.

Mueller, W.S. (1974) 'Cognitive complexity and salience of dimensions of person perception', *Australian Journal of Psychology, 26*, 173–82.

Munden, A. (1982) 'Eating Problems amongst Women in a University Population', unpublished dissertation, University of Southampton.

Muntz, H.J. and Power, R. (1970) 'Thought disorder in the parents of thought-disordered schizophrenics', *British Journal of Psychiatry, 117*, 707–8.

Muzekari, L.H. and Bates, M.E. (1977) 'Judgement of emotion among chronic schizophrenics', *Journal of Clinical Psychology, 33*, 662–6.

Nawas, M.M. and Landfield, A.W. (1963) 'Improvement in psychotherapy and adoption of the therapist's meaning system', *Psychological Reports, 13*, 97–8.

Needleman, J. (1968) *Being-in-the-World: Selected Papers of Ludwig Binswanger*, Harper Torchbooks, New York.

Needs, A. (1988) 'Psychological investigation of offending behaviour' in F. Fransella and L. Thomas (eds.), *Experimenting with Personal Construct Psychology*, Routledge & Kegan Paul, London.

Needs, A. (1990) 'Some issues raised by the application of personal construct psychology to the sexual abuse of children' in P. Maitland (ed.), *Personal Construct Theory Deviancy and Social Work*, Inner London Probation Service/Centre for Personal Construct Psychology, London.

Neimeyer, G.J. (1984) 'Cognitive complexity and marital satisfaction', *Journal of Social and Clinical Psychology, 2*, 258–63.

Neimeyer, G.J. (1985) 'Personal constructs in the counseling of couples' in F. Epting and A.W. Landfield (eds.), *Anticipating Personal Construct Psychology*, University of Nebraska Press, Lincoln.

Neimeyer, G.J. (1987a) 'Personal construct assessment, strategy, and technique' in R.A. Neimeyer and G.J. Neimeyer (eds.), *Personal Construct Therapy Casebook*, Springer, New York.

Neimeyer, G.J. (1987b) 'Marital role reconstruction through couples group therapy' in R.A. Neimeyer and G.J. Neimeyer (eds.), *Personal Construct Therapy Casebook*, Springer, New York.

Neimeyer, G.J. and Banikiotes, P.G. (1980) 'Flexibility of disclosure and measures of cognitive integration and differentiation', *Perceptual and Motor Skills, 50*, 907–10.

Neimeyer, G.J., Banikiotes, P.G., and Ianni, L.E. (1979) 'Self-disclosure and psychological construing: a personal construct approach to interpersonal perception', *Journal of Social Behavior and Personality, 7*, 161–5.

Neimeyer, G.J., Behnke, M., and Reiss, J. (1983) 'Constructs and coping: physicians' responses to patient death', *Death Education, 7*, 245–64.

Neimeyer, G.J. and Ebben, R. (1985) 'The effects of vocational interventions on the complexity and positivity of occupational judgements', *Journal of Vocational Behavior, 27*, 87–97.

Neimeyer, G.J. and Fukuyama, M. (1984) 'Exploring the content and structure of cross-cultural attitudes', *Counselor Education and Supervision, 23*, 214–24.

Neimeyer, G. and Hall, A.G. (1988) 'Personal identity in disturbed marital relationships' in F. Fransella and L. Thomas (eds.), *Experimenting with Personal Construct Psychology*, Routledge & Kegan Paul, London.

Neimeyer, G.J. and Hudson, J.E. (1985) 'Couples' constructs: personal systems in marital satisfaction' in D. Bannister (ed.), *Issues and Approaches in Personal Construct Theory*, Academic Presss, London.

Neimeyer, G.J. and Khouzam, N. (1985) 'A repertory grid study of restrained eaters', *British Journal of Medical Psychology, 58*, 365–8.

Neimeyer, G.J. and Merluzzi, T.V. (1979) 'Group structure and group process: explorations in therapeutic sociality', paper presented at 3rd International Congress on Personal Construct Psychology, Breukelen.

Neimeyer, G.J. and Merluzzi, T.V. (1982) 'Group structure and group process: personal construct therapy and group development', *Small Group Behavior, 13*, 150–64.

Neimeyer, G.J. and Metzler, A. (1987a) 'The development of vocational schemas', *Journal of Vocational Behavior, 30*, 16–32.

Neimeyer, G.J. and Metzler, A.E. (1987b) 'Sex differences in vocational integration and differentiation', *Journal of Vocational Behavior, 30*, 167–74.

Neimeyer, G.J. and Neimeyer, R.A. (1981a) 'Functional similarity and interpersonal attraction', *Journal of Research in Personality, 15*, 427–35.

Neimeyer, G.J. and Neimeyer, R.A. (1981b) 'Personal construct perspectives on cognitive assessment' in T. Merluzzi, C. Glass, and M. Genest (eds.), *Cognitive Assessment*, Guilford, New York.

Neimeyer, G.J. and Neimeyer, R.A. (1986) 'Personal constructs in relationship deterioration: a longitudinal study', *Social Behavior and Personality, 14*, 253–7.

Neimeyer, G.J., Nevill, D.D., Probert, B., and Fukuyama, M.A. (1985) 'Cognitive structures in vocational development', *Journal of Vocational Behavior, 27*, 191–201.

Neimeyer, R.A. (1978) 'Death anxiety and the Threat Index: an addendum', *Death Education, 1*, 464–7.

Neimeyer, R.A. (1980) 'George Kelly as therapist: a review of his tapes' in A.W. Landfield and L.M. Leitner (eds.), *Personal Construct Psychology: Psychotherapy and Personality*, Wiley, New York.

Neimeyer, R.A. (1981) 'The structure and meaningfulness of tacit construing' in H. Bonarius, R. Holland, and S. Rosenberg (eds.), *Personal Construct Psychology: Recent Advances in Theory and Practice*, Macmillan, London.

Neimeyer, R.A. (1984) 'Toward a personal construct conceptualization of depression and suicide' in F.R. Epting and R.A. Neimeyer (eds.), *Personal Meanings of Death: Applications of Personal Construct Theory to Clinical Practice*, Hemisphere/ McGraw-Hill, New York.

Neimeyer, R.A. (1985a) 'Personal constructs in clinical practice' in P.C. Kendall (ed.), *Advances in Cognitive-Behavioral Research and Therapy* (vol. 4), Academic Press, New York.

Neimeyer, R.A. (1985b) *The Development of Personal Construct Psychology*, University of Nebraska Press, Lincoln.

Neimeyer, R.A. (1985c) 'Actualization, integration, and fear of death: a test of the additive model', *Death Studies, 9*, 235–44.

Neimeyer, R. (1985d) 'Personal constructs in depression: research and clinical implications' in E. Button (ed.), *Personal Construct Theory and Mental Health*, Croom Helm, London.

Neimeyer, R.A. (1985e) 'Group psychotherapies for depression: an overview', *International Journal of Mental Health, 13*, 3–7.

Neimeyer, R.A. (1986a) 'The threat hypothesis: a conceptual and empirical defense', *Death Studies, 10*, 177–90.

Neimeyer, R.A. (1986b) 'Personal construct therapy' in W. Dryden and W. Golden (eds.), *Cognitive Behavioural Approaches to Psychotherapy*, Harper & Row, London.

Neimeyer, R.A. (1987a) 'Core role reconstruction in personal construct therapy' in R.A. Neimeyer and G.J. Neimeyer (eds.), *Personal Construct Therapy Casebook*, Springer, New York.

Neimeyer, R.A. (1987b) 'An orientation to personal construct therapy' in R.A. Neimeyer and G.J. Neimeyer (eds.), *Personal Construct Therapy Casebook*, Springer, New York.

Neimeyer, R.A. (1987c) 'Personal construct theory and the cognitive-behavioral therapies: assimilation or accommodation?', paper presented at 7th International Congress on Personal Construct Psychology, Memphis.

Neimeyer, R.A. (1988a) 'Integrative directions in personal construct therapy', *International Journal of Personal Construct Psychology, 1,* 283–97.

Neimeyer, R. (1988b) 'Clinical guidelines for conducting Interpersonal Transaction Groups', *International Journal of Personal Construct Psychology, 1,* 181–90.

Neimeyer, R.A. (1988c) 'The origin of questions in the clinical context', *Questioning Exchange, 2,* 275–80.

Neimeyer, R.A. (1989) 'Constructivist contribution to psychotherapy integration', paper presented at 8th International Congress on Personal Construct Psychology, Assisi.

Neimeyer, R.A. and Chapman, K.M. (1980) 'Self–ideal discrepancy and fear of death: the test of an existential hypothesis', *Omega, 11,* 233–40.

Neimeyer, R.A., Davis, K., and Rist, P. (1986) 'The future of personal construct psychology: a Delphi poll', *British Journal of Cognitive Psychotherapy, 4,* 37–44.

Neimeyer, R.A. and Dingemans, P.M. (1980) 'Death orientation in the suicide intervention worker', *Omega, 11,* 15–23.

Neimeyer, R.A., Dingemans, P.M., and Epting, F.R. (1977) 'Convergent validity, situational stability and meaningfulness of the Threat Index', *Omega, 8,* 251–65.

Neimeyer, R.A., Fontana, D.J., and Gold, K. (1984) 'A manual for content analysis of death constructs' in F. Epting and R.A. Neimeyer (eds.), *Personal Meanings of Death: Applications of Personal Construct Theory to Clinical Practice,* Hemisphere/ McGraw-Hill, New York.

Neimeyer, R. and Harter, S. (1988) 'Facilitating individual change in Personal Construct Therapy' in G. Dunnett (ed.), *Working with People: Clinical Uses of Personal Construct Psychology,* Routledge, London.

Neimeyer, R.A., Heath, A.E., and Strauss, J. (1985) 'Personal reconstruction during group cognitive therapy for depression' in F. Epting and A.W. Landfield (eds.), *Anticipating Personal Construct Psychology,* University of Nebraska Press, Lincoln.

Neimeyer, R.A., Klein, M.H., Gurman, A.S., and Greist, J.H. (1983a) 'Cognitive structure and depressive symptomatology', *British Journal of Cognitive Psychotherapy, 1,* 65–73.

Neimeyer, R.A. and Mitchell, K.A. (1988) 'Similarity and attraction: a longitudinal study', *Journal of Social and Personal Relationships, 5,* 131–48.

Neimeyer, R.A. and Moore, M.K. (1989) 'Assessing personal meanings of death: empirical refinements in the Threat Index', *Death Studies, 13,* 227–45.

Neimeyer, R.A. and Neimeyer, G.J. (1983) 'Structural similarity in the acquaintance process', *Journal of Social and Clinical Psychology, 1,* 146–54.

Neimeyer, R. and Neimeyer, G. (1985) 'Disturbed relationships: a personal construct view' in E. Button (ed.), *Personal Construct Theory and Mental Health,* Croom Helm, London.

Neimeyer, R.A., Neimeyer, G.J., and Landfield, A.W. (1983b) 'Conceptual differentiation, integration and empathic prediction', *Journal of Personality, 51,* 185–91.

Nelson, R.E. and Craighead, W.E. (1977) 'Selective recall of positive and negative feedback, self-control behaviors, and depression', *Journal of Abnormal Psychology, 86,* 379–88.

Nemiah, J.C. and Sifneos, P.E. (1970) 'Affect and fantasy with psychosomatic patients' in O.W. Hill (ed.), *Modern Trends in Psychosomatic Medicine* (vol. 2), Butterworth, London.

Neuringer, C. (1961) 'Dichotomous evaluations in suicidal individuals', *Journal of Consulting Psychology, 25,* 445–9.

Neuringer, C. (1967) 'The cognitive organization of meaning in suicidal individuals', *Journal of General Psychology, 76,* 91–100.

Neuringer, C. and Lettieri, D. (1971) 'Cognition, attitude and affect in suicidal individuals', *Life-Threatening Behavior, 1,* 106–204.

Nevill, D.D., Neimeyer, G.J., Probert, B., and Fukuyama, M. (1986) 'Cognitive structures in vocational information processing and decision making', *Journal of Vocational Behavior, 28*, 110–22.

Nidorf, L.J. and Crockett, W.H. (1965) 'Cognitive complexity and the integration of conflicting information in written impressions', *Journal of Social Psychology, 66*, 165–99.

Nietzsche, F. (1969) *The Genealogy of Morals*, Vintage, New York.

Noble, G. (1970) 'Discrimination between different forms of televised aggression by delinquent and non-delinquent boys', *British Journal of Criminology, 11*, 230–44.

Noble, G. (1971) 'Some comments on the nature of delinquents' identification with television heroes, fathers and best friends', *British Journal of Social and Clinical Psychology, 10*, 172–80.

Norcross, J.C. (1986) 'Eclectic psychotherapy: an introduction and overview' in J.C. Norcross (ed.), *Handbook of Eclectic Psychotherapy*, Brunner/Mazel, New York.

Norris, H. and Makhlouf-Norris, F. (1976) 'The measurement of self-identity' in P. Slater (ed.), *The Measurement of Intrapersonal Space by Grid Technique. Vol.1. Explorations of Intrapersonal Space*, Wiley, London.

Norris, M. (1977) 'Construing in a detention centre' in D. Bannister (ed.), *New Perspectives in Personal Construct Theory*, Academic Press, London.

Norris, M. (1983) 'Changes in patients during treatment at the Henderson Hospital therapeutic community during 1977–81', *British Journal of Medical Psychology, 56*, 135–44.

Norton, G.R., Allen, G.E., and Hilton, J. (1983) 'The social validity of treatments for agoraphobia', *Behaviour Research and Therapy, 21*, 393–9.

Norton, K., Evans, C., and Sperlinger, D. (1988) 'Object relations, repertory grids and anorexia nervosa: a replication and extension of Feldman's technique', paper presented at 17th European Conference on Psychosomatic Research, Marburg.

Nuzzo, M.L. and Chiari, G. (1987) 'A constructivist framework for exploring malignancies', paper presented at 7th International Congress on Personal Construct Psychology, Memphis.

Oatley, K. and Hodgson, D. (1987) 'Influence of husbands on the outcome of their agoraphobic wives' therapy', *British Journal of Psychiatry, 150*, 380–6.

O'Donovan, D. (1964) 'Polarization and Meaningfulness in 6,300 Value Judgements', unpublished MS, University of Missouri.

O'Donovan, D. (1965) 'Rating extremity: pathology or meaningfulness', *Psychological Review, 72*, 358–72.

O'Donovan, D. (1985) 'Computer dream analysis' in F. Epting and A.W. Landfield (eds.), *Anticipating Personal Construct Psychology*, University of Nebraska Press, Lincoln.

O'Hare, D.P.A. and Gordon, I.E. (1976) 'An application of repertory grid technique to aesthetic measurement', *Perceptual and Motor Skills, 42*, 1183–92.

O'Keefe, B.J. and Delia, J.G. (1978) 'Construct comprehensiveness and cognitive complexity', *Perceptual and Motor Skills, 46*, 548–50.

O'Keefe, B.J. and Delia, J.G. (1979) 'Construct comprehensiveness and cognitive complexity as predictors of the number and strategic adaptation of arguments and appeals in a persuasive message', *Communication Monographs, 46*, 231–40.

O'Keefe, B.J. and Sypher, H.E. (1981) 'Cognitive complexity measures and the relationship of cognitive complexity to communication', *Human Communication Research, 8*, 72–92.

Oliver, D. and Landfield, A.W. (1962) 'Reflexivity: an unfaced issue of psychology', *Journal of Individual Psychology, 18*, 114–24.

O'Loughlin, S. (1989) 'Use of repertory grids to assess understanding between partners in marital therapy', *International Journal of Personal Construct Psychology, 2*, 143–7.

Olson, J.M. and Partington, J.T. (1977) 'An integrative analysis of two cognitive models of interpersonal effectiveness', *British Journal of Social and Clinical Psychology, 16*, 13–14.

O'Mahony, P.D. (1982) 'Psychiatric patient denial of mental illness as a normal process', *British Journal of Medical Psychology, 55*, 109–18.

O'Reilly, J. (1977) 'The interplay between mothers and their children: a construct theory viewpoint' in D. Bannister (ed.), *New Perspectives in Personal Construct Theory*, Academic Press, London.

Orford, J. (1974) 'Simplistic thinking about other people as a predictor of early drop-out at an alcoholism halfway house', *British Journal of Medical Psychology, 47*, 53–62.

Osgood, C.E., Suci, G.J., and Tannenbaum, P.M. (1957) *The Measurement of Meaning*, University of Illinois Press, Urbana.

O'Sullivan, B.O. (1984) 'Understanding the Experience of Agoraphobia', unpublished PhD thesis, University of Dublin.

O'Sullivan, B. (1985) 'The experiment of agoraphobia' in N. Beail (ed.), *Repertory Grid Technique and Personal Constructs: Applications in Clinical and Educational Settings*, Croom Helm, London.

O'Sullivan, B. (1988) 'Feminism and PCT' in F. Fransella and L. Thomas (eds.), *Experimenting with Personal Construct Psychology*, Routledge & Kegan Paul, London.

Ourth, L. and Landfield, A.W. (1965) 'Interpersonal meaningfulness and nature of termination in psychotherapy', *Journal of Counseling Psychology, 12*, 366–71.

Pallis, D.J. and Stoffelmayr, B.E. (1973) 'Social attitudes and treatment orientation among psychiatrists', *British Journal of Medical Psychology, 46*, 75–81.

Panayotopoulos, D.J. and Stoffelmayr, B.E. (1972) 'Training preferences, social attitudes and treatment orientation among psychiatrists', *Journal of Clinical Psychology, 28*, 216–17.

Pardes, H., Papernik, D., and Winton, A. (1974) 'Field differentiation in inpatient psychotherapy', *Archives of General Psychiatry, 31*, 311–15.

Parker, A. (1981) 'The meaning of attempted suicide to young parasuicides: a repertory grid study', *British Journal of Psychiatry, 139*, 306–12.

Partington, J.T. (1970) 'Dr. Jekyll and Mr. High: multidimensional scaling of alcoholics' self-evaluations', *Journal of Abnormal Psychology, 75*, 131–8.

Pask, G. (1975) *Conversation, Cognition and Learning*, Elsevier, Amsterdam.

Patterson, C.A. (1980) *Theories of Counseling and Psychotherapy* (3rd edition), Harper & Row, New York.

Pederson, F. A (1958) 'Consistency Data on the Role Construct Repertory Test', unpublished MS, Ohio State University.

Pennebaker, J.W. (1985) 'Traumatic experience and psychosomatic disease: exploring the roles of behavioral inhibition, obsession, and confiding', *Canadian Psychology, 26*, 82–94.

Penrod, J.H., Epting, R.F., and Wadden, T.A. (1981) 'Interpersonal cognitive differentiation and drug of choice', *Psychological Reports, 49*, 752–6.

Pepper, S.L. (1942) *World Hypotheses*, University of California Press, Berkeley.

Perls, F.S. (1969) *Gestalt Therapy Verbatim*, Real People Press, Lafayette, California.

Persons, J.B. and Burns, D.D. (1986) 'The process of cognitive therapy: the first dysfunctional thought changes less than the last one', *Behaviour Research and Therapy, 24*, 619–24.

Persons, J.B. and Foa, E.B. (1984) 'Processing of fearful and neutral information by obsessive-compulsives', *Behaviour Research and Therapy, 22*, 259–65.

Pervin, L. (1973) 'On construing our constructs. A review of Bannister and Fransella's Inquiring Man: the theory of personal constructs', *Contemporary Psychology, 18*, 110–12.

Pervin, L.A. (1980) *Personality: Theory, Assessment and Research* (3rd edition), Wiley, New York.

Peter, H. and Hand, I. (1987) 'Expressed emotion and agoraphobia in the Camberwell family interview', paper presented at 18th Annual Meeting of Society for Psychotherapy Research, Ulm.

Peterfreund, E. (1983) *The Process of Psychoanalytic Therapy*, Analytic Press, Hillsdale, NJ.

Philip, A.E. and McCulloch, J.W. (1968) 'Personal construct theory and social work practice', *British Journal of Social and Clinical Psychology, 7*, 115–21.

Phillips, E.M. (1985) 'Using the repertory grid in the classroom' in N. Beail (ed.), *Repertory Grid Technique and Personal Constructs: Applications in Clinical and Educational Settings*, Croom Helm, London.

Phillips J.P.N. (1975) 'A note on the scoring of the Grid Test of Schizophrenic Thought Disorder', *British Journal of Social and Clinical Psychology, 14*, 99–100.

Phillips, J.P.N. (1977) 'On the incorrect investigation of interactions', *British Journal of Social and Clinical Psychology, 16*, 249–52.

Phillips, W.M. (1976) 'Role construct repertory technique: some relationships with personality, psychopathology and intelligence for neuropsychiatric patients', *Psychological Reports, 38*, 951–5.

Platt, S. and Salter, D. (1987) 'A comparative investigation of health workers' attitudes towards parasuicide', *Social Psychiatry, 22*, 202–8.

Polanyi, M. (1958) *Personal Knowledge*, University of Chicago Press, Chicago.

Pollock, L.C. (1986) 'An introduction to the use of repertory grid technique as a research method and clinical tool for psychiatric nurses', *Journal of Advanced Nursing, 11*, 439–45.

Poole, A.D. (1976) 'A further attempt to cross-validate the Grid Test of Schizophrenic Thought Disorder', *British Journal of Social and Clinical Psychology, 15*, 179–88.

Poole, A.D. (1979) 'The Grid Test of Schizophrenic Thought Disorder and psychiatric symptomatology', *British Journal of Medical Psychology, 52*, 183–6.

Pope, M. and Keen, T. (1981) *Personal Construct Psychology and Education*, Academic Press, London.

Potamianos, G., Winter, D., Duffy, S.W., Gorman, D.M., and Peters, T.J. (1985) 'The perception of problem drinkers by general hospital staff, general practitioners and alcoholic patients', *Alcohol, 2*, 563–6.

Presley, A.S. (1969) 'Slowness and performance on the Grid Test of Schizophrenic Thought Disorder', *British Journal of Social and Clinical Psychology, 8*, 79–80.

Press, A.N., Crockett, W.H., and Rosenkrantz, P.S. (1969) 'Cognitive complexity and the learning of balanced and unbalanced social structures', *Journal of Personality, 37*, 541–53.

Preston, C. and Viney, L.L. (1983) 'Self and ideal self perception of drug addicts', *International Journal of Addictions, 20*, 35–42.

Procter, H.G. (1981) 'Family construct psychology: an approach to understanding and treating families' in S. Walrond-Skinner (ed.), *Developments in Family Therapy*, Routledge & Kegan Paul, London.

Procter, H. (1985a) 'A construct approach to family therapy and systems intervention' in E. Button (ed.), *Personal Construct Theory and Mental Health*, Croom Helm, London.

Procter, H. (1985b) 'Repertory grids in family therapy and research' in N. Beail (ed.), *Repertory Grid Technique and Personal Constructs: Applications in Clinical and Educational Settings*, Croom Helm, London.

Procter, H.G. (1987) 'Change in the family construct system: therapy of a mute and withdrawn schizophrenic patient' in R.A. Neimeyer and G.J. Neimeyer (eds.), *Personal Construct Therapy Casebook*, Springer, New York.

Procter, H.G. (1989) 'Aspects of hypnosis and personal construct theory', paper presented at 8th International Congress on Personal Construct Psychology, Assisi.

Procter, H.G. and Brennan, J. (1985) 'Kelly and Erickson: towards a personal construct hypnotherapy', paper presented at 6th International Congress on Personal Construct Psychology, Cambridge.

Procter, H. and Parry, G. (1978) 'Constraint and freedom: the social origins of personal constructs' in F. Fransella (ed.), *Personal Construct Psychology 1977*, Academic Press, London.

Rachman, S. (1983) 'The modification of agoraphobic avoidance behaviour: some fresh possibilities', *Behaviour Research and Therapy, 21*, 567–74.

Rachman, S. and Hodgson, R. (1974) 'Synchrony and desynchrony in fear and avoidance', *Behaviour Research and Therapy, 12*, 311–18.

Rachman, S. and Levitt, K. (1985) 'Panics and their consequences', *Behaviour Research and Therapy, 23*, 585–600.

Rachman, S. and Lopatka, C. (1986a) 'Match and mismatch in the prediction of fear – I', *Behaviour Research and Therapy, 24*, 387–93.

Rachman, S. and Lopatka, C. (1986b) 'Match and mismatch of fear in Gray's theory – II', *Behaviour Research and Therapy, 24*, 395–401.

Radley, A.R. (1974a) 'Schizophrenic thought disorder and the nature of personal constructs', *British Journal of Social and Clinical Psychology, 13*, 315–28.

Radley, A.R. (1974b) 'The effect of role enactment upon construed alternatives', *British Journal of Medical Psychology, 47*, 313–20.

Rainey, L.C. and Epting, F.R. (1977) 'Death threat constructions in the student and the prudent', *Omega, 8*, 19–28.

Randall, M. and Thomas, L. (1988) 'Developing a learning culture in a bank' in F. Fransella and L. Thomas (eds.), *Experimenting with Personal Construct Psychology*, Routledge & Kegan Paul, London.

Rapaport, D. (1959) 'The structure of psychoanalytic theory – a systematizing attempt', in S. Koch (ed.), *Psychology: A Study of a Science, 3*, McGraw-Hill, New York.

Ravenette, A.T. (1973) 'Projective psychology and personal construct theory', *British Journal of Projective Psychology and Personality Study, 18*, 3–10.

Ravenette, A.T. (1975) 'Grid techniques for children', *Journal of Child Psychology and Psychiatry, 16*, 79–83.

Ravenette, A.T. (1977) 'Personal construct theory: an approach to the psychological investigation of children and young people' in D. Bannister (ed.), *New Perspectives in Personal Construct Theory*, Academic Press, London.

Ravenette, A.T. (1980) 'The exploration of consciousness: personal construct intervention with children' in A.W. Landfield and L.M. Leitner (eds.), *Personal Construct Psychology: Psychotherapy and Personality*, Wiley, London.

Raz-Duvshani, A. (1986) 'Cognitive structure changes with psychotherapy in neurosis', *British Journal of Medical Psychology, 59*, 341–50.

Rehm, L. (1971) 'Effects of validation on the relationship between personal constructs', *Journal of Personality and Social Psychology, 20*, 267–70.

Reid, F. (1979) 'Personal constructs and social competence' in P. Stringer and D. Bannister (eds.), *Constructs of Sociality and Individuality*, Academic Press, London.

Reid, W.A. and Holley, B.J. (1972) 'An application of repertory grid techniques to the study of choice of university', *British Journal of Educational Psychology, 42*, 52–9.

Reiss, D. (1981) *The Family's Construction of Reality*, Harvard University Press, Cambridge, MS.

Reker, G.T. (1974) 'Interpersonal conceptual structure of emotionally disturbed and normal boys', *Journal of Abnormal Psychology, 83*, 380–6.

Resnick, J. and Landfield, A.W. (1961) 'The oppositional nature of dichotomous constructs', *Psychological Record, 11,* 47–55.

Rice, L.N. (1974) 'The evocative function of the therapist' in D.A. Wexler and L.N. Rice (eds.), *Innovations in Client-Centered Therapy,* Wiley, New York.

Richardson, F.C. and Weigel, R.G. (1971) 'Personal construct theory applied to the marriage relationship', *Experimental Publication System, 10,* MS No. 371–5.

Ricoeur, P. (1970) *Freud and Philosophy,* Yale University Press, New Haven.

Riedel, H.W. (1970) 'An investigation of personal constructs through nonverbal tasks', *Journal of Abnormal Psychology, 76,* 173–9.

Riedel, H.W. (1972) 'Schizophrenia, personal constructs, and Riedel's constructs: a rejoinder', *Journal of Abnormal Psychology, 79,* 151–2.

Rigdon, M.A. (1983) 'Death threat before and after attempted suicide: a clinical investigation', *Death Education, 7,* 195–209.

Rigdon, M.A. and Epting, F.R. (1983) 'A personal construct perspective on an obsessive client' in J. Adams-Webber and J.C. Mancuso (eds.), *Applications of Personal Construct Theory,* Academic Press, Toronto.

Rigdon, M.A., Epting, F.R., Neimeyer, R.A., and Krieger, S.R. (1979) 'The Threat Index: a research report', *Death Education, 3,* 245–70.

Riley, S. and Palmer, J. (1976) 'Of attitudes and latitudes: a repertory grid study of perceptions of seaside resorts' in P. Slater (ed.), *The Measurement of Intrapersonal Space by Grid Technique. Vol. 1. Explorations of Intrapersonal Space,* Wiley, London.

Rilke, R.M. (1946) *Selected Letters of Rainer Maria Rilke, 1902–1926,* Macmillan, London.

Ritter, E.M. (1979) 'Social perspective-taking ability, cognitive complexity, and listener-adapted communication in early and late adolescence', *Communication Monographs, 46,* 40–51.

Rivers, C. and Landfield, A. (1985) 'Personal construct theory and alcohol dependence' in E. Button (ed.), *Personal Construct Theory and Mental Health,* Croom Helm, London.

Robertson, I.T. and Molloy, K.J. (1982) 'Cognitive complexity, neuroticism and research ability', *British Journal of Educational Psychology, 52,* 113–18.

Robinson, P.J. and Wood, K. (1984) 'Fear of death and physical illness: a personal construct approach' in F.R. Epting and R.A. Neimeyer (eds.), *Personal Meanings of Death,* Hemisphere/McGraw-Hill, Washington, DC.

Rodney, Y. (1981) 'The Effects of Mood on Self and Person Perception', unpublished MS, Brock University.

Rogers, C.R. (1951) *Client-Centered Therapy,* Houghton Mifflin, Boston.

Rogers, C.R. (1956) 'Intellectual psychotherapy', *Contemporary Psychology, 1,* 357–8.

Rollnick S. and Heather, N. (1980) 'Psychological change among alcoholics during treatment', *British Journal of Alcohol and Alcoholism, 15,* 118–123.

Romney, D. (1969) 'Psychometrically assessed thought disorder in schizophrenic and control patients and in their parents and siblings', *British Journal of Psychiatry, 115,* 999–1002.

Romney, D. and Leblanc, E. (1975) 'Relationship between formal thought disorder and retardation in schizophrenia', *Journal of Consulting and Clinical Psychology, 43,* 217–22.

Rona, D.C. (1986) 'Closure of institutions and the role of psychologists', *Clinical Psychology Forum, 4,* 11–13.

Rosch, E. (1978) 'Principles of categorization' in E. Rosch and B.B. Lloyd (eds.), *Cognition and Categorization,* Erlbaum, Hillsdale, NJ.

Rosenbaum, R.L. (1982) 'Paradox as epistemological jump', *Family Process, 21,* 85–90.

Rosenberg, S. (1977) 'New approaches to the analysis of personal constructs in person perception' in J.K. Cole and A.W. Landfield (eds.), *1976 Nebraska Symposium on Motivation*, University of Nebraska Press, Lincoln.

Ross, M.V. (1985) 'Depression, self-concept, and personal constructs' in F. Epting and A.W. Landfield (eds.), *Anticipating Personal Construct Psychology*, University of Nebraska Press, Lincoln.

Rotter, J.B. (1966) 'Generalized expectancies for internal versus external control of reinforcements', *Psychological Monographs, 80*, 1, whole no.

Rowan, J. (1976) *Ordinary Ecstasy: Humanistic Psychology in Action*, Routledge & Kegan Paul, London.

Rowan, J. (1981) 'Humanistic therapy', *New Forum, March*, 63–4.

Rowe, D. (1969) 'Estimates of change in a depressive patient', *British Journal of Psychiatry, 115*, 1199–200.

Rowe, D. (1971a) 'Poor prognosis in a case of depression as predicted by the repertory grid', *British Journal of Psychiatry, 118*, 297–300.

Rowe, D. (1971b) 'An examination of a psychiatrist's predictions of a patient's constructs', *British Journal of Psychiatry, 118*, 231–44.

Rowe, D. (1971c) 'Changes in the perception of relationships in the hypomanic state as shown by the repertory grid', *British Journal of Psychiatry, 119*, 323–4.

Rowe, D. (1973a) 'The use of the repertory grid in the study of object relations', *British Journal of Projective Psychology and Personality Study, 18*, 11–19.

Rowe, D. (1973b) 'An alternative method in the use of repertory grids', *Australian Psychologist, 8*, 213–19.

Rowe, D. (1976) 'Grid technique in the conversation between patient and therapist' in P. Slater (ed.), *The Measurement of Intrapersonal Space by Grid Technique. Vol.1. Explorations of Intrapersonal Space*, Wiley, London.

Rowe, D. (1978) *The Experience of Depression*, Wiley, Chichester.

Rowe, D. (1980) 'Logical limitations', *New Forum, August*, 6–9.

Rowe, D. (1982) *The Construction of Life and Death*, Wiley, Chichester.

Rowe, D. (1983a) *Depression: The Way Out of the Prison*, Routledge & Kegan Paul, London.

Rowe, D. (1983b) 'Metaphors and metaphysics' in J. Adams-Webber and J.C. Mancuso (eds.), *Applications of Personal Construct Theory*, Academic Press, Toronto.

Rowe, D. (1983c) 'Resistance to change' in E. Karas (ed.), *Current Issues in Clinical Psychology* (vol. 1), Plenum Press, New York.

Rowe, D. (1985a) 'Depression is a prison' in F. Epting and A.W. Landfield (eds.), *Anticipating Personal Construct Psychology*, University of Nebraska Press, Lincoln.

Rowe, D. (1985b) *Living With the Bomb: Can We Live Without Enemies?*, Routledge & Kegan Paul, London.

Rowe, D. (1987) *Beyond Fear*, Fontana, London.

Rowe, D. (1989) *The Successful Self*, Fontana/Collins, London.

Rowe, D. and Slater, P. (1976) 'Studies of the psychiatrist's insight into the patient's inner world' in P. Slater (ed.), *The Measurement of Intrapersonal Space by Grid Technique. Vol.1. Explorations of Intrapersonal Space*, Wiley, London.

Rowles, G.D. (1972) 'Choice in Geographic Space: Exploring a Phenomenological Approach to Vocational Decision-Making', unpublished MSc dissertation, University of Bristol.

Rudikoff, E.C. (1954) 'A comparative study of the changes in the concepts of the self, the ordinary person, and the ideal, in eight cases' in C.R. Rogers and R.F. Dymond (eds.), *Psychotherapy and Personality Change*, University of Chicago Press, Chicago.

Runkel, P.J. and Damrin, D.E. (1961) 'Effects of training and anxiety upon teachers' preference information about students', *Journal of Educational Psychology, 52*, 254–61.

Rutter, D.R., Draffan, J., and Davies, J. (1977) 'Thought disorder and the predictability of schizophrenic speech', *British Journal of Psychiatry, 131*, 67–8.

Rychlak, J.F. (1968) *A Philosophy of Science for Personality Theory*, Houghton Mifflin, Boston.

Rychlak, J.F. (1977) *The Psychology of Rigorous Humanism*, Wiley-Interscience, New York.

Rychlak, J.F. (1981) *Introduction to Personality and Psychotherapy: A Theory-Construction Approach*, Houghton Mifflin, Boston.

Rycroft, C. (1968) *Anxiety and Neurosis*, Allen Lane, London.

Rycroft, C. (1970) 'Cause and meaning' in S.G.M. Lee and M. Hubert (eds.), *Freud and Psychology*, Penguin, Harmondsworth.

Ryle, A. (1967) 'A repertory grid study of the meaning and consequences of a suicidal act', *British Journal of Psychiatry, 113*, 1393–403.

Ryle, A. (1969) 'The psychology and psychiatry of academic difficulties in students', *Proceedings of Royal Society of Medicine, 62*, 1263–6.

Ryle, A. (1975) *Frames and Cages: The Repertory Grid Approach to Human Understanding*, Sussex University Press, London.

Ryle, A. (1978) 'A common language for the psychotherapies', *British Journal of Psychiatry, 132*, 585–94.

Ryle, A. (1979a) 'The focus in brief interpretive psychotherapy: dilemmas, traps and snags as target problems', *British Journal of Psychiatry, 134*, 46–54.

Ryle, A. (1979b) 'Defining goals and asessing change in brief psychotherapy: a pilot study using target ratings and the dyad grid', *British Journal of Medical Psychology, 52*, 223–34.

Ryle, A. (1980) 'Some measures of goal attainment in focused integrated active psychotherapy: a study of fifteen cases', *British Journal of Psychiatry, 137*, 475–86.

Ryle, A. (1981) 'Dyad grid dilemmas in patients and control subjects', *British Journal of Medical Psychology, 54*, 353–8.

Ryle, A. (1982) *Psychotherapy: A Cognitive Integration of Theory and Practice*, Academic Press, London.

Ryle, A. (1985) 'The dyad grid in psychotherapy research' in N. Beail (ed.), *Repertory Grid Technique and Personal Constructs: Applications in Clinical and Educational Settings*, Croom Helm, London.

Ryle, A. (1989) 'George Kelly: should we follow his footsteps or stand on his shoulders?', *International Journal of Personal Construct Psychology, 2*, 463–6.

Ryle, A. (1990) *Cognitive-Analytic Therapy: Active Participation in Change: A New Integration in Brief Therapy*, Wiley, Chichester.

Ryle, A. and Breen, D. (1971) 'The recognition of psychopathology on the repertory grid', *British Journal of Psychiatry, 119*, 317–22.

Ryle, A. and Breen, D. (1972a) 'A comparison of adjusted and maladjusted couples using the double dyad grid', *British Journal of Medical Psychology, 45*, 375–82.

Ryle, A. and Breen, D. (1972b) 'Some differences in the personal constructs of neurotic and normal subjects', *British Journal of Psychiatry, 120*, 483–9.

Ryle, A. and Breen, D. (1974a) 'Change in the course of social work training: a repertory grid study', *British Journal of Medical Psychology, 47*, 139–47.

Ryle, A. and Breen, D. (1974b) 'Social-work tutors' judgement of their students', *British Journal of Medical Psychology, 47*, 149–52.

Ryle, A. and Lipshitz, S. (1974) 'Towards an informed countertransference – possible contribution of repertory grid techniques', *British Journal of Medical Psychology, 47*, 219–25.

Ryle, A. and Lipshitz, S. (1975) 'Recording change in marital therapy with the reconstruction grid', *British Journal of Medical Psychology, 48*, 39–48.

Ryle, A. and Lipshitz, S. (1976a) 'An intensive case- study of a therapeutic group', *British Journal of Psychiatry, 128*, 581–7.

Ryle, A. and Lipshitz, S. (1976b) 'Repertory grid elucidation of a difficult conjoint therapy', *British Journal of Medical Psychology, 49*, 281–5.

Ryle, A. and Lunghi, M. (1969) 'The measurement of relevant change after psychotherapy: Use of repertory grid testing', *British Journal of Psychiatry, 115*, 1297–304.

Ryle, A. and Lunghi, M. (1970) 'The dyad grid – a modification of repertory grid technique', *British Journal of Psychiatry, 117*, 323–7.

Ryle, A. and Lunghi, M. (1971) 'A therapist's prediction of a patient's dyad grid', *British Journal of Psychiatry, 118*, 555–60.

Ryle, A. and Lunghi, M. (1972) 'Parental and sex role identification of students measured with a repertory grid technique', *British Journal of Social and Clinical Psychology, 11*, 149–61.

Sadowski, A. (1971) 'Personal Construct Organization: Correlates in Behavior and Experience', unpublished Master's thesis, University of Missouri.

Salmon, P. (1963) 'A Clinical Investigation of Sexual Identity', unpublished case study.

Salmon, P. (1969) 'Differential conforming as a developmental process', *British Journal of Social and Clinical Psychology, 8*, 22–31.

Salmon, P. (1970) 'A psychology of personal growth' in D. Bannister (ed.), *Perspectives in Personal Construct Theory*, Academic Press, London.

Salmon, P. (1976) 'Grid measures with child subjects' in P. Slater (ed.), *The Measurement of Intrapersonal Space by Grid Technique. Vol.1. Explorations of Intrapersonal Space*, Wiley, London.

Salmon, P. (1979) 'Children as social beings: a Kellyan view' in P. Stringer and D. Bannister (eds.), *Constructs of Sociality and Individuality*, Academic Press, London.

Salmon, P. (1990) 'Kelly then and now', paper presented at 2nd British Conference on Personal Construct Psychology, York.

Salmon, P., Bramley, J., and Presley, A.S. (1967) 'The Word-in-Context Test as a measure of conceptualization in schizophrenics with and without thought disorder', *British Journal of Medical Psychology, 40*, 253–9.

Salter, A. (1949) *Conditioned Reflex Therapy*, Farrar, Straus, New York.

Sanderson, C. (1990) 'Mad, bad or normal. An investigation into how abused and non-abused subjects construe child sexual abusers' in P. Maitland (ed.), *Personal Construct Theory Deviancy and Social Work*, Inner London Probation Service/Centre for Personal Construct Psychology, London.

Sarason, I.G. (1978) 'Three lacunae of cognitive therapy', *Cognitive Therapy and Research, 3*, 223–35.

Sarbin, T.R. (1977) 'Contextualism: a world view for modern psychology' in J.K. Cole and A.W. Landfield (eds.), *1976 Nebraska Symposium on Motivation*, University of Nebraska Press, Lincoln.

Sarbin, T.R. and Mancuso, J.C. (1980) *Schizophrenia: Medical Diagnosis or Moral Verdict?*, Pergamon, New York.

Sartre, J.-P. (1948) *Existentialism and Humanism*, Methuen, London.

Satir, V. (1967) *Conjoint Family Therapy*, Science and Behavior Books, Palo Alto.

Scarlett, H.H., Press, A.N., and Crockett, W.H. (1971) 'Children's descriptions of their peers', *Child Development, 42*, 439–53.

Schachter, S. and Singer, J.C. (1962) 'Cognitive, social and physiological determinants of emotional states', *Psychological Review, 69*, 379–99.

Schafer, R. (1976) *A New Language for Psychoanalysis*, Yale University Press, New Haven.

Schaible, R. (1990) 'Persönliche Konstrukte in der Beschreibung interpersonaler Bezlehungen bei Frauen mit Agoraphobie', *Newsletter of German Grid Group*, p. 8.

Schmittdiel, C., Landfield, A., and Rivers, C. (1981) 'Personal constructs of individuals arrested for driving while intoxicated: a clinical analysis', paper presented at 4th International Congress on Personal Construct Psychology, St. Catharines, Ontario.

Schnolling, P. and Lapidus, L.B. (1972) 'Arousal and task complexity in schizophrenic performance deficit: a theoretical discussion', *Psychological Reports, 30,* 315–26.

Schonecke, O.W., Schuffel, W., Schafer, N., and Winter, K. (1972) 'Assessment of hostility in patients with functional cardiac complaints. Part 1', *Psychotherapy and Psychosomatics, 20,* 272–81.

Schroeder, H.E. and Rakos, R.F. (1983) 'The identification and assessment of social skills' in R. Ellis and D. Whittington (eds.), *New Directions in Social Skills Training,* Croom Helm, London.

Schüffel, W. and Schonecke, O.W. (1972) 'Assessment of hostility in the course of psychosomatic treatment of three patients with functional disorders. Part II', *Psychotherapy and Psychosomatics, 20,* 282–93.

Schwartz, R.M. (1986) 'The internal dialogue: on the asymmetry between positive and negative coping thoughts', *Cognitive Therapy and Research, 10,* 591–605.

Schwartz, R.M. and Garamoni, G.L. (1986) 'A structural model of positive and negative states of mind: asymmetry in the internal dialogue' in P.C. Kendall (ed.), *Advances in Cognitive-Behavioral Research and Therapy* (vol. 5), Academic Press, New York.

Schwartz, R.M. and Garamoni, G.L. (1987) 'States of mind model: the golden section and psychopathology', paper presented at 7th International Congress on Personal Construct Psychology, Memphis.

Schwartz, R.M. and Gottman, J.M. (1976) 'Toward a task analysis of assertive behavior', *Journal of Consulting and Clinical Psychology, 44,* 910–20.

Schwartz, R.M. and Michelson, L. (1987) 'States-of-mind model: cognitive balance in the treatment of agoraphobia', *Journal of Consulting and Clinical Psychology, 55,* 557–65.

Scott, R.D. and Alwyn, S. (1978) 'Patient–parent relationships and the course and outcome of schizophrenia', *British Journal of Medical Psychology, 51,* 343–55.

Scott, R.D. and Ashworth, P.L. (1969) 'The shadow of the ancestor: a historical factor in the transmission of schizophrenia: a family study', *British Journal of Medical Psychology, 42,* 13–32.

Scott, R.D., Ashworth, P.L., and Casson, P.D. (1970) 'Violation of parental role structure and outcome in schizophrenia: a scored analysis of features in the patient–parent relationship', *Social Science and Medicine, 4,* 41–64.

Scott, R.D., Fagin, L., and Winter, D.A. (1990) 'Family relationships and outcome in schizophrenia and the often unperceived role of the patient', in preparation.

Scott, R.D. and Montanez, A. (1972) 'The nature of tenable and untenable patient–parent relationships and their connexion with hospital outcome' in D. Rubinstein and Y.O. Alanen (eds.), *Proceedings of IVth International Symposium on Psychotherapy for Schizophrenia,* Excerpta Medica, Amsterdam.

Scott, W.A. (1963) 'Cognitive complexity and cognitive balance', *Sociometry, 26,* 66–74.

Sechrest, L.B. (1962) 'Stimulus equivalents of the psychotherapist', *Journal of Individual Psychology, 18,* 172–6.

Selby, G. (1988) 'Occupational therapy: from soft toys to Personal Construct Theory' in G. Dunnett (ed.), *Working with People: Clinical Uses of Personal Construct Psychology,* Routledge, London.

Seligman, M. and Johnston, J. (1973) 'A cognitive theory of avoidance learning' in J. McGuigan and B. Lumsden (eds.), *Contemporary Approaches to Conditioning and Learning,* Wiley, New York.

Selvini-Palazzoli, M., Boscolo, L., Cecchin, G., and Prata, G. (1980) 'Hypothesizing-Circularity-Neutrality: three guidelines for the conductor of the session', *Family Process, 19,* 3–12.

Semerari, A. (1989) 'The construction of therapeutic relationship: a theoretical model', paper presented at 8th International Congress on Personal Construct Psychology, Assisi.

Semerari, A. and Mancini, F. (1987) 'Recursive self-invalidation in neurotic processes', paper presented at 7th International Congress on Personal Construct Psychology, Memphis.

Shapiro, D.A., Caplan, H.L., Rohde, P.D., and Watson, J.P. (1975) 'Personal Questionnaire changes and their correlates in a psychotherapeutic group', *British Journal of Medical Psychology, 48*, 207–16.

Shapiro, D.A. and Shapiro, D. (1982) 'Meta-analysis of comparative therapy outcome studies: a replication and refinement', *Psychological Bulletin, 92*, 581–604.

Shapiro, M.B. (1961) 'A method of measuring psychological changes specific to the individual psychiatric patient', *British Journal of Medical Psychology, 34*, 1–5.

Shapiro, S.A. (1981) *Contemporary Theories of Schizophrenia*, McGraw-Hill, New York.

Shaw, M.L.G. (1980) *On Becoming a Personal Scientist: Interactive Computer Elicitation of Personal Models of the World*, Academic Press, London.

Shaw, M.L.G. and Gaines, B.R. (1981) 'Recent advances in the analysis of a repertory grid', *British Journal of Medical Psychology, 54*, 307–18.

Shaw, M.L.G. and Mancuso, J.C. (1987) 'Modeling cognitive processes' in J.C. Mancuso and M.L.G. Shaw (eds.), *Cognition and Personal Structure: Computer Access and Analysis*, Praeger, New York.

Sheehan, M.J. (1977) 'Constructs and Conflict in Depression', unpublished MSc thesis, University of Surrey.

Sheehan, M.J. (1981) 'Constructs and "conflict" in depression', *British Journal of Psychology, 72*, 197–209.

Sheehan, M.J. (1985a) 'A personal construct study of depression', *British Journal of Medical Psychology, 58*, 119–28.

Sheehan, M.J. (1985b) 'The process of change in the self-construing of a depressed patient' in N. Beail (ed.), *Repertory Grid Technique and Personal Constructs: Applications in Clinical and Educational Settings*, Croom Helm, London.

Sheerer, E.T. (1949) 'An analysis of the relationship between accept for and respect for self and respect for others in ten counseling cases', *Journal of Consulting Psychology, 13*, 169–75.

Shlien, J., Mosak, H., and Dreikurs, R. (1962) 'Effect of time limits: a comparison of two psychotherapies', *Journal of Counseling Psychology, 9*, 31–4.

Shorts, I.D. (1985) 'Treatment of a sex offender in a maximum security forensic hospital: detecting changes in personality and interpersonal construing', *International Journal of Offender Therapy and Comparative Criminology, 29*, 237–50.

Shubsachs, A.P.W. (1975) 'To repeat or not to repeat? Are frequently used constructs more important to the subject? A study of the effect of allowing repetition of constructs in a modified Kelly Repertory Test', *British Journal of Medical Psychology, 48*, 31–7.

Shultz, R. and Brenner, G. (1977) 'Relocation of the aged: a review and theoretical analysis', *Journal of Gerontology, 32*, 323–33.

Silverman, G. (1977) 'Aspects of intensity of affective constructs in depressed patients', *British Journal of Psychiatry, 130*, 174–6.

Skenderian, D. (1983) 'Psychological aftermath of stroke: reflections of a personal construct psychologist', paper presented at 5th International Congress on Personal Construct Psychology, Boston.

Skene, R.A. (1973) 'Construct shift in the treatment of a case of homosexuality', *British Journal of Medical Psychology, 46*, 287–92.

Slade, P.D. and Sheehan, M.J. (1979) 'Measurement of "conflict" in repertory grids', *British Journal of Psychology, 70*, 519–24.

Slade, P.D. and Sheehan, M.J. (1981) 'Modified Conflict Grid Program', unpublished MS., Royal Free Hospital, London.

Slater, P. (1965) 'The use of the repertory grid technique in the individual case', *British Journal of Psychiatry, 111*, 965–75.

Slater, P. (1968) 'Summary of the Output from DELTA', unpublished MS, Institute of Psychiatry, London.

Slater, P. (1969) 'Theory and technique of the repertory grid', *British Journal of Psychiatry, 115*, 1287–96.

Slater, P. (1970) 'Personal questionnaire data treated as a form of repertory grid', *British Journal of Social and Clinical Psychology, 9*, 357–70.

Slater, P. (1972) 'Notes on INGRID 72', unpublished MS, Institute of Psychiatry, London.

Slater, P. (1974) 'The Reliability and Significance of a Grid', unpublished MS, St. George's Hospital Medical School, London.

Slater, P. (1976) 'Monitoring change in the mental state of a patient undergoing psychiatric treatment' in P. Slater (ed.), *The Measurement of Intrapersonal Space by Grid Technique. Vol. 1. Explorations of Intrapersonal Space*, Wiley, London.

Slater, P. (1977) *The Measurement of Intrapersonal Space by Grid Technique. Vol.2. Dimensions of Intrapersonal Space*, Wiley, London.

Slater, P., Chetwynd, J., and Farnsworth, J. (1989) 'Analyzing disagreement with logical equivalence matrixes', *International Journal of Personal Construct Psychology, 2*, 443–57.

Slater, P. and Makhlouf-Norris, F. (1983) 'An adaptation of PCP for analysing disagreements', paper presented at 5th International Congress on Personal Construct Psychology, Boston.

Smail, D.J. (1970) 'Neurotic symptoms, personality and personal constructs', *British Journal of Psychiatry, 117*, 645–8.

Smail, D.J. (1972) 'A grid measure of empathy in a therapeutic group', *British Journal of Medical Psychology, 45*, 165–9.

Smail, D.J. (1978) *Psychotherapy: A Personal Approach*, Dent, London.

Smail, D.J. (1987) *Taking Care: An Alternative to Therapy*, Dent, London.

Smith, M., Hartley, J., and Stewart, B. (1978) 'A case study of repertory grids used in vocational guidance', *Journal of Occupational Psychology, 51*, 97–104.

Smith, M.L. and Glass, G.V. (1977) 'Meta-analysis of psychotherapy outcome studies', *American Psychologist, 32*, 752–60.

Smith, M.L., Glass, G.V., and Miller, T.I. (1980) *The Benefits of Psychotherapy*, Johns Hopkins University Press, Baltimore.

Smith, S. and Leach, C. (1972) 'A hierarchical measure of cognitive complexity', *British Journal of Psychology, 63*, 561–8.

Soldz, S. (1983) 'Hostility in the severely disturbed personality: clinical considerations', paper presented at 5th International Congress on Personal Construct Psychology, Boston.

Soldz, S. (1986) 'Construing of others in psychotherapy: personal construct perspectives', *Journal of Contemporary Psychotherapy, 16*, 52–61.

Soldz, S. (1987a) 'The flight from relationship: personal construct reflections on psychoanalytic therapy' in R.A. Neimeyer and G.J. Neimeyer (eds.), *Personal Construct Therapy Casebook*, Springer, New York.

Soldz, S. (1987b) 'Integrating personal construct and psychoanalytic psychotherapies', paper presented at 7th International Congress on Personal Construct Psychology, Memphis.

Soldz, S. (1988) 'Constructivist tendencies in recent psychoanalysis', *International Journal of Personal Construct Psychology, 1*, 329–47.

Soldz, S. (1989) 'Do psychotherapists use different construct subsystems for construing clients and personal acquaintances? A Repertory Grid study', *Journal of Social and Clinical Psychology, 8*, 97–112.

Soldz, S. and Soldz, E. (1989) 'A difficulty with the Functionally Independent Construction measure of cognitive differentiation', *International Journal of Personal Construct Psychology, 2*, 315–22.

Southwell, E.A. and Merbaum, M. (eds.) (1971) *Personality: Readings in Theory and Research*, Brooks/Cole, Belmont.

Space, L.G. (1976) 'Cognitive Structure Comparison of Depressives, Neurotics and Normals', unpublished PhD thesis, Wayne State University.

Space, L.G. and Cromwell, R.L. (1978) 'Personal constructs among schizophrenic patients' in S. Schwartz (ed.), *Language and Cognition in Schizophrenia*, Lawrence Erlbaum, Hillsdale, NJ.

Space, L.G. and Cromwell, R.L. (1980) 'Personal constructs among depressed patients', *Journal of Nervous and Mental Disease, 168*, 150–8.

Space, L.G., Dingemans, P.M., and Cromwell, R.L. (1983) 'Self-construing and alienation in depressives, schizophrenics, and normals' in J. Adams-Webber and J.C. Mancuso (eds.), *Applications of Personal Construct Theory*, Academic Press, Toronto.

Spelman, M., Harrison, A., and Mellsop, G. (1971) 'Grid test for schizophrenic thought disorder in acute and chronic schizophrenics', *Psychological Medicine, 1*, 234–8.

Sperber, J.C. (1977) 'Personal constructs and child psychiatric diagnosis – A pilot study', *British Journal of Medical Psychology, 50*, 65–72.

Sperlinger, D.J. (1971) 'A Repertory Grid and Questionnaire Study of Individuals Receiving Treatment for Depression from General Practitioners', unpublished PhD thesis, University of Birmingham.

Sperlinger, D.J. (1976) 'Aspects of stability in the repertory grid', *British Journal of Medical Psychology, 49*, 341–7.

Spindler Barton, E., Walton, T., and Rowe, D. (1976) 'Using grid technique with the mentally handicapped' in P. Slater (ed.), *The Measurement of Intrapersonal Space by Grid Technique. Vol. 1. Explorations of Intrapersonal Space*, Wiley, London.

Spitzer, R.L., Andreasen, N., Endicott, J., and Woodruff, R.A., Jr. (1978) 'Proposed classification of schizophrenia in DSMIII' in L.C. Wynne, R.L. Cromwell, and S. Matthysse (eds.), *The Nature of Schizophrenia: New Approaches to Research and Treatment*, Wiley, New York.

Spotnitz, H. (1976) *Psychotherapy of Preoedipal Conditions*, Jason Aronson, New York.

SPSS INC (1988) *SPSS-X User's Guide* (2nd edition), SPSS Inc., Chicago.

Stanley, B. (1985) 'Alienation in young offenders' in N. Beail (ed.), *Repertory Grid Technique and Personal Constructs: Applications in Clinical and Educational Settings*, Croom Helm, London.

Stefan, C. (1977) 'Core role theory and implications' in D. Bannister (ed.), *New Perspectives in Personal Construct Theory*, Academic Press, London.

Stefan, C. and Linder, H.B. (1985) 'Suicide, an experience of chaos or fatalism: perspectives from personal construct theory' in D. Bannister (ed.), *Issues and Approaches in Personal Construct Theory*, Academic Press, London.

Stefan, C. and Molloy, P. (1982) 'An investigation of the construct validity of the Bannister-Fransella Grid Test of Schizophrenic Thought Disorder', *British Journal of Clinical Psychology, 21*, 199–204.

Stefan, C. and Von, J. (1985) 'Suicide' in E. Button (ed.), *Personal Construct Theory and Mental Health*, Croom Helm, London.

Stephenson, W. (1953) *The Study of Behavior: Q-Technique and its Methodology*, University of Chicago Press, Chicago.

Stewart, V. and Stewart, A. (1981) *Business Applications of Repertory Grid*, McGraw-Hill, London.

Stojnov, D. (1990) 'Construing HIV positivity amongst heroin addicts' in P. Maitland (ed.), *Personal Construct Theory Deviancy and Social Work*, Inner London Probation Service/Centre for Personal Construct Psychology, London.

Strachan, A. and Jones, D. (1982) 'Changes in identification during adolescence: a personal construct theory approach', *Journal of Personality Assessment, 46*, 529–35.

Strickland, B.R. (1978) 'Internal–external expectancies and health-related behaviors', *Journal of Consulting and Clinical Psychology, 46*, 1192–211.

Stringer, P. (1972) 'Psychological significance in personal and supplied construct systems: a defining experiment', *European Journal of Social Psychology, 2*, 437–47.

Stringer, P. (1976) 'Repertory grids in the study of environmental perception' in P. Slater (ed.), *The Measurement of Intrapersonal Space by Grid Technique. Vol.1. Explorations of Intrapersonal Space*, Wiley, London.

Stringer, P. (1979) 'Individuals, roles and persons' in P. Stringer and D. Bannister (eds.), *Constructs of Sociality and Individuality*, Academic Press, London.

Stringer, P. and Bannister, D. (eds.) (1979) *Constructs of Sociality and Individuality*, Academic Press, London.

Stringer, P. and Terry, P. (1978) 'Objective constructs and cognitive structure', *British Journal of Medical Psychology, 51*, 325–33.

Sundberg, N.D., Taplin, J.R., and Tyler, L.E. (1983) *Introduction to Clinical Psychology: Perspectives, Issues and Contributions to Human Service*, Prentice-Hall, Englewood Cliffs, NJ.

Tajfel, H. and Wilkes, A.L. (1964) 'Salience of attributes and commitment to extreme judgements in the perception of people', *British Journal of Social and Clinical Psychology, 3*, 40–9.

Takens, R.J. (1981a) 'Commonality, sociality and therapeutic accessibility' in H. Bonarius, R. Holland, and S. Rosenberg (eds.), *Personal Construct Psychology: Recent Advances in Theory and Practice*, Macmillan, London.

Takens, R.J. (1981b) 'Sociality and empathy in the therapeutic dyad', paper presented at 4th International Congress on Personal Construct Psychology, St. Catharines, Ontario.

Takens, R.J. (1987) 'Personal construct theory and client-centered therapy: two sides of a coin', paper presented at 7th International Congress on Personal Construct Psychology, Memphis.

Tamaka-Matsumi, J. and Marsella, A.J. (1976) 'Cross-cultural variations in the phenomenological experience of depression: word association studies', *Journal of Cross-Cultural Psychology, 7*, 379–96.

Tarrier, N., Vaughn, C.E., Lader, M.H., and Leff, J.P. (1979) 'Bodily reactions to people and events in schizophrenics', *Archives of General Psychiatry, 36*, 311–15.

Taylor, F.G. and Marshall, W.L. (1977) 'Experimental analysis of a cognitive-behavioral therapy for depression', *Cognitive Therapy and Research, 1*, 59–72.

Thomas, L.F. (1976) *The FOCUS Technique: 'Focusing the Repertory Grid'*, CSHL Technical Paper, Brunel University.

Thomas, L.F. (1979) 'Construct, reflect and converse: the conversational reconstruction of social realities' in P. Stringer and D. Bannister (eds.), *Constructs of Sociality and Individuality*, Academic Press, London.

Thomas, L. and Harri-Augstein, S. (1983) 'The self-organized learner as personal scientist: a conversational technology for reflecting on behavior and experience' in J. Adams-Webber and J.C. Mancuso (eds.), *Applications of Personal Construct Theory*, Academic Press, Toronto.

Thomas, L.F. and Harri-Augstein, S. (1985) *Self-Organised Learning: Foundations of a Conversational Science for Psychology*, Routledge & Kegan Paul, London.

Thomas-Peter, B.A. (1990) 'Construct theory and cognitive style in personality disordered offenders' in P. Maitland (ed.), *Personal Construct Theory Deviancy and Social Work*, Inner London Probation Service/Centre for Personal Construct Psychology, London.

Tibbles, P.N. (1988) 'Changes in Personal Construing of Mildly Depressed Out-Patients Following Assessment for Dynamic Psychotherapy', unpublished MSc thesis, University of Surrey.

Tobacyck, J. (1984) 'Death threat, death concerns, and paranormal belief' in F. Epting and R.A. Neimeyer (eds.), *Personal Meanings of Death: Applications of Personal Construct Theory to Clinical Practice*, Hemisphere/McGraw-Hill, Washington, DC.

Tobacyck, J. and Eckstein, D. (1980) 'Death threat and death concerns in the college student', *Omega, 11*, 139–65.

Todd, N. (1988) 'Religious belief and PCT' in F. Fransella and L. Thomas (eds.), *Experimenting with Personal Construct Psychology*, Routledge & Kegan Paul, London.

Todd, T. (1973) 'An experimental investigation of Kelly's fixed role therapy with hysterical and obsessive personalities', *Dissertation Abstracts International, 33*, 5527–8.

Traue, H.C., Gottwald, A., Henderson, P.R., and Bakal, D.A. (1985) 'Nonverbal expressiveness and EMG activity in tension headache sufferers and controls', *Journal of Psychosomatic Research, 29*, 375–81.

Tripodi, T. and Bieri, J. (1963) 'Cognitive complexity as a function of own and provided constructs', *Psychological Reports, 13*, 26.

Trower, P. (ed.) (1984) *Radical Approaches to Social Skills Training*, Croom Helm, London.

Trower, P., Bryant, B. and Argyle, M. (1978) *Social Skills and Mental Health*, Methuen, London.

Truax, C.B., Schuldt, W.J., and Wargo, D.G. (1968) 'Self-ideal concept congruence and improvement in group psychotherapy', *Journal of Consulting and Clinical Psychology, 32*, 47–53.

Truax, C.B., Wargo, D.G., and Silber, L.D. (1966) 'Effect of group psychotherapy with high accurate empathy and nonpossessive warmth upon female institutionalised delinquents', *Journal of Abnormal Psychology, 71*, 267–74.

Tschudi, F. (1977) 'Loaded and honest questions: a construct theory view of symptoms and therapy' in D. Bannister (ed.), *New Perspectives in Personal Construct Theory*, Academic Press, London.

Tschudi, F. (1984) 'Operating Manual for: Flexigrid Version 2.1. August 1984. An Integrated Software System for Eliciting and Analyzing Grids', unpublished MS, University of Oslo.

Tschudi, F. and Rommetveit, R. (1982) 'Sociality, intersubjectivity, and social processes: the sociality corollary' in J.C. Mancuso and J.R. Adams-Webber (eds.), *The Construing Person*, Praeger, New York.

Tschudi, F. and Sandsberg, S. (1984) 'On the advantages of symptoms: exploring the client's construing', *Scandinavian Journal of Psychology, 25*, 69–77.

Tully, J.B. (1976) 'Personal construct theory and psychological changes related to social work practice', *British Journal of Social Work, 6*, 481–99.

Turbiner, M. (1961) 'Choice discrimination in schizophrenic and normal subjects for positive, negative and neutral affective stimuli', *Journal of Consulting Psychology, 25*, 92.

Turnbull, M.J. and Norris, H. (1982) 'Effects of Transcendental Meditation on self-identity indices and personality', *British Journal of Psychology, 73*, 57–68.

Turner, J.B. (1964) 'Schizophrenics as judges of vocal expressions of emotional meaning' in J.R. Davitz (ed.), *The Communication of Emotional Meaning*, McGraw-Hill, New York.

Tutt, N.S. (1970) 'Psychiatric nurses' attitudes to treatment in a general hospital', *Nursing Times, 66*, 137–9.

Twentyman, C.T. and Zimering, R.T. (1979) 'Behavioural training of social skills: a critical review' in M. Hersen, R.M. Eisler, and P.M. Miller (eds.), *Progress in Behavior Modification* (vol. 7), Academic Press, New York.

Tyler, F.B. and Simmons, W.L. (1964) 'Patients' conception of the therapist', *Journal of Clinical Psychology, 20*, 112–33.

Tyler, L. (1985) 'Personal construct theory and the rest of psychology' in F. Epting and A.W. Landfield (eds.), *Anticipating Personal Construct Psychology*, University of Nebraska Press, Lincoln.

Vacc, N.A., Loesch, L.C., and Burt, M.A. (1980) 'Further development of the adapted modified role repertory test', *Measurement and Evaluation in Guidance, 12*, 216–22.

Vaihinger, H. (1924) *The Philosophy of 'As If'*, Routledge & Kegan Paul, London.

Van den Bergh, O., DeBoeck, P., and Claeyes, W. (1981) 'Research findings on the nature of constructs in schizophrenics', *British Journal of Clinical Psychology, 20*, 123–30.

Van den Bergh, O., DeBoeck, P., and Claeys, W. (1985) 'Schizophrenia: what is loose in schizophrenic construing?' in E. Button (ed.), *Personal Construct Theory and Mental Health*, Croom Helm, London.

Van der Kloot, W. (1981) 'Multidimensional scaling of repertory grid responses: two applications of HOMALS' in H. Bonarius, R. Holland, and S. Rosenberg (eds.), *Personal Construct Psychology: Recent Advances in Theory and Practice*, Macmillan, London.

van Deurzen-Smith (1984) 'Existential therapy' in W. Dryden (ed.), *Individual Therapy in Britain*, Harper & Row, London.

Vannoy, J.S. (1965) 'Generality of cognitive complexity–simplicity as a personality construct', *Journal of Personality and Social Psychology, 2*, 385–96.

Varble, D. and Landfield, A.W. (1969) 'Validity of the self–ideal discrepancy as a criterion measure for success in psychotherapy: a replication', *Journal of Counseling Psychology, 16*, 150–6.

Varela, F.J. (1979) *Principles of Biological Autonomy*, North Holland, Oxford.

Vaughn, C.E. and Leff, J.P. (1976) 'The influence of family and social factors on the course of psychiatric illness', *British Journal of Psychiatry, 129*, 125–37.

Vicary, S. (1985) 'Developments in mothers' construing of their mentally handicapped one-year-olds' in N. Beail (ed.), *Repertory Grid Technique and Personal Constructs: Applications in Clinical and Educational Settings*, Croom Helm, London.

Villegas, M. and Feixas, G. (1985) 'Personal construct theory and the existential-phenomenological approach: a research into autobiographical texts', paper presented at 6th International Congress on Personal Construct Psychology, Cambridge.

Villegas, M., Feixas, G., and Lopez, N. (1986) 'Phenomenological analysis of auto-biographical texts: a design based on personal construct psychology', *Phenomenological Inquiry, 10*, 43–59.

Viney, L.L. (1980) *Transitions*, Cassell, Melbourne.

Viney, L.L. (1981) 'Experimenting with experience: a psychotherapeutic case study', *Psychotherapy, 18*, 271–86.

Viney, L.L. (1983a) 'The assessment of psychological states through content analysis of verbal communications', *Psychological Bulletin, 94*, 542–63.

Viney, L.L. (1983b) *Images of Illness*, Krieger, Malabar.

Viney, L.L. (1983c) 'Experiencing chronic illness: a personal construct commentary' in J. Adams-Webber and J.C. Mancuso (eds.), *Applications of Personal Construct Theory*, Academic Press, Toronto.

Viney, L.L. (1985a) 'Physical illness: a guidebook for the kingdom of the sick' in E. Button (ed.), *Personal Construct Theory and Mental Health*, Croom Helm, London.

Viney, L.L. (1985b) 'Humor as a therapeutic tool' in F. Epting and A.W. Landfield (eds.), *Anticipating Personal Construct Psychology*, University of Nebraska Press, Lincoln.

Viney, L.L. (1986) 'The Development and Evaluation of Short Term Psychotherapy Programs for the Elderly: Report to the Australian Institute of Health', unpublished MS, University of Wollongong.

Viney, L.L. (1987a) 'Psychotherapy in a case of physical illness: "I have a choice"' in R.A. Neimeyer and G.J. Neimeyer (eds.), *Personal Construct Therapy Casebook*, Springer, New York.

Viney, L.L. (1987b) 'Constructivist and psychoanalytic psychotherapies: two models for therapeutic research', paper presented at 7th International Congress on Personal Construct Psychology, Memphis.

Viney, L.L. (1990) 'A constructivist model of psychological reactions to physical illness and injury' in G. Neimeyer and R. Neimeyer (eds.), *Advances in Personal Construct Psychology* (vol. 1), Jai Press, New York.

Viney, L.L. and Bazeley, P. (1977) 'The affective responses of housewives to community relocation', *Journal of Community Psychology, 5*, 37–45.

Viney, L.L., Benjamin, Y.N., and Preston, C. (1988) 'Constructivist family therapy with the elderly', *Journal of Family Therapy, 2*, 241–58.

Viney, L.L., Benjamin, Y.N., and Preston, C.A. (1989b) 'An evaluation of personal construct therapy for the elderly', *British Journal of Medical Psychology, 62*, 35–42.

Viney, L.L., Benjamin, Y.N., and Preston, C. (1989c) 'Mourning and reminiscence: parallel psychotherapeutic processes for the elderly', *International Journal of Aging and Human Development, 28*, 239–49.

Viney, L.L., Clarke, A.M., Bunn, T.A., and Benjamin, Y.N. (1985b) 'Crisis-intervention counseling: an evaluation of long- and short-term effects', *Journal of Counseling Psychology, 32*, 29–39.

Viney, L.L., Clarke, A.M., Bunn, T.A., and Benjamin, Y.N. (1985c) 'An evaluation of three crisis intervention programmes for general hospital patients', *British Journal of Medical Psychology, 58*, 75–86.

Viney, L.L., Clarke, A.M., Bunn, T.A., and Benjamin, Y.N. (1985d) 'The effect of a hospital-based counseling service on the physical recovery of surgical and medical patients', *General Hospital Psychiatry, 7*, 294–301.

Viney, L.L., Clarke, A.M., Bunn, T.A., and Teoh, H.Y. (1985e) 'Crisis intervention counseling in a general hospital: development and multi-faceted evaluation of a health service', *Australian Studies in Health Care Administration, 5*.

Viney, L.L., Henry, R., Walker, B.M., and Crooks, L. (1989a) 'The emotional reactions of HIV antibody positive men', *British Journal of Medical Psychology, 62*, 153–61.

Viney, L.L. and Tych, A.M. (1985) 'Content analysis scales measuring psychosocial maturity in the elderly', *Journal of Personality Assessment, 49*, 311–17.

Viney, L.L. and Westbrook, M.T. (1976) 'Cognitive anxiety: a method of content analysis of verbal samples', *Journal of Personality Assessment, 40*, 140–50.

Viney, L.L. and Westbrook, M.T. (1979) 'Sociality: a content analysis scale for verbalizations', *Social Behavior and Personality, 7*, 129–37.

Viney, L.L. and Westbrook, M.T. (1981) 'Measuring patients' experienced quality of life: the application of content analysis scales in health care', *Community Health Studies, 5*, 45–52.

Viney, L.L. and Westbrook, M.T. (1982) 'Psychological reactions to chronic illness: do they predict rehabilitation?', *Journal of Applied Rehabilitation Counselling, 13*, 38–44.

Viney, L.L. and Westbrook, M.T. (1984) 'Coping with chronic illness: strategy preferences and associated psychological reactions', *Journal of Chronic Diseases, 106*, 1–14.

Viney, L.L. and Westbrook, M. (1986–7) 'Is there a pattern of psychological reactions to chronic illness which is associated with death?', *Omega, 17*, 169–81.

Viney, L.L., Westbrook, M.T., and Preston, C. (1985a) 'The addiction experience as a function of the addict's history', *British Journal of Clinical Psychology, 24*, 73–82.

von Foerster, H. (1981) *Observing Systems*, Intersystems Publications, Seaside, CA.

Walker, B.M., Ramsey, F.L., and Bell, R.C. (1988) 'Dispersed and undispersed dependency', *International Journal of Personal Construct Psychology, 1*, 63–80.

Walton, H.J. and McPherson, F.M. (1968) 'Phenomena in a closed psychotherapeutic group', *British Journal of Medical Psychology, 41*, 61–72.

Warr, P.B. and Coffman, T.L. (1970) 'Personality, involvement, and extremity of judgement', *British Journal of Social and Clinical Psychology, 9*, 108–21.

Warren, N. (1966) 'Social class and construct systems: examination of the cognitive structure of two social class groups', *British Journal of Social and Clinical Psychology, 4*, 254–63.

Warren, W.G. (1983) 'Personal construct theory and psychoanalysis: an exploration', paper presented at 5th International Congress on Personal Construct Psychology, Boston.

Warren, W.G. (1985a) 'Personal construct theory and "the cognitive": a philosophical investigation', paper presented at 6th International Congress on Personal Construct Psychology, Cambridge.

Warren, W.G. (1985b) 'Personal construct psychology and contemporary philosophy: an examination of alignments' in D. Bannister (ed.), *Issues and Approaches in Personal Construct Theory*, Academic Press, London.

Warren, W.G. (1989) 'Personal construct theory and mental health', paper presented at 7th International Congress on Personal Construct Psychology, Assisi.

Warren, W.G. and Parry, G. (1981) 'Personal constructs and death' in H. Bonarius, R. Holland, and S. Rosenberg (eds.), *Personal Construct Psychology: Recent Advances in Theory and Practice*, Macmillan, London.

Watson, J.P. (1970a) 'A measure of therapist–patient understanding', *British Journal of Psychiatry, 117*, 319–21.

Watson, J.P. (1970b) 'The relationship between a self-mutilating patient and her doctor', *Psychotherapy and Psychosomatics, 18*, 67–73.

Watson, J.P. (1970c) 'A repertory grid method of studying groups', *British Journal of Psychiatry, 117*, 309–18.

Watson, J.P. (1972) 'Possible measures of change during group psychotherapy', *British Journal of Medical Psychology, 45*, 71–7.

Watson, J.P. (1985) 'Reply to Bryant', *Journal of Family Therapy, 7*, 259–60.

Watson, J.P., Gunn, J.C., and Gristwood, J. (1976) 'A grid investigation of long-term prisoners' in P. Slater (ed.), *The Measurement of Intrapersonal Space by Grid Technique. Vol.1. Explorations of Intrapersonal Space*, Wiley, London.

Watts, F.N., and Sharrock, R. (1985) 'Relationships between spider constructs in phobics', *British Journal of Medical Psychology, 58*, 149–54.

Watzlawick, P., Weakland, J., and Fisch, R. (1974) *Change*, Norton, New York.

Weeks, D.J. (1985) 'Conceptual structure in hypochondriasis, arthritis and neurosis', *British Journal of Clinical Psychology, 24*, 125–6.

Weigel, R.G., Weigel, V.M., and Richardson, F.C. (1973) 'Congruence of spouses' personal constructs and reported marital success: pitfalls in instrumentation', *Psychological Reports, 33*, 212–14.

Weiner, B. (1980) *Human Motivation*, Holt, Rinehart, & Winston, New York.

Weinreich, P. (1979) 'Ethnicity and adolescent identity conflict' in V. Saifullah Khan (ed.), *Minority Families in Britain*, Macmillan, London.

Weinreich, P. (1983) 'Emerging from threatened identities: ethnicity and gender in redefinition of ethnic identity' in G. Breakwell (ed.), *Threatened Identities*, Wiley, Chichester.

Weinreich, P., Doherty, J., and Harris, P. (1985) 'Empirical assessment of identity in anorexia and bulimia nervosa', *Journal of Psychiatric Research, 19*, 297–302.

Weiss, J., Sampson, H., and the Mount Zion Psychotherapy Research Group (1986) *The Psychoanalytic Process*, Guilford, New York.

Wessler, R. (1984) 'Cognitive-social psychological theories and social skills' in P. Trower (ed.), *Radical Approaches to Social Skills Training*, Croom Helm, London.

Westbrook, M.T. (1976) 'Positive affect: a method of content analysis for verbal samples', *Journal of Consulting and Clinical Psychology, 44*, 715–19.

Westbrook, M.T. and Viney, L.L. (1977) 'The application of content analysis scales to life stress research', *Australian Psychologist, 12*, 157–66.

Westbrook, M.T. and Viney, L.L. (1980) 'Measuring people's perceptions of themselves as origins and pawns', *Journal of Personality Assessment, 44*, 157–66.

Wexler, D.A. (1974) 'A cognitive theory of experiencing, self-actualization, and therapeutic process' in D.A. Wexler and L.N. Rice (eds.), *Innovations in Client-Centered Therapy*, Wiley, New York.

Widom, C.S. (1976) 'Interpersonal and personal construct systems in psychopaths', *Journal of Consulting and Clinical Psychology, 44*, 614–23.

Wijesinghe, O.B.A. and Wood, R.R. (1976a) 'A repertory grid study of interpersonal perception within a married couples psychotherapy group', *British Journal of Medical Psychology, 49*, 287–93.

Wijesinghe, O.B.A. and Wood, R.R. (1976b) 'A repertory grid study of interpersonal perception within a married couples psychotherapy group – study II', unpublished MS, Claybury Hospital.

Wile, D.B. (1981) *Couples Therapy: A Nontraditional Approach*, Wiley, New York.

Wilkins, G., Epting, F., and van de Riet, H. (1972) 'Relationship between repression-sensitization and interpersonal cognitive complexity', *Journal of Consulting and Clinical Psychology, 39*, 448–50.

Wilkinson, D. (1982) 'The effects of brief psychiatric training on the attitudes of general nursing students to psychiatric patients', *Journal of Advanced Nursing, 7*, 239–53.

Williams, E. (1971) 'The effect of varying the elements in the Bannister-Fransella Grid Test of Thought Disorder', *British Journal of Psychiatry, 119*, 207–12.

Williams, E. and Quirke, C. (1972) 'Psychological construing in schizophrenics', *British Journal of Medical Psychology, 45*, 79–84.

Williams, J.M.G., Watts, F.N., MacLeod, C., and Mathews, A. (1988) *Cognitive Psychology and Emotional Disorders*, Wiley, Chichester.

Willutzki, U. (1989) 'Problem-specific cognitions: what do therapists know about their clients' perspective?', paper presented at 1st European Congress of Psychology, Amsterdam.

Wilson, G.D. (1975) *Manual for the Wilson-Patterson Attitude Inventory (WPAI)*, NFER, Windsor.

Winer, D. and Gati, I. (1986) 'Cognitive complexity and interest crystallization', *Journal of Vocational Behavior, 28*, 48–59.

Winer, J.L., Cesari, J., Haase, R.F., and Bodden, J.L. (1979) 'Cognitive complexity and career maturity among college students', *Journal of Vocational Behavior, 15*, 186–92.

Winer, J.L., Warren, G.D., Dailey, K.C., and Hiesberger, J. (1980) 'Complexity of judgement of occupational titles among Holland types', *Vocational Guidance Quarterly, 29*, 12–24.

Winter, D.A. (1971) 'The Meaningfulness of Personal and Supplied Constructs to Chronic Schizophrenics and Normals', unpublished BSc dissertation, University of Durham.

Winter, D.A. (1975) 'Some characteristics of schizophrenics and their parents', *British Journal of Social and Clinical Psychology, 14*, 279–90.

Winter, D.A. (1982) 'Construct relationships, psychological disorder and therapeutic change', *British Journal of Medical Psychology, 55*, 257–70.

Winter, D.A. (1983) 'Logical inconsistency in construct relationships: conflict or complexity?', *British Journal of Medical Psychology, 56*, 79–88.

Winter, D.A. (1985a) 'Repertory grid technique in the evaluation of therapeutic outcome' in N. Beail (ed.), *Repertory Grid Technique and Personal Constructs: Applications in Clinical and Educational Settings*, Croom Helm, London.

Winter, D.A. (1985b) 'Neurotic disorders: the curse of certainty' in E. Button (ed.), *Personal Construct Theory and Mental Health*, Croom Helm, London.

Winter, D.A. (1985c) 'Personal styles, constructive alternativism and the provision of a therapeutic service', *British Journal of Medical Psychology, 58*, 129–36.

Winter, D.A. (1985d) 'Group therapy with depressives: a personal construct theory perspective', *International Journal of Mental Health, 13*, 67–85.

Winter, D.A. (1987) 'Personal construct psychotherapy as a radical alternative to social skills training' in R.A. Neimeyer and G.J. Neimeyer (eds.), *Personal Construct Therapy Casebook*, Springer, New York.

Winter, D.A. (1988a) 'Constructions in social skills training' in F. Fransella and L. Thomas (eds.), *Experimenting with Personal Construct Psychology*, Routledge & Kegan Paul, London.

Winter, D.A. (1988b) 'Reconstructing an erection and elaborating ejaculation: personal construct theory perspectives on sex therapy', *International Journal of Personal Construct Psychology, 1*, 81–99.

Winter, D. (1988c) 'Towards a constructive clinical psychology' in G. Dunnett (ed.), *Working with People: Clinical Uses of Personal Construct Psychology*, Routledge, London.

Winter, D.A. (1989a) 'An alternative construction of agoraphobia' in K. Gournay (ed.), *Agoraphobia: Current Perspectives on Theory and Treatment*, Routledge, London.

Winter, D.A. (1989b) 'Group therapy as a means of facilitating reconstruing in depressives', *Group Analysis, 22*, 39–48.

Winter, D.A. (1990a) 'Psicopatologia della costruzione di significati' in F. Mancini and A. Semerari (eds.), *Conoscenzo Individuale e Psicopatologia*, Nuova Italia Scientifica, Rome.

Winter, D.A. (1990b) 'A personal construct theory view of social skills training' in P. Maitland (ed.), *Personal Construct Theory Deviancy and Social Work*, Inner London Probation Service/Centre for Personal Construct Psychology, London.

Winter, D.A. (1990c) 'Therapeutic alternatives for psychological disorder: personal construct psychology investigations in a health service setting' in G.J. Neimeyer and R.A. Neimeyer (eds.), *Advances in Personal Construct Psychology* (vol. 1), Jai Press, Greenwich, Connecticut.

Winter, D., Baker, M., and Goggins, S. (1991) 'Into the unknown: transitions in psychiatric services as construed by clients and staff', *International Journal of Personal Construct Psychology*, in press.

Winter, D. and Gournay, K. (1987) 'Constriction and construction in agoraphobia', *British Journal of Medical Psychology, 60*, 233–44.

Winter, D.A., Shivakumar, H., Brown, R.J., Roitt, M., Drysdale, W.J., and Jones, S. (1987) 'Explorations of a crisis intervention service', *British Journal of Psychiatry, 151*, 232–9.

Winter, D.A. and Trippett, C.J. (1977) 'Serial change in group psychotherapy', *British Journal of Medical Psychology, 50*, 341–8.

Wojciszke, B. (1979) 'Affective factors in organization of cognitive structures in the context of interpersonal perception', *Polish Psychological Bulletin, 10*, 3–13.

Wolff, S. and Barlow, A. (1979) 'Schizoid personality in childhood: a comparative study of schizoid, autistic and normal children', *Journal of Child Psychology and Psychiatry, 20*, 29–46.

Wood, K. and Robinson, P. (1982) 'Actualization and fear of death: retesting an existential hypothesis', *Essence, 5*, 235–43.

Wood, R.R. (1977) 'Empathy and Similarity of Perception in a Married Couples' Psychotherapy Group: a Repertory Grid Study', unpublished Dip Clin Psychol dissertation, British Psychological Society, Leicester.

Woodfield, R.L. and Viney, L.L. (1985) 'A personal construct approach to bereavement', *Omega, 16*, 1–13.

Woog, R.A. (1978) *An Evaluation of the Role of Extension in the Autralian Pig Industry*, University of Melbourne, Melbourne.

Woolfson, R.C. (1979) 'Consensus in construct identification', *British Journal of Medical Psychology, 52*, 169–74.

Wooster, A.D. (1970) 'Formation of stable and discrete concepts of personality by normal and mentally retarded boys', *Journal of Mental Subnormality, 16*, 24–8.

Worsley, A. (1981) 'In the eye of the beholder: social and personal characteristics of teenagers and their impressions of themselves and fat and slim people', *British Journal of Medical Psychology, 54*, 231–42.

Wright, D.M. (1973) 'Impairment in abstract conceptualization and Bannister and Fransella's Grid Test of Schizophrenic Thought Disorder', *Journal of Consulting and Clinical Psychology, 41*, 474.

Wright, K.J.T. (1969) 'An Investigation of the Meaning of Change in Phobic Patients using Grid Methods', unpublished MPhil thesis, University of London.

Wright, K.J.T. (1970) 'Exploring the uniqueness of common complaints', *British Journal of Medical Psychology, 43*, 221–32.

Wylie, R. (1961) *The Self Concept*, University of Nebraska Press, Lincoln.

Yalom, I.D. (1970) *The Theory and Practice of Group Psychotherapy*, Basic Books, New York.

Yalom, I.D. (1980) *Existential Psychotherapy*, Basic Books, New York.

Yardley, K.M. (1976) 'Training in feminine skills in a male transsexual: a pre-operative procedure', *British Journal of Medical Psychology, 49*, 329–39.

Yorke, D.M. (1985) 'Administration, analysis and assumptions: some aspects of validity' in N. Beail (ed.), *Repertory Grid Technique and Personal Constructs: Applications in Clinical and Educational Settings*, Croom Helm, London.

Yorke, M. (1989) 'The intolerable wrestle: words, numbers, and meanings', *International Journal of Personal Construct Psychology, 2*, 65–76.

Zaken-Greenberg, F.Z. and Neimeyer, G.J. (1986) 'The impact of structural family therapy training on conceptual and executive therapy skills', *Family Process, 25*, 599–608.

Zalot, G. and Adams-Webber, J. (1977) 'Cognitive complexity in the perception of neighbours', *Social Behavior and Personality, 5*, 281–3.

Zelhart, P.F. and Jackson, T.T. (1983) 'George A. Kelly, 1931–1943: environmental influences on a developing theorist' in J. Adams-Webber and J.C. Mancuso (eds.), *Applications of Personal Construct Theory*, Academic Press, Toronto.

Ziller, R.C., Megas, J., and De Cencio, D. (1964) 'Self-social constructs of normals and acute neuropsychiatric patients', *Journal of Consulting Psychology, 28*, 59–63.

Zukav, G. (1979) *The Dancing Wu Li Masters: An Overview of the New Physics*, Fontana, London.

Zweig, J.P. and Czank, J.Z. (1975) 'Effect of relocation on chronically ill geriatric patients of a medical unit', *Journal of the American Geriatric Society, 23*, 132–6.

# Index